SECOND EDITION

PUBLIC RELATIONS
WRITING

SECOND EDITION

PUBLIC RELATIONS WRITING
Principles in Practice

DONALD TREADWELL
JILL B. TREADWELL

SAGE Publications
Thousand Oaks ■ London ■ New Delhi

Exhibits

This edition retains the basic "principles to practice" structure of the previous edition with chapters reordered and with some change in emphasis in the light of reviewers' comments. Instructors may choose to focus primarily on the "applied," writing chapters (8–16) or to emphasize the preliminary "principles" chapters. The text is suitable for both graduate and undergraduate writing courses and terms of any length.

To support your teaching, you can now access a companion web site and an updated instructor's manual for teaching tips, suggested learning objectives and assessment ideas, and quiz content.

We have also updated the companion workbook. It has two new clients and many new assignments that build on the textbook theme of blending principle and practice.

We position public relations writing as a two-way, relationship-building process and therefore appreciate dialogue (albeit indirect) with instructors and reviewers. We look forward to receiving your comments (c/o Sage Publications) on this edition of the text.

For Students

If there are two things that predict your career success, it is your ability to communicate effectively and to manage relationships.

We hope that in the complex and challenging world of public relations writing, this book will help you develop both of these abilities. We hope that it will become your habit to consider all the factors that lead to that combination of message strategy, language, and medium that will foster your organization's relationship with its publics. Therein lies your success as a writer.

Our approach is also framed by what many see as the workplace of the future. Few will deny that the workplace is changing. In contrast with traditional models in which individuals worked for one employer for their lifetimes, you will likely change employers several times during your career. This may reflect your changing interests and expertise as well as changing working conditions. Even within organizations, you may find yourself working in a team that dissolves and reinvents itself as projects change. It is also increasingly possible that your primary employer will be you—as you work in a contract or freelance capacity for many clients from your laptop at a distance.

We can predict with some certainty that the workplace of the future will be an environment of global competition and global communication. Participation in the global communication environment will not be limited to multinational companies with billion-dollar budgets, but rather will be open to organizations of all sizes— even to individuals—with the knowledge and skills to forge relationships between even disparate organizations and audiences.

If this sounds like a public relations writer, you are correct. You will bring to the workplace a unique combination of broad-based strategic thinking and document-specific abilities that will make you attractive to employers and essential if you decide to "go it alone." The ability to understand your organization's environment and its multiple publics and how to communicate effectively with them is a prerequisite not just for your success as a public relations writer but also more generally for success in your career.

Finally, we hope you will find that public relations writing is fun. The cut and thrust of debate over which headline is the most persuasive or which analogy will most successfully cross cultural boundaries is part of the creative challenge you will come to enjoy. This presupposes, and requires, that you have a love of language. We hope that this book equips you for a successful writing career and enthuses you with that passion for language that is the hallmark of all professional writers.

Please contact us care of Sage Publications to let us know what you think of the text and related materials.

We look forward to hearing from you.

With Appreciation

Two things we have learned are that writing a text is an ongoing process and that it is always improved by the input, criticism, and encouragement of the many people who take the time to read, review, offer suggestions, and provide information. The following people were instrumental in producing this second edition.

- ✦ The Sage Publications development team for their confidence in the text. We thank especially Margaret Seawell, editor *par excellence,* and Claudia Hoffman and Kate Peterson, our unparalleled production team, for their professional support and active collaboration in all phases of the project.
- ✦ The reviewers who joined us in the debate over issues as broad as "how big should the big picture be?" and as specific as the order or title of chapters. We have considered all of your ideas carefully and adopted many of them. The book is unquestionably stronger for your input. Thank you for your participation: Professors Robert Brown (Salem State College), Gladys McKie (Northeastern University), Karen Miller Russell (Grady College of Journalism and Mass Communication, University of Georgia), Bruce E. Konkle (University of South Carolina at Columbia), Joseph Massey (California State University at Fullerton), R. Brooks Garner (Oklahoma State University), Marijane Wernsman (Texas Tech University), Michael Kent (Montclair State University), and Bonita Dostal Neff (Valparaiso University).
- ✦ The many organizations that graciously consented to our reprinting their materials and/or provided guidance and assistance, including

  Ad Council
  Alteon Training, LLC
  AMC Entertainment
  American Hospital Association
  American Red Cross
  Amtrak
  Coalition to Protect America's Health Care
  Cornell University
  ExxonMobil
  Girls Inc. of Holyoke
  Hasbro, Inc.

The Hill

Johnson & Johnson

Loomis Communities

The *New York Times*

Phoenix Coyotes

Pfizer, Inc.

PR Newswire

PRWeek magazine

Public Relations Society of America

The Republican

Six Flags New England

United Nations

U.S. Environmental Protection Agency

Vanguard Communications

◆ Special thanks to those professionals whose assistance went above and beyond the call of duty: Patricia Banas, Pam Blasé, Brandi Dobbins, Corinne Ebbs, Damon Markiewicz, Mark Morris, Blake Smith, and MaryAnn Stebbins-Burns.

◆ As always, our students, whose insights continue to amaze and inspire us, especially Jill Monson, our reviewer-in-residence.

◆ The teachers and professional colleagues whose example, encouragement, and critical challenges have shaped our writing and fueled our enjoyment of words and their potential: Des Donovan, Dick Dale, Martin Singer, Tom Miller. John Thomson, and Gary Frazier.

◆ Thanks to Alan Plater and Alan Bates, whose *Oliver's Travels* reminds us what a pleasure language can be.

◆ To Bonnie for moral support and many laughs, and Caroline and Elizabeth, who we hope will carry our enthusiasm for writing into the future.

◆ Finally, a special thank you to the five people who really made it all possible— Norm and Betty, and Tom, Jean, and Helen—each one inspiring in a special way.

Theoretical Influences on Public Relations Writing

KEY PRINCIPLES

1. Public relations writing initiates and sustains the relationships between an organization and its publics.

2. Public relations writing has a role in every organization.

3. The goals of public relations writing are to inform and to effect attitude and behavioral change.

4. The public relations writer has three audiences: the organization, the organization's publics, and the media.

5. Public relations writing is based on theories of behavior and attitude change.

Public relations writing is writing designed to initiate, develop, or sustain positive relationships with groups of people who can affect an organization or individual's well-being.

If public relations is about developing and maintaining relationships between an organization and its publics, then public relations writing is about applying language (and design) to fostering those relationships.

But far from being a simple, linear process of "write it and they will act," effective, successful, strategic public relations writing is a complex process. It brings together theories of human behavior, motivation, and organizational culture, as well as the practices of writing and design, and often the latest technology. It aims to foster behavior that is in the mutual interests of both organizations and their publics.

This chapter provides an overview of that combination of theory and practice required to become an effective public relations writer in the context of modern business and nonprofit, political, and social environments. It outlines the public relations sector and two theoretical foundations of effective public relations writing as a prelude to the specifics of writing practice in Chapter 2.

Public Relations in the 21st Century

Several late-20th- and early-21st-century events and developments have had a profound effect on the way we look at organizations and opinion leaders in modern society.

✦ The September 11, 2001, terrorist attacks on the World Trade Center and the Pentagon, popularly referred to as "9/11," led to a reexamination of how governments, companies, and nonprofit organizations alike respond to crises and how those responses can be improved.

✦ Technological advances—notably digital technology—made access to and dissemination of information easier and faster (for those with the budgets to enter the digital world).

✦ After a decade of investment frenzy, a series of high-profile business failures precipitated by the dot-com bust put ethics on a par with finances in the public's view of (especially) American business and businessmen and -women. Names such as Enron, Tyco, ImClone, and Parmalat became household names generally associated with all that is bad in modern business practice.

✦ The rise and fall of celebrities as role models has precipitated a discussion of the values and principles on which our society is based and of the role and influence of the news and entertainment media on societal values.

✦ Respected media outlets such as the BBC and *New York Times* struggle to maintain or restore credibility in the face of their own ethical blunders.

✦ Even nonbusiness institutions generally regarded as the foundations of society—the church and the government—have come under well-deserved scrutiny for questionable ethics and practices.

✦ Charitable giving reached unprecedented levels, led by high-profile major donors such as Ted Turner and Bill and Melinda Gates, but fueled also by companies joining a social-responsibility movement that has an increasingly global reach and by the more than 70% of American households that responded to pleas from more than 1.4 million charities (American Association of Fundraising Counsel, 2003).

✦ Business has responded to charges of ethical irresponsibility and self-interest with industry and organizational codes of conduct and a formal focus on moral business practices.

✦ Public relations, advertising, and marketing practitioners have begun to recognize their common purposes and publics and increasingly to work together. This is blurring the traditional distinctions among them. The combined disciplines are commonly referred to as integrated communication (IC) or integrated marketing communication (IMC).

Introducing the Public Relations Industry

Public Relations Agencies

The following is a list of the major international public relations agencies. You will hear their names again and again as you enter and monitor the public relations world. As you study them more closely, you will see that they or their affiliates are involved in media and government relations, crisis and event management, public affairs, brand marketing, corporate responsibility programs and reputation management, advertising, marketing, and integrated communication services, among others.

Public relations sees a unique role for itself in this mix. At the same time, it recognizes its commonalities with advertising, marketing, and other communication specializations. Together these specializations offer a world of opportunity for the talented public relations writer.

The Major Players

Burson-Marsteller	Ketchum
Edelman	Ogilvy PR Worldwide
Fleishman-Hillard	Porter-Novelli International
GCI Group	Universal McCann
Hill and Knowlton	Weber Shandwick Worldwide
Incepta Group	

You will find this a relatively stable list but their revenues, clients, rankings, and affiliations (in the form of mergers and acquisitions) all change with the economy and as new business opportunities emerge. There are also hundreds, perhaps thousands, of smaller international, regional, and local public relations agencies as well as individual practitioners. You may find your public relations niche at any of these levels and with any of the above specializations.

Interest Groups

The Public Relations Coalition is a partnership of major organizations with public relations interests. The following list shows some of the many Public Relations Coalition organizations whose members have public relations as a common interest:

Arthur W. Page Society
Conference Board Council on Communications Strategy
Corporate Communication Institute at Fairleigh Dickinson University
Council of Communication Management
Council of Public Relations Firms
Global Public Affairs Institute
Hispanic Public Relations Association
Institute for Public Relations
International Association of Business Communicators (IABC)
International Public Relations Association (IPRA)
National Black Public Relations Society
National Investor Relations Institute
National School Public Relations Association (NSPRA)
Public Affairs Council
Public Relations Society of America (PRSA)
Women Executives in Public Relations (WEPR)

Finding Your Niche

For those seeking the challenge of joining the ranks of 21st-century public relations practitioners, the news is good. The Commission on Public Relations Education reported in 1999 that a lack of trained people to meet the expanding demand for public relations services and counsel might well be public relations' next crisis. The report called for graduates who are grounded in the liberal arts and sciences, prepared in theory and practice, and equipped with the writing, thinking, and analytical skills that will allow them to carry out their "fundamental responsibility of building understanding, credibility and trust between organizations and their publics" (Commission on Public Relations Education, 1999, p. 2).

Where you use these skills will vary considerably, as will what you write about. You might find your niche in public relations writing defined by the following:

- *The type of organization*—government, nonprofit, private enterprise, international agency
- *The organization's sector or interest*—health care, education, technology, entertainment or leisure, culture, finance, retail
- *The type of communication you will specialize in,* including both the segment of the industry and the type of product/s you may be responsible for:

> *Broadcast media*—public service announcements, video news releases, media satellite tours
>
> *Print media*—news releases, annual reports, newsletters, marketing materials
>
> *Internet communications*—web page design, e-mail/newsgroup announcements, newsgroup monitoring, web newsletters
>
> *Events*—display design, speechwriting, collateral materials
>
> *Publicity*—obtaining media coverage
>
> *Advertising*—paid advertising placements to promote an image or argue a position on an issue

Exhibit 1.1 shows the sectors in which PRSA members were employed in 1997 (Public Relations Society of America, 1997). Although a new survey had not been published at the time this text was published, there is little reason to think that the 1997 data is not still valid. It is reasonable to believe that most PRSA members still work in corporations or public relations firms, and that human services sectors such as health care and education are a growing area for public relations. After all, the competition for funding is more intense as tax-supported agencies face budget cuts and closer examination of exactly how they use their funds.

Theoretical Foundations of Public Relations Writing

Public relations may still be defining its roles, relationships, and disciplinary bases, but that does not mean it does not draw on a solid foundation of theory. Indeed, the multitude of theories on which it can draw is one of its strengths.

EXHIBIT 1.1	Public Relations Society of America (PRSA) professional, compensation, and demographic statistics based on a PRSA survey.

*Demographics of Public Relations
Society of America members (in percentages)[a]*

Where they work

Corporations	29
Public relations firms and agencies	28
Health/welfare	10
Education	9
Trade/professional associations	7
Government/military	6
Sole practitioner	4
Not-for-profit	3
Advertising agencies	2
Miscellaneous	2

What they earn per year

< $45,000	32
$45,000 to $75,000	43
> $75,000	25

Who they are

Male	40
Female	60

Source: Reproduced with permission of the Public Relations Society of America.
a. Total membership as of January 1, 1997, was 17,626.

Public relations in general and public relations writing in particular are well grounded in rhetorical, communication, organizational, and behavior and attitude change theory. In itself, the range of applicable theories demonstrates the wonderfully cross-disciplinary nature of the profession. In particular, we suggest that systems theory provides the overview and rationale for public relations and public relations writing and that persuasion theories provide the basis for effective communication on behalf of your employer.

Systems Theory: Looking at the "Big Picture"

The Significance of Relationships

The underpinning theory for understanding the relationships between organizations and their publics is systems theory. Using living organisms as the analogy, systems theory takes as its basis the need for organisms to connect to and monitor resources in their environments. Organisms must be able to take in air, water, and nutrients or they will die. They must be able to monitor their environments to locate these essentials and to identify threats such as predators and temperature changes. They must also be able to respond to such changes.

As with organisms, so is it with organizations. Every organization has multiple publics or groups of people who share a common interest in the organization. Just as organisms need positive relationships with the systems that can affect their survival, so the organization needs positive relationships with its relevant publics, each of which has its own views of how the organization should behave. Ultimately, the health of the organization depends on the strength and nature of the relationships it has with its publics, both internal and external.

The most basic definition of public relations comes simply from inverting the term. Public relations is relations with publics.

Public relations writers operate as links in a system. They link organizations to external systems such as their industry sectors, government(s), the news media, and stakeholders and to internal systems such as their employees and research, personnel, and legal offices. In turn, they also link these systems back to the organization. The health of the organization depends on the practitioner's ability to develop and maintain relationships with all of these systems, and more.

Public relations writers initiate, develop, and sustain such relationships through the power of language (and design). Systems thinking and professionalism both require us to monitor the environment and the effects of our messages. This means that our relationships with publics should be two-way rather than one-way. We should spend as much time listening and questioning as we do designing and disseminating messages.

The systems concept of interconnectedness means that a shift in one set of relationships can have a major impact on other relationships. For example, the unwillingness of legal counsel to immediately clear a news release may result in a story not reaching the media in time to make the evening broadcast and the organization losing an opportunity to respond effectively to a crisis. This is an example of an internal system component affecting a much larger external system. And, as any politician knows, even the most carefully crafted message aimed at strengthening relationships with one public may have the unintended effect of alienating another public. Any proposal to change tax rates, for example, meets with approval from one public and disapproval from another.

Systems theory also proposes that there is more than one way to achieve a result. Just as organisms meet the great goal of survival by adopting different survival strategies, so also do public relations writers find alternate ways of communicating with publics. The writers have the option (and indeed obligation) to consider outcomes, ethics, time, and budget in deciding what combination of research, messages, and communication methods will most effectively develop relationships with particular publics.

It is the challenge of public relations writers to find both the communication strategy and the communication content that will initiate, nurture, or sustain relationships with key publics. To do this, the writers move between theory and practice and between macro-level analysis of relationships and micro-level word-by-word thinking about message design. For any given public relations problem, the writers will consider the organization and how it is perceived, the message design and methods of communication that will effectively reach multiple internal and external publics, and the desired message outcomes. All of this takes place within the context of the organization's broad social, economic, and political environment.

Exhibit 1.2 shows these considerations as a writing "preflight" checklist of factors to consider when applying writing to relationship building. It is similar in concept to a classic model of communication developed by Claude Shannon and Warren Weaver (1949). The model is, of course, simplistically linear; public relations thinking in practice means recognizing that all these components of communication interact with each other simultaneously within the broad social context we referred to earlier.

The Nature and Quality of Relationships

Each communication decision you make implies a decision about the nature of the relationships you are trying to establish, improve, or maintain. As Grunig and Hunt (1984) have suggested, relationships may represent a wide range of

| EXHIBIT 1.2   **Communication issues suggested by the Shannon-Weaver (1949) model.** | | | | |

Direction of communication to publics ⟶

⟵ Direction of planning and of feedback from publics

Source	Message	Channel	Receiver	Outcome
Spokesperson	Logic	Best message exposure	Psychographic	Knowledge
Expertise	Emotion	Purpose of message	Demographic	Attitude
Charisma	Appeals	Inform	Interest level	Behavior
Sincerity	Timing	Demonstrate	Education level	
	Readability	Persuade	Active or passive seeker of information	
	Memorability	Detail		
	Length	Does message need to be retained?	Knowledge	
	Balance	Time-frame (when)	Attitude	
	Detail	Cost	Behavior	

attitudes toward truth and participation. At one extreme is "press agentry" (one-way propagandistic communication with scant regard for the truth). At the other are full two-way, symmetrical relationships. They are founded on mutual understanding in which key publics are regarded as partners capable of providing valuable input that will help the organization. Between these two extremes lie the "public information" mode based on journalistic principles and the "two-way, asymmetric mode."

While the Grunig and Hunt analysis reflects an historical perspective, it also reflects the quality or ethics of relationships, and therefore has implications for public relations writers. Exhibit 1.3 summarizes these perspectives.

Persuasion Theories and Their Implications

If systems theory suggests the importance and the nature of an organization's relationships with its publics, then persuasion theories suggest the importance of understanding how people think and behave. In turn this provides the basis for how to apply language to fostering relationships on behalf of your client. The rest of this chapter looks at the second theoretical foundation of public relations writing—persuasion. More specifically, it looks at theories of attitude and behavior change.

With systems theory as our reference, it is clear that the aim of virtually all public relations communications is to manage relationships with publics in the organization's environment. The purpose is to secure positive behavior toward the organization and/or its causes. You might, for example, want the public to support,

EXHIBIT 1.3   Grunig and Hunt (1984) model applied to public relations writing issues.

Model	View of publics	Writing and ethical implications	Desired outcomes
Press agentry/publicity	Publics as targets of one-way hyperbole, and perhaps questionable truths	Persuasive. Write what works regardless of the ethics of process or outcome.	Behavior, e.g., voting, purchasing
Public information mode	Publics as consumers of information	Convey the facts honestly. Professional journalism standards.	Informed publics
Two-way/asymmetrical communication	Publics as targets of persuasion based on truth and accuracy	Persuasive/informative. Use what you know about your publics to shape organizational communication policy, content, and style.	Publics aligned behaviorally and/ or attitudinally with employer
Two way/symmetrical communication	Publics as partners in dialogue to mutual benefit	Persuasive/informative. Adapt writing to meet needs of both employer and publics.	Behavior and attitudes of both employer and client aligned for mutual benefit

buy, give money, stay in school, volunteer, vote, switch brands, or stop smoking, to name but a few possible outcomes.

Even damage-control messages written in response to a crisis have the underlying purpose of restoring public confidence in the organization so that it can proceed successfully with its operations. In the case of groups that oppose the organization, simply persuading them against active opposition may be a positive result. No wonder the ability to write a persuasive message ranks so high among the skills employers look for in the writers they hire (Treadwell & Treadwell, 1999).

In the following sections, we introduce some persuasion history and theories about persuasion that will help you understand public relations writing.

Centuries of Persuasion

Most likely, we can date public relations writing and its criticisms back to the first evocative message carved on a wall—and to the cave-critic who thought she could do better. We can date the first systematic study of persuasion to classical Greece, where the Sophists (tutors who trained others in the art of persuasive messages) were much in demand because persuading a jury of one's peers was integral to the judicial system of the 5th century B.C.E. This art of public speaking was referred to as rhetoric. Aristotle viewed rhetoric as a system of logic by which the truth of a situation might be approached. He developed three persuasive approaches still in use today: *ethos, pathos,* and *logos.* Ethos—the expression of character in discourse—is an appeal to credibility or authority, pathos is an appeal to the emotions, and logos is the appeal of a logically developed argument.

Roman rhetoricians including Cicero and Quintilian considered rhetoric an important component of citizenship and governance. The character of the speaker was important to credibility and effectiveness. They believed that public speakers should have a subject matter mastery as well as strong moral character. The ideal orator was a "good man speaking well." To cultivate and maintain their public images, Roman emperors used what we might now think of as public relations techniques—including the minting and distribution of coins with the emperor's likeness.

The communication techniques associated with the rise of Christianity may help to account for its widespread ability to persuade people to join its ranks. The early Christian church used symbols (e.g., cross and fish) that were easy to reproduce and identify. The church also used storytelling, metaphors, and analogies to help people understand a new and perhaps difficult theology.

And certainly the American colonists made use of what we now recognize as public relations techniques—slogans, symbols, demonstrations/events, and the colonial press—to convey the message of independence from England. The term "Boston Massacre" illustrates the "labeling" technique that public relations pioneer Edward Bernays called "semantic tyranny." Semantic tyranny is based on the idea that events cannot help but get a name. Whoever names (or labels) an event exercises some control over the long-term perception of that event. In this case, although the death toll was only five, the label "massacre" clearly evokes sympathy for those massacred and antipathy toward those who massacred them. It is interesting to speculate how His Britannic Majesty's representatives in the colonies might have labeled the Boston Massacre for home consumption had they had a public relations bent. The words *skirmish* and *police action* come to mind.

The technique of semantic tyranny is still widely used as government agencies, corporations, and individuals seek the appropriate label for events. Government agencies and the military especially have gained some reputation for the technique, often referred to as "bureaucratese." Without the aid of government spin-doctors, would "collateral damages" have come to mean civilian casualties, or "productivity enhancements" to mean "firing people"?

This continues today. The *New York Times Magazine* devotes a weekly column (William Safire's "On Language") to unraveling the rise and fall of words and phrases in common usage and their misappropriation. In the late 1990s, Securities and Exchange Commission (SEC) chairman Arthur Levitt campaigned against the complex words and sentences commonly found in corporate financial reports—a sin he referred to as "gobbledygook."

From the Sophists to the SEC, the debate continues over the role, ethics, and efficacy of language in moving segments of society to a specific attitude or behavior. The debate raises as many questions as it answers, as the following discussion questions suggest.

DISCUSSION   1

Is persuasive communication merely the application of shallow appeals to move popular sentiment, an essential component of democratic society, or a mechanism by which society ultimately arrives at agreed truths? Why?

Whose needs take priority for public relations writers: their audiences or their employer? Or do they act in the public good?

Do public relations writers need a mastery of communication techniques only, or do they also need a solid mastery of their subject?

When, if ever, do communication means justify the ends?

To what extent should moral character and standards be a prerequisite for public relations practitioners?

Whereas critics may cite consumer advertising and public relations as examples of all that's wrong with persuasive communication, the reasonable responses are that, in a democratic society, organizations, causes, and individuals are entitled to a voice and that promoting and that debating positions in the court of public opinion are how, ultimately, we arrive at consensus. In some respects, this is the position of the Greek rhetoricians, who argued that truth may be understood by rhetoric, the exchange of well-argued ideas.

As a professional wordsmith, the public relations writer continues a long history of advocacy and of contributing directly or indirectly to the democratic process. The PRSA Code of Ethics positions public relations as serving the public good. It sees public relations as building relationships rather than as one-sided propaganda.

The following sections look at some theories related to behavioral and attitudinal change and show how they influence the public relations writer's thinking.

Theories of Behavior and Attitude Change

Theories of behavior and attitude change suggest the influences in people's decisions to act on a message. In this section, we discuss some models of persuasion and finish with a discussion of their implications for persuasive writing.

Fishbein: Theory of reasoned action

Bandura: Social learning theory

Petty and Cacioppo: Elaboration likelihood

Festinger: Cognitive dissonance

Katz, Blumler, and others: Uses and gratifications

Witte: Extended parallel process model

McGuire: P-A-C-Y-R-A persuasion process

Theory of Reasoned Action (Fishbein)

Martin Fishbein's theory of reasoned action (see, e.g., Bowman & Fishbein, 1978) proposes that an intention to behave results from the person's attitudes toward the behavior and toward the social norms related to it (e.g., Is it a good thing to do *and* will my friends think it's cool?). Think of the peer approval that is so often used as the basis for advertising consumer products.

> *Interpretation: The Fishbein model suggests that to be persuasive writers, we need to identify and consider not only people's attitudes toward the behavior or action itself, we also need to understand their beliefs and social influences and the strengths of those beliefs and influences. People can share beliefs but have different evaluations of those beliefs. For example, two people may both believe that an organization is environmentally responsible, but one may find this very important and the other may rate it as irrelevant.*

Social Learning Theory (Bandura)

Albert Bandura's social learning theory (1986) adds two important ideas to our persuasion tool kit. The first is that people learn from their observation of others. For example, the social behavior of people who are heavy television viewers may be based on the social behaviors that they see modeled on television. The second notion is *self-efficacy* or the belief in one's own ability to carry out a particular behavior.

> *Interpretation: The Fishbein model suggests that an individual might, say, quit smoking if she believes that it would be good for her future and that people important to her would approve of her doing this. Bandura adds to this the idea that she must also have confidence in her ability to quit before that behavior will happen.*
>
> *Bandura's work suggests to us as writers that, first, we must show or model the behaviors that we are trying to get others to adopt and, second, we must convince readers and listeners that they have the ability to adopt these behaviors.*

You can often see the application of these ideas in advertising. Ads for new foods show people looking in the dairy case of a supermarket because this is a behavior they must adopt in order to find the product. Ads showing everyday "you and I" characters announcing that "they did it and you can do it too" boost the confidence of the audience toward trying out a new product or behavior.

Elaboration Likelihood (Petty and Cacioppo)

Petty and Cacioppo's theory of elaboration likelihood (1986) addresses the important idea that audiences do not process all messages equally; rather, they see some as more relevant and engaging than others. Messages that require critical analysis or elaboration are processed through what Petty and Cacioppo call the "central route." Messages that are less relevant and do not get full elaboration or analysis are processed through the "peripheral route."

The central route implies careful processing of the message argument. The peripheral route implies less attention to the message and more to influences from peripheral or environmental factors such as the reputation of the source or the views of significant others. The route taken is a function of one's ability and motivation to be critical of content and argument.

> *Interpretation: The implications for writing are that publics you know to be motivated to read your messages and that have the ability to analyze them critically require messages that focus on content, logic, and argument. Publics that are less motivated or that have less ability to analyze arguments can be reached more successfully by using peripheral cues. Metaphors, analogies, and human interest stories may be more effective than "just the facts."*

Cognitive Dissonance (Festinger)

Festinger's theory of cognitive dissonance (1957) belongs with a set of theories called balance theories, which attempt to explain how people deal with information that is conflicting for them. Dissonance is a common occurrence for most of us, and balance theories suggest that we work to reduce it. For example, two equally important research papers due on the same day compete for your attention; that digital camera you were going to buy now has a more attractive—and more expensive—competitor; there is a party tonight and a tutoring session for a test—each with its rewards. In each of these cases, how will you make—and rationalize—your decision?

Cognitive dissonance theory is also helpful in understanding people's responses to persuasive writing. Festinger argues that any two perceptions held by an individual will have one of three possible relationships: irrelevance, consonance, or dissonance. Persuasive communications first must be relevant, or you will ignore them as irrelevant. Assuming they are relevant, you will see the messages as consonant if they provide information and arguments that you agree with or as dissonant if they do not.

Generally, we try to reduce dissonance. Although you may do so by changing your behavior or attitude in the direction of the message, many other things can also happen that will have the same effect. You may avoid the information. You may seek information consonant with your own position. Or you may reduce the importance of the overall issue by derogating the message or its source or by distorting the message so it aligns with your beliefs. For example, you may rationalize your decision to prefer the party over the tutoring session by deciding that you deserve a break from all the hard studying you have been doing or that you will do better on your tests if you are relaxed, or perhaps by deciding that the test isn't really that important.

> *Interpretation: Cognitive dissonance suggests that people will work to avoid your messages if they conflict with their current beliefs. On the other hand, the astute public relations writer who can create a level of dissonance may lead readers to seek out new information about the writer's client and to shift their attitudes toward the client. Consider, for example, sales appeals for hybrid cars, which can be higher priced than their gas-powered*

equivalents. An appeal to fuel economy may have no impact on buyers who feel that they are entitled to spend their money as they please. However, an appeal based on reducing environmental pollution may create dissonance in buyers with an environmental conscience. They may then reduce the dissonance and the so-called buyer's remorse that follows by rationalizing that even though they paid more for a vehicle than they should have, they are making a contribution to a cleaner environment.

Uses and Gratifications (Katz, Blumler, and others)

The fact that people are active in how they use media is the foundation of what is called "uses and gratifications" research (Blumler & Katz, 1974). This approach posits that people are not simply passive consumers of media messages, but rather they are active and selective. They use media in different ways for entertainment, as a substitute for interpersonal relationships, as a source of information, or to compare their personal lifestyles and values to those of the perceived (media) world. The research reminds us that people do not just sit back and receive messages but actively process them according to their needs for information or entertainment.

> *Interpretation: A public relations writer therefore needs to understand not only theories of message construction but also how people use the information they receive. Surveys, focus groups, and interviews can provide answers to such questions with a view to strengthening our writing.*

Extended Parallel Process Model: Fear Versus Threat (Witte)

Many writers have to deal with lifestyle issues, and a conventional, often controversial, and frequently inappropriate tactic is to base persuasion on fear. Kim Witte's extended parallel process model (1992) suggests that we need to draw a distinction between fear and threat. Fear is an emotional response to a perceived threat when individuals believe that they have little control over what they can do. Threat is the thoughts one has about danger or harm. It is something people can deal with if they believe they have the ability to so. Like Bandura, Witte suggests self-efficacy or one's belief in one's own ability is a critical issue. Arousing fear as a reaction may be undesirable as people may avoid fear by deciding to ignore the problem.

> *Interpretation: Problems presented to people must be presented in such a way that people feel they are able to handle them.*

Persuasion Process (McGuire)

William McGuire (1989) has written extensively on persuasion. He proposes that, in the process of being persuaded, individuals go through six steps from first awareness to final behavioral response. These steps are presentation, attention, comprehension, yielding, retention, and action. There are practical implications for writing and design at each step.

Presentation. The target public must be exposed to your message at the optimum time and place if it is to see or hear the message. The presentation strategy must use relevant media or a combination of media that reaches the target public—perhaps direct mail, targeted advertising, or a personal visit to direct potential clients to the site. If your public consists of heavy readers, there is little point writing for broadcast media, and even though web pages may be a logical way of attracting clients, if the prospects do not have web access or are unfamiliar with the Web, the presentation is doomed before it starts.

Attention. Having targeted your audience by using appropriate media, you must grab the public's attention. It is the classic challenge of advertising. With all the direct mail coming into your mailbox every day, how does an organization make its message stand out above the others for you? Some of the answers for writers include the following:

Classic news determinants. Material that is timely, relevant, unusual, or proximate or that has human interest will appeal to people.

Structure and style. Intriguing leads, good use of metaphor, analogy, and human interest will attract and retain readers' attention.

Relevant vocabulary. Advertisers face a constant challenge of ensuring that *grunge, radical,* and *extreme* are relevant terms to the adolescent market at the same time as they research what the inevitable replacement terms are going to be.

"Power words." Words such as *success, love, power, money, fear, save,* and *approved,* among others, are power words. They have an inherent appeal that attracts attention and motivates action.

Design. Page layout, typography, and graphics help grab readers' attention and lead the reader through the message (see Chapter 7).

Comprehension. This does not occur merely because you have the reader's attention. To ensure comprehension, your writing must use the idioms and vernacular of the reader. Sometimes it must literally be in the language of the reader. More typically, comprehension means writing at the level of your reader or in the vocabulary of your reader. As a college student, you would expect graduate school materials to be written at your level of education, not below.

Comprehension does not mean writing to the lowest common denominator, "the cat sat on the mat" level. Rather, it means writing at an appropriate level for the audience. For example, medical and health personnel will find polysyllabic medical terminology entirely appropriate and accurate. It may require a trained medical communicator to write effectively for such a group. On the other hand, the same topic written for the general public will require "translating" the medical terms into common usage.

Yielding. This is the stage at which your persuasive writing skills are most tested. Your writing has no effect until people yield to your argument. This is where the theories in this chapter come into play. How can you use the public's values and beliefs, peer opinion, modeling, and notions of self-efficacy, for example, to shape a persuasive argument?

Retention. Readers must remember and implement persuasive messages on a continuing basis. A health maintenance organization (HMO) may launch an awareness campaign for a new telephone information line that is successful in the short term. But unless consumers internalize the phone number so that they dial it automatically when they need health information, the campaign may not be judged successful in the long term.

Action. Action is the ideal finale. Although we may not expect immediate action as a result of routine communications such as a news release, action is always the ultimate goal. As Bandura's (1986) theory reminds us, we may have to show specific behavior so people can emulate it.

> *Interpretation: The McGuire model suggests that we must select appropriate media and write attention-grabbing, persuasive, and memorable copy at an appropriate level. It suggests that all these stages of persuasion need to happen, in sequence. Persuasive appeals alone are insufficient. Instead, successful presentation and audience targeting are essential prerequisites without which the other stages cannot take effect.*
>
> *Each stage also requires a delicate balance between too much and too little emphasis. Spectacularly eye-catching graphics will grab attention but may detract from the message. The detail of a well-written argument may be persuasive but simply look too lengthy or boring as to deter the public from reading it. The successful writer gives equal attention to all phases of the persuasion process.*

Thinking About Message and Source

The public relations writer can control two aspects of writing in translating theory into practice. These are the source (who says it) and the message. A third aspect, message distribution, is dealt with chapter by chapter as we discuss print, broadcast, and electronic media.

Thinking About Source Credibility

Collectively, the above theories have less overt interest in the question of "who says?" than did the Greek and Roman rhetoricians. However, "Who says it?" remains an important question for public relations writers as they choose source or spokespersons for an organization's messages.

Research has identified three main components of source credibility: expertise, dynamism or charisma, and sincerity. No message can be effective if it is seen to come from a source that is not deemed credible. Audiences will be more receptive to speakers or authors who demonstrably know what they are talking about, who have appealing personal qualities, and who are sincere in their beliefs. Depending on your message, audience, and medium, you can choose sources for their expertise, charisma, sincerity, or all three.

For example, your university or college is seeking donors to fund the construction of a state-of-the art student center. From whom should the fundraising letter come—the president, head of student affairs, the president of the alumni association, a current student, VIP alum, or all of the above? The same issue applies, but with even more urgency during a crisis. Who can, and who should, speak on behalf of the organization? The issue is one of finding a source with the maximum credibility, and it is an issue you will deal with frequently and at many levels.

Aristotle's concept of ethos as character also has ethical implications. We alluded earlier in the chapter to product spokespersons whose character and credibility have "come undone" in the light of legal actions against them. Writers may need to go on an "ethics watch" to ensure that their organization speaks with an authentic, credible, and consistent voice.

Thinking About Message Development

Aristotle also wrote of two basic message concepts—pathos, or the appeal to emotions, and logos, or the logic or structure of messages. His writing foreshadowed much of contemporary thinking about message design.

Pathos: The appeal to emotions. The appeal to pathos or appeal to the emotions can be interpreted as an appeal based on finding a connection or emotional link to the audience. It can be seen as advertisers, direct mail specialists, and fundraisers seek the emotional appeal behind a product or cause that will have you respond to it. Your college or university, for example, will not base a development campaign for a new student center on the fact that it needs money. Of course it needs money. What emotional bond with your alma mater will persuade you to donate that money? Is it the sentimental appeal of good days with friends? The value you see in higher education? The potential embarrassment of knowing that yours is the only name missing from the donor list for your class? Or the competitive sense that the class of '05 can beat the class of '04 at fundraising?

Logos: The appeal to facts and logic. The concept of logos, logic, or the structure of argument addresses the idea that it is possible to build successful persuasive messages on evidence and logic alone. The structure of logical persuasion should always be clear and in itself logical. It should flow smoothly from beginning to end, from claim to proof to restatement of claim, question to answer, or premise to conclusion.

Press or broadcast editorials are good examples of the appeal of logic and the use of logical structure in a persuasive message. A typical editorial structure is to describe the writer's position, provide supporting evidence, raise the opposing point of view and then refute it, and then come back to recapitulate the writer's position—as the only logical solution, it is hoped. The classic news release, on the other hand, requires a structure that meets the logic of news editing; that is, the story should move from the most important to the least important items.

Imagine a lending agency trying to persuade you to repay your student loan. Aristotle provides useful options for developing effective messages. For example, the agency will have information at its fingertips to support an appeal to logic. Government regulations, repayment agreements, and repayment notices all validate the agency's "facts" about the benefits of prompt repayment and the penalties for not paying. Financial institutions will likely be able to recommend students "just like you" who are willing to testify to the benefits of repayment—and whom you will regard as credible sources. If facts and credible sources fail to convince you, the agency may resort to appeals based on your desire to further your education (you won't be able to get additional loans if you are in default) or your intent to purchase a house (and your need for a good credit rating). These appeals focus on your needs, and push your emotional "buttons."

Strategic Foundations of Public Relations Writing

As a writer, you have a responsibility to consider how your writing can best help establish, develop, and maintain positive and ethical relationships with your organization's publics. This implies a process in which communication is a deliberate strategy, informed by research and grounded in a solid theoretical foundation for what you are doing. It results from clear and careful planning, and the key elements of communication strategy—publics and outcomes—logically arise from the fundamentals of strategic planning:

Remember, of course, that your writing will always take place within the framework of the organization as a whole. Your employer will have objectives that generally relate to becoming bigger, better, or more efficient. Typically, and more specifically, such objectives may call for increasing enrollment, membership, or market share by a specific amount within a specific time frame. The organization should also be clear (at the management level) about why it wishes to communicate in the first place. Your role as a public relations counselor will include helping the organization define these purposes and the publics that relate to them. It is a good example of why public relations belongs on the management team.

Publics

Key among the elements of public relations thinking is the issue of publics. Systems theory and public relations thinking mean that automatically you are thinking about publics, determining the nature of the relationships you have with them, and assessing how the relationships might be improved or strengthened through communication.

Generically, you as a public relations writer have multiple publics starting with your employer and your employer's publics (of course). To the extent that you will use them to reach many other publics, the news media will also be one of your publics. Your challenge will be to balance the needs of these two latter publics as you meet the needs of your employer's publics.

Your Employer's Publics

Your primary concern will always be the publics with which your organization has, wants, or needs a relationship. These publics are the raison d'être of public relations practice and the focus of all of your efforts. You will begin by identifying and defining them and then develop strategies that will target them with messages aimed at initiating, sustaining, or changing their relationships with the organization.

A related issue will be organizing the publics into some sense of priority. Typically, you cannot deal with all of them simultaneously or equally, nor will you need to. While your college or university sees all its publics as equally vital to its health, at any given time some will be more important than others. Families and graduates take priority at commencement, faculty when academic policy changes are needed, all employees when a major restructuring takes place, news media when a campus emergency occurs, trustees and legislators when statutory changes affect the institution, and so on.

Prioritizing publics is a necessary part of effective public relations research and planning. See Chapter 5 for a discussion of ways in which you can look at these publics and prioritize them into manageable, identifiable segments.

Focusing on the knowledge, attitude, and behavior of your employer's publics will help you make decisions regarding appropriate media and messages. Knowing what your audience reads, for example, will help you choose styles that suit that public's reading level and use analogies and other stylistic devices to which the public will relate. Part of the reason why the *New York Times* and *USA Today* do not share a common readership is the different writing styles, that is, the grade level of the copy, the length of stories, the complexity of the leads, and, in some cases, the topics presented.

Understanding and prioritizing publics are also critical dimensions of managing your own resources. Few organizations have the time, money, and personnel to communicate regularly with all of their publics. But the fact is, they don't need to. Part of the art of public relations is knowing what relationships you need with various publics. This will help you determine when you should communicate with which publics to meet your organization's communication goals. You must understand which publics have priority both overall and in specific situations.

Your Employer

As you make decisions and execute strategies to communicate with your employer's publics, you will also have to deal with your employer as one of *your* publics. In fact, your employer may be the most challenging of all the audiences you write for.

To begin with, your employer pays your salary and justifiably expects that you will consider its needs first when determining communication strategy and tactics. What you write, how you write it, and how you distribute it will be driven by the organization's culture and vision of its relationship to its publics. You may also find yourself confronting management's attitude toward the media and messages you propose to use, even if these attitudes are not consistent with sound communication strategy.

It is a fact of public relations life that organizations often forget their goals when faced with the tantalizing prospect of "making the six o'clock news." They assume that having a public relations writer on staff means that they can expect to see the organization's name in the media frequently. This may be publicity, but it is not public relations. Such employers act as if "PR" stands for press release rather than public relations. On the other hand, we recognize the propensity of editors to view releases from public relations sources as suspect based on a stereotypical misconception that such stories are the product of devious "spin doctors" who engineer pseudo-events to generate false publicity that would not exist had not these public relations types masterminded the whole thing in the first place.

Given these two positions, the public relations writer frequently has to reconcile an employer's insistence on promoting the company name against the media perspective that the name itself is not news; rather, the news is what the name did. Sometimes it is difficult to persuade a proud company president that leading a media release with the headline "XYZ Company president announces new product" is less likely to attract an editor's attention than "New product competes successfully on national market." Educating your employer about the media may be as much a part of your job as educating the media about your employer.

The News Media

If you need to reach large numbers of people quickly and inexpensively, the news media themselves will be publics for you. You will want to know and be able to interpret to your employer a sense of the mass media's values and requirements for accuracy, balance, and deadlines so that releases meet media needs as well as serve employer interests. Writers must also be able to interpret their employer's organization to the media, especially local media, in a way that is seen to be relevant to them. Developing good working relationships with the media will be a wise strategy for you personally as you learn what stories your local media will use—and why or why not.

Other forms of media—for example, newsletters, brochures, client mailers, and web sites—do not have external gatekeepers to pass judgment on your story before it reaches the reader, so these media are not in themselves a separate audience.

Outcomes

Knowing what you want to have happen as the result of your communication is as critical to your decision making as knowing whom you are communicating with; you need to understand the outcome you want from the message.

Broadly speaking, there are three possible outcomes of communication: knowledge or awareness (K), attitude change (A), and behavioral change (B). Many practitioners use the K-A-B typology of outcomes to decide the basic purpose of their writing. Be aware, however, that although knowledge, attitude, and behavior are interrelated, it is a mistake to assume that merely informing people will automatically lead to their being persuaded and changing their behavior.

The K-A-B options have the beauty of all being measurable. With pre- and post-surveys as the typical methodology, you can assess whether targeted audiences have changed their level of awareness, attitude, or behavior. With controlled experimental conditions of exposure to your message(s), you can even make a reasoned assessment of whether your communications can take credit for the change.

Grunig and Hunt (1984) have identified five outcomes that are more specific to the responsibilities of the public relations writer. They suggest that people can

- ✦ *Receive* the message.
- ✦ *Remember* the message.
- ✦ *Believe* the message.
- ✦ *Have an intent to act* on the message.
- ✦ *Act* on the message.

Obviously, these outcomes are listed in increasing order of difficulty for the public relations writer to achieve. You receive hundreds of advertising messages a day, but how many of those do you believe or act on? This is where the theories we have discussed above can maximize your chances of success. You may succeed in disseminating messages without a theoretical foundation, but having people act on them requires both a macro-level understanding of behavior and attitude change, planning, and the micro-level mastery of writing skills we introduce in Chapter 2.

Some rhetoricians suggest that the main outcomes of communication are to inform, to persuade, and to entertain. At a minimum, public relations writers hope to see their audiences informed; in the ideal, they hope to see them persuaded; but many forget the potential for entertainment. Public relations writing can attract with humor. Even the usually serious *New York Times* may accept a little light public relations humor around April 1st. Humor can lighten a heavy subject and may be the means to a more serious goal of persuasion.

Summary

Our tour of theory has taken us from considering the nature and purpose of organizations' relationships to their publics to thinking about how we respond to messages, and from the rhetoricians of another age to contemporary persuasion theory.

We can see that while miscommunication and misunderstandings can occur at any point in the persuasion process, theories provide guidance for anticipating and counteracting these problems. Message appeals based on building self-confidence, removing threat, appealing to human needs, providing role models, and suggesting peer or societal approval are all "classics." These theories, based on research, listening, and understanding people's needs and how they use information, predict a good probability of success. You will use them to your benefit.

One of the best techniques for the beginning writer is to emulate copy that has worked for your organization in the past. Many corporate announcements such as new appointments, promotions, and financial reports are formulaic; if the formula works, why not repeat it? At best, you should identify why it worked (or didn't) so you can apply (or avoid) the same principles in your writing.

At some point, you will move beyond the routine and formulaic and will need to develop a sense of what comprises an effective message. This is where your understanding of your audience and the theories of persuasion come to the fore. They will provide a basis for selecting and developing appeals that reach and persuade your audience.

Refer again to Exhibit 1.2, which illustrates the relationship of message and source to other components of public relations thinking, that is, communication methods and audience/public. The main components, along with the addition of "outcome," suggest a checklist for planning public relations writing. Note that the process of communication runs left to right while the process of planning runs right to left—that is, in planning, you start with the outcomes you want and work back through the steps. Starting with a thorough knowledge of your publics, you should be able to plan messages, communication methods, and spokespersons to maximize your chances of achieving knowledge, attitude change, or behavior change in your audience.

This information alone will not guarantee success, but it will greatly increase the likelihood that you will select a spokesperson (source), decide on an appeal and develop content (message), and choose a medium (channel) that will effectively influence the organization's relationship with its publics.

ON THE TEXTBOOK WEB SITE

✦ Go to www.sagepub.com/treadwell for web exercises, study hints, case studies, and additional examples appropriate to this chapter and chosen or developed to supplement the chapter content.

REFERENCES

American Association of Fundraising Counsel. (2003, June 23). *Charity holds its own in tough times* [Press release]. Retrieved February 11, 2004, from www.aafrc.org/press_releases/trustreleases/charityholds.html

Bandura, A. (1986). *Social foundations of thought and action.* Englewood Cliffs, NJ: Prentice Hall.

Blumler, J. G., & Katz, E. (Eds.). (1974). *The uses of mass communications: Current perspectives on gratifications research.* Beverly Hills, CA: Sage.

Bowman, C. H., & Fishbein, M. (1978). Understanding public reaction to energy proposals: An application of the Fishbein model. *Journal of Applied Psychology, 8*(4), 319–340.

Commission on Public Relations Education. (1999). *Public relations for the 21st century: A port of entry.* Retrieved June 14, 2004, from http://www.prsa.org/_Resources/resources/pre21.asp

Festinger, L. (1957). *A theory of cognitive dissonance.* Stanford, CA: Stanford University Press.

Grunig, J. E., & Hunt, T. (1984). *Managing public relations.* New York: Holt, Rinehart & Winston.

McGuire, W. J. (1989). Theoretical foundations of campaigns. In R. E. Rice & C. K. Atkin (Eds.), *Public communication campaigns* (pp. 43–66). Newbury Park, CA: Sage.

Petty, R. E., & Cacciopo, J. T. (1986). *Communication and persuasion: Central and peripheral routes to attitude change.* New York: Springer-Verlag.

Public Relations Society of America. (1997). *Member survey.* Retrieved January 5, 1998, from http://www.prsa.org/survey97.html

Shannon, C., & Weaver, W. (1949). *The mathematical theory of communication.* Urbana: University of Illinois Press.

Treadwell, D. F., & Treadwell, J. B. (1999). Employer expectations of newly-hired communication graduates. *Journal of the Association for Communication Administration, 28*(2), 87–99.

Witte, K. (1992). Putting fear back into fear appeals: The extended parallel process model. *Communication Monographs, 59,* 329–349.

RESOURCES

Public Relations Agencies

Burson-Marsteller .... www.bm.com

Edelman .... www.edelman.com

Fleishman-Hillard .... www.fleishman.com

GCI Group .... www.gcigroup.com

Hill and Knowlton .... www.hillandknowlton.com

Incepta Group .... www.incepta.com

Ketchum .... www.ketchum.com

Ogilvy PR Worldwide .... www.ogilvypr.com

Porter-Novelli International .... www.porternovelli.com

Universal McCann .... www.universalmccann.com

Weber Shandwick Worldwide .... www.webershandwick.com

Coalition Members

Arthur W. Page Society .... http://www.awpagesociety.com

Conference Board .... http://www.conferenceboard.org/pdf_free/councils/157.pdf
    Council on Communications Strategy

Corporate Communication Institute .... http://www.corporatecomm.org/
    at Fairleigh Dickinson University

Council of Communication Management .... http://www.ccmconnection.com/

Council of Public Relations Firms .... http://www.prfirms.org/

Global Public Affairs Institute .... http://www.gpai.org/

Hispanic Public Relations Association .... http://www.hprala.org/

Institute for Public Relations .... http://www.instituteforpr.com

International Association of Business .... http://www.iabc.com
    Communicators (IABC)

International Public Relations Association (IPRA) .... http://www.ipra.org

National Black Public Relations Society .... http://www.nbprs.org

National Investor Relations Institute .... http://www.niri.org

National School Public Relations Association (NSPRA) .... http://www.nspra.org

Public Affairs Council .... http://www.pac.org

Public Relations Coalition ...... http://www.awpagesociety.com/resources/pr_coalition.asp

Public Relations Society of America .... http://www.prsa.org

Women Executives in Public Relations (WEPR) .... http://www.wepr.org

Sending the Message

Writing for Style, Flow, and Credibility

KEY PRINCIPLES

1. **Every document has a public relations purpose.**

2. **Public relations writing links audience needs with organizational goals.**

3. **Credibility is a public relations writer's greatest ally.**

4. **Style and flow give public relations writing character and professionalism.**

5. **Parallel structure and transitions lead a reader through the text.**

6. **Public relations writing is fun.**

THE PRINCIPLES IN PRACTICE

Cover letters for job applications—the client is *you*.

In Chapter 1, we discussed the theories that underpin effective public relations writing. On a conceptual level, these theories help you understand what makes your publics "tick." On a practical level, they emphasize the importance of knowing the audiences you are writing for, the approaches that may help align their interests with those of your organization, and the need to select appropriate media and adapt your writing to those media.

In this chapter, we move from the macro to the micro, from an introduction to the foundation theories to an introduction to the foundation practices.

Where Does Public Relations Writing Originate?

Public relations writing has its roots in the goals and objectives of the organization, particularly its strategy for establishing and managing relationships with its publics.

Organizational Goals

In the hierarchy of organizational planning, your organization will have objectives that generally relate to becoming bigger, better, or more efficient at whatever the organization does. Ideally, public relations practitioners will be represented at management level and play a role in setting these objectives as well as in meeting them.

At management level, you will identify publics and advocate for those publics when appropriate. You will ensure that the organization's communication program supports its mission and objectives and meets ethical and professional standards. On a day-to-day level, you will develop and implement strategies based on the organization's goals. Your plans for individual projects will be part of the overall public relations plan that, in turn, will be part of the organization's strategic plan.

Publics

Your writing is always grounded in the relationships the organization has or wants to have with its publics. Your choices of media and content and timing will be based on the needs and values of your publics and of your organization. Generally speaking, knowledge is the key to effectiveness: The more you know about a public, the more certain you can be that your messages will reach that public. In Chapter 5, we discuss the many ways you can look at and learn about these publics.

"Whom are you writing to?" will be the first question you ask at the start of *every* writing project. It will be part of formal project planning (discussed in Chapter 8) and something you should ask yourself even if you do not produce a written plan.

Thinking About Writing: Style and Flow

Public relations writing always has an agenda. Its aim is always to inform, persuade, or influence behavior. This is why we included theories of persuasion in Chapter 1. The public relations writer shapes words (and sometimes graphics) to achieve these aims.

The first test of good public relations copy is if it can easily be read, heard, and understood. Few pieces of writing will persuade anyone to do anything if the reader leaves them on the shelf, tosses them into the wastebasket, changes stations, or exits the web page. You don't want your carefully crafted résumé ending up in the "thanks, but no thanks" pile, or your employer's annual report relegated unread to the ubiquitous "circular file."

How, then, do you write copy that will achieve your persuasive aim? The answer returns to the issue of your audience. You must write *to* your publics, using the grammar and sentence structures that they use, choosing words that they understand and that are appropriate to your message, and writing in a style that suits both the public and your choice of media.

The following sections discuss some of the basic principles that you should master to succeed in public relations writing (and indeed in most other writing). Although audiences vary greatly, the principles are sound for all types of professional writing.

Fundamentals of Style

What Is Style, and How Can You Master It?

Of all the issues related to public relations writing, style is arguably the least definable, the most contentious, and the most likely to make your writing memorable. The word *style* has many meanings ranging from "unique" to "better than the rest" to "a particular way of doing things." Style helps signal to the reader what the communication is about and why it should be attended to. It defines the character of the organization or individual behind the communication. Style reinforces the seriousness of a strategic business proposal or alternatively the warmth of an article about the organization's new family health initiative.

More important, style is the way you establish a relationship with your audience, using the words, phrasing, sentence structures, and sometimes idioms that they understand and find credible. This is *not* a license to forget the rules of grammar and syntax you have learned since starting school. They are still valid, and following them is the mark of a professional writer. Rather, public relations style encourages you to think beyond the rules to type, layout, and graphic treatments that will help make your communication clear, effective, and memorable. It frees you to use stylistic devices such as headings and bullet points that are discouraged in much academic writing.

You should recognize that in breaking the rules, you will enter the ongoing debate between grammar purists and pragmatists. On one hand, as shown by the frequent letters to the editor decrying a reporter's misuse of punctuation or capitalization, there exists a core of people to whom traditional rules of sentence structure, grammar, and punctuation are little short of sacred. Anything less than perfection is viewed as a reflection on the writer's education and the loose standards of the publication that published the article.

On the other hand, there are pragmatists who argue that writing and speech should always reflect the current practice of social communication and give priority to meeting audience needs. Idioms and slang enrich the writing and make it more colorful as well as more intelligible to readers and listeners.

By and large, 21st-century public relations writers (and most writers for the general public) adopt a middle ground. They generally adhere to tried-and-true rules of grammar, but they feel free to break them when necessary to reflect changing societal usages and conventions, and *always* as the result of a deliberate, strategic decision. Rightly or wrongly, the concern of public relations writers is effective communication rather than grammatical perfection. They assume that style must suit the needs of their defined publics.

This applies to all your writing, from the cover letter you send with a résumé to the annual report you produce for shareholders of a public company. No matter how good it looks or sounds, if the writing style does not suit the audience, it is likely that the readers/viewers/listeners will tune out. When they do, your opportunity to inform, persuade, or affect their attitude or behavior is gone.

House Style

Apart from general styles and the styles peculiar to the media or specific documents are the style issues internal to every organization. Insofar as it reflects an organization's hard-earned (and possibly expensive) image, this is the style that will most affect your writing. It should be consistent across the many types of writing you and others do for the organization, from employee newsletters, brochures, and advertising copy to position papers, annual reports, and, of course, media releases.

An organization's accepted style is usually referred to as its "house style." It is likely that you will learn about your employer's house style from the writing done by your predecessors and through internal style manuals. In small organizations, house style is often passed down from public relations writer to public relations writer and includes little more than how the president wants her name presented and whether you must spell out the full company name or whether you can refer to it by initials alone.

While you might never use the first name of Dr. J. G. McLeod, chief executive officer (CEO) of a large hospital, the young entrepreneur who heads a start-up Internet company may be uncomfortable having you refer to her as "Ms." Even the issue of whether to use abbreviations reflects the culture of the organization and is a way in which writing style reflects this culture. These may seem like minor issues, but they are likely to cause significant management wrath if they are not defined and used consistently. In cases where there has been a merger or a legal action regarding the company name, there may be contractual and legal implications in ensuring everyone uses the name, logos, and symbols correctly.

As organizations grow, it is likely that they will develop a written style manual, often quite lengthy and technical, to which all members of the organization must adhere. You may well find yourself developing, revising, and promoting such a manual. Defining a house style ensures that everyone in the organization knows how to present information consistently and that all documents, including those designed for the Web, share a common, professional, identifiable image. It may land you willingly in the role of educator, teaching your fellow employees about the importance and methods of using a common style, and less willingly in the role of style-monitor, ensuring that the house style is used universally.

House style manuals routinely address the use of the company name and registered logos, trademarks, and servicemarks as well as "rules" for capitalization, color, typefaces, and even paper selection. The LEGO® Company information sheet discussed in Chapter 6 is distributed as part of the company's press kit so that the media know how to use the corporation's many registered names. Typically, house style manuals also set standards for using graphics and logos on stationery, advertising, vehicles, and signage and web applications.

E X E R C I S E   1

Find out if your college or university has a style manual. What topics does it cover? How is it distributed to all personnel who might need it? What evidence can you find that the style manual is used? What evidence can you find that it is not used?

Industry Style

Many industries or disciplines, such as the American Medical Association (AMA), have common styles that govern (especially) publishing in that discipline. You may be familiar with the American Psychological Association (APA) style manual, which covers writing in all social science disciplines (including this text). If you are writing for professional publications in a particular field, you should be aware of the publishing guidelines for that field. It is easier to write in an acceptable style from the beginning than to adjust style later to meet the requirements of a publication or publisher.

Successful public relations writers also have a good understanding of the styles prevalent in the public relations and communication industries in general. Start a file or box of public relations clippings and samples that you like (or don't like). Most professionals maintain such a file (called a resource file or more casually a "swipe file") throughout their careers and refer to it for inspiration (not for plagiarizing). They also refer to it for guidance on how other organizations handled a situation and the styles they adopt in various situations.

Media Style

When you are writing for the press or broadcast, you will also be subject to media style. The media have conventions for formatting, length, structure, and, in the case of broadcast, punctuation and spelling that you should follow to maximize the likelihood that your release will be printed or broadcast. See Chapters 9 and 11 for detailed discussion of these conventions and how to use them to your public relations advantage.

With regard to the debate between "rules" and "style," media generally adopt a middle ground that errs on the side of the rules. But be aware that all media do not necessarily adopt the same middle ground; each newspaper, magazine, and radio or television station has its own standards of style. The most a public relations writer can do is to learn the styles of the media to which you most commonly send releases or pitch stories. Learning these styles should be part of developing a profile of the media you work with.

Personal Style

Even while focusing on your audience and following the conventions of your organization and the media, you will develop your own writing style. It will likely reflect the types of writing that you enjoy, find challenging, and indeed succeed at. Some writers thrive on producing light, humor-filled copy; others cannot write humor to save their lives. Some specialize in narratives, others in clear technical information and facts. Some write easily for broadcast media, others for print, or advertising or for reports or grant proposals.

Part of your aim in this course should be to test a range of writing styles for a range of purposes. We hope you will find one or more that enthuses you or sparks a career interest.

Style Decisions: Writing for Credibility

Why spend so much time on the issues of style? Because style influences credibility, which is key to effective communication. Little has changed since Aristotle chose ethos (the appeal to a speaker's character) as the most significant of his three persuasive appeals. We still believe those we trust, and we trust those we find credible.

Most public relations writing decisions are based on securing an organization's credibility so that target publics see its messages as truthful, reliable, and believable. What will make a message credible to your target public? The level of detail, readability, word choice, sentence and paragraph structure, logic, and appeals can all work for or against the credibility of a message. Your task as a public relations writing student is to learn to use them to your advantage.

Detail

Credibility often comes from a level of detail that is relevant to your audience. While ponderous technical detail will turn off most readers or listeners, it may sometimes be required, as for example, by SEC requirements for financial reporting. Human interest detail that colors a feature piece may be essential to the article's success.

The level of detail you offer by way of drawing conclusions for the audience should relate to the level of education of the audience. A relatively uninformed audience may need conclusions spelled out for them. On the other hand, highly informed audiences may be able and want to form their own conclusions. Indeed, there is some evidence that the psychological investment of doing so will improve their recall of the message.

The level of detail you can or should provide also relates to the audience's interest in your message or your organization. Purchasing agents who are looking for your employer's product or services may want, and be willing to read, a lengthy proposal with detailed specifications and processes. On the other hand, casual prospects will be satisfied with just a brief overview or fact sheet. And you may be content to just put a company's name and business in front of people who are, for now, satisfied with their current supplier or servicer.

Readability

Credibility is closely bound to readability (or, for electronic media, "understandability"). Readers/viewers/listeners/users who cannot understand your message will probably fail to act as you wish. As important, they may come to believe that your organization does not care enough about them to ensure that messages are shaped with them in mind. This is a message you surely do *not* want to send.

In practice, the level of writing is generally equated with the educational level of the reader. Formulae such as the Flesch readability scores give an unbiased sense of what grade level would understand the copy. Generally, such scales use word length, sentence length, and sentence structure for their assessments; long sentences with multisyllabic words equate to a higher level of readability. You can often make copy more readable just by making long sentences shorter, by dividing them into two or more sentences, or by editing them to take out the unnecessary words.

Most word processing programs have checks to help you assess the reading level of your copy. It is always a good idea to use these checks to ensure that your copy is written at the level your audience can understand. We discuss the issue of readability scales in more detail in Appendix A.

Vocabulary

How do you determine what is an appropriate level of vocabulary? It will help to know how your audiences speak, write within your vocabulary limits, understand the importance of strong and active words, and learn to "hear" what you write.

Know How Your Audiences Speak

Generally, we are most comfortable with and find the greatest credibility in people who use our language. This is an important lesson for the public relations writer struggling to establish a relationship with one or more publics.

You can most confidently select vocabulary if you know how your audiences speak. What would they write if they were in your position? What words do they use? What is their general level of education? Do they understand terms from the art, industrial, scientific, math worlds? What about terms from the Internet world of e-mail, file swapping, and chat rooms? Or references to sports, sitcoms, cartoons, rock or jazz music?

The issue is not only finding the right word for the right audience in the way that *Scientific American* writes about insects and *Reader's Digest* about bugs. It is also that the same word can take on multiple meanings: For example, *mice* are rodents to a zoologist and computer-input devices to a computer programmer (who also has a unique, high-tech meaning for the term *bugs*).

Consider too the different readerships of William F. Buckley and Dave Barry and of *People Magazine* and *The New Yorker*. People return to the publications, programs, and web sites that have articles/pages on topics that interest them and that they can easily understand. What they will read may be an even greater issue on the Internet where publishers of online magazines are still testing the styles and articles that will attract and hold the attention of their readers (or should it be viewers? or users?).

Every occupational or demographic group has an expectation that it will be spoken to in its own language. Persuasive communicators especially face a constant challenge of using relevant jargon to establish "street cred" in the youth market. At the same time, they face the task of researching what the (inevitable) replacement phrases are going to be. But youth jargon is not the only jargon to consider. Plumbers, physicians, programmers, and other occupational or linguistic groups all have vocabulary that has special meaning to them and, as important, that positions you as an insider. Public relations writers are well advised to knowledgeably adopt such jargon if their writing is to be credible. And they must be prepared to change the jargon as they adapt the same message for multiple audiences.

Some words and phrases emerge out of hard work in a specific context, such as a presidential speech or movie script. Others emerge spontaneously from in-group shorthand developed by specific industries or disciplines. The software, human relations, and marketing disciplines as well as the sports and entertainment industries are responsible for many such terms. "Show me the money," baby boomers, proactive, empowerment, netspeak, and blogging are but a few that come to mind. More enter the world nearly every day.

Some phrases quickly infiltrate popular speech. Using them may initially mark the writer as knowledgeable and part of the group (i.e., credible). But such phrases have a natural life cycle and quickly move from current to passé. It may be better to avoid the terms than to be caught using last week's term, especially if your audience is teenagers, whose jargon changes as quickly as their clothing preferences.

Continuing debates over politically correct speech (see Appendix E) have their roots in the style used by particular publics with whom one misstep (or misusage) can have disastrous results. As a writer tasked with effective liaison between your organization and its publics, you must be sensitive to the language choices and patterns used by those publics. Anything less and you risk being seen as writing in a "foreign" or possibly offensive language.

Use Language *You* Understand

Big words are not always impressive, especially if you do not use them correctly. For example, we're still not sure what one job applicant had in mind when she wrote in her cover letter: "My proficiency, administrative/managerial skills and detailed acclimated are traits I have always valued and will continue to maintain." She went on to assure the reader that "this career-adapted company is what I have been searching for." We hope she found it, but to the company that received it, it was clear that she did not understand what she was writing.

As a writer, it is easy to hide behind big words and to make copy *sound* important even if you do not understand the subject. Unfortunately, this often leads to longer and longer sentences and weaker and weaker copy. In themselves these are certain giveaways that you are not comfortable with your subject or perhaps even that you do not understand it. And if you, as a writing professional, do not understand what you are writing, it is likely that many others will also not understand. (This also holds true in writing essays for academic classes.)

Note that crossword puzzles and similar word games are good exercises in learning about words.

Use the Correct Word, and Use Words Correctly

Using words correctly is a hallmark of a true professional. It is our experience that many novice writers do not appreciate the importance of correct word usage either for their organization or for their own credibility. When you use the wrong word or use a word incorrectly, you look silly. You call into question your own education, professionalism, and yes, credibility, not to mention that of your employer.

"I can't ever remember the difference between *affect* and *effect* (or *personnel* and *personal*, or *who's* and *whose*, etc.)" is an excuse we have heard often. Frankly, if you really want to be a public relations writer, it is time that you learned the difference. At a minimum, you should have a list of words that you have trouble with so that you can refer to it whenever you start to write them. Such words and their differences are as close as an online dictionary. Using words incorrectly in your application will cost you the interview; using them incorrectly in your employer's communications will cost you the job.

Appendix E includes many of the words that consistently trip up student writers, and there are many more. We suggest that you review this appendix carefully to ensure that you understand how to use all of them. We also suggest that a good dictionary and thesaurus should be well-thumbed parts of your writing arsenal.

Choose Active Words

Choosing active words is a basic premise for all writing because active words make your copy interesting and involve the reader in what you are doing/selling/promoting.

If you can involve the reader, you have gone halfway toward reaching your goal of informing, persuading, or influencing attitude or behavior. On a personal level, this is especially relevant to a résumé and cover letter.

Active words are "doing" words; they are immediate and important. In contrast, passive words are tentative and less interesting. It is the difference between playing in the game and being a spectator.

Generally, active words are verbs and verb forms that are *not* preceded by *is/are/were/have/has/had*. For example:

Passive	*Active*
The meeting *was attended* by all staff.	All staff *attended* the meeting.
The machine *is being run* by Sue.	Sue *runs* the machine.
I *was taught* grammar rules.	I *learned* grammar rules.

Passive structure often emphasizes the wrong part of the sentence. In the first two examples, the emphasis is on the meeting and the machine, neither of which did anything interesting, rather than on the staff and Sue, who did. The third example gives the impression that you let things happen to you (i.e., that someone taught you) rather than that you took an active a role in your (presumed) success. This will be personally important when writing job applications, in which you want to demonstrate what you can do,

Passive voice removes both information and people from a statement. You should prefer the active voice because it provides information and a "people presence" (e.g., "Sue," "he," or "staff") that make the statement more interesting.

Note that passive voice is sometimes public relations strategy for avoiding blame and responsibility—as happens with the stereotypical "mistakes were made" announcement. Such strategies not only have style, human interest, and news implications, they also have ethical implications.

Choose Strong Words. Closely related to the issue of active words is that of strong words and phrases. Seek words that clearly describe a situation or differentiate between or emphasize the most important points. This demands that you master the nuances of words and phrasing, which is a sign of a skilled professional. Consider, for example, the very different messages sent by the following descriptions of your involvement with a student group that helped clean up a local park after a storm.

I *helped* clean up Stanley Park after a storm.

I *worked with a group* that cleaned up Stanley Park after a storm.

I *led a group* that cleaned up Stanley Park after a storm.

I *directed a group* that cleaned up Stanley Park after a storm.

I *worked with a team* that cleaned up Stanley Park after a storm.

I *led a team* that cleaned up Stanley Park after a storm.

I *led a team of volunteers* that cleaned up Stanley Park after a storm.

DISCUSSION 1

What is the strength of "leading" versus "working with"? What are the different connotations of "leading" and "directing"? Why might prospective employers prefer to see that you worked with a team rather than a group? What does the fact that this was a volunteer team say about you? Why is even the least of these better than "Stanley Park was cleaned up after a storm"?

Although you should generally be wary of too many adjectives in professional writing, when used judiciously, they can help you differentiate your message from the ordinary or, perhaps, your competitors. For example, on a personal level do you "write copy," or do you "write clear, crisp copy"? As well as being alliterative (*look it up*), the adjectives *clear* and *crisp* demonstrate that you understand two important traits of good copywriting.

Choosing the strongest words requires that you understand what differentiates your organization from its competitors. Does your agency "operate in the health education field," or does it "promote positive health practices"? It is likely that thousands of organizations, some of which are only peripherally involved, could make the first claim. The second claim, however, sends the message that your organization is proactive and results oriented.

If necessary, read your copy aloud and see if the words engage your attention. If they do not, it is unlikely they will engage the attention of anyone less interested in them than you are. There are other examples in Appendix E.

Grammar

Like sentence structure and vocabulary, grammar is a function of education, culture, and medium. You can include or exclude readers, viewers, listeners, or users simply by your choice of tools, in this case, grammatical tools. Long sentences with many phrases or clauses are simply harder to understand than short, simple sentences. This is of special concern if you are writing for broadcast.

Choose grammar as carefully as you choose words. If you are writing a health bulletin with important, immediate news for a large population (e.g., an audience with many levels of education and reading abilities), stay with short sentences and simple words. The message must be understood by as many people as possible as quickly as possible. Alternatively, if you are writing a grant proposal that will be read by technical experts, it may be appropriate to use industry jargon and more complex sentence structures. And if you have the occasional luxury of writing an ad or promotional direct mail piece, you will seek colorful phrasing that will be memorable. Your choices depend on the medium and, of course, the audience.

Sentence Structure

Grammar, of course, involves correct sentence structure, which you have learned since grade school. Good sentence structure is a sign first of an educated writer and ultimately of a professional writer. As with using the correct word, it involves understanding the nuances of what you are writing.

Consider, for example, what a difference the word *only* makes depending on where it is added to the four-word sentence "I wrote the copy."

Only I wrote the copy .... No one else is to blame; I did it by myself.

I *only* wrote the copy .... Don't blame me; I didn't even see the photos.

I wrote *only* the copy .... The headline and captions are the editor's responsibility.

I wrote the *only* copy .... If you want copy, you'll have to use mine.

I wrote the copy *only* .... I did nothing else.

EXHIBIT 2.1	**Samples of excess words and their alternatives. Omitting the underscored words or choosing the concise phrase will make your writing easier to understand.**

Common examples of excess words

all of the different
an actual fact
another one
at the time when
by means of
close proximity
first of all, last of all
for the purpose of
hour of noon
in order to
intents and purposes
in the city of Auburn
seem to be
short space of time
somebody or other
small sized
together with

Wordy	Concise
at the present time	today or now
at which time	when
for the reason that	because
inasmuch as	because
in the event that	if
in the nature of	like
on the basis of	by
prior to	before
relinquished his position	resigned
utilize	use
with regard to	about
with the result that	so that

In particular, you should master the ability to write a variety of grammatical structures, including both simple and complex sentences, phrases and clauses, and the punctuation that goes with them. This will give your writing the variety needed to keep it fresh, interesting, and flowing smoothly.

Sentence construction and especially punctuation are complex issues. Few writers manage them perfectly without occasionally referring to a good grammar book. We suggest you always have one handy for easy reference, and we have suggested several classic options at the end of this chapter.

There are situations—such as writing to reach teens—in which writing colloquially may dictate some structural "looseness." But this is neither the norm nor a reason not to master the rules of good grammar. Writing colloquially should be a deliberate and occasional breaking of the rules, *not* an excuse for not learning them.

Sentence Length

There are few pieces of writing that will not benefit from a prudent editing, usually to express a thought more concisely and sometimes to clarify its meaning, and few readers who will not appreciate the editing effort. For example, there are 37 words in the previous sentence. The same thought could be expressed as "Readers appreciate the clear, concise ideas that result from careful editing"— only 11 words.

Excess Words

Using many words to express a simple thought is a common stylistic problem. Sometimes the extra words are just that—extra. The words *different* and *various* come to mind. For example, we often see "there are many *different* approaches to the problem" rather than "there are many approaches." Some extra words have no justification at all. *Unique,* for example, is an absolute; there is no such thing as "very unique." Look at your copy carefully to ensure that every word adds to the meaning.

Sometimes writers deliberately use extra words because they sound important. In such cases, substituting their humbler synonyms might please the busy reader. See Exhibit 2.1 for common examples in which you can either omit the excess words and leave the meaning intact or substitute one word for many.

Often extra words find their way into copy as writers struggle for content or flow. If the former, the excess words and the long paragraphs that result often signal that the writer is unsure of the facts or argument. He or she is trying too hard to persuade.

If the latter, the excess words may help lead the reader through the copy and may be assets rather than liabilities. Some extra words or phrases add color and subtle meaning even if they are grammatically unnecessary. An extreme but eloquent example is the opening line of Abraham Lincoln's "Gettysburg Address": "Four score and seven years ago, our fathers brought forth upon this continent. . . ." Would we remember it as well if it began, "Eighty-seven years ago, our ancestors founded a country . . ."? Your task is to choose judiciously and use extra words only for emphasis and strength.

E X E R C I S E   2

The following statements about web site design are confusing by virtue of too many words. Rewrite them to express the meaning as simply as possible. Do not try to do it all in one step. Working on them step-by-step will help you understand the language and structures you are working with.

Because you can archive the publications, your web site visitors can have access to all issues through a simple search long after they may have discarded any print versions.

Comment screens capture informal opinions and perhaps some demographic data from visitors. You should be aware, however, that people who respond to comment screens are unlikely to be representative of the overall visiting public.

Paragraph Length

Paragraph length goes hand in hand with sentence length, but with a difference. Paragraph length also plays a design role capable of having an important psychological effect on the reader. Think of the impression you have about documents just from their appearance. Compare, for example, an essay in which the first paragraph extends through two pages *(it happens)* with an average newspaper feature article. How does the solid page of type compare with the multiple paragraphs of the feature? Which seems easier on the eye? Would you actually read them both? (*Be honest.*) Except in formal academic writing (and perhaps even there), long paragraphs impede understanding at best and deter people from reading further at worst.

Arguably, we were all taught to start a new paragraph whenever we introduced a new idea and to write a strong topic sentence at the beginning of every paragraph. This is still true, but from a public relations point of view there is more to it. Topic sentences not only forecast the paragraph contents, but perhaps more important, they also act as bullet points for readers who want to scan the text. What this means for the public relations writer is that anything you want to emphasize should be in a lead or topic sentence.

A second case for short paragraphs is that readers are easily bored and often distracted. Because they have no inherent reason to read your copy, you must persuade them that you have something worth reading. Few of them will return to the beginning of a long paragraph to get the gist if they lose your train of thought. Points in the third quarter of a paragraph are likely to be missed. If the point is important, it should be in an important place.

What is a long paragraph? For most public relations writing, four- or five-sentence paragraphs are long enough; three may be better. For web sites, two inches of text are usually considered the maximum.

Overall Message Length

In most cases, there are practical limits on the length of copy. For example, news releases are typically no longer than a few paragraphs, and there is evidence that listeners tire of a speech after 20 minutes. Many experts recommend that copy destined for the Web should be presented in one-screen bites so that users do not have to scroll too much. They also suggest that it should be up to 40% shorter than the same copy written for other media.

For some formats, the length will be dictated by the medium. For a 20-second public service announcement (PSA), you must work to 20 seconds and accommodate information and argumentation to meet that time frame. Computer media such as CDs, flash drives, and DVDs may dictate the maximum length of a multimedia presentation.

A general guideline is that if you have provided all the facts a public needs, developed well-structured arguments, and paid attention to the needs and constraints of the medium, then the length will be appropriate.

The Fundamentals of Flow

What Is Flow, and Why Is It Important?

As a general rule, people do not like uncertainty. Just as they seek street signs and directional arrows to guide them on trips, so they seek markers to indicate where they are and what is to come in a communication. If style is the element that helps you relate to your reader, flow is the way you guide the reader or listener through the text. Flow is what makes readers comfortable with the document and surprised when they reach the end so quickly.

For you as a writer, flow is the quality that will increase the likelihood that your golden words will be read in full. Losing the flow interrupts the reader's engagement with your message. At that point, you risk losing his or her attention. The ability to write public relations copy that flows smoothly differentiates experienced writers from novices. It is a skill worth developing

Four key attributes of flow are rhythm, transitions, parallel structure, and headings.

Rhythm

Just as dancers follow the rhythm of music, so readers or listeners follow the rhythm of words. This is especially obvious in spoken copy, but it holds true as well in written text. You want the reader to "get into" the rhythm of your words.

Think about speeches that are regarded as classic: Lincoln's "Gettysburg Address," Martin Luther King, Jr.'s "I have a dream" speech, and John F. Kennedy's "Ask not what your country can do for you" speech, for example. They grab you immediately and the rhythm compels your attention. The rhythm draws you through the speech, never letting go.

Establishing rhythm involves using transitions and parallel structure to set up expectations of what is to come and then to make clear that you are meeting these expectations. It involves learning to "hear" what you write and to recognize when a phrase or sentence needs editing or restructuring to maintain the rhythm. Remember that once lost, it is as difficult to reestablish a rhythm in your copy as it is for dancers to recover after missing a beat.

Transitions

Transitions are textual cues. They relate copy to what has come before and they forecast what will follow. They establish relationships between words, sentences, paragraphs, or sections, and they help readers understand the points being made. Furthermore, they help readers become comfortable with the document. Acting as road signs, they help readers understand where you, the writer, are heading and make it easy for them to join you for the ride (or read).

Transitions between sections usually take the form of paragraphs. Transitions between paragraphs usually occur in the first sentence. And transitions between sentences usually occur near the beginning of the sentence.

Transitions are especially important in speechwriting, in which you do not have the benefit of graphic techniques such as headings to signal a change of subject or introduce a topic. See Exhibit 2.2 for a description of the "directions" you can achieve through the strategic use of transitions.

Parallel Structure

Parallel structure is central to professional writing. It is the way writers establish the relationship between two or more ideas. It subtly provides information the reader needs to understand the point, and it helps establish the rhythm of your writing.

Parallel structure ranges from matching the plurality of subjects, pronouns, and verbs to writing multiple phrases or clauses with the same subject/verb/object

---

EXHIBIT 2.2   The uses of transitions to provide guidance for the reader.

Transitions, the road signs of public relations writing

Function	Examples—Use these words and phrases
Forecast examples	to illustrate, for example
Indicate that what follows is a continuation of what has gone before	e.g., furthermore, in addition, another
Establish a cause-effect relationship	because, since, as a result
Indicate a sequence or time relationship	then, before, after, finally, previously
Signal a concession	although, even though, granted that
Introduce a comparison, i.e., that what follows will have elements in common with what has come before	in comparison, likewise, similarly
Introduce a contrast, i.e., that what follows will be new, different from, or opposite to what has come before	although, but, however, in contrast, on the other hand
Emphasize or reinforce a point	indeed, in fact, obviously, clearly
Signal that the author is restating a point	to summarize, in other words, in brief
Introduce consequences or conclusions	accordingly, as a result, therefore
Introduce a summary of the contents	in conclusion, summing up

form. It involves recognizing grammatical pairs, such as "not only/but also," and "either/or," and ensuring that you write both halves of the pair. As readers, when we see the word *either*, we recognize a choice and we expect that a second option will follow after the word *or*. If the writer fails to provide the second option, that is, fails to meet our expectation, then the flow of the idea will be broken and the communication interrupted.

Parallel structure is also at the heart of one of the public relations writer's best friends: the bullet point (see Exhibit 2.3). Bullet points are a way to summarize, to provide information quickly, to highlight important points, and to meet the needs of a general audience accustomed to sound bites and instant information. For bullet points to be effective, they must be parallel so the elements both stand out on their own and work together to make or support a central point. Every point in a bulleted list must flow smoothly from the heading or answer a question people might have about the topic.

Reading your copy aloud will help you identify parallel structure problems. Ideally, by reading it aloud you will settle into the rhythm of the words and it will be obvious when the rhythm (i.e., the parallel structure) has been broken. When a sentence doesn't make sense or when you begin to trip over a section, look closely to see if parallel structure is the problem. See Appendix E for a more detailed discussion of parallel structure.

EXHIBIT 2.3   Bullet point basics.

The Bullet Point: A Visual Sound Bite

There is a high probability that whatever you write will have a readership/"listenership" that is pressed for time and/or conditioned by the fast-paced, quick-answer, "pop-up video," sound-bite style of communication. Even if they are seeking the information, they want it *now* and they want it *fast*.

Bullet points are a common—and effective—technique for conveying information quickly and for attracting attention to important issues. When used well, they direct readers to the important points quickly and act as a road map through a document. They are a useful stylistic device for most media except perhaps, news writing.

Bullet Points as a Graphic Technique

Bullet points are a graphic technique in which phrases, sentences, or even paragraphs are made obvious by setting them apart from the margin-to-margin copy technically by bullets (●), but in practice by numbers, asterisks, diamonds, boxes (1,*,◆,■), or other graphic symbols. You may even use the organization's logo or special graphics as bullets to set apart sections that you want the reader to notice.

Bullet Points as a Writing Technique

For bullet points to be effective, they must meet the readers' implicit expectations that the information after the bullet is important and that it merits their special attention. This means that you must use bullet points well—and sparingly.

Implicitly, bullet points set off a list of words, phrases, sentences, or short paragraphs. Regardless of the length, the information after the bullets must be parallel in structure. They should follow from the heading, or "lead," in the way that the Beatitudes from the Bible each completes the phrase "Blessed are . . . ," to use a familiar example.

In the following chart see how each of the bullets follows from the opening phrase. In column 1, all of the bullets are qualities, each consisting of a modifier and noun. In column 2, each bullet begins with an active, past-tense verb to complete the phrase "During my college career, I. . . ." In column 3, each bullet is a noun phrase.

As evidence of the importance of this, consider what happens when they don't match, for example, "During my college career, I editor of campus newspaper" or "While at Central College, I was a played on the women's varsity soccer team."

Qualities required for PR writing position:	During my college career, I:	While at Central College, I was a/an:
◆ Relevant knowledge	◆ *Majored* in public relations and media writing	◆ Public relations *major* specializing in writing
◆ Writing experience	◆ *Edited* the campus newspaper	◆ *Editor* of campus newspaper
◆ Work experience	◆ *Interned* in the PR Department of Noble Hospital	◆ Public relations *intern* at Noble Hospital
◆ Academic excellence	◆ *Earned* Dean's List grades for six consecutive terms	◆ *Dean's list student* for six consecutive terms
◆ Extracurricular activities	◆ *Played* on the women's varsity soccer team	◆ *Goaltender* on women's varsity soccer team

E X E R C I S E   3

Identify the examples of parallel structure in this parallel structure section. There are many examples.

Headings and Subheads

Grounded in principles of design, headings (and subheads) facilitate both scanning and understanding. Generally, headings have some graphic distinction—size, color, and special effects—that set them apart from the text of a document. They are the staple of brochures, fact sheets, and direct mail, but they are equally effective in reports, proposals, and newsletters. They make it possible for readers to see at a glance the points being made and the structure of a document. They help readers quickly find the material that interests them. On web sites, headings act as links and buttons, directing us quickly to new content or pages.

Over time, we have all come to understand the "language" of headings. We understand that the biggest or brightest heading is the most important or most encompassing. The lead story of the daily newspaper has the biggest headline; chapter titles are larger than section titles, which are larger than subsection titles. Maintaining such a clear hierarchy of headings is important in making the structure of your message clear.

From a writing point of view, maintaining this hierarchy involves parallel structure. If a level-one heading is a question, then ideally all level-one headings should be questions; if a level-two heading is a phrase, then all level-two headings should be phrases.

How Do You Learn About Style and Flow?

Read Other Writing and Listen to Others' Speech

It could be argued that if you do not know what a newspaper is, you will have difficulty writing for the press. The same goes for all types of public relations writing. There are good ideas and bad ideas, and you can avoid some pitfalls by getting accustomed to what good public relations writing (and design) looks like and sounds like.

In particular, good public relations writing is so tightly written that the reader is hard-pressed not to finish the article. It is easy to find examples of copy that flows. Think, for example, about the opinion-editorial (op-ed) columns written by William Safire, George Will, Molly Ivins, or *Sports Illustrated* columnists Steve Rushin and Rick Reilly. They are all opinion pieces, and the writers want you, the reader, to read completely through the text. The writers have to write tightly to accommodate the restrictions of newspaper or magazine space and to move readers through the logic of argument to a conclusion. Their writings are generally good models of the principles of style and flow.

On a verbal level, pay attention to the speech of people who speak well, such as most college professors, politicians, and broadcast announcers. Their speech will attune you to the rhythms of speech that you can emulate in your own speaking and writing. This will be an especially important type of research in speech writing.

Learn to "Hear" What You Write

Once you know what good writing "sounds like," you should be able to hear what *you* write. Start if you must by actually reading the text aloud. With a little practice, you will find that you can "hear" the text as you write it. The object is to identify sentences that are too long, that do not flow together, or that do not make sense. In particular, you will start to hear problems with flow and small differences in the choice or position of words that can make a big difference in what the reader understands.

Revise, Revise, Revise

It is a long-held joke among writers that the primal human urge is neither love nor hate; rather it is one person's desire to "~~edit, amend, rewrite, cut, add to, improve, tweak~~ . . . revise another's copy." It is the habit of good writers to exercise this desire using their own writing.

Even the best professional writers seldom if ever produce finished copy on the first try. Furthermore, they do not regard this as a failure. Instead, they enjoy working with the text, revising everything from individual words to entire sections. They "play" with words and rhythms, shaping them to fit time and space limitations and to bring together the interests of the organization and its publics.

Developing Your Own Style

Ultimately, part of your success as a public relations writer will depend on your ability to create your own style. This will influence the type of writing you do best and likely the type of position in which you are comfortable. In addition to whether you prefer factual over creative writing, advertising over news writing, or print over broadcast, for example, your personal style will relate to how you handle deadlines, and even how you approach a writing project.

If you work best under deadlines, then projects with long time frames may not be your forte. But you might thrive in a busy department that specializes in media relations with daily release deadlines. Do you outline before writing, produce a rough draft for extensive revision, or write close-to-perfect final copy the first time? If you think extensively before writing, you may frustrate a supervisor who expects you to produce polished copy off the top of your head. Understanding your personal style will help you find that public relations niche in which you can succeed.

Style Resources

Although the above sections address the most common style issues, you will learn about others from careful analysis of documents your employer has produced previously. There will also be times that you want to refer to a style authority either to validate your instincts or to provide guidance on style issues you do not deal with every day, such as legal citations or research footnotes.

For general style, a classic guide is Strunk and White's *The Elements of Style,* a brief, popular source of practical grammar and style guidelines. For anyone preparing copy for the news media, *The Associated Press Stylebook and Briefing on Media Law* and perhaps a stylebook specific to broadcast copy such as *The Associated Press Broadcast News Handbook* will be essential.

For specific styles, you will refer to your house style guide and possibly to the style guides for major sectors or industries. The voluminous *Chicago Manual of Style* is a definitive source of information that you will find useful for reports, annual reports, and documents that may be published. APA style is familiar to anyone writing in the social sciences as is the Council of Biology Editors (CBE) style for the biological sciences.

Generally, you should have access to general style guidelines, sector-specific style guidelines, and client-specific style guidelines. Many of them are available in the reference section of your neighborhood bookstore and library.

Putting Theory and Fundamentals Into Practice: Writing a Cover Letter for Your First Client—You

Enough talking—it is time to put these fundamentals into practice by writing the first document related to your budding career as a public relations writer: the cover letter that lands you your first interview. This section walks you step-by-step from the thinking about audience needs and your assets that should precede the letter to the specifics of letter writing and formatting.

There are many types and formats for letters and résumés. Each of them presents a particular applicant's attributes (and masks his or her weaknesses) better than the others. What these formats have in common is the discipline they demand. They make you *think* about your attributes and use the format that presents them (and *you*) best to *your* publics—that is, prospective employers. This is the same process you will go through to present your employer to *its* publics.

What Will You Write?

Before you start writing this or any other document, take time to plan what you have to say. Consider the publics you will address and the outcomes you hope to achieve.

Identifying the public's needs comes first. In the case of application letters and résumés, this requires thinking what skills the organization wants an entry-level writer to have. Rather than thinking that a résumé leads to a job, thoughtful writers recognize that the job requirements lead to the résumé.

Audience Needs

As with all other types of public relations writing, the more you know about the audience, the easier it will be for you to appeal directly to that audience. In this case, you will want to know the job requirements, the organization's culture (to help you make wise decisions about style and design), and, if possible, something about the decision maker's concept of public relations.

How do you gather this information? Ideally, your network of public relations contacts includes someone in the organization who can advise or even recommend you. With 70% to 80% of positions being filled through personal contact or internal promotion, you cannot network enough or know too many people.

If you do not have a personal contact, you can research the annual report, obtain brochures, or even visit the company if possible. Visit the web sites for information about the organization's goals, vision, employment practices, activities, and locations. Is there an employee newsletter or archive of news releases? Is there a community initiative that relates to your volunteer experience? Look for a "link" you can use to establish a relationship with the organization. It will set you apart from applicants who do not have such a link.

In many cases, however, especially for first jobs, you will make some "apply–don't apply" decisions based only on an advertisement in the newspaper or online. Every ad (or any other documents that organizations write about themselves) provides clues to the qualities that organizations want in their employees. They will help you make decisions about what experience (even classes) will have the strongest appeal.

DISCUSSION 2

Look at the ads in Exhibit 2.4. What do they tell you about the advertisers? Pay special attention to the tone of the ads. Which do you believe are the most/least conservative? How will this relate to the tone of your cover letter and your choice of words? For example, on which advertiser should you risk a really creative cover letter? In this case, the creativity of the Channing L. Bete, Inc., ad opens the door to creativity on your part; you might even admit that one of your parents won the Kentucky Derby (i.e., acknowledge that you really are "half beast"). What skills are most important to each advertiser? What personal traits?

Your Experience

The other side of identifying what prospective employers want is identifying your strengths. This is the evidence you will present to support the argument that you are the best candidate for the job.

Once you look at your experience in relation to employer, you will see what makes your experience unique compared to other applicants. Bringing this "uniqueness" to the fore is what you are trying to achieve in a résumé, and especially in a cover letter. For hints on looking at your experience, see Exhibit 2.5, "Identifying and framing your assets." You are developing the answer to the question, "How will my skills benefit that organization?"

As you refine your skills into benefits, remember the jargon that is appropriate to the industry. Refer to "copy" rather than text, "layout" rather than page design, and "screens" or "frames" rather than pages for the Web. And if the web site you designed was "interactive," make this clear.

EXHIBIT 2.4   Sample ads for public relations writing.

Senior Copywriter, Direct Mail Advertising

HALF MAN, HALF BEAST

The normal half of the man or woman in this unique position attends marketing meetings while remaining responsibly alert and in an upright position, tracks his or her writing time on campaigns; styles Word documents to enable designers to flow them into Quark; digs up and reuses existing copy to save time and so on. This is the stuff you willingly brave in order to get to that other part of the job . . .

The fun half. The creative beast with the copy-writing talent and experience to bring life to the next new direct marketing campaign. We write catalogs, collateral and targeted cover letters. Lots of cover letters. So show us your scintillating headlines. Your energetic, cohesive, benefit-oriented body copy. Show us agility with ad copy that would make Ogilvy proud, if he ever read our stuff, which, as far as we know, he doesn't. But thousands of business-to-business customers nationwide do.

We're an in-house ad agency at an established educational publisher. We're employee-owned, Macintosh (Word 6) based, web-connected (see us at channing-bete.com) and truly team-oriented. All in a contemporary facility here in balmy (for now) Western Mass.

Ad Copywriting experience is a must for this senior position. Mac experience would be helpful. You'll need a bachelor's degree or equivalent. Many of our products are related to health education; knowledge in this area would be an asset, though it's not required. Above all, show us your creative ability as an ad copywriter.

We offer health and dental plans, 401(k), profit sharing, an employee stock ownership plan, and much more. Please send a resumé, cover letter, salary history, and three non-returnable work samples when responding to:

Director, Human Resources — Dept. SR

Channing L. Bete Co., Inc.
200 State Road, South Deerfield, MA 01373-0200

DIRECTOR OF PUBLICATIONS

The College, a national leader in nontraditional adult higher education, seeks a highly organized & energetic individual to join our advancement team at the Coordinating Center, Saratoga Springs.

Responsible for design, composition & printing of major publications, including bulletins, viewbooks, recruitment materials & newsletters; serve as designer/layout editor of the EMPIRE State College News magazine, an alumni publication; maintain an annual publications plan & production schedule; supervise freelance writers, designers & interns; & assist in marketing, advertising, promotional & special event efforts.

Three years of publications management/design experience; a bachelor's degree in graphic design or related field; desktop publishing expertise; strong organizational skills; good writing/editing skills; & strong interpersonal abilities. Photography skills a plus. Letter & resumé to: **Kirk Starczewski, Dir. of College Relations, SUNY ESC, 1 Union Ave, Saratoga Springs, NY 23866. AA/EOE**

Empire State College

NEWSPAPER REPORTER WANTED:

Fast, organized, reporter who likes people and small towns. Someone who can see and quickly write obvious hard news, subtle community stories, and human interest features. Must have strong writing skills, and be assertive, precise, inquisitive and accurate.

Write to:
Editor Tim Blagg
The Recorder
Box 1367
Greenfield, MA 01302

The **Recorder**

Source: Reproduced with permission of Channing L. Bete, Co., Inc., South Deerfield, Massachusetts; SUNY Empire State College, Saratoga Springs, New York; and *The Recorder,* Greenfield, Massachusetts.

EXHIBIT 2.5   **Identifying and framing your assets.**

Turning Lemons Into Lemonade

We often hear students say they have nothing to put in a résumé, as if all their experience has given them nothing but "lemons." *Wrong*. Just because you do not have commercial public relations writing experience does not mean that you do not have what an employer is seeking, especially for entry-level positions. In such cases, the employer is likely looking for relevant knowledge, enthusiasm, fresh ideas, and the willingness to learn, work hard, and fit in with the public relations team. Remember, every employer's basic question is: "What can this applicant bring to our organization?"—a variation on "What's in it for me?" Focusing on this will help you turn your "lemons into lemonade."

Recognizing Your Assets

Look at your experience as broadly as possible. Following are some hints for examining the most common categories.

Education

Of course, your education is important, and if you have excellent grades, say so, but be selective in discussing the classes you have taken.

- ✦ Focus on upper-level courses that relate to the position or the employer.
- ✦ Define what makes your experience different from the "same" course of study taken by other applicants. How did the courses prepare you for the job?
- ✦ Don't forget academic honors, but what you can *do* is more important.

Extracurricular Activities

Generally, it is harder to reject a person you know than a stranger. Extracurricular activities introduce you as a person, with interests and values and experiences that demonstrate your breadth and desirability. Remember, however, to stay professional and to steer clear of personal details.

- ✦ Think about your social activities (clubs, sororities, and fraternities), sports.
- ✦ Focus especially on community and volunteer activities, which will likely have great appeal as organizations increase their own social responsibility.
- ✦ Identify your leadership roles.

Work Experience

Even if your summer jobs were all in fast-food service, for example, they still demonstrate that you know how to conduct yourself in a business environment. And don't forget that you wrote articles about your local branch for the corporate newsletter, or designed flyers for the food drive.

Internships

In today's job market, the word internship has appeal in its own right. Many of the respondents to our survey cited "previous work experience" as something they consider critical, even in a new graduate (Treadwell & Treadwell, 1999). And several public relations executives we know admit that they would be unlikely to look at a new graduate without internship experience.

EXHIBIT 2.5   (Continued)

Intangible Assets

Of course, you want a potential employer to know that you are responsible, hard-working, trustworthy, creative, and so forth, but since we all think this about ourselves, it is less than credible when we make the claim ourselves.

✦ Find a way to let others say it for you. Quote your internship supervisor.
✦ Provide details that demonstrate these qualities.

Framing Your Assets

Having identified your assets, you need to relate them to the target organization, that is, to "frame" them so they are clearly relevant to the reader. As a communication tactic, *framing* means interpreting facts in a context that makes them relevant and persuasive. It can be as simple as interpreting the value of a media writing class for the reader who does not know, for example, that it had a heavy concentration on writing for broadcast (which is the mainstay of the organization's communications). On a more subtle level, it may involve interpreting a summer job as "customer service," or your campus club leadership as business management. Choosing strong, active words, such as *led* or *directed* rather than *belonged to* is also a key part of framing your experience.

DISCUSSION   3

Sometimes it is helpful to have a third party interpret your skills for an employer. List six things you would want a prospective public relations employer to know about you. What evidence do you have that you are good at these things or that you even have these skills or attributes? Who can testify to this? How can you work this third-party testimony into an application letter?

Résumé Versus Cover Letter

Once you have identified your attributes and how they will benefit an organization, you will present them in two formats: a résumé and a cover letter. Résumés are an exercise (albeit a good one) in organization and brevity. They present all of your *relevant* experience and skills in an outline format, and they challenge your ability to present as much information as possible as succinctly as possible.

Cover letters introduce you as a person and highlight what the reader can expect to find in the résumé and tempt the reader to turn to the résumé for details. They emphasize skills or experiences you especially want the reader to notice. You might think of cover letters as "advertisements" for the résumé and for your writing abilities.

The companion web site to this text contains some guidance on thinking about and writing effective résumés. For this chapter, we will limit our discussion to the cover letter because it provides a good first exercise in writing.

The Cover Letter

You may not always be able to judge a book by its cover, but first impressions count, and you get only one chance to make that first impression. That first impact comes from your cover letter, the first thing your reader will see. Accordingly, cover letters should be as carefully crafted as any document you would write for an employer. They should "sell" *you* as strongly as you would sell the organization to which you are sending the letter.

The cover letter is a sample of your writing ability and your understanding of your audience and how to attract that audience. It may include only two or three of your assets, but those two or three should be the strongest and most appealing. As with the résumé, the cover letter will be grounded in the planning you did to identify your skills, the organization's needs, and the common ground between them.

To look at it from a negative point of view, if you can't even promote yourself effectively, how can an organization expect you will promote its interests effectively? See Exhibit 2.6 for hints on getting started off right.

Following are some principles (as well as some practical hints) for writing business letters that will help you look and sound professional while presenting your assets to the greatest advantage. You will revisit these principles in Chapter 8, from the viewpoint of a writer for an organization.

Selecting a Format: Rifle Approach Versus Shotgun Approach

There are two standard application letter formats, commonly referred to as the shotgun approach and the rifle approach. They are named after the ammunition and shot pattern of the respective firearms, and their uses reflect these strategies. Although most commonly used to describe letters, insofar as they focus on the different approaches needed for mass audiences and individuals, they could apply to most public relations writing.

The shotgun approach. A shotgun sprays ammunition (shot) in a wide pattern. It is not precise but achieves its goal through the volume of ammunition discharged and the breadth of the target area. Anything in the target area may be "caught."

Shotgun letters are typically sent to many (possibly hundreds of) organizations, much the way a salesperson makes "cold calls" to many prospects hoping that several will give him time to present his sales pitch. Shotgun letters may also be posted at online job search web sites that employers can access when they are hiring.

Since you are not responding to a known vacancy, shotgun letters must identify the job you are seeking as well as the skills you offer. It helps to be aware of the titles and descriptions for positions in various industries so that even in a shotgun letter you can discuss your abilities in relevant terms. For example, although the term "corporate communication" might make your public relations skills appealing in a commercial environment, the same terminology would have less appeal to nonprofit organizations.

Although shotgun letters can maximize your reach in a job search, beware of thinking of them as simple "one size fits all" documents that you can send out for

EXHIBIT 2.6   Writing professional headings for business letters.

Business letters are formal documents. Even if it is not your "natural" style, your employer will expect you to use it. Chief among the conventions for business letters are those for the address panel and the greeting.

The Masthead

Just like the masthead of a publication, the masthead of a letter includes information about the sender. Organizations typically have stationery printed with the masthead, including name, possibly logo, address, and contact information (e.g., phone, fax, URL). Your letters should have the same information about you.

The Address Panel

Business letters typically open with information about the recipient in the upper left corner of the letter under the masthead. In order, enter the recipient's name, position/job title, department (if appropriate), organization/company name, and address. If you do not know the recipient's name (and cannot learn it), begin with the position and department (e.g., Manager, Public Relations Department). The recipient's name should *always* include Mr., Ms., Mrs., Dr., Rev., etc., followed by the first name or initials and surname (e.g., Dr. Alison Campbell). This panel should be repeated on the envelope.

The Greeting

Following the address panel is the greeting, commonly known as the "Dear _____:" line. Think of it as the written equivalent of a "hello _____."

This raises the question of how you will refer to the recipient. On a case-by-case basis, the answer varies with the individual to whom you are writing, but the following points made by communication managers we surveyed should help you make informed and wise decisions.

◆ As a general rule, unless you know the reader personally, begin with "Mr. (or Ms., Dr., General, etc.) followed by the surname (e.g., Mr. Anderson). You may be comfortable calling relative strangers by their first names, but people may not welcome such familiarity. Why risk offending the reader on the first line when a simple "Mr. (or Ms.) Surname" will open the letter accurately and professionally?

◆ Do not use the person's first name in the greeting. It is unlikely that you would walk up to a person and say, "Hello Doctor John Smith." Similarly, you would not greet him as "Dear Dr. John Smith." Simply write, "Dear Dr. Smith."

◆ What if you don't know the recipient's name? Call the company receptionist to ask the name and job title of the department manager. This demonstrates both your professionalism and your ability to research. It will also ensure that your letter is delivered directly into the correct hands.

◆ "Sir or Madam" is still acceptable but usually deemed excessively formal in today's more casual workplace. Reserve it for times when you cannot identify the reader's name.

any job in any industry. Doing so may actually make you look silly. For example, it is unlikely that a human resources manager who receives a letter like the following true example would know which of the company's many vacancies the writer wanted to apply for. It is equally unlikely she would try to find out.

"Thank you for submitting/posting the information on this position. I have a deep interest regarding the duties allocated and could possibly begin soon. Being aware of the job definition, I feel I would be the best candidate to carry out the functions required. I am ready for challenges, training and I am very open-minded."

Even shotgun letters benefit from some degree of targeting. Shotgun letters build relationships based on links you can identify and capitalize on. If you take the trouble to modify them for an industry or a geographic area, you may be able to use what you know about the industry or region to help establish a relationship with the recipient.

The rifle approach. A rifle shoots individual bullets at specific, known targets. It is precise and targeted. Similarly, rifle-approach letters are appropriate responses to public ads or as the result of referrals or contact with the organization. You will know what the organization does and what the job requirements are. Rifle letters build relationships based on your knowledge of the hiring organization's specific needs.

Although you may develop a basic rifle letter that highlights your primary attributes, each rifle letter that you send should be revised to focus on the known requirements of the specific organization and/or job being offered. What you know about the company, the position, the industry, and possibly the contact person will allow you to find common ground with the reader, that is, to establish a relationship.

For example, if the job you are seeking is to support the fundraising department of a nonprofit organization, it would be wise to highlight your volunteer fundraising experience. On the other hand, if the job is to produce newsletters for a corporation, you would instead highlight the newsletters you produced for a campus club and your summer job in a corporate office.

Many jobseekers prepare both types of letters, sending a shotgun version to multiple prospects and posting it online, and reserving a basic rifle letter for specific targeted employers as the job search identifies them. Both of these letters will typically be accompanied by a résumé with more detail.

Sell Your Assets

Regardless of the format you choose, a cover letter is not the place to identify your failings. Instead, write your cover letter to highlight the most exciting, interesting, or relevant aspects of the résumé. You alone know which of your many skills relate best to the prospective employer's needs, so highlight them in the cover letter.

One way to think about the points to emphasize in your cover letter is to consider what three points you would include in a "highlights" section at the top of the résumé. If you put these highlights into prose form and relate them to the employer's needs, your cover letter will be a strong one.

A way of selling your assets that was especially popular in the 1990s and that still has advocates is to present your skills as a two-column comparison of the job requirements and the skills you offer. For shotgun letters, this allows you to define both the skills needed and the skills you have. It provides a framework for your attributes. The same format can be effective for rifle letters although the table would match your skills with the requirements described in the ad.

Support your claims. Concrete evidence is always your best ally. Saying you are diligent, talented, and energetic is just an idle claim unless you can back it up with details of the projects you have done, the results you achieved, what you have learned, and what your employers, internship supervisors, and professors thought of your work. You should have identified this specific evidence during the planning process.

Be creative but not cute. We know this is a fine line, but it is one you had better not cross. The same manager who only laughed at the letter that began: "When it comes to communications, I can leap tall buildings at a single bound" gave serious consideration to the application from a veteran communicator who pointed out that his 20 years of experience made him "four times as good" as those with only the required 5 years of experience. He then detailed four areas in which he was especially competent. A gimmick? Perhaps, but it was well done, brief and relevant.

A word of warning about creativity: Even while you are being creative, be sure to sell yourself. Creativity may be at the heart of the Channing Bete culture (that led to the Half Man, Half Beast ad shown in Exhibit 2.4), and you may want to be equally creative in your response. But you can bet the company is deadly serious about producing top-quality, on-time work for its clients and the company's first interest is in evidence that you can do the same.

Always suggest the next step. This is generally a good "sales" technique that you will want to remember for nearly every letter you write as a professional. Are you available for an interview? Say so. Will you call to set an appointment? Can you provide work samples or references? Let the reader know. And then follow up on your questions and promises.

Say thank you. It never hurts to show your appreciation for a reader's time and consideration of your qualifications.

Sign the letter. This may sound unnecessary, but be sure to sign your letters. Failure to do so makes you look careless, calls your credibility into question, and is likely to cost you an interview.

Proofread—for accuracy. Organizations understand that you may be applying for many jobs with many companies, but this does not excuse you from paying careful attention to accuracy. We know of many cases in which busy applicants have responded to one ad with the information required for another, sometimes referring to the wrong company by name. It takes excellent organizational skills to ensure accuracy, but if you confuse letters and companies and names, it will be at your peril.

Proofread again—for spelling and grammar. After writing and editing a document, you are often too close to it to notice errors that are obvious to another reader. Do not depend on spell check or hesitate to have an objective third party proofread it for you. Even errors that appear to be simple typographic mistakes (commonly called "typos") may give the reader a reason to eliminate you from consideration.

EXHIBIT 2.7   Examples of standard business letter layouts. At left is a block format and at right is an indented format.

Your Name Address Phone number	**Your Name** Address Phone number
Date	Date
Recipient's name *(Preceded by Mr./Ms./Mrs./Dr.)* Position (Job title) Company/Organization Address City, State Zip	Recipient's name *(Preceded by Mr./Ms./Mrs./Dr.)* Position (Job title) Company/Organization Address City, State Zip
Dear Mr/Ms/Mrs. _____: *(called the greeting or salutation)*	Dear Mr/Ms/Mrs. _____: *(called the greeting or salutation)*
The first paragraph should state what position you are looking for, where you saw the ad or how you learned about the organization (if appropriate). If you have been referred by someone who knows you *and* the organization, state this in the first paragraph. It establishes a link between you and the reader, which is always good.	The first paragraph should state what position you are looking for, where you saw the ad or how you learned about the organization (if appropriate). If you have been referred by someone who knows you *and* the organization, state this in the first paragraph; it establishes a link between you and the reader, which is always good.
In the middle paragraph(s) tell the reader why you should be considered for a/the position. Highlight the points of your resumé that are particularly relevant to the organization and/or the job for which you are applying. Provide further details, including specific achievements. Numbers and results are always important. Remember to use strong adjectives, active verbs and specific nouns.	In the middle paragraph(s) tell the reader why you should be considered for a/the position. Highlight the points of your resumé that are particularly relevant to the organization and/or the job for which you are applying. Provide further details, including specific achievements. Numbers and results are always important. Remember to use strong adjectives, active verbs and specific nouns.
Close by offering your availability for an interview. Tell the reader how he/she can reach you, and when (if you are not there all of the time). Thank the reader for his or her time.	Close by offering your availability for an interview. Tell the reader how he/she can reach you, and when (if you are not there all of the time). Thank the reader for his or her time.
Sincerely, *(called the closing)* *Your SIGNATURE* Your name typed	Sincerely, *(called the closing)* *Your SIGNATURE* Your name typed

---

For example: A publications manager would conceivably learn all she needed to know about an applicant's editing ability from the following sentence: "I want a career that focuses on the writing andediting aspect of public relations." An unfortunate typo indeed.

Then, when you have proofread the letter thoroughly, do it again. A trick many seasoned writers use is to read documents from the end forward. Read each sentence carefully, stopping between sentences. This effectively isolates the sentences and stops you from reading what you *think* you have written rather than what is actually on the page.

Cover Letter Formats

Exhibit 2.7 illustrates the two basic layout formats for cover letters: block and indented. The block format has all of the type (except the closing and signature) flush to the left margin. There are no indents. The text is fully justified. This is a design term meaning aligned both left and right. If you choose a block format, be certain to put a space between paragraphs so that the copy does not run together into one long block.

Indented copy starts like this paragraph; the first line is indented, usually between .25 and .5 inches. Although it is still a good idea to put a space between paragraphs, it is not essential because the indents signal the paragraph breaks.

Appearance Counts

We know you are trying to get a writing job and agree that what you say and how you say it are the most important aspects of the cover letter and the résumé, but if you ignore the appearance of either one, you will shortchange even the best copy. Over 94% of the respondents to our survey said that the appearance of a cover letter was important or very important for applicants for communication positions. We suggest you begin now to develop sensitivity to the ways in which design can help you communicate more effectively and professionally.

If a package looks professional, readers subconsciously expect it to be professional. This is a good start. In addition, a cover letter that looks professional demonstrates your careful attention to your own communications and implicitly the attention you will pay to the organization's communications.

For a very professional look, you may choose to use special stationery, usually with your name prominently at the top, in large, bold, or special type with your address, telephone and fax numbers, and e-mail address printed under the name. Use a good-quality bond paper.

Do not fold a résumé and cover letter. Instead, send them flat in a large, preferably white, envelope. Not only will they look more impressive and professional, but also, if the résumé is scanned, folds can interfere with the scanning.

You do not have to be a graphic artist or professional designer to produce a professional-looking résumé and cover letter. Attention to three simple points—format, type/graphics, and position—should help you achieve professional results.

Attracting attention. Many books discuss how to make your document stand out by using headlines, colored paper, artwork, and even personal photos, for example. There is an appropriate place for each of these techniques, but if the organization you are applying to isn't that place, then you are wasting your time.

We have seen many unusual résumés and cover letters in newsletter format or with many illustrations on brightly colored paper. Some include clip art or multiple typefaces in an attempt to stand out from the rest. Innovative? Perhaps, although clip art is generally tacky. Eye-catching? Yes. Classy and professional? Usually not. Appropriate for a conservative company in which professionalism is a priority? Definitely not, even though the basic idea may be a good one. Contrary to your intent, sending a hot pink, cartoon-filled letter may advertise that you do not understand what constitutes a professional communication.

On the other hand, that hot-pink presentation, especially with artwork done by the sender, may well land an interview with a public relations agency known for its offbeat creativity. The message, once again, is to learn as much as possible about your audience in order to tailor your presentation for that audience. See Exhibit 2.8 for tips about using type to make your letter stand out, while still looking professional. Keep it simple is generally a good rule.

Simple layout. The position of a letter on the page is one of the most common demonstrations that an applicant does not understand the importance of

---

EXHIBIT 2.8   Tips for text and type.

With few exceptions, cover letters should be only one page, so you should make type, margin, and positioning decisions to achieve this. Remember, however, that the first objective for your letter and résumé is to have them read.

For better or worse, word processing has made it possible for you to use many styles, sizes, and effects of type in a document. As every professional communicator that we know will tell you, "just because you can, doesn't mean it's a good idea."

The following tips will help your documents look professional:

- ✦ Choose 10-point or 12-point type; 12 is better, but 10 is acceptable.
- ✦ Choose an easy-to-read typeface, such as Times/Times New Roman, Helvetica, Arial, Palatino, or faces in the **Bodoni** or Schoolbook families. Limit yourself to one typeface for text and a second for headings.
- ✦ Stay with "roman" type (as in this sentence) for body text. Save special effects such as *italic,* **boldface,** and ***bold italic*** for headings.
- ✦ *Carefully* increase or decrease margins to create a balanced appearance. A general rule of type is that the smaller the typeface (or the type size), the shorter your line should be. Long lines in small type are very difficult to read.
- ✦ Try to avoid "widows" (when one line extends to the next page) and "orphans" (when the last word of a paragraph extends onto a new line). Although justifying the type (so that it is aligned on both left and right) will achieve this, doing so results in a very formal appearance. Judicious editing is a better solution.

Do edit or use some of the above techniques to fit it onto one page, especially if your letter extends only one or two lines onto a new page. Few things look less professional than a second page with almost no type on it.

Web Tips

If you are posting your résumé on a web page, be certain to use standard typefaces that are available on most browsers, such as Times New Roman, Arial, and Verdana. Test the page using several browsers and operating systems to ensure it looks the way you want it to look. If you do not want the layout to change, consider posting it as a .pdf file.

---

professional appearance. You have an entire sheet of paper—use it. You would be unlikely to print the entire letter on the right half of the page, so why would you print it all at the top?

Professional letters are balanced on the page, with equal or nearly equal right and left margins, and a top margin .25 inch less than the bottom margin. Use the print preview feature of your word processing program to see how the letter will look on the page before you print it.

After the Letter

Congratulations on being asked to come in for an interview. Your letter and résumé did their jobs. But do not make the mistake of thinking your writing demonstration is over. Most organizations give applicants a writing or editing test as part of the interview process. This is in addition to the résumé, cover letter, and any writing samples you may have provided.

It pays to go to the interview prepared to write a news release, newsletter article, or pitch letter, for example, and maybe to take a spelling, editing, or grammar test. Especially creative interviewers may test your abilities by having you write an advertisement or even a letter of reference on yourself. Remember: Identifying audience needs is always a good place to start.

After the Interview

It is hoped you have "nailed" the interview, but even that isn't the end. Just as you want to make a good first impression, you also want to make a good last impression. A simple note, thanking the interviewer for his or her time, is a good tactic for many reasons. It is polite and professional. It allows you to remind the interviewer of your strengths. And it gives you the opportunity to provide or offer additional information.

But keep it brief. Refer to the interview to be sure the reader knows who you are, express your enthusiasm for the organization, and say thank you. Write it as carefully and professionally as everything else you have done.

ON THE TEXTBOOK WEB SITE

✦ Go to www.sagepub.com/treadwell for web exercises, study hints, case studies, and additional examples appropriate to this chapter and chosen or developed to supplement the chapter content.

WRITING WRAP-UP

1. Write a brief report that discusses the knowledge and skills needed for a successful career in public relations writing.

2. Write a cover letter and résumé applying for any of the jobs advertised in Exhibit 2.4. The cover letter should demonstrate your ability to identify and present your strengths in a format relevant to the employer.

3. Write a second cover letter applying for another of the positions. This letter should demonstrate your ability to adapt the information in your previous letter to the needs and interests of different employers.

REFERENCE

Treadwell, D. F., & Treadwell, J. B. (1999). Employer expectations of newly-hired communication graduates. *Journal of the Association for Communication Administration, 28*(2), 87–99.

Books

American Psychological Association. (2001). *Publication manual of the American Psychological Association* (5th ed.). Washington, DC: American Psychological Association.

Goldstein, N. (Ed.). (2004). *The Associated Press stylebook and briefing on media law.* Reading, MA: Addison-Wesley.

Gordon, K. E. (1993). *The DeLuxe transitive vampire: The ultimate handbook of grammar for the innocent, the eager, and the doomed.* New York: Pantheon.

Kalbfeld, B. (2000). *The Associated Press broadcast news handbook.* New York: McGraw-Hill.

Strunk, W., & White, E. B. (2000). *Elements of style* (4th ed). Needham Heights, MA: Longman.

University of Chicago Press. (2003). *The Chicago manual of style* (15th ed.). Chicago and London: University of Chicago Press.

Williams, J. M. (2002). *Style: Ten lessons in clarity and grace* (7th ed.). Reading, MA: Longman.

Web Sites

NASA Handbook for Technical http://stipo.larc.nasa.gov/sp7084/index.htmll
Writers and Editors

Onelook Dictionaries .... www.onelook.com

Purdue University Online Writing Lab .... http://owl.english.purdue.edu

Strunk, W., Jr., *Elements of Style* http://www.bartleby.com/141

SUNY New Paltz .... http://www.newpaltz.edu/styleguide/editorial/about.html
Style On-line Guide

U.S. Government .... http://www.gpoaccess.gov/stylemanual/index.html
Printing Office

Xerox Corporation Style Guide .... http://www.xids.com/corpid/

Ethical Influences
on Public Relations Writing

1. **Public relations writing requires ethical decisions.**

2. **Public relations writers have an obligation to act ethically.**

3. **Public relations writers have an obligation to help their employer act ethically.**

4. **Societal, sector, organizational, and personal standards help resolve ethical dilemmas.**

5. **The PRSA Code of Ethics provides guidelines for ethical action for all public relations practitioners.**

The law, subject to interpretation though it may be, ultimately decides what you must *not do* with respect to communication content, timing, and process. So what governs what you *should do?* When all the communication options are legal, how do communication decisions get made on a day-to-day basis?

Welcome to the world of ethics, the discipline that focuses on right and wrong rather than legal and illegal. Ethics are debated in Congress, churches, school committees, and neighborhoods on the level of values. The differences of opinion revealed in such debates are testimony to the difficulty of identifying a code of behavior that can be applied across time, cultures, and disciplines, not to mention public relations. At the heart of such debates is the attempt to develop consistent standards of behavior that will guide organizations in their relations with publics and therefore provide a framework for the content and nature of their communications with these publics.

Ethics are the standards of behavior—personal, organizational, and societal— that guide decisions about what is right and what is wrong. As such, they influence all aspects of an organization's operations, including the content and process of its communications.

The problem is that ethics are seldom black and white. Rather, they operate in a gray area between true and false, accurate and "technically accurate," good and bad, moral and immoral (or amoral), and honorable and dishonorable. Ethical standards help public relations writers resolve dilemmas such as if and when including or omitting certain facts crosses the line between simple selection and deliberate misrepresentation. Ethics help them determine when "stretching the truth" is akin to outright lying, and where to draw the line between fact and promotion.

Ethics periodically become a hot media topic as lapses in ethical standards by government and businesses enter the limelight. Individuals who have been charged with ethical misconduct range from the presidents of energy and financial services companies to the president of the United States, from members of the clergy to members of the military, and from college athletes to once-certain Hall of Fame baseball players. Issues on which organizations themselves may be subject to ethical scrutiny include the ethics of insurance companies restricting medical services to patients or a manufacturer's obligation to recall a defective product if the defect does not affect the health or safety of the user.

The ethical principles you will bring to the table are shaped at several levels: the ethics of the society or culture in which you operate, the ethics of the public relations discipline, the ethics of your organization, and your personal sense of ethics. Together they will shape your public relations writing.

Theories of Ethical Action

The ethical codes adopted by individuals, organizations, disciplines, and governments result from and contribute to the ethical standards of the society in which they operate. Some of these ethical codes are the products of philosophical reasoning or the world's great religions. They have stood the test of time over many centuries. Others are more recent attempts to reflect the rapidly changing, situational nature of 21st-century society. All of them represent an effort to identify universal standards by which activities can be evaluated and decisions can be made with a common grounding.

Christians, Fackler, and Rotzoll (1995) identify the great universal models of ethics as the following:

♦ A*ristotle's "golden mean."* The golden mean is an average, "meet in the middle" solution between two extremes. It is the solution that opposing parties might eventually agree on. It will perhaps offend the least number of people.

A public relations practitioner might use the golden mean as an operating policy with respect to disclosing information about a client—operating somewhere between revealing every detail and saying or revealing nothing.

♦ *Mill's principle of utility.* Philosopher John Stuart Mill argued that ethical decisions should be based on achieving the greatest good for the greatest number. Public relations practitioners might put this into practice by releasing information that maximizes benefit for the greatest number of people.

This is a useful notion except for the possibility that what is good for the greatest number may not be good for the organization. Although product safety recalls represent the greatest good for the greatest number, they are expensive and at least in the short term, embarrassing for the manufacturer.

✦ *The Judeo-Christian ethic.* The Judeo-Christian ethic is expressed as "do unto others," that is, treat others as you would want to be treated. If you don't want your private life revealed, why would you insist on including such information in a feature story about the organization's new chief scientist?

✦ *Kant's categorical imperative.* Philosopher Immanuel Kant took the position that what is right for one is right for all. The test of behavior or values is that they should be universally applicable. Thus, if attack advertising is legally acceptable and you are prepared to launch attack ads against your competition, then you should be willing to be the target of such ads yourself.

Insofar as they provide a clear basis for decision making that will stand over time, these ethical models come as close as we may get to universal models.

DISCUSSION   1

Almost any decision about communication involves ethical decisions at some level. Here are three scenarios:

✦ To meet a marketing deadline you are asked to prepare and release publicity for a consumer product that has not yet been fully tested.
✦ A new start-up company asks you to put the projected rather than the actual number of employees on its web site so that the company will appear larger than it is.
✦ You work for a company you know to be heading into financial trouble. Company executives ask you to stay out of any executive meetings so that you can then "honestly" deny any knowledge of the company's problems.

How should you respond to each of three situations. What theories of ethical action outlined above support your reasoning?

The Situational Approach to Public Relations Ethics

In many respects, ethics and communication strategies must be situational, varying as they do with the importance of the situation, the publics affected, the purpose of the communication, and the resources available to deal with the issue.

The situational model argues essentially that communication strategies can be determined only in light of such basic questions as, "Whom do we need to reach?" and "About what, when, where, how, and why do we want to reach them?" It is fair to say that these questions are the basis for both the activities of many public relations writers and the criticism that because "it depends on the situation," there is no underlying ethic.

Situational ethics reflect the systems notion that there is more than one way of arriving at a solution. They also reflect postmodernist notions that truth depends on perspective, that is, that because there are multiple perspectives we may not ever be able to arrive at "the" answer.

In practice, any of these ethical models is unlikely to be found as a pure type at any level of society. Organizations, individuals, governments, and other entities seldom have a communication code of practice or corporate philosophy based on a "pure" or specific ethical principle. In addition, the attempt to implement such models may be confounded in practice by deadlines and pragmatism. Like people, organizations may buy into the principle of Judeo-Christian ethics or Kant's categorical imperative or even situational ethics but practice it only when it is convenient. As St. Augustine of Hippo put it, "Give me chastity and continency, but not yet" (Partington, 1992).

The idea that a single ethical model will ever standardize communication practice goes against the basic tenet that effective communication requires segmenting, targeting, or differentiating a global audience into groups so that messages will be maximally effective.

Strategic communication implies discrimination in the best sense of the word, that is, formulating communication strategies according to the attributes and needs of a defined public. To the extent that publics differ in their expectations of appropriate organizational behavior, a single ethic may actually lead to inappropriate messages and methods. The categorical imperative that what's right for one is right for all actually clashes head-on with communication practice.

Defining Ethical Standards

In the same way that you, as a public relations writer, operate in an environment with many audiences, so you will operate in an environment with many levels of ethics. Each of them will affect what you can write and how you will write it. These levels range from societal ethics (e.g., as set out in the Bible, Koran, and Torah) to your personal ethical standards. Between these, a range of sector and organizational ethical standards present their own special challenges. You may find yourself juggling the various levels especially as you work in a global professional environment increasingly concerned with ethics and ethical business conduct.

The high-profile business scandals and failures of the late 20th and early 21st centuries gave rise to widespread distrust of business and of business practices and practitioners on the part of the publics on whom these businesses depend. This has led to a high level of self-examination on the part of business and a renewed emphasis on establishing and acting in compliance with formal ethical standards. Nonprofits, many of which suffered their own public embarrassments, have followed suit.

The public relations industry has been at the forefront of efforts to establish and promote the ethical standards of organizations and their governing bodies, starting with its own associations.

Public Relations Ethics

Public relations practitioners have wrestled with the need for a code of practice since at least 1906 when journalist-turned-publicist Ivy Ledbetter Lee worked for mine operators involved in a bitter struggle with miners striking for improved conditions. Lee persuaded his mine-owner clients to communicate with the press and issued the "Declaration of Principles" stressing that the information provided by the mine owners would be prompt, accurate, newsworthy, and of value and interest to the public. Lee's commitments form the core of most public relations statements of ethics.

The PRSA, International Association of Business Communicators (IABC), Society for Professional Journalists (SPJ), and other professional communication groups have attempted to identify such universals as a basis for their specific standards of practice. The PRSA Code of Ethics (provided in Appendix B) sets out the standards to which PRSA members are expected to conform. Expressing values of advocacy, honesty, expertise, independence, loyalty, and fairness, the code recognizes that all members of the profession contribute to the image of the profession as a whole by the ethical standards they apply as individuals. Six provisions provide guidance on specific ethical behaviors to ensure that public relations activity is undertaken in the public interest.

Ultimately, of course, codes of practice are voluntary. Although you can be removed from the PRSA if you are found to have seriously violated its professional code, that doesn't prevent you from writing or practicing public relations. Wilcox, Ault, and Agee (1998) estimate that only about 10% of the estimated 157,000 public relations professionals in the United States are members of the PRSA, which leaves 90% of public relations practitioners unaffected by even stringent enforcement of the PRSA code. Nevertheless, these codes and the principles they espouse provide guidance for any public relations writer wrestling with the ethics of specific decisions.

As the discipline of public relations matures, we can expect these professional organizations will continue to develop an underpinning of ethical standards that transcend time and place. This expectation gains validity in light of a study that found that public relations practitioners' self-reported beliefs and behaviors about ethics correlated with the respondents' age, gender, and income (Pratt, 1992). This suggests perhaps that demographic attributes may explain ethical values and that it may therefore be difficult to influence these values. The study also revealed a significant correlation between the respondents' attitudes toward ethics and their PRSA accreditation. This suggests that membership in professional organizations and peer support may be mechanisms through which a common approach to public relations ethics may develop.

Recently, the PR Coalition—a group of academic and industry communication specialists that formed in the wake of many disclosures of corporate malpractice—has affirmed the need to restore trust in the minds of publics, employees, and other stakeholders (Arthur W. Page Society, 2003). It proposed a three-part action plan:

- ✦ Restore trust in business
- ✦ Adopt ethical principles
- ✦ Pursue transparency and disclosure in operations

The PR Coalition recognized that all businesses must enjoy public approval if they are to succeed. Given that trust is based on relationships and relationships are effected through communication, it is clear that public relations writers have an important role to play in restoring trust.

DISCUSSION 2

A public relations counselor is the best person to provide advice to management on ethical behavior. What arguments can you find for and against this position?

Professional Ethics

The issue of trust in relationships is not confined to the public relations industry or to the United States. In an era of instant global communication, many national and international organizations also are at work addressing this issue. A quick web search for the term "codes of ethics" will yield hundreds, perhaps thousands, of ethical codes, which govern the practices of professions as diverse as medicine, engineering, architecture, education, behavioral science, and computer programming, to name but a very few. Generally, these codes are grounded in professional societies and oversight organizations. Since 1958, even the U.S. government has had a code of ethics that governs the actions of federal employees.

There may be an increased convergence on global ethical standards for public relations as multinational corporations link business practices in many countries and as the Internet expedites discussion and understanding among practitioners. Since 1986, a group of international business leaders known as the Caux Round Table (CRT) has attempted to promote principled business leadership as a way to defuse international tensions associated with trade imbalances. The CRT's first emphasis is on establishing "what" rather than "who" is right. Its principles are set out in the Caux Round Table Principles for Business (CRT, 2003).

In 2003, the UN Convention Against Corruption formalized global efforts to combat graft and corruption. More than 100 countries were involved in this global action (Transparency International, 2003). And the World Bank has identified corruption as the single greatest obstacle to economic and social development. "[Corruption] undermines development by distorting the rule of law and weakening the institutional foundation on which economic growth depends." The bank has launched an aggressive anticorruption program (World Bank Group, n.d.).

Efforts have been as widespread on the U.S. business scene. In 2004, the Business Roundtable, an association of U.S. chief executive officers (CEOs), established the Business Roundtable Institute for Corporate Ethics at the University of Virginia, one of many similar institutes at educational institutions throughout the United States. The mission of the institute is to enhance ethical behavior of business leaders in the conduct of day-to-day business decision making.

Because the adoption of such standards depends on how effectively they are communicated at organizational, sector, national, and international levels, public relations writers may well play a vital role in the evolution and adoption of even international codes of behavior. Nations and organizations continue to hold to their own cultures, values, and ways of doing things, so it remains to be seen whether public relations standards remain culturally relative or over time converge on one internationally accepted set of standards (Kruckeberg, 1998).

DISCUSSION 3

We propose that as communication technology increasingly links countries and cultures, one internationally agreed-on code of ethics for public relations practice will develop. What arguments can you find in favor of and against this statement? How do you feel about it?

Organizational Ethics

Just as public relations professionals are subject to ethical standards governing their conduct, so too are organizations subject to ethical standards established by management, industries or sectors, and regulatory agencies. In some organizations, these standards are detailed, written, and public. In others, they are informal and possibly unwritten. On one level, they govern business decisions in which the public relations practitioner may or may not be involved. On another level, they affect the organization's communications and will intimately involve the public relations writer.

You should be aware that you might find yourself being asked to issue communications about actions you personally believe are unethical. Although rare, it can occur. If and when it does, it will severely challenge your personal sense of ethics and your loyalties to your organization and your profession.

Organizational Ethics as Mission, Values, and Vision

There are many bases for organizational ethics. They range from doing what is necessary to protect the bottom line to exercising a social responsibility to employees, communities, and even the broader society. Generally, ethical standards are codified in the organization's mission, values, or vision statements and express the standards under which the organization will relate to its many publics. Such statements reveal much about the organization's priorities toward its activities and its publics. Accordingly, public relations writers will find them a source of guidance about the publics the organization considers important and about themes that will echo throughout the organization's communications.

Johnson & Johnson, which is historically named at the top of corporate responsibility polls, has its values espoused in the "Credo" shown in Exhibit 3.1. Notice in particular how the four sections of the Credo address the company's key publics—medical personnel and consumers, employees, communities, and stockholders. It sets out the values under which the company operates: fair business practices, respect for employees, commitment to making the world a better place, and maximizing shareholder investments.

These values have clear relevance for Johnson & Johnson public relations writers. They provide guidance on whom they will communicate with, the tone and style they will use, and the purpose of the communications.

By contrast, the U.S. Food and Drug Administration (FDA) has an extremely broad mission—the health of the U.S. public. Shown as Exhibit 3.2, the agency mission statement is very broad, focusing on what the agency will do rather than on specific publics it will address. It provides direction to public relations writers with regard to public relations themes they will be expected to reflect in their messages, such as concern for the public, safety, innovation, and a commitment to providing accurate, science-based information.

Organizational Ethics as Social Responsibility

Ideally, a comparison of social responsibility activities and organizational mission statements will reveal a confluence. Social, political, community, and environmental aims will be reflected in company policy and actions. But words are just

---

EXHIBIT 3.1   "Our Credo."

Johnson & Johnson
Our Credo

We believe our first responsibility is to the doctors, nurses and patients, to mothers and fathers and all others who use our products and services.
In meeting their needs everything we do must be of high quality.
We must constantly strive to reduce our costs in order to maintain reasonable prices.
Customers' orders must be serviced promptly and accurately.
Our suppliers and distributors must have an opportunity to make a fair profit.

We are responsible to our employees, the men and women who work with us throughout the world.
Everyone must be considered as an individual.
We must respect their dignity and recognize their merit.
They must have a sense of security in their jobs.
Compensation must be fair and adequate, and working conditions clean, orderly and safe.
We must be mindful of ways to help our employees fulfill their family responsibilities.
Employees must feel free to make suggestions and complaints.
There must be equal opportunity for employment, development and advancement for those qualified.
We must provide competent management, and their actions must be just and ethical.

We are responsible to the communities in which we live and work and to the world community as well.
We must be good citizens—support good works and charities and bear our fair share of taxes.
We must encourage civic improvements and better health and education.
We must maintain in good order the property we are privileged to use, protecting the environment and natural resources.

Our final responsibility is to our stockholders.
Business must make a sound profit.
We must experiment with new ideas.
Research must be carried on, innovative programs developed and mistakes paid for.
New equipment must be purchased, new facilities provided and new products launched.
Reserves must be created to provide for adverse times.
When we operate according to these principles, the stockholders should realize a fair return.

Source: Reprinted with permission of Johnson & Johnson.

---

words. As important as looking at an organization's stated values is looking at whether it puts these values into practice. Much of the focus on ethical practice now relates to the organization's social responsibility, also referred to as its corporate citizenship.

The aforementioned Caux Round Table (CRT) is one of the international organizations spearheading social responsibility movement. CRT is based on *kyosei*, the ethical principle of "living and working together for the common good" and human dignity. Writing in the *Harvard Business Review*, Ryuzaburo Kaku (1997), former chairman of Canon, Inc., and a founding member of CRT, proposes that companies can be classified into four types:

♦ *Economic survival.* Management and owners share the benefits of operation and care little for employees.

♦ *Cooperating with labor.* Managers and workers are united in working for the prosperity of the corporation and both share in the profits. The company does little to solve problems in the local community.

♦ *Cooperating outside the company.* The company respects the interests of its own stakeholders (customers, staff, shareholders, suppliers, competitors, and the local community), but this is geographically limited.

♦ *Global activism.* The company cares for all its direct stakeholders and beyond. Such organizations experience no labor disputes, exist harmoniously with local communities, and strive to fulfill their obligations on a global scale.

Recognizing that it is idealistic, Kaku also proposes a fifth category—the government as kyosei partner—that is, a company that actively seeks to change the world for the better and that recruits other organizations to do likewise. He sees this as necessary as companies evolve into ethical social institutions.

This concern for working actively to change the world for the better is growing quickly as organizations respond to their publics' concerns and the pressures they exert. Consider, for example, the number of organizations (businesses and institutions alike) that reexamined their investments and business interests in then-apartheid South Africa or in tobacco companies as the result of tacit or explicit threats by shareholders or donors to withdraw funds or vote a change in management.

Companies large and small have recognized the corporate benefits of adopting causes that support the communities in which they operate (locally and globally). For example, both Starbucks and Green Mountain Coffee Roasters have been named to many "most socially responsible" lists as a result of their commitment to supporting sustainable harvesting practices and to purchasing beans under Fair Trade conditions. Vermont-based premium ice cream manufacturer Ben & Jerry's has gained a reputation for its support of social and political issues. Its commitment to social responsibility is reflected in the values of product integrity and economic soundness and what it calls "linked prosperity" (Ben & Jerry's, n.d.)

A variation on the social responsibility theme is the commercial world's public concern for the environment, arguably sparked by Rachel Carson's book *Silent Spring.* Businesses have been spurred on, no doubt, by the increasingly vocal concern of their publics for the environment and by the legislation these publics have been able to effect that, in turn, affects the businesses. Pollution control, no-lead gasoline, and materials recycling are but a few of the issues that come to mind. Closer to home for the public relations writer, the direct mail industry has come under criticism because of the volumes of paper it is seen to use.

Publics increasingly seek information about and make decisions (including investment decisions) based on an organization's social responsibility. To this end, organizations worldwide put as much time, effort, and money into reporting on their social responsibility as on their financial responsibility. The reporting ranges from responsibility sections in financial reports to sections of web sites to elaborate, formal printed reports on corporate environmental, social, community and health initiatives.

Johnson & Johnson demonstrates fulfillment of its Credo through web links to pages on diversity, environment, governance, health and safety, international initiatives, policies, and publications. Such pages notably demonstrate the company's transparency—its willingness to be subject to and respond to public scrutiny of its practices.

The public relations writer may well be called on to help develop policies for responding to public pressure on social issues and to create messages publicizing the organization's efforts. You may also participate as you plan environmentally responsible communication strategies such as using electronic media in lieu of print media and selecting recycled papers for print documents and product packaging.

The move toward social responsibility seems to be having an effect. In 2003, the PRSA conducted a survey of organizations that issue formal social-responsibility reports. The survey showed that not only do the organizations see a need to continue such reporting, but also they are planning to expand the practice (Public Relations Society of America, 2003). The European Union and individual countries are considering mandating such reporting.

In addition, a number of annual surveys—such as those by *Business Ethics Magazine* and *Fortune Magazine*—include questions on corporate responsibility and rank companies on reputation, corporate citizenship, and employment practices. Categories include, for example, best company for minorities, for women, or for parents.

Being listed among the "top 10" in such categories has become as prestigious as being listed among the 10 largest or most profitable companies—and it is arguably more realistically attainable for most organizations. Companies use their rankings in such surveys to help combat the negative image that "big business" has acquired from the high-profile scandals and business failures at the turn of the century. For example, Pfizer reports such rankings in its annual report (see Exhibit 16.1 in Chapter 16) and on its web site.

All of the publicity about an organization's good deeds logically raises the question of whether social concerns are really just another way of looking out for a company's bottom line. In some cases, the answer is surely "yes." Without implying that Nike's interest in social responsibility is insincere, it is clear that few have failed to notice that the company's very public advocacy of fair employment practices did not occur until after the company was itself charged with the exploitation of child labor forces in Southeast Asia. The company found itself embroiled in a lawsuit that challenged the limits of corporate speech over just this issue. (See Chapter 6.)

The efforts of such organizations as Transparency International to bring accountability and openness to governments and corporations alike must also have an influence on major organizations. But for many organizations, social responsibility and "green marketing" are a way of life and the organizations gain both popular and financial support from their investments in social issues. The investment industry has responded to this trend by ranking companies by their concern for environmental, minority, and other social issues and by creating mutual funds that limit investments to companies that meet defined criteria for social responsibility.

E X E R C I S E   1

Look at the "Press Room" or "News Release" section of corporate web sites. Do they publicize their good works? Some would say that this dilutes the sincerity of the activities and that the deeds should be a reward in their own right. Others claim that companies seeking the goodwill of their publics should promote their good deeds in an effort to involve the public in these activities and to establish relationships based on them. In other words, it is good public relations. What do you think? Why?

Organizational Ethics as Reputation Management

Another way of looking at organizational ethics is to see them as a vehicle for or expression of what Fombrun (1998, p. 5) calls "reputation management." Fombrun says that reputations are "an outgrowth of a company's identity, an external crystallization of what the company does, how it does it, and how it communicates with its stakeholders," that is, a direct reflection of its ethical principles.

If, as Fombrun asserts, building a strong reputation means that a company must do more than just manipulate its external image through public relations and advertising—that is, it must build its reputation from the inside out—then it can be inferred that an organization's ethics are at the heart of its organizational identity and integral to its future. Ethics will form the basis of its long-term relationships.

Fombrun (1998) suggests that "the greater the transparency with which a company conducts its business, the more likely it is to be perceived as genuine and credible" (p. 7). Its public relations are less likely to be categorized as "spin doctoring," and its communications more likely to be seen as full and open disclosure. Public relations will focus on close contact and rapport with stakeholders in a concerted effort to make the company transparent and legitimate.

The aim of this is to convert stakeholders into advocates so that you can measure success by their supportive behaviors. This builds what Fombrun refers to as "reputational capital," which is measured by the extent to which the organization becomes the first choice for buyers, investors, and clients. Think, for example, of the reputational capital earned by Avon, Inc., not only as the result of product quality but also as a result of its close association with the "Race for the Cure" of breast cancer, a cause dear to the hearts of especially the company's key female publics.

Many organizations have assigned responsibility for developing and enforcing standards of performance that reflect the organization's ethical values to total quality management (TQM), human resources, or ethics departments (Fitzpatrick, 1996). One would expect to find public relations professionals closely involved with such departments because of their shared interest in answering the question, "Why is the organization doing this?" When this does not happen, it leaves the public relations department in the position of expressing ethical standards it has had little or no role in developing and that accordingly may have little relation to the standards or expectations of the organization's publics.

Organizational ethics are often represented in advertising, both in what the ads say and in what they don't. For example, for many years there was an implicit if not official code that an organization would not malign a competitor in its advertising. Today, however, companies routinely point out their competitor's weaknesses or condemn the competition with faint praise, through comments such as "X is an excellent product but I wanted something faster acting" (or "more modern," or "better for my health"). Even the legal profession has been torn by debates over the advertising undertaken by personal injury lawyers. Organizations must not only decide whether these messages are ethical in themselves but also weigh whether the tactic reflects ethical standards that the organization wants to promote.

As organizations recognize the sense of an integrated approach to communication, the question of "what are our organizational ethics?" will be increasingly shared among advertising, marketing, corporate ethics, and public relations departments. This will succeed only if all parties have a common understanding not only of what they are doing (performance) but also of why they are doing it (standards of performance).

Personal Ethics

The level of ethics that is likely to be most familiar will be your personal sense of ethics, a product of your education, religion, and family and community values. The better you understand your own ethical roots, the easier it will be to identify organizations in which you will be ethically comfortable.

Regardless of where your ethical standards come from, they provide you with help on decisions that will not go away for most public relations practitioners. The following questions present typical dilemmas for public relations writers. They will help you understand the breadth of ethical issues you may face and clarify your own position on public relations ethics.

- ✦ Where do your obligations lie? To your employer? To the public? The PRSA code specifies that public relations serves the public good. What happens when the public interest and an organization's interests collide? Is it inevitable that they will collide?
- ✦ What obligations do you have to stockholders, the media, government agencies, consumers, your industry colleagues, yourself?
- ✦ What are the ethical implications of giving a story as a "special" to one reporter and not all?
- ✦ Can you write as a freelance professional for one organization and also in the same capacity for its competitors? If so, must you tell each of them?
- ✦ How do you handle the tension between sexual exploitation and the knowledge that a sexy ad will attract precisely the audience you want?
- ✦ Should you use fear tactics in an appeal?

Some organizations have little regard for anything except the bottom line and take an expedient or short-term view of ethics in order to achieve quick results. As a public relations writer for such an organization, you may find yourself pressured to strategically omit some facts and produce documents that are "technically correct" rather than 100% truthful.

Even if your organizational ethical standards do not address such issues, the PRSA Code of Ethics (see Appendix B) may help you in all of these situations. In advocating truth and honesty, avoiding conflicts of interest, and providing the public with *all* information necessary for informed decision making, the code provides clear guidelines for responsible and ethical action. It also advises that you act as an advocate *to* the organization, conveying the need and responsibility for full truth and accuracy, as well as *from* the organization to its publics.

Ethics and Public Relations Writing

As a public relations writer, you will frequently be faced with situations that require you to make ethical decisions. You will have an ethical basis for recommending that your CEO does (or does not) address expected losses in a speech to the local chamber of commerce, and ethics will almost certainly play a part in your decision to print, or not to print, articles on sexual harassment in the employee or client newsletter. It is important therefore to understand why a statement may be unethical, where the organization stands on the issue and the ethics, and where you stand personally.

There is an inevitable diversity in how communication professionals behave as a result of their individual and/or organizational interpretations of codes. All practitioners do not balance their concurrent loyalties to client, self, the profession, publics, and society in the same way.

The public relations writer putting words to paper is at the nexus of societal, sector, employer, and personal definitions of appropriate and ethical behavior. Writers must resolve the many roles that organizations have assigned to public relations practitioners over time and determine how they will adopt or how they will mix or balance them.

Exhibit 3.3 illustrates several of the roles that organizations typically require a public relations practitioner to fill and the implications these roles may have for public relations writing. To work effectively in an organization, you must be able to accept the role you are given and its ethical implications or be willing to work at changing the organization's values. You must be comfortable supporting the organization's ethics or internally advocating for a change in those ethics. Either way, your own ethical standards will determine your comfort in an organization.

Four broad ethical issues that the public relations writer will face frequently are the following:

✦ Truth (getting the facts) and accuracy (correctness or freedom from error).
✦ Full versus partial disclosure of information. This might be described as being "technically honest"—not providing false information but also not providing full information that might change the reader's perception of the organization or situation. Do you think this is ethical? If not, is it always unethical? Are there situations in which it really does not matter?
✦ Initiating disclosure versus responding to demands for information. Is the organization proactive or reactive?
✦ Reconciling organizational versus other interests. Does your obligation to promote the public interest conflict with the organizational interest?

As a public relations writer, the ethical decisions you make about content and process will usually come back to one of these issues. Assume that you are tasked with producing a new view book for your college or university. Unfortunately, your campus suffers from one problem that students complain about on many campuses: the quality of food at the campus cafeterias and snack bars. Intuitively, you believe that incoming students should be well informed about what they are facing—after all, you wish you had known about the greasy burgers—but should you tell them about the food?

EXHIBIT 3.3	**The ethical implications of the roles a public relations practitioner might assume in an organization.**

Potential roles for public relations practitioners and their practical and ethical implications

Role	Implications	Ethical position
Spokesperson for the organization	Public relations is neutral. It is a channel by which the organization's views are conveyed to the public(s).	Ethically neutral. Ethical standards and motivations lie with the employer.
Conscience of the organization	Public relations ensures that constituencies' concerns are heard by management and that organizational actions conform to accepted standards of behavior.	Public relations acts as an advocate for ethical standards of organizational behavior.
Boundary spanner	Public relations ensures that constituencies' views are heard and considered by management and vice versa. It facilitates/interprets dialogue between the organization and its publics.	Ethically appropriate behavior is the negotiated outcome of dialogue among parties.
Advocate for the organization	Public relations ensures the organization's position is effectively argued and that publics are persuaded of the organization's position.	Loyalty to the organization is the driving value and persuasion the basic strategy.
Information specialist	Public relations ensures that facts about the organization are communicated successfully without overt advocating.	Situational ethics are underpinned by journalistic standards. The information is truthful, but facts are selected depending on the issue, public(s) and purpose of the communication.

The Judeo-Christian ethicist on your right shoulder says, "It is your duty to tell your potential colleagues about the inedible campus food." But the advocate on your left shoulder rightly notes that such negative information might deter a student from enrolling, which means that your brochure will be counterproductive if you publish it with this information. And the food really isn't *that* bad.

At this point, it is likely in practice that the organization's hierarchy if not its ethics will take precedence and the brochure would not be published with the negative information even if you wrote it that way. At worst, this may leave you feeling that you have committed the sin of omission rather than commission.

This is a relatively superficial, albeit real, example. If the issue is more important, you may not feel as comfortable with the decision or, if you are at a management level, as comfortable making the decision that conforms to the organization's interests rather than to your own standards of truthful full disclosure.

EXHIBIT 3.4	**Common strategies for crisis responses. Which do you think are ethical?**

Strategies for crisis responses

Ignore it
Deny it
Divert the public's attention
Scapegoating (blame someone else)
Stonewall
Rationalize
Minimize the problem
Cite legal constraints
Release information selectively
Brazen it out; go on the offensive
Collaborate with critics
Accept responsibility

Consider some of the genuinely important issues we commonly see affecting organizations: environmental catastrophe, product safety recalls, financial mismanagement, and sexual harassment. Although the events and issues themselves may not be cause for concern, in practice for the public relations writer, what the organization chooses to say about them is directly related to the writer's job and may even involve the writer in an ethical dilemma depending on the organization's stance on truth, disclosure, and self- versus other interests.

These strategies shown in Exhibit 3.4 will usually be executed by corporate spokespersons and reflected in a common message across all media. No doubt you can identify many more.

EXERCISE 2

Exhibit 3.4 includes a list of common strategies used as public relations responses to crisis situations. In light of the high-profile ethical dilemmas experienced recently by political, educational, religious, business, and nonprofit organizations, they should be strikingly familiar. This does not mean they are good, effective, or ethical strategies.

Choose a crisis (environmental disaster, financial malfeasance, etc.) for a company you know. Assume that the crisis occurred yesterday and the media has approached you for comment on the situation. To this point, nothing has been said. Write a one-sentence response demonstrating each of the strategies.

By contrast, Baker and Martinson (2002) argue that persuaders can act ethically if they so desire. They developed the TARES test for communicators concerned about the justifiability of their persuasive efforts. TARES is an acronym for five principles of ethical public relations writing. It bears a striking resemblance to parts of the PRSA and other codes of ethical practice.

✦ *Truthfulness*—providing substantially complete information. Are you providing sufficient information so that people can make fully informed choices?
✦ *Authenticity*—personal integrity. Are you prepared to be identified as the source of the information? Do you believe that others will benefit if they accept your message?
✦ *Respect.* Do you respect the recipients of your messages or see them merely as means to an end?
✦ *Equity.* Are you treating people fairly? For example, do you make complex financial information understandable if you know the audience won't understand it?
✦ *Social responsibility*—the social implications of your communications. Is the broader public interest served by your communications?

Baker and Martinson argue that the TARES model can help practitioners weigh the consequences of their actions from the point of view of their organizations, society, and their own personal integrity.

Ethical decisions pervade every aspect of public relations and public relations writing. Because ethics is so important, we have included an Ethical Issues panel in all of the following chapters. The panels present topical and relevant ethical situations, and we hope they will help you understand both the continuing issues and the many resources available to help you manage these issues.

ON THE TEXTBOOK WEB SITE

◆ Go to www.sagepub.com/treadwell for web exercises, study hints, case studies, and additional examples appropriate to this chapter and chosen or developed to supplement the chapter content.

WRITING WRAP-UP

1. A recent newspaper column (fictitious, we hope) suggests that public relations ranks low as an ethical profession. Write a letter to the newspaper's editor arguing that public relations professionals are, in fact, well equipped and positioned to be ethical consultants for their employers. Draw on the resources in this chapter and elsewhere to build the strongest argument you can.

2. Assume that you are about to form your own PR agency. Write the mission statement for this agency. Do not forget the convergence of values and publics when you write it. Why have you chosen the values that you did?

REFERENCES

Arthur W. Page Society. (2003). *Restoring trust in business: Models for action.* Retrieved January 10, 2004, from http://www.prsa-counselors.org/docs/prcoalition.pdf

Baker, S., & Martinson, D. L. (2002). Out of the red-light district: Five principles for ethically proactive public relations. *Public Relations Quarterly, 47*(3), 15–19.

Ben & Jerry's, Inc. (n.d.). *Our mission statement.* Retrieved December 9, 1998, from www.benjerry.com

Caux Round Table. (2003). *Principles for business.* Retrieved June 10, 2004, from http://www.cauxroundtable.org/principles.html

Christians, C. G., Fackler, M., & Rotzoll, K. B. (1995). *Media ethics: Cases and moral reasoning* (4th ed.). White Plains, NY: Longman.

Fitzpatrick, K. R. (1996). The role of public relations in the institutionalization of ethics. *Public Relations Review, 22*(3), 249–259.

Fombrun, C. J. (1998, September). The art and science of reputation management. *International Public Relations Review,* pp. 4–8.

Kaku, R. (1997, July-August). The path of kyosei. *Harvard Business Review,* pp. 55–63.

Kruckeberg, D. (1998, Spring). Future reconciliation of multicultural perspectives in public relations ethics. *Public Relations Quarterly, 43*(1), 45–48.

Partington, J. (Ed.). (1992). *The Oxford dictionary of quotations* (4th ed.). New York: Oxford University Press.

Pratt, C. B. (1992). Correlates and predictors of self-reported ethics among U.S. public relations practitioners. *Psychological Reports, 70*(1), 259–267.

Public Relations Society of America. (2003). *Survey projects future of corporate social reporting.* Retrieved June 14, 2004, from http://www.prsa.org/_News/press/pr111203.asp

Transparency International. (2003, December 8). *UN launches new global convention against graft on December 9th, henceforth International Anti-Corruption Day.* Retrieved February 2, 2004, from http://www.transparency.org/pressreleases_archive/2003/2003.12.08.un_anti_corruption_day.html

Wilcox, D. L., Ault, P. H., & Agee, W. K. (1998). *Public relations strategies and tactics* (5th ed.). New York: Longman.

World Bank Group. (n.d.). *Anticorruption.* Retrieved February 2, 2004, from http://www.worldbank.org/publicsector/anticorrupt/index.cfm

RESOURCES

Books and Articles

Baker, L. W. (1994). Putting ethics to work in public relations. *Executive Speeches, 9*(1), 62–64.

Esrock, S. L., & Leichty, G. B. (1998). Social responsibility and corporate web pages: Self-presentation or agenda-setting. *Public Relations Review, 24*(3), 305–320.

Kruckeberg, D. (1996). A global perspective on public relations ethics: The Middle East, *Public Relations Review, 22*(2), 181–189.

Nelson, R. A. (1994). Issues communication and advocacy: Contemporary ethical challenges. *Public Relations Review, 20*(3), 225–231.

Thomsen, S. R. (1998). Public relations and the tobacco industry: Examining the debate on practitioner ethics. *Journal of Mass Media Ethics, 13*(3), 152–164.

Weber Shandwick. (2003, December 8). Corporate communications role increases in complexity and stature, survey finds. Retrieved March 20, 2004, from http://www.webershandwick.com/newsroom/sub/newsrelease.cfm?contentid=10978

Weston, A. (1997). *A practical companion to ethics.* New York: Oxford University Press.

Web Sites

Business Roundtable Institute .... http://www.darden.virginia.edu/corporate-ethics/
for Corporate Ethics

Caux Round Table .... www.cauxroundtable.org

Direct Marketing Association (DMA) .... www.the-dma.org

DMA Ethical Guidelines (search for "Guidelines .... www.the-dma.org
for Ethical Business Practice")

Ethics Resource Center.. http://www.ethics.org

Food and Drug .... http://www.fda.gov/opacom/morechoices/mission.html
Administration

Global Reporting Initiative .... www.globalreporting.org

Institute for Global Ethics.. http://www.globalethics.org

International Association of .... www.iabc.com
Business Communicators (IABC)

IABC Code of Ethics for .... www.iabc.com/members/joining/code.htm
Professional Communicators

PRSA.. www.prsa.org

PRSA Code of Ethics.. www.prsa.org/_about/ethics

Social Marketing Institute .... www.social-marketing.org

The Social Marketing Institute was created to advance the use of commercial marketing
concepts to influence individual and societal well-being.

Society of Professional Journalists .... www.spj.org
(SPJ) Code of Ethics

SPJ Ethical Standards (select "Ethics Info") .... www/spj.org

U.S. government code of ethics .... usgovinfo.about.com/blethics.htm

Cultural Influences on Public Relations Writing

1. **All organizations operate in a multicultural environment, influenced by global, national, industry, organizational—and now Internet—cultures.**

2. **Cultures affect public relations writers as they identify and define audience needs and characteristics.**

3. **Cultural values affect what and how a public relations writer will write.**

4. **Public relations writers play a role in influencing cultural values.**

5. **Public relations writers play a role in linking cultures.**

On March 3, 2003, U.S. Secretary of State Colin L. Powell announced the resignation of Charlotte Beers, undersecretary for Public Diplomacy and Public Affairs, for health reasons. Appointed in October 2001 in the wake of 9/11 to a job variously described by outsiders as "marketing America to hostile Muslims abroad," "selling Uncle Sam, " "Muslim propaganda chief, " "heading the propaganda war," and "propaganda czar," the tenure of the ex-Ogilvy and Mather head at the State Department was not, by all accounts, marked by success, even given her multi-million-dollar operating budget (Paine, 2003).

What Is Culture?

Culture—the way groups of people collectively think and act—may explain some of the tensions in the short-lived relationship described above. From a public relations perspective, the undersecretary's position involved managing relationships among a variety of cultures at a variety of levels: organizational, sector, national, ethnic, and religious. Her mission required an understanding of ethnic and religious cultures, appreciating the differences between Muslim cultures and Arab cultures, among others. At the same time, her State Department activities were located within the culture of diplomacy with its subtle and nuanced approaches to language. This was a far cry from the creative and extroverted language she enjoyed during her advertising career. Simply put, the cultures of diplomacy and advertising have different ways of analyzing problems—the thought processes of "Foggy Bottom" are not those of Madison Avenue.

This culture clash is just one example of the many that can surround and involve public relations writers as they strive to represent their organizations and organizational cultures with sensitivity and relevance to publics that may or may not share their cultural values.

At their most general, cultures are groups of people who share values, ethics, behaviors, and experiences that are important to them. For the public relations writer, understanding cultures is a way to understand the values and motivations of publics that are important to an organization. Understanding their cultures will help you determine what communication strategies, arguments, and vocabulary are appropriate to reach those audiences. Understanding an organization's culture will help you understand why its communications have a particular style and are produced according to particular procedures and standards.

A common link running through ethics, culture, and public relations is the issue of values and the evaluation of relationships. What in a relationship is of value? What behaviors are appropriate, or most important? How does one decide? If understanding ethics helps us with such decisions, then understanding culture helps us identify the values on which groups (or cultures) make decisions and take action.

The Fluid Nature of Cultures

Cultures are fluid, overlapping, interactive, and important. Shared values bring individuals together (as a culture), and in turn the individuals help the culture to evolve in nature and purpose. An ethnic culture may bring people together to celebrate their heritage or to mobilize for change. Organizational cultures shape office dress codes, social rituals, and, of course, the language and methods the organization uses to establish relationships with its employees and external publics.

The members of any culture, be it ethnic, religious, or occupational, are also a part of many other cultures, such as the city in which they live (e.g., "blue collar," "white collar," "artsy"). Individuals will also be influenced by the cultures of their religion, their education, and, of course, their workplaces.

And these cultures will influence each other. Consider, for example, whether the dot-com phenomenon of the 1990s would have developed the same reputation for informality if it had started in the northeastern or midwestern United States rather than in California. The culture of Texas has clearly been influenced by its proximity to Mexico, of Miami to its large Cuban population, and of Dearborn, Michigan, by its ties to the automotive industry.

Culture: Why It's Important

Culture is an important concept to public relations writers because their work is aimed at influencing relationships between cultures at many levels. You need to identify and understand cultures for three reasons:

✦ To identify how they influence their members' values, expectations, and predispositions toward the writer's client

✦ To identify each culture's communication behaviors to effectively establish relationships with members of that culture

✦ To identify the culturally sensitive, micro-level tactics that will facilitate the building of relationships

As we argued above, the cultures of both organizations and publics are themselves products of many other cultures, which implies that you must understand these as well.

In this chapter, we look at culture from the global level down to the level of the individual public relations writer. Each culture is nested within an other or others. We argue therefore that public relations writers must understand the cultures of sender and of receivers at all levels—global, societal, sector, and organizational—if their writing is to be effective.

The Global Audience

As Grunig, Grunig, and Dozier (2002) point out, because most organizations are affected by organizations in other countries, all public relations is global or international. Fueled by unprecedented advances in communication technology, the concept of cross-cultural relationship building increasingly applies on a global level.

What Does Having a Global Audience Mean?

At one level, we can think of communication by organizations whose mission truly is global, notably the United Nations, but also organizations such as the Red Cross/Red Crescent and Doctors Without Borders, whose concerns transcend national and cultural boundaries. At another level, global communication operates between smaller cultures as nation addresses nation, U.S. business addresses Asian consumers, or German environmental activists link with their counterparts on other continents.

As a public relations writer, you may find yourself representing an overseas organization or government in the United States or a U.S. organization overseas. If you develop web sites, you will engage in perhaps unintended global communications simply by virtue of the technology. Global strategies may involve masterminding worldwide communications from a single head office or delegating offices in individual countries to plan and implement their own communication strategies. At both extremes, it involves understanding the potential for establishing relationships with publics in every corner of the world.

World events such as the continuing growth of the European Union; pressures to expand NAFTA (North American Free Trade Agreement); political rivalries on the Indian subcontinent; the polarization of Muslim, Christian, and Jewish communities; and the emergence of trade pacts in Southeast Asia continue to redefine the players on the global stage. Coupled with new communication technologies, such trends present challenges, opportunities, and the need for new sensibilities for public relations practitioners.

It is tempting to envisage one global marketplace brought about by communication technologies and geographic and economic alliances, but the reality for public relations is a significant increase in the number of culturally diverse publics that practitioners must be able to deal with. As national boundaries blur and change, publics will be more clearly identified with cultures than with nationality, and the need for cultural sensitivity and cross-cultural research and communication skills can only become more important.

Sriramesh and White (1992) propose that to communicate successfully in the global marketplace, public relations practitioners will have to become sensitive to the cultural heterogeneity of their audiences and tailor their public relations techniques to suit different cultures. "The result will be the growth of a culturally richer profession" (p. 611).

Public relations writers who focus their communications on their publics and who routinely make decisions with those publics in mind will have an advantage when it comes to cross-cultural communication. They will already be attuned to looking at their publics' values, interests, communication behaviors, and demographics.

For example, with business interests in more than 125 countries on six continents, ExxonMobil Corporation routinely issues media releases for distribution in both the United States and other interested countries. As a company spokesperson explains, the company has a sound audience-focused strategy for doing so. The company does not alter the message of releases when circulating them in more than one country but they "may put a greater or lesser emphasis on different points depending on the audience." They also may "include additional information in one country's release if we feel that the audience requires more detail" (Lauren Kerr, Mobil Corporation, e-mail correspondence, November 23, 1998).

The Influence of the Internet

Cross-cultural connections are increasingly facilitated by that global medium of instant cultural exchange: the Internet. As technology increasingly lowers the cost and raises the speed and level of sophistication with which we can reach audiences around the globe, the public relations writer is obliged to consider its macro- and micro-level implications.

While it may be tempting to see the Internet as the realization of McLuhan's global village, it probably has a diversifying effect. The Internet makes it possible for individuals to form a huge array of virtual cultures defined by common interests and perhaps language. Effectively, it thus fragments traditional societies and makes the task of identifying relevant publics even more difficult. And as the Internet includes millions of individual e-mail addresses as well as hundreds of thousands of web sites, public relations practitioners may need to view the Internet increasingly as a medium of interpersonal rather than mass communication.

At the same time, the Internet does facilitate global communication. For example, many search engines offer translation services from their home pages. Users can search, retrieve, and translate web search results to and from English and many European and Asian languages. In addition to web page and e-mail translation, the technology can be used for the automatic translation of newspaper articles, worldwide tourist information, and academic, marketing, and health research. It has the potential to speed information flow among divisions of multinational corporations operating in different countries and suggests the possibility that as the technology matures it may become unnecessary to design web sites in multiple languages.

If all or part of your responsibility is to communicate internationally, you will also want to be aware of the standards of practice for public relations in the countries in which you operate. For a full listing of associations worldwide, visit the International Public Relations Association (IPRA) and other web sites listed at the end of this chapter.

You will see that each site has a particular emphasis. IPRA emphasizes professional development and the ethical, moral, and social responsibility of the profession. Some countries' sites discuss quality performance, professional training, international client servicing, and the integration of public relations with related disciplines such as advertising and sales promotion. And still others focus on enhancing the image of the profession and providing an "umbrella" for practitioners from education, journalism, management, and marketing. Together they illustrate the global breadth and potential of public relations philosophy and practice.

Managing Global Communication

One way to think about the intersection of communication and culture is to look at it in terms of the management of communication strategies. This is especially relevant when thinking in terms of global communication.

Wind, Douglas, and Perlmutter's (1973) discussion of international marketing suggests that organizations have four options for managing a global communication process.

- ✦ They can develop an *ethnocentric* "we're right" position with plans for overseas communication developed in the home office.
- ✦ They can develop a *polycentric* "they're right" position based on local, independent operations that honor national borders.
- ✦ If they reach the point at which markets cross national boundaries, they may adopt a *regiocentric* approach that develops plans within regional markets rather than political boundaries.
- ✦ This may in principle extend to the fourth option, a *geocentric* approach based on a worldwide orientation that ignores national boundaries.

The approach adopted by an organization to manage cross-cultural communications will shape everything about those communications from the choice of content and spokespersons to the style of writing and the selection of graphics.

Societal Cultures

There are many ways to look at cultures and their influence. In addition to the global and virtual cultures discussed above, public relations writers may find it necessary to understand (1) the culture of the nation(s) in which they work and (2) the potentially unlimited number of subcultures within that nation. Such cultures form around and reflect shared political, religious, social, and demographic characteristics.

All of these cultures have the potential to influence public relations practice. Prevailing community cultures and their standards shape the priorities and discourse of candidates running for public office, local news coverage, and advertising aesthetics and standards. National cultures shape and frame everything from the way the nation describes itself through the level of sexual explicitness acceptable in advertising (or perhaps Super Bowl half-time shows) to the laws governing public relations, advertising, and marketing practices.

Public relations practitioners understand the need to work within the constraints of culture at these different levels and to align organizational messages with cultures of interest. There are two important reasons for this: to align messages with priority publics as specifically as possible and to make best use of an always-limited communication budget.

Although it is tempting to define cultures by national origin, it is easy to see that most cultures have little to do with political or geographic boundaries. Although they may be influenced by national cultures, societal cultures coalesce on a wide range of demographic and attitudinal attributes, and situational issues and experiences. Accordingly, there are many ways of identifying these cultures. Most of the methods represent a combination of the "classics" we raise in Chapter 5—demographics, psychographics, and geography—but they often provide us with very different views.

For example, researchers trying to get a picture of the United States based on demographic data from the U.S. census over time would see increasing ethnic and racial diversity, and especially a growing Hispanic minority. Some public opinion pollsters see "two Americas"—defined ideologically and geographically—in which the "red" states (that in 2004 voted for George W. Bush) and the "blue" states (that voted for John Kerry) also differ in their positions on abortion, same-sex unions, religious affiliation and practice, and gun ownership ("America Culturally Divided," 2004). And still others suggest that, in a country the size of the United States, there are regional cultures defined by language and behavior that transcend state boundaries (Allen & Schlereth, 1990).

Another way to segment and prioritize U.S. subcultures that is popular with marketers and politicians is to identify groups that have a growing political or economic clout or voice, such as mature, Latino, African American, gay, and Asian cultures. There are also cultures based on lifestyle and special needs. Thus, to the above list of U.S. subcultures we could add the disabled, Internet users, country music fans, and vegetarians to name but a very few.

D I S C U S S I O N   1

What would a public relations writer moving to your state need to know about customs, values, and language in order to write effectively for a state-based client?

Sector Cultures

Sector cultures influence organizational cultures and vice versa. While businesses compete for customers and nonprofits compete for contributions, volunteer time, and public awareness, there comes a time when similar organizations work together under a sector "umbrella"—whether they wish to or not. In turn, they are affected by the actions and image of that sector.

For example, as investors looked with increased skepticism at all investment firms following the SEC clampdown on mutual fund brokers, even companies unaffected directly by the problems found themselves battling the image of a few. They were uniformly viewed as operating in a culture of fraud and self-interest. John J. Brennan (2004) chairman of the Vanguard Group, acknowledged this in a message to the company's fund-holders, saying, "In the long run, no firm can benefit if it operates within a tarnished industry" (p. 4).

Sector cultures have three implications for public relations writers. First, at times of crisis you may need to align yourself with organizations that would normally be competitors in order to protect a common interest. You will do this even while differentiating yourself from the individuals or organizations responsible for the breakdown in public(s) confidence.

Second, there will be elements of style common to all organizations within the sector. Every sector has a distinctive vocabulary and way of using it. Walker Gibson (1966), for example, distinguished between the "sweet talk" of modern advertising, the "stuffy talk" prose of organizations, and the (modified) "tough talk" of journalism. These adjectives correlate closely with Deal and Kennedy's (1982) description of organizational cultures.

Third, the approaches that you bring as a public relations writer seeking to initiate, develop, or sustain relationships will be influenced by the sector in which you operate. For example, while writing for a university, you will strive to give that institution a unique and attractive image. But generally your writing style will be similar to that used by other universities and different from that used in business-to-business communications, the high-tech sector, or health care marketing.

Professional organizations also have a particular way of viewing and talking about their sector. For example, for reasons of history (i.e., the Gillett Amendment of 1913), the National Association of Government Communicators (NAGC) refers to its members as information officers, press officers, public affairs experts, communications specialists, or press secretaries, rather than as public relations or publicity experts.

As with organizational culture, sector cultures are shaped by their members and therefore directly or indirectly by your work as a public relations professional.

Organizational Cultures

Of all levels of culture, the culture of the organization that employs you will probably have the most profound impact on your writing.

Organizational culture can be understood in a variety of ways—how the organization does things, what it holds to be important, the values and activities that differentiate it from other organizations, the stories and jokes that people tell about it, and the rites, rituals, and routines that people in the organization engage in. To the extent that organizational culture means how the organization does things, it will also define the nature of your writing.

Clues to an organization's ethical standards can be found in its culture. How the organization interacts with its employees and expects its employees to behave and to interact (or not) with external publics will tell you something about how it values people. For example, in a highly publicized case, the report of the Columbia Accident Investigation Board (CAIB) named the NASA culture as a contributory factor in the in-flight breakup of the space shuttle *Columbia* in February 2003. The report suggested that safety issues had been subrogated to budgets and schedules. It blamed a culture in which the administration's "we can do it" attitude may have inadvertently sent to employees the message that efficiency took precedence over safety—or process over people (CAIB, 2003).

Ironically, this charge came on the heels of praise that the NASA public relations team had learned the lessons from its 1987 *Challenger* debacle in which NASA refused to even comment on the disaster for several hours. As part of the NASA response to the CAIB report, the organization adopted measures for reporting safety concerns under the slogan "If it's not safe, say so!"

Types of Organizational Cultures

Organizational culture has attracted attention from scholars as well as managers and executives because it is thought to explain or predict organizational performance. In a widely read study of organizations, Deal and Kennedy (1982) identify four types of organizational culture:

✦ *The tough-guy, macho culture* with tough, competitive, high-risk career tracks such as advertising, surgery, and entertainment. The heroes are tough risk takers.

✦ *Work hard, play hard cultures* where there is small risk and quick feedback. The heroes are valued for outcome such as sales figures, not risk. Deal and Kennedy cite McDonald's and Mary Kay as examples.

✦ *Process bureaucracies,* such as government agencies, where there is little risk and little feedback. The values are technical perfection and the processes are slow.

✦ *"Bet your company" cultures,* high-risk, slow-feedback organizations such as NASA and oil exploration companies. Results may be a long time coming but they are large and gratifying if and when they happen. The organization focuses more on the future than the present.

Clearly, these categories describe very different organizational cultures with very different values. Depending on where an organization falls in these categories, a public relations writer could expect to communicate with very different publics on very different subjects, using very different styles of writing.

EXERCISE 1

Refer to the four culture types above set out by Deal and Kennedy (1982). Write four job descriptions for an entry-level public relations writer to suggest the specific communication standards of each culture. What skills will each culture regard as most important? How will each culture deal with issues of disclosure of information, deadlines, and relative tolerance for typographical errors, for example?

From your own experience, identify other organizational cultures not identified by Deal and Kennedy.

In some ways these organization types reflect the Grunig and Hunt (1984) typology of public relations discussed in Chapter 1: press agentry, public information, two-way/asymmetrical, and two-way/symmetrical.

Researchers continue to study organizational cultures in an attempt to define the characteristics that differentiate them. For example, Hofstede, Neuijen, Ohayv, and Sanders (1990) define six scales on which organizations may be characterized:

✦ Process-oriented versus results-oriented
✦ Employee-oriented versus job-oriented
✦ Parochial versus professional (whether employees identify with the organization or with their job)
✦ Open versus closed (whether it is welcoming and inclusive or cold and exclusive)
✦ Loose versus tight control (whether it is casual or formal, including strong, unspoken dress and behavior codes)
✦ Normative versus pragmatic (whether it is driven by organization rules or by the market)

These are not cultures, per se, but rather dimensions on which it is possible to map out or compare cultures. Using these tools and others will allow you to describe the organizational culture you are looking at and to assess issues of professional concern such as image (desired and actual), ethical standards, and practices including the organization's position on social responsibility.

At the writing level, a formal organizational culture will most likely predict formal language, while a results-focused organization may be less concerned with standards for writing than with its effects. An employee-focused organization will place emphasis on employee communications in addition to external communications.

Cultural dimensions and the way they are expressed in public relations writing may informally predict the ability of organizations to work together. For example, in the 1980s two of New Zealand's largest companies merged to form Fletcher-Challenge, Inc. Challenge Corporation, the more conservative of the two with its roots in the country's agricultural industry, had values based on its relationships with employees and clients. Public relations staff focused on internal communications, producing newsletters and annual reports to keep employees informed and motivated, and informational materials to help farmer clients prosper. In contrast, Fletcher Holdings, founded as a family-held company in the higher-risk building and construction industries, had a hierarchical structure and an external focus. Its communications focused on government lobbying, news releases, and advertising, almost to the exclusion of its internal publics.

These divergent public relations strategies are evidence of values and cultures that ultimately proved incompatible. "Turf" issues abounded as the merged public relations staffs, including one of this textbook's authors, tried to maintain their own previous focus while at the same time working for a new organizational culture. The culture clash among the public relations staff was symptomatic of the culture clash within management, and indeed the company as a whole. Although not a direct result of cultural differences, within 20 years the company had first risen to great heights on an international scale and then in 2001, dissolved altogether.

How Do You Learn About an Organization's Culture?

You will come to understand an organization's culture through listening, questioning, and close observation. Many organizations commit their vision of the ideal to paper or web site, often as part of mission or vision statements. They do so because they need employees and other publics to know the kinds of relationships they can expect to have with the organization, and because they want to position the organization as unique and special in a world of, perhaps, many similar organizations. Sometimes you will infer an organization's position on ethical and cultural issues from a formal code of social responsibility.

You can begin learning about corporate cultures from the employment ads an organization places. After the ads, you will learn about the corporate culture by the content and tone of the interview and first days in the organization, that is, from other employees. Did they give you a tour of the whole enterprise? Were you introduced to senior executives? Is there a training or mentoring program? Did you have the opportunity to ask questions? As Deal and Kennedy (1982) suggest, finding out the organization's heroes and villains, rites and rituals, dress and language will also give you insight on its values and generally how things get done. Chapter 5 discusses the research of organizational cultures in more detail.

All material about your employer—written, spoken, and graphic—reveals something about its culture as it relates to public relations. This includes especially the advertising and public relations documents that have been produced by your predecessors or colleagues.

Look, for example, at the mission statements of the Public Affairs Offices of the U.S. Army and the U.S. Navy shown in Exhibit 4.1. These are the departments responsible for public relations functions for their organizations.

These offices serve the same function and their missions reflect similar commitments to informing the U.S. public, but notice the different emphases. If the Army's mission "to establish the conditions that lead to confidence in America's Army" sounds like a public relations mission, it should, but it pays no attention to other than a general public. In contrast, the Navy's statement addresses multiple publics, beginning with its own personnel and their families and continues with a tone that is far more "user friendly" and less "military" than the Army mission. What do these missions say about the cultures of the two branches?

How Do Organizational Cultures Affect the Public Relations Writer?

The adjectives used by Deal and Kennedy (1982) and others, for example, "macho," "high/low risk," "slow feedback," are well-accepted descriptions of organizational cultures. But how do they translate into public relations plans and specific writing projects? What do they mean to the public relations writer in practice?

First and most important, they will affect what you can write. Next they will influence whom you are writing to and finally how you write or present it. In fact, prevailing

EXHIBIT 4.1   The mission statements of the offices that handle "public relations" for the U.S. Army and U.S. Navy. Remember, entities affiliated with the U.S. government do not have public relations departments under that name.

U.S. Army Public Affairs Office

Mission

Public Affairs fulfills the Army's obligation to keep the American people and the Army informed, and helps to establish the conditions that lead to confidence in America's Army and its readiness to conduct operations in peacetime, conflict and war.

Navy Office of Information

Mission

Our job is to inform Navy men and women, their families and the American public on key issues relating to the Navy-Marine Corps team.

We are also charged with working with national and international media, and community relations on a national level, and providing public affairs policy and guidance to public affairs officers, Navy journalists and civilian public affairs specialists serving the Navy worldwide. CHINFO is also responsible for production of print and broadcast internal information products through its subordinate command, the Naval Media Center who produces and distributes its products such as Navy News, *All Hands* magazine, and the *Navy-Marine Corps News*, a weekly half-hour television program seen across the U.S. on many cable outlets.

Source: U.S. Army Public Affairs Office, http://www4.army.mil/ocpa/resources/mission.php; Navy Office of Information, http://www.chinfo.navy.mil/navpalib/chinfo/chinfo.html.

cultures and their attributes will influence everything from the frequency of the employee newsletter to whether you use the president's full name in media releases.

To appreciate the relationship between organizational cultures and public relations writing, consider the cultural attributes a public relations writer might use to express organizations from a communications standpoint. Many of these reflect the terminology of Hofstede et al. (1990). These attributes might include polarities such as "open/closed," "formal/informal," "people-focused/product-focused," "forward-looking/grounded-in-the-past," "involved/isolated," "impulsive/cautious," "optimistic/pessimistic," or "flexible/rigid."

Where the organization stands between such polarities says a great deal about the topics a public relations writer will be allowed, required, or encouraged to write about (or not, as the case may be). It will help determine whether the organization's relationship with the media is cordial and cooperative or antagonistic. It also hints at what audiences an organization may consider most important and, by implication, the types of public relations "products" (e.g., news, features, broadcast, newsletters) the organization will want produced.

And finally, dimensions such as "formal/informal," "optimistic/pessimistic," and "people/product" suggest how a public relations writer will be expected to write. They will determine the accepted style, vocabulary, and tone of the writing and who will be allowed to speak for the company, even in the staff newsletter.

For example, the organizational culture will be reflected in management's willingness (or lack thereof) to "go on record," to communicate frequently and openly, and to initiate communications. In turn, this will affect your relations with local media, the level of disclosure in the annual report, the choice of communication methods, and even your readiness to manage a crisis, to name but a few situations.

Formal and traditional organizations may not want you to use a vernacular that is entirely appropriate for your audience but does not reflect the image the organization wants to portray. Part of your job may be mediating a clash of cultures between, for example, your trendy and avant-garde public relations agency and your formal and conservative management.

Ethical Issues

Ethics and Cross-Cultural Public Relations

Diversity is a desirable goal of U.S. colleges and universities. However, representing this diversity is a challenge for the institutions' public relations departments. The dilemma is how to achieve this aim when the actual level of diversity has not reached the desired level of diversity.

Some institutions have resorted to altering photos in order to increase the sense of cultural diversity on the campus. Because research shows that high school students look to brochures and videos seeking students with whom they will be culturally comfortable, it is clear why an institution would want to maximize the appearance of diversity in these documents. And we do not suggest that the commitment to diversity on these campuses is insincere. However, when they have been "caught" altering photos—even to reflect the actual level of diversity—the publicity has been immediate and negative.

The jury is still out on whether this practice is ethical. On one side is the argument that as long as the institution's population is accurately represented overall, photos that are doctored to include students of color, for example, are no worse than photos that are staged to reflect the same level of diversity, or indeed than stock photos purchased for use in admissions materials. On the other side are those who argue that the implicit "need" to doctor the photos is symptomatic of a lack of serious effort to make campuses more welcoming to diverse populations.

In deciding whether to adjust photos, even to represent accurate situations, the public relations writer might be guided by the PRSA Code of Ethics. Of particular interest are the provisions that require truth and accuracy in order to help publics make informed decisions. Another way to look at the issue is to ask yourself whether the benefits of one or two doctored photos are worth the cost to your or the university's credibility—always a high price to pay.

As Michael Schoenfeldt, Vanderbilt University vice chancellor for public affairs, commented in the *Chronicle of Higher Education,* "Every time doctoring does happen, it will be exposed. People are savvy. Ultimately, manipulating the truth never works" (Jacobson, 2001).

How Does the Public Relations Writer Affect Corporate Culture and Ethics?

Public relations writers can have a powerful, if sometimes indirect, effect on how people choose to behave in organizations. Employees' perceptions of their organization, their models for behavior, and their organization's standards and value are implicit or explicit in everything the public relations writer becomes involved with from employee newsletters and annual reports to employees to communications with clients or news coverage of the organization. Public relations writers may help shape organizational culture and values as much as they are shaped by them.

The Macro-Focus: Understanding Cultures

Cross-cultural communication can succeed or fail at either or both of the two levels we emphasize in this book: the macro-level thinking that develops communication strategy and the micro-level thinking about words, communication style, and delivery methods.

In one attempt to define the dimensions of national cultures, Kluckhohn and Strodtbeck (1961) suggest that cultures could be compared on the basis of the following:

- ✦ Their evaluation or assumptions about human nature *(evil-mixed-good)*
- ✦ The relation of people to the environment (*subjugation-harmony-mastery*)
- ✦ Their orientation in time *(past-present-future)*
- ✦ Their orientation to activity *(being-doing)*
- ✦ The relationships among people *(hierarchical-collateral-individual)*

In studies that have spanned four decades, Geert Hofstede (2001) has explored the dimensions on which cultures can be differentiated. Over the course of his studies, he has identified five variables: power distance, uncertainty avoidance, individualism, masculinity, and long-term orientation. He found that these dimensions show significant and meaningful correlations with geographic, economic, demographic, and political/national indicators. They are shown with their implications for public relations writing in Exhibit 4.2.

Such dimensions are important because they suggest how organizations influenced by a national culture might think about their relationships with their publics—short term, exploitive, proactive or reactive, dominating or collaborative, and so on.

Because communication expresses, preserves, and transmits culture, we can expect that such dimensions will predict the type of communication that is practiced and acceptable in different cultures, be they organizational or national. For example, many Asian cultures have in common an emphasis on relationships within family and society. Such a group-centered orientation may make U.S.-oriented appeals based on individualism inappropriate.

The cultures of organizations and publics will also influence communication methods. Because organizations are culture-bound, their values about authority, government, business, the environment, or the socially disadvantaged will vary in response to their cultures. In cultures that place great emphasis on personal interaction to establish a sense of trust, mutual understanding, and loyalty, relations may focus very heavily on interpersonal communication. The same is true of cultures in which there is distrust of government-owned/controlled media.

U.S. theories of communication cannot necessarily be exported or, if exported, will inevitably be transposed into versions of the original. Clearly, it is important to know a partner culture well before you attempt to communicate with and in that culture.

Look, for example, at Exhibit 4.3, an op-ed piece prepared by (then) Mobil Corporation as part of its ongoing corporate advocacy program. Distributed in the

EXHIBIT 4.2   Application of Hofstede's (2001) categories to culture and public relations writing.

Hofstede's categories	Cultural and organizational characteristics	Possible implications for public relations writing
Power Distance Indicator (PDI): Gauges human equality or inequality with respect to laws, privilege, prestige, wealth, and power.	Characterized by obedience, conformity, paternalism, protection of the wealthy, and autocratic government. Organizations with a high PDI are likely to be centralized and hierarchical, with a large number of supervisors.	✦ Public relations as a means of control. ✦ One-way, inside-out communication. ✦ Less room for creativity. ✦ Writer may work under direction rather than as a team member.
Uncertainty avoidance: Gauges the culture's need for certainty versus uncertainty or ambiguity.	Nationalistic, "tight" societies with more elaborate legal systems and emphasis on expertise overlay competence. Organizations are structured with rules and rituals and an emphasis on memos, reports, accounting planning and control systems, and the use of experts.	✦ Public relations as a routine, systematized activity. ✦ Informative, factual information. ✦ Initiated by subject matter experts. ✦ Process is important. ✦ Writer is subject to many checks and balances.
Individualism	Encourage individual initiative. Enjoyment appeals over duty, and there is greater social mobility.	✦ Creativity. ✦ Competition of ideas. ✦ Need to rise above a diversity of messages in the marketplace of public opinion. ✦ Writer must have ability to argue a position successfully.
Masculinity dimension: Assesses cultures as assertive versus nurturing.	View money as more important than people, achievement more than service, independence more than interdependence, excelling more than leveling, rewards for performance, more job stress and more industrial conflict.	✦ High performance work ethic. ✦ Deadlines and productivity important. ✦ Public relations as a business tool more than as a service to society. ✦ Deadline driven or not.
Time Horizon	The degree to which group members will defer present gratification to meet long term goals.	✦ Quality *or* results will take priority. ✦ Ethical standards may be compromised by short-term goals. ✦ Time available for research will vary. ✦ Decisions may or may not be fully informed.

EXHIBIT 4.3   Op-ed article as distributed to the U.S. press in support of trade negotiations with China.

Opening more doors with China

1

2   **As President Clinton prepares for his visit to China it's a good time to reflect on this growing force in international trade.**

3   Mobil's ties to China began in 1880 when **clipper ships** delivered kerosene for the Mei Foo (beautiful, trustworthy) lamps that brought light to people's homes throughout the country.   Before long, we opened trading offices in Shanghai and Hong Kong.   Today, **4** **as the leading international marketer** of finished lubricants in China, Mobil supplies products that help power China's industrialization. Mobil is proud of our heritage in China, and we are excited about the progress the country is making on many fronts.

For example, China has expressed a desire to move to cleaner-burning fuels and technologies to meet the increasing energy demands of its populace.   Last October, it signed the Energy and Environment Cooperation Agreement with the United States and followed that up with an Energy Conservation Law that sets effective targets for various sectors of the economy.

In Hong Kong, China is using natural gas in power generation, and it's building pipelines to feed an expanding gas network that is being developed for Beijing and Shanghai.   This grid will enable more residents to move to natural gas.   In the fast-growing coastal provinces which lack sufficient reserves of gas, China is giving strong consideration to importing liquefied natural gas (LNG).

Mobil can help China with its development and use of cleaner-burning energy.   We're discussing several integrated energy projects including exploration and development of indigenous natural gas and suppling LNG for power plants. Gas is not only clean burning, but also more efficient in today's combined-cycle gas turbines.

We're eager to develop storage and distribution facilities for liquefied petroleum gas — a clean, efficient source of fuel used for cooking — and recently completed our second and third lubricant-blending plants in China.

Mobil is promoting environmental awareness too.   We've recently donated $1.2 million to establish the Mobil China Environmental Education Fund, which will publicize the government's environmental protection plans and educate officials on matters of environmental importance.

5   **Trade is likely to be a key issue as the leaders of our two countries meet. Some would argue that the West's approach to trade with China should be more conditional, that trade links should be tied to improvement in human rights. While there is no denying the importance of human rights, attempts to change another nation's policies by choking off trade are ineffective because they undermine the leverage and influence that trade provides in bringing about change.**

The fresh air of dialogue and engagement holds greater promise.   Global commerce promotes dialogue and prosperity, which together often foster increased political and personal freedoms.   We're beginning to see evidence of that in China. **We urge the U.S. government** **6** **to grant permanent status as a Most Favored Nation to the country.**   At the same time, the international community should promote China's inclusion in the World Trade Organization on internationally accepted conditions.

7   **China has entered a new era of growth and development. The U.S. and others can choose to be partners in that growth and work constructively for progress, or they can turn their backs on a nation that is home to 22 percent of the world's people.**

8   **We believe the answer is clear. It's time to open more doors.**

Mobil ®The energy to make a difference ™

http://www.mobil.com   ©1998 Mobil Corporation

EXHIBIT 4.4 **The heading and first paragraph of the Mobil Corporation op-ed article as printed in the Chinese press. Following that are the key areas in which edits were made to the piece before it was printed in Chinese.**

美孚愿紧跟中国改革开放的步伐

美孚公司自 1880 年起开始进入中国，当时快速帆船为美孚（取美好而可靠之意）灯运来了煤油，为中国家庭的照明提供了方便。不久以后，美孚在上海和香港开设了贸易公司，而今，作为中国市场上成品润滑油的主要国际供应商，美孚为中国的工业提供了源源不断的动力。美孚为其在中国进行的努力而骄傲，更为中国在许多方面的飞速发展而感到欣喜。

1. Headline changed to: Mobil will keep step with the Chinese economic reform.

2. First paragraph omitted.

3. Clipper ships changed to: high-speed sailboats.

4. The leading international marketer changed to: one of the leading international marketers.

5. Paragraph omitted.

6. Sentence omitted.

7. Paragraph changed to: Mobil helps the Chinese people know Environmental Protection in more detail.

8. Paragraph changed to: Mobil will keep in step with Chinese Economic Reform and best times are ahead.

Source: Reproduced with permission of Mobil Corporation, Inc., Fairfax, Virginia.

Note: The numbers coincide to the numbers and bold/underscored sections on the original op-ed shown as Exhibit 4.3.

U.S. press in June 1998, the piece appears to be an excellent example of the public relations writer successfully treading that fine line between supporting the organization's interests and writing copy that will be acceptable to the media and readership in foreign countries in which it will also be distributed—in this case China.

The writer succeeded to the point that the piece did run in the Chinese press (see Exhibit 4.4), but not without substantial edits described in the exhibit, to make it conform to Chinese media standards for advertising. "Chinese advertising regulations prohibit the use of superlatives or comparisons in ads," explained company spokesperson Lauren Kerr. "Also China prohibits any and all 'political' messages in advertising. Therefore, all references to President Clinton and the U.S. were deleted from this ad, as were mentions of national policies" (L. Kerr, Mobil Corporation, e-mail correspondence, November 23, 1998).

This should leave you with the ideas that national and cultural values do affect public relations practice, both process and content; that cultures do differ on the basic values, which to some extent predict communication practice; that research on a country's culture and communication and public relations practices is essential; and that operating in more than one country requires a basic strategic decision as to whether to centralize or localize communication.

The Micro-Focus: Language and Vocabulary

On a micro- or message level, successful cross-cultural communication involves sensitivity, empathy, flexibility, tolerance for ambiguity, and a high level of respect for the nuances of language.

For example, in 2003 Hispanics officially replaced African Americans as the largest minority population in the United States. Looking at the communication challenges associated with this population reveals many of the micro-level issues that will affect your efforts to establish relationships with any culturally distinct public.

A report by *Hispanic Business* magazine (2003, p. 3) shows that 37% of total Hispanic income is earned by people age 15–34. The same report cites Nielsen predictions that the Hispanic teen population will grow 62% by 2020. This means that much of the buying power for this demographic group rests in the youth market. So, if your employer provides goods or services or wants to mobilize the youth vote in areas with large Mexican, Cuban, or Puerto Rican communities, providing information in Spanish, choosing Spanish-language media, and certainly using examples and metaphors that have meaning and impact for Hispanic teens may be necessary to cultivate a relationship with those teens.

But even defining this "Hispanic" public presents a challenge. Debate continues to rage over whether this population should be referred to as "Hispanic" or as "Latino/Latina," reflecting earlier debate over "Black" and "African American." Many people of Hispanic origin see themselves as, for example, Cuban American or Mexican American rather than Hispanic or Latino. Writers must understand the cultural background of the specific Hispanic public for which they are writing.

If you are writing broadcast copy for this market, be certain that you know whether the pronunciation is "kyew-ban" or "koo-ban." It makes a difference. The wrong word or the wrong pronunciation may position your organization as an outsider in a cultural community at exactly the time you are trying to position it as a member, supporter, or sympathizer of that community.

In the United States, it would be an oversimplification to assume that a Hispanic public dictates Spanish-language communication. Not only does the preference for Spanish vary by group, but so also do media preferences. Some Hispanics may prefer Spanish-language radio but watch television or read in English (Tharp, 2001). There are similar analogies in other ethnic communities.

DISCUSSION 3

We recall a spirited debate over the headline of an ad that was targeted for the *Wall Street Journal* to announce that the N.Z. Company had been listed on the New York stock exchange. The artwork was a photo of a racehorse crossing the finishing line well ahead of its competitors. The debate raged over whether the headline should read "making the pace" or "setting the pace." Which would you recommend? Why?

Vernacular and style must "translate" into other languages or even other versions of English. You must use *programme* and *labour* to meet the expectations of Commonwealth readers, and remember that much of the world (and the United Nations) writes dates as day-month-year rather than the U.S. convention of month-day-year. This can have a significant effect on whether international guests arrive for your grand opening on February 3rd (02/03/05) or four weeks late on March 2nd (03/02/05), for example. When in doubt, spell it out.

The international communication consulting firm InterSol, Inc. (1998) cautions that you must pay attention not only to accurately translating copy but also to seeing that graphics, brand names, examples, and metaphors are culturally appropriate before you use them. The business world is rife with stories—some documented, some apocryphal—of failed attempts to "translate" product names, slogans, and copy directly into languages other than the original. For example, the first attempt to translate the name Coca-Cola into Chinese allegedly resulted in a phrase that means "bite the wax tadpole," and General Motors had to rename its Chevy Nova for the South American market because in Spanish *no va* means "won't go." Such marketing miscommunication myths remind us of the need for cultural and linguistic sensitivity and for homework, homework, and more homework.

Even colors and numbers are culturally ambiguous at best and culturally sensitive at worst. Although in English the word *periwinkle* means blue, in German it is the dark green color of the plant's leaves. The color of mourning in the United States is traditionally black, in Asia it is white; in Brazil, purple; and in Mexico, yellow. In some parts of Asia, the numbers four and nine are unlucky. Innocently printing brochures in the wrong color or packaging products in groups of four could cost you sales.

Cultural blunders send the message that your organization either does not understand the local customs, culture, or audience needs or, perhaps worse, does not care. In either case, they contribute to the problems you face in persuading the audience to accept the organization's message and adopt the behavior the organization wants.

Not surprisingly, the United Nations, that most cross-cultural or geocentric of bodies, developed a house style to accommodate the multicultural demands on media releases issued by its Department of Public Information. Stylistically, the United Nations adopted a compromise between American English and British English, using the "u" in *labour* and *colour*, but a "z" in *capitalization* and *organization* (except for the International Labour Organisation, whose official name is spelled with an "s") (United Nations, 1998).

UN staff caution that the issues involved in communicating the actions of a multicultural body are far more complex than simple spelling choices and require special attention to the details of cultural differences. George Parker, former chief, News Coverage and Accreditation Service, UN Department of Public Information, said that "writing for 185 member-state bosses . . . is somewhat like walking on a tight rope during the entire workday" (G. Parker, UN Department of Public Information, personal communication, October 7, 1998). He cited three situations as typical and problematic:

◆ *Spelling.* Even difficult names such as former Mongolian Ambassador Jargalsaikhany Enkhsaikhan have to be spelled correctly—every time. Regardless of their rank, people do not like having their names spelled incorrectly. "It ruins their moment in the sun," Parker notes.

◆ *Reflecting the sensitivity of international names.* Since 1990, fifteen countries have changed their names as the result of war, merger, independence, or evolution. Some returned to versions of previous names, such as Zaire back to Congo. UN reporters must be particularly sensitive to the rancor that using an old name can raise.

◆ *Maintaining strict neutrality.* UN writers take pains to avoid "loaded" phrases such as "he alleged" and even "he claimed" in favor of "he said," which Parker acknowledges is drab but necessary.

Public relations writers must be sensitive to similar issues in their own day-to-day cross-cultural projects. A content-free example is that specifying 8.5″ × 11″ paper will mark you as an outsider in most other countries where the international standard "A-4" is used.

Culture and Its Implications for Public Relations Writing

It should be clear that as a public relations writer you will work at the intersection of many cultures, starting with three cultures with which you have an immediate relationship. They are your organization's culture, the culture of the sector in which the organization operates (e.g., health care, technology, nonprofit), and the culture of the public relations sector as a whole.

Cultures will affect your career at many levels. First, you will bring to any position the influences of your own culture. The cultures in which you were raised, that is, your family, educational, social, and spiritual communities, and the values they instilled all influence your first employment decision. For example, many students might be opposed to working for a tobacco company on the grounds of health and concern for others. Others see no difficulty and in fact find interesting challenges in promoting this perfectly legal product.

Once in a position you will begin to understand your organization's values and culture and how they relate to the values held by the industry sector. Professionally, you will also be influenced by the values of the public relations sector. The values or standards of behavior of public relations professionals are set out in, for example, the PRSA Code of Ethics (see Appendix B) and the International Association of Business Communicators Code of Ethics for Professional Communicators. They articulate the values of a profession but may or may not be followed by your employer. Governing many of your activities ultimately will be the legal system, itself a product of a nation's culture. We discuss law and the public relations writer in Chapter 6.

Culture can affect your writing in both large and subtle ways. On a large scale, it will affect decisions on strategy. For example, in Saudi Arabia the message source may carry far greater significance than the message itself (Zaharna, 1995); thus, a key element in public relations strategy is selecting credible spokespersons.

Cultural sensitivity is also required at the level of word use. For example, Spanish is a language in which pronoun use depends on a speaker's relationship to the public. Thus, Tharp (2001) explains that in addressing U.S. Latino consumers "Budweiser, in keeping with its positioning as the 'King of Beers,' uses the respectful *usted* [rather than the more intimate *tu*] to address Budweiser consumers" (p. 137).

Clearly, cultures influence communication strategies, the definition of key publics, and the nature of the relationships to be developed with those publics as well as the linguistic subtleties required for effective message design.

Public relations writers must also pay attention to the influence of culturally based factors of which the audience may not even be aware. For example, taste is a cultural phenomenon. What is trendy in the United States may be seen as distasteful in other countries. The same problems may occur if you try to export what is "in" in New York City to the upper Midwest, rural South, or even rural upstate New York. Humor too is culturally based; generally, it does not translate well from culture to culture and therefore is not a smart idea in cross-cultural communication.

Facilitating Cross-Cultural Communication

Cross-cultural communication is not necessarily difficult in spite of the well-documented misfires of less than culturally sensitive organizations and governments that failed to rely on local expertise and/or to pretest their communications. There are many resources to help organizations understand their target cultures and to help them create effective messages that are also culturally sensitive.

One solution is to make use of multinational public relations agencies with offices in many countries. Even public relations firms without their own overseas offices are often part of an international network or affiliation such as Interlink through which they can access necessary international expertise. Organizations with less frequent communication needs may use an international translation service.

The aim is to employ a professional with experience in the target market who can guarantee not only the accuracy but also the appropriateness and fluency of the translation. To be effective, translators should be fluent in both English—preferably in your organization's industry so that they fully appreciate the nuances of the message—and the target culture so they effectively translate those nuances (or warn against them).

Given the subtleties of human persuasion, a competent local professional remains the best bet, but as the original writer you can do much to ensure accuracy in translation. Begin with simple text without embellishments, technical terms, or especially idioms. Include facts that are relevant to the target audience, but avoid metaphors and speech that you think is colorful. It may be misunderstood or not translate easily. Let a translator who understands the local culture insert the metaphors.

We caution, however, that simple word translations, such as those provided by web sites, do not substitute for the oversight of someone who can also translate with cultural nuances and sensitivities in mind.

E X E R C I S E   2

To test the effectiveness of web translations, try submitting a random paragraph of text from the newspaper into one of the services. Have it translated from English to a language you know. Does it make sense in the foreign language? Does it have the same color and cultural "flavor"? Now have the translation translated into a third language, and then a fourth and fifth. At this point, have it translated back into English. How does it differ from the original? What aspects did and did not translate accurately?

In principle, public relations writing for international audiences is the same as writing for domestic audiences. Both require analyses of publics, cultures, and appropriate communication strategies with a view to strengthening relationships. For the public relations writer, the difference is the level of attention required to understand the relative importance of different publics, and the linguistic subtleties and cultural values that shape message design and relationship building. As Grunig et al. (2002) suggest, the principles of successful public relations must be adapted to local conditions including culture/language, the political, economic and media systems, economic development and the extent and strength of local values.

ON THE TEXTBOOK WEB SITE

✦ Go to www.sagepub.com/treadwell for web exercises, study hints, case studies, and additional examples appropriate to this chapter and chosen or developed to supplement the chapter content.

WRITING WRAP-UP

1. Assume you have just been hired as a consultant by one of the following organizations to develop guidelines to be given to new entry-level public relations writers in the organization.

   ✦ A public university
   ✦ A major (research and patient care) medical center
   ✦ A defense industry contractor

Write a letter to the head of the public relations department about communication standards that you believe capture the organization's way of doing things with respect to deadlines, accuracy, frequency, responsiveness, and disclosure of information. Remember that the organization has many audiences, including external, internal, and the media. Will the standards change depending on the audience?

REFERENCES

Allen, B., & Schlereth, T. J. (Eds.). (1990). *Sense of place: American regional cultures.* Lexington: University Press of Kentucky.

America culturally divided; blue vs. red states, Democrats vs. Republicans—Two separate nations, new O'Leary Report/Zogby Poll reveals. (2004, January 6). Retrieved February 15, 2004, from http://www.zogby.com/search/ReadNews.dbm?ID = 775

Brennan, J. J. (2004, Winter). Vanguard chairman on 2003 . . . and 2004. *In the Vanguard, Voyager edition.* Vanguard Group.

Columbia Accident Investigation Board. (2003, August). Organization, culture and unintended consequences. In *Report of the Columbia investigation.* Retrieved October 12, 2003, from www.caib.us/news/report/chapters.html

Deal, T. E., & Kennedy, A. A. (1982). *Corporate cultures: The rites and rituals of corporate life.* Reading, MA: Addison-Wesley.

Gibson, W. (1966). *Tough, sweet and stuffy: An essay on modern American prose styles.* Bloomington: Indiana University Press.

Grunig, L. A., Grunig, J. E., & Dozier, D. M. (2002). *Excellent public relations and effective organizations: A study of communication management in three countries.* Mahwah, NJ: Lawrence Erlbaum.

Grunig, J. E., & Hunt, T. (1984). *Managing public relations.* New York: Holt, Rinehart & Winston.

Hispanic Business, Inc. (2003). *US Hispanic consumers in transition: A descriptive guide.* Santa Barbara, CA: Hispanic Business.

Hofstede, G. H. (2001). *Culture's consequences: Comparing values, behaviors, institutions and organizations across nations* (2nd ed.). Thousand Oaks, CA: Sage.

Hofstede, G., Neuijen, B., Ohayv, D. D., & Sanders, G. (1990). Measuring organizational cultures: A qualitative and quantitative study across twenty cases. *Administrative Science Quarterly, 35,* 286–316.

InterSol, Inc. (1998, July 2). Writing for translation. *Global Advisor Newsletter* Retrieved October 6, 1998, from www.intersolinc.com

Jacobson, J. (2001, March 16). In brochures, what you see isn't necessarily what you get. Scandals raise larger issues about how diversity is portrayed. *Chronicle of Higher Education, 47*(27), A41, 2p, 2c. Retrieved March 2, 2004, from http://chronicle.com/weekly/v47/i27/27a04101.htm

Kluckhohn, F. R., & Strodtbeck, F. L. (1961). *Variations in value orientations.* Evanston, IL: Row, Peterson.

Paine, K. D. (2003, March 28). Can this reputation be saved? *Measurement Standard, the International Newsletter of PR Measurement.* Retrieved February 28, 2004, from http://www.themeasurementstandard.com/issues/303/eng/repsaved303

Sriramesh, K, & White, J. (1992). Societal culture and public relations. In J. E. Grunig (Ed.), *Excellence in public relations and communication management.* Hillsdale, NJ: Lawrence Erlbaum.

Tharp, M. C. (2001). *Marketing and consumer identity in multicultural America.* Thousand Oaks, CA: Sage.

United Nations. (1998). *Provisional handbook for United Nations press releases.* New York: UN Department of Public Information.

Wind, Y., Douglas, S. P., & Perlmutter, H. V. (1973, April). Guidelines for developing international marketing strategies. *Journal of Marketing, 37,* 14–23.

Zaharna, R. S. (1995). Understanding cultural preferences of Arab communication patterns. *Public Relations Review, 21,* 241–255.

International Public Relations Organizations

The starting point for national public relations organizations is the list compiled by the International Public Relations Association. Its web site is listed below with some English-language sites where you will be able to compare standards of practice and definitions of public relations.

Canadian Public Relations Society, Inc. .... www.cprs.ca
    (English and French versions)

German Public Relations Consultants .... www.gpra.de
    Society (German and English versions)

Institute of Public Relations—U.K. .... www.ipr.org.uk

Institute of Public Relations of Singapore .... www.iprs.org.sg

International Public Relations Association .... www.ipra.org

Public Relations Institute of Australia .... www.pria.com.au

Public Relations Institute of New Zealand .... www.prinz.org.nz

Support for Cross-Cultural Communications

AltaVista "Babel Fish" Translation Service .... www.world.altavista.com

InterSol, Inc. (translation services) .... http://www.intersolinc.com/

Trade Show Exhibitors Association .... http://www.tsea.org/

5

Research Influences
on Public Relations Writing

1. **Effective public relations writing is based on research.**

2. **Public relations writers must know what, how, and why to research.**

3. **Important research topics for public relations writing are** **environment, organization, publics, media, messages, and message effects.**

4. **Public relations writing involves ethical decisions.**

What Is Research?

Research thinking is the ability to formulate useful questions and to answer them with confidence toward the goal of improving an organization's relationships with its publics.

Whether or not you realized it at the time, you have been doing informal research for many years. When you decided to go to college or university, you initially identified a "universe" of possible institutions. You then ruled out a number of them based on cost, location, majors, and entry requirements. Then you worked through a short list focusing on majors you were interested in and quality-of-life issues such as housing and recreational and social facilities. Finally, you visited the campus, spoke with faculty and admissions representatives, sat in on a class, sampled the food, and met students before making a final decision. You developed a systematic way to answer an important research question, "What is the best institution for my educational needs?"

So you already have an instinct for research. You know how to ask questions and find answers. You have discovered that research is simply an objective, systematic way of gathering information to answer questions. At an intuitive level, you should come to do the same with your writing, assessing it with respect to vocabulary, choice of medium, design, and likely effects on audience.

As you proceed in your career, you will learn that professional research involves finding out the bad news as well as the good news. You will also discover a reciprocal relationship between research and planning. You do research so that you can plan effectively. At the same time, the planning you have already done will dictate the kind of research and writing that you will need to do.

Public relations research recognizes that the basis of public relations is two-way relationships. It is fundamentally a process of listening to the voices of an employer and the employers' publics in order to strengthen relationships between them.

Public relations writers and public relations managers/directors/planners share many of the same research interests. All of them need to understand audience demographics, psychographics, lifestyles, values, attitudes toward the organization, and media use. All need to assess whether their communications had any effect and whether and how their programs could be improved. The chief difference is that the public relations writer has a more specific interest in message content and presentation.

Research Components

Lerbinger (1977) defines six elements of public relations in which research plays an important role:

✦ *The organization's environment*—the outside world in which it operates
✦ *The organization's structure*—the internal world it has created
✦ *The organization's publics*—internal and external
✦ *The message*—the communication content
✦ *The media*—available to and used by the organization to disseminate its messages
✦ *The effects of the program* on the audiences/publics—did the program achieve its aim?

These categories represent the many levels of thinking needed by a public relations writer, from understanding broad environmental issues to choosing among specific media/messages and responsibly trying to assess the impact or effects of one's writing. This chapter looks at these categories answering the following three questions for each one.

✦ Why/how is this important to the public relations writer?
✦ What will you research (the research question)?
✦ How can you conduct the research (the research method)?

Researching the Environment

The environments in which an organization operates will affect many public relations writing decisions. You must understand these environments so you can help the organization be sensitive and respond to its environment, even to relationships that on the surface may not be obvious or seem important. For example, a poor growing season in Colombia may seem a remote issue, but Colombia exports coffee, and if you write for a chain of coffee shops you may have to explain to customers why the cost of their daily latte is going up.

Environmental research for public relations focuses on the economic, political, regulatory, social, cultural, technological, energy, marketing, financial, and legal components of the organization's environment. We would also add the environment of public opinion. For example, if the public doesn't care about toxic sludge, why should you spend time writing a news release that promotes the company's responsibility in installing new filtering equipment? And if you don't know who your competitors are, what they are saying, and whether they are successful, how can you write copy that positions your organization as unique in its competitive environment?

The Environment: What to Research

An important part of researching the environment is identifying the influences on public opinion for or against the organization even without your knowledge or participation.

Chief among these resources are political bodies that control the legal and regulatory environment in which the organization operates. At the minimum, you should know which legislators represent your district(s) and what their positions are on issues that affect your employer. It also means knowing and maintaining contact with all of the legislators who sit on committees directly related to the organization.

You will also want to know and understand local government and business associations, especially if your organization does most of its business or receives most of its support locally. You will need to research the benefits of belonging to Rotary, Kiwanis, or other service clubs or to the chamber of commerce to be part of the network of local business leaders that influences both local politics and public opinion.

Don't forget the professional and industry codes of ethics and conduct that influence the way the organization behaves. You will learn informal codes of behavior from attending conferences and networking with colleagues. You will also learn about formal codes from sector associations and indeed, from your organization itself.

And, of course, you will want to gain knowledge of competitors to position your organization successfully against them in the marketplace and to be able to work with them when outside forces threaten the industry. They will readily become colleagues when you all need to address regulatory changes affecting the sector as a whole. Insofar as nonprofits compete for the same volunteers and donor dollars, even they have "competitors" of which you should be aware.

One of the most important environmental issues you may research will be the laws and regulations that apply to your employer's sector. For example, SEC regulations regarding financial disclosure will affect your writing for public companies, and failure to observe them may result in penalties.

Even more encompassing are the regulations of the U.S. Postal Service (USPS). They govern everything from the size and shape of envelopes to the position of the address to the use of adjectives by nonprofit organizations. Missteps regarding postal regulations can have a serious impact on your message distribution and your budget.

The Environment: How to Research

For some researchers, environmental scanning refers to specific techniques. For our purposes, we think of it simply as trying to "read" the environment for issues, trends, and changes that may affect an employer and the writing you will need to do. It involves becoming a consumer of the national and local media as well as media that service your organization's business sector. It also involves listening, and generally paying attention to what is going on in your employer's world.

Media scanning will help you answer the "Where do we stand now?" question for your organization. It sets the scene within which your writing takes place.

Media Scanning

Media scanning can be both informal and formal. Informally, you read newspapers, magazines, and journals (national, local, and industry specific) to keep current on issues in the forefront of the public or media. You can get a feeling for public sentiment by the adjectives used and of your organization's relevance by the amount of print space or broadcast time it receives.

You can also scan formally and regularly by using professional services to systematize the process. At one time, press clipping actually meant cutting articles from publications to get a crude measure (in column inches) of press attention. Today, scanners and a variety of analytic software make it possible to measure and assess media coverage electronically. They can also help answer questions about the tone of media coverage, that is, positive, neutral, or negative.

On the Web, meta-search applications can search all major Internet search engines at once. This is handy for monitoring issues across many sources. Other search engines examine Internet discussion groups for content that may be relevant to your employer.

A related forecasting method is to scan the media for new words as they appear. Tracking and predicting what words are "dying" or appear to be growing in use by your publics will help you choose appropriate vocabulary. There is a school of thought that believes language in the media predicts trends in consumer activity. Think of how the terms *solar power*, *Generation X*, and *disco* have waxed and waned over time. The theory is that such terms appear in the media before they gain wide popular usage and therefore may predict trends in consumer adoption. Professional forecasters using this technique assume that "in the beginning was the word." Voracious media scanning should become a professional habit. It puts you in a position to identify and capitalize on trends in public opinion.

Databases: Where, Who, and What

The explosion of Internet and CD-ROM-based databases coupled with private, public, professional, and library-based research services is changing the face of communication practice, especially direct mail. We use the term *database* somewhat loosely to indicate any set of information that you can research. This includes, for example, media directories that list key contact people at media outlets and media calendars that list the special topics that upcoming issues will center on. You will find this useful when scheduling media placements.

It is not necessary that you become an expert in the detailed geography of a specific data set. What is important is that you understand where to turn for the information you need.

Tips for Database and Web Site Searches

The objective of any data search is to maximize the number of relevant hits and minimize the number of irrelevant hits. Therefore:

✦ *Select the most appropriate databases* for information about your organization. For example, ERIC (Educational Resources Information Center) is a likely source if your employer is a college, but you will also want to access a source that reports on public attitudes to education, such as the *Chronicle of Higher Education.*

✦ *Use word combinations and quotation marks to narrow the search.* A search for "McDonald" may yield anything from McDonald's hamburgers to Old McDonald's farm to the genealogy of the clan McDonald. Combination terms such as "clan McDonald" will narrow the search, for example, to your Scottish ancestors. Combination terms are bounded by quotation marks " " and direct the search engine to give you only those results that include all of the words in the search.

✦ *Think larger, or smaller, than the first term you try.* For example, the terms "public relations," "marketing," and "advertising" may be too broad; depending on what information you are seeking, you may need to search using "public relations for nonprofits," "marketing to seniors," "advertising in China," and the like. And in the commercial world, the brand may not be the company. For example FritoLay is Pepsico; KFC is Yum! Brands.

✦ *Use technology to save and transfer information.* Accessing the Internet from a personal computer means you can download information that you can analyze or use to build your own reference file in a customized database. You can also export your findings to colleagues or collaborate on projects electronically.

✦ *Don't ignore print.* Many sources, including much federal government information, may be available online but they may still be available in print, especially if it is historical information. For example, census data are made available in the *Statistical Abstract of the United States,* the U.S. Commerce Department publishes information on consumer trends, and the federal Centers for Disease Control and Prevention (CDC) publishes mortality and morbidity statistics.

The Web

The World Wide Web (WWW) provides access information on most topics and will be especially useful in helping you research environments if you do so wisely. The Web can be a good, but not perfect, source of information. From experience you should know that the reliability and credibility of material on the Internet need to be reviewed critically. Also, web sites are ephemeral; the information you download on Tuesday may change on Wednesday, and the host site itself may disappear by Thursday.

You can access information on your organization's sector and its publics from searches for web sites hosted by organizations, companies, and private individuals. The results you get will vary with the search engine. Search engines—not to be confused with databases—are tools that search web sites for words you enter or select. Because search engines use different criteria and access different types of online material, you must develop the ability to refine your selection to narrow the results to a manageable number. A good reference librarian will be able to help you get maximum results from a search. See the "Tips for Database and Web Site Searches" box.

E X E R C I S E   1

Explore the differences in search engines by using a common search term such as "public relations writing" on three different search engines.

Now try using the terms "printer," "printing," and "commercial printing" on one search engine. You will notice a great difference in the search results. What does this tell you about the importance of keywords in searches and in creating web sites of your own?

Sources of information about federal legislators, their committees, and their opinions can be found through the congressional web site thomas.loc.gov/ (after Thomas Jefferson) and the individual member web sites linked to it. The thousands of web sites sponsored by advocacy groups will also provide information, both pro and con, about issues that may affect your organization. There are many directories for these sites.

You can find information about your competitors from many sources including newsletters or online mailing lists hosted by your competition and perhaps joining or subscribing to them. This has some ethical implications; you will need to find out from the discussion moderator or mailing list operator how membership operates and what the ground rules for discussion sites are. If anyone can join the discussion, obviously you will be able to do so; if membership requires approval, you may or may not get it. List membership is a two-way street: If your list is uncontrolled, there is no reason why competitors—and the media—cannot subscribe to yours as well.

Government web sites. You can access laws and regulations, publications, and educational materials through federal, state, and local government web sites. They generally include indexes and search engines to assist your research and are also usually linked to other web sites.

Begin your search for federal government web sites through firstgov.gov (note: no "www") or www.fedworld.gov. From these home pages, you can access the web sites of all federal departments and agencies and some state web sites.

Similarly, state or city web sites can often be accessed by the state or city name or abbreviation. If not, try to access state information through a federal web site and city information through the state.

Web Site Credibility: The Need to Evaluate

Web site credibility is an issue for anyone seeking information on the Web, from students conducting research for term papers to professional researchers conducting a literature review for a research report. The question is, "To what extent can you rely on the information you get from a web site given the multitude of authors, institutions, agencies, and biases or personal agendas on the Web?" Basically, the same criteria you use in evaluating print media apply to evaluating web sites. The more important issue is that you understand the need to evaluate them rigorously before you commit your employer's resources to a project based on an outdated web site. See the "Evaluating Web Sites" box for a discussion of web evaluation standards.

Evaluating Web Sites

We suggest you answer the following questions when evaluating a web site's content. They are the same questions that visitors to your employer's web site may be asking. They should give you thoughts about web design for your employer.

- ◆ *Ownership*—Whose web site is it? Is it sponsored by an identifiable person or organization?

- ◆ *Authorship*—Who wrote it? What are the qualifications, experience, reputation, and longevity of the author(s) and/or host institution?

- ◆ *Purpose*—What appears to be its purpose: information, persuasion, or entertainment?

- ◆ *Bias*—Can you see an agenda or mission (explicit or implicit)? In itself, an agenda, such as promoting conservative or liberal political issues, does not lower the site's credibility and does not mean that the information provided is not true. It may mean, however, that the web site presents only one side of an issue and that to see the full picture you will need to seek out web sites presenting the other side or at least the full spectrum of opinions.

- ◆ *Authority*—Is the content reviewed? Are there identifiable criteria or reviewers or editors by which material is screened or chosen for the web site?

- ◆ *Links*—Are there credible links? What sites (if any) that you know to be credible and reliable link to this web site?

- ◆ *Currency*—Is the information up to date? "Old" material as such is not an issue, but dated material that clearly should be updated reflects negatively on the professionalism of the author or web manager and the credibility of the site.

Researching the Organization

You cannot know too much about your employer's organization. Its history and background, problems and successes, values, attitudes, and culture all influence your writing because they tell you "how things get done around here." In due course, they also explain *why* things get done the way they do. The way in which an organization chooses to talk about itself often is the product of an emotionally important history, the influence of a founder with a strong personality, or perhaps a significant merger or restructuring.

In addition to understanding the organization's culture and history, you will need to know its structure and lines of communication, its media relations, and its key publics. Understanding the reasons behind the terminology, the relationships, and the processes will help you relate more easily to the organization and secure maximum assistance with your writing.

The Organization: What to Research

First, it is critical that you understand the organization's history.

For example, knowing the origin of the organization's name may help you predict and defuse resistance to a proposed name change. You will quickly come to understand that, for management at least, there may be an important emotional or sentimental difference between the shorthand "Dorn" and the full "Dorn and Sons," or between "Fletcher-Challenge Corporation" and "Challenge-Fletcher Corporation." If you want a real-life understanding of the emotional debate that can arise from a simple name change, consider the rancorous debate over whether Rutgers University should change its name to the State University of New Jersey. The solution was a compromise: Rutgers, The State University of New Jersey (Mclarin, 1994).

Organizational research should also give you a sense of overall public relations and writing strategy. Does the organization want a high or low profile? Is there terminology it prefers (or hates)? For example, many organizations now refer to "associates" or "partners" rather than to "employees." And a female CEO may choose to be called "chairwoman" because she is female, "chairman" because (rightly or wrongly) she believes it puts her on an equal footing with other corporate leaders in the industry, or the gender-neutral "chairperson." If she heads a university department, she might even opt for just "chair." Such terminology may be a rule that you will follow or raise questions for which you must suggest a solution. You will need to grasp the importance of such terminology.

There are at least three other organizational attributes that will help you understand the organization: mission, structure, and culture. The organization's mission-vision-goals-objectives spell out its values regarding the relationships that your writing supports. Directly or indirectly, your writing will be evaluated on the contribution it makes to the organization's mission.

Structure, the division of responsibilities and linkages among units in the organization, will be important because it will tell you where key decisions get made and how the organization communicates internally.

Culture, that complex amalgam of attitudes, behaviors, values, and vocabulary that defines the organization, is what makes it unique. Culture explains "why" as well as "how" things get done. It drives many aspects of your writing. As a writer, you will be expected to reflect the organization's culture in the way you write about it.

The Organization: How to Research

External Sources

Unless you commission research, you probably will not find public opinion related specifically to your organization, but you will likely find public opinion about relevant issues in the industry. From this you can draw conclusions about the organization. You may also find public opinion about the sector in which the organization operates.

Internal Sources

Internal sources include colleagues and supervisors, and of course, archives and files. You will find useful information in mission, philosophy, or core value statements. These are typically provided to new employees during their orientation.

Annual reports, employee communications, and archives are additional sources of organizational information. So are product specifications, organization charts, employee bios, and bulletin boards (electronic and hard copy).

Large organizations may have professional historians or archivists. Depending on the organization's level of technological evolution, historical documents may be on a web site, intranet, microfiche, or basement shelves.

It is as likely that you will work for organizations that have yet to realize the importance of retaining historical documents. They will realize the importance of this when that 50th anniversary celebration comes around and there are no archives of annual reports, maps, or photos. You may find yourself educating management on the value of such records to secure the allocation of resources to support an archive project.

Organizational Culture Research

Why do physicians and scientists insist on using technical, scientific terminology that laypeople may not understand? Why might they object to your attempts to "translate" this vocabulary into something more easily understood? For example, your study of science or medicine as culture will reveal core values related to precise language, to avoiding generalizations that cannot be supported, and to vocabulary as a measure of professionalism. Organizations and occupations have defined ways of doing things. They must be understood if your writing is to effectively relate the organization to its publics.

The tools of organizational culture research are attentive listening and observation of language, use of space, rituals, dress, superior-subordinate relationships, values, and taboos. Open listening can elicit how management believes the organization should be represented, how it differs from competitors, how they identify core values and important publics, and what ethical standards do and should apply.

Deal and Kennedy (1982) suggest several ways to understand organizational cultures. For example, you can read what the company says about its culture, interview employees, observe how people spend their time, assess the content of what is being discussed or written about, or pay attention to the anecdotes and stories.

Spradley (1979) suggests three broad categories of questions that will help you understand organizational cultures:

- ✦ *Descriptive questions*—"Tell me about . . ."
- ✦ *Structural questions*—"What are all the different kinds of . . . ?"
- ✦ *Contrast questions*—"Explain the difference between . . ."

As a wordsmith, you will share Spradley's interest in "folk terms," that is, the terminology that is unique to or has a special meaning for the organization. You will be able to use these terms as well as descriptive, structural, and contrast questions to discover the broad cultural themes that run through the organization.

You will likely discover basic ideas that drive the organization whether or not they are expressed formally. For example, you should be able to learn a great deal from statements such as "People think we're a software company, but we really sell productivity tools" (a software developer) or "We have a reputation for attacking people who can't pay their bills, but what no one understands is that we can help resolve debtors' problems and keep them out of further trouble" (a collection agency).

When validated as representing issues that are important to the organization, such statements provide a framework and basis for writing. For example, the quotes above suggest that the software developer will want statements about software framed in terms of the results it can achieve for customers rather than in terms of technical specifications. And the collection agency will want its activities presented as assistance rather than as confrontation.

D I S C U S S I O N   1

Following are quotes from three organizations.

✦ *HMO*–"The future of health care lies in technology."
✦ *Internet service provider*–"We're betting our future on the fact that simplifying the web interface for customers will guarantee greater market share."
✦ *College*–"The future of higher education is in off-campus, distance learning and customized programs for people already at work."

What do these quotes suggest about how the organizations might position themselves to their publics? The type of relationships they seek with publics? The type of writing they might prefer (e.g., formal–informal)?

After synthesizing the information you have gathered, you will need to anticipate your publics' questions about the organization. Taking a journalistic approach, you will ask the classic "who, what, when, where, why, and how" questions.

Much of your research about the organization may be informal information gleaned from conversations with other employees, managers, and sometimes outside sources. This informal research may provide you with the questions for your formal research. In addition, you may want to take advantage of a rarely acknowledged but essential skill if you really want to know what's going on in your organization—the ability to read upside down!

Researching Publics

A public is an identifiable group of people with attributes in common that can affect the well-being of an organization. Publics are the reason for every organization's existence. Without the support of key publics, established and maintained through communication, organizations might not survive.

Accordingly, you will need to understand the publics that are important to its success and survival. "Public" in this context need not imply large. A public can be small but very significant, such as a group of legislators, a single donor, or a board of directors.

As a public relations writer, you will want to know how your publics feel about the media you might select for your messages and whether your message gives them the information they want and need. These questions are the basis for the customer service response cards that you receive from vehicle manufacturers after a service check and the content surveys run periodically by many magazines. They will also be the topics of surveys that you may run for employee and client newsletters to identify ways to improve these communications.

Publics: What to Research

There are five things about publics that you will typically need to research to maximize the impact of your writing:

+ *Demographics*—Age, sex, income, occupation, location, and the like are demographic attributes. It is information that the U.S. census typically obtains.
+ *Psychographics (or attitude)*—How do they feel about your organization (or its programs)?
+ *Knowledge*—What do they know about your client?
+ *Behavior*—How do they act toward your organization or its products and services?
+ *Media use*—What do they read, view, listen to?

You will also need a good understanding of their K-A-B—knowledge, attitudes, and behavior—and as discussed in Chapter 4, the culture and values of occupational or cultural sectors to which they belong.

The answers to such generic questions about an organization's publics will influence the strategy and tactics of your writing. Publics that are barely aware of the organization clearly need to be made aware before they can develop positive attitudes or behaviors. Publics that are on your side need communication content that keeps them that way. Hostile publics clearly need all your persuasion skills to reduce and ideally eliminate the level of hostility. As a public relations professional, you will be more interested in behaviors than attitudes because behaviors are the ultimate measure of your success as a writer.

Publics: How to Research

Information about external publics comes from four sources: database research, publicly available information, proprietary research, and do-it-yourself research. Information about internal publics usually comes from do-it-yourself research.

Database Research

Experience should tell you that demographic and psychographic breakdowns of publics overlap. People living in a geographic area are usually demographically similar, with attitudes, lifestyles, and media use in common. Understanding how they overlap and what this means to communication and especially persuasion is the foundation of a very 21st-century discipline: database research. Database research is the analysis of information held in one or more databases to identify common themes, patterns of activity, and communication behavior in a public. It will help an organization manage its relationships with that public.

For example, market researchers have become skilled at overlaying information about individuals with census data about zip codes to build a profile of that area's demographics, attitudes, and lifestyles. You can find examples of this process at the claritas.com web site where you can type in your home zip code and obtain a demographic profile of your area. The U.S. Census Bureau provides a similar service on its web site.

Many commercial services have developed database analysis systems to help organizations understand and maximize results from their publics. For example, both the Republican and Democratic parties developed extensive databases after the 2000 presidential election, preparing to apply such "market analysis" techniques to targeting political messages in the 2004 race, even to the level of being able to send different messages to several members of a single family (Gertner, 2004).

Although they differ in detail, these segmentation programs, as they are called, are all based on the analysis of information gathered and held in commercial and public databases including the U.S. census. They have growing relevance to public relations as practitioners strive to understand their publics more thoroughly.

The VALS™ (Values, Attitudes, Lifestyles) system developed by SRI International classifies individuals into eight broad categories based on an individual's self-orientation (principle-, status-, or action-oriented) and resources (the personal, demographic, and material resources individuals have to draw upon). The Yankelovich "MindBase" lifestyle categorization is a similar service.

The PRIZM® Segmentation System developed by Claritas, Inc., classifies communities on two criteria: urbanization (country/city) and income. Based on census data and analytical measures developed by Claritas, it is continually updated to reflect population shifts and changing demographics. PRIZM and its related system Microvision® help marketers identify the zip codes in which their target audiences live, allowing the marketers to develop effective media-buying strategies.

The PRIZM cluster analysis divides the population into 67 clusters or neighborhood types. Each of the thousands of zip codes in the United States can be described by one of the neighborhood types. The PRIZM analysis sample shown in Exhibit 5.1 is an overview of four clusters within the "Urban Midscale" social group. Claritas describes this group as the middle-income, urban-fringe neighborhoods of America's major metropolitan areas. Claritas describes these clusters as sharing "high population densities, ethnic diversity, public transportation and all the perks and risks of urban life."

Even with the limited information presented in Exhibit 5.1, you can see that defining your target group can help you determine whether to write at college or grade school level, whether to place an article in fashion or sports magazines, or possibly even whether English would be the most appropriate language. Going one step further, if the characteristics of, say, the "Mid-City Mix" segment describes your target audience, PRIZM can tell you the zip codes that are predominantly this category. This will tell you where to target your messages and avoid unnecessary time and expense.

DISCUSSION 2

Exhibit 5.1 is a summary of the PRIZM data available for four clusters in the "Urban Midscale" social group: "Urban Achievers," "Old Yankee Rows," "Mid-City Mix," and "Latino America." The information includes some demographic characteristics, lifestyle indicators, and media preferences. Use these data to predict which, if any, of these cluster groups would be a likely target audience(s) for information about each of the following products and services:

✦ Information on a referendum to build a new fitness center
✦ Information on a referendum to turn the riverfront into a park
✦ Fundraising appeals
✦ A mailing promoting "high tech" electronic devices
✦ A mailing promoting new cable TV services
✦ Information on a new line of clothing by black designers
✦ PSAs promoting successful parenting

EXHIBIT 5.1   Excerpts from the clusters in the PRIZM U2 "Urban Midscale" social group.

Nickname	Urban Achievers	Old Yankee Rows	Mid-City Mix	Latino America
Demographics	Mid-level, white-collar, urban couples	Empty-nest, middle-class families	African-American, singles/families	Hispanic middle-class families
Predominant adult age range	24–34, 65+	65+, 35–44	Under 18, 25–34	Under 18, 25–34
Key education level	College grads	Grade school, high school	Grade school, high school, some college	Grade school
Predominant employment	Professional, white-collar	White-collar, service	Service, white-collar	Service, blue-collar
Key housing type	Renters, multi-unit 2–9, multi-unit 10+	Renters, multi-unit 2–9	Renters/owners, multi-unit 2–9	Renters, multi-unit 2–9
Lifestyle preferences	Attend pop/rock concerts	Belong to union	Use 3-way calling feature	Visit Disney theme park
	Own electronic organizer	Believe ad campaigns	Shop at T.J. Maxx	Do weight training
	Use debit card	Buy mutual fund through a bank	Use postal money orders	Bought life ins. from mail ad
	Watch *ABC News Nightline*	Watch pay-per-view movies	Watch *The NAACP Image Awards*	Read baby magazines
	Read *New York Magazine*	Read men's magazines	Read *Muscle and Fitness*	
Socioeconomic rank	Middle	Middle	Middle	Middle
Key ethnic/ racial type	White/Asian/ Hispanic	Mix	Black/Hispanic	Hispanic

Source: ©1998, Claritas Inc. PRIZM and Claritas Inc. are registered trademarks of Claritas Inc. The PRIZM Cluster names such as "Mid-City Mix" are trademarks of Claritas Inc. Reproduced with permission.

Proprietary Research

There is also a body of consumer opinion that has been captured but that is not publicly available. This information is the result of proprietary research and forms the basis of strategic marketing for the organization that commissioned it and therefore owns it. It is information you protect rather than release for your competition to access. As an employee, you may well have access to this information but only under conditions of confidentiality.

Proprietary research may become publicly available after it has become dated and has lost its immediate relevance, topicality, or commercial value. This makes the data of little value if you want to track fast-changing issues, but if you are prepared to assume that public attitudes toward higher education or donating blood may not change significantly over time, then such data can be cost-effective.

Publicly Available Information

There are also many sources of publicly available information. This is good news for organizations especially with limited budgets or projects that do not require special surveys.

The first source is your library. Public, academic, and corporate libraries have access to many databases. Many relevant databases as well as journals such as *Public Opinion Quarterly* and *American Demographer* are potentially available. Consult with a reference librarian to ensure that your search for information will be as efficient as possible.

A second credible source is the U.S. census, a common source of information about publics down to city block level. The Bureau of the Census web site includes census data and maps about the size and income of households, education levels, and race.

The news media, especially major newspapers and television networks, frequently run surveys on topical or political issues such as candidate preferences or foreign policy. They then publish the results. Such polls may be statistically sound or simply "call-in snapshots" of public opinion with no claim to represent the opinion of the wider community.

Interest groups also run and publish survey results on topics as diverse as men's necktie preferences and handgun control. Such surveys provide insight on issues and may be valid from a research point of view. Be aware, however, that they may have been commissioned with an agenda in mind. You will want to seek information on who commissioned and conducted the survey, on the methods and questions used, on the sample size and demographics, and perhaps whether the survey was reviewed or refereed.

You may also find research results on web sites such as www.pollingreport.com that summarize the results of other surveys.

Do-It-Yourself Research

Do-it-yourself research ranges from informal questions around the water cooler to focus groups of newsletter readers to web site response forms to full-fledged, formal surveys. If you can't find information that is relevant, and a hired research firm is an approach you don't need or cannot afford, you might choose to conduct your own research. You have available any or all of the methods that might be used by professional research companies, including telephone, mail, and web-based surveys, focus groups, and interviews.

Conducting effective research is difficult and, especially, time-consuming. It requires an understanding of sampling, statistics, interview techniques, and question development. Regardless of the method you choose, the basis of all research should be the organization's goals for communicating with its publics: that is, knowledge, attitude, and behavior. For example, the Red Cross likely wants people to know that giving blood is important. It also wants them to have a positive attitude toward giving blood and ideally to engage in the behavior of giving blood. As a writer for the Red Cross, you would be particularly interested in research that assesses messages and how people respond to them.

Such goals, as well as budget and the time you have available for research, will influence your choice of research methods and design right down to the questions you ask. If you want a behavioral outcome, you will need research that measures this—probably observation or respondent's self-reports of their actions. Alternatively, measuring attitude or attitude change almost certainly requires interviewing people and giving them an opportunity to express themselves.

Researching Messages

The fundamental question about any piece of writing is its acceptability. Acceptability should be understood in terms of the three audiences that a public relations writer must consider: the organization, the organization's publics, and the media.

The way these audiences affect the writer can be seen in the classic public relations news release that must satisfy all three publics simultaneously. First, the release must meet organizational standards. These range from ethical and value standards ("we don't use that kind of language in this organization") through strict legal standards where the release is formally cleared for compliance with SEC standards of disclosure or for potential copyright violations. Second, it must meet media requirements for content and style. Finally, it must meet the requirements of the reading-viewing-listening public. Consider how a new product release for an auto company would, or should, differ depending on whether the release is targeted to the daily press, *Car and Driver* magazine, or *Consumer Reports*.

Messages: What to Research

For the public relations writer, message research addresses subject, style, and technique, more specifically, readability, recall, and design. You will want to know whether newsletter readers find the articles readable, comprehensible, reliable, credible, useful, relevant, and memorable.

Message research answers questions such as "Does this article answer the public's questions?" "Does active voice have more appeal than passive voice?" "What appeals will attract the public?" "What metaphors would be useful?" "How can this message reach the unmotivated reader?"

Readability

Readability research helps you determine if your audience will find your writing interesting and written at an appropriate educational level. One test of this is the quick readability check available through most word processing programs. Readability scores relate to comprehension. Text that scores at a grade 12 level will not be fully understood by anyone who reads at the level of eighth graders.

Design

As discussed in Chapter 7, design plays a key role in guiding the reader through a text. Type, layout, color, and graphics support your writing and make it stand out from competing messages. Wise use of graphics may even reduce the amount of writing you have to do.

You will want to research design because aesthetics can attract reader attention and make the document memorable. As important is the fact that seemingly mundane features such as typography, use of white space, column width, and the level and number of headings can all influence how easily readers make their way through your copy. As with messages, you may want to pretest design alternatives in focus groups.

Messages: How to Research

Professionals research messages at two stages: before they are launched to determine that the messages will work and after they have been released to see that they reached the intended audience and achieved the desired objective. Pretesting methods range from focus groups to get broad reader reaction to readability and grammar checks to help avoid the embarrassment of misspelled words and reader confusion.

Readability Tests

Readability tests help you assess how comprehensible your writing will be to people of differing educational levels. It is a function of vocabulary, word length, sentence length, and of the correct use of grammar. Grammar use can also be assessed through software programs that identify verb-subject (mis)matches and excessive use of the passive rather than active voice. We do not recommend relying on grammar checks any more than you would rely solely on a spell check.

Another way to measure readability or comprehension is the "Cloze" procedure in which readers receive copy with words deleted and are asked to fill them in. The theory is that if the copy has a logical flow and is relevant and comprehensible, then readers will be able to fill in the blanks. The more blanks successfully filled in, the more readable the copy.

Measuring recall. If you need readers, listeners, or viewers to recall a message, you will have to research whether this happened or not. Public relations writers with an interest in what leads to recall may assess the recall of previous copy before setting out on a new project.

In many cases, informal research will be enough to meet your needs. Comments heard around the office and solicited from key employees will tell you what you need to know about staff reaction to the employee newsletter. Similarly, although thousands may read a media story, a phone call to local editors may be all the feedback research you need to do. After all, it is the editors rather than the readers who make the decision to publish.

There are times when formal research is required. For example, publishers would likely choose to formally survey their thousands of readers for their opinions on the content and design of a monthly magazine or a web site. In such cases, the survey form is inserted into every copy of the publication, posted to the web site, or e-mailed to subscribers. The sample is the entire population of subscribers and purchasers. Although "pass along" readers may not have the opportunity to respond to the survey, their opinion may not be that important if they are not the target audience.

At the extreme of formal research, carefully designed surveys and rigorous sampling may be needed to understand people's responses to advertising messages. Follow-up focus groups may be needed as well to learn why people responded the way they did.

Content Analysis

The broad approach for message research is content analysis. Content analysis is a quantitative method for assessing the frequency of words or phrases and for making inferences about the message source. It can be used, for example, to assess whether an article is positive or negative toward an organization or whether the organization's writing is inward or outward, or future- or past-focused. It has an extensive body of literature.

Content analysis is also used to assess the writing of others, such as when you examine press coverage to determine how much coverage your organization received and the kind of coverage it was. The former is an indirect measure of public interest and the latter an indirect measure of media attitudes toward your organization. When done with some level of sophistication, content analysis can trace very subtle changes in a writer's predispositions.

To assess audience response to message content, broadcast media research often assesses the responses of participants who push a button or keypad to record their reactions to a televised speech or commercial. Because such devices can record consumer response in real time—microsecond by microsecond—it is possible to gauge consumer reaction at word level and to excise offending words so that the speech, program, or commercial becomes more persuasive.

Researching messages also means keeping up-to-date with what is being said in the industry, media, and general public by and about your organization and its competitors.

EXERCISE 2

There are many formulae for calculating readability. Check your word processing software for such a capability. It is usually under "Tools." Run the program on a piece of your writing and get a score. What does this score tell you, or not tell you, about probable reader response to your writing?

Ethical Issues

Ethics and Public Relations Research

There are many ethical issues with regard to research, including issues of timing, use of budget, and indeed, purpose. A particular charge is that you can manipulate research to get any results you want and sadly, this is true. That does not mean that you should do so, however.

The most common ethical problems relate to the wording of survey questions. In many cases, these are just badly written questions but insofar as they have the potential to produce the results you want rather than the results that are accurate, they are ethically suspect, not to mention poor research. For example:

Leading Questions

"Would you rather study public relations or be taken outside and shot?" Presumably, this question will produce a very large percentage of respondents in favor of studying public relations.

However, the question has obviously been loaded, that is, written to obtain the results the researcher needed to support his or her case for a public relations program.

Most leading questions are not as obvious as this. Instead, they suggest an appropriate response, for example, "Like other responsible citizens, do you watch network news?"

Just as you are ethically obliged to give out true and accurate information, so should you feel obliged to seek true and accurate information.

Yes/No Questions

"Should we send the employee newsletter to your home?" Although yes/no questions such as this provide fast answers, they do not necessarily give respondents the opportunity to express their real feelings. On many issues, people are somewhere in the middle and want the opportunity to tell you that.

The yes/no format (or indeed any question that provides only polar opposite options) may force them into a position they do not feel strongly about and may misrepresent their true feelings. This is especially dangerous from a research viewpoint if you use their answers to justify a decision they do not support. For example, your employer would surely want to know that while 70% of the respondents answered "yes" to the question about company newsletters, most of them would have said they were "neutral" if you had given them that option. In this case, the company might decide to save the considerable expense of mailing the newsletters home.

The point is not limited to yes/no questions, but rather applies to any set of options that are simply black or white. Even that very simple demographic question "Sex: Male ____ Female ____" does not provide some individuals the opportunity to record their sexual preference, which your organization may want to know.

One remedy for these problems is to pretest questionnaires carefully to ensure that respondents understand the questions, that they are answering the question you think you have written, and that they have the opportunity to give you the fair and accurate results you are seeking.

Researching Media

As a public relations writer, you will be expected to understand the media in general and in the specific context you will use it. You will have to know the strengths and limitations of all forms of media, including the Internet. For example, it is likely that you will be asked to recommend how the media can be used to reach the maximum number of people in the most cost-effective manner. Understanding the complete range of available media will help you answer questions such as "Should web pages replace our in-house bulletin boards?" "Should we e-mail the employee newsletter?" or "Should we start a monthly newsletter or post information on our web site?"

Fundamentally, you must try to identify which, of all media options, will be the best choice to meet your organization's objectives and then conduct the monitoring and evaluation research to confirm your choices.

Media: What to Research

You will need to research the following about any medium:

◆ What public(s) does it reach?
◆ How frequently does it reach them?
◆ What are its attributes—visual? storable? retrievable? color? audio? interactive?
◆ What is its cost and cost-effectiveness? These two concepts are rather different. For example, television advertising is relatively inexpensive per capita, but it reaches a large number of people you may not need to reach; on the other hand, direct mail can be relatively expensive per piece, but if it is well targeted, there may be much less waste.

Media: How to Research

There are several ways to research these questions: published media directories, informal networking, and formal research.

Published media directories. These provide contact information for the media as well as editorial calendars and deadlines. Information published by specific media outlets will provide information on their reach, including audience size and characteristics.

Informal networking. Informal networking with editors, journalists, and public relations colleagues will help you find out what works and doesn't in practice. You will also learn the realities of media selection. For example, if a local newspaper editor has a long-running feud with your organization, you may not be able to anticipate positive editorial responses to your messages. It may be better to take your message (and your money) to the paper's business department and buy advertising space.

Networking with your colleagues in advertising and marketing for whom media comparisons, media shopping, and media costing are a routine practice will give you more precise answers to media selection questions. Cost will not be the only factor. If people need to retain the message, broadcast media can probably be excluded. If movement is critical, your choices will include CDs, video, or the Web.

Formal research. Formal research such as broadcast audience ratings and print media circulation provide accurate measurements of audience size and attributes.

Measures of media impact include *penetration* statistics that show the number or percentage of your target audience that received the message and how many times (*frequency*). A similar measure is *impressions*: the number of times a story appeared in print. You will also, of course, be interested in the *reach* of a medium, that is, what media reach what percentage of your target publics?

You might also assess the *vehicle effect* of your placements. The vehicle effect is the effect of the specific medium (vehicle) on your message. The same topic covered by the *New York Times* and by an elementary school newspaper has, we assume, more credibility in the *New York Times*. Public relations writers try to place stories in the most credible media for the audience. Research on media placements may give a subjective weighting to stories that make it into more credible media.

Communication Audits

One tool that embraces both message research and media research is the communication audit. Like content analysis, the communication audit is a rather specific procedure, but in general use it has come to mean almost any set of questions that assesses the adequacy or effectiveness of communications. Communication audit questions aimed at employees might ask for information such as "Think of information you remember getting at work over the last week . . ."

+ What was it?
+ When did you get it?
+ How did you get it?
+ How relevant was it?
+ What was your level of satisfaction with it?
+ What level in the organization did you get it from (superior, colleague, subordinate)?
+ Did you request it or did it come to you unsolicited?

Respondents might also be given diaries and asked to record their communication activity such as the amount of time they spend reading, in meetings, or on the phone. This line of questioning can be very helpful for an employee communication specialist seeking to find out whether the employee newsletter is getting good distribution and whether it is useful to employees. Another useful question might be, "Who else read the issue?" If families do not read the newsletter, you might recommend saving the cost of mailing by distributing it at the office.

In public relations practice, the communication audit has come to mean two things. The first is assessing the difference between how your publics see the organization and how the organization wishes to be seen. Second is trying to assess how differences could be bridged by changing the content or methods of communication.

Some practitioners describe a "media audit" as regular phone contact with editors to check that they are getting the organization's releases and their level of satisfaction and usage of the material. It will tell you, for example, whether editors prefer to receive releases by mail, e-mail, fax, PR Newswire, Business Wire, or other medium.

EXERCISE 3

Media comparisons: Bring to class a national newsweekly, a national newspaper, and a local newspaper that all cover the same topic. How do the stories differ in amount of coverage, bias/opinion, if any, and style of writing? Can you see input from public relations practitioners in any of these stories? What is their purpose in the story? What is the public relations message they are telling?

Researching Effects

Effects research is bottom-line research. It measures results in order to answer the questions, "Did your communication succeed?" and "Did you reach your objectives?" Effects research is the basis of your next round of decision making and sometimes the next round of research. If the brochure did not result in sales or if the direct mail letter prompted no responses, it is time to find out why and so you can reliably adopt a different strategy or choose another medium with the next project.

Effects Research: What to Research

Effects research tries to measure whether and how publics respond to messages. The three basic outcomes are knowledge, attitude, and behavior, so the aim of effects research is to assess whether the message achieved any or all of these outcomes. You want to know, as outlined by Grunig and Hunt (1984), whether your publics

- ✦ Received the message
- ✦ Understood the message
- ✦ Remembered the message
- ✦ Believed the message
- ✦ Acted on the message

In the case of media releases, you will also want to know how many media carried your story as well as if, when, and how they changed it. You will want to know if the story prompted other stories by other writers. Many public relations professionals also measure the number of negative stories about their organizations and record the nature and number of rebuttals they made on their organization's behalf.

Public relations writers also have an interest in the story content itself. For indirect stories, that is, those written about an organization by the media, what topics were covered, and was the treatment favorable, unfavorable, or neutral? By analyzing news "slants" by geographic location or type of media, for example, you can find out whether attitudes to your client are regional and/or whether the slant varies from press to TV to radio. One way to track such placements is to use commercial or web-based press clipping services.

Effects Research: How to Research

How do you know whether your audience received, understood, remembered, believed, or acted on the information? How do you know *when* they got it? Are there bottlenecks in the distribution system? Do employees take the staff newsletter home?

One way to assess whether publics received and understood the message is through recall research. Recall research is usually done in an interview or focus group with unprompted questions such as "In the last week do you remember reading-hearing-seeing any stories about Internet services?" If the answer is "no," your Internet service client has a problem with either message design or delivery. If the answer is "yes," then open-ended questions can follow up and explore what messages were memorable and why.

The Web offers some precise measurements of audience response to writing. Web technology allows you to record responses to web page content. Options include the number of hits a page receives, when the hits occur, the order in which a visitor works through the site, which links get revisited, and the last page hit before the visitor places an order or requests information. The assumption is that this last hit is what triggered a purchase or request for action and is therefore an especially motivational part of the site. The time spent on each page or part thereof can be taken as a surrogate measure of visitor interest.

Awareness, recall, comprehension, and persuasion/attitude change can be measured by surveys, interviews, focus groups, and message pretesting as appropriate. Behaviors are often measured by unobtrusive measures that do not intrude on the survey subjects. For example, a New England Subaru dealership determines where to place its radio advertising by having its service staff turn on the car radios of every vehicle brought in for service. Recording the stations that the radios are tuned to tells the dealership what their customers are listening to.

A classic type of unobtrusive publication research is to place different versions of the publication in a display rack and count how many copies of each version get taken. This will tell you which version is preferred, but not, of course, why it is preferred.

Although effects research typically comes after the project is complete, the research questions should be defined in advance. They will be driven by the aims of the communication and the public(s) to whom it is addressed.

Researching Relationships

The above areas of research focus on strengthening relationships between an organization and its publics by using messages and media. Recently, however, researchers and practitioners have begun to assess the actual strength and nature of the relationships themselves. This research is informed by the idea that relationships are two-way. It emphasizes reciprocity and mutual understanding. Researchers try to assess whether the public is satisfied with the relationship as well as whether the organization is satisfied (Hon & Grunig, 1999).

Research and the Web

Because the Web can be both a research tool and a subject of research, because it is both a mass medium and an individual medium (via e-mail), and because it combines all communication modes—documents, video, audio, and graphics—it presents some unique challenges and opportunities for research.

The Web Challenges

The first challenge is the Web's enormity. In 2002, Paine estimated that the Web has 3 billion web pages, some 80,000 newsgroups, and approximately 15,000 editors and reporters writing for the Web. Web growth continues.

The second challenge is the ephemeral, changing nature of web content. As any user knows, content can change on a minute-by-minute basis. This is useful for dealing with emergencies but can make research such as tracking content difficult. For example, newspapers that typically produce news once a day in print format may produce multiple versions of the same story as they update their web sites, sometimes on a real-time basis. This makes tracking messages over time significantly more difficult.

A challenge that the Web shares with other media is that of trying to relate an individual's use of the Web to messages you may post on it and their subsequent responses (if any) to your writing.

Nonetheless, researchers look increasingly to the Web as a research tool. They now use dedicated web sites and real-time "chat" to organize focus sessions with participants at distant locations. This both increases their pool of participants and lowers the cost of research. The Web can also be used to post or deliver surveys, and to monitor public opinion in addition to accessing search engines and databases for formative research and tracking web use.

The Web: What to Research

Paine (2002) proposes several types of information that web research can provide. It can be summarized as follows:

✦ Information about what is being published about you (and your competitors) on the Web
✦ Information about the size of the audience you are reaching
✦ Information about what your publics are saying and thinking, and what actions they are taking in relation to you

The Web: How to Research

Information—or misinformation—that is being published about your organization can often be located with a search engine. There is, however, an "unknown Web" that may not be identified by search engines and routine searches. This includes discussions and materials that are password protected. Proprietary software may be needed to track all relevant content in a timely and regular fashion.

Information about what publics are saying about your organization will usually come from monitoring discussion and chat groups. Proprietary services can track and record postings to such groups. Proprietary software called "conversation trackers" can also produce a summary picture from the participant comments in newsgroups, mailing lists, and message boards.

Information about the size and nature of your audience is essentially a ratings question. A number of companies including Jupiter Research and Nielsen attempt to provide this information, but a precise measure remains elusive.

Psychographically, there are two major web publics for any organization: those with a keen interest in getting information and those with merely a peripheral interest, perhaps cruising the Web for its entertainment value. The first public has two divisions—supporters and opponents—both of which may be equally keen to visit your site.

Organizations of all sizes and with a range of budgets conduct web-based research using their own web sites or intranets to capture data about their web publics. As this is a relatively inexpensive and increasingly common research method, it is something you as a public relations writer should be familiar with.

Most researchers agree that for many research purposes "hits aren't it." The problem is that hits on your web site provide little information about why the user came to the site or whether he or she is satisfied with it. One person visiting a thousand times is still an audience of one. Hits do not measure the importance or influence of a site to any given public or visitor (Paine, 2002). Hits provide quantitative but not qualitative information that tells you about attitudes.

There are several approaches to answer "why?" as well as to obtain information about visitors' attitudes. You can ask them to voluntarily provide information, require them to answer questions as a condition of access to your site, or, if you have a targeted list of individuals, you distribute a questionnaire to be completed and returned electronically.

Also, it is increasingly easy to design and post surveys to a web site or to design questionnaires for e-mail distribution. The caveat with such research is the question of how you find respondents. Obviously, self-selected respondents may have a different point of view from those whom you need to solicit actively. You may be able to locate lists of individuals through discussion groups, mailing lists, e-zines, Internet service providers (ISPs), and the like.

While there are sophisticated users who will be comfortable providing some basic information if they see that the information return from your site is good, suspicions about web security run high and many users remain concerned about providing information. They are concerned about providing credit card numbers to online merchants, and with what happens to information once they have provided it. The fact that you may be developing a database to better serve visitors to the site may have negative, "big brother" connotations for those same visitors if they find out about it.

You may be able to improve your response rate to a request for visitor information by running online contests or quizzes or offering prizes. Even obtaining a zip code (that can be compared to a PRIZM matrix, for example) can give you a number of demographic attributes of your web public.

The question of assessing the influence of your writing on a public's behavior is as difficult if not more so on the Web than for traditional media. Proprietary services can provide some detailed answers. For example, you can track which sites people came from to place an order or request information at your site. This will tell you which sites were most powerful in driving them to your site. You can also measure the change in traffic at a site after a major promotion and, all other things being equal, deduce that your communications initiated the change.

DISCUSSION 3

Web sites can be powerful research tools for accumulating information on visitors' browsing habits and interests. Some data collection is obvious—for example, the web site posts a questionnaire. Other research is invisible to visitors as the web site records their time on the site and patterns of usage. What are the ethical implications of this "invisible" research? What are the advantages and disadvantages of a web site for collecting information on public opinion, behavior, and demographics?

ON THE TEXTBOOK WEB SITE

✦ Go to www.sagepub.com/treadwell for web exercises, study hints, case studies, and additional examples appropriate to this chapter and chosen or developed to supplement the chapter content.

WRITING WRAP-UP

1. Identify a campus club or organization that you believe needs public relations support. Conduct a small research project to identify information you will need in order to write effectively for this new client. Write a set of questions that will assess how well known it is, its image on campus, and the types of people most likely to join it.

2. Briefly describe how you will administer the survey and how you will select the participants.

3. Write a covering letter to the head of the organization seeking approval to proceed with the survey.

REFERENCES

Deal, T. E., & Kennedy, A. A. (1982). *Corporate cultures: The rites and rituals of corporate life.* Reading, MA: Addison-Wesley.

Gertner, J. (2004, February 15). The very, very personal is the political. *New York Times Magazine,* pp. 42–47.

Grunig, J. E., & Hunt, T. (1984). *Managing public relations.* New York: Holt, Rinehart & Winston.

Hon, L., & Grunig. J. E (1999). *Guidelines for measuring relationships in public relations.* Institute for Public Relations Commission on PR Measurement and Evaluation. Gainesville, FL. Retrieved January 5, 2004, from www.instituteforpr.com

Lerbinger, O. (1977). Corporate uses of research in public relations. *Public Relations Review, 3,* 11–19.

Mclarin, K. J. (1994, February 20). Rutgers seems to like its stately, shapeless image. *New York Times,* Metro section, p. L5.

Paine, K. D. (2002). *Measures of success for cyberspace.* Retrieved January 5, 2004, from http://www.instituteforpr.com/pdf/2002_onlinemeasurement.pdf

Spradley, J. P. (1979). *The ethnographic interview.* New York: Holt, Rinehart & Winston.

Public Relations Research

Broom, G. M., & Dozier, D. M. (1996). *Using research in public relations: Applications to program management.* Englewood Cliffs, NJ: Prentice Hall.

Journal of Public Relations Research. A quarterly publication of the Public Relations Division of the Association for Education in Journalism and Mass Communication. Mahwah, NJ: Lawrence Erlbaum.

Public Relations Quarterly. Published quarterly by Public Relations Quarterly.

Public Relations Review. Published five times a year by Elsevier.

Stacks, D. W. (2002). *Primer of public relations research.* New York: Guilford.

Web Resources

Claritas .... www.claritas.com

PollingReport.com .... www.Pollingreport.com

SRI International .... www.sri.com

U.S. Census Bureau .... www.census.gov

Yankelovitch MONITOR .... http://secure.yankelovich.com/solutions/shortform_p01.asp
MindBase

Zip code search (select "You are where you live") .... www.claritas.com

6

Legal Influences on Public Relations Writing

1. **Public relations writing is a unique combination of commercial speech and free speech.**

2. **Public relations writers must understand both legal and public relations approaches to communication.**

3. **The Internet brings new legal issues that may affect the public relations writer.**

4. **Public relations writers may be held legally accountable for what they write.**

5. **Federal regulations relating to intellectual property, copyright, privacy, disclosure, and financial reporting may affect public relations writing.**

Generally, a broad constitutional right underpins corporate as well as individual speech, but as with individuals and the media, it is not an unlimited right. There are restrictions and limits. As a public relations writer, you should know the law because ultimately there are legal constraints on what you can write, and these constraints change over time.

Like individuals, organizations are limited in the extent to which they can defame others, intrude on the privacy of individuals, use the work of others without permission, and violate contracts or the regulations of statutory agencies. Often there is a fine line between legality and a violation. The main message of this chapter is that it is better to check before you cross that line than to be sorry later. This is especially so since corporations (especially) may be seen as having "deep pockets," and may be particularly vulnerable to expensive legal actions.

While there are constraints on advertising in particular, recent years have seen increasing acknowledgment that commercial or corporate speech does enjoy some legal protection. For example:

✦ In 1976 in *Virginia State Board of Pharmacy v. Virginia Citizen's Consumer Council* (425 U.S. 748), the Supreme Court held generally that "commercial speech" was not wholly outside the protection of the First and Fourteenth Amendments and specifically that statutory bans on advertising prescription drug prices violated these amendments.

✦ In 1978, the Court in *First National Bank of Boston v. Bellotti* (435 U.S. 765) overruled a Massachusetts law that businesses could speak only on issues that materially affected them. A Massachusetts statute had held that banks and businesses could not spend money to influence voting other than on questions that materially affected their property, business, or assets. The Court decided that the expression of views on issues of public importance does not lose First Amendment protection simply because the source is a corporation that cannot prove that the issues materially affect the corporation's business.

✦ In 1980, the Court in *Consolidated Edison Company of New York, Inc. v. Public Service Commission of New York* (447 U.S. 530) ruled that the commission could not prohibit utility companies from mailing bill inserts that discussed controversial issues of public policy. Suppression of these inserts was held to infringe the freedom of speech protected by the First and Fourteenth Amendments.

✦ In a similar-sounding case, a 1986 ruling in *Pacific Gas and Electric Company v. Public Utilities Commission of California* (475 U.S. 1) upheld the right of the utility to refuse to include messages in its mailings. The commission had required the utility to include the newsletter of a third party in its mailings. The Court held that this order penalized the utility's expression of opinion and was not justified by the state's interest in promoting speech to make a variety of views available to customers.

✦ And although *Nike v. Kasky* (a high-profile 5-year case that ended in 2003) resulted in an out-of-court settlement, it demonstrated the continuing debate over what constitutes free versus commercial speech. The issue arose over whether Nike's public relations campaign to counter negative publicity about its overseas employment practices misled the public, in violation of the California "truth in advertising" law. At stake was whether the campaign statements were commercial speech (regulated by the law) or not commercial speech and therefore protected under the First Amendment.

A number of commentators have addressed the potentially chilling effect on corporate public relations if corporate critics were able to level their criticisms under First Amendment protections while businesses were at legal risk of responding for fear that all their communications would be regarded as commercial speech (Jenkins, 2003). It is likely this issue will recur as companies adopt more public relations strategies to promote their corporate social responsibility programs.

Ethical Issues

Ethics and Public Relations Law

. . . but Is It Ethical? . . . or Legal?

Does legal mean ethical? Does ethical mean legal? These questions are at the heart of many dilemmas facing business, and ultimately their public relations practitioners as they advocate internally for legal and ethical practices and sometimes try to repair the damage done by practices that do not meet these standards. The reality is, of course, that legal and ethical are not the same and that neither side is always right. Consider the following examples.

Ethical but Not Legal

In 2002, the international aid organization Doctors Without Borders publicly announced that it would begin to purchase generic drugs in foreign countries at a considerably lower cost than brand-label U.S. drugs. The aim was to procure more medicine for the same money, but the effect was to violate U.S. patent laws. Was this legal? No, but few would argue it was unethical. The drug companies did not pursue the issue in the courts, presumably wary of a public relations backlash, and Roche, the manufacturer of one of the AIDS drugs in question, subsequently agreed to reduce its prices to poor countries (Bowing to Pressure, 2003).

Legal but Not Ethical

The reverse situation put sportswear giant Nike in the crosshairs of a similar ethical/legal dilemma. At issue was the company's use of child labor in its overseas manufacturing facilities.

Although the company was not breaking child labor laws in the countries involved, and although U.S. labor laws do not apply to overseas manufacturing, the company endured a serious backlash from groups decrying the ethics of this practice. Nike, and other companies with similar policies, adopted child labor policies for international operations that reflected U.S. laws and ethical standards.

As typically happens in battles between ethics and the law, neither of these situations is completely resolved. The legal argument for patent laws (and protection of U.S. pharmaceutical companies) is currently being carried by U.S. government efforts to make enforcement of the patent laws a condition of trade negotiations with many third-world countries—and the ethical issue remains. And Nike's sincerity and ethical practices are still under heavy scrutiny despite public relations strategies ranging from letters to customers to corporate social responsibility reporting in print and on the Web. The question remains whether the company is not living up to its words or whether its words have not been communicated effectively.

The lesson is that ethics, and sometimes the law, are situational. You will have to weigh the values of the ethical codes that guide your actions to determine the course of action to follow. At best in both situations above, you should be guided by the PRSA code provision that you act as an advocate for the public interest and uphold the reputation of the profession.

Generally, there is support for the idea that the First Amendment protects both the marketplace of ideas and the public's interest in receiving information, including from institutional or corporate sources. One exception to this is the U.S. government itself, which is prohibited from using appropriated funds to pay "publicity experts" unless the funds are specifically appropriated for that purpose (5 U.S.C. §3107). This so-called Gillett Amendment of 1913 addressed legislators' concerns that the government might use publicity techniques to propagandize its own citizens.

A related school of thought argues that government agencies obtain their policy direction from the public they serve via their elected representatives. It follows that because the agencies technically receive their direction from the public, they should have no need to "sell" themselves or their programs to the public (Tuerck, 1978).

In practice, public information offices abound in government, and citizens reasonably expect that government agencies will inform the public of their work. Nevertheless, you will search in vain for a federal government office door that has "Public Relations" on it. Note, for example, the mission statements we have printed from the U.S. Army and Navy in Chapter 4 and the Food and Drug Administration in Chapter 3. All of them originate from "public affairs" or "information" offices.

Protecting Organizational Interests: Working With Lawyers

Conceptually, the roles of corporate legal counsel and corporate public relations counselor are identical. They are both employed to advocate effectively on behalf of the organization, to give the organization sound advice, and to protect the organization's image. Lawyers do so in a legal setting; public relations counselors do so in the court of public opinion.

Despite these common aims, the paths of lawyers and public relations counselors often diverge with respect to disclosure, especially in times of crisis when their respective reflex actions may be diametrically opposed. There may be an occupational difference of philosophy between the legal propensity for "no comment" and the public relations instinct toward open and early response. Communication professionals are all too aware that silence in the court of public opinion may be interpreted as "having something to hide." They understand that if the organization's story is not made public quickly, then someone else's version may become the cornerstone of the public perception.

It is the job of public relations practitioners to ensure that they and their employer's legal advisors share a common approach to issues and crisis resolution before problems arise. This means being able to work with lawyers and having enough legal knowledge to give legal counsel confidence that day-to-day public relations writing will present no legal and expensive embarrassments.

Management should recognize that legal and public relations inputs are equally important in formulating policy. A short-term legal victory at all costs may not translate into a public relations victory in the long term. Although the decision of what to do may well rest with management personnel other than either legal or public relations professionals, it is the job of both groups to see that the decision makers are well advised regarding both the short- and long-term impacts of any decision. This is why legal and public relations counsel should be represented at the same level of management, reporting at some point to the same executive.

In any major forward-thinking organization, these relationships and procedures most likely will be well established and not present an immediate issue for an entry-level public relations writer. However, it may be necessary for a beginning writer or a practitioner in a small organization not only to demonstrate the importance of public relations input at the policy-making level but also to prove that law and public relations counsels should have equal claims to management's attention with regard to communication policy.

Especially in the area of litigation public relations, attorneys and public relations specialists increasingly recognize the contribution that the other can make to a client's reputation. There is increasing recognition that proceedings in the courtroom cannot be kept separate from proceedings in the media. There is a conceptual shift from efforts to keep the news media from influencing justice to the idea that an organization's advocates, be they attorneys or public relations specialists, have an obligation to speak in public if their organization's reputation is to be protected (Watson, 2002).

One area in which it is essential that public relations work closely with legal counsel is in the area of crisis planning. In the event of an emergency, both professions can make a major contribution to planning who will make what statements to what audiences, when, and how. There is a clear partnership here that can be extended into other common interest areas such as contracts, manuals, and procedures, or any medium or forum in which the client's position is publicly voiced.

Public relations practitioners who contract externally for writers, photographers, printers, models, or research or mailing services should have contracts that specify the conditions of performance and subsequent ownership and use of all materials. These contracts should, at least initially, be cleared through legal counsel. The process itself provides an opportunity for the public relations writer to work with legal colleagues, establish relationships, and open paths to mutual understanding of communication policy and practice.

Legal and public relations counselors can avert turf disputes by developing protocols or procedures that cover routine information work. Routine news releases can go through a standard clearance procedure that will protect against any legal problems. Legal and public relations counsel can develop their common interests by ensuring that new employees know and understand procedures for dealing with the media.

Public relations writers should be aware of the legal issues, laws, and agencies that typically affect writing. How well you write (or don't) may have legal implications. Familiarity with communication law will not only support your own professionalism but also protect the rights of your employer. For example, Petrini and Shea (1992) identify 52 cases in which poor writing actually created legal problems. The issues included unclear purpose, unfocused writing, poor organization, difficult language, excess verbiage, improper or ineffective choices of words, and grammatical errors that mislead readers. The major concerns for public relations writers are discussed in the section titled "The Issues."

Protecting Your Own Interests: Contracts

At some point, you will likely enter into a contract to provide services to a company or you will contract with someone else for services to you or your organization. Typically, these will be photographic, writing, and printing contracts. As an employee, you may be asked to sign an employment contract when you are first employed.

The first three types of contracts essentially cover what is to be provided and at what cost. Issues include who owns the rights to the photographs, how many times you may use them and under what conditions, or at what point in the printing process do errors in spelling or photo placement become your problem rather than the printer's. Do you know if the printer can substitute paper stock without consulting you or if you can be charged for storage if you don't take delivery immediately? Standard agreements cover most of these questions, but it is your responsibility to ensure high standards of performance at an agreed-on price by specifying *your* standards and requirements in a contract and then ensuring they are met.

Employee contracts typically bind you to confidentiality about your organization and its clients and your salary. It may also set out reasons for dismissal and will most likely have a "non-compete" clause that says you can't take existing clients with you or solicit their business when you leave.

Contracts are especially important for freelance public relations writers, especially those involved in producing user manuals or publicity pieces based on information provided by your client. Unlike physicians, lawyers, and the clergy who enjoy "privilege" and typically cannot be required to reveal client confidences, public relations counselors do not enjoy this status. If you work for a party involved in a lawsuit, you may well be subpoenaed and required to disclose information you have about your client.

Similarly, while you are in principle responsible for checking all content given to you by a client, this may be difficult in practice and in some cases you may not have the technical expertise to do so. To protect themselves against liability in the event of product failure or charges of fraudulent publicity, many writers include "hold harmless" clauses in their contracts with clients. Such clauses make the client responsible for the accuracy of the content. It is also wise to require clients to officially review and sign off on all documents before they are printed and distributed. Keep a copy of all such approvals.

The bottom line is that if you are writing copy for any outside organization, as a freelancer, consultant, or small business, you should consult an attorney and have a standard contract prepared that you will sign with all clients. Such a contract should define the responsibilities you will undertake as well as the responsibilities of the client. It will define deadlines and define responsibilities for proofreading and signing off on final copy. This may save you considerable headaches later when a client refuses to pay because of a typographic error or missed deadline.

The Issues

Legal issues related to public relations writing usually focus on ownership and access to information. Who owns the rights to text, photographs, logos, slogans, web designs, even the special "look" of a publication or product (referred to as *trade dress*)? Who has the right to access and use information, especially on the Internet?

Ownership rights are addressed in law under copyright, trademarks, service-marks, and domain names (collectively referred to as *intellectual property rights*) and under freedom of information and privacy. As a public relations professional, your task is to protect the intellectual property rights of your employer (and yourself) while also respecting the rights of other companies, authors, designers, or composers, for example. This means that whenever you use material originated by someone else, you should review the existing copyright laws, consult an attorney as necessary, and obtain any permissions you believe are necessary. It is always safe to obtain permission from the copyright holder.

On the advice of their legal counsel, many organizations ask new employees (or new students, etc.) to sign releases that allow the organization to use photos of the person in press releases and other documents promoting the organization.

Legal Definitions and Symbols

Federal Laws

Federal laws are the result of congressional actions. They must be passed by both sections of Congress and signed into law by the president. Laws may be described as "Public Law" (P.L.) or as part of the United States Code (U.S.C. or U.S. Code). These are simply two different ways of organizing the laws. The code of public laws is organized by content. The U.S. Code is organized by Title. For example, laws relating to education are all included as part of Title 20; laws relating to copyrights are under Title 17. You can view a list of titles through the FedLaw web site, http://www.thecre.com/fedlaw/default.htm.

Federal Regulations

If laws are "what must be done," then regulations are "how it will be done."

After the laws are passed, the relevant departments and agencies identify the regulations they need to ensure that the law is put into effect. Typically, regulations include time frames, conditions, and procedures. The Code of Federal Regulations (C.F.R.) contains all regulations put in place by federal departments and agencies to implement the laws.

Pending Federal Legislation

All bills proposed in Congress are given numbers by which they can be identified and on which you can search. Bills introduced into the House of Representatives begin with H.R. (House Resolution); bills introduced into the Senate begin with S.R. (Senate Resolution).

Legal Decisions

Legal decisions resolve a dispute or conflict. Depending on your institution's resources, you can search legal decisions by the names of the parties, the exact legal citation, and/or the court (Supreme Court; federal, district, circuit, or state court, etc.). Your best asset for legal research is a good research librarian.

Symbols

Most common legal symbols can be produced using standard word processing software and common fonts (typefaces). Following are the guidelines for finding the symbols discussed in this chapter using both Macintosh and PC computer systems. After these explanations, we have included a brief table of the key commands used for each symbol.

(Continued, next page)

Copyright: ©   Trademark: ™   Registered: ®   Section (for laws and regulations): §

Key Commands for Commonly Used Legal Symbols

Following are the key commands for the common symbols shown above. These may not apply to all typefaces and all software programs. If they do not work, refer to your software manual.

Key commands	Symbol in words	Symbol Macintosh	PC
Copyright	©	Option + g	Control + Alt + c
Trademark	™	Option + 2	Control + Alt + t
Registered	®	Option + r	Control + Alt + r
Section (for laws and regulations)	§	Option + 6	See symbols menu

At the end of this chapter, we have provided a list of sources for up-to-date and more specific information on intellectual privacy issues as well as on personal privacy and freedom of information. We urge you to become familiar with these and other sources to help you stay current with issues that will affect your own work and your employer's rights. To help you interpret some of these documents, the "Legal Definitions and Symbols" box gives a brief introduction to some of the abbreviations and notations found in legal research and citations. It also provides instructions for producing many of the legal symbols, such as ™ ©, and §, on your computer.

Copyright, ©

Ideas are just that: ideas. But once they are fixed in tangible form such as a web page, a photograph, a piece of music, or an employee magazine, they can be copyrighted. It is wise to consider anything published (including Internet materials) as copyrighted and to seek the permission of the copyright holder for permission to use it. This is especially the case if the copyright is to be used for commercial purposes. Copyright is protected under Title 17, U.S. Code. This law presumes copyright of material from the moment it is created. Formal registration with the U.S. Copyright Office ensures full legal protection.

The "fair use" provision of the copyright law allows some copyrighted material to be reproduced without the holder's permission under some circumstances. To claim reproduction rights under the fair-use provision, you will potentially have to prove all of the following:

✦ You have credited the source.
✦ You have not taken the material out of context.

◆ The usage will not significantly affect the original market for the material (i.e., you are not taking sales or profit away from the copyright holder).
◆ The use is for educational, research, or legitimate news purposes (in principle, nonprofit uses).
◆ Only a small portion of the original document is used.

As a general rule, it may be easier and wiser to obtain permission to use the material than to hope that you will be able to defend a fair-use lawsuit. Note that federal government documents are not copyrighted, but like any copyright material they need to be used in context. Do not use them to promote or advertise a client, for example.

E X E R C I S E   1

There is a close link between plagiarism, typically an academic infraction, and copyright infringement. Review your institution's position on plagiarism in relation to the basic ideas of copyright outlined in this chapter. How does the policy reflect copyright concerns? How does it differ? Could copyright law be used to deal with problems of plagiarism on college campuses?

Copyright laws apply to all media, including print, music, art, and photography. A 1989 Supreme Court decision, *Community for Creative Non-violence v. Reid* (490 U.S. 730), determined that independent contractors own copyright in their own work. In practice, therefore, the ownership and use of a freelancer's work are negotiable. Typically, you will negotiate a price with independent contractors—such as photographers, artists, videographers, composers, and musicians—based on the nature and frequency of use of the artwork, photographs, videos, or music.

In some respects, copyright permission is simply a common courtesy. You do not want other people using your best creative efforts without your permission, so seek permission for use of their materials.

One area that can be a concern for public relations writers is when they submit ideas, public relations plans, creative ideas, and writing samples to a prospective client. What happens if you don't get the contract, but the recipient uses your ideas anyway? This is a difficult area. You can put a copyright symbol "©" on your proposal along with restrictions on its use but then you may offend a potential client. If the worst happens, you are stuck with the problem of demonstrating copyright violation. Remember that copyright covers only the exact expression of an idea, not the underlying idea itself.

Trademarks and Servicemarks, ™ ® SM

Trademarks (TM) and servicemarks (SM) are conceptual cousins of copyright except that they are covered by trademark rather than copyright laws. Trademarks and servicemarks are short—usually the names of companies, products, slogans, and services. They protect property that is part of the organization's public image. Trademarks and servicemarks are protected under local, state, and federal laws. Only registration of a mark with the Trademark Office of the Department of

Commerce, however, allows the holder to use a registration mark ® and to claim trademark protection nationwide.

Organizations work hard to ensure that their carefully and expensively developed trademarks and servicemarks are not abused. For example, *Polo Magazine* and the Ralph Lauren organization went to court over rights to the word *Polo*, essentially asking the question, "Is polo a sport or a shirt?" (Anthony, 1998). After many appeals, the courts ruled in 2002 that *Polo Magazine* may continue publication under that name, but must publish the disclaimer "Not affiliated with Polo Ralph Lauren" whenever the magazine uses the word "Polo" (*Westchester Media Co. L.P. v. PRL USA Holdings Inc.* [48 Fed Appx. 917 5th Cir. 2002], 2002).

And in 2003, the World Wildlife Fund (WWF) won a highly publicized battle with the World Wrestling Federation (now World Wrestling Entertainment) over the "WWF" designation.

You can monitor lawsuits such as this through Westlaw or other legal sites listed at the end of this chapter.

In a similar vein is the issue of trademarks that become "too familiar." You might think, for example, that Kimberly-Clark would be glad that people think all tissues are "Kleenex" and that the Xerox Corporation would be glad that consumers think that all copiers are "Xeroxes." Instead, as Exhibit 6.1 shows, to companies that enjoy such success in getting their names into the public lexicon, the issue is very serious. Xerox Corporation went to federal court to stop a California company from using the Xerox trademark on its toner and other copier and printer supplies.

In contrast, meat processing company Hormel, Inc. says it does not object to the use of the generic slang word *spam* to describe unsolicited commercial electronic mail because no one confuses it with the company's famed meat product. However, it draws the line at companies that seek to trademark products using the Hormel trademark "SPAM" (Hormel, 2003).

The problem is that, once a trademark becomes generic, the brand name product is no longer distinctive. Theoretically, if all copiers are "Xerox" then it doesn't matter what copier you buy. But all copiers aren't Xerox, and the company doesn't want you to think they are. Because its name is associated with hard-earned product quality and market share, it is important for an organization to protect its product names—hence trademarks. A web-related example is the often used "listserv" or "list serve." "LISTSERV" is a trademarked name of L-Soft International, which objects to the name being used generically. Use "mailing list" instead.

A good rule to follow is that most trademarks are adjectives, not nouns or verbs. Use trademarks as modifiers as in "Kleenex tissues" or "Xerox copiers." Similarly, trademarks are not verbs—you can copy on a Xerox machine, but you cannot "xerox" anything. If you have questions about the correct spelling or usage of another organization's trademark or name, ask them. They will be pleased to help.

Occasionally, the issue becomes clouded when organizations trademark otherwise common words. For example, the heavy metal band of the same name holds the trademark on the word "Anthrax." In 2001, this became a problem when anthrax scares sent scores of people to the Web in search of information on the health issue. The band members realized they had a problem when they were inundated with calls from the media. For a while, they linked their web site to the Centers for Disease Control and Prevention (CDC) so that people searching for "anthrax" would find a ready link to the information they wanted (Zielbauer, 2001).

EXHIBIT 6.1   **Ad produced by Xerox Corporation to educate the public on infringement of the Xerox trademark.**

When you use "Xerox"
the way you use "aspirin,"
we get a headache

Boy, what a headache! And all because some of you may be using our name in a generic manner. Which could cause it to lose its trademark status the way the name "aspirin" did years ago. So when you do use our name, please use it as an adjective to identify our products and services, e.g., Xerox copiers. Never as a verb: "to Xerox" in place of "to copy," or as a noun: "Xeroxes" in place of "copies." Thank you. Now, could you excuse us, we've got to lie down for a few minutes.

THE DOCUMENT COMPANY

XEROX

XEROX,® The Document Company,® and the digital X are trademarks of XEROX CORPORATION. 36 USC 380.

Source: Reprinted with permission of Xerox Corporation, Stamford, Connecticut.

Note: The Xerox Corporation has run this ad for many years. This version includes the Olympic symbol and rings, recognizing the company's official sponsorship of the 2000 Olympic Games. The Olympic name and symbol are among the most carefully guarded trademarks in the world. As many companies have found to their chagrin, the International Olympic Committee (IOC) will take legal action against any organization that refers to itself as "Olympic" unless it is officially sanctioned to do so by the IOC—as Xerox was in 2000.

A trademark—denoted by ™—says that use of the name is restricted to the trademark's owner and that it must be used in a special way defined by the owner. Coca-Cola Corporation insists that Coke™ has a capital "C"—always. A servicemark— denoted by SM—is generally used for services rather than products. Both trademarks and servicemarks are denoted by ® when they are registered with the Copyright Office. Part of a public relations writer's job is to know how an employer's logos, trademarks, and slogans should be designated to protect them.

Exhibit 6.2, taken from a LEGO Company press kit, demonstrates how LEGO Company wants its name used, and it is very specific. This message is part of all of the company's media kits. Note that the Public Relations Department is the contact point about use of the logo. Not surprisingly, Xerox Corporation takes its corporate identity just as seriously, maintaining a Corporate Identity Office to protect the corporation's image. Exhibit 6.3 from the manual *Basic Graphic Standards* explains why Xerox Corporation takes its image so seriously (Xerox, 1997a, p. 1).

The manual, produced in full color with careful attention to exact color matches, also addresses the use of the corporate signature, the Digital X brand mark, and affiliate signatures (see Exhibit 6.4). The manual establishes rules for the use of the signature and the Digital X including the size, typeface, accepted layouts, and relative sizes for the signature and brand mark, and the use of the signature and brand mark on documents, signage, packaging, and advertising. It also specifies the exact colors that can be used for the various elements. A discussion of the legal issues related to the use of the signature and symbols begins "The name 'Xerox' is our most valuable asset" (Xerox, 1997b, p. 9). This is correct—and the company's efforts to protect it are well founded.

EXHIBIT 6.2   Instructions for use of LEGO corporate name and logo.

Use of LEGO® Trademarks

We at LEGO Systems, Inc. appreciate your help in protecting our valued trademarks. The following rules will help you use our trademarks correctly.

1. The word LEGO® and our five major brand names: LEGO® PRIMO, LEGO® DUPLO®. LEGO® SYSTEM, LEGO TECHNIC® and LEGO DACTA® should be written in CAPITAL letters.

2. Please use our trademarks as adjectives, not as nouns. For example, refer to our products as "LEGO® toys" or "LEGO® DUPLO® sets." LEGO products should not be referred to in a generic way, such as "LEGOS," "LEGO's or "legos."

3. If there is a need to reproduce a LEGO logo, please contact the Public Relations Department regarding the trademark's graphic design.

Thank you for your cooperation.

LEGO, LEGO PRIMO, LEGO DUPLO, LEGO SYSTEM, LEGO TECHNIC, LEGO DACTA, LEGOLAND, Unitron, Blacktron, Space Police, Control Lab, the LEGO Maniac and LEGO Imagination Center are trademarks of the LEGO Group.

Source: Reprinted with permission of LEGO Company, Enfield, Connecticut.

EXHIBIT 6.3   Xerox Corporation graphic standards.

Xerox Graphic Standards

Graphic standards and guidelines are critical elements of a corporate identity program. They help ensure the successful application of logos, colors and typography across the corporation. The consistent designs that result are what build brand value and strengthen the image of Xerox...

...The effective and consistent use of our new corporate identity is vital to building the leadership image of Xerox Corporation. For it is through identity that we express ourselves. And it is through these expressions that the public forms an image of us.

The strong interdependence of identity and image is why this Basic Graphic Standards Manual has been developed. It provides the kind of helpful information and guidance that will enable every Xerox employee to speak to our various constituencies—customers, shareholders, suppliers and partners—with one voice.

This integrated cohesive approach to corporate identity and design is intentional. In fact, it is a business imperative. In today's age of information overload, only the clearest, most consistent messages leave lasting impressions.

Source: Reprinted with permission of Xerox Corporation, Stamford, Connecticut.

You should note that infringements are not limited to copy alone. Publishers such as *Time* magazine and *National Geographic* have registered respectively their distinct red and yellow borders, their trade dress. It is as illegal to appropriate this look or style as it is to appropriate the name.

Web Rights

The explosive growth of the World Wide Web has brought with it innumerable new issues related to the protection and use of copyright, trademarks, and servicemarks and to privacy. The fact that the Internet makes it possible to disseminate and access vast amounts of information instantaneously also makes it exponentially more difficult to control the ownership and use of that information.

It is fair to say that the ability to stretch the limits of existing law has far outpaced the ability of courts to predict or control commerce on the Internet, for which few of the laws were written. To date, four primary issues related to Internet commerce have dominated the courts: trademarks/domain names, links and frames, dilution, and meta-tags. Given the still relative infancy of Internet commerce, these issues may prove to be only the tip of the iceberg.

Trademarks Versus Domain Names

Since April 1999, the Internet Corporation for Assigned Names and Numbers (ICANN) has been responsible for the formal assignment of Internet domain names in the United States. ICANN coordinates the activities of the many ISPs and other companies that register domain names. (A *domain name* is an organization's trade name on the Web. For example, in the URL http://www.sagepub.com, the domain name is sagepub.)

This is in the United States only. Many foreign countries have their own authorities for issuing domain names, and alternative domain name registration systems have been proposed in the United States. Many of these systems include a geographic designation in the name such as .com, .us, .org, or .jp (for Japanese sites).

From the beginning, the overriding and often sole criterion for domain name acceptability was whether it had already been assigned. In practice, this led to a "first come, first served" policy that left many companies with well-recognized trade names prohibited from using those trade names as their domain names. Microsoft, Avon, Hasbro, Planned Parenthood, and the Better Business Bureau (BBB) are but a few of the organizations that have had to resort to legal action to secure their registered trade names for the Web. In light of the previously discussed trademark battle between the World Wildlife Fund and the (now) World Wrestling Entertainment, it is interesting to note that wwf.com leads to a wrestling forum site and that the World Wildlife Fund can be found under panda.org. This is a good example of the confusion that can result from trademarks and domain names.

Multiple court decisions involving both U.S. and foreign courts have done little to resolve the overall issues. These cases have raised such diverse defenses as the date of trademark registration, the public's awareness of the trade name, the potential for confusion, the intent of the domain name registrant, and the potential for dilution of the trademark holder's business.

EXHIBIT 6.4   A Xerox specialty signature. The digital X and "XEROX" are printed in the corporate red and "The Document Company" is printed in black.

Source: Reprinted with permission of Xerox Corporation, Stamford, Connecticut.

Regulations preventing one person from registering multiple domain names have stopped opportunistic "webpreneurs" from registering domains solely with the aim of tying up recognized trade names and ultimately selling the rights to use those names on the Web back to their original holders. The future of controls over domain name registration as well as other issues of cyberspace regulation will rest with ICANN (in the United States) and internationally with the World Intellectual Property Organization (WIPO) in Geneva, Switzerland. WIPO is the agency of the United Nations responsible for the promotion of international standards for intellectual property.

Links and Frames

A second area of concern in which the courts have already been called in to try to regulate web commerce is the issue of *links* and *frames* to another web site. Users who click on a link automatically open the linked site. Framing is a variation of this in which the original site imports all or part of another web site into its own. Although the secondary site has no control over how its site is used on the parent site, it is inevitably linked with it.

Think, for example, of a travel agent that links to airline and hotel sites. Depending on the type of link, the travel agent's site may or may not show the URL of the airline or hotel. The content may be clearly identifiable as originating from the airline or hotel or it may appear to be part of the travel agent's site. If the same travel agent "frames" these same airline and hotel sites, pages from the airline and hotel sites will be imported into the travel agent's site, framed by the travel agent's identification. The problem arises not with the information provided, but rather with the impression it leaves, that is, that the travel agent is an official agent (or possibly the only agent) for the airline and hotels.

A secondary problem is whether or not the travel agent also brings into its site the advertising that the airline or hotel may already have on its own site and that has been paid for by the advertisers. As the courts wrestle with these issues and their effect on Internet commerce, web site designers are beginning to address the problem on their own by writing code that either prevents unlimited linking or framing.

Dilution

Under U.S. trademark antidilution statute 15 U.S.C. §1125(c), *dilution* is the use of a trademark in such a way as to "dilute" or tarnish the image of the mark, even if consumers know that there is no association between the trademark holder and the entity misusing the trademark.

Trademark dilution was at the heart of a 2003 U.S. Supreme Court decision (*Moseley d/b/a Victor's Little Secret v. V Secret Catalogue Inc.*, 01–1015) involving a small lingerie specialty store called Victor's Little Secret and the lingerie giant Victoria's Secret. The court ruled in favor of "Victor," concluding that even though Victoria's Secret may own a famous mark with a strong association in consumer minds, the use of the name Victor's Little Secret did not confuse consumers and was unlikely to do so (Regehr, 2003). The decision suggests that dilution cases will require brand owners to find evidence (e.g., using public awareness surveys) that their trademark has been harmed.

Meta-tags, Keywords, and Other Search Cues

Meta-tags are part of the programming of every web site that allows search engines to find the site during searches. Web site designers have become skilled at including keyword meta-tags that will be picked up during searches regardless of whether or not they relate to or are representative of the site. Some advertising rates, for example, are based on the number of "hits" or visits to a site, so maximizing their identification during searches can have an impact on the site-owner's bottom line.

However, as of the time of printing, many of the largest search engines, including Google, Yahoo!, and MSN, had moved from using meta-tags to other methods of identifying relevant sites. Although refusing to identify their methods of searching, there generically seems to be a reliance on keywords—in titles or content. Because this will clearly continue to change, we suggest that you consult the organization that hosts your web site for advice on making your web site rise to the top of a search query.

The issue that may have precipitated this uncertainty is the number of lawsuits regarding the inclusion of keywords with potentially fraudulent intent, such as the use of hidden meta-tags (perhaps written in white type on white background or black type on a black background). They may be repeated hundreds of times unseen in the background but because of their frequency, may move the site to the top of the search results. For example, in a 1997 decision, *Playboy Enterprises, Inc. v. Calvin Designer Label* (No. C-97–3204; N.D.Cal., Sept. 8, 1997), a U.S. district court decided in favor of the plaintiff, Playboy Enterprises, against the publisher of a pornography web site. The site was ordered to shut down after a judge determined that the Playboy trademarks used in the site's URL, and hidden as meta-tags in its computer codes, influenced search engines to identify the site even though it has no affiliation with Playboy Enterprises.

As a writer, your role in protecting your employer's web rights is to ensure that you are not misappropriating others' material and/or misrepresenting your organization or its products and services.

Privacy

The issue of privacy in web communications has raised its ugly head again and again as reports of hackers raise the specter of a big brother presence in all our lives, as private citizens object to organizations gathering and sometimes selling information about visitors to corporate web sites, and as the privacy of e-mail comes under scrutiny.

The U.S. Congress and state legislatures have responded to calls for Internet privacy protection with laws designed to curb the invasion of personal privacy. Watchdog groups such as the Electronic Privacy Information Center (EPIC) and the Electronic Frontier Foundation, to name just two, have sprung up to provide information about Internet privacy and to monitor and sometimes lobby for legislation and legal decisions related to these issues.

On the other side, industry organizations including the Direct Marketing Association and the BBB are attempting to implement self-controls among their members that will nevertheless protect their interests in obtaining and using information. The Online Privacy Alliance, which includes many U.S. business leaders, promotes Internet privacy among its member sites including the posting of privacy policies or information practice policies on the sites where consumers can see them. BBBOnline, TRUSTe, and the CPA WebTrust have established "seal" programs that validate the privacy practices of approved web sites.

Because the problems, issues, and legislation regarding online privacy change almost daily, it is difficult to talk about them with any long-term validity. We suggest you monitor both government web sites and the sites of privacy and industry organizations to keep abreast of changes in legislation that may affect your employer and your writing.

Spamming

Closely related to privacy in the public mind is the issue of unsolicited e-mail, *spamming.* Congress tackled this issue with the "Can-Spam Act" of 2004 (P.L. 108–187); however, the jury is still out, so to speak, on whether the law will resolve or contribute to the problem. The law purports to crack down on spam by imposing stiff penalties on those convicted of spamming and promises to investigate the creation of a national "do not spam" list.

A survey by the Pew Internet & American Life Project (*Can-Spam Act,* 2004) project reported an increasing displeasure with unsolicited e-mail. Nearly 30% of respondents reported reducing their use of e-mail and over 85% said that they had some level of distress—both as the result of spam (pp. 1–2). Despite criticism that the Can-Spam law actually legalizes spam, continued public dissatisfaction is likely to lead to even greater restrictions. This may affect the ability of public relations writers to reach target publics.

DISCUSSION 1

The Internet raises new complications in the area of intellectual property rights as they relate to public relations. Do you think the government should be involved in domain name registration? Why or why not? Should domain name registration be done on a "first come, first registered" system? Should domain name registration be tied to trademark registration? Should names be auctioned to the highest bidder?

Should it be illegal for other sites to link to yours without your permission? Should you be able to freely use any material posted on the Web without violating copyright and/or paying a fee?

Increasingly, public relations practitioners need to be aware of "gripe" sites or "anti-" sites that may conduct smear campaigns against an organization. The legal responses to this can be complicated. Regulation is made difficult by the fact that the individuals disseminating defamatory material may often hide behind screen names and other identities. Public relations responses range from addressing the concerns raised on such sites to regarding the sites as valuable (and free) focus groups from which you can gain valuable insights on an organization's performance (Casarez, 2002).

Defamation, Libel, and Slander

Public relations and journalism tend to meet in the public mind when the issue is the high-stakes defamation or alleged defamation of a public figure. The victim does not have to be a public figure, however, to be defamed through libel or slander. It is just that the scenario becomes higher profile and more difficult for public figures because they carry a higher burden of proof and their attackers or defamers have several defenses against the charges of defamation.

The defenses against accusations of defamation are truth, privilege, and fair comment. Truth is what actually happened or was said. Privilege generally covers comment made by government or judicial officers in the course of proceedings. Fair comment covers the public expression of opinion on matters of public interest. It is what prevents restaurant critics from getting sued as long as they can back up allegedly defamatory statements with fact. In addition, public figures must prove not only defamation per se but also malice on the part of the individual or medium alleged to have defamed them.

If defamation is what has happened, that is, the victim's name, reputation, or image has been publicly defamed, then libel and slander are how the defamation occurred.

A quandary for public relations writers is that the same efforts that promote their employers effectively may take the employer from "non–public figure" to "public figure" and therefore paradoxically make the employer less able to demonstrate that it has been defamed.

Freedom of Information, Privacy, and Sunshine Laws

Few communication issues have been more contentious or public in recent years than the issues of freedom of information and privacy. The examples are many and span nearly every aspect of modern society. They include privacy of and the public's access to the following:

- ✦ Corporate and private files (including e-mail) in an era of increasing government surveillance and subsequent public suspicion
- ✦ Medical records in an age of increasing AIDS awareness and fear
- ✦ Student records as the National Collegiate Athletic Association (NCAA) reacts to accusations of fraud in athletic departments
- ✦ Financial records as the Internet can make credit card information readily available (legally or not) to at least seasoned hackers and scam artists as well as legitimate businesses

✦ Records of consumer purchasing behavior at a time when the sale of mailing lists and the use of automated dialing equipment make it possible for vendors to enter the privacy of a consumer's home with unwanted solicitations and with every mail delivery

Even as issues of freedom of information and privacy have captured the public's imagination and as the U.S. Constitution and Bill of Rights have been repeatedly examined for interpretations that protect the extreme positions of right to access and right to privacy, Congress has enacted laws to address specific privacy issues. Perhaps the best demonstration of how these issues may be seen as two sides of the same coin is the fact that provisions governing both of them are couched in the same statute: Title 5, U.S.C. §552, which is generally called the Freedom of Information Act (FOIA). Within this act, §552(a) is usually referred to as the Privacy Act and §552(b) as the Sunshine Act. Note that many states have also enacted their own FOI, privacy, and sunshine laws.

You should always be familiar and comply with the statutes of the state(s) in which your employer conducts its operations. For a brief introduction to the laws and to additional sources of information, see the Federal Citizen Information Center (FCIC) web site.

Freedom of Information Act

The Freedom of Information Act (FOIA) (Title 5, U.S.C. §552 by P.L. 104–231, 110 Stat. 2422) requires information on the activities of the federal government to be made available on request. Exceptions include trade secrets and information related to criminal proceedings and national security.

This open scrutiny by the public also applies to government contracts and contracting. Corporations bidding for government contracts may have their proposals scrutinized by their competitors under FOI laws after contract award. Public relations writers involved in marketing communications should be aware of this potential scrutiny.

Privacy Act

The Privacy Act, Title 5, U.S.C. §552(a), as amended, limits the disclosure of information gathered and/or held on individuals by the federal government including departments, agencies, and organizations acting on behalf of these departments and/or agencies. This includes, for example, information about your student loans held by colleges and/or collection agencies, Medicare records held by hospitals, and tax returns filed electronically by tax return companies.

Federal rules of evidence (Rule 501, 28 U.S.C.A.) as well as state laws protect the privacy of communications between lawyer and client, psychotherapist and patient, and husband and wife, for example. These *privileged communications* must generally be kept in confidence.

Sunshine Act

The Sunshine Act (1976), 5 U.S.C. §552(b), and equivalent state and local statutes open the meetings of federal and public agencies to the public. This may influence your media release tactics if your employer is a public agency. If, for example, you know or can assume that media representatives will routinely attend meetings of your government agency employer, you may need only to provide relevant background information at the time rather than trying to write and release a full report of the meeting yourself.

PATRIOT Act

The USA PATRIOT Act (2001), P.L. 107–56, also has implications for privacy and communication, yet to be fully assessed. It is fair to say that the act expands the ability of law enforcement agencies to conduct surveillance, to require the disclosure of information by, for example, colleges and universities, and in some instances to impose a gag order prohibiting individuals from even discussing a search with others.

Issues such as the tracking of foreign students, releasing library user records, and intercepting Internet data such as e-mail addresses have been some of the concerns raised in response to this act.

The bottom line: Consult a knowledgeable counsel.

What Does This Mean to the Public Relations Writer?

In addition to these acts, there are freedom and privacy protections in many other laws to regulate the actions of specific industries, the dissemination of specific types of information, and/or access to information. For example, the Children's Online Privacy Protection Act of 1998 (COPPA) was designed to protect the privacy rights of children on the Web, and the associated regulations mandated the disclosure of privacy policies by government bodies. Nevertheless, opponents continue to use the free speech rights of adults to challenge the law's constitutionality. This debate will likely continue.

The highly publicized "do not call" list, and "Can-Spam" acts are likely to be the tip of the iceberg for privacy legislation, much of it related to the collection and use of information on the Web. Many organizations already disclose their policies on their web sites. This is an area of legislation you will want to watch carefully.

This is not to say that all or even most information you may want to publicize is protected by privacy laws; however, it is a cautionary warning of the need to be aware of the possible repercussions of using specific or identifiable people or organizations in copy without the express, possibly written, permission of the individual or organization.

For example, in a 1998 legal action, a student who had received no financial aid from his college sued the institution after his photograph was used in a college financial aid brochure. He charged the institution with invasion of privacy, unauthorized appropriation of his image, and portraying him in a false light ("Lafayette College Sued," 1998). The writing implications are to be careful with how employees (or students, clients, etc.) are described and to keep writing focused on the employee's work rather than personal characteristics.

A routine issue for public relations writers is obtaining permission to use employee statements, photographs, or biographical information in company releases, videos, annual reports, and/or promotional materials. It is a good idea to obtain release/consent forms whenever you need to use employee information. Many colleges do this when students enroll each year with a view toward keeping students' local papers alerted to the student's graduation, for example, and/or to use photos of students in the college view book and other publications. Conversely, hospitals generally refuse requests to photograph patients, citing privacy laws as their reason.

DISCUSSION 2

There is a common misconception that the "do not call" list means you will get *no* telephone solicitations. This is not true.

Conduct a search using FedLaw or Westlaw, for example, for the wording of this law and the status of proposed amendments. What does this law actually say? What organizations and purposes are exempt? Why is this a good idea? Why not? Do the same for the "Can-Spam" law or other laws affecting public relations.

Financial Reporting and Insider Trading

Financial reporting is arguably the most heavily regulated of all organizational communication efforts. The relevant federal agency in this case is the SEC. The agency's general position on the release of financial information is that investors must have accurate information as soon as possible and as simultaneously as possible. The SEC's financial reporting requirements are very precise. To meet some of them, public relations writers *must* work closely with legal counsel and financial executives on precise wording and release mechanisms and timing.

Insider trading means taking advantage of financial or market information about an organization that the general public does not have. For example, in 1964 Texas Gulf Sulphur (TGS) discovered a major mineral deposit in Canada. The initial TGS press release led the SEC to charge the company with violations of the Securities Exchange Act. A federal court found that the release had led reasonable investors to believe that there was no ore discovery, or if so, that it was not as rich as rumored to be and that shareholders were therefore influenced to sell their stock because of the release. The court found the release to be misleading and that due diligence was not exercised in drafting and releasing it (*Securities and Exchange Commission v. Texas Gulf Sulphur Company,* 312 F.Supp. 77, 1964).

This decision has two implications for public relations writers. First, news releases must state the truth as it is known at the time of the release. Second, public relations personnel are "insiders"; they are responsible as corporate officers for any violations of laws relating to financial disclosure. The TGS case defined an insider as anyone with access to information that, if disseminated, might influence the price of a stock. In 1997, the definition of insider trading widened to include almost anyone who has access to such information—including, in 2003/2004, Martha Stewart.

This definition reinforces the care the public relations writer must take regarding the release or use of information. Because writers should be aware of "inside" information in a general sense, they are especially vulnerable to accusations of misuse of information and arguably even of conspiracy.

A rule of thumb has been "tell nobody and then tell everybody." The Web and newswires and business wires have made it possible to "tell everybody" quickly and simultaneously. Rapid and potentially worldwide disclosure can occur independently of whether standard newswires such as AP and Reuters release the story. Ted Pincus, former CEO of the investor relations firm Financial Relations Board, calls this a "two tier" system that creates uncertainty as to the point at which the information becomes public. In this sense, Web junkies with constant feeds are privileged over investors who have to rely on their local paper to carry a newswire story (Pincus, 1997).

The Agencies

Securities and Exchange Commission

Public relations writers must be aware of Securities and Exchange Commission (SEC) requirements for full and timely disclosure of any information that might affect the price of a client's publicly traded stock, the recently expanded definition of insider trading, and the very specific reporting and format requirements for financial information, especially annual reports and 10-K information.

The SEC has also become increasingly concerned that the intent of disclosure regulations not be frustrated by what former SEC chairman Arthur Levitt called "legalese and gobbledygook." The SEC web site now posts an online guide for reporting firms called "How to Create Clear SEC Disclosure Documents."

The intricacies of financial disclosure are detailed and changing. For more information, check with the SEC and the PRSA web sites and updates and commentary in, for example, the *New York Times, Business Week,* the *Wall Street Journal, Public Relations Review,* and *Public Relations Quarterly.*

Federal Trade Commission

The Federal Trade Commission (FTC) has oversight of advertising content, but its oversight may also include product news releases, photographs, and infomercials. Increasingly, the FTC has held responsible not only the manufacturer of a product but also the advertising, public relations, and production people responsible for information and publicity about the product. Even celebrities who endorse products have been held responsible for the claims they make.

It is obvious that a great deal of creativity and artistic license is permissible in advertising—thank goodness—but the FTC demands that ultimately you must be able to substantiate claims made in advertising. It can require that any false claims be dropped from future advertising and even that corrective advertising be run to correct previously misleading information. If you have had a part in making and publicizing false claims, you are legally responsible for them. It is your responsibility to see that product or service claims you make are accurate and can be substantiated.

Many states have their own "truth in advertising" statutes. It was such a law that Nike fell afoul of in the *Nike v. Kasky* case discussed earlier.

Food and Drug Administration

From a communication point of view, the Food and Drug Administration's (FDA) concern is with drugs, over-the-counter medicines, and cosmetics. It came into the public eye in the 1990s as it entered the debate over whether it has authority to control nicotine as a drug. It has also gained increased awareness as a result of food poisoning scares and its attempts to increase its authority to police food production and distribution.

The FDA's concerns with advertising and news releases are that they be accurate, that there be no false claims, and that unauthorized uses of a drug or medicine not be promoted. Clearly, "wiggle words" such as *could*, *may*, and *possible* have the potential to clarify or mislead the public about a product. They provide both ethical and legal challenges for writers, who may be held liable if the FDA finds that misleading or false statements have been made.

Current FDA regulations require that information about a drug's potential hazards and/or side effects be made available to the public. This accounts for the fine print you see at the bottom of many television and print ads for pharmaceuticals. Even the fine print is controlled. In 1997, the FDA required the manufacturers of the drug Claritin to change their television ad on the grounds that side-effect information and contact information for more details were presented in a confusing fashion (Wijnen, 1997b).

In the late 1990s, the FDA eased some requirements with respect to the advertising of pharmaceuticals on television (Wijnen, 1997a). Although broadcast ads must still be truthful and contain information about associated health risks, the summary of the side effects may be brief if manufacturers provide a toll-free phone number or Internet address for detailed information.

While this may be even more helpful for consumers seeking information, manufacturers and direct marketers now face another public relations issue: ensuring the privacy of those who choose to call for information. Calling an 800 number for information on drugs has been described by one consultant as "the marketing equivalent of putting a tattoo on your forehead announcing your medical condition" (Campanelli, 1997).

Federal Communications Commission

The Federal Communications Commission (FCC) regulates broadcasting and telecommunications including phone, computer, and satellite networks. It is probably fair to say that its recent emphasis has been more on industry regulation than broadcast content.

The FCC relates to the public relations practitioner in two ways: public service announcements (PSAs) and political communication. PSAs are essentially commercials carried at no cost for nonprofit and usually uncontroversial agencies. Radio and TV stations once used them to demonstrate that they were broadcasting in the public interest. However, as broadcasting has become increasingly deregulated by the FCC, public service time has become more difficult to obtain. Nevertheless, the FCC still requires stations to operate in the public interest and stations still see value in being seen as "good neighbors" and running PSAs that have great value for nonprofit organizations.

On a related issue, although broadcast stations are not required to give time to political candidates, the FCC's equal-time rule requires them to provide equal time to all qualified candidates if it is requested. News and interview shows are exempt from this calculation. Stations are also required to sell time to qualified candidates for federal office. You and your candidate, not the media, are legally responsible for the content of your political advertising.

U.S. Postal Service

The U.S. Postal Service (USPS) prohibits you from mailing material that would incite riots, murder, or assassination. In the light of the post-9/11 anthrax scares, this includes sending suspicious envelopes containing unidentified white powders.

Given that the thoughtful and ethical public relations writer has no such intent, why might the USPS be an agency to be concerned with? The answer lies in the more mundane world of postal regulations. For example, the size and weight of direct mail pieces directly affect the cost of mailing them. Presorting and barcoding mail reduce the cost of bulk mailers. On the other hand, special treatments such as nonstandard sizes, extra-weight card stock, and "self-mailers" that must be held closed with tape or a sticker (called a wafer-seal) add to the cost. There are also restrictions on the size and placement of address panels if you want to qualify for reduced rates.

Clearly, you can cost your employer a lot of money if you don't consider USPS regulations when designing and writing direct mail pieces. That extra 5¢ per piece adds up when you have a mailing of even 1,000 pieces. You would be wise to talk with your printer and to know the *Postal Service Manual.*

For some industries, other regulations also have an effect on even routine mailings. The Fair Debt Collection Practices Act (FDCPA; PL 95–109), for example, prohibits collection agencies from identifying the nature of their business on envelopes mailed to debtors because this would infringe on the debtor's privacy. It also decrees particular language and rights that must be given to debtors on the first written contact. You need to be aware of any such restrictions related to your employer's industry.

You should also be aware of public reactions to direct mail (if you want it) or junk mail (if you don't). Direct mail usually represents an attempt by an organization to solicit your business or to raise money. Consumers have a right to decide whether they want such mail. It is a subjective issue, but many people who don't like junk mail change their minds at the thought of being cut off from all such offerings, so it seems that many objections are to specific content rather than the process itself.

We leave this chapter with a legal case memorable for its name alone—Pig 'n Whistle. In this case, the value of Pig 'n Whistle restaurant and motel chain stock rose as a result of press releases made by its public relations agency. A federal court concluded that the agency had not verified the truth of the information provided by Pig 'n Whistle and that it should have done so. The agency was required among other things to establish procedures for selecting and accepting new clients that would not place the agency in a position of violating federal securities laws and for obtaining information from clients that would also prevent violation of securities laws (*Securities and Exchange Commission v. Pig 'n Whistle*, 359 F.Supp. 219 and 1972 WL 309, N.D.III).

The bottom line is that you as a public relations writer are responsible for both content and media decisions. As Morton and Loving (1994) point out, courts consider even entry-level public relations practitioners to be corporate officers and therefore liable for communications that breach the securities act. "Even communication technicians are liable for investor communications if they are noted as contact persons on releases or have primary control of communications in their releases" (p. 129).

It is always wise to monitor laws and regulations that affect your organization to ensure that you are interpreting them accurately and that your own writing complies with them. And, returning to the first theme of this chapter—consult with your legal allies when necessary. Topics of special interest to the public relations writer include privacy, confidentiality, disclosure, and postage, to name but a few. Fortunately, the Web has made it much easier to keep abreast of these laws. The FedLaw web site is a good starting point.

ON THE TEXTBOOK WEB SITE

✦ Go to www.sagepub.com/treadwell for web exercises, study hints, case studies, and additional examples appropriate to this chapter and chosen or developed to supplement the chapter content.

WRITING WRAP-UP

1. Using the resources in this chapter and elsewhere, write a set of legal guidelines for a new public relations appointee to your college or university. The guidelines should summarize the major regulations, agencies, and court decisions that could affect the employee's day-to-day work as a writer and specifically any work in media relations and communication. *Hint:* Think of this as a précis writing exercise on this chapter.

REFERENCES

Anthony, T. (1998, July 19). Lawsuit prompts question: Is "Polo" a shirt or a sport? *Sunday Republican,* p. E11.

Bowing to pressure, Roche cuts price for AIDS drug [Press release]. (2003, February 13). Retrieved March 19, 2004, from http://www.doctorswithoutborders.org/pr/2003/02-13-2003_pf.html

Campanelli, M. (1997, August 18). Will marketing bonanza lead to privacy legislation? *DM News, 19*(31), pp. 1, 50.

Can-Spam Act has not helped most email users so far. (2004, March 17). Research report, Pew Internet & American Life Project. Retrieved March 19, 2004, from http://www.pewinternet.org/reports/toc.asp?Report=116

Casarez, N. B. (2002, Summer). Dealing with cybersmear: How to protect your organization from online defamation. *Public Relations Quarterly, 47*(2), 40. Retrieved March 5, 2004, from EBSCO Host Communication and Mass Media Complete database

Hormel, Inc. (2003). *Spam and the Internet.* Retrieved October 1, 2003, from http://www.spam.com/ci/ci_in.htm

Jenkins, A. (2003, April/May). What would you do? *Communication World, 20*(3), 14. Retrieved March 5, 2004, from EBSCO Host Communication and Mass Media Complete database

Lafayette College sued over photo in financial-aid brochure. (1998, June 26). *Chronicle of Higher Education,* p. A39. Retrieved June 14, 2004, from http://chronicle.com/prm/che-data/articles.dir/art-44.dir/issue-42.dir/42a03902.htm

Morton, L. P., & Loving, B. (1994). In the stocks: Perilous press releases. *Public Relations Review, 20*(2), 127–139.

Petrini, C., & Shea, G. F. (1992, January). A case for clear writing. *Training and Development, 46*(1), 63–66.

Pincus, T. (1997, September 7). When news is in the timing. *New York Times,* p. F14.

Regehr, P.C. (2003). US Supreme Court dilution case–Victoria's Secret. Moseley d/b/a Victor's Little Secret v. V Secret Catalogue Inc., 01–1015. Retrieved June 14, 2004, from Findlaw for Professionals: http://library.lp.findlaw.com

Tuerck, D. G. (Ed.). (1978). *The political economy of advertising.* Washington, DC: American Enterprise Institute for Public Policy Research.

Watson, J. C. (2002, Winter). Litigation public relations: The lawyers' duty to balance news coverage of their clients. *Communication Law and Policy, 7*(1), 77. Retrieved March 5, 2003, from EBSCO Host Communication and Mass Media Complete database

Wijnen, R. (1997a, August 18). Agencies expect DRTV drug bonanza. *DM News, 19*(31), 1, 50.

Wijnen, R. (1997b, September 8). FDA recalls Claritin DRTV ad, cites lack of information. *DM News, 19*(33), 1, 62.

Xerox Corporation. (1997a). Introduction. In *Basic graphic standards.* Stamford, CT: Xerox Corporation.

Xerox Corporation. (1997b). Specialty signatures. In *Basic graphic standards.* Stamford, CT: Xerox Corporation.

Zielbauer, P. (2001, December 27). What's in a band's name? Plenty if it's Anthrax. *New York Times.* p. E1. Retrieved March 21, 2004, from LexisNexis.

RESOURCES

Information on Copyright/ Trademark/Servicemark/Patent Law

Copyright Basics, a brief review of copyright law available from the Copyright Office, http://www.copyright.gov/circs/circ1.html

Copyright Law of the United States of America. (2003, June). United States Copyright Office. Library of Congress Circular 92.

Web searches for topics such as "trademark," "copyright," "intellectual property," "cyberlaw," "domain names" and "privacy" on common search engines will lead to hundreds of sites for government departments and agencies, law search organizations and libraries, public interest groups, and law firms. Through these sites you can access the laws themselves as well as a lay person's explanations, interpretations, and opinions on the laws. Following is a representative sampling of these sources. Inclusion in the list does not imply the authors' endorsement of any of the sites listed or criticism of any sites not listed.

Information on Laws, Regulations, Congressional Actions, and Court Rulings

Cornell Law School, Legal Information Center .... www.law.cornell.edu

Emory University .... www.law.emory.edu

Federal Law Information Center (FedLaw) .... www.thecre.com/fedlaw/default.htm

FedLaw includes searchable sections on laws and on regulations as well as bills before current and recent sessions of Congress.

FindLaw .... www.findlaw.com

Georgetown University .... www.georgetown.edu

Internet Legal Research Group... www.ilrg.com/caselaw

THOMAS web site of the Library of Congress .... thomas.loc.gov

The THOMAS web site is a source of legislative information on the Internet. From this site you can access information about members of Congress, committees, bills, public laws (by number), and historical documents.

Information on Freedom of Information (FOI) and Privacy

Electronic Privacy Information Center (EPIC) .... www.epic.org

Online Privacy Alliance .... www.privacyalliance.org

Information on the Legal Issues Regarding the Internet and World Wide Web

American Lawyer Media's law.com .... www.law.com

BBBOnline (A Better Business Bureau Program) .... www.bbbonline.org

CPA WebTrust .... www.cpawebtrust.org

Electronic Frontier Foundation .... www.eff.org

Electronic Privacy Information Center (EPIC) .... www.epic.org

ICANN (Internet Corporation for Assigned Names and Numbers) .... www.icann.org

TRUSTe .... www.truste.org

World Intellectual Property Organization (WIPO) .... www.wipo.org

Government Departments and Agencies Related to Legal Issues Discussed in This Chapter

Department of Commerce .... www.doc.gov

Department of Education .... www.ed.gov

Department of Health and Human Services .... www.hhs.gov

Department of Homeland Security .... www.dhs.gov

Department of Justice (DOJ) .... www.usdoj.gov

DOJ Freedom of Information http://www.usdoj.gov/04foia/index.html
and Privacy Act page

DOJ Office of Information and Privacy .... www.usdoj.gov/oip/oip.html

Federal Bureau of Investigation (FBI) .... www.fbi.gov

Federal Communications Commission (FCC) .... www.fcc.gov

Federal Citizen Information Center (FCIC) .... fic.info.gov

Federal Trade Commission (FTC) .... www.ftc.gov

Food and Drug Administration (FDA) .... www.fda.gov

Library of Congress .... www.loc.gov

Securities and Exchange Commission (SEC) .... www.sec.gov

U.S. Copyright Office of the Library of Congress .... www.loc.gov/copyright

U.S. Patents and Trademark Office .... www.uspto.gov

U.S. Postal Service .... www.usps.gov

7

Design Influences on Public Relations Writing

1. **The strongest public relations documents result from a marriage of writing and design to send a common message.**

2. **Good design is simple.**

3. **Public relations writers need to understand the basics of design—layout, typography, color, use of graphics—to maximize the effectiveness of their writing.**

Which Is More Important, the Copy or the Design?

If ever there was a contentious issue, this is it, ranking right up there with "which came first, the chicken or the egg?" "Turf" disputes abound between writers and designers. The fact is that the best communications result from collaboration between the two in which text and design complement each other from the start.

Effective communications result from design that supports the copy so naturally that it is, for all intents, invisible. Good design gives a document personality, direction, and attitude. It makes a reader say, "I'll open this now," instead of "I'll put it aside for later." But it should not be so obvious that the message is secondary to the layout, however unique.

Communication Is the Key

Award-winning designer and design consultant Jan V. White (1982) says that "working editors and designers . . . must never forget that the only thing that matters is the story and the context within which the story will be perceived. . . . Of prime concern must always be the fundamental function of editing/designing—communication" (p. x).

This is not a design text. What we offer is an introduction to the principles, terms, and techniques that will help you create simple and effective documents in which text and design work toward a common communication aim and effectively express the organization's culture and image as well as the message. We hope to convince you that with attention to some basic principles, do-it-yourself design *can* be a recipe for success, not to mention that it is fun.

If you have no sense of visual balance or no interest in visual presentation, by all means find a good designer who understands your employer's style, culture, and mission and who shares your concern for effective communication. Whether you do it yourself or employ a professional artist, the important issue is that you plan the design as carefully as you plan your writing.

Thinking of design from the start of every project will challenge you to write better copy and encourage you to think for presentation. It will result in a product that combines the best of words and pictures, space, type, graphics and color in an appealing, effective, and successful communication.

Design as a Public Relations Tactic

Readers are impatient creatures. We receive thousands of visual messages every day, and we look for design cues that help us determine what is critical, important, relevant, or interesting and what we can ignore.

These design cues are not necessarily the work of professional artists. For example, assembly instructions are numbered; so are the steps in a recipe. The fine print of a contract is just that, *smaller, harder-to-read type.* It is placed at the end or the bottom for a reason. Question-and-answer columns use large *Q*'s and *A*'s or different type to distinguish the questions from the answers. Many state highways code their signage by color: blue or black for traffic information and directions, red or yellow for warnings, green for scenic attractions, and brown for historic sites.

Designers create these visual cues by strategically using the following four design elements to support the text: space, type, graphics, and color. Understanding how these elements work will help you ensure that your own projects include not only effective copy but also the design cues to help readers or viewers interpret or use that copy.

A good way to develop your own design ability is to pay attention to the visual cues you receive every day. Collect samples of documents you particularly like (or don't like)—ads, brochures, annual reports, newsletters, printouts of web pages, anything that attracts you. In the industry, this is unabashedly called a "swipe file," although you should think of it as a samples or resource file.

You will find the samples useful as a stimulus when you are suffering from "designer's block," when you want to see what a particular type style looks like as a headline, how photos look on textured papers, or even as a barometer of which techniques are being overused. You should regard your swipe file as a resource for design research, as a way of helping you learn from the best. It is not a license to steal other people's designs.

White (1982) cautions against using unexplained examples when producing design books because "the outward form of the examples is often grafted onto material that is unsympathetic to that form. . . . It is not enough to show a good solution without defining what makes it good—and what it is good for" (p. xi). Exercise this same concern with regard to your swipe file. It is not enough to know that you like a design or even that it won multiple awards. You must also be sure that it was a successful communication—not just an interesting design—and understand why it was successful. Only then can you determine if the concept is appropriate for your own project.

If design becomes a large part of your job, we suggest taking a design course or enrolling in one of the hundreds of seminars offered each year by software companies, computer and design magazines, and consultants.

Communicating With Space

How space is used in a layout is the first impression, conscious or not, that a reader has of a document. Space has direction, personality, and attitude. It can lead you into a story, straight to a highlight, or off the page. Large spaces are bold and confident, small ones weak and timid. Irregular spaces are interesting and challenging, regular ones comfortable and safe.

If the space is filled top to bottom, margin to margin, it may signal that the article is "boring," on one hand, or simply "too much," on the other. If the space is too empty . . . actually we don't know what the reader's reaction would be in this case; it never happens.

If you as a designer do not fill the space, you may be sure someone else will. One of the most difficult aspects of design is creating areas of white space so natural that no one sees them as areas to be filled. You may well find yourself in the position of defending and protecting the white space in your layout.

In this text, we shall instead focus on format, balance, and symmetry as the spatial concepts that form the basis of your design or layout.

Format

By spatial format we mean horizontal or vertical. Horizontal formats are referred to as *landscape* and vertical formats as *portrait*. The most common format is portrait. Letters, memos, most newsletters, and this text have pages in a portrait format. If we receive a document in a landscape format, we notice it; it stands out from the rest immediately. Although *individual* pages may be portrait format, you can achieve great impact by treating *adjacent* pages as a landscape format. It is difficult to create a horizontal "feel" on a portrait format or to use vertical art on a landscape page. Artwork that is very strong or critical to the story may dictate a particular format.

When designing for TV and the Web, you must always "think landscape" because that is the format of most TV and computer screens. TV art is traditionally designed in a landscape 4:3 ratio; however, as the widescreen/HDTV format (which has a 16:9 ratio) gains in popularity, it is likely that the 4:3 ratio will slowly disappear.

Computer screens present a greater problem. Although a single screen is a landscape format, a "page" is actually two screens long, giving a total usable area *for one page* that is a portrait ratio.

Balance

All good layouts are balanced.

Unbalanced layouts will appear to be tilting; one side appears heavier than the other. They will be irritating to readers or viewers. Unbalanced layouts also call attention to the design at the expense of the copy—for all the wrong reasons.

Balance may be symmetric or asymmetric. A simple analogy for balance is a child's seesaw. When both children weigh the same, the seesaw balances if they sit the same distance from the center, which is the balance point (see Exhibit 7.1, left).

EXHIBIT 7.1   Balance. The example on the left is symmetric, balanced equally from the center. The example on the right is asymmetric, balanced unequally from the center.

When the children do not weigh the same, the seesaw cannot balance unless the heavier child moves toward the balance point (Exhibit 7.1, right).

These same principles also apply to layout. Regardless of the size, shape, or document (ad, newsletter, chart, graph, etc.), the layout must balance; the elements must appear to "weigh" the same or have the same strength on both sides of a balance point.

If you are not sure whether a layout is balanced, try looking at it upside down. This helps you see the elements as relative visual strengths rather than being distracted by the actual words and photos.

Symmetric Layouts

In symmetric layouts such as the one in Figure 7.2, the balance point lies in the center and the halves are positioned as mirror images. Symmetric layouts are not bad or wrong but they tend to be formal and predictable. The relationship between the elements is obvious, which may make them boring. For beginning designers, symmetric layouts are generally easier to create but more difficult to make interesting. You must make good use of type and graphics to add interest and variety. But it can be done.

Asymmetric Layouts

Asymmetric layouts such as Exhibit 7.3 also have equal weight on both sides of the balance point, but the elements on each side are not equally positioned from the center.

Asymmetric layouts are inherently interesting because the relationships among the elements are not obvious. You achieve visual balance by adjusting the position and/or strength of elements in relation to each other until the elements to the left balance those on the right. Sometimes this is a matter of moving the elements as we moved the child on the seesaw. Sometimes you can achieve the same impact by increasing the size of a headline or photo, setting type in bold, or putting captions close to photos so they are seen as one strong element rather than many small ones.

Asymmetric layouts are surprisingly flexible. They can accommodate many small photos or one large one, lists of names, lengthy interviews, and the demands of documents as diverse as simple brochures and multipage annual reports. Even lengthy annual reports are usually based on one or two basic layouts that unify the document. Photos, charts and graphs, and perhaps quotes from the CEO create variety and make the pages appear fresh despite the common layout(s).

Asymmetric layouts are more challenging—some would say more risky—to create than symmetric layouts, but they are infinitely more interesting for the reader and satisfying for the designer. If you are not a confident designer, we suggest you begin with a simple asymmetric layout, perhaps for an advertisement that includes

EXHIBIT 7.2 **Symmetric layout.**

EXHIBIT 7.3 **Asymmetric layout.**

only a few blocks of text and one graphic element. Then graduate to longer and more complex documents.

Spreads

Spread is the term for crossing a column, fold, margin, or gutter with a layout. Double-column spreads span two columns. Double-page spreads are two facing pages. Centerspreads are facing pages printed on one sheet of paper. There is only one centerspread per document and it lies, obviously, in the center. Saddle-stitched documents are stapled through the centerspread.

Spreads provide wonderful layout opportunities, but you must regard the two columns or two pages as a single entity; you cannot ignore the fold or gutter. Rather, you must design with it in mind, with lines and direction that make it obvious that the text and graphics on the right page (the *recto*) are a continuation of the text and graphics on the left page (the *verso*). Although technically you *can* print half of a photo on one page and half on the next, or continue a line across the gutter, you must be certain your printer can *register* (align two or more printing plates exactly), trim, and assemble the pages precisely.

The only safe time to print graphic elements across the center is on a true centerspread. Even then, be careful to crop and size the photo so that the fold falls between rather than across people or important objects. Using this criterion, you could print Exhibit 7.4 on facing pages as well as on a centerspread. Exhibit 7.5, however, requires a centerspread to ensure that lines of type and photos cannot be misaligned.

EXHIBIT 7.4   Symmetric layout across two pages.

Symmetric layouts have
equal visual weight on
both sides of a center line,
often the gutter on
double-page spreads.

Sectetuer adipiscing elit, sed diam nonummy nibh euismod tincidunt ut laoreet dolore magna aliquam erat volutpat. Ut wisi enim ad minim veniam, quis notsrud exerci tation ullamcorper suscipit lobortis nisl ut aliquip ex ea commodo consequat. Duis autem vel eum iriure dolor in hendrerit in vulputate velit esse molestie consequat, vel illum dolore eu feugiat nulla.

Facilisis at vero eros et accumsan et iusto odio dignissim qui blandit praesent luptatum zzril delenit augue duis dolor te feugait nulla facilisi. Lorem ipsum dolor sit amet, consectetuer adipiscing elit, sed diam nonummy nibh euismod tincidunt ut laoreet dolore magna aliquam erat volutpat. Ut wisi enim ad minim veniam, quis notsrud exerci tation ullamcorper suscipit lobortis nisl ut aliquip ex ea commodo consequat. Duis autem vel eum iriure dolor in hendrerit in vulputate velit esse molestie consequat, vel illum dolore eu feugiat nulla facilisis at vero eros et accumsan et iusto odio dignissim qui blandit praesent lup-

tatum zzril delenit augue duis dolor te feugait nulla facilisi.

Lorem ipsum dolor sit amet, consectetuer adipiscing elit, sed diam nonummy nibh euismod tincidunt ut laoreet dolore magna aliquam erat volutpat. Ut wisi enim ad minim veniam, quis notsrud exerci tation ullamcorper suscipit lobortis nisl ut aliquip ex ea commodo consequat. Duis autem vel eum iriure dolor in hendrerit in vulputate velit esse molestie consequat, vel illum dolore eu feugiat nulla.

Lorem ipsum dolor sit amet, consectetuer adipiscing elit, sed diam nonummy nibh euismod tincidunt ut laoreet dolore magna aliquam erat volutpat. Ut wisi enim ad minim veniam, quis notsrud exerci tation ullamcorper suscipit lobortis nisl ut aliquip ex ea commodo consequat. Duis autem vel eum iriure dolor in vulputate velit esse molestie consequat, vel illum dolore eu feugiat nulla facilisis at vero eros et accumsan et iusto odio dignissim qui blandit praesent luptatum zzril delenit augue duis dolor te feugait nulla facilisi.

Lorem ipsum dolor sit amet, consectetuer adipiscing elit, sed diam nonummy nibh euismod tincidunt ut laoreet dolore magna aliquam erat volutpat. Ut wisi enim ad minim veniam, quis notsrud exerci

quis notsrud exerci tation ullamcorper suscipit lobortis nisl ut aliquip ex ea commodo consequat. Duis autem vel eum iriure dolor in hendrerit in vulputate velit esse molestie consequat, vel illum dolore eu feugiat nulla facilisis at vero eros et accumsan et iusto odio dignissim qui blandit praesent luptatum zzril delenit augue duis dolor te feugait nulla facilisi.

Lorem ipsum dolor sit amet, consectetuer adipiscing elit, sed diam nonummy nibh euismod tincidunt ut laoreet dolore magna aliquam erat volutpat. Ut wisi enim ad minim veniam, quis notsrud exerci tation ullamcorper suscipit lobortis nisl ut aliquip ex ea commodo consequat. Duis autem vel eum iriure dolor in hendrerit in vulputate velit esse molestie consequat, vel illum dolore eu feugiat nulla facilisis at vero eros et accumsan et iusto odio dignissim qui blandit praesent luptatum zzril delenit augue duis dolor te feugait nulla facilisi.

Lorem ipsum dolor sit amet, consectetuer adipiscing elit, sed diam nonummy nibh euismod tincidunt ut laoreet dolore magna aliquam erat volutpat. Ut wisi enim ad minim veniam, quis notsrud exerci tation ullamcorper suscipit lobortis nisl ut aliquip ex ea commodo consequat. Duis autem vel eum iriure dolor in hendrerit in

Lorem ipsum dolor sit amet, consectetuer adipiscing elit, sed diam nonummy nibh euismod tincidunt ut laoreet dolore magna aliquam erat volutpat. Ut wisi enim ad minim veniam, quis notsrud exerci tation ullamcorper suscipit lobortis nisl ut aliquip ex ea commodo consequat. Duis autem vel eum iriure dolor in hendrerit in vulputate velit esse molestie consequat, vel illum dolore eu feugiat nulla facilisis at vero eros et accumsan et iusto odio dignissim qui blandit praesent luptatum zzril delenit augue duis dolor te feugait nulla facilisi.

Lorem ipsum dolor sit amet, consectetuer adipiscing elit, sed diam nonummy nibh euismod tincidunt ut laoreet dolore magna aliquam erat volutpat. Ut wisi enim ad minim veniam, quis notsrud exerci tation ullamcorper suscipit lobortis nisl ut aliquip ex ea commodo consequat. Duis autem vel eum iriure dolor in hendrerit in vulputate velit esse molestieLorem ipsum dolor sit amet, consectetuer adipiscing elit, sed diam

EXHIBIT 7.5   Asymmetric across two pages. Ideally, this would be a centerspread, thereby avoiding registration problems with the photo and the headlines that run across the gutter.

CENTERSPREADS ARE IDEAL FOR HORIZONTAL LAYOUTS

Erat volutpat. Ut wisi enim ad minim veniam, quis notsrud exerci tation ullamcorper suscipit lobortis nisl ut aliquip ex ea commodo consequat. Duis autem vel eum iriure dolor in hendrerit in vulputate velit esse molestie consequat, vel illum dolore eu feugiat nulla facilisis at vero eros et accumsan et iusto odio dignissim qui blandit praesent luptatum zzril delenit augue duis dolor te feugait nulla facilisi.

Lorem ipsum dolor sit amet, consectetuer adipiscing elit, sed diam nonummy nibh euismod tincidunt ut laoreet dolore magna aliquam erat volutpat. Ut wisi enim ad minim veniam, quis notsrud exerci tation ullamcorper suscipit lobortis nisl ut aliquip ex ea commodo consequat. Duis autem vel eum iriure dolor in hen-

erat volutpat. Ut wisi enim ad minim veniam, quis notsrud exerci tation ullamcorper suscipit lobortis nisl ut aliquip ex ea commodo consequat. Duis autem vel eum iriure dolor in hendrerit in vulputate velit esse molestie consequat, vel illum dolore eu feugiat nulla facilisis at vero eros et accumsan et iusto odio dignissim qui blandit praesent luptatum zzril delenit augue duis dolor te feugait nulla facilisi.

Lorem ipsum dolor sit amet, consectetuer adipiscing elit, sed diam nonummy nibh euismod tincidunt ut laoreet dolore magna aliquam erat volutpat. Ut wisi enim ad minim veniam, quis notsrud exerci tation ullam-

erat volutpat. Ut wisi enim ad minim veniam, quis notsrud exerci tation ullamcorper suscipit lobortis nisl ut aliquip ex ea commodo consequat. Duis autem vel eum iriure dolor in hendrerit in vulputate velit esse molestie consequat, vel illum dolore eu feugiat nulla facilisis at vero eros et accumsan et iusto odio dignissim qui blandit praesent luptatum zzril delenit augue duis dolor te feugait nulla facilisi.

Lorem ipsum dolor sit amet, consectetuer adipiscing elit, sed diam nonummy nibh euismod tincidunt ut laoreet dolore magna aliquam erat volutpat. Ut wisi enim ad minim veniam, quis notsrud exerci tation ullam-

erat volutpat. Ut wisi enim ad minim veniam, quis notsrud exerci tation ullamcorper suscip- it lobortis nisl ut aliquip ex ea commodo consequat. Duis autem vel eum iriure dolor in hendrerit in vulputate velit esse molestie consequat, vel illum dolore eu feugiat nulla facilisis at vero eros et accumsan et iusto odio dignissim qui blandit prae- sent luptatum zzril delenit augue duis dolor te feugait nulla facilisi.

Lorem ipsum dolor sit amet, consectetuer adipiscing elit, sed diam nonummy nibh euismod tincidunt ut laoreet dolore magna aliquam erat volutpat. Ut wisi enim ad minim veniam, quis notsrud exerci tation ullam- corper suscipit lobortis nisl ut aliquip ex ea commodo conse- quat. Duis autem vel eum iriure dolor in hendrerit in vulputate velit esse molestie

erat volutpat. Ut wisi enim ad minim veniam, quis notsrud exerci tation ullamcorper sus- cipit lobortis nisl ut

Even the secondary story supports the layout!

Erat volutpat. Ut wisi enim ad minim veniam, quis notsrud exerci tation ullamcorper suscipit lobortis nisl ut aliquip ex ea commodo consequat. Duis autem vel eum iriure dolor in hendrerit in vulputate velit esse molestie consequat, vel illum dolore eu feugiat nulla facilisis at vero eros et accumsan et iusto odio dignissim qui blandit praesent luptatum zzril delenit augue duis ullamcorper suscipit lobortis nisl ut aliquip ex ea com- modo consequat. Duis autem vel eum iriure dolor in hendrerit in vulputate velit esse molestie consequat.

Lorem ipsum dolor sit amet, consectetuer adipiscing elit, sed diam nonummy nibh euismod tincidunt ut laoreet dolore magna aliquam erat volutpat. Ut wisi enim ad minim veniam, quis notsrud exerci tation ullam- corper suscipit lobortis nisl ut aliquip ex ea commodo conse- quat. Duis autem vel eum iriure dolor in hendrerit in vulputate velit esse molestie consequat, vel illum dolore eu feugiat nulla facilisis at vero eros et accumsan et iusto odio dignissim qui bland- it praesent luptatum zzril delen- it augue duis dolor te feugait

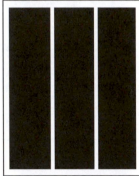

Columns

Columns are particularly related to balance and symmetry. Columns (vertical strips of text) can make a designer's task much easier or much more difficult depending on whether the number and widths of the columns are chosen with the document contents in mind. This is especially important when working with multipage documents with many articles, photos, and graphic elements, such as newsletters and annual reports.

Exhibit 7.6 illustrates four of the most common column formats: equal two-column, equal three-column, unequal two-column, and unequal three-column. Most letter-sized newsletters (page size 8.5″ × 11″) are set in two or three columns. Two is more formal and often more boring. Three columns provide more opportunity for interesting layouts and make it easier to use photos of varying sizes and to accommodate stories of different lengths. A variation is to use one fairly wide column or two equal columns with a narrow column at the left. The narrow column can be useful for captions, comments, or lists of names such as new employees or contest winners without wasting space in a wide column.

Layout Relationships

Regardless of their symmetry, successful layouts are based on relationships and on organizing elements to make these relationships clear. The following rules will help you create interesting layouts for ads, brochures, newsletters, annual reports, and web sites.

✦ *Keep it simple.* The key to good design is restraint. Consider whether a new element makes it easier to follow the flow and understand the message or whether it competes with the rest of the layout to confuse and deter the reader from reading further. Every element in a layout should be there for a reason, and with few exceptions, that reason should be something other than "because it looks nice."

✦ *Organize copy blocks* so readers know instantly where they must go to continue the article. Be wary of placing photos so they cut off a column if it means the reader doesn't know whether to continue the story under the photo or at the top of the next column.

✦ *Remember that the natural flow* of a document is from top left to bottom right. This same principle applies to small parts of a design, such as a newsletter article or a bar graph.

◆ *Ensure that the most important part of the article is obvious.*

◆ *Place photos, artwork, and charts and graphs close to text they support.*

◆ *Start columns at the same level.* This is much more important than having them end at the same level.

◆ *Try to minimize the number of elements you see.* This is not necessarily the same as the number of elements in the layout. By grouping photos or setting captions at the same width as a photo, you can fool the eye into seeing the group or the photo and caption as a single element that fills a regular space. In contrast, using photos of different sizes and shapes and positioning them all over a layout leaves readers with no idea which is the most important or where to look first.

◆ *"Think alignment"* whenever you add an element. Ask yourself how the element relates to the elements and spaces around it. Placing elements at random heights, for example, leads the viewer's eye all over the place and interrupts the natural flow of communication. Notice how the horizontal "feel" of the layout in Exhibit 7.5 is carried out not only by the headlines and the height of all of the columns in the lead story but also by the fact that the caption under the photo at right ends at the same height as the secondary headline. This subtly continues that line throughout the layout as well.

◆ *Pay attention to the details.* Whenever you add an element to a layout, assess how it relates to the height and width of all other elements. Moving a photo up or down even 1/8 inch can make the difference between a layout that tells a story and one that simply has a lot of elements.

◆ *Keep spacing consistent.* The need for precision and consistency extends to the spacing between elements. Look closely at your daily newspaper or any magazine and you will see that the distance between headlines and copy or photos and captions and copy is always the same. Because of this, the space "disappears" in the layout. If the spacing changes each time, it becomes obvious and intrusive.

◆ *Create patterns with text or graphics.* You could, for example, size multiple head-and-shoulders photos to the same size and print them with a short quote all at the top or bottom or in a row across several (but not all) columns of the layout. Or you could print several short articles across a layout, starting all of them at the same height with the same number of lines in the headline but different lengths of copy. Be careful not to make the patterns too regular or too obvious.

◆ *Create interest by deliberately breaking one relationship* that you have established. If your layout is well planned and you have made it easy for the reader to follow the story, then breaking one relationship will surprise the reader and add interest. For example, Exhibit 7.5 allows one column of copy to flow to the bottom of the page, creating one vertical line in an otherwise horizontal layout. Two long columns would have destroyed the horizontal feel, and none would have been boring.

Exhibit 7.7 illustrates how breaking column or margin relationships can turn staid, boring layouts into pages with interest and focus. On the left page, a *pull quote* breaks into the center vertical line between columns. Pull quotes are

EXHIBIT 7.7   Pull quotes and bleed photos are simple ways to break up and add interest to an otherwise dull, two-column layout.

Chairman's Report, continued from page 1

Lorem ipsum dolor sit amet, consectetuer adipiscing elit, sed diam nonummy nibh euismod tincidunt ut laoreet dolore magna aliquam erat volutpat. Ut wisi enim ad minim veniam, quis notsrud exerci tation ullamcorper suscipit lobortis nisl ut aliquip ex ea commodo consequat. Duis autem vel eum iriure dolor in hendrerit in vulputate velit esse molestie consequat, vel illum dolore eu feugiat nulla facilisis at vero eros et accumsan et iusto odio dignissim qui blandit praesent luptatum zzril delenit augue duis dolor te feugait nulla facilisi.

Lorem ipsum dolor sit amet, consectetuer adipiscing elit, sed diam nonummy nibh euismod tincidunt ut laoreet dolore magna aliquam erat volutpat. Ut wisi enim ad minim veniam, quis notsrud exerci tation ullamcorper suscipit lobortis nisl ut aliquip ex ea commodo consequat. Duis autem vel eum iriure dolor in hendrerit in vulputate velit esse molestie consequat, vel illum dolore eu feugiat nulla facilisis at vero eros et accumsan et iusto odio dignissim qui blandit praesent luptatum zzril delenit augue duis dolor te feugait nulla facilisi.

Lorem ipsum dolor sit amet, consectetuer adipiscing elit, sed diam nonummy nibh euismod tincidunt ut laoreet dolore magna aliquam erat volutpat. Ut wisi enim ad minim veniam,

" *Pull quotes are useful stylistic devices. They help provide white space and interesting copy shapes.* "

quis notsrud exerci tation ullamcorper suscipit lobortis nisl ut aliquip ex ea commodo consequat. Duis autem vel eum iriure dolor in hendrerit in vulputate velit esse molestie consequat, vel illum dolore eu feugiat nulla facilisis at vero eros et accumsan et iusto odio dignissim qui blandit praesent luptatum zzril delenit augue duis dolor te feugait nulla facilisi.

Lorem ipsum dolor sit amet, consectetuer adipiscing elit, sed diam nonummy nibh euismod tincidunt ut laoreet dolore magna aliquam erat volutpat. Ut wisi enim ad minim veniam, quis notsrud exerci tation ullamcorper suscipit lobortis nisl ut aliquip ex ea commodo consequat. Duis autem vel eum iriure dolor in hendrerit in vulputate velit esse molestie Lorem ipsum dolor sit amet, consectetuer adipiscing elit, sed diam nonummy nibh euismod tincidunt ut laoreet dolore magna aliquam erat volutpat. Ut wisi enim ad minim veniam, quis notsrud exerci tation ullamcorper suscipit it lobortis nisl ut aliquip ex ea commodo consequat. Duis autem vel eum iriure dolor in hendrerit in vulputate velit esse molestie

Lorem ipsum dolor sit amet, consectetuer adipiscing elit, sed diam nonummy nibh euismod tincidunt ut laoreet dolore magna aliquam erat volutpat. Ut wisi enim ad minim veniam, quis notsrud exerci tation ullamcorper suscipit lobortis nisl ut aliquip ex ea commodo consequat. Duis autem vel eum iriure dolor in hendrerit in vulputate velit esse molestie consequat, vel illum dolore eu feugiat nulla facilisis at vero eros et accumsan et iusto odio dignissim qui blandit praesent luptatum zzril delenit augue duis dolor te feugait nulla facil

Lorem ipsum dolor sit amet, consectetuer adipiscing elit, sed diam nonummy nibh euismod tincidunt ut laoreet dolore magna aliquam erat volutpat. Ut wisi enim ad minim veniam, quis notsrud exerci tation ullamcorper suscipit lobortis nisl ut aliquip ex ea commodo conse-

Chairman's Report
continued from page 1

Lorem ipsum dolor sit amet, consectetuer adipiscing elit, sed diam nonummy nibh euismod tincidunt ut laoreet dolore magna aliquam erat volutpat. Ut wisi enim ad minim veniam, quis notsrud exerci tation ullamcorper suscipit lobortis nisl ut aliquip ex ea commodo consequat. Duis autem vel eum iriure dolor in hendrerit in vulputate velit esse molestie consequat, vel illum dolore eu feugiat nulla facilisis at vero eros et accumsan et iusto odio dignissim qui blandit praesent luptatum zzril delenit augue duis dolor te feugait nulla facilisi.

Select caption widths to complement the layout.

Lorem ipsum dolor sit amet, consectetuer adipiscing elit, sed diam nonummy nibh euismod tincidunt ut laoreet dolore magna aliquam erat volutpat. Ut wisi enim ad minim veniam, quis notsrud exerci tation ullamcorper suscipit lobortis nisl ut aliquip ex ea commodo consequat. Duis autem vel eum iriure dolor in hendrerit in vulputate velit esse molestie consequat, vel illum dolore eu feugiat nulla facilisis at vero eros et accumsan et iusto odio dignissim qui blandit praesent luptatum zzril delenit augue duis dolor te feugait nulla facilisi.

Subhead One

Lorem ipsum dolor sit amet, consectetuer adipiscing elit, sed diam nonummy nibh euismod tincidunt ut laoreet dolore magna aliquam erat volutpat. Ut wisi enim ad minim veniam, quis notsrud exerci tation ullamcorper suscipit lobortis nisl ut aliquip ex ea commodo consequat. Duis autem vel eum iriure dolor in hendrerit in vulputate velit esse molestie

Lorem ipsum dolor sit amet, consectetuer adipiscing elit, sed diam nonummy nibh euismod tincidunt ut laoreet dolore magna aliquam erat volutpat. Ut wisi enim ad minim veniam, quis notsrud exerci tation ullamcorper suscipit lobortis nisl ut aliquip ex ea commodo conse-quat. Duis autem vel eum iriure dolor in hendrerit in vulputate velit esse molestie consequat, vel illum

Subhead Two

Lorem ipsum dolor sit amet, consectetuer adipiscing elit, sed diam nonummy nibh euismod tincidunt ut laoreet dolore magna ali-quam erat volutpat. Ut wisi enim ad minim veniam, quis notsrud exerci tation ullamcorp-er suscipit lobortis nisl ut aliquip ex ea com-modo consequat. Duis autem vel eum iriure dolor in hendrerit in vulputate velit esse molestie Lorem ipsum dolor sit amet, con-sectetuer adipiscing elit, sed diam nonummy nibh euismod tincidunt ut laoreet dolore magna aliquam erat volutpat. Ut wisi enim ad minim veniam, quis notsrud exerci tation ullamcorper suscipit lobortis nisl ut aliquip ex ea commodo consequat. Duis autem vel eum iriure dolor in hendrerit in vulputate velit esse molestie

Lorem ipsum dolor sit amet, consectetuer adipiscing elit, sed diam nonummy nibh euis-mod tincidunt ut laoreet dolore magna ali-quam erat volutpat. Ut wisi enim ad minim veniam, quis notsrud exerci tation ullamcorp-er suscipit lobortis nisl ut aliquip ex ea com-modo consequat. Duis autem vel eum iriure dolor in hendrerit in vulputate velit esse molestie consequat, vel illum dolore eu feugiat nulla facilisis at vero eros et accumsan et iusto odio dignissim qui blandit praesent lup-tatum zzril delenit augue duis dolor te feugait

---

phrases or sentences pulled from the article and used as graphic elements. In addition to creating visual interest, well-chosen pull quotes highlight important issues in the text.

The pull quote does not cut the columns off completely nor does it break into them evenly. This alone turns a symmetric layout into an asymmetric one. For the pull quote to be effective, the type on both adjacent columns must be justified to leave a clear rectangle of white space. A particular advantage of the pull quote technique is that it is free; you create a graphic from the text of the article.

On the right page, the photo breaks the top margin and bleeds off the edge of the page. The photo in the upper third of the page is balanced by the subhead in the lower third of the page and by the headline that is set flush right. Setting the text ragged right (see Exhibit 7.12) softens what would otherwise be a dominant vertical gutter between columns. Both of these layouts were created by creatively position-ing a single graphic element.

◆ *Keep it simple.* We know we said this before, but it is important. Your aim is to communicate by holding the readers' attention and guiding them through the message.

Communicating With Type

Type can be your best friend or your worst enemy. At best it is an inexpensive design element, something you can manipulate to create visual impact and support your message. At worst it can actually disrupt your communication.

Type font, style, size, alignment, and color are the subjects of pages of description in the style manuals of many large organizations. Organizations that make an investment in researching and developing an identifiable style and having it implemented on documents, buildings, and vehicles have an equal interest in seeing that style used and the image maintained.

Fonts

EXHIBIT 7.8   Sample fonts organized to demonstrate differences in style and size.

Serif fonts, 10 point

Times
Times New Roman
Bodoni
New Century Schoolbook
Palatino

Sans serif fonts, 12 point

Helvetica
Arial
Verdana

Display fonts, 14 point

Bodoni Poster
Charcoal
Textile

Script fonts, 14 point

Lucida Handwriting
Edwardian Script

Fonts are typefaces. Like space, they add direction, attitude, and personality to your design. Exhibit 7.8 illustrates several of the most common fonts. Although only a small sample, they illustrate many of the aspects that give type personality and character, for example, height, slope, roundness, delicacy, simplicity, and density.

Some fonts are casual, inviting readers into the document; others are formal, sending the message that the text is difficult or academic. This ability of fonts to express character is why you must select carefully when choosing typefaces for your communications. Xerox Corporation (1997) explains the significance of its signature typeface as follows: "Xerox Corporation stands for exceptional quality, design and engineering. The typography selected for our corporate signature is the result of careful study to identify a font with those characteristics and with a modern, classic look that will carry us into the future" (p. 13). The company's choice of typeface is Walbaum.

While there are hundreds, maybe thousands, of fonts, relatively few of them are suitable for text or body copy. Many of the fonts that come with computers are well-designed with a high degree of readability. Including Times, Times New Roman, Helvetica, and Arial, they are commonly known as text or body faces. Stay with them, or with the Bodoni, Cheltenham, Palatino, or Univers families for text. Reserve special fonts, often called "display" faces, for special emphasis.

Display typefaces should be complementary to the typeface chosen for body copy. Two elaborate typefaces may conflict with each other, and two sans serif faces may be boring. An extra bold display face will look out of proportion with a very light, delicate body face.

Considering that you will have multiple styles available in each font (bold, italic, underscored, caps, etc.), limit your selection to two fonts (or font families) per document, one for text and the other for emphasis. A routine but effective division of fonts is to use a very readable font such as Times New Roman for body copy, a bold version for headlines, and a sans serif font such as Helvetica for captions, subheads, and graphics.

Your choice of font will be based on your organization's style, the personality of the fonts, and what you know about the audience(s) who will receive the document. Print several paragraphs in each face you are considering and compare their readability, image, and personality. The body text of this book is Minion Regular, and the exhibits are Quay Sans Book.

Type Size and Spacing

Type is measured in points and picas. There are approximately 12 points to a pica and approximately 6 picas to an inch. Exhibit 7.9 illustrates the relationship between typical type sizes set in the Helvetica font. Body copy is usually set in 10-point or 12-point type. Subheads are set in 12-, 14-, or 18-point type and headlines in a larger size selected to suit the importance of the story and the width of the columns.

Leading

Leading, pronounced "ledding," is the space between lines of type as illustrated in Exhibit 7.10. It is named for the lead spacing strips that were inserted between lines of hand-set type for letterpress printing. Like type, leading is measured in points.

Leading is specified as "type size"/"type size + leading." For example, 12/14 is 12-point type with 2-point leading; 12/16 is 12-point type with 4-point leading. This is read as "12 on 14" or "12 on 16." Setting 12/12 or 14/14 is described as "setting solid" and is generally not a good idea. Two- to 3-point leading is a general guide for 10- or 12-point body copy.

EXHIBIT 7.9   Common type sizes. The sizes are printed below each letter.

7 8 9 10 12 14 18 24 30 36 42 48 54 60

EXHIBIT 7.10   Samples of type set with different leading: (from left) 10/10, 10/13, 10/18.

Lines of type that are too close together are difficult to read. This is 10-point type set with no (0) point leading (10/10).

This 10-point type set with 3 points of leading (10/13) is pleasant and easy to read. A good rule of thumb is to set the leading at 20 percent to 30 percent more than the point size of the type.

Lines of type that are too far apart are difficult to read. This is 10-point type set with 8-point leading (10/18). Although the effect is interesting, it should be limited to small amounts of copy.

EXHIBIT 7.11   Examples of kerning to improve the appearance of type. The top row is set without kerning. The bottom row has been kerned to eliminate awkward spaces.

YOYO   yoyo
YOYO   yoyo

Kerning

Kerning is the spacing between letters. For most purposes, the proportional spacing that is automatic with most computers and fonts is sufficient. In some cases, however, you may want a special effect or be unhappy with the kerning of specific letters. Exhibit 7.11 shows the effect of kerning changes between especially problematic letter combinations.

Alignment

Type can be aligned (also called justified) in four ways as shown in Exhibit 7.12: left, right, centered, and both left and right (justified). Each alignment has its advantages and purposes. You also have several indentation options: indent, no indent, or hanging indent. Regardless of your choice of alignment, you may have to manually adjust word or character spacing or even rework the text to ensure that the lines remain fairly even with no awkward gaps. This is especially true with justified columns. Note the obvious gaps in the justified example.

Type Styles

Exhibit 7.13 includes examples of many of the type styles available on word processing and page layout programs. It is a common misconception that these techniques, capital letters especially, are a useful stylistic device. In fact, they are hard to read, especially in long lines, and should be limited to short lines or words only. If you want to emphasize something, bold or italic type is the best choice.

EXHIBIT 7.12   Alignment.

Left justified is the most common alignment. It is also called flush left or ragged right. The right side remains uneven, which gives it an informal look.

Right justified type, also called ragged left or flush right, is the rarest alignment. It is usually reserved for captions or headlines to emphasize a strong vertical line.

Centered type is usually reserved for captions or headlines. Try to keep the lines fairly even for ease of reading.

Justified columns are aligned on both sides. This is the most formal alignment. You may have to adjust spacing or rewrite the text to avoid awkward gaps, especially with narrow columns.

EXHIBIT 7.13   Type styles.

BOLD, bold

ITALIC, italic (or oblique)

BOLD ITALIC, bold italic

UNDERSCORED, underscored

ALL CAPS (uppercase)

SMALL CAPS

CAPS AND SMALL CAPS

Because software may automatically change underscored (underlined) type to active Internet links, be especially wary of underscoring.

You should also be familiar with the typographic symbols that are available on most computers to add emphasis. These graphic elements are most often used to set bullet points off from the rest of the text. They include these symbols ✳ ■ ● ◆ ▼ ★ → ✔ ☞ plus many more.

On Macintosh computers, these symbols can be found as the Zapf Dingbats or Wingdings typeface. On PCs, check out the "Symbol" option on the "Insert" menu. The symbols available on your system will depend on your software, the fonts you have loaded, and the printer you are using, but most systems and both ink jet and laser printers accommodate some special symbols or characters.

Special Type Effects

You can also set type in curves and wavy lines, stretch it, elongate it, or squeeze it. As a writer, you should be conscious of how changing the text, especially in a headline, can create the opportunity to use such special effects. For example, changing "Closing the Gap" to "Bridging the Gap" allows you to use the type treatment shown in Exhibit 7.14. These effects require sophisticated software and excellent graphic and computer skills, so it is a good opportunity for writer and designer to work together to enhance a message.

You can also create visual interest by indenting paragraphs, increasing spacing between paragraphs, or inserting subheadings using bold or a different size type.

Display Initials and Drop Caps

Large initial letters at the start of a paragraph attract attention and clearly tell the reader where to start. Although we do not recommend using too many of these,

EXHIBIT 7.14   Samples of special type effects. There are many type management and art programs to help you create such effects. Use them sparingly.

Bridging THE GAP

One, two, three, STRETCH!

WAVY LINES ARE CLEAREST WHEN SET IN ALL CAPS.

you may be able to make them part of your publication's identifiable style by using very large letters, at least three lines high, to lead the most important articles and smaller capitals (perhaps two lines deep) for all other articles. Before you adopt this as a newsletter style, look at several issues to determine whether too many small articles will simply make this technique look busy.

As shown in Exhibit 7.15, display initials can be just that, large initials. They can be drop caps in which the letter extends down into two or three (or more) lines of type, or they can sit on their own in the margin next to the first paragraph (called a hanging initial). Large initials and hanging initials are more casual and more interesting because they leave interesting areas of white space above or next to the paragraph. Drop caps are more formal with the top flush with the top of the paragraph and the rest surrounded by a regular white shape. Regardless of the letter, you must ensure that the first word continues on as normal; there should not be a large amount of white space between the initial and the rest of the word.

If you use them sparingly, display initials may be an opportunity to consider special typefaces and/or very large sizes that complement the subject matter of the article. For example, for an article on spring weddings, consider either a script face normally associated with wedding invitations or a special font in which the initial is entwined with flowers. At the other extreme, an article on engineering might benefit from initial caps with a technological or construction feel. Used this way, the initials echo the theme of the document and become a supportive graphic element.

EXHIBIT 7.15   Drop caps and other display initials draw attention to the paragraph.

ANY letter can be used as a large initial to create interest and direct the reader to the start of the story.

DROP caps are inset into the first two or three lines of type. They must be the exact height of those lines.

LETTERS such as "L" require special treatment when used as drop caps to avoid awkward spacing.

SOMETIMES drop caps can be set in reverse out of a black or colored background.

INITIALS that lie in the margin are called "hanging" initials. They are most effective with very large or very tall letters.

EXHIBIT 7.16   **Text wrap. The text is shaped to the contour of the graphic.**

Many software programs allow you to wrap text around graphics to add visual interest, as we have wrapped this paragraph around the right edge of Exhibit 7.16. Used selectively and carefully, this is generally a very effective technique. In most cases, the text wraps around one side of a simple picture or a regular graphic, but it is also possible to have the text follow the contour of your logo or other irregular shape. To get a smooth contour, you will need to justify the text against the side of the wrapped object.

Text Wrap and Shapes

A particularly difficult technique, and one that is probably best left to the experts because it must be done very well in order to succeed, is to set the type in the shape of an object. This is usually a very painstaking project, requiring much manipulation of type sizes, leading, and kerning to eliminate awkward spaces in the middle of lines and keep a uniform grayness to the copy. The shape should stand out, not the spaces or closely set lines. Check your software manual for instructions on using all typographic and graphic techniques.

Communicating With Graphics

Many of the techniques discussed in "Communicating With Type" are really ways of using type as graphic elements. This section discusses the role of other graphic elements, including rules, screens, photographs, and art to enhance successful communication.

EXHIBIT 7.17   **Rules (lines). Most of these can be made with simple word processing and layout programs.**

Hairline:
1 point:
2 point:
4 point:
8 point:
12 point:
Double:
Dotted:
Dashes:
Multiple:
Arrows:

Rules

There was a time when inserting lines between columns of type or between articles meant drawing the lines with ink or stripping them on with layout tape during the paste-up. Today, most software offers a range of styles and widths of lines (called rules), borders, and shadows that can be inserted to separate and add emphasis and interest. Many options are shown in Exhibit 7.17. As with novelty type styles, rules are effective ways to emphasize copy, but don't overuse them. Select two or three widths of rule, define their use, and use them consistently.

Screens

Screens are shades of a color or black. They draw attention to articles or sections of charts or graphs. You can print screens in any color, but be prepared for how different a bright solid color will look when printed as a screen. For example, thousands of designers have realized to their horror that screens of red are always pink.

Be careful to select a screen density that allows type printed on top of it to be read easily. Exhibit 7.18 shows screens of black from 10% to 100%. Each block contains a line of type (12-point bold) printed in 100% black, and a line printed in 100% white. As you can see, if you are printing in black, it is best to use screens less than 40%. White type requires a screen of at least 70% to be easily read. This differs with other colors. Variations on this are blends in which the color moves smoothly from one color to another or gradations in which the color moves smoothly from a light screen to a dark screen as shown at the bottom of Exhibit 7.18.

Screens can also add depth to a design. As shown in Exhibit 7.19, a screen positioned behind even a simple shape or a single letter results in a three-dimensional effect. Be careful to position all such screens equally (e.g., all to the lower right) in relation to the objects or you will confuse the reader.

Photographs

If your method of reproducing a document allows photographs, it is a good idea to use them, especially if they are photos of the people and activities relevant to the message—and as long as they are clear and in focus. Acceptable methods include offset printing, postscript-compatible printers, and some high-quality copiers.

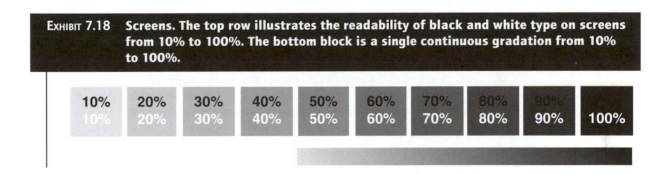

EXHIBIT 7.18   Screens. The top row illustrates the readability of black and white type on screens from 10% to 100%. The bottom block is a single continuous gradation from 10% to 100%.

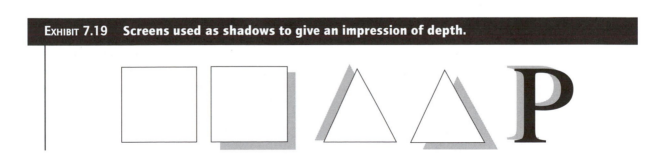

EXHIBIT 7.19   Screens used as shadows to give an impression of depth.

The best photos tell a story. Especially for external use, photos must be of high quality—so hiring a professional photographer may be wise. Look for a photographer who specializes in news or business photography rather than portrait photography. And don't underestimate the value of the commercial press. Always order a copy of any photos of your staff or activities that appear in the press.

Arguably, you may be able to use photos of lesser quality in internal newsletters where the staff know the people in the photos and where the photos may have been taken and submitted by other staff members such as photos of the holiday parties at branch offices.

You can also purchase disks or CD-ROMs with professional photographs. Sometimes you can download photos online. All such photos come with permissions and/or conditions for use. Depending on the subject, they may be less expensive than hiring a photographer and photo stylist.

The output from digital cameras allows the designer to manipulate photographic content and treatment as part of the publication process. The quality of digital images is ever improving, but as with images taken on film or transparency, you must be certain they are of an acceptable standard for the quality of your production.

Following are some hints for using photos effectively:

✦ People should look into the layout, not out of it—unless your aim is to direct readers to the next page.

✦ Photos should add to the story. Readers can tell when photos are just filler and they will respond by ignoring them.

✦ Scale photos to make relationships obvious. The relative sizes of photos tell readers something; the most important photo should be the biggest.

✦ Enlarge or reduce photos of people so all of the heads are the same size. This is essential if the photos will be printed at the same level in the layout. The same is true of buildings or equipment. Exhibit 7.20 illustrates how two cityscapes printed at the same scale and at the same level create a unified look.

✦ Resize photos to set up relationships. For example, use small photos of questioners and a large photo of the respondent to support a Q&A forum.

✦ Try to catch people in action, gesturing or speaking expressively rather than staring into the camera. Other than allowing people to put a face to a name, routine headshots add little to a story. The same is true of the clichéd "grip and grin" photos of presentations and award ceremonies. Even so, because they record history, they are often must-use photos.

✦ Align the horizons on side-by-side landscape photos. See Exhibit 7.20.

✦ Cutting people off when cropping photos—should you or shouldn't you? There used to be a rule that you never cut off even the top of a head, for instance, but as times, styles, and communication design values have changed, it is now regarded as a potentially valuable technique. Strategic cropping (e.g., of extra people, the top of a head, someone's back, or the scenery) can change a routine shot into a dramatic graphic that focuses attention on an interesting detail that goes unnoticed in the full shot. Just be sure that the cropping is not disturbing, such as an arm without a hand.

EXHIBIT 7.20   It is important to maintain the same scale for photographs and to print them so they appear to have the same horizon.

✦ You can also crop and print photos in various shapes and surround them with plain boxes, shadowed boxes, or even elaborate frames. This can be effective if the photo has a very light background with little contrast from the paper. Be restrained. Very bold or elaborate frames may call more attention to themselves than to the photo or artwork they surround. Simple, hairline or 1-point boxes can be very elegant and, when used consistently in an article, can add very subtle style and focus.

Sizing Photos

Sizing (or *scaling*) means reducing or enlarging a graphic (photograph, chart or graph, line art). There are many reasons to resize a graphic. The original may be too large or too small to achieve the balance and/or symmetry of the design. You may want to create relationships between photos, making one more important than another. You might not have the space to use a graphic full size (or it is not important enough to be used in its original size). Or you may simply want to have all heads appear the same size.

As Exhibit 7.21 illustrates, sizing must be proportional. If an image is sized in only one direction (vertically or horizontally), for example, it will be distorted in one direction. Correct sizing must be done in *both* directions, that is, must be proportional.

To avoid distortion, all resizing must be proportional. As shown in Exhibit 7.21, if you lay reduced or enlarged photos on top of each other, one corner matching, a diagonal drawn through one will also be the diagonal for the others. Exhibit 7.22 shows what happens when an image is resized in only one direction.

> **EXHIBIT 7.21   Photo and artwork sizing. In the examples, B is the original size (2.5" × 2"), A is a 50% reduction (to 1.25" × 1"), and C is a 120% enlargement (to 3" × 2.375"). When proportionally sized photos are laid on top of each other, the same diagonal line will stretch through all of them.**

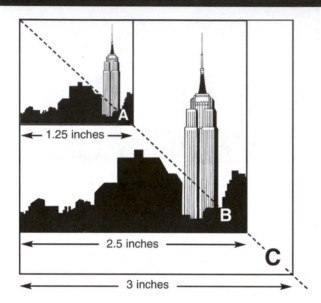

Many computer drawing and desktop publishing programs allow you to select the graphic and specify the new size as a percentage (from 10% to 1000%), and the graphic will automatically resize. To do this manually, select the graphic and hold down the shift key while you drag one of the corner boxes diagonally.

Photo Handling

There are several ways to send a photo to a printer. First, the photo can be scanned as a halftone and inserted directly in the layout. Crop or resize the photo in the art or page layout program. Although photos may look grainy on your printer, it will look much finer and less grainy if a printer or commercial service bureau processes them.

A second way is digital transmission. Saving files in portable document format, know as PDF, allows you to send them via e-mail. Recipients can open and view them, or printers can use them in layouts.

> **EXHIBIT 7.22   Photo reductions or enlargements must be in proportion to the original.**

Original Size

Vertical Reduction Only

Horizontal Reduction Only

What is done traditionally—and what you must do if you do not have a scanner—is to insert a black box of the correct size where the photo will go in the layout, for placement only. Key the photo to the correct black box and indicate on a tissue overlay how it should be cropped and whether it should be printed full size (100%) or reduced/ enlarged (and by how much).

You can create special photo effects using screens and filters. Some are available as options on the scanner and/or in drawing programs (e.g., Illustrator™) or image processing programs (e.g., PhotoShop™). Such techniques include mezzotint, line screens, and posterization. We mention them so you are aware that they exist, but we recommend leaving them to professional designers.

Line Art

Line art is the collective term used to describe graphics other than photos. Line art includes cartoons, charts, and graphs (except those that include photos). Chances are your employer's logo will be line art. As with photos, you can either place line art directly into your layout or provide it separately for the printer to size and insert. It is easier to scan line art successfully than to scan photographs.

There are many sources of artwork to liven up a publication. If you are very fortunate, you will have an artist or cartoonist on staff or find a talented amateur to provide artwork just for the exposure or at relatively little cost.

The most common source of line art is known as *clip art*, which you can buy as hard copy, disk, or CD-ROM or download from the Internet. Clip art includes collections of art that are either in the public domain or have been specially assembled for distribution and reproduction to users like you. It includes drawings, cartoons, and symbols that you can use to create interest and call attention to copy.

Clip art comes with limited permission to reproduce it without crediting the source. Depending on the type of art, you may even be able to modify it for your own organization. For example, you may be able to print your own copy in the voice balloons of clip art cartoons.

Caution: There is no doubt that, when used wisely and in moderation, visuals can make an important difference in a publication's appearance and its effect. However, too much artwork that does not clearly relate to a story may become unprofessional or tacky.

Do not under any circumstances simply photocopy and reproduce cartoons or artwork without permission.

Charts and Graphs

Charts and graphs are the backbone especially of financial reporting. They translate numbers into visual images and, if done well, can save pages of complicated explanations because they make relationships immediately obvious. If done poorly, they may convey the wrong information.

Many software programs make it easy to take numbers from a database and convert them to charts and graphs. This will save you from time-consuming calculations and from the detail of creating the charts, but it does not change the fact that you must understand the concepts you want to illustrate and the type of chart that will best illustrate those concepts.

EXHIBIT 7.23   Sample charts and graphs.

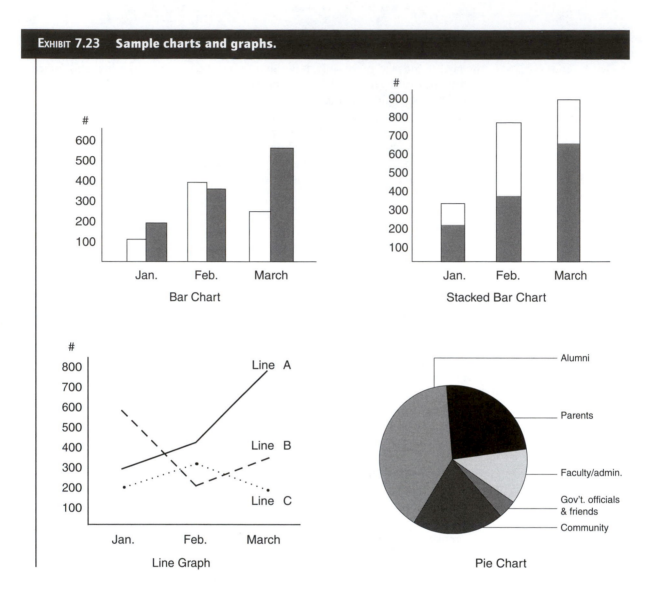

There are four basic formats for charts and graphs as well as variations on each of them (see Exhibit 7.23). Each one is useful for presenting a particular type of information.

✦ *Bar charts* are useful for expressing comparisons of the same category at several points, of different categories at the same time, or sometimes of multiple categories over time. By using multiple bars for each time period, for example, you can compare the growth of two elements as well as show their relationship to each other.

✦ *Stacked bar charts* show the cumulative effect of many elements. For example, you could illustrate both the total annual fund donors in each of the past three years and how these totals were divided between men and women.

✦ *Line graphs* show change over time, such as the change in share prices. Multiple lines illustrate relative change among variables, such as the average prices of shares on the New York and NASDAQ stock exchanges, or the change in price of XYZ Company compared to the Dow Jones average.

Each line in a line graph must be distinct and clearly labeled, preferably on the line itself rather than requiring the reader to associate the line with a key. Unless the aim of the chart is to show what a tangle the share prices have become, it is best to limit the number of lines to three or four. More than that simply dilute the message.

✦ *Pie charts* illustrate the relationships among elements to each other, that is, the "wedges," and to the whole, that is, the "pie." Although pie charts don't have to be circles, it is more difficult for the reader to understand the relationship if the segments are pulled from an ellipse or other irregular shapes that distort the relative areas of the segments and present information inaccurately. This is a criticism of many annual report charts.

Selecting the appropriate chart requires that you understand the message you want to send and can isolate one or two relationships to illustrate this message. For example, your management has requested a report summarizing the results of a reader survey conducted about an employee newsletter. The purpose of the survey was to determine if the changes based on last year's survey made a difference. Can you use charts to summarize this and make the point that the changes were effective? We think so, based on the survey results in Exhibit 7.24.

The first step is to determine what information is relevant to the chart. The second is to determine what format will present this information effectively. Following is the thinking used to make these decisions.

EXHIBIT 7.24   Readership survey results for charts and graphs case example.

Employee newsletter readership survey

Total employees: 600 both years

Questions	Total "yes" answers		"Yes" answers by level		
	Last year	*This year*	*Managers*	*Part time*	*Full time*
1. It is easy to read	200	600	50	150	400
2. It has an interesting appearance	510	520	35	185	300
3. My department is covered well	400	450	155	80	215
4. Too much management news	100	550	0	200	350
5. I usually take it home	200	500	20	80	400
6. My family reads it	150	510	10	100	400

✦ Your aim is to demonstrate whether you are improving. Accordingly, you want to compare this year with last year, not managers to staff, so the "Managers," "Part time," and "Full time" categories are irrelevant for this purpose. You will use only the information in the top box.

✦ You must provide two results (last year and this year) for each category.

✦ You are comparing numbers of employees.

✦ You are illustrating the answers to questions one through four only.

The multiple-column bar chart allows us to express all of these comparisons clearly. The vertical axis is the number of staff who agreed with each of the statements. The horizontal axis shows the categories: reading ease, appearance, department coverage, and management coverage. (The fifth set of columns in Exhibit 7.25 is explained below.) We can express the comparison between last year and this year by using two columns for each category. Exhibit 7.25 is the resulting chart. It clearly demonstrates that the changes we made last year to increase readability, appearance, and department news have paid off.

But there is a problem with the fourth set of bars. We understand the "language" of bar charts so that that higher is better—and indeed the first three questions bear this out. But question four is a category in which more people are *dis*satisfied with the newsletter. Instead of looking at question four and thinking, "Wow, we did something right," you should be thinking, "Whoa, we did something wrong." It would be easier to understand this if the results were presented as shown in the fifth set of bars, which clearly demonstrate that satisfaction has gone down for this category.

The employee readership survey also tells us how responses differ by employee type. We could use this information to plot a pie chart that shows the percentage of answers made by managers and part-time and full-time staff. Let's look, for example, at the topic "I usually take it home." You will use only the information in the bottom box. The total number of people who said they take it home is 500. The total staff is 600, so 100 do not take it home. This is 17% of the total ($100/600 = .17 = 17\%$). The 400 full-time staff represent 2/3 or 67% of the total of 600. The 80 part-time staff represent 13%, and the 20 managers represent 3%. ($17 + 67 + 13 + 3 = 100\%$). These percentages are represented by the pie chart in Exhibit 7.26.

Design Points for Charts and Graphs

You may find it a challenge to create headings, captions, and keywords for charts and graphs because they must clearly define the category while being short and relatively equal in length. If you are not using automated charting software, you will need to know how to use three common spacing options: leading (which we have already discussed), "space before/after," and tabs. The "space before/after" option puts a uniform amount of spacing before or after each paragraph. This is in addition to any leading you already have in place. Use this spacing command as part of a style sheet so that you can easily change spacing for many lines or paragraphs without making individual adjustments.

Style sheets hold the type specifications for a document, for example, body copy, large headlines, subheads, and captions. After setting the styles, you can then position the curser in a paragraph and click on a style, and the paragraph will automatically format to that style. If you change the specifications of a style, all

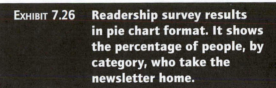

EXHIBIT 7.25   **Readership survey results in bar chart format. It shows the people who answered "yes" to each of the survey questions.**

EXHIBIT 7.26   **Readership survey results in pie chart format. It shows the percentage of people, by category, who take the newsletter home.**

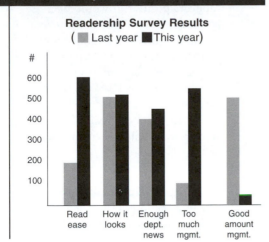

Readership Survey Results
(▪ Last year ▪This year)

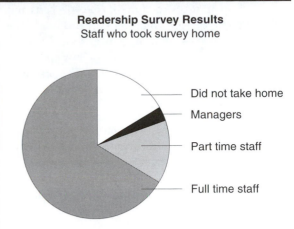

Readership Survey Results
Staff who took survey home

paragraphs set in that style will automatically reformat. Styles and style sheets are very useful for maintaining consistency across a document and from one document to another. Learn to use them.

Hitting the space bar should *never* substitute for a tab. Because of proportional spacing, tabs are the only way you can guarantee that columns will line up, and they are critical to charts, graphs, and all types of columns. You can set tabs for left, right, or center alignment or to align the decimal points, which is critical when setting the columns of financial statements. They save time because you can change the spacing on all lines of a column with a simple change in tab style or position. Learning to use tabs effectively will immediately increase the professionalism of all your publications.

This is a good time to point out that there are wide differences of opinion on which to present first in a chart: the earliest or latest information. Advocates of most recent" point out that this information is new and, therefore, what people want to see. Their opponents argue that time is linear and should be presented that way—that is, oldest to newest, left to right—so readers can easily identify the changes. For charts and graphs, we fall with the "earliest year first" camp (see Exhibit 7.25). For financial information, however, we believe readers are accustomed to seeing the current year first and agree it is the most important information.

The rules of good layout also apply to charts and graphs. Think of them as small layouts and balance them just as you would page layout. With pie charts in particular, be especially conscious of the need to read from left to right, top to bottom. It is a good idea to bring all of the headings to one side so they can be read easily. It also gives you control over what part the reader sees first (see Exhibit 7.26).

And keep it simple. The reason you are using a chart is to simplify complex numbers. Don't let a complicated graph defeat the purpose.

Ethical Issues

Charts and Graphs Ethics

It is often said that you can prove anything with statistics, and produce the chart or graph to back it up. In many cases this is true. All charts and graphs depend on the selective inclusion—and exclusion—of information, and the choices you make can prove your own point or disprove someone else's. But this freedom to pick and choose comes with a responsibility to be accurate as well as truthful.

In 1998, the SEC recognized the potential for graphic treatments to skew messages in an organization's favor, and the SEC provides guidelines on avoiding this in its landmark Guide to Plain English. Key issues include the following:

◆ *Selectively omitting important information.* For example, in the readership survey discussed as Exhibit 7.24, most staff think the newsletter has too much management news. It might be tempting to avoid this in a report to a board of directors that last year approved your recommendation to increase the newsletter size to include more management news.

◆ *Inaccurate comparisons.* Exhibit 7.25, which reports the results of questions one–four, inadvertently falls into this trap. In the first three sets of bars, "this year's" numbers are good. Staff are more satisfied with the reading ease, appearance, and coverage of their departments than they were last year. The reader implicitly expects that the fourth set of bars will follow suit.

But the fourth set of bars reports a huge increase in the number of people who are *dis*satisfied with the level of management news. The bars represent a negative trend, but it appears positive. It would be more consistent to present this information as the number of people who were satisfied with the amount of management information, that is, 50 rather than 550. The fifth set of bars shows how this would result in a very different but more easily understood picture of employee satisfaction and dissatisfaction.

◆ *Graphs that do not have zero as their starting point.* Implicitly we expect that the intersection of the X axis and Y axis signifies zero.

◆ *Hiding behind percentages.* Percentages can be deceptive; 80% can be as low as 4 out of 5 or 8 out of 10, or it could be 80,000 out of 100,000. Knowing the baseline is key to understanding the percentage. Is the board of directors more likely to fund a new full-color version of the employee newsletter based on the preferences of 80% of 1,000 staff or 80% of 45 managers?

◆ *Distorting the scale.* Widely spaced lines demonstrate growth more dramatically. Conversely, narrowly spaced lines help minimize negative results. Avoid changing the scale or proportions of a graph to manipulate the viewer's understanding. If you are presenting many graphs, keep the scale consistent for easy understanding.

These principles should apply to any graphic treatment of numbers and statistics.

Jazzing It Up

Charts and graphs present wonderful opportunities for creativity. After you are certain that you understand the purpose and know the relationships you have to work with, consider special treatments that will create interest and support the message.

◆ *Use color* to help you make the point. Just be careful that too many colors or effects don't interfere with the message.

◆ *Think beyond boxes and circles.* Use line art as symbols to create more interesting effects. A common and still effective treatment divides up dollar bills or coins to illustrate income and expenses. Any circular object that can be divided into wedges, for example, a pizza or an orange, is a possibility for a pie chart.

◆ *Column charts do not have to be squared off at the top.* You can stack boxes, use different sizes of people or pencils, or create a skyline of carefully sized buildings.

◆ *Think dimension and movement.* Many charts and graphs use a three-dimensional effect. This is a technique best left to professional artists, but it is a good opportunity to make use of their talents. You can also pull out slices of a pie (make them the most important slices), let a rocket or piles of coins reach different heights, or present the results as a race, using horses, racecars, or runners, for example.

◆ *Create a special effect.* Illustrate the difference between two quantities as thermometers, partially filled glasses, or contrasting spots on a grid. Customize a stacked column chart by dividing a photo or object such as a dollar bill into the appropriate segments (see Exhibit 7.27). AMC Entertainment Inc., for example, used stacked drink cups—almost an icon of the movie-going experience—to illustrate revenue growth in a recent annual report.

You can find many other ideas in a good design book and from examples in your swipe file. Finding an appropriate symbol for a chart is often difficult, but when you do, it is worth the effort.

EXERCISE 1

Return to the survey data shown as Exhibit 7.24. Create a bar chart and a pie chart using the data not used in the samples. Try to think of creative graphics for these charts. If the "staff and managers" descriptions do not inspire you, consider instead students, faculty, athletes, and cafeteria staff, for example.

Diagrams

Like charts and graphs, diagrams make the complex simple and help you avoid long descriptions that may not do the job as well as a visual aid. Diagrams are typically used to illustrate processes (how things work). Perhaps the most common is the humble map that substitutes for pages of directions.

The U.S. Occupational Safety and Health Administration (OSHA) uses diagrams to illustrate occupational safety hazards. One OSHA series aimed at teens

EXHIBIT 7.27   Creative charts and graphs add interest and help explain the subject. It helps to provide numbers or a grid to help readers understand the charts.

Total Revenues
(\$ in Millions)

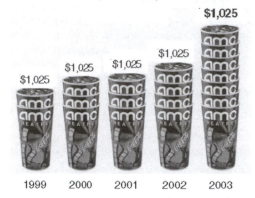

1999   2000   2001   2002   2003

Allocation of public relations budget by audience

Alumni (57%)   Students (23%)   Faculty (13%)   State (7%)

How employees prefer to receive information

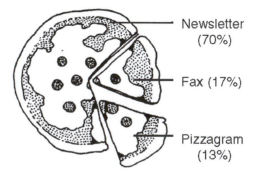

Newsletter (70%)

Fax (17%)

Pizzagram (13%)

working in fast food restaurants uses diagrams to demonstrate the most ergonomically safe way to do their jobs such as carrying heavy trays of food, reaching across hot grills, or as shown in Exhibit 7.28 standing for long periods of time.

Diagrams also make clear the relationships between parts and help explain scientific and engineering concepts. For example, until TWA Flight 800 exploded off the coast of Long Island in July 1996, few in the general public knew or cared about the configuration of fuel tanks in the belly of a 747. Following the disaster, however, as speculation focused on a mechanical problem, many publications and TV news broadcasts ran diagrams showing the location of the fuel tanks and electrical lines and diagramming how the disaster might have occurred. And suddenly we understood.

Probably the most common form of diagram—after the map—is the common organizational chart that sets out the organizational hierarchy and illustrates how divisions relate to each other. Exhibit 7.29 is an example of such a chart. The vertical axis is the hierarchy, setting out reporting structures (who reports to whom). The horizontal axis describes the organization of divisions and units at the same level in the organization. Imagine trying to describe in words the interactions made so clear by this chart. Software programs including PowerPoint and Excel have user-friendly modules to help you create organizational as well as other charts and graphs.

You may find that spending part of your budget to commission a special graph or piece of artwork may be wise if it quickly gets across a message it would otherwise take several paragraphs—or pages—to explain.

Communicating With Color

There was a time not long ago when using color in a document required a large budget and/or a large print run. Fortunately, color has been a focus for hardware and software developers, with the result that cost-effective color options are now available to all organizations for all sizes of print runs.

EXHIBIT 7.28   **Diagram from OSHA "Drive-Thru" guidelines. The accompanying text is: "Avoid static postures by continually altering your position. Use a foot rest bar or a low stool to help alter your posture by raising one foot and then the other."**

For small print runs such as handouts for a client meeting, printing multiple copies on a color laser or ink jet printer or making copies on a color photocopier may be cost-effective and adequate. If you don't have such equipment in your own office, commercial copy shops, printers, and office services offer this service.

For larger or more complex projects such as newsletters, annual reports, and brochures, time, quality, folding, paper choice, and distribution requirements make laser printers and photocopiers impractical. Instead documents using colored, glossy, heavy, or textured papers that are folded and/or stapled, that have colored photos and charts and graphs, and that are distributed outside the organization are usually produced using an offset printing process.

♦ *Process color* is used for reproducing photographs, paintings, and other artwork in which there are many colors or the colors are not unique and distinct. Think of the difference between Leonardo da Vinci's *Mona Lisa* and artwork of the American flag. Whereas the flag could be reproduced using just red and blue ink, the *Mona Lisa* has an infinite number of colors and shades that flow together with no separation. Reproducing the *Mona Lisa* requires process color.

With process color, only four inks—usually cyan (a blue), magenta (a pink/red), yellow, and black—are used to create all of the other colors. The colors are created on the printing press as dots of the four-process colors lie side by side. Expanses of grass, for example, will have many dots of yellow and blue, with the shades coming from more dots of blue or a few dots of magenta or perhaps black. The human eye does not see the individual ink dots, but rather the combined color, green.

Process color is costly and time-consuming. The photo processing must be done carefully and well and the printing process itself must be carefully monitored to ensure the proper flow of ink and correct registration of the printing plates. You must also be certain that the paper stock will hold process colors well.

♦ *Spot color* is the mainstay of most public relations documents, both internal and external. In comparison to the four inks of process color, with spot color the ink you print is the color you will see.

You will be able to identify spot color printing projects wherever you look. Bumper stickers, most corporate stationery, packaging that does not include photos, and business cards are all usually spot color. So are most logos and many posters. Look, for example, at the logo of your favorite college or professional sports team.

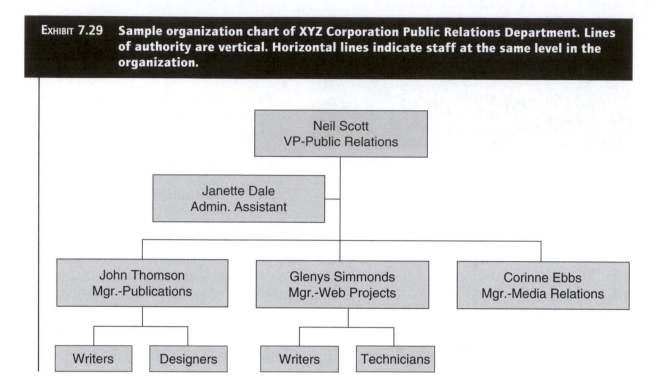

EXHIBIT 7.29   Sample organization chart of XYZ Corporation Public Relations Department. Lines of authority are vertical. Horizontal lines indicate staff at the same level in the organization.

The printing industry relies on standardized colors to ensure exact color matches across batches of ink, time, and projects. The most common standard is Pantone or PMS (Pantone Matching System), but other systems are starting to appear. You can obtain swatch books showing all of the inks. All inks certified under the PMS system are created from recipes of 10 other inks: white, black, yellow, warm red, rubine red, rhodamine red, purple, reflex blue, process blue, and green. PMS #300, a fairly common bright blue, is composed of 13 parts process blue and 3 parts reflex blue.

This recipe is important when printers open a new container of ink halfway through your project, when you allow distant offices to order stationery from a local printer, or when you want to exactly match a particular color. Specifying the PMS color directs the printer to the exact color you want and the exact recipe to make this color. The beauty of spot color is that it can be translated into many media, even including the silk-screen and embroidery techniques used to reproduce logos onto hats, T-shirts, banners, and displays.

Be aware that in all types of printing, the paper choice will affect the final color. Work closely with your printer to ensure the result you want is the result you get.

Selecting the Right Color

Selecting organizational colors is a decision that usually rivals changing the organization's name. The CEO will have preferences, the board will demand approval, and long-time employees will want to stay with the colors they have used for years. Your job will be to steer the decision to colors that will be well received by your employer's audiences and that will reproduce well in all of the media you are likely to use.

Colors have attributes that can help or hinder communication. Choosing the right ones can express or enhance organizational personality just as clothing enhances a person or interior design a room. Keyes (1993) defines three attributes of color that strengthen or weaken visual presentations: it focuses attention, it groups objects, and it creates focal points or "information targets" that grab attention before other information. This points to the need to choose wisely both the colors used and what will be colored. Using color on unimportant material wastes the impact of the color and confuses the readers, who expect the colored material to be important. On the other hand, using color with care and logic can guide the reader through the text and ensure that the important message is noticed.

Colors have the ability to suggest qualities such as taste, shape, temperature, weight, and smell. Color preferences are influenced by age, social class, and their traditional association with specific products. Clearly, what you know about your audience will help you select colors that will attract their attention and appeal to them. Following are some attributes commonly associated with colors. Do you agree with them? What others can you define?

- ✦ Strong colors—black, red.
- ✦ Weak colors—yellow and all pastels and screens.
- ✦ Warm colors—red, yellow, orange.
- ✦ Cool colors—blue, green, purple.
- ✦ Outdoor colors—green, yellow, brown, blue.
- ✦ "Important" colors—purple, black, red, royal blue, gold.
- ✦ Holiday colors—red/green, Christmas; red/pink, Valentine's Day; lilac/turquoise/light yellow, Easter; orange/black, Halloween; brown/orange/gold, Thanksgiving; red/white/blue, Independence Day or Memorial Day.
- ✦ Receding/advancing colors—dark objects appear smaller, light colors appear larger.

Traditionally, some colors are regarded as feminine (pink and lilac) and some as masculine (brown and gray). Thankfully these stereotypes seem to be changing as fashion designers promote tan and gray styles for women and a rainbow of colors, both bright and pastel, for men's shirts, for example. The issue for you as a communicator is to identify how color choice may affect your audience and choose accordingly.

As discussed in Chapter 4, color may also be a cultural issue. You should also be aware of the colors used by your employer's competitors so you can avoid them.

Legibility of Type on Background

Legibility is the ability to physically see and read the type. Legibility is a complex result of type size, weight and density, the use of background space, and color attributes including adjacent colors, the number of colors per page, and the reader's psychological responses to colors. Color combinations as they affect type legibility are also a function of the medium.

EXHIBIT 7.30 **This chart lists in order of decreasing legibility color combinations used in print documents.**

1. Black on white
2. Black on yellow
3. Green on white
4. Red on white
5. Blue on white
6. White on blue
7. Yellow on black
8. White on red
9. White on green
10. White on black
11. Red on yellow
12. Green on red

Exhibit 7.30 shows a common ranking of color combinations for legibility in a print medium. ("Use Color Effectively," n.d.). Typically, black on white or yellow has the maximum contrast and visibility. However, Keyes (1993) explains that many other factors can also affect legibility. For example, other combinations can overtake black on white if the type has a greater stroke thickness (is set in bold). Changing the hue, value, or intensity (saturation) of a color, such as dark green instead of bright green or light violet instead of dark violet, will also change legibility or contrast.

Use Color Sparingly

In most cases, color is an option, not a necessity. A well-designed black-and-white ad will stand out in a sea of colored ads while "yet another" colored photo will be lost on the same page. Depending on the message, a single, well-chosen spot of color has more impact than an overwhelming proliferation of colors. Color is a valuable tool. Make it work for you.

Color Separations

Spot color printing is achieved by producing a separate printing plate for each color. These are called *separations*. Exhibit 7.31 illustrates the color separations that would be used in printing a drawing of the U.S. flag using two spot colors, red and blue. The white will come from the paper. If you actually want a red, white, and blue flag, you cannot use colored stock unless you are prepared to pay for white ink as well as the red and blue.

When you send a project to the printer, you must either provide the separations in paper or film form or specify what elements should be printed in what color. You can produce separations automatically from most art and page layout programs.

DISCUSSION 1

Color is fun. Be careful, however, that it does not take over the design and confuse the viewer about your message. Color should also express an organization's culture and support its image.

Think, for example, about organizations you know and their corporate color, such as United Parcel Service (UPS) or your own or rival colleges and universities. What do these colors say about the organization? Do they match the organization's image? Why or why not? Why do you think these colors were chosen?

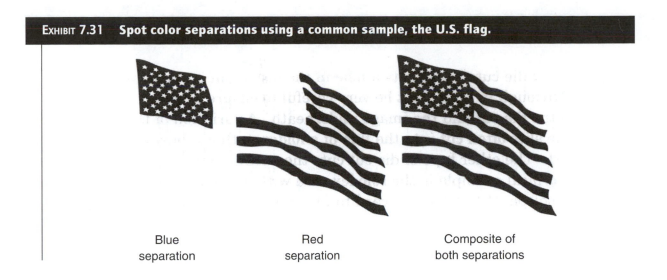

EXHIBIT 7.31   Spot color separations using a common sample, the U.S. flag.

| Blue separation | Red separation | Composite of both separations |

Special Options

Following are several other design options that can have a tremendous impact on the visual appeal of a document. Although effective, some of them require special treatment, extra production time, and much additional cost.

Formats and Folding

Format is likely to be one of your first creative decisions when you start a new project. Some formats are obvious, such as booklets for programs. In other cases, you may have the option to be more creative, usually for brochures and sometimes annual reports. Unusual formats and folds can attract attention or make it difficult to find what you want. Formats that are too clever steal attention from the message.

Some readers find lengthy accordion folds difficult to follow, especially if a light paper stock allows them to fall open awkwardly. They may prefer a small booklet that they can leaf through easily.

Following are some of the standard formatting options you will encounter, organized by number of folds, from least to most complex. They are illustrated in Exhibit 7.32.

◆ *Booklet* is the common, single-fold format we are all familiar with from programs, newsletters, and annual reports. Booklets have a minimum of four pages, including front and back covers. Pages increase in multiples of four.

Multipage booklets may be stapled—called saddle stitching—to hold the pages together. Common booklet sizes take advantage of common paper sizes, 8.5″ × 11″ or 11″ × 17″, which fold neatly to 5.5″ × 8.5″ or 8.5″ × 11″ booklets, respectively.

EXHIBIT 7.32   **Common formats and folding options.**

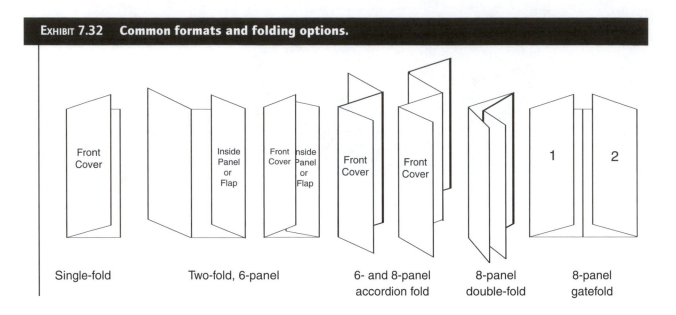

Most page layout software allows you to set up layouts in page spreads, for example, pages 1, 2, 3, 4 through 20, and then automatically reorganize the pages into what are called printer spreads (page 1 next to page 20, page 2 next to page 19, etc.) needed to produce the booklet. The newest generations of digital photocopiers, which allow you to send copying directly from computer to copier, automatically create booklets from single-page layouts.

◆ *Short sheets* are a series of flat pages of different heights that stack together and fit into a folder (see Exhibit 7.33). Individually the sheets are fact sheets about products, services, or locations. Together they present a detailed picture of the organization. Because they are presented in a folder, new or additional information such as price lists can be inserted to meet the needs of individual recipients and to accommodate changes.

To be successful, short sheets require considerable planning. Except for the front sheet, the heading is the only part that should be visible when the sheets are stacked. If any additional information is visible, it will be distracting.

The front (smallest) sheet is usually used for an introduction, a brief description of the organization, a mission statement or message from the CEO. It may be difficult to limit this information to the shortest of the sheets although technically you can use both sides.

◆ *Folded mailers* start with a single flat sheet of paper and are folded into a smaller size. The most common finished sizes fit into a standard business envelope, a #10 envelope that measures 9″ × 4.25″. You will find many ideas for creative folds and sizes as well as for color combinations and graphics in the documents you receive. Pay attention to the brochures you receive in the mail and add

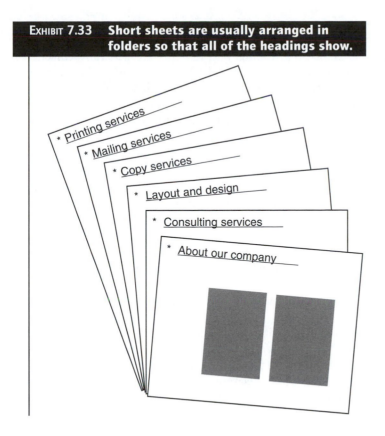

EXHIBIT 7.33   Short sheets are usually arranged in folders so that all of the headings show.

* Printing services

* Mailing services

* Copy services

* Layout and design

* Consulting services

* About our company

the most interesting to your resource file. Exhibit 7.32 illustrates several of the most common format and folding options.

Self-mailers include an address panel and are mailed without an envelope. They must meet postal requirements for weight and positioning of the address panel, and have a seal to keep them closed (called a wafer-seal).

Folded mailers are extremely versatile and offer many options for paper stock, color, and presentation. Accordion folds especially are easy to expand by increasing the paper size and adding folds to accommodate additional information. Gatefolds are effective if panels #1 and #2 that form the "gate" are a single picture or message that can be cleanly divided in half. These panels should relate to each other or the effect is wasted.

Remember that you can turn any of these formats 90° and have them open down rather than left to right. This works best with the single-fold, double-fold, or accordion styles.

Die Cuts

There are two types of die cuts—so called because the printer uses a *die* to cut a special shape. One puts a hole in the document so that an image can be seen through it. You must be very careful to ensure precise positioning of both the die cut and the image underneath. A variation is the slits of cut into the flap of a folder so that a business card can be inserted. The other type of die cut cuts the entire document into a special shape. A typical example is the Rolodex card with a tab at the top and notches at the bottom that allow the card to fit into a roll or file.

Embossing

Embossing creates texture by pressing an image into the paper. To be successful, the image must be very sharp and the paper stock must be carefully selected for both weight and finish. Some papers will not hold an imprint well and the finish on others will crack if they are embossed.

Foil Stamping

Foil stamping is a heat process used to apply a metallic foil to a specific design, often a logo or organization name. The foil can be any color, but it will have a metallic look. It is possible to test this effect on a laser printer using foils that are available from many computer products suppliers.

Techniques such as embossing, foiling, and die cuts are generally considered expensive. This will conflict with the image of frugality and sound financial management that nonprofits attempt to project. On the other hand, silver or gold foiling on high-quality stock may perfectly convey the image of financial strength that is expected of companies bidding for particular high-value contracts.

The Presentation Folder

Many organizations regard presentation folders as one of their flagship publications, ranking right up there with annual reports for unit cost and sophistication of technique.

The simplest presentation folder is 15″ × 18″ folded to 9″ × 12″ with a 3″ pocket along the bottom of both inside panels. In many cases, the pocket has die-cut slits into which a business card can be inserted. A smaller version will fit into a standard #10 business envelope. More sophisticated folder designs also abound, with embossed or die-cut panels, foldouts, and booklets saddle-stitched into the folder.

Because of their cost, folders are often considered a major project, especially for small organizations. For the same reason, they are often multipurpose, with the same design having to be appropriate for use by management, sales and marketing, human resources, and certainly public relations, such as for press and information kits. Folders are likely to have a long shelf life as multiple departments work their way through print runs large enough to be seen as cost-effective—usually at least 1,000.

Folders are printed on what is known as cover stock, that is, heavy paper that will hold its shape when other documents are inserted. If you are looking for an expensive, high-quality image, this may be a good opportunity to use foiling, die cuts, or embossing, especially because these techniques require heavy paper stock.

It is wise to make routine, general-use folders as timeless as possible. We know of a company that printed 2,000 presentation folders including the company's mission statement and president's signature on the inside of the folder. It seemed like a good idea at the time, but when the president left the company a few months later, the organization was left with hundreds of unused—and unusable—folders and a high unit cost for those that had been used. Without that signature, the folders would still be usable.

Design Issues for the Web

Just as writing for the Web shares the principles of good writing for print, so designing for the Web makes use of the same principles of good design for print documents. If anything, these principles are even more important because of the relationship between text and design in web communication.

It is especially difficult to separate writing for the Web and design for the Web because many of the web writer's necessary concerns—navigation/directions, length, and style—are so closely linked to the web site design and to the site's success. If the text and the design support each other, the web site will be easy to navigate. If they do not, the visitor will quickly become lost and frustrated and probably leave the site.

One of the easiest ways to acculturate yourself to good web design is to pay attention to the web sites you visit. What do you like about them? If you leave them quickly, why? What makes them easy or difficult to navigate? Do the graphics support or impede your understanding of the content? Answering these questions will help you understand how to design a web site and how it and the text together determine its success. Just as you maintain a print document swipe file, we suggest you monitor the many web awards programs and visit the winning sites. A routine search using the words "web awards" will yield many options.

Good web site design is difficult. Although many programs automatically translate text into HTML, this does not in itself make the result a good web page. To the contrary, successful web design requires intimate knowledge of the capabilities of many systems and of the ways to effectively link pages, documents, topics, and sites. To maximize the effect of your organization's investment in web technology, consider working with a web designer who can make your copy work effectively in cyberspace. Do-it-yourself web sites are often a disaster.

Even if you do this, it will still benefit you to understand how the design principles we discussed earlier in this chapter apply also to design for the Web. All good web site designs have a concern for balance, layout, type, color, and graphics—principles you already know. To this you will necessarily add navigation, that all-important foundation of successful web sites. Following is a review of these principles with special attention to how they apply to web design.

Layout

Think of web layouts as fluid, with the path of your words restricted by browser limitations, operating systems, screen width, and resolution (the clarity of what you see). You can set your computer monitor for various resolutions, ranging from 640×480 to 1152×768 or higher. The higher the numbers, the greater the resolution, that is, the finer and less grainy an image will be. You will be able to see more of the screen at one time, but the type gets progressively smaller.

As a general rule, you will be designing for a 13″ to 17″ diagonal screen or for a succession of screens if one page flows beyond a single screen length. If the text must flow beyond one screen, ensure that this is obvious or the user may not see the end.

Web layout is closely linked to navigation and organization; it must support visitors' efforts to quickly find the information they came for. At the same time, it should invite them to stay and provide obvious reasons for doing so. If you think this suggests a simple design with obvious bullet points, you are right.

A single-column layout with navigational buttons along the side is often the most practical format. Single columns allow you to flow text onto additional screens. They also allow you to present material as tables, charts and graphs, or photos without awkward breaks.

As important as designing the layout is the need to use it consistently throughout the site. Users should be able to find the navigational buttons in the same place on every page so that they can easily find their way around the site. They should always be able to return to the home page to start again. Establish this layout theme on the home page, including any key graphic images and colors that will repeat throughout the site.

Balance

As with print documents, well-designed web sites will be balanced, symmetrically or asymmetrically. However, as Bohle (1995) points out, balance does not necessarily work the same on the Web as it does in print. In web design, what the designer sees is not necessarily what the viewer will see.

Alignment is a particular problem thanks to the limitation of some web design software to align elements exactly where you want them. This may be overcome by specifying the size (e.g., of photos or graphics) as percentages of a total screen size rather than as absolute sizes (e.g., 200 pixels × 400 pixels—pixels being the common unit of measurement on the Web). This means that a photo specified at a 50% size will take up 50% of the screen width regardless of what the width actually is. The same photo specified as absolute pixels may take up all of a very small screen or very little of a large screen. Either way, it may destroy your layout.

Another solution is to work with graphic techniques over which you have more control, such as different weights of type (size and boldness) and colors to create visual balance and interest in a single-column format instead of trying to position multiple text blocks that may not be successful.

Always try to view the web site on multiple systems with old and new browsers, on both PC and Macintosh platforms, and in multiple resolutions to see what problems occur. Then decide what you want to change if you can and what you will have to live with.

Type

Web sites are a visual medium, but one that the user often sees in the worst possible conditions. Eyestrain and backaches are common complaints that could cause the user to leave your site if it takes too long to load or is too difficult to search. This is additional to the concerns we discussed before about typefaces that are too small or otherwise difficult to read and lines that are too long.

You may find yourself sacrificing the special typeface that is part of your organization's signature when it comes time to use it on the Web. If users do not have that typeface on their computers (and it is likely they will not), then the system will default to a typeface that may well be larger or smaller than you want. This will interfere with even the most carefully designed web layout. The worst-case scenario is a default to a monospace font such as Courier. Check several browsers to see what is available as standard typefaces (the standards we discussed above: Times New Roman, Arial, Helvetica, Times, and now Verdana are generally safe options).

Just as bold type acts as a traffic sign in print layouts, so it does in web design. Set headlines, bullet points, and other navigational cues in larger and/or bolder type, perhaps even in color, to take advantage of the contrast they provide and the attention they attract.

Do *not* use underscores for emphasis. On the Web, underscored type indicates a hyperlink. This is part of the web language we have come to understand.

Color

Color on the Web is different from color in print. The former is projected color; the latter is reflected. The color you put on the Web is not necessarily the color the user will see. In this case, the problem is the capability of the monitor and its settings. You may want to design color and graphics for the lowest monitor display capability—256 colors—even though this limits the sophistication of the graphics.

Another guideline is to stay with the default colors provided on your system. They are supported by many systems and provide the best assurance that the average user will see them accurately, although one cannot be 100% certain. Again, check the web site on multiple monitors to get a feel for what viewers will see under all possible conditions.

Color also affects the size of a file. Suffice it to say that it increases it (possibly a lot), which will in turn increase the time it takes to load the file. This is not to suggest that you should not use color; to the contrary, the Web was made for color. It does, however, suggest that you should use color judiciously, choosing perhaps two or three colors and staying with them throughout the presentation. Just as too many colors can interfere with a clear printed message, too many colors on a computer screen may also distract the user. The colors compete for the viewer's attention.

Always check the readability of type on colored backgrounds. Background colors can have a significant effect on how easy it is to read copy, especially if it too is set in color. Web guru Jakob Nielsen (www.useit.com) also cautions against the color blue for type, even headings. On the Web, blue is most commonly used for hyperlinks. Our understanding for the web language is that words set in blue will be links. Even if it plays havoc with your design, find another color.

Navigational Support

There are several ways to provide users with navigational cues, including hypertext links, buttons, and search screens. Hypertext links usually come directly from the text or from bulleted lists. The convention—which users universally understand, even expect—is to set such links in blue, usually underlined. Clicking on the colored type automatically brings up the linked screen. After you access a hyperlink, it changes color to signal that you have been there.

Graphic elements such as buttons or boxes attract attention, but it must be clear where the viewer should click—on the button or the text or preferably either. Although clever graphic buttons may attract attention, they may also increase download time and try your viewer's patience. Whatever style you select, stay with it for all buttons to conserve memory and reduce the download time. More important than the button appearance is the clarity of the text describing where the link leads.

For long documents or complex web sites, you may also want to provide a search capability so that the viewer can search for topics of special interest.

Graphics on the Web

Web visitors should be able to rapidly and easily access all pages of a web site. In this context, graphics require careful thought. While in print, pictures may be worth 1,000 words, as graphic files they are memory hogs, especially if they are animated. Not everyone has a blazing high-speed machine, and on anything less, the download time for large graphic files may be a deterrent, especially for the casual visitor. Evidence and your own experience should suggest that anything more than a 10- to 15-second wait will cause visitors to leave the site, one argument for text over graphics.

You may be able to reduce download time by choosing alternate file formats for graphics. JPEG and GIF are two of the most common, but they have different benefits for the web designer. JPEG, which scrolls the artwork line by line, can accommodate millions of colors but not large color blocks. On the other hand, GIF can handle only 256 colors but is well suited for animation, and its method of downloading the artwork—presenting a blurred image that gradually becomes clearer—allows viewers to understand the graphic while it is being drawn on the screen.

Web site graphics should be important enough to warrant the download time. It helps to also describe complex graphics in text that visitors can read before or during the download time. It is also wise to include a text alternative to accommodate users whose browsers cannot handle large graphics or who do not want to wait for the download.

Again: Keep It Simple

What makes an effective web graphic? First, simplicity—the simpler the better. Graphs that summarize important but lengthy financial reports, organizational charts that illustrate the corporate structure, and flowcharts that substitute for process descriptions are all useful web graphics as long as they fit onto one page. The visitor should be able to view and understand the entire graphic on one screen. The second aspect of good web graphics is color—for accent and understanding. Although multiple colors increase download time, just a few in key places will help to reinforce your message and the web site structure.

There are now many sources of graphics for web sites, many of them available online and many of them free. A search for the words "online clip art" or "web graphics" will yield many options.

There is no doubt that graphics assist attention, understanding, and retention. However, until such time as you are confident that all of your target visitors can successfully handle large graphic files, there is also some argument that, remembering Jakob Nielsen's admonition that web copy should be half the length of print copy, "500 words are worth a picture." This is good news for writers. And the fewer the words, the stronger the argument.

HTML, the Language of the Web

The language you use to create web text from text and graphics files is HTML—hypertext markup language—or its newer versions XML and XHTML. HTML is a standard generalized markup language (SGML) in wide use.

HTML commands, or *tags,* indicate positioning, alignment, typeface and style changes, links, and navigation tools. For example, <b>, <br>, and <h3> indicate bold font, paragraph break, and a level of heading, respectively.

Many software packages, including word processing and page layout programs, will translate your pages into HTML. Not all of them do it well or efficiently. This is yet another case of "just because you *can* do it, doesn't mean it's a good idea."

Some sophisticated programming languages create web pages that can be changed without special programming. A web master can open any pages created in these languages and enter new information or change the old information and immediately have it posted on the web site. This technology allows for simple, dynamic fact sheets that always contain up-to-date facts and statistics. Some of the programs are also interactive—likely the wave of the future.

ON THE TEXTBOOK WEB SITE

✦ Go to www.sagepub.com/treadwell for web exercises, study hints, case studies, and additional examples appropriate to this chapter and chosen or developed to supplement the chapter content.

WRITING WRAP-UP

1. The club or organization you identified in the "Writing Wrap-Up" for Chapter 5 requires a visual identity to provide a consistent and identifiable image in all its communication. Thinking of the organization's purpose and culture, write a set of guidelines for all the media you expect the organization to use. The guidelines should include color specifications, use and placement of the logo, and type specifications for its print media. If the organization has no logo, what would you suggest? Set out your specifications as pages of a manual and present them with a covering letter to the head of the organization seeking approval of your recommendations.

REFERENCES

Bohle, R. (1995). Principles of web design. *Web Review.* Retrieved September 27, 1998, from www.webreview.com

Keyes, E. (1993, November). Typography, color, and information structure. *Technical Communication, 30*(4), 638–654.

Use color effectively [Photocopy]. (n.d.). Department of Communication Arts, Cornell University.

White, J. V. (1982) *Editing by design* (2nd ed.). New York: R. R. Bowker.

Xerox Corporation. (1997). Typography. In *Basic graphic standards.* Stamford, CT: Xerox Corporation.

RESOURCES

Books

Favre, J. P., & November, A. (1979). *Color and, und, et Communication.* Zurich: ABCVerlag.

Tufte, E. R. (2001). *The visual display of quantitative information* (2nd ed.). Cheshire, CT: Graphics Press.

White, J. V. (1982). *Editing by design* (2nd ed.). New York: R R. Bowker.

White, J. V. (1991). *Graphic idea notebook* (Rev.). Rockport, MA: Rockport Publishers.

Magazines

Communication Arts and its online version including .... www.commarts.com
search capability and links to other databases

Dynamic Graphics and *STEP inside design* (to subscribe) .... www.dgusa.com

Publish and its online cousin *Publish* ....www.publish.com
RGB (magazine on Web publishing)

Magazines published and sent to registered users by most graphic and desktop software companies, including Adobe, PageMaker, Corel, and PhotoShop

Sources of Royalty-Free Clip Art and Photos

(Note: "Royalty-free" does not necessarily mean free. You may still have to pay a fee for accessing these graphics.)

Jupiterimages (online photo and graphics)........................... http://www.jupiterimages.com/

Sources of Free Online Clip Art

#1 Free Clip Art (be certain to heed the.. www.1clipart.com
ownership disclaimer in this site)

Animation Factory's MediaBuilder... www.mediabuilder.com

Clip-Art.com (free clip art)... www.clip-art.com

Clip Art Connection .... www.clipartconnection.com

Mining Co. (free clip art) .... webclipart.miningco.com/library

Original Free Clip Art.. www.free-clip-art.net

Design Magazines on the Web

Communication Arts .... www.commarts.com

Publish RGB... www.publish.com

Testing Color Combinations on the Web

Color Schemer Online.. http://www.colorschemer.com/online.html

ZSPC Super Color Chart... http://www.zspc.com/color/index-e.html

8

From Principles to Planning to Practice

Business Writing, Fact Sheets, and Bios

1. Media can be differentiated by the degree of control they afford over content, timing, and distribution.

2. The level of control public relations writers want or need over a message is a key factor in media selection.

3. Public relations writers must plan for audience, outcomes, media, budget, and timing.

4. Even routine business and informational documents carry public relations messages and play a role in public relations strategy.

1. Business letters, memos, and reports—individual audiences.

2. Fact sheets, backgrounders, bios, and boilerplates—mass audiences.

The Planning

In previous chapters, we reviewed the principles that feed into effective public relations writing. Translating these principles into practice is a process first of planning and then of implementation.

At the macro level, a good public relations plan will define the communication strategies to be followed and the resources needed to assist an organization in reaching its goals.

EXHIBIT 8.1	The relationship of public relations writing to overall public relations and organizational goals.

Organizational plans, objectives, mission statements

↓

Goals that can be influenced by communication
(With whom must you communicate, how, when and about what, to influence these goals?)

↓

Public relations plans
(that can be implemented with resources available)

↓

The public relations writing plan
(Content - Format - Media - Scheduling)

↓

Org. Culture ↘   ↙ Ethics
                    ↙ Public(s)
Purpose → **PR WRITING** ← Resources
Time ↗   ↖ Legal
                    ↖ Industry
                    standards/practices

At the micro (or document) level, a public relations writing plan sets out content, design, and media/method strategies needed to support the public relations plan.

To be effective, all of the plans should be grounded in the plan(s) that address organizational goals. Organizational goals provide a framework for public relations plans that in turn frame public relations writing plans. In reverse, the successful execution of the writing plan helps the public relations department and ultimately the organization meet their broad, strategic goals for, say, increased membership or market share. Exhibit 8.1 illustrates the relationship among these plans.

The arrows in the diagram show the influences on public relations writing plans. However, most of the relationships shown are reciprocal. Writing/communication plans should affect the allocation of resources for communication as much as the allocation of resources will affect the plans.

For complex projects such as campaigns, annual reports, and events, there are many tools to help you plan and schedule. Some of the most important are described on the textbook web site. In this chapter, we focus on developing a planning mind-set for writing rather than project management. Because this mind-set is important to all public relations documents, we provide a "reminder" Planning panel in each of the following writing chapters.

Everything you know about ethics, law, persuasion, research, design, and particularly audience(s) feeds into the communication decisions that make up a public relations writing plan.

The typical public relations writing plan has seven components: publics, outcomes, media, budget, timing, evaluation—and, of course, message content.

In this chapter, we consider each of these components, introduce basic business writing formats that you will inevitably be required to master early in your career, and invite you to consider how addressing the above elements of planning can increase the effectiveness of your writing. The questions raised will apply to all your public relations writing projects from the most basic to the most complex.

Planning for Publics: Audience-Based Decision Making

The organization's publics should be at the center of all thinking, planning, and execution. But the public relations writer always has at least one additional audience: the organization you are working for. And to the extent that your duties involve writing for the mass media, you have an audience of media gatekeepers, the editors and reporters who determine whether to use your story and if so, how and when. You cannot write effectively without considering all of these audiences and their sometimes conflicting requirements. One test of your skill as a writer will be your success in resolving any conflicts and meeting the needs of all three audiences simultaneously.

Audience 1: The Organization's Publics

What you know about your target publics and their relative importance to your organization is at the heart of public relations planning because it affects your decision making on many levels. Identifying the target publics as clearly and prominently as possible in the plan will help ensure that these publics and their attitudes and needs do not get lost in the thrill of selecting new media and that your budget is appropriately spent.

As discussed in Chapter 5, publics are commonly segmented and defined by geographic, demographic, psychographic, media use, and/or lifestyle characteristics and criteria.

Prioritizing publics. Because you cannot deal with all publics simultaneously or equally, you will need some criteria to determine their relative importance. You need to answer the question, "Given a specific objective, which of all your organization's publics is the most important?" Sometimes the most important public will be self-apparent such as the committee that decides who will win the contract your organization is seeking. More often, however, many different publics will compete for your attention.

There are many ways of determining your most important publics. One consideration would be your ability to influence that public—and vice versa. At one extreme is a public that cannot affect your employer and that you cannot influence. This public has a low priority for your attentions. At the other extreme, a public that can seriously affect your organization and that can be persuaded or affected by the organization obviously has a high priority. Shareholders, employees, and potential donors usually fall into this category. In between are the organization's other publics.

In prioritizing publics, you will have to consider their attitudes toward your organization. It will be more difficult to move publics with a negative attitude to a positive stance than it will be to reinforce existing positive attitudes in another public.

Other factors that will influence your prioritization are the resources available to work effectively with a public, the time you can devote to that public, the public's relevance to organizational goals, and whether the situation could be considered a crisis, which might change the priority level of some publics.

The criteria for ranking or evaluating publics will depend on the time frame the organization has in mind and the specific outcomes you are seeking. Whereas a development office may rate groups by donor potential, a public affairs office might rate the same groups in terms of their political influence. Public relations writers working on an image campaign may decide that their most important publics are the news media and rate their importance on a "prestige" scale.

Note that while research gives you the information on which to base a decision, it does not make the decision for you. Each of the above decisions is a value judgment typically with ethical implications.

What you know about publics will influence, sometimes dictate, whether or not you communicate with them (and when), the media you use to reach them, the appeal you use to ensure the message resonates with them, the grammar you choose to ensure the copy will be understandable, and even the colors that will attract attention.

Audience 2: The Organization

An organization's attitudes about itself and about its relationships with publics will tell you a lot about how the organization wants to be presented. For example, the following statements clearly help to position and differentiate the four companies from each other.

- To maximize returns to shareholders in a socially responsible manner
- To engage in ethical business practices while protecting the environment
- To maximize the potential for all employees
- To become the technological leader in widget production within five years

These statements and the values they express tell the writer three important things: how to position the organization in communications, what messages take priority, and whether mass media are viable options for reaching the organization's publics. Because the first company seeks to balance profit with social responsibility, the public relations strategy will be to highlight its overall corporate responsibility. The second company has a concern for ethical business practice and will want its messages to emphasize its commitment to the environment. The third will presumably attempt whenever possible to credit employees for its corporate triumphs and to emphasize its internal training and employee support programs. It will expect you to position it as a committed employer with an enviable working environment.

Meanwhile, the widget manufacturer will likely view news about a new support system for single-parent employees as an important message for an internal audience of employees, but would not give it priority for a public media release because it does not promote the organization as a technological leader. This does not mean that the company would not release the story to the media, only that it will not take priority over public relations activities that promote the organization's technological expertise.

Audience 3: The Mass Media

Working with the mass media is always a delicate balance between promoting your organization's interests and meeting media requirements for content, style, and especially neutrality. On one hand, the mass media are indispensable if you need to reach large audiences relatively quickly. They make it easy to disseminate your message locally, regionally, nationally, or even internationally. And if you use a wire service such as PR Newswire or Bizwire, you can reach specialty media that in turn reach audiences specifically interested in your message.

The mass media also have the advantage that (except for video news releases) they are low cost or no cost. You will pay a high price, however, for treating the mass media as a source of "free advertising." Rightly or wrongly, many editors have a propensity to view releases from a public relations source as suspect based on a stereotypical misconception that such stories are the product of devious corporate "spin doctors" engineering pseudo-events to generate false publicity that would not exist had not these public relations types masterminded the whole thing in the first place. You will not do your organization or the public relations sector any favors by contributing to this impression.

Being seen to waste the media's time will also cost you your credibility—a high price to pay indeed. Media trust is invaluable in a crisis when you need to get *your* side of the story into the public eye/ear quickly. Alternatively, if you are seen as a cooperative and reliable source, the media may approach you for comment on issues relevant to your industry. Media trust is a valuable commodity and you risk it foolishly.

Exhibit 8.2 illustrates how these three categories of publics differ with regard to the classic elements of a news story: "who, what, when, where, why, and how." It highlights the range of interests you will have to balance in each document you write.

Planning for Outcomes

A key part of planning is specifying the outcomes or results expected from communication with the target publics. In Chapter 1, we suggested a number of ways to look at communication purposes or outcomes. The overall public relations plan should specify the knowledge, attitudinal, or behavioral changes expected from specific publics. Writing plans then look at the combination of message content, communication methods, and timing that will result in publics not only receiving the message but also remembering, believing, and acting on it.

Outcomes can be written "soft" or "hard." Soft outcomes are generalities (e.g., "to establish relationships with the community"). Soft outcomes are generally acceptable; who could disagree with them? They also have the virtue of strategic ambiguity; they express noble goals but no indication of what is to happen. Soft outcomes are common in mission and vision statements.

On the other hand, hard outcomes are quantitative, specific, and measurable. They specify precisely what is going to happen, with whom, when, and typically what will define a measurable degree of improvement or change. The hard-outcome statement that "at least 85% of American women over the age of 40 will have annual mammograms by the end of the decade" spells out precisely who (American women over age 40), what action (will have annual mammograms), when (by the end of the decade), and by how much (at least 85%).

The advantage of hard outcomes is that the results are measurable. Through research, we can know precisely whether the desired outcome happened. The difficulty, of course, is that many factors contribute to most outcomes. In the example above, the best writing in the world may have no impact if the target group is low income, has no access to health care, or has deep religious or cultural convictions against breast examination. A public relations message aimed at persuading a public to change its behavior clearly requires a different level of sophistication and complexity than one aimed just at achieving a basic level of awareness or one aimed at having people carry out a set of instructions.

EXHIBIT 8.2	How news interests differ by organization, audience, and media.

Question	Client concerns	Audience concerns	Media concerns
Who	are our publics? do we *want* to communicate with? do we *have* to communicate with? e.g., by regulations	is interesting? do we want to hear about?	interests our audience?
What	is our purpose or agenda: knowledge, attitude change, behavior change? do we *want* to tell our public(s)? do we *have* to tell our public(s)? e.g., under SEC regulations	do we know … and want to know about this organization? interests us? affects us?	is this organization's purpose or agenda? is news about this organization? is not being told in this situation that may be of interest or concern to our audience?
When	should we release this information?	do we need this information? (if it is necessary)	should this be published? does our audience need the story?
Where	should we place the story? what media? what region(s)?	would we expect to find the story?	will our audience be most interested?
Why	do we *want* to issue this release? do we *need* to issue this release? e.g., to meet regulations, counter negative opinion or protect the public	do we need (or want) this information? what's in it for me?	was this release issued? should we publish/air it? should we give this priority over other stories?
How	should we position the organization in this release? should (can) we temper bad news?	do we respond to this news? in attitude? in behavior?	do we handle this editorially? will this story affect (hopefully maximize) our audience's interest in our publication or broadcast?

Note that the terminology of outcomes is inconsistent. You may read about key results areas, strategic aims, or simply outcomes, as well as goals and objectives. You will have to find out precisely what each of these means to your organization. In this text, we refer to broad, soft outcome statements as goals, and to specific, targeted, measurable hard-outcome statements as objectives.

Planning for Media and Methods

The choice of media for any public relations situation will be a function of the publics you identify as important, the message you need to send, and the available budget and time. Clearly, you should only choose media that reach your target publics, especially for paid advertising. If the message needs to be retained or referenced, broadcast media make little sense. If the message must demonstrate a procedure or a skill, you will need to choose a visual medium, with diagrams, photographs, or even live demonstrations.

Planning helps you choose the *best* medium or media mix for your purpose. Understanding your audiences and the purpose of your messages must precede decisions about which media to select and how to take advantage of them. For example, knowing that your audience is large (e.g., all adults in your state) will steer you to the mass media; knowing it is small (e.g., the Board of Directors) will steer you to memos or letters; knowing it is widely scattered will lead you to newsletters or e-mail.

Message purpose also clearly affects media choice. Urgent messages relating to public safety demand the news media; introducing clients to a new billing procedure needs a targeted mailing; and providing visitors with general information can be done through a standard fact sheet that is designed not to go out of date or a web page that is easily updated.

Planning for Cost or Budget

It costs money to print materials and manage distribution channels, much less so to produce news releases or host news conferences. There is an obvious tradeoff between uncontrolled media, which, with the exception of video news releases (VNRs), cost relatively little to produce but have no guarantee of reaching an audience, and controlled media, which guarantee a defined audience at a given time and control of content but almost always at a cost.

A primary advantage of the mass media, in addition to the number of people who can be reached, is cost. The placement of stories in the mass media is essentially free, other than the cost of your time; the mass media make it possible to reach large numbers of people at low cost.

Generally speaking, the larger the budget the more media options you have and/or the more sophisticated your communications can be and/or the more people you can reach. We have used "and/or" to describe these options because choosing one (such as reaching a large mailing list) may limit another (e.g., sophistication), even with a very large budget.

Budget also enters into creative decisions. A large budget does not mean that a high level of sophistication is automatic or advisable. Nonprofit or public agencies, even with substantial budgets, may be well advised to produce material of modest cost to avoid the aura of high-level funding and "money to burn" that may displease taxpayers and supporters.

In theory, planning drives the budget. You specify the end product (public service announcement, direct mail letter, or bumper sticker) in the requisite numbers plus production and distribution costs, and a good supporting argument will secure the funding you need. Typically, you have a fixed budget, and the number of predictable writing projects is divided into that budget to arrive at the sum available for a particular project.

Generally, there is a reciprocal relationship between planning and budgeting. The number, quality, and distribution of your writing products are affected by your budget, but a good plan with a good supporting argument is needed to get the budget you want.

Planning for Timing

Timing is a critical element of every public relations writing plan. Deadlines dictate what you may or may not be able to produce, and time of year dictates the topicality of many stories. Length/size, format, treatment, and content of writing are often functions of how much time you have to write.

The theory is that with careful planning you will have all the time you need, and for some publications this is true. Work on many corporate annual reports starts the day after the current report is released if not before, and the editor has a year to conceptualize, plan, research, write, design, and edit. By contrast, a media release about an organizational crisis may be drafted on your laptop on the train between the 3 a.m. phone call you get at home and the 7 a.m. crisis response meeting at the office.

Public relations writers, especially in the fields of fashion, food, and cosmetics, may have a seasonal calendar of events in which photographs and copy for a December magazine issue are initiated during the summer and finished by September to meet production deadlines. A similar situation exists in sports public relations.

Timing and its importance in media selection are generally related to the urgency of the message. There will be times when control over content and distribution will be less important than control of (or by) timing. Emergency statements relating to public health and safety will dictate the use of the news media because of their ability to disseminate messages rapidly.

On a smaller scale, you may choose to use e-mail or fax rather than standard mail to deliver urgent messages rapidly to important but less numerous publics. Documents such as fact sheets, backgrounders, and brochures deliberately omit time-sensitive content so that they remain valid for a long time without constant updating.

Web sites may or may not be driven by timing. On one hand, they have the potential to be updated minute-by-minute, which gives credibility to the messages. Many financial services companies opt for real-time posting of stock prices and interest and exchange rates. This requires a commitment of resources and talent that may be unnecessary for organizations that do not have constantly changing information to disseminate. On the other hand, even if you have the capability to "push" information to your target publics in a timely fashion, you have little control over when or even if they will see the information.

Planning for Evaluation

Because planning takes place to ensure that you meet designated outcomes, writing plans should identify how you will evaluate success. In some cases, this will be easy. If the purpose of a campaign is to recruit new members, you will be able to measure whether this happened. If the only communication was a direct mail letter, then you can reasonably assume that the letter was responsible for the change.

The more specific the outcome statements, the more easily you will be able to determine whether the public relations plan worked. This is the fundamental advantage of writing hard outcomes over soft outcomes. The continuing challenge will be determining the specific contribution your writing made to the outcome.

Planning for Control

Throughout this discussion we have alluded to the issue of control, specifically control of content, timing, and distribution. Control is a key issue when choosing media whose varying levels of control make them more or less appropriate for specific audiences and situations.

Control is especially important when the news is bad, embarrassing, or of crisis proportions. Psychologically, the organization may want total control so that as few people as possible know, an attitude that may be reinforced by legal counsel who want time to develop a legal position and reduce the organization's legal exposure. Against this, public relations counsel will probably argue for full and open disclosure to preserve the organization's credibility and prevent erroneous or fictitious versions of events from circulating, as they inevitably will if the organization adopts a "no comment" stance.

The difference between controlled and uncontrolled media is simple and important. Controlled media allow you to control message content, distribution, and timing. Any medium in which you, the public relations writer, can ensure that your content will be distributed unchanged has a high degree of content control. Any medium in which external gatekeepers (e.g., editors or reporters) play a role in determining whether the story will run and/or what the final content will be has a low level of control over content and timing.

At one extreme is that public relations classic—the news media. Once you involve the mass media, you generally lose control over how, when, where, or even if the message goes any further. One advantage of the mass media that may tempt you to risk losing control over content and timing is that readers/viewers see news coverage as valid and unbiased because its apparent source is journalists and editors rather than advertising or public relations executives. To the extent that the news media have credibility, so too does their coverage of your news. If published or broadcast, your releases will reach your publics as news or program content, rather than as advertising. There is an implicit endorsement that the content has news value, and implicitly a higher level of credibility for the reader or viewer. In addition, news releases cost almost nothing.

A disadvantage of news releases is that you have little or no control over what information will be presented adjacent (in time or space) to yours. This may work to your benefit or detriment. Although you do not want the grand opening of a hamburger restaurant printed next to an article on an outbreak of *E. coli*, having a your dean's list announcement printed next to a feature story on rising college test scores is an implicit endorsement of your institution's quality.

At the other extreme in control is paid advertising—the only way to guarantee control of message content, timing, placement, and appearance. Your advertising dollar buys exposure in a specific medium at a specific time for the message you have written and designed. Advertising also offers the potential for attention-grabbing design and content that you may not have when writing to news criteria. However, your communications may be regarded as "only" advertising and therefore as biased or one-sided.

Between these extremes lie many choices of media, each of which has its own advantages and disadvantages related to content, timing, and distribution. Exhibit 8.3 lists the wide choice of media that public relations writers have available for any

EXHIBIT 8.3   Chart demonstrating the level and types of control you have using a range of media available to public relations writers.

Medium	Distribution Control	Timing Control	Content Control	Options/decisions/comments
Advertising (paid)	Yes	Yes	Yes	Used for image, issue, and advocacy messages when you are willing to pay for control.
Annual reports	Yes	Yes	Yes	To shareholders, employees, alumni, etc. Some content is dictated by SEC regulations.
Backgrounders	Yes	Yes	Yes	Typically distributed as part of press kits or information packages to targeted recipients.
Biographies	Yes	Yes	Yes	Typically distributed as part of press/information kits to known or targeted recipients.
Broadcast news	No	No	No	Radio and television (not advertising).
Brochures, flyers, etc.	Yes/No	Yes/No	Yes	Control relates to whether brochures can be picked up by general public or are sent to individuals.
Bulletin boards	Yes	Yes	Yes	Company, industry, magazines, newsletters. Trade association publications.
Correspondence (indiv.)	Yes	Yes	Yes	Letters, memos, e-mail to individuals.
Correspondence (mass)	Yes	Yes	Yes	Letters, mail-merge, and e-mail to newsgroups and targeted lists.
Employee publications	Yes	Yes	Yes	You can target distribution to encourage or discourage "pass-on" readership.
Direct mail	Yes	Yes	Yes	Used for prospecting, soliciting.
Events: Sponsored by	Yes	Yes	Yes	Distribution controlled by invitation list organization.
Events: Sponsored by other organization	Limited	Yes	Yes	You may know generally who will be at the event but you cannot control who visits your exhibit.
Fact sheets	Yes	Yes	Yes	Typically distributed as part of press/information kits to known or targeted recipients.
Fax: Targeted	Yes	Yes	Yes	You send fax to individual or bulk "mailing list."

(Continued, next page)

EXHIBIT 8.3 (Continued)

Medium	Distribution Control	Timing Control	Content Control	Options/decisions/comments
Handbooks/manuals	Yes	Yes	Yes	Provided individually to known persons, usually employees.
Information racks	Limited	No	Yes	You can control where the distribution racks are located, but not who accesses them or when.
Magazine articles	Limited	No	No	Consider specialized publications, generally to known demographic groups. Options include sponsored (e.g., airline) magalogs.
Media advisories	Yes	Yes	Yes	Sent to targeted mailing list.
Newsgroups/ chat rooms	Yes	Yes/No	Yes	You should know generally the nature of the group so your reply can be targeted.
Pitch letters	Yes	Yes	Yes	Sent to targeted mailing list.
Position papers	Yes	Yes	Yes	Typically distributed as part of press/ information packages to known or targeted recipients.
Posters	No	No	Yes	Generally mass rather than targeted audience.
Press conferences	Yes/No	Yes	Yes/No	Full control over prepared statements but not over questions posed by the press.
Press: newspapers	No	No	No	PR writers must determine whether a story merits news or feature writing.
Proposals, reports	Yes	Yes	Yes	Typically produced for known audience.
Satellite links, media tours	Yes	Yes	Yes	Treat as for the press. The audience is the media.
Specialty items	No	Yes	Yes	E.g., pens, clothing, candy, and other novelties.
Speeches	Yes	Yes	Yes	Audience usually known generally.
Web cast	Yes/No	Yes	Yes/No	Can restrict access via password. See also Press conferences.
Web pages	No[a]	No	Yes	Used for e-mail.
Videos/DVDs	Yes	Yes	Yes	Used for employee training, education, sales, and marketing support.

a. Except with controlled access by password access codes.

given message and the controls over content, distribution, and timing usually associated with each. It should help you see the advantages and disadvantages associated with the various media and why some media lend themselves to some audiences and some purposes.

Ethical Issues

Ethics and Business Writing

Public relations writers face ethical decisions on a daily basis—even with routine "business" correspondence. Some examples follow.

What Gets Written—and What Doesn't

It is obvious that you cannot include every piece of information in every document, nor should you want to. But how do you choose what *not* to print? Brevity generally aids the reader and makes communication more effective but it comes at the price of "lost" information.

Persuasive writing tends to leave out the bad news and include the good news. This may be understandable and defensible if you are promoting yourself in a job application letter, but what if you are writing a report on which your employers will be making a major policy decision? In such a case, they need to know the consequences of both a "yes" and a "no" decision and you will shortchange them unless your report discusses both the negatives and the positives of a situation.

The PRSA Code of Ethics provides some useful guidance for this decision. The principle regarding the free flow of information requires that you provide "accurate and truthful information that . . . [contributes] to informed decision-making" (PRSA code).

The Use and Abuse of Adjectives and Appeals

The use of language is a second issue of ethical concern. While there are some legal constraints (e.g., SEC regulations) on some financial reporting, the major determinant of much writing is the writer's ethical standards with respect to describing a client, product, or service. There are advertising copywriters who can comfortably describe their client's monthly sales as "once in a lifetime opportunities." As a conscientious writer, can you describe an event as "significant" if it isn't?

Again, you can find some guidance in the PRSA code's call for truth and accuracy, as well as in your own obligation to enhance the profession of public relations by building respect and credibility with the public. You cannot do this if you are seen to exceed the boundaries of credibility in what you write.

Planning: Finding the Middle Ground

Planning is part of the process of finding a middle ground among the ideal, the practical, and the affordable. While highly desirable in principle, planning may be difficult in practice for a number of reasons, not the least of which is that the daily pressures of phone calls and meetings can make it difficult to set aside time for planning.

From an evaluation point of view, it can be difficult to know precisely how writing contributes to outcomes. The fact that you wrote a wonderful fundraising piece and your organization subsequently raised record donations last year does not necessarily mean that there is a relationship between the two.

Also, writing may be driven by factors other than your organization's goals or your own planning. Traditional one-way models of public relations are driven by organizational goals, but contemporary models emphasize a two-way relationship with publics. Thus shareholders, interest groups, statutory agencies, and the media may all demand, want, or be entitled to information. Common sense says that you will respond to these requests. This means that a lot of communication effort will be driven by what your constituencies need and that you may unable to predict or plan for this.

For reasons such as these, few public relations writing professionals produce a written plan for routine projects such as news releases or even regular newsletters, but be assured that they do go through a mental planning process.

Exhibit 8.4 is a planning sheet for developing effective copy. It is a written version of the mental checklist that most public relations writers go through, consciously or unconsciously, before sitting down at the keyboard. You may find it helpful to actually use this as a checklist; eventually, as your experience grows, these considerations will become second nature, although using it occasionally will help keep your planning skills sharp.

Refer to the list again when you conduct the postwriting evaluation; it may help you define where you may have gone wrong (e.g., what assumptions could have been different or what research you should have done) and revise your thinking for the next project.

Summary

Like research and ethics, planning should be a mind-set in which you constantly try to anticipate organizational developments and public responses to the organization so that appropriate messages, media, and relationships with important publics are in place before they are needed.

Planning for message timing, as well as for content and distribution, all get back to the fundamental identification of your audience and purpose and your need for control of message, medium, and timing.

The planning mind-set makes public relations desirably proactive rather than reactive.

DISCUSSION 1

Think of a public relations campaign you might be interested in managing or are currently aware of. Specifically, how would a failure to consider each of the following weaken the writing for the campaign: publics, outcomes, media, budget, timing, evaluation, and message content?

The Practice: Beginning With the Basics

Although entry-level public relations writers may see themselves spearheading the organization's communication strategy and execution, the reality is that a lot of

EXHIBIT 8.4   Checklist for public relations writing.

Purpose:
What is your aim?
_____ To inform
_____ To persuade
What outcome/s do you want:?
_____ Knowledge
_____ Attitudinal
_____ Behavioral

Legal:
What constraints do you have e.g.
copyright? privacy?
Should you consult legal counsel?

Ethical:
What harm, if any, might come from
the message?
_____ Is the message truthful?
_____ Is the message accurate?
_____ Is the message in violation
      of any client code of con-
      duct or PRSA Standards of
      Practice?

Culture:
How will your employer's culture
shape your writing?

How will audience cultures affect
how your message is received?

Research:
What should you research?
_____ Environment
_____ Client
_____ Publics
_____ Media
_____ Message

What techniques will work best?
_____ Interviews
_____ Archive searches
_____ Web searches
_____ Surveys
_____ Focus groups
_____ Content analysis
_____ Other

Publics:
Have you considered:
_____ Geographics
_____ Demographics
_____ Psychographics
_____ Media use

Medium:
Which will most effectively . . .
(a) reach your public?
(b) convey the message?
_____ Mail
_____ Press
_____ Radio
_____ Television
_____ Multimedia
_____ Web page
_____ E-mail
_____ Display ads
_____ Special media e.g., t-shirts
_____ Other

Message:
Is it clear what message your
publics are to get; and the consequences to them of accepting or
rejecting the message?

Can the message be misunderstood?

Appeals:
If the writing is to persuade people,
what appeal and what level of
appeal will be used?
_____ Fear
_____ Self-improvement
_____ Personal testimony
_____ Celebrity testimonials
_____ Peer appeals
_____ Expertise/authority
_____ Status/recognition
_____ Independence
_____ Patriotism
_____ Family

Style:
Have you considered:
_____ News
_____ Feature
_____ Q & A
_____ Speech
_____ Advertising
_____ Direct mail

Interactivity:
Do people need to be able to
respond to this message? If so,
have you considered:
_____ 800-numbers
_____ Order forms
_____ Reply-cards
_____ Reply-paid envelopes
_____ Web sites

Position/Approach:
How will this piece of writing position the organization in the public's
mind?

Deadline/Scheduling:
What is the timing for the project?
_____ Crisis
_____ Immediate/urgent
_____ Medium term e.g. monthly
      newsletter
_____ Long term e.g. annual
      report

Evaluation
How will you assess the outcomes
of your message?

hard work and learning must take place before you will be able to fill these roles comfortably and professionally. With this in mind, before looking at the mainstream public relations media, all of which are subject to judgments about audience, reach, objectives, cost-effectiveness, and writing style, we look at some perhaps less exciting but no less important modes of communication that essentially help you learn about your organization and develop a style appropriate to it.

These include routine communications (memos, letters, and reports) plus such standard public relations pieces as fact sheets and personnel biographies. They are typical of the first projects an entry-level public relations writer may be given simply because they will help you learn about the organization and give you practice in the style and terminology that reflect your organization's culture.

Most of these documents are essentially factual. Their purpose is to convey information as directly and simply as possible. This is not to say you may not want to persuade someone with your report or that the "facts" in your fact sheet may not be chosen to appeal to a particular audience, only that they are not overtly persuasive or argumentative. You will soon come to appreciate that types of writing—informative, news, feature, and persuasive—are seldom exclusive. The importance is that you learn to balance the styles and use them strategically to achieve your employer's aims.

As you start to write, consider how asking questions about publics, outcomes, media and methods, content and design, cost, timing, and evaluation might improve the final product.

Letters

One of the first tests of your understanding of the organization's culture will be in memos or letters you write to other personnel and possibly to outside sources. Chapter 2 reviewed principles of writing in general and of letter writing in particular as they related to applying for a job. These principles do not change just because you are writing to ask a guest to speak at a function, to pitch a news story, or to respond to a shareholder who has a grievance or suggestion. Letters have as many purposes as an individual has in communicating. They may inform, acknowledge, or confirm an action or service; challenge an organization; seek redress; or attempt to persuade.

Following is a quick review of the important points discussed in detail in Chapter 2. We suggest you review that chapter for more detail regarding formats, appearance, style, and content.

- ◆ *Use appropriate style.* Letter style, beginning with whether you use "Dear Sir" or "Dear John" as a salutation and continuing through to whether you sign them "John D. Rockefeller" or "John," is always a function of how well you know the person you are writing to.
- ◆ *Be specific.* Be clear about why you are writing. Many letters now adopt the memo style of "Re: followed by a subject or title" printed just before the salutation. Your organization's style may encourage or discourage this option.
- ◆ *Be concise. Always* assume that the reader is busy and wants to read your letter as quickly as possible. Do not waste time with digressions, unnecessary details, or needlessly technical language.
- ◆ *Suggest the next step.* Do not leave readers wondering what you want them to do. Airline officials who deal with customer complaints often comment on the number of letters they receive that make no mention of redress or compensation. After a page of detailed complaints about a flight, the

customer does not leave the airline with any sense of what he actually wants, such as a refund, another ticket, or a new suitcase. If you need action by a specific date, be sure to include the deadline.

✦ *Proofread.* Check spelling, grammar, and sense.
✦ *Proofread again.*
✦ *Appearance.* Business letters are always typed. Use letterhead paper and mail them in envelopes with a return address. The only handwriting should be your signature.

And remember, letters have the potential to become part of the organization's permanent records (files or archives). They are usually driven by the organization's need to explain or document its decisions and to retain a "paper trail" or "electronic trail" of these decisions or actions. Be aware of this permanence and of any possible secondary readership when you write anything related to your employer. This may guide some style and content decisions.

Memos

Think of memos as mail sent internally; with rare exceptions, memos do not go outside the organization. For this reason, most recipients will be familiar with the sender, the topic, and the context of the memo, thereby making detail and elaboration unnecessary.

In terms of format and style, memos are the simplest of all written communication. The headings are clear, the content brief and to the point, and the length seldom longer than one physical page. Memos may be informative or persuasive. They are used for internal business such as announcing new policies or holiday schedules or urging employees to take advantage of free cholesterol testing or to pick up their tax forms. Typically, the memo advises staff how and where to obtain detailed information rather than providing it in the memo itself.

Memos can be sent to individuals, posted on a bulletin board or intranet, or put on a circulation list so some employees see the memo before others. Enclosing them with employee paychecks is an effective distribution mechanism for memos sent to all employees.

Many people complain about an (over-) abundance of memos and e-mail. Because this may result in indifference or information overload, you cannot assume that receivers will automatically read your memo. It helps to be conscious of the potential for grabbing readers' attention through typography, borders, or making the sender's name very obvious. With mail merge as a standard word processing tool, there is no reason in principle that memos sent to a mailing list cannot be individualized for each recipient. Some organizations have a system of color-coded memos to distinguish urgent from routine from social, for example.

Memo Style

As shown in Exhibit 8.5, memo headings are always "Date:" "To:" "From:" and "Subject (Re:)." The order and layout of the headings will be a matter of house style. In the absence of such guidelines, most word processing software has memo templates that prompt you through memo creation. Because many people file memos by date, we suggest having the date at the top as with a business letter.

Memos are not signed. Instead, the writer acknowledges authorship by initialing next to his or her name in the "From" heading.

EXHIBIT 8.5   Sample memo on the subject of smileys and emoticons for e-mail.

Date: January 10, 2005
To: Martin T. Supervisor
From: Susan P. R. Writer
Re: Suitability of "smileys" for professional e-mail

It is my opinion that encouraging the use of emoticons (also called "smileys") and particularly e-mail shorthand such as "ROFL" is not consistent with professional communication. I understand that their aim is to support text in the way gestures and facial expressions augment speech—for example, the smiley face ☺. However, because they are not universally accepted or understood, they have the potential to be seen as disrespectful and unprofessional. Furthermore, they demand extra work on the part of the reader to interpret them. I believe they interfere with rather than support the message.

Accordingly, I suggest we make it clear to all staff that the use of "smileys" should be reserved for personal e-mail only.

Please advise. Thank you.

As with all other communications, the level of formality is determined by your relationship with the recipient (i.e., your public) and the seriousness of the topic (your purpose). Memos sent to senior management are likely to be filed as part of the organization's official records. They should reflect your professionalism, with full sentences and careful explanations. In contrast, memos sent to your fellow social club committee members may be casual, even conversational.

Do not, however, fall into the trap of thinking that informal equals unimportant. Memos may be simple and informal, as in "I am confirming our meeting on May 21st at 4 p.m. in the conference room; see you there." Or they may be as formal as the "smileys" memo provided as Exhibit 8.5.

E-mail

We have already discussed e-mail and the Internet as research tools. E-mail also has potential for employee, client, and media communication and allows text, graphic, audio, and video files to be sent as e-mail attachments and viewed or listened to by any receiver who has the software and systems to access them. E-mail makes possible the electronic distribution of news releases via such services as Business Wire and PR Newswire. And e-mail to discussion groups such as PRForum allows public relations writers to seek advice or provide information worldwide.

The appeal of e-mail is clearly seen in the fact that most people have it. Even those who do not have access directly often have it indirectly through friends, relatives, or businesses.

Undeniably, e-mail has many benefits. It can be instantaneous or nearly so, allowing you to respond to questions—even across the country—in real time. It is as easy to send mail to 100 people as to one. You can keep a record of both outgoing and incoming mail, and you can sort or search e-mail instantly by date, topic, recipient, or sender. "Address books" make it possible to prepare e-mail for distribution without having to remember cumbersome addresses. It is even possible to configure mailers to strip out those long headers or to put them at the bottom of the incoming message so you can go straight to the message itself.

A primary benefit of e-mail is its ability to link people in their own time. You can send a message at your convenience, confident that receivers will be able to log on and receive it at their convenience. This is useful for keeping in touch with people whose availability for phone calls is uncertain and/or when time zone differences make personal contact inconvenient. From many recipients' viewpoints, e-mail, especially for messages that do not require a response, helps avert the phone calls that punctuate and interrupt a business day.

For the public relations writer, e-mail has enormous potential for collaborative writing and long-distance client servicing. Draft speeches, releases, or even publication layouts can be sent to colleagues in any corner of the world to be reviewed/revised and returned. It is also changing the way we think about client servicing as your clients can be geographically diverse and as public relations consultants from outside your area can just as readily prospect for your clients.

This is not to say that e-mail is without problems. Attorneys may advise you not to use it for legal documents, instead requiring traditional hard copies that can be put physically in the recipient's hands. Also consider that e-mail is not available to everyone and that not everyone likes or wants to use it. Many people do not like to read material on screen, especially long documents, and while it is true that they can print hard copies, it seems presumptuous to require them to do the work.

In a recent study (*Can-Spam Act*, 2004), many people reported reducing their e-mail use because of the increase in spam. Nearly two-thirds reported that spam made them less trusting of e-mail. Clearly, the success of antispam legislation will play a role in your decisions about using e-mail as a medium for sending messages externally.

Many managers complain that e-mail has resulted in a proliferation of unnecessary and time-consuming copies of e-mail. Just because you *can* copy your boss on every e-mail you send doesn't mean you should. To the contrary, you can increase the likelihood of a recipient reading your messages if you have the reputation of only sending messages that are important.

From the privacy point of view, be aware that your e-mail may leave an "electronic paper trail" that potentially may be part of judicial proceedings. For example, the question has arisen of what now constitutes a meeting. If the trustees of a state university discuss issues by e-mail, are they holding a meeting in violation of state sunshine laws and can the media demand access to records of the e-mail exchanges?

Style Considerations for E-mail

Perhaps the major drawback with regard to e-mail is style. Most e-mail is mercifully brief. But for some writers, the prospect of sending an electronic rather than hard-copy memo results in a spur-of-the-moment, stream-of-consciousness style that resembles neither news nor feature in style, nor much else in structure. Except in a few, very informal corporate cultures, stream-of-consciousness style is not appropriate for business communications.

With regard to quality, two issues are important: First, the informality of e-mail is often inconsistent with a professional image. Second, if visual layout is important (and we argue that it should be), be aware that you have little control over whether the recipient can even open the message, much less view it in all its well-designed glory.

Although e-mail seems ideal for quick messages, one-line comments and notes that you can leave on another computer for the user to read as time permits, this brevity may lead to an informality that is less than professional. And, of course, if you need a paper trail to support what you actually said, send a memo.

The issue of design is one of software and system compatibility. The only way you can be certain that your receiver will see exactly what you send is to know that the receiver has an identical system to yours, including the same browser/version and software. If the user has to resort to "plug-ins," the result may or may not look like your original document. If appearance is important, it is wise to assume the reader does not have compatible software and instead to send a short e-mail alerting the reader that you are sending a fax of the formatted document.

As a sender, you have some control over capitalization and paragraphing, but your control over design techniques such as typeface, boldface, underscores, or special characters that you normally use to add emphasis varies with the e-mail program. Special characters may print out on different systems as completely unrelated letters or numbers. Such issues become especially important when sending—or receiving—any type of graphic content, including PowerPoint presentations.

One way of recapturing some of the expression you can achieve in print with boldface and italics is through the use of what are termed "emoticons" or "smileys." These combinations of standard typographic symbols and punctuation marks are used to give the text some emotional overtones as in :-) designating the classic happy face. There is an e-mail shorthand in which acronyms substitute for frequently used phrases; for example, ROFL and IMHOP, respectively, mean "rolling on the floor laughing" and "in my humble opinion." As you can see from the sample memo (Exhibit 8.5), opinion is divided regarding the place of such netspeak in professional communications. We point out that these options are available, but they are far from universal. We suggest that you err on the safe side and reserve them for personal communications when you know the recipient speaks the same e-mail "language" that you speak.

DISCUSSION 2

The acceptability and conventions of e-mail are closely related to an organization's culture. Consider the cultures of your college or university, a large hospital, a bank, and a new software development company to answer the following questions.

Which do you think would be most likely to endorse, even encourage e-mail? Which would be least likely to do so? Why? What correlation can you see between the culture you assume these organizations will have and the attitudes to e-mail you identified above? What purposes do you think each of them would use e-mail for?

Reports (other than annual reports)

Reports will be a way of life for many public relations writers, especially as you progress into communications strategy and management. You will write reports to propose new public relations activities, to update management (or a client) on the progress of a project, and to present the results of your public relations work.

In many large organizations, report format and sometimes style are dictated by the house style to ensure that all departments provide consistent information in a consistent format. Other organizations have no such restrictions, although the following three types are generally accepted as comprehensive ways of presenting material.

Basic Reports

The basic report format is simple: introduction, body, and conclusion. It parallels a basic speech formula described as "tell them what you're going to tell them, tell them, and then tell them what you just told them." The busy reader needs to know what it is about, relevant details, and your conclusions/recommendations.

Keep in mind that there are conventions in report structure that audiences need and that your purpose should dictate. While "Introduction, Body, Conclusion" is common, "Introduction, Conclusion, Body" may save a reader time, and "Conclusion, Introduction, Body" may save a busy executive even more time.

Expanded Reports

As a public relations professional, you may write expanded reports when proposing a new budget or a public relations plan or when reporting the results and evaluation of your public relations work. It includes more detail about the process leading up to the report and, because it may be relatively long, it also typically includes a clearly marked "Executive Summary" to give the busy reader a preview of the report.

Research or Technical Reports

Research reports present the results of research done by you or a consultant on issues that affect your employer. Research results are usually written up in a format that includes a review of literature and the research question, hypothesis, and methodology. They may conclude with extensive resource lists and appendixes to clarify or provide greater detail. One of your jobs may well be to rewrite such a technical report into a public relations plan or proposal, a summary document for management, or a simplified document for a general readership.

The research report format is often very detailed and oriented toward formal research. True research reports seldom deviate from this format, which is well established in scholarly circles. Although public relations writers may produce a report with this level of detail, such as when they conduct a formal reader survey, in most cases public relations research reports omit the sections on literature review, research question or hypothesis, and citations. The format will be much closer to the expanded report format but with the inclusion of the research methods.

You may also have to produce progress reports for projects or research unfolding over a period of time, and end-of-project or evaluation reports when the project ends. All can usually follow the expanded report format.

EXERCISE 1

Read a research report from *Public Relations Review* or *Public Relations Quarterly*. What are the major headings? Why do you think the report is formatted the way it is? How would the report need to be rewritten to attract attention from the news media?

Report Style

Almost without exception, report style is direct, factual, and relatively formal. This does not mean the report must be filled with big words and long, complicated thoughts. To the contrary, it should be written in an easy-to-read style devoid of adjectives and descriptive phrases. If the report uses jargon unique to your employer's industry, consider either explaining each term the first time it appears and/or providing a glossary of terms to assist readers who are not familiar with the contents and terms.

Even interested readers seldom have the time to read long reports, so the writer's challenge is to help readers quickly find and absorb the information that is important to them while also communicating what is most important to the writer—a typical public relations challenge.

Many readers never go deeper than the executive summary and/or the conclusions and recommendations. They are willing to assume the methodology is professional or to leave criticism of it to those with more expertise. Their primary questions are, "What does this mean?" "What should I/we do as the result of this report?" and possibly "What will this cost?" Consider addressing all of these issues in your conclusions.

Readers will be helped by an obvious structure in the body of the report. The narrative structure should make it clear whether you are presenting a pro/con view of marketing options, describing the history of a campaign, or introducing new technology that you want the organization to adopt. Use heads and subheads to guide the reader through the structure.

Executive summary. The executive summary, referred to as an abstract in academic and technical writing, is basically a "report at a glance." It should include all of the key points including the conclusions. The executive summary is *not* the introduction to the report; it is simply a quick recap of the highlights.

Writing an executive summary is a good exercise in focusing your thinking to key issues and in condensing your writing. It is also a good place to make use of the bullet point techniques we introduced in Chapter 2 and that we return to again and again as a valuable technique for public relations writing.

Stylistic devices. Take advantage of stylistic devices to make reports easy to follow and digest. Devices that have been used successfully include starting each chapter with a short summary and printing key phrases in the margins to attract attention and act as a road map through the subject matter—a variation on the pull quotes discussed in Chapter 7. And, of course, bullet points make even the most complex information appear manageable.

Even titles can help the reader find the important points of a report and help you send public relations messages about the report. The report title should make it clear what the report is about and the chapter and section titles should be equally descriptive.

D I S C U S S I O N   3

Following are four examples of titles for a report on a public relations research project. What differences can you determine among the titles? What benefits does each one have?

✦ The ABC Company Public Awareness Campaign
✦ A Review of Progress in the ABC Company Public Awareness Campaign
✦ Results of a Survey of the ABC Company Public Image
✦ Media Coverage of ABC Company by Frequency and Type of Mention, 1st Quarter 2005

Fact Sheets, Backgrounders, Boilerplates, and Bios

As you learn about the organization for which you are writing, you may be asked to produce some of the basic support documents that organizations keep on hand. They include such informational documents as fact sheets, backgrounders, and bios of organizational VIPs. As long as the information is current, the organization can distribute them in display units, send them out in response to queries for information, and include them in media kits, which we will discuss in greater detail in Chapter 9.

Fact sheets and *backgrounders* are general-purpose documents that provide routine information about an organization or issue and that answer the most anticipated questions about the organization or issue. *Bios* are fact sheets about people.

Traditionally, single- or double-page printed documents, fact sheets, backgrounders, and bios have made a natural and easy transition to the World Wide Web, which is increasingly positioned—and used—as a source of information. Especially valuable to many organizations is the fact that the Web can accommodate technical specifications and price lists, both of which can change rapidly, as well as audio and video content and interactive capabilities. All of these can be implemented (or not) to suit a web site visitor's needs.

Even topic- or audience-specific fact sheets have a home on the Web. Although they may be coded into HTML (the language of the Web), they are often presented as .pdf (portable document format) files that users can download and print for easy reference. Because .pdf files retain the formatting of the original document, text, layout, graphics, and photographs remain intact without special programming and formatting. So even though we deal with them as "documents," the thinking about purpose, content, and general presentation of fact sheets will not change even if you are developing them with the Web in mind.

Fact Sheets

One of the beauties of fact sheets is their multipurpose nature; you can develop fact sheets about the organization as a whole as well as fact sheets about specific programs, products, or activities. Audiences for general-purpose fact sheets range from new employees to visitors to media representatives at a press conference to students writing for information for a school report. At special events such as the opening of a new facility, you may develop special fact sheets with answers to what you anticipate will be the most commonly asked questions.

In the investment community, fact sheets are well defined. They are high-quality, glossy, full-color documents produced with the aim of attracting investments. In addition to information about the company, its products or services, and perhaps executives, such fact sheets typically include growth statistics and an overview of the company's financial status. The SEC monitors them closely for accuracy and false claims.

Many organizations also develop fact sheets for each of their products, programs, or audiences. This is a simple, often inexpensive way to provide information for specific publics with specific interests. For example, in addition to its corporate fact sheet, Texas Instruments, Inc. (TI) has a series of fact sheets dedicated to—in increasingly targeted focus—its commitment to education, to higher education, and to higher education in Texas, the company's home. TI has similar fact sheets to support its commitment to the community, the environment, and minority opportunity development.

Another way to look at fact sheets is by audience or public. Public relations writers for pharmaceutical companies may find themselves shaping the same information into fact sheets for physicians, nurses, parents, and perhaps even children.

Because they are relatively easy to produce and can often double as introductory brochures, fact sheets are common even to small organizations.

Developing general-purpose fact sheets. When developing a general fact sheet, it may be useful to ask yourself the question: "What 10 topics would I cover if I were giving a 5- or 10-minute speech introducing the organization to the local chamber of commerce?" Your answers might include the organization's mission or vision, age, form of ownership, size, activities, geographic operations, products or services, and social involvement with the community. These are all good topics for general-purpose fact sheets. Start by listing these topics and continue by fleshing them out with one or two facts from the organization's history or operations.

Fact sheets have traditionally taken a question-and-answer format, and this is certainly acceptable especially if the purpose is to answer questions for the press. But they may also take a "5W+H" (who, what, when, where, why, and how) or chronological format, or set out brief technical specifications of a new product or facility.

The first pages from the Federal Emergency Management Agency (FEMA) booklet-format fact sheet shown as Exhibit 8.6 demonstrate some typical fact sheet content and treatment. It begins with a description of FEMA, its mission, and a bulleted list of its activities. Additional pages describe FEMA programs in greater detail and list the FEMA regional offices. It proves that fact sheets have moved well beyond the standard single-page flat-sheet format.

In support of this agency-focused fact sheet, FEMA also produces fact sheets on the hazards that the agency typically deals with, including earthquake, wildfire, floods, terrorism, and more than a dozen others. These fact sheets provide guidelines for public action in the event of such a hazard, answering the question of "what do I do now?"

Part of your challenge as a public relations writer often will be turning what could be a list of technical specifications understood only by industry specialists into interesting statistics the public can understand and identify with. For example, when it was launched in January 2004, the *Queen Mary 2* was the largest passenger ship ever built. What does that mean? ABC News (2004) described it in terms familiar to its U.S. audience—"almost as long as the Empire State Building is high, more than twice the length of Seattle's Space Needle, and longer than four football fields . . . a quarter of a mile from bow to stern." Looking at the comparisons more globally, the ship's owners describe its length in relation to the Washington Monument, the Eiffel Tower, Big Ben, and "41 double-decker London buses" (Cunard Line, 2004). These are good examples of selecting facts to suit the target audience. Any of them would be appropriate in a fact sheet about the giant liner.

DISCUSSION 4

Recent research (McCabe, 2001) indicates that

✦ more than 30% of college students admit to repetitive serious cheating on exams
✦ 15% have submitted a paper obtained in large part from a term paper mill or web site
✦ 52% have copied a few sentences from a web site without citing the source

For your campus, relate each of these to the population of dorms, the size of departments, the capacity of a classroom/gym/auditorium/cafeteria, and the number of students receiving awards at commencement.

EXHIBIT 8.6   Sample pages and excerpts from the text of the fact sheet of the Federal Emergency Management Agency (FEMA).

What is FEMA?

FEMA is an independent federal agency with about 2,500 full-time employees stationed in Washington, D.C., and across the country, and nearly 4,000 standby disaster assistance employees who are available to help out after disasters.

FEMA's mission is to:

reduce the loss of life and property and protect our nation's critical infrastructure from all types of hazards, through a comprehensive emergency management program of risk reduction, preparedness, response and recovery.

While FEMA was not created until 1979, it can trace its beginnings to 1803, when the first disaster legislation was passed, to provide assistance to a New Hampshire town following an extensive fire. FEMA was formed by executive order from the many separate disaster-related functions and agencies that had existed previously.

The new agency developed an all-hazards approach that treated civil defense and natural hazards preparedness as similar emergencies. Since its creation, FEMA has responded to hundreds of disasters in all 50 states, Puerto Rico, Guam, the Pacific Island Trust Territories and the U.S. Virgin Islands.

What does FEMA do?

One way to look at what FEMA does is to think about the disaster cycle. Emergency managers prepare for emergencies and disasters, respond to them when they occur, help people and institutions recover from them, work to reduce future risk of losses and prevent disasters, when possible, from occurring in the first place.

Some specific things FEMA does:

• Work with state and local officials to determine the scope of the disaster and essential needs in the impacted area;
• Create and staff federal/state Disaster Field Offices and coordinate with other federal agencies under the Federal Response Plan;
• Make disaster aid available;
• Educate the public about preparing for and reducing risk from disasters;
• Fund emergency planning in all 50 states;
• Sponsor emergency preparedness exercises;
• Train firefighters and set firefighting standards;
• Administer the National Flood Insurance Program;
• Credential urban search and rescue teams;
• Develop consequent management plans for domestic terrorism.

This is FEMA

Disaster can strike at any time, anywhere. They can be an act of nature or an act of terrorism. They can strike suddenly, or build over days and weeks before bringing catastrophe. No matter how they come, disasters put millions of Americans in danger every year, and destroy billions of dollars worth of property. But every year, FEMA employees are there — helping communities reduce their risk, helping emergency officials prepare for the inevitable or helping people get back on their feet after their lives are torn apart.

What is FEMA?

FEMA is an independent federal agency with about 2,500 full-time employees stationed in Washington, D.C., and across the country, and nearly 4,000 standby disaster assistance employees who are available to help out after disasters.

FEMA's mission is to:

reduce the loss of life and property and protect our nation's critical infrastructure from all types of hazards, through a comprehensive emergency management program of risk reduction, preparedness, response and recovery . . . Since its creation, FEMA has responded to hundreds of disasters in all 50 states, Puerto Rico, Guam, the Pacific Island Trust Territories and the U.S. Virgin Islands.

What does FEMA do?

One way to look at what FEMA does is to think about the disaster cycle. Emergency managers prepare for emergencies and disasters, respond to them when they occur, help people and institutions recover from them, work to reduce future risk of losses and prevent disasters, when possible, from occurring in the first place.
Some specific things FEMA does:
• Work with state/local officials to determine . . . essential needs in impacted area;
• Make disaster aid available;
• Educate the public about preparing for and reducing risk from disasters;
• Sponsor emergency preparedness exercises;
• Train firefighters and set firefighting standards;

Partnerships

FEMA doesn't do its important work alone; it works with 26 other agencies that are part of the Federal Response Plan, ranging from the U.S. Small Business Administration to the Department of Defense.

Disaster Myths

Myth 1: A disaster will never happen to me.
Myth 2: If a disaster does happen, there's nothing I can do about it.
Reality: Upwards of a million Americans a year learn that disasters DO happen. Every state in the U.S. is at risk for some natural disaster, and all are at risk for manmade disasters. But you CAN do something about preventing damage and safeguarding lives. FEMA wants everyone to be knowledgeable about the risks they face and what measures to take. For more information, visit the FEMA web site, at www.fema.gov.

FEMA's Regions (10 listed)

Backgrounders

Although sometimes interchangeable with fact sheets, backgrounders have more defined purposes and audiences. Backgrounders are written for people who want or need more information on a subject. They typically include more details, statistics, and possibly technical jargon if your target audience will understand it.

From the public relations writer's viewpoint, backgrounders are often written for reporters seeking additional information to understand your industry or as background for a story. For example, FEMA supports each of its "hazards" fact sheets with a backgrounder on the hazard itself. Whereas the fact sheet on "terrorism" focuses on preparation and response, the supporting backgrounder deals with terrorism in general, including facts about chemical and biological weapons, terrorism prior to September 11, 2001, and terrorism in the United States. Reporters might easily seek such information to flesh out articles they are writing. Similarly, they might turn to the tables of statistics on recycling aluminum cans provided as backgrounders by the Aluminum Association.

Backgrounders may also take a more historical slant than fact sheets to explain how the organization, product, or service has evolved and to help the reader understand the relationship of the new product or service to the industry or society. Historical backgrounders are often developed as time lines. The U.S. Food and Drug Administration (FDA) distributes a historically oriented backgrounder, "Milestones in Food and Drug Law History." It reviews legislation from 1820 and could be easily used as an index of laws by writers seeking an understanding of the topic.

Fact sheets and backgrounders as public relations documents. While grounded in information, both fact sheets and backgrounders are part of an organization's persuasive strategy to develop relationships. Even when you are providing information, you are doing so with a purpose related to the organization's goals. It is your choice, for example, what topics to include and what facts and examples you choose to support them. As important, it is your choice to use words that support the organization's image and overall message.

Fact sheets typically focus on organizational strengths and identify unique attributes to differentiate the organization from its competitors. Choose examples that position the organization as uniquely worth developing a relationship with.

As important as choosing examples is your ability to organize them effectively. Even multipage fact sheets address only three or four key issues. But if the issues are clearly identified (by headings and graphic treatments) and the examples are convincing, the fact sheet will have done its job of providing basic information. Remember, fact sheets are generally not aimed at the already committed but rather at newcomers to the organization. And since information (knowledge) is the first step in the process of persuasion, the role of the fact sheet as an introduction should not be underestimated.

Boilerplate Descriptions

A variation of the fact sheet is the single-paragraph description often referred to as a *boilerplate*. The boilerplate describes in about 100 words what the organization is and does, that is, it summarizes a general fact sheet. It includes such information as the organization's years in operation, address and/or locations, business structure (e.g., public corporation, partnership), size, and activities.

While the boilerplate may have some promotional or persuasive elements, it is first and foremost a statement of facts. Its purpose is to provide a snapshot of the organization to quickly answer the questions, "What does the organization do?" and ideally "How does it stand out from similar or competing organizations?"

Because you may not be able to anticipate all possible uses for such a paragraph, it should be written broadly and at a level to be understood by a very wide audience. Because boilerplate paragraphs frequently are used in news releases, they must also meet media criteria for brevity, accuracy, and fact.

Organizations use boilerplate paragraphs at the end of news releases, in conference programs, and in brochures and flyers, that is, whenever a brief description of the organization is needed. When accompanying media releases, they provide the reporter and editor with information about the organization that is not included in the release. When used in conference programs, they help attendees select vendors with services of interest.

Recognizing that the use for boilerplates varies greatly, theme park Six Flags New England provides four versions of a boilerplate as part of its standard media kit. This "editorial description" is shown as Exhibit 8.7. The versions range from a simple location statement, to 30-, 50- and 100-word boilerplate descriptions. This helps ensure that a description acceptable to Six Flags can be used regardless of the space or time available.

Like the fact sheet and backgrounder, even the humble boilerplate has a public relations aim. Boilerplates present a special challenge as you choose words and phrasing even more carefully to achieve that aim in one paragraph.

EXERCISE 2

Using the two pages of the FEMA fact sheet in Exhibit 8.6 as a basis, write a boilerplate paragraph that FEMA might use at the end of media releases. Consider whether FEMA would also be able to use it as a description in the program of trade shows it might attend. Why would it be appropriate? Why not?

The Bio (biography)

Bios (biographies) are fact sheets about people, and like fact sheets they are common components of media kits and web sites. Bios usually take one of three forms: the data sheet, the straight chronological bio, and the narrative bio.

The first is the information that employees provide on joining the organization or that public relations writers compile in liaison with the human resources office when an employee is promoted to a position that will be publicly prominent. Data sheets typically include date of hire, position(s) within the company, educational qualifications, and civic activities and memberships. Data sheets are not for public distribution but, with the consent of the employee, can be used to answer media inquiries or to flesh out a media release involving the individual. Many colleges and universities have incoming students complete data sheets (including parents' names and local newspapers) that allow the institutions to distribute articles about students to their local press, subject to the legal constraints of the Family Education Rights and Privacy Act (FERPA), of course.

EXHIBIT 8.7   Editorial descriptions used as part of the Six Flags New England media kit.

Six Flags New England

EDITORIAL DESCRIPTION

Contact: Mary Ann Stebbins ~ Marketing Communications Manager ~ (413) 786-9300, ext 3358

30-Word Description

Six Flags New England in Agawam Massachusetts is New England's largest Theme Park featuring eight roller coasters plus **Hurricane Harbor** Water Park. Call (413) 786-9300 or www.sixflags.com for more information.

50-Word Description

Six Flags in Agawam Massachusetts, New England's largest theme park, features the expanded **Hurricane Harbor** Water Park with a wave pool, nine slides and more. One low price includes all rides includes the water park, eight roller coasters, spectacular shows and most attractions. Call (413) 786-9300 or log on www.sixflags.com.

100-Word Description

Six Flags is located in Agawam Massachusetts and is New England's largest theme and water park featuring the expanded **Hurricane Harbor** with over one dozen new attractions including a second wave pool, nine cool new slides, a kids area and more.

Check out eight super thrilling, high lifting roller coasters including **Batman-The Dark Knight**, and **Superman-Ride of Steel**. Enjoy entertaining shows like the **Batman Thrill Spectacular**, attractions, restaurants and gift shops. It's two great parks for one low price. Open weekends April 19-Memorial Day, daily through Labor Day and weekends November 2. Call (413) 786-9300 or log on to www.sixflagscom.

Location

Six Flags is located on Route 159 (Main Street) in Agawam, MA, between Springfield and Hartford. Just 30 minutes from Hartford and 90 minutes from Boston.

Source: Reproduced with permission from Six Flags New England.

If written up as a backgrounder, the data sheet will likely be a chronological listing of the subject's career, education, and related activities. Chronological bios share concept and format with the standard résumé. They are often included in media kits, providing reporters with background information about organizational VIPs and possibly guest speakers. The bio serves as raw material for the reporter's story.

Not all bios follow this "just the facts" style. Rather, many are "featurized" with color or quotes or develop themes in a narrative style. This is often at the expense of detailed attention to comprehensiveness, dates, and places. Narrative bios tell a story and usually introduce the subject as a person rather than just reciting the facts. You might, for example, use a personal quote from the CEO on her philosophy of customer service or write a brief summary of projects she led in order to give readers an understanding of her interests and how she works.

This brings up the question of how much personal information to include in a bio. The answer depends on the purpose of the bio and the personality of the subject. "Official" bios of company directors written for the annual report will focus entirely on business activities. Bios of the same executives for a new-employee orientation package may be both more informal and more personal to reflect the organization's employee-friendly culture.

Narrative bios are also written as introductions for guest speakers or award recipients.

To see the differences in bio style, compare the excerpts from the NASA biographies of three of the most famous U.S. astronauts, Neil Armstrong, Scott Carpenter, and Sally Ride shown as Exhibit 8.8. Although much of the Armstrong bio is written in full sentences, it nevertheless has the feel of a data sheet, simply firing facts at the reader as quickly as possible. You should be able to imagine the same information being presented in bullet-point format.

In contrast, the Carpenter bio, which is entirely narrative, has the feel of a life story. The opening paragraph establishes a theme and grabs the reader's attention. It avoids the technical jargon common to most other NASA bios, substituting reader-friendly terms such as propeller-driven fighters, attack planes, and seaplanes. You might be able to "hear" this bio being used to introduce Carpenter at an award ceremony.

As the first woman in space, Ride became a role model for American girls and has cultivated a "user friendly," approachable image. She is often quoted on space issues and has a reputation for educating through her public appearances. The personal details at the beginning of her bio reflect this willingness to be seen as a person rather than just as an astronaut.

Bios as Public Relations Documents

Remember that even informal bios say something about the organization and that in doing so they are part of your public relations message. They also say something about the audiences. The bios of executives of companies listed on the stock exchange focus clearly on their experience and expertise—aiming at shareholders and potential shareholders seeking information that will affect their investment decisions. Bios for the same people sitting on the board of a nonprofit might emphasize their leadership in community and philanthropic programs. This time, the target might be the decision makers of funding organizations who want assurance that the nonprofit is managed effectively and responsibly. The essential message is the same for both the corporation and nonprofit, but the evidence used to support the message will be very different.

You may well have several bios on hand for the organization's VIPs, each with a special emphasis for a particular audience.

DISCUSSION 5

It is likely that your college or university public relations department maintains a file of bios on campus spokespersons. Whose bios would you expect to find in that file? Who might have multiple bios? Why? For what purpose would these bios be used?

EXHIBIT 8.8 **Excerpts from the bios of National Aeronautics and Space Administration (NASA) astronauts Neil Armstrong, Scott Carpenter, and Sally Ride.**

Excerpts From NASA Astronaut Bios

Neil A. Armstrong

Personal Data: Born August 5, 1930 in Wapakoneta, Ohio. Married. Two sons.

Education: [B.S.] degree in aeronautical engineering from Purdue University; [M.S.] degree in aerospace engineering from University of Southern California. He holds honorary doctorates from a number of universities.

Special Honors: He is the recipient of many special honors, including the Presidential Medal for Freedom in 1969; . . . and the Congressional Space Medal of Honor, 1978.

Experience: From 1949 to 1952, he served as a naval aviator; he flew 78 combat missions during the Korean War. During 1971-1979, Armstrong was professor of aerospace engineering at the University of Cincinnati. . . . Currently serves as Chairman, AIL Systems, Inc. Deer Park, N.Y. [continued]

Scott Carpenter

Scott Carpenter, a dynamic pioneer of modern exploration, has the unique distinction of being the first human ever to penetrate both inner and outer space, thereby acquiring the dual title, Astronaut/Aquanaut.

He was born in Boulder, Colorado, on May 1, 1925, the son of. . . . He attended the University of Colorado from 1945 to 1949 and received a [B.S.] degree in Aeronautical Engineering.

Carpenter was commissioned in the U.S. Navy in 1949. . . . During the Korean War he served with patrol Squadron Six, flying anti-submarine, ship surveillance, and aerial mining, and ferret missions in the Yellow Sea, . . . He attended the Navy Test Pilot School and . . . flew tests in every type of naval aircraft, including multi- and single-engine jet and propeller-driven fighters, attack planes, patrol bombers, transports, and seaplanes. . . .

. . . On leave of absence from NASA, Carpenter participated in the Navy's Man-in the-Sea Project as an Aquanaut in the SEALAB II program. . . . During the 45-day experiment, Carpenter spent 30 days living and working on the ocean floor. [continued]

Sally K Ride (Ph.D.)

Personal Data: Born May 26, 1951, in Los Angeles, California. Her parents, Dr. and Mrs. Dale B. Ride, reside in Encino, California. She enjoys tennis (having been an instructor and having achieved national ranking as a junior), running, volleyball, softball & stamp collecting. . . .

. . . Dr. Ride has written a children's book, *To Space and Back*, describing her experiences in space, has received the Jefferson Award for Public Service, and has twice been awarded the National Spaceflight Medal. [continued]

Note: The full bios of these and all other NASA astronauts can be found on the web site of the Johnson Space Center, http://www .jsc.nasa.gov/people.

ON THE TEXTBOOK WEB SITE

✦ Go to www.sagepub.com/treadwell for web exercises, study hints, case studies, and additional examples appropriate to this chapter and chosen or developed to supplement the chapter content.

WRITING WRAP-UP

The campus organization you worked for in the "Writing Wrap-Up" in Chapters 5 and 7 requires a boilerplate paragraph that can be in the campus viewbook and on its web site, and a fact sheet for the new-student orientation packet.

1. Write the boilerplate paragraph.

2. Write and design a one-page fact sheet.

3. Also write a covering letter to the head of the organization briefly explaining the documents and seeking approval for their use.

REFERENCES

ABC News. (2004, January 20). *World's largest cruise ship set for first transatlantic luxury voyage*. Retrieved January 26, 2004, from http://www.cruisemates.com/articles/CMpress/ABCNEWS_com,%20January%2013,2004–1.htm

Can-Spam Act has not helped most email users so far. (2004, March 17). Research report, Pew Internet & American Life Project. Retrieved March 19, 2004, from http://www.pewinternet.org/reports/toc.asp?Report=116

Cunard Line. (2004). *About QM2, ship facts, some comparisons*. Retrieved January 26, 2004, from http://www.qm2-uk.com/

McCabe, D. (2001, November). *An overview of research on academic integrity*. Keynote address, Center for Academic Integrity, Texas A&M University.

RESOURCES

Featured Organizations

FDA	www.fda.gov
FEMA	www.fema.gov
NASA	www.nasa.gov
Six Flags New England	www.sixflags.com

Out of Your Control . . . or Is It?

Newswriting for the Press

1. **The media are looking for news. Public relations is a large and valid source.**

2. **Ensure that your news is really news; don't waste the media's time.**

3. **News releases *can* carry public relations messages.**

4. **Following journalism standards for topic, style, and format will maximize the likelihood of having your release printed.**

5. **Cultivating personal and positive relationships with the media will pay off.**

6. **If you help the media do their jobs, they may help you do yours.**

1. **News releases for the press—from choice of topic to style and format.**

2. **Pitch letters and media advisories—maximizing media coverage.**

Underlying all chapters in this book is the principle that all communication should serve a strategic purpose to foster beneficial, two-way relationships for an organization. The issuance of a news release is no exception. From a public relations writing point of view, the reason to issue a news release is that doing so fits your communication plan and will effectively help you meet the organization's goals. This is assuming, as we discussed in Chapter 8, that the news media are appropriate to your audience, your communication purpose, and your willingness to risk loss of control, especially over timing and content. News releases should be an option when the following are true.

♦ *Immediacy is important.* If you need to reach an audience that is served by an identifiable daily medium, placing a story in that medium will let you get the news out within hours or days of your writing it.

♦ *You don't need control of timing.* Releases based on other news determinants, particularly human interest, proximity, or possibly rarity or the bizarre, often have no *immediate* news value but nevertheless qualify as "news."

This lack of timeliness may be an advantage because the media often keep these stories on file and use them when they have space or time. Weekend TV news broadcasts and the Sunday paper typically include many more "soft" news stories than might be used during the week when business interests usually fill the extra space or time.

♦ *You can afford to risk the loss of control over content.* It is likely that an editor will change the content of a release to fit available space and time or to meet other media requirements for brevity, neutrality, and accuracy. Most stories can be edited without loss of information value, especially if the story is written in inverted-pyramid style that puts the most important information at the top. In such cases, the mass media are indisputably a cost-effective way to reach large numbers of people simultaneously.

However, in some cases the loss of control to the news editor is something you cannot or do not want to risk. A release on a breakthrough product may prompt an editor to invite comment from your competitors, to bury the story in a regional roundup, or to preface the story with the organization's technological failure a year ago. In such cases, releasing the news to the media may not be the best strategy for reaching your publics. You might opt instead or as well to use a newsletter, mailer, or web site to ensure that no one "messes with the message."

Generally, there are two types of writing for the mass media: news (including press and broadcast) and feature. Newswriting is done by the media's own reporters and correspondents and by public relations writers employed by businesses and organizations. Feature stories may be based on an idea from a public relations writer but they are usually researched and written or delivered by a media staff member. This is not to suggest that public relations writers do not write feature stories, but rather that their features are as likely to be used in controlled media such as newsletters, annual reports, and specific, targeted trade publications as in the news media. For this reason, we will deal with feature writing in Chapter 10.

This chapter focuses on newswriting as a means of disseminating information that your organization wants (or in some cases is required by law or regulations) to disseminate. Usually, this will be good news, the story of a successful project or person. Sometimes it will be routine such as the annual releases issued by colleges to their graduates' local press, and in other cases—it is hoped, rare—it will be negative, even of crisis proportions.

It is true that editors and journalists in both the press and broadcast arenas view material from a public relations source as potentially biased—as well they should. Some would argue that public relations writing *should* be biased; after all, public relations writers have a responsibility to promote their employers and are evaluated on how well they do it.

This does not mean that public relations writing and newswriting are incompatible. In fact, good public relations writing may have a high news value, conveying valuable information that is both of interest to the public and in the public interest. If the news value is real, and the writer makes an effort to be factual, accurate, timely, and professional, articles from a public relations source will likely be printed or broadcast.

Most media are hungry for information. They have a commitment to regular, scheduled deadlines and a defined amount of time or space to fill. Accordingly, the source of material is less important than its content and potential audience interest. If public relations writers can provide relevant content and do it to deadline, they are providing news and a news service.

Planning

Deadlines, Deadlines, Deadlines

Generally speaking, the media wait for no one, so if ever there was a reason for planning, it is so that you do not miss media deadlines. These deadlines can be immediate or in what seems like the distant future, but they are nevertheless firm and important.

General media planning should be part of your routine so that releases are prepared, cleared, and distributed with plenty of time for the media to respond (if necessary) and, it is hoped, to schedule coverage. It is also an argument for having boilerplate paragraphs that you can attach to the end of releases to provide information about the organization.

Planning for getting in tomorrow's morning paper (literally) means knowing the relevant editors and reporters, their deadlines, and their contact numbers, especially for genuinely late-breaking news.

Planning for distant deadlines generally requires knowing what they are and scheduling so that you have all of the information available when you need it. For example, getting your college's schedule of events for a month-long celebration of women printed in the March 1st issue of the *Women's Times* requires that you know all details well in advance of a mid-February deadline. Your planning will also involve making your sources aware of their deadline for providing you with information.

Many magazines and newspaper supplements are typically planned and put to bed months in advance, so if a particular issue is critical for your organization, such as to meet seasonal issues, then advance planning will be critical.

While it is tempting to fantasize about writing great news stories that get coverage on the national news—and indeed some organizations have teams of writers to handle newswriting and media liaison on this grand scale—this is not the reality of newswriting for most public relations practitioners. Instead, you may well find your newswriting routine, primarily announcing events, new products, or key appointments or, if you work for a college or university, sending news about students to their local media.

Do not be deceived into thinking that "routine" means unimportant, however. If such releases are part of the organization's plan to reach key publics, then they are as important in maintaining relationships as the once-in-a-lifetime "breakthrough" announcement. And it is as challenging to blend an organization's public relations message into a routine release as into a special one. In fact, if you enjoy working with words and understand the nuances of language and style, writing news releases that convey public relations messages while meeting media requirements for objectivity and brevity is a challenge that you may enjoy.

Using the Media Effectively: More Than "Making the Six o'Clock News"

Regardless of whether they choose news or feature, press or magazines, or radio or television, by cultivating positive relationships with the media, public relations writers can improve the likelihood that their releases will be used. The better you know the editors, reporters, and correspondents who will act as gatekeepers for your releases, the better you will be able to position releases to pass through those gates easily.

Close and mutually respectful relationships with the media will also help ensure that your organization is always treated fairly by the media, especially in circumstances over which you have no control. Reporters who know they can rely on you to provide accurate, timely cooperation when asked and who recognize that you do not waste their time with spurious releases unrelated to their interests, audiences, or local areas are likely to approach you for a story if they hear something positive. Perhaps more important, they may warn you or ask you for comment before printing something negative. Ensuring that your organization receives fair treatment may be as close as you can come to controlling media content.

If you work with the media regularly, it will be your job to help shape the organization's attitudes toward and relationships with the media. Approaching the media with the idea that they work for you or that they are there to give you free publicity may be counterproductive in the long term. On the other hand, approaching the media with the idea that you are helping them to do their job will get their attention and help establish long-term relationships.

One radio executive we know maintains that the primary goal of a radio station is "to keep as many listeners as possible for as long as possible" (James, 2004). The same would be true for television stations, and the press clearly has an equivalent in terms of fostering reader loyalty. Accordingly, the media look to you, the public relations writer, to help them do this, that is, to meet the needs and satisfy the wants of *their* reading/listening/viewing publics. Writing media releases, or proposing news or feature topics that strengthen their relationships with their publics, will strengthen their relationships with you. For example, a television series on women's health produced by a local medical center and a local TV station provides a benefit to the station's viewers, the station, and the medical center. More to the point, it would not be possible with the station or medical center's public relations office working alone.

Ethical Issues

The Truth, the Whole Truth, and Nothing but the Truth

The decision of whether to tell the truth should be easy, as should telling nothing but the truth. You have an obligation to yourself, to your organization, to the public relations industry, to the media, and to the public not to lie. The dilemma usually arises over the question of whether to tell the *whole* truth.

There are two circumstances where you may be unable to tell the whole truth.

♦ You may know the whole truth but be unable to reveal it for legal or ethical reasons. The legal decision is easy. If under law you cannot reveal, for example, the names of accident victims or a patented industrial process, you may not do so.

Where there is no such legal constraint, however, you face ethical dilemmas such as loyalty to your employer versus the public good. This is frequently a tension for public relations writers called to defend their organization's practices in the form of news releases and statements. The PRSA Code of Ethics regarding the need to be accurate as well as true may help. Does withholding information still allow the public to get an *accurate* picture of the situation?

♦ You do not know the whole truth. Especially in crisis conditions, the media and affected publics will expect full disclosure. While you may be able to provide a "who," "what," "where," and "when," you may unable to provide a "why" and "how" because nobody knows, for example, the cause of the accident. You may be unable to provide an informed comment for some time but you should still be as forthcoming and transparent as possible.

Alternatively, employers may withhold information from you so that you can write for the media in all honesty while withholding information that is part of the story. The public relations writer may or may not be aware this is happening. This places the writer in the position of being a writing technician rather than a communication strategist.

Even media planning has its ethical implications. On one hand, it may pay you to release good news on a slow news day to maximize the chance it will be covered. On the other hand, a common strategy for bad news is to release it just in time for the media to report it but close enough to news deadlines that they have no opportunity to fully investigate the story. Another is to release bad news on Friday afternoon, confident that many people will miss the story in the weekend news and that the media will have focused on other issues by Monday. Are these techniques ethical?

Ideally, every organization will have a strategic position with respect to media relations. Will it be open and frank to encourage frequent media coverage? Will it be essentially a low-profile strategy? Or will it be regrettably but necessarily combative to deal effectively with media that have an editorial predisposition in conflict with your employer's position?

As a public relations writer, you will be in the front line of executing whichever strategy your organization chooses. An open and frank relationship implies active communication that seeks to inform and educate your publics through the media. Maintaining a low profile implies limited media writing because you have determined that active use of the mass media is not an appropriate way to reach your publics and/or not the best use of your communication resources.

A combative strategy may sometimes be necessary to combat widespread misinterpretation of your client. Beginning in the 1970s, for example, (then) Mobil Corporation became well known for aggressively addressing what it saw as erroneous media coverage of its activities. The company purchased space in which it ran "advertorials" advocating its own position. It still maintains an active media advocacy program about issues that affect the company and its operations worldwide. After media coverage accusing Nike of tolerating sweatshop conditions in the Asian factories where its shoes are made, Nike fought back with press releases, advertisements, and letters to the editor.

There are times when even the best relationships in the world are not going to get your release published. For example, you are probably never going to succeed in placing an article for handgun control in *Guns & Ammo*. In such cases, your task is to find media with compatible editorial aims and policies in which to place the story or to adopt other channels for delivering the message.

Where to Place News Releases: Media Selection

Depending on your employer's business sector, one or more of the news media may be routinely interested or uninterested in your releases. This means that you must target not only the publics you hope will read your message but also the specific media that will reach these publics. For example, health, educational, and financial institutions are the subject of daily stories in most media; TV stations and daily papers usually have reporters specifically assigned to health, education, and finance "beats," reflecting what the media perceive as strong public interest in stories from these sectors. Public relations writers in these sectors generally have a good placement ratio for releases they issue. The media may also approach your health, education, or finance employer for information.

Most organizations, however, seek and receive media coverage much less often and find it much more difficult to place anything but a crisis story. Accordingly, it is the job of public relations writers to interpret their employer's organization to the (usually local) media in a way that is seen to be relevant.

News does not deal only with issues that are important, weighty, national, or regional; it does not even have to impact most of the population. Most articles in local newspapers, especially "freebie" giveaway papers, are about local people dealing with local and domestic issues that other families, individuals, or groups have to deal with. A story does not have to be nationally significant, "hard," or even "new" to become a viable news story in the right medium, especially if it is local or targeted toward an industry sector, for example.

Sometimes "the right medium" does not even include the local press or broadcast stations, because their reach is far beyond the publics the organization wants to reach. Specialized publications (and possibly broadcast stations or shows) often offer a cost-effective way to reach targeted publics without wasting effort on masses of people who have no interest in the subject. Even a generally low-profile organization may want a high profile in its own sector.

Media services, directories, and press release software can help you target media by topic, interest, or locale. For example, eNR Services, Inc., formerly the Campus Release Network (CRN) used by college and university public relations offices to target releases to media in the hometowns of their students, alumni, or prospects, allows institutions to request media information by zip code, medium, geographic area, and subject. If your news is of truly national interest (if not importance) or you are not certain of the individual media that may be interested, services such as PR Newswire will, for a nominal fee, put your story in front of thousands of media outlets, national, regional, local, and industry- or sector-specific.

There are many directories of U.S. and international print and broadcast media. Look for names such as Bacon's and Burrelle's in your library or conduct a web search to obtain more. Typically, such directories are also available via the Web or on CD-ROM. The advantage of running a CD-ROM directory on your own computer is, of course, that you can compile, customize, and update mailing lists to meet your exact needs.

EXERCISE 1

To understand the role of public relations in providing information to the mass media, you should pay close attention to the sources of articles in media you read and see regularly. For example, refer to a weekday issue of the major daily newspaper serving the town or city in which your campus is located.

✦ How many stories are in the business section of the paper, including stories/columns?
✦ How many stories are about local people, issues, letters, or companies?
✦ How many stories may have been sent in or initiated by a public relations release?

Writing and Placing News Releases

Having determined that your organization has a message to communicate and that the media may be interested in the message, you can increase the chances of having the story used by packaging it to suit media requirements.

Your first aim is to target the story to at least the media you consider most important. Make it obvious that the story will interest their readers/listeners/viewers and that it fits their "mix." It also helps to write the story in a style that is consistent with the style used in the target media and to present it in a format that is easy for the media to use. On a busy day in the newsroom or at the station, the fact that your story follows correct press or broadcast conventions could make the difference between seeing it in print or on the evening news and having it tossed aside.

Newswriting for the Press: Content

At this point, we will begin to focus on the press, as the media most likely to use stories written by public relations writers if only because there is considerably more space in the print media than on even 90 minutes of local television news. We will look at writing for broadcast media in Chapter 11. Be forewarned, however, that many of the principles discussed in this chapter—especially those related to determining "what is news"—apply also to writing for broadcast.

News Values or Determinants

A look at any newspaper will show that despite their common aim of conveying news, news releases vary greatly in purpose. They may announce a new product, management changes, the winning of an award, or showing up well in survey results. They may direct readers and viewers to an event or service, or they may be openly political as elected officials try to publicize their track records as they look toward reelection.

Whatever their content (or bias), releases that are printed always meet some basic news criteria—the so-called news determinants. The media and the public relations writer (although not necessarily the organization) can usually find common ground on what determines "news."

Classic determinants of news or news values are the following:

♦ Timeliness
♦ Relevance
♦ Proximity
♦ Prominence
♦ Rarity
♦ Trendiness
♦ Human interest

As the eyes and ears of the media in your organization, you should be aware of these determinants and keep them in mind as you observe the organization. Developing this media mind-set will help you identify relevant story topics for both external and internal media.

Timeliness

Timeliness generally implies that the event is new—that it is, literally, *news.* Public relations writers may stretch this to include stories and events with a seasonal or topical relevance. For example, hospital education programs focusing on hypothermia and the common cold are clearly more appropriate in December than July. Similarly, if your financial services employer wants to be positioned as helpful in resolving the delicate issue of unpaid student loans, graduation may be a more effective time than March to get the message out. What is timely may depend on what is happening in the world as well as within your own organization.

Relevance or Consequence

People listen to one radio station—WIIFM—"what's in it for me?" Accordingly, the media seek news that answers this question for their readers or viewers. Events and organizations have relevance if the media can see a potential impact on their audiences. An organization becomes relevant if its activities affect people's incomes, health, lifestyles, or relationships, for example. The organization's mission statement may bring to light areas, such as concern for the environment, that are appropriate to specialized media that, in turn, may be interested in your articles.

Proximity

Proximity means nearness. A story is more likely to be considered news if it is local or has a local connection. For obvious reasons, local media cover local events. But consider too how they search for local connections to even national and international events and why local reporters seek interviews with the locally based distant cousin or former college roommate of a celebrity or disaster victim.

The lesson is simple: Make the issue locally relevant and you increase the news value of a release. For example, just prior to the Salt Lake City Olympics, the Atlanta-based Centers for Disease Control and Prevention (CDC) received several columns of coverage in a central Massachusetts paper for a new antismoking campaign using Olympic athletes. The "hook" was that one of the campaign designers was in town to attend a local college alumni function. The media interviewed her, and the campaign received publicity.

Educational institutions and the military are especially adept at localizing news. The fact that Mary Smith of Sheboygan, Wisconsin, graduated from Cornell University in Ithaca, New York, is not likely to be of major interest to the residents of Ithaca, but it will be of interest to people in Sheboygan. If part of Cornell's mission is to attract students from all parts of the country, then distributing the release to the Sheboygan paper helps to meet that goal.

Many public relations writers operate on the principle that "all news is local," and "localize" wherever possible. Especially for multiple or routine releases, this localizing task is made easier by the mail merge capability of many software programs, as discussed in Appendix A.

Prominence: The VIP Effect

Generally, people attract attention, and important people attract more attention. This is why one popular public relations strategy is to use VIPs as spokespersons. An organization may elect to speak through a newsworthy spokesperson who will attract attention to events, media releases, mailers, or advertising campaigns.

Public relations writers often gain attention for an organization by riding a wave of interest in a prominent person. For example, awareness of prostate and testicular cancer has been heightened by the personal testimony of politicians, athletes, and entertainers who have come forward to promote early detection and treatment. Bob Dole, John Kerry, Rudy Giuliani, Colin Powell, Joe Torre, Lance Armstrong, Robert DiNiro, and Jerry Lewis are but a few of the men whose experiences with these cancers have "put a face" on a disease that not too long ago no one talked about.

Many organizations, typically colleges and universities, health organizations, and historical/arts societies, offer speakers' bureaus through which they make experts available to provide interpretations or background information or to speak with the media whenever a topic becomes popular or newsworthy. The organization effectively turns its own staff or members into VIPs and gives the media reason to come to the organization for information. This often spins off into generally improved relations with the media as well.

Rarity/the Unusual/the Bizarre

We all enjoy a break from the routine, and so do the media. Small unusual events lighten a page or a program and help the media fill empty time or space. Make a point of looking at the media around April 1st to see this news determinant at work. Stories on macaroni farming, pickle trees, a left-handed Whopper, and the Taco Bell Liberty Bell have all made it to print or broadcast on April Fools' Day, even in the usually formal *New York Times*.

If you find a little-known fact or oddity about your organization, you may be able to exploit it to obtain publicity of this kind. The strategic question is whether you would recommend it. Such stories may backfire, especially if they misrepresent the organization or if the media have been taken in by the joke. With a view toward protecting its own and its members' images, PR Newswire refuses to release such articles. It gets back to the issue of what image the organization wants to cultivate.

Trendiness

This is a relatively new category of news determinant, but we see it often as editorial choices are driven by the public interest in what is current, new, cool, or just "happening." Research organizations release stories about teenagers' changing eating habits or apathy about voting, "temp" agencies release stories about trends in workplace dress standards, and medical researchers report on study results with a regularity that brings to mind the "disease of the month." These trends often receive further coverage in op-ed columns, opinions, and feature stories as the subject becomes a "trend" in which we are presumably interested.

DISCUSSION   1

Media coverage of trends gives rise to questions about whether the news media report the news or whether by virtue of their reporting, they create the news. What do you think? Why?

Human Interest

We are all interested in other people. The daily work, triumphs, tragedies, and relationships of people being people have an inherent reader or viewer interest. For the public relations writer, this frequently translates into a case study or example style of writing. For example, although new Internet technology may not have wide interest per se, if the writer can show how the technology is being used by the disabled to electronically attend school or how students can understand and research weather by taking meteorological data from remote locations, the technology becomes relevant and interesting. Public relations writers who can find one or more of these attributes in their employers' activities have great potential for media coverage.

News Determinants in Action

The following example demonstrates that editors do indeed use these news determinants to help their decision making. The science editor of a medium-size daily paper (circulation: 95,000 daily, 140,000–150,000 Sunday) received 20 releases during a two-week period. He printed only four of them. His reasons for not printing the remaining 16 are a litany of "don'ts" for the savvy public relations writer:

+ *"No link to our area"* (comment made on nine of the releases). He noted on one of the releases that it might lead to a story, that is, the subject had some interest, but the company that sent it wouldn't be mentioned because it had no link to his area.
+ *"No interest"* or *"Who cares?"* (comment made on three releases).
+ *"The wires will probably do this story."* The story had such news value that the national wire services would likely distribute it, and the paper would use it from the wire services; there was no reason for the editor to put effort into it.
+ *"Good background"* (comment made on two releases). There is no news value in the release; he will not use it but may keep it for background if another story comes along.
+ *"Company bias"* (the cardinal sin for a public relations writer).

Exhibit 9.1 includes excerpts from the four releases he chose to print. They clearly illustrate the local interest and attempt to find news value that led to the editor's approval. Note how Smith College clearly defined the local interest, the DEP and UMass related technical issues to important human interest concerns, and the DEM concisely issued a public health/safety warning. The writers of all four releases paid attention to what editors look for, and they were rewarded by seeing their articles in print.

In the broadcast arena, the competition is even hotter because of extreme time limitations. A news editor for a small- to medium-size local TV station may receive upward of 30 video news releases (VNRs) and an equal number of releases and have the opportunity to take more than 200 satellite feeds from multiple networks—every day. The editor must whittle these down into the 10 minutes (perhaps) of news that the station will air during a half-hour broadcast. The challenge for public relations writers is to write stories that float successfully above this flood of releases that reach editors' desks every day.

This means—and it may be difficult for a publicity-conscious CEO to understand—that you must find and make obvious the *real* news value in a story. Overzealous writers do themselves and their employers a disservice by overemphasizing the organization's name at the expense of the news or by promoting the organization at the beginning of the story and so diluting its news value. For example, the news media and your employer may agree that opening or expanding a facility to provide 24-hour service for customers is newsworthy, but they will differ on the newsworthiness of the following leads for the release.

Ms. Jane Jones, Vice President of XYZ Corporation, announced today that the corporation would take several initiatives to improve customer servicing.

Twenty-four-hour service will come to XYZ Corporation customers next week as a result of several technological innovations.

EXHIBIT 9.1   Four excerpts from media releases.

Smith (College) Receives Grant for Mill River Research

NORTHAMPTON, MA — Smith College has recently been awarded a $115,000 grant from the Krusos Foundation, Inc., of Cold Spring Harbor, New York, to support its environmental science program and specifically to underwrite a collaborative research project involving the Mill River watershed in the towns of [names].

Through collaboration with the Silvio Conte National Fish and Wildlife Refuge of the U.S. Fish and Wildlife Service, interdisciplinary teams of Smith College and other Five College faculty and students will gain hands-on knowledge as well as "contribute valuable expertise to an important conservation project," says Tom Litwin, [title]. . . .

Smith College

Massachusetts Notifies EPA of Intent to Sue Over Clean Air Petition

Massachusetts officials today notified U.S. Environmental Protection Agency administrator Carol Browner of their intent to file suit against EPA for its failure to act on the state's petition demanding that strict emission standards be imposed on Midwest and Southeast power plants. The petition, filed on August 14, required EPA to make a finding within 60 days. That 60-day deadline expired on October 13 with no action by EPA.

"More than 750,000 Massachusetts citizens suffer from respiratory ailments that are made worse by smog. Their health is hanging in the balance," said Governor Paul Cellucci. . . .

Massachusetts Department of Environmental Protection

UMass Professor Wins $1.4 Million Grant From National Science Foundation

Computer-linking research could eventually be used in development of air traffic control, patient monitoring systems.

AMHERST, Mass. — George Avrunin, professor of mathematics and statistics at the University of Massachusetts, has received a $1.4 million grant from the National Science Foundation for research on the effective linking of computer systems. The grant will fund a four-year project Avrunin is working on in conjunction with UMass computer science professors Lori Clarke and Leon Osterweil. The group's research could eventually be used in the development of computer systems used in areas such as air traffic control, airline reservation systems, and the monitoring of hospital patients. . . .

University of Massachusetts at Amherst

State Issues Wildfire Advisory

The Massachusetts Department of Environmental Management (DEM) has issued a Statewide Wildfire Advisory due to lack of rainfall and an increase in the number of fires reported.

"We are asking that individuals be especially careful when extinguishing their cigarettes, discarding ashes from their woodstoves or just enjoying the outdoors in general," said DEM Commissioner Peter Webber. . .

The DEM is responsible for the detection of wildfires throughout the Commonwealth's lands through a system of fire towers, aided by ground patrols within each district. . . .

Massachusetts Department of Environmental Management

Source: Reprinted with permission from Smith College, Northampton, Massachusetts; the Massachusetts Department of Environmental Protection, Boston; the University of Massachusetts at Amherst, Amherst; and the Massachusetts Department of Environmental Management, Boston.

The first lead is "source driven"; Ms. Jones is understandably keen to see her name and her company name up front in the news. The second lead is "receiver driven"; it comes from considering not only what the media receivers of the release (i.e., editors) look for as news but also what their receivers (i.e., the readers) see as a priority.

It is a good skill to be able to switch between a public relations focus and an editorial focus to get a sense of what the media like and dislike in a news release. Consider, for example, the differing focuses evident in a news release distributed by Girls Inc. of Holyoke and the article as it ran in the local newspaper.

The release announced an annual dinner and silent auction. This is a typical subject for public relations releases, especially for nonprofit organizations that want the public to attend, contribute, and/or volunteer. It is good news that should interest the public, but such topics are also where the interests of the organization and the media often clash.

DISCUSSION 2

Review the Girls Inc. media release in Exhibit 9.2 in light of the news determinants discussed in this section.

+ Refer to the criteria used by the editor who was quoted at the beginning of this section. Do you think he would run this story? Why or why not?
+ What aspect/s of this release do you think will interest the news media? What news determinants do they represent?
+ What, if anything, do you think will be less important to the media? Why?
+ If you were writing the release, what, if anything, would you do differently?

Exhibit 9.3 is the article as it appeared in the local paper under the byline of a Holyoke beat reporter. Both the public relations writer and the newspaper writer are true to the aims of their employers and present their stories accurately. However, the Girls Inc. writer's concern for emphasizing the organization and the newspaper writer's for the interests of the paper's readers result in very different leads and story emphases.

DISCUSSION 3

Review the Girls Inc. article in Exhibit 9.3.

+ How does the article differ from the media release in Exhibit 9.2? What did you expect to see in print that was not in the article, and vice versa? What indication do you have that the reporter was familiar with the area?
+ What topics have received more (or less) emphasis? Why do you think this occurred?
+ What does this tell you about what editors do or do not look for in media releases?

You might have noticed two errors in the newspaper article. One is the spelling of an honoree's name, and the second is the price of dinner tickets. What would you have done if you were the public relations writer in this situation?

EXHIBIT 9.2   Media release from Girls Inc. of Holyoke.

Girls Inc. to Host Celebration Dinner

A dinner and silent auction will be held on March 21st at the Log Cabin Banquet and Meeting House to celebrate the Girls' Bill of Rights.

The Girls' Bill of Rights asserts that girls have the right:

◆ to be themselves and to resist gender stereotypes.
◆ to express themselves with originality and enthusiasm.
◆ to take risks, to strive freely, and to take pride in success.
◆ to accept and appreciate their bodies.
◆ to have confidence in themselves and to be safe in the world.
◆ to prepare for interesting work and economic independence.

The Celebration Dinner enables members of the Greater Holyoke community to celebrate these rights, as well as the accomplishments of six local women. The six honorees are chosen for their individual accomplishments, in addition to their personal philosophies and presence in the community, which inspire girls to be strong, smart, and bold.

Honorees for the 2002 Celebration Dinner include: Kathleen G. Anderson, mayoral aide; Gladys Lebron-Martinez, Director of Health and Human Services at Nueva Esperanza, Inc. Also being honored are Francesca Maltese, Development Manager at O'Connell Development Group; Dr. Sonia Nieto, Professor of Education at the University of Massachusetts; Doris M. Ransford, President of the Greater Holyoke Chamber of Commerce; and Ellen Story, State Representative.

The Celebration Dinner will feature live music, as well as a silent auction with a wide variety of items for bid including a hot air balloon ride, driving lessons, and many gift certificates from area merchants.

This year's event is sponsored in part by Appleton Dental Associates and Peoples Bank. The emcee will be Kathy Tobin of WGGB-TV News 40.

Social hour begins at 5:30. Tickets are available at $35 and tables of ten can be reserved for $350. To make a reservation please contact Karen Kakley at (413) 532-6247.

Source: Reprinted with permission from Girls Inc. of Holyoke, Holyoke, Massachusetts.

Newswriting for the Press: Structure

Identifying the news, the news value, and appropriate lead ensures that you have a story that will interest the media, but that is only part of the challenge of getting the release printed. The rest is writing the release so that it is media-friendly. This means following media conventions for structure and style, even while you are sending a public relations message.

Media Structure: The Inverted Pyramid

Regardless of whether they are written by a reporter or a public relations writer, news stories follow the classic *inverted pyramid* structure and the "5W+H" checklist for content. Inverted pyramid structure means writing from most important to least important facts and answering the following media questions:

Who? What? When? Where? Why? How?

EXHIBIT 9.3   The Girls Inc. article as it appeared in the newspaper.

Girls Inc. Honorees Accomplished Women

By Mike Burke, *Staff writer*

HOLYOKE—Girls Inc. of Holyoke will honor six area women at its annual celebration dinner and silent auction beginning 5:30 p.m. March 21, at the Log Cabin Banquet and Meeting House.

Officials at the Girls Inc. said the six women are chosen for their individual accomplishments, in addition to their personal philosophies and presence in the community which inspires girls.

The honorees include Kathleen G. Anderson, mayoral aide and director of the Management Assistance Program in City Hall; Gladys Lebron-Martinez, director of health and human services at Nueva Esperanza; Frances Maltese, development manager at O'Connell Development Group; Dr. Sonia Nieto, professor of education at the University of Massachusetts; Doris M. Ransford, president of the Greater Holyoke Chamber of Commerce; and State Rep. Ellen Story, D-Amherst.

The six honorees also represent the Girls Inc. Bill of Rights in the community: girls have the right to be themselves and resist stereotypes; express themselves with originality and enthusiasm; take risks; strive freely; and take pride in success.

Also, they have the right to accept and appreciate their bodies; have confidence in themselves and be safe in the world; and to prepare for interesting work and economic independence.

The celebration dinner, in addition to honoring the above, will also include a live auction fundraiser with many items up for bid.

The event is sponsored in part by Appleton Dental Associates and Peoples Bank.

The emcee for the evening will be Kathy Tobin, news director of Channel 40.

Tickets are $10 each. For information call Karen Kakley at 532-6247.

Source: Reprinted with permission from *The Republican*.

The Lead

The news lead should tell the story in the first sentence or two. A mental tool for developing an effective news lead is the "20-second rule." If you had only 20 seconds to tell a friend about your story, what would you say? Write that down, and you have the first draft of a summary lead.

Who, what, when, where, why, and how are also leads; a writer could use any of these as the "hook" for the article. This is where an organization's interest in self-promotion may clash with the media definition of what makes news. An organization may see "who" as a lead whereas the key question for the media is "what," because what happened is usually more important than who did it.

There are obvious exceptions to this rule. Sometimes the VIP effect or a "prominence" news value makes "who" an obvious lead. Consider, for example, the lead to Exhibit 9.4 in which both the Red Cross and the Basketball Hall of Fame names have the ability to attract the attention of both editors and readers. And if the bare facts of a new product release appear less than enthralling, a

---

EXHIBIT 9.4   Media release from the American Red Cross of Western Massachusetts.

January 13, 2002

Hall of Fame & Red Cross Team For Blood Drive

— Event to be held on January 17 at the Basketball Hall of Fame —

The Naismith Memorial Basketball Hall of Fame and your American Red Cross are teaming up to help save lives. Winter storms and a higher incidence of colds and flu make collecting enough blood to meet patient needs especially challenging this time of year. Springfield area residents who are 17 years of age or older, weigh at least 110 pounds and are in good health are invited to a take time out and give blood at the Basketball Hall of Fame, located at 1000 West Columbus Avenue, on Friday, January 17. Donor hours are 10 a.m. to 4:00 p.m.

According to the Red Cross, giving blood is a "slam dunk." The entire procedure, including paperwork and refreshments, takes about an hour. The actual donation, which takes about 10 minutes, is easy and virtually painless. Donations are used for surgery, trauma, cancer treatment, hemophilia and many other life-threatening conditions.

The Naismith Memorial Basketball Hall of Fame is pulling out all the stops to make this event an enjoyable way for the Springfield community to keep the blood supply plentiful for everyone. Potential donors will receive a coupon for free admission to the Hall of Fame and Reebok will offer a 30% coupon, redeemable at their Hall of Fame store.

"The American Red Cross is issuing a full court press to eliminate blood shortages," said Katie Lariviere, Director of Western Massachusetts Operations, "and we are grateful to the Basketball Hall of Fame for their generous offer to sponsor this blood drive in their fantastic new facility."

Blood donations of all blood types are urgently needed at this time. Please call the American Red Cross at 785-0901, or log on at www.newenglandblood.org, for more information about giving the Gift of Life.

Together, we can save a life.

Source: Reprinted with permission from the American Red Cross—New England.

---

circuitous "how the product was developed" lead may attract greater editorial curiosity and attention.

The Body

Generally, public relations releases begin with a summary lead (the important facts), followed by a reason to read further (why the story is important), the story details, and an interpretation or response (what does it mean, what should I do?). It ends with a boilerplate paragraph about the organization. The public relations writer and the media can probably agree on the lead and the importance: There must be news value and a summary to begin a story and reasons for the reader/viewer to find the story relevant.

However, the same story written by a public relations writer and a journalist might vary on the interpretation and boilerplate. Journalists seldom write to influence behavior (other than in columns and editorials). Nor do they include background facts about an organization if the facts have no news value. On the other hand, public relations writers usually write for results: They want readers to call the client's 800 number, buy a product, or donate money. Exhibit 9.7 later in this chapter illustrates one way of writing to the inverted pyramid.

Typically, the media has no objection to organizational background, but its proper place is at the end of the release. It is often provided through the boilerplate paragraph discussed in Chapter 8.

Exhibit 9.4 is a release issued by the American Red Cross of Western Massachusetts announcing a blood drive at the Naismith Memorial Basketball Hall of Fame. The Red Cross issues versions of this release regularly, and making them interesting is often a challenge.

Note how the writer used the location at the Basketball Hall of Fame to attract attention to the story and then carried it through the release, even in the organization's message about the blood drive. Phrases such as "time out," "slam dunk," and "full court press" continue the theme without overshadowing the news or the Red Cross message.

This release also follows the inverted pyramid structure well. The first paragraph contains all of the key details including the urgency of the need, and the key details about donor eligibility and the blood drive. Although the rest of the release provides interesting and valuable detail about donating blood and the Hall of Fame event, if an editor chose to print only the first paragraph, the Red Cross would have been satisfied that the key message had been disseminated.

Newswriting for the Press: Style

After determining that your story is news, identifying the media that will consider it so, and determining the relative importance of facts, you can increase the likelihood of having the story used by writing the release in a style that is compatible with the style used by the media you have chosen.

Why use media style? Because it makes life easier for busy deadline-driven editors. Demonstrate in your writing that you "speak the language" of news and understand news cultures and your releases will gain a higher level of acceptance.

Journalism Style

Arguably, the most important aspect of writing for the press is neutrality. The basis of good journalism is accuracy and honesty, reflected in presenting all sides of an issue without bias toward one side or the other.

The media understand that news provided by public relations sources has an agenda: You want the readers to choose your product, service, event, or cause over all other options competing for their interest, time, or money. And the media do not expect that you will call attention to negative stories about your organization, such as a lawsuit unrelated to the issue at hand. But they do expect (and your adherence to the PRSA Code of Ethics demands) that the information you provide is honest and accurate and that it does not distort the truth even if it does not present all sides.

For example, the news media routinely report statements released by attorneys in high-profile trials. The media recognize that the statements may well be biased in favor of a client but they otherwise meet standards of newsworthiness and, when used in conjunction with other sources of information, will present a complete picture.

Word Choice for Journalism Style

Chapter 2 discussed the importance of choosing words that have character and attitude, especially strong verbs and descriptive adjectives. News releases are one exception to this practice (annual reports are another). On the K-A-B (knowledge-attitude-behavior) scale (see Chapter 1), the primary goal of newswriting is knowledge. The news media arguably would see it as the *only* goal.

Accordingly, news style is informational, based on facts. It uses neutral (rather colorless) verbs that simply tell what happened rather than being leading or attitudinal. It uses emotionally neutral attributions such as "announced" or "stated" rather than the emotionally charged "accused" or "attacked" to describe what a person said.

News style also avoids adjectives and adverbs—unless they are facts. Quantitative modifiers may be acceptable; qualitative ones seldom are. Dr. Louise Jackson may be described as "director of Central University Bioresearch Program" (a demonstrable fact), but she should not be described as "the most innovative director that Central University Bioresearch Program ever had," which is editorializing on your part. If you want this description in the release, find a way to quote a credible source on the subject. It is still an opinion but clearly so, and if the source carries weight, it is a valid and newsworthy one.

Does this mean that you cannot promote the organization in a news release? To the extent that by promotion you mean overt persuasion, the answer is that you should not do it. Save persuasive copy for paid advertisements or brochures. But to the extent that every public relations release says something about the organization's image, you *will* be able to send public relations messages in news releases, and indeed you should try to do so. The mere fact that the Avon Corporation sponsors the "Race for the Cure," for example, sends a positive message about Avon without the need for lengthy persuasive or descriptive wording about how wonderful the company is. It is likely that writers for Avon will try to mention the sponsorship in most documents.

Reconciling Public Relations and Media Interests

The releases shown as Exhibits 9.5 and 9.6 pay clear attention to their organizations' public relations interests. Exhibit 9.5 was issued by the Phoenix Coyotes National Hockey League (NHL) team to announce the introduction of an automated fan feedback system at its home rink. Exhibit 9.6 was issued by Alteon Training to announce the receipt of an award from the Korean government. The writers used many of the following techniques for conveying their public relations messages.

◆ *Remember the organization's aim or mission.* Seize opportunities to include it in a release. Note how both the Phoenix Coyotes and Alteon Training releases cite

---

EXHIBIT 9.5   Media release from the Phoenix Coyotes hockey club.

COYOTES LAUNCH FANTRAK TO GIVE THE FANS A VOICE

FOR IMMEDIATE RELEASE:

Wednesday, March 24, 2004

SCOTTSDALE, ARIZONA — The Phoenix Coyotes announced today the launch of FanTrak, a new technology that enables the club to solicit feedback from fans during home games and then access the results immediately after each game over the web, from any computer in the world.

"FanTrak provides us with the ability to immediately know what our fans are thinking, and will allow us to track fan behavior and interaction and provide us invaluable feedback," said Coyotes Executive Vice President of Business Operations Brian Byrnes. "Our top priority is to deliver outstanding service and exceed our fan's expectations. We look to develop long-term relationships with our fans and this program will help us understand what our fans want so we can react to their needs and suggestions quickly. FanTrak will allow our fans to have a voice in the process and an interaction with the team on a consistent basis."

FanTrak, owned by Turnkey Sports, enables sports teams, events and venues to intercept and survey fans in attendance at games and other events and receive results overnight. The system captures survey information from attendees on Palm Pilots. After each event, the Palm Pilots are "hot-synched" and the data instantly uploads to a robust, user-friendly reporting site. Clients can access their data from anywhere in the world immediately. The FanTrak reporting site puts more control in the marketers' hands because it contains intuitive, user-friendly tools for marketers to sort, cross-tabulate and analyze any piece of data with any other piece of data, instantly.

"I'm excited about implementing FanTrak because we believe it will be an extraordinary asset to the Coyotes," added Byrnes. "FanTrak will give the fans a powerful new voice and will provide us with a traceable history to make sure the games are enjoyable and fun for everyone."

The Coyotes have entered into a FanTrak License with Turnkey Sports, the owner of FanTrak. Turnkey Sports focuses its business on market research, executive search and new facility feasibility. Turnkey Sports currently is completing a year-long, League wide market research study for the National Football League (NFL) and has performed market research assignments for clients across sports and entertainment. For more information, visit www.turnkeysports.com or www.fantrak.com.

Source: Reprinted with permission from the Phoenix Coyotes.

---

the organizations' missions, positioning the announcement as evidence of that mission. In doing this, Alteon's use of the phrase "is *further* recognition" conveys the message that this level of achievement is routine for the company. The public relations message in the Coyotes' release focuses on the technology as a means of strengthening the club's relationships with its fans, clearly a mission-based public relations message.

◆ *Use quotes to convey your purpose, mission, and message.* When used wisely, statements from credible sources can be a valuable tool. Sometimes quotes are a way to let someone else talk about the organization's merits. Alteon's decision to quote the Korean director general lends credibility to the company's claims. Of all the quotes in the release, this is the most likely to be used.

Alteon Receives Award for Contribution to Aviation Safety

SEATTLE, April 14 /PRNewswire/ — Alteon Training, a wholly owned subsidiary of The Boeing Company (NYSE: BA), recently received an award for the company's contribution to overall aviation safety in Korea over the last five years from the South Korean Ministry of Transportation, through the Korean Civil Aviation Safety Authority (CASA). CASA Director General Chong-Kook Kim presented the award to Alteon management during a recent visit to Korea.

"We are very proud of this award," said Pat Gaines, Alteon president. "It is further recognition that we are on the right path to fulfilling our mission of improving worldwide aviation safety."

"Alteon has been doing important, high-quality work in Korea and is viewed as an important contributor to the advancement of our industry," said Director General Kim.

"We share this award with Korean Airlines and Asiana," said John Albrecht, Alteon vice president for Sales and Business Development. "It was through their executive management's progressive vision of training and safety that we were asked to partner in Korea. And it is through their dedication, commitment and foresight that we have been able to achieve what we have."

Alteon Training is the world's preferred aviation training partner and the industry leader in providing customer-focused aviation training solutions. The company provides customers an expanding and integrated services portfolio that includes flight, technical and cabin-crew training, and training materials.

Alteon is a wholly owned subsidiary of The Boeing Co. within Boeing Commercial Airplanes' Commercial Aviation Services group. The training organization supports the world's aviation community with more than 70 full-flight simulators in 20 locations around the world.

Source: Reprinted with permission from Alteon Training, LLC.

At other times, quotes help personalize the public relations message. Paragraph two of the Coyotes' release would have been awkward if written in the third person: "The club's top priority is to deliver. . . ." However, when presented as a quote from a senior executive, words such as "*Our* priority," "so *we* can react to their needs," and especially "*our* fans" give the message and the organization warmth and conviction.

The second paragraph of a release is generally a good place for that strong, active public relations quote. It does not interfere with the news, but still has a position of importance in the release.

✦ *Choose and frame information to reflect the organization's image.* It is clear that the Phoenix Coyotes have a business interest in installing the FanTrak system and that it will benefit the club as well as the fans. Nevertheless, "framing" the system as a way to help the club serve its fans and to involve the fans in the club's future is a good public relations strategy, especially as technology can be suspect with regard to privacy and cost.

✦ *Follow the same guidelines for interviews.* If you are being interviewed for broadcast, a skilled practitioner will find ways to accomplish the same aims, or will coach the interview subject to be sensitive to the organization's public relations aims when responding to media questions.

Brevity

Good news style celebrates sentence brevity, for print as well as for electronic media. Short sentences help readers read quickly. Long sentences may confuse them. There are many rules of thumb for media writing. Although they vary in detail—for example, not more than 30 words, three sentences, or five lines—they share a call for brevity.

EXERCISE 2

It is often difficult to write succinctly while including all of the information the organization demands. Sometimes the writer is "trapped" by long, but necessary, titles and names. Sometimes there is a contractual or "political" need to represent more than one organization. Many of the examples cited in this chapter fall afoul of this principle at some point, even while they accomplish other aims very well. Try the following exercises using the media releases shown as Exhibits 9.4, 9.5, and 9.6 as the basis.

✦ Identify sentences and paragraphs that violate the principle of brevity. Rewrite them to include the necessary information, but in a simpler style.
✦ All three releases involve two organizations. Rewrite the releases as if they had been issued by the other organization, that is, the Basketball Hall of Fame, Turnkey Sports, and the Korean government. How will you change the headline and first paragraph? Why? What facts will be more (and less) important?
✦ The Phoenix Coyotes release in particular has the potential for a featurized treatment using a lead other than the news. Rewrite the first paragraph using prominence, rarity, trendiness, and human interest news determinants.

Style Resources

Although individual media may have their own style conventions, fortunately there are generally accepted styles for both press and broadcast writing. If you don't know the style of the media to which you want to send a release, following these generic styles is usually a safe bet.

AP (Associated Press) style and UPI (United Press International) style are arguably the most common of the media styles. These styles govern the writing of journalists, and by association they should govern public relations writers who hope to have releases accepted by print media. Stylebooks of individual media contain the particular style rules used by that paper's journalists.

The Associated Press Stylebook and Briefing on Media Law and the *UPI Stylebook and Guide to Newswriting* are common stylebooks for writing for the press. They will help you deal with names, titles, addresses, stock prices, percentages, meteorological data, years, and highway numbers, each of which has its own style. Another advantage is that they help you track the constantly changing words and usages that are (or are not) deemed politically correct at a given time.

Some media, including *Science Magazine* and British newspapers *The Times* and *The Guardian,* publish their style guides online for the benefit of journalists and writers who want to submit articles. It is likely that this practice will increase. The point is that you should find out what style your target publication uses, and then use it.

A self-styled "journalist's bible," the *AP Stylebook* provides guidance on more than 150,000 topics of grammar, spelling, punctuation, and usage. Of special interest to the public relations writer are the sections on punctuation, the use of business names, how to present time and numbers, and the overview of copyright, Freedom of Information, and libel laws. Writers concerned with economy of writing should also become familiar with style on abbreviations and acronyms. For example, "FBI" and "mph" are both acceptable on first reference, whereas "WHO" and "mpg" should be defined on first reference before they can stand alone.

These style manuals are useful references for determining how to do the following:

◆ *Refer to people.* AP style generally uses the person's first and last names for the first mention and subsequently uses only his or her last name. In contrast, the perhaps more genteel *New York Times* continues to use an older style, which precedes names with "Mr.," "Mrs.," or "Ms." Still other papers include a middle initial for all names, at least in stories written by their own reporters. Knowing the requirements of your own local media will help.

◆ *Write titles.* If the title appears before the name, use commonly accepted abbreviations such as "Gen." for general, "Adm." for admiral, or "police Sgt." for police sergeant. Spell out long, unfamiliar titles or those that could be confused, such as "Commander," "Commissioner," or "Commissar." In press copy, short titles precede the name while long titles follow the name: "President Bush"; "Bonnie Simpson, assistant editor of arts and entertainment."

◆ *Write numbers.* Numbers from one through nine are generally spelled out and those 10 and greater are written as numerals. Numbers that are measurements may also be written as numerals (e.g., 5 minutes). Numbers that start a sentence are always spelled out, with the exception of years. For example, "2000 was an election year" is correct but "2,000 people cast votes" is not; instead write, "Two thousand people cast votes."

If the number is especially complex, such as 12,345,678, it may be wiser to restructure the sentence or, as in broadcast style, to use an approximation such as "just over 12 million" than to spell out the entire number. If spelled out, the style is "twelve million, three hundred forty-five thousand, six hundred seventy eight." For dollar amounts, the style is either "$3,456,789" or "more than $400 million." Numbers used in proper names follow the style for the name: "3M," "1st Union Bank."

These style issues are complex—and important. Keep your style manual handy for easy reference, and use it.

E X E R C I S E   3

One way to understand media styles is to compare them. Select four publications of different types such as a local daily newspaper; a news magazine such as *U.S. News & World Report*; a public general interest magazine such as *People* or *Reader's Digest*; a specialized "literary" magazine such as the *New Yorker*; a special interest publication such as *Rolling Stone, Psychology Today, Sports Illustrated, Soap Opera Digest,* or *Field and Stream*; or an online publication such as *Slate*.

- Describe the style of each publication (formal/casual, stilted/conversational, informative/entertaining, etc.).
- Describe the vocabulary of each publication (technical, scientific, graduate, high school, etc.).
- What education level do you think would be needed to understand most of the articles in the publication?
- Rank the publications in order of readability.
- What audiences read each of the publications? Does this correlate to reading level?

Write a one-paragraph review of your campus food service in the styles of at least three of the media you reviewed above. Try to capture each publication's vocabulary, phrasing, and style.

Newswriting for the Press: Formatting

There are generally agreed-on ground rules that can increase the probability that your release will make it to print. Although some editors argue that they will use a release handwritten on brown paper if the content is good, it is obvious that your chances are much better if the paper is plain bond and the content is typed and printed by a laser or ink-jet printer.

The point of following these media conventions is to approximate as closely as possible the article as it might be printed in the media and to give busy editors all of the information they need in one concise document. Following these conventions will demonstrate that you are both media-friendly and professional. Exhibit 9.7 illustrates the format that provides the media with information they need.

Contact Information

At the top of the first page include all of the contact information you can provide: office phone, cell phone, home phone, pager, fax, and e-mail, postal and street addresses. If possible, also provide the name of another contact who can cover for you if you're not around.

Remember that journalists do not work a standard eight-to-five day. You may be taking a well-deserved early leave from the office at 4 p.m., but you are doing so at the time that many journalists are coming to work to plan, write, and put together tomorrow morning's paper. It is not uncommon for a journalist to contact you anywhere between 5 p.m. and the wee small hours of the morning. Public relations writers with frequent media contact carry pagers and are never off duty.

Page Numbering

Pages should be numbered to ensure that if the release gets disassembled, the editor would know how many pages to look for. One convention is to use a 1/4, 2/4, 3/4, 4/4 style of numbering to indicate pages 1, 2, 3, or 4 of a total of four. Often, writers use one or two identifying words along with the page number so the style becomes "Charity walk 1/2," "Charity walk 2/2."

Pages other than the last should have the word "more" centered at the bottom and the release should end with "Ends," "30," or "XXX" after the last sentence.

EXHIBIT 9.7   Template for media releases showing required information and formatting.

Model press release

ORGANIZATION NAME *(use letterhead if you wish)*
ADDRESS

DATE: _____

CONTACT: Name   _____
                Phone   _____   Home phone   _____
                Cell   _____   Fax   _____
                E-mail   _____

ALTERNATE: Name   _____
                Phone   _____   Alternate   _____
                Fax   _____
                E-mail   _____

NEWS RELEASE: FOR IMMEDIATE RELEASE
            or **("EMBARGOED UNTIL: Date _____")**

(SPACE FOR EDITOR TO WRITE HEADLINE)

HEADLINE *(optional)*

LEAD PARAGRAPH–NEWS STORY: The lead paragraph must capture the editor's interest immediately. It must encapsulate the story and make the editor aware of why his or her readers would be interested. Always double-space the story. Use the traditional "news pyramid" format, writing from most general to greatest detail. Following is a typical news release structure.

First paragraph: Who, what, when, where, why, how.

Second paragraph: Quote from a spokesperson.

Third paragraph: More detail about subject.

Fourth paragraph: Yet more detail.

Fifth paragraph: Quote from
(another) spokesperson.

Sixth Paragraph:
Contact Info.

Boilerplate

"ENDS," "30," or "XXX" at bottom of last page

PAGINATION: Key word and page number/total pages
(e.g., Fan Trak 1/4)

Spacing

Releases should be double spaced on plain bond paper, one side only, with margins of 1.5 inches on all sides. When releases were typed on a typewriter, double spacing gave a full blank line between each line of type.

Word processing programs and printers allow you to also space at 1.5 lines. For the purposes of press releases, this is acceptable spacing. The point is to give the editor space to make edits on the original document and send it directly for layout.

Release Date

All releases should carry a release date, usually "immediate" meaning that the media can use the release as soon as they get it. Sometimes, however, you may want the release to be used on a specific day, perhaps to coincide with a new-product launch or an annual meeting. The phrases "Embargo until" or "Do not use before" tell the media not to use the release until the specified date.

Why would you send out a release in advance of an event and risk an early news leak? You might do so to ensure that as many media outlets as possible get the release, to ensure that journalists have an opportunity to ask questions before they use it, or perhaps because you will be so busy on "the day" that anything you can prepare in advance is just good planning.

Embargoes

How can you guarantee that an *embargo*, or hold, will be honored? You can't. The media are intensely competitive, and each one has professional and economic reasons to be first with the news. Whether embargoes are respected is a function of the relationship you build with the media.

News professionals may honor an embargo for two reasons. First, no professional wants to "break" the story of your CEO's speech in advance only to discover that he canceled at the last minute and the speech was never given. Second, public relations executives do have some redress; media outlets that leak embargoed material will probably find that their public relations sources dry up and their ability to gather news is adversely affected. However, given the competition for news, it is wise to assume that embargoes will not be honored and to use them as your experiences with local media suggest.

To Headline or Not to Headline

The first reason that you would write a headline for a release is the same reason that the press puts a headline at the top of the story: to attract the reader's (in this case, editor's) attention. The second reason is that if you are really lucky and a newspaper uses the release unchanged you will have not only written tomorrow's news story, you will have written the headline as well.

But this is a hot debate. Headlines are an editor's responsibility and editors are seldom predisposed to have others writing headlines for them. Furthermore, for the print media, headlines are an exercise in layout; they need to be a specific size and length to fit a column or a page layout. This alone makes it unlikely that your headline will be used as written. Some public relations writers provide editors the courtesy of a blank space to work in by starting their release one-third of the way down the first page.

Most writers probably write a headline anyway. The worst that can happen is that it doesn't get used. This is more than offset by the potential that a well-crafted headline that effectively highlights the news value of the story may be instrumental in drawing editorial attention to the story. Note how the writers of the Red Cross, Phoenix Coyotes, and Alteon Training releases (Exhibits 9.4, 9.5, and 9.6, respectively) all used headlines to capture an editor's attention.

Distributing Your Release: How to Get the Word Out

Distributing Releases to the Press

The releases are written; where possible they are localized, perhaps using mail merge software. How do you get them to your media contacts? The best answer is to talk with your media contacts and find out. Here are some generalities.

Mail

Mail is generally reliable and inexpensive and it provides hard copy. Editors still prefer it for unsolicited releases that are not time-sensitive. Mail also lets you include ancillary material such as fact sheets, photographs, or the program for the concert you are trying to publicize. However, we all know that sending messages by mail does not guarantee instant delivery or let you answer media questions immediately. If you need to reach news editors immediately, use the following options.

Fax

Some editors prefer fax because it combines the virtues of hard copy with immediacy. Some fax machines have a "broadcast" option whereby you can store fax numbers in memory and then send one fax to all those numbers at the push of a button. It is a handy way of automating the distribution process as long as you don't develop a reputation for "junk fax."

One potential problem is that a news office may share one fax machine among many writers. Faxing to a number does not guarantee that the fax will get to a specific individual. Fax also cannot handle enclosures, and there is a loss of print quality. In addition, it is easy for the pages of a lengthy fax to get out of order, a clear case for page numbering.

Newswires

Wire services such as Associated Press have local reporters, or "stringers." If this local contact decides that your story has news value, she will forward it to the wire service for distribution to subscribers. Don't expect routine releases to be carried by the wire services, but stories of regional or national value or even interesting or novel features might get coverage.

An alternate way of reaching journalists electronically is through networks such as the PR Newswire ProfNet service, MediaNet, a journalist-operated reporting tool, or eNR used by many colleges and universities. These services help journalists find, for example, industry experts, case studies, in-house documents, opinion, or alternate points of view.

Public relations writers should pay particular attention to PR Newswire, which focuses on disseminating public relations information. Although founded to help public companies meet SEC obligations to release information simultaneously to all business media, PR Newswire now serves nonprofit, government, and educational organizations as well as business. For a membership fee, organizations can post news within instant reach of thousands of business, industry, and consumer media outlets.

E-mail

E-mail distribution of releases is tempting and logical. You simply develop a mailing list in your computer and at the press of a button send releases to the media contacts on your list. It is instant and you save trees, right? Unfortunately it's not that simple. Many editors prefer working on hard copy. Others feel that they are already drowning in e-mail. Avoid cluttering up their e-mail boxes with information they did not request.

On the other hand, there are editors who accept e-mail as long as the headers and subject titles indicate a clearly relevant release from a legitimate and recognized source. PR Newswire, for example, accepts all releases electronically—but with strict controls to ensure they are legitimate. The pros and cons of using e-mail for distributing media releases involve issues of software compatibility and, of course, providing the information that the recipient (in this case, the editor) wants and needs.

One strength of computer-to-computer communication is that it allows you to send not only text but also audio and video. With the necessary software, recipients can edit your text online and then drag the content straight into page layout software. Audio and video producers can similarly drag this content into a news production as *actualities* (audio material). In practice, software and hardware incompatibilities, economic realities, and editorial preferences for "hands on" may make this scenario unlikely for some media sources. Check before you adopt these methods.

The Web

An alternate to this scenario is posting releases on the organization's web site. Web posting ensures that the information is accessible to the public regardless of whether the media prints or airs the story. The pages are typically referred to as "Press Room," "Media Releases," "News," or "For the Media."

Web pages can also provide audio and video that is not available with other distribution methods. When the Phoenix Coyotes hockey team announced the recipients of it charitable grants, the web posting of the release allowed visitors to click on a link to photos of the grant recipients.

Releases posted on a web site serve as an ongoing resource for web visitors seeking information on a topic. For some organizations, web posting provides a lasting public service. It is likely that travelers may refer to web archives of releases from the U.S. Departments of State or Homeland Security as they plan international and domestic travel.

Releases posted on the Web can also be delivered directly to anyone who opts to be on an e-mail list, or posted on a staff intranet to keep employees informed. Look for such news options on the web sites you visit.

Customizing News Releases

Think back to the news determinants we discussed earlier, and to the need to make news releases relevant to the audiences of the media you have chosen for distribution. Mail merge and e-mail software simplify this process, allowing you to tailor releases for a range of local markets. It is an adaptation of the personalization used by the direct mail and marketing industries.

Mail Merge

For many organizations, the majority of releases are routine, standard information that repeats year after year and is made newsworthy simply because it is personalized to individual media outlets. Think, for example, of an annual list of graduates or contest or charity race winners. Using mail merge software, you can customize a generic message for the graduates' or winners' local media. Mail merge is discussed in more detail in Appendix A.

E-mail Software

You can also find e-mail software to help you customize releases for electronic distribution to media that will accept distribution this way.

Why Are *You* Writing the Release or Producing the Video? (and the tools to help you avoid it)

For an internal audience, you may be author, editor, and publisher combined, in which case you have no choice but to write all stories. However, for external release, a welcome alternative is to alert the media to a story that may interest them and then provide opportunities for journalists to develop the story themselves. As a general rule, if the media come to you, the story will be published/aired. The challenge is to get them to come to you.

There are some advantages to having the media write (or produce) the story. First, you will know ahead of time that the story will likely be used, and therefore you may save time and money in producing articles that may never be used. Second, the media may be attracted because they have control over the story and can give it the treatment they prefer. The downside is that you and your organization lose control over the final content and treatment; however, such control is always a media prerogative anyway.

If you have cultivated positive relations with the local media, arranging coverage may be as simple as calling to alert the journalist or editor to the event, new product, chairman's speech, charity promotion, or whatever you want to promote. One public relations executive in the cosmetics industry spends much of her time on the phone maintaining relations with a multitude of beauty editors, providing them with advance notice of her clients' activities and special events. Even if a particular "tip" does not itself lead to coverage, she considers it time well spent because it helps establish her and her clients in the editors' minds. This often leads to the editors approaching her and offering her clients what is essentially free coverage in stories that are not seen as public relations.

If the story meets the media's criteria for news and their timing and scheduling, they will either send a reporter or request that you provide specific content such as text of the speech, photos/videotape, or other actualities. Either way, you will probably get coverage.

More typically, your task will be limited to promoting the story through a media alert or pitch letter and providing the writer/reporter with relevant supporting information in the form of backgrounders, position papers, and/or biographies (bios). You may also have to provide facilities such as parking and/or interview rooms.

And don't ever forget the value of a good "photo op." The press always needs good photos, and many otherwise routine events have made the papers purely on the basis of a good photo. Animals and children have such photographic potential that organizations such as zoos and day care centers may have to do little more than send the media a copy of the flyer announcing an event to have a photographer show up, or at least to have the photo editor call for further information. Your organization may seem less photogenic, but if you can find a photo op, make sure the press knows about it.

The formats used to draw media attention to a potential story are the pitch letter and the media alert/advisory.

The Pitch Letter

The pitch letter is the most overt or aggressive of written overtures to the media. It is a clear attempt to target editors and to promote an organization's event, personnel, or product as worthy of news coverage. It identifies aspects that you believe the receiver of your letter will be interested in, and it explains why readers/viewers would be interested. It also suggests precisely how the media can access the story, that is, whether the topic is a potential interview, live event, interview, speech, or demonstration. Finally, it details the time, date, and place of any events so that the media can plan to attend. Note that a pitch letter does not have to be an actual letter; it may take the form of a fax or e-mail message.

Exhibit 9.8 is an example of a letter pitched to the editors of campus newspapers asking them to print an accompanying editorial about animal research. Note how the letter emphasizes the appeal of the "product" (in this case an op-ed) to the editor's readers.

Recognizing that "exclusivity" is a "hot button" for media that pride themselves on being the first, or preferably only, outlet with a story, pitch letters are commonly sent to the outlet most likely to run the story and that best serves your target audience and communication objectives. If this is the case, make it clear in the letter.

If you can identify more than one appropriate medium, develop a different story idea for each media, and send them directly to the editors responsible for that "beat." For example, the opening of a new arts center might have appeal to a lifestyle editor for its focus on home decor, to a business editor for its potential to revitalize a neighborhood, or to an arts editor for the artists who will exhibit there. Do not rely on the media to determine the appeal of a story; spell it out so they understand how your story will appeal to their readers.

On an even more media-friendly note, a medical center news director we know provides his local TV channel with a monthly calendar of events at the hospital *and* of special interest dates that the media might find interesting as they try to

EXHIBIT 9.8   Pitch letter sent with an op-ed article.

Date

Dear Editor:

I am submitting the enclosed opinion editorial regarding the harmful use of animals in education on behalf of Dr. Jonathan Balcombe, a biologist and associate director for education on Annual Research Issues for The Humane Society of the United States (HSUS). The HSUS is the nation's largest animal protection organization.

We are certain that this editorial will interest many of your readers. It is intended to spark debate on your campus about the use of animals in science education. The issue of animal use in education is a growing concern among American college students. Scores of animal rights groups have sprung up on campuses during the past decade, and The HSUS receives dozens of calls each month from college students seeking humane alternatives to classroom dissection or vivisection assignments.

If you prefer an electronic version of the piece, I can send it to you on disk or e-mail it to your newsroom. In addition, you can find more information about dissection in the classroom on our World Wide Web site at www.hsus.org. Please do not hesitate to call me if you have any questions. Thank you in advance for considering "Students: Refuse Animal Dissection."

Sincerely,

Colleen Dermody
Public Relations Director

Enclosure

The Humane Society of the United States
2100 L Street, NW, Washington, DC 20037
(202)452-1100 FAX (202)778-6132
Printed on recycled paper

Source: Reprinted with permission of the Humane Society of the United States, Washington, D.C.

fill 90 minutes of local news each night. Such topics include National Sports Injury Awareness Week, the anniversary of the first heart transplant, or the "official" start of the flu season. When the media find local interest in one of these topics, or sometimes when they need filler, they turn to the hospital for expertise—good coverage with minimal effort. Other organizations, including the American Red Cross, do the same on a national basis.

The Media Alert or Advisory

The media alert or advisory is usually a two- or three-paragraph message to editors identifying a news opportunity. If the event has sufficient news value, such as a visiting VIP, or if it is an event of community interest such as a grand opening or college commencement ceremony, the advisory may use a simple 5W + H format.

Alternatively, it may set out the facts of the event with a brief explanation of why it is relevant to media audiences.

Exhibit 9.9 is a media advisory that was used effectively by Six Flags New England to attract local media to the opening of the new Hurricane Harbor water park. Although brief, it gives editors of both print and electronic media many reasons for covering the event: the novelty and human interest of six weddings, the exotic setting, and opportunities for visual and interview material. Note particularly

---

EXHIBIT 9.9   Media alert issued by Six Flags New England to announce the opening of the Hurricane Harbor water park.

MEDIA ADVISORY

Six Adventurous Couples to Wed in Six Flags'
Hurricane Harbor Water Park June 21st

First Day of Summer Kicks off with Newlyweds taking the real plunge

MEDIA INVITE

WHAT: Six Flags New England celebrates the expansion and opening of Hurricane Harbor water park with a wedding! Six Flags will provide a FREE wedding to six couples that have committed to "take the plunge" and exchange vows in the newly expanded Hurricane Harbor water park. Six Flags will provide the romantic setting in the tropical paradise of Hurricane Harbor, a Justice of the Peace and a beautiful reception that will take place in the picturesque River's Edge Picnic Grove.

Couples from Connecticut and Massachusetts will stand among friends and family in Hurricane Harbor water park as they exchange vows and legally become Husband and Wife.

WHEN: Friday, June 21, 2003 — First Day of Summer!

11AM — Wedding in Hurricane Harbor

12noon-4PM — Wedding reception in the River's Edge Picnic Grove

WHERE: Six Flags New England — Hurricane Harbor
1623 Main Street — Agawam, MA
For more information call (413) 786-9300, ext. 3358

VISUAL & INTERVIEW OPPORTUNITIES:

✦ Six couples exchanging vows in Hurricane Harbor Water Park
✦ Newlyweds taking the "official plunge" on the all-new Geronimo Falls and Zooma Fails water slide
✦ Family and Friends watching as each couple becomes Husband and Wife
✦ Newlyweds and their guests enjoying a wedding reception complete with food, music, champagne toast and wedding cake

TECHNICAL/Materials:

✦ Interviews with couples available.

SIX FLAGS and all related indicia are trademarks of Six Flags Theme Parks Inc. ®,™ and ©2003. (s03).

Source: Reprinted with permission of Six Flags New England.

how clearly these opportunities are spelled out. The advisory resulted in coverage by both television and the press.

Wire services may include it on their daybooks (calendar of events) if they consider it sufficiently newsworthy. Editors track these daybooks for interesting stories and may schedule your event into a reporter's or photographer's schedule even if you have not sent an advisory to that medium.

Supporting the Media

Merely attracting the media's attention isn't the end of a public relations writer's job. You must also provide additional information that reporters and editors need to complete the story to their satisfaction. Think of this as just "part of the service."

Media Kits

Media kits, also called press kits, are the most common way of providing the press with background information about an organization. Press kits are an assemblage of an organization's informational material, usually prepared to support an event such as the opening of a new facility, a presidential inauguration, or the launch of a new product or development campaign. Typically, they include any or all of the writing formats discussed in this book as well as photographs, maps, and diagrams as appropriate.

Press kits range from the quick and simple, assembled totally from existing material, to the elaborate and expensive using special folders and full-color material prepared especially for the occasion.

Some organizations make their media kits more permanent and comprehensive. The Boston Celtics media kit is a paperbound book, produced annually and containing schedules, player and team statistics, policies, and contacts for all teams in the National Basketball Association (NBA). Sports reporters who cover the Celtics presumably keep it on a shelf over their desks and refer to it often. For ease and speed of delivery, an entire press kit can also be put on CD-ROM and mailed or made available as part of a satellite media tour.

To the extent that press kits are produced to inform the media only, they may be becoming a dinosaur of public relations writing. To the extent that they are produced to support a specific event, they will continue to be a physical "take home" presence at news conferences and product launches, and an easily accessible information source on the Web. "Press kit" describes one common purpose; the content is better described as information kit or information package.

Even if the kit is assembled for a specific press conference, much of the content is likely to be the materials you have prepared previously: fact sheets, bios of executives and keynote speakers, backgrounders, position papers, news releases, speeches, technical specifications, photographs, and the like. To this standard material you can add information prepared specifically for the occasion, such as a copy of the CEO's speech, floor plans of the new building, or the results of a marketing survey about the new product. The aim is to give the media as much information as possible about the organization and the subject or event.

Camera-ready artwork and photographs that can be used to illustrate an article are also important. Ensure that you have model releases for all photos you distribute. To meet the needs of electronic as well as print media, include a list of available actualities and the formats in which they can be provided.

Media kits are increasingly finding their way onto organizational web sites, particularly for organizations that find themselves in the news or that receive frequent media inquiries. For example, "The Jason Project," an ongoing science education program, maintains an extensive media kit on its web site. Reporters (and others) can refer to it for facts, history, comments, statistics, and photos whenever students in their area participate in the project.

Another benefit of the Web for media kits is that you can post photographs, actualities, and video clips for downloading. In principle, any of the above can also be archived into a database so that a history of organizational events also becomes available. Announcements that involve a corporate office or technical expert can be linked to the individual's own home page providing perhaps a brief bio and a point of contact for e-mail questions. The major constraint on the use of web-based press kits is, of course, the extent to which the recipients have the hardware and compatible software to permit the effortless downloading of files, especially memory-hungry graphics files.

Position Papers

We have previously discussed the fact sheets, backgrounders, and bios that form the basis of most media kits. Another common enclosure is the position paper—often called a "white paper"—that sets out the organization's position on a topical issue on which the organization wishes to take a public stance. Examples of topics might include corporate taxation, a new technology, affirmative action, or legislation mandating stricter environmental controls. Typically, the position paper takes the form of an editorial; it is factual, presenting both sides of the argument and then a concluding argument in favor of the employer. See Chapter 14 for a fuller discussion of opinion-editorial (op-ed) articles, of which the position paper is one example.

Prepared Statements

A briefer form of the position paper is the prepared statement, which the organization may make in response to a contentious issue or to questions from the media. Prepared statements are brief and because of this they are criticized as ambiguous. This may be a deliberate strategy; often it is the only statement that an organization is able to make in the early stages of a developing situation. Prepared statements also have an important internal function of giving employees a quick organizational viewpoint or guideline that they can use if questioned.

Success

Ideally, a well-written, well-placed release will get your organization space on the front page of the paper, or lifestyle or business section, as appropriate. Sometimes, however, success comes in less dramatic fashion than 12 column inches or a 3-minute TV spot. Take for example, Exhibit 9.10, a media alert inviting the media to an event at which the Milton Bradley president was to launch the Children's Giving Tree Program, and, below the release, the text of the coverage this alert received on a local radio station.

EXHIBIT 9.10   Media release advisory (top) and the way a local radio station used it (bottom).

CHILDREN'S GIVING TREE KICKS OFF FOURTEENTH YEAR WITH OPENING CEREMONY ON TUESDAY, NOVEMBER 25 AT 10 A.M.

WHO: Members of the Springfield Golden Age Club, students from the Springfield Day Nursery and Milton Bradley's Vice President of Human Resources Michael Niziolek.

WHAT: Special opening of the Fourteenth Annual Children's Giving Tree.

WHEN: Tuesday November 25, 1997 at 10:00 a.m.

WHERE: Tower Square in downtown Springfield.

WHY: To kick off the fourteenth annual Giving Tree. Children from local schools provide holiday gifts for needy children in the Springfield area by making and donating ornaments to the Tree. For every ornament placed on the Tree, Milton Bradley donates a toy or game to one of three local children's charities.

HOW: The toys and games are distributed in time for Christmas by local branches of the United Way, the Salvation Army Toy for Joy and the Marine Corps Toys for Tots. Representatives from each organization will be on-hand for the opening ceremony.

For more information, contact Earl Donahue at Milton Bradley Company, (413) XXX-XXXX, extension XXXX.

Excerpts From WRNX Script:

It's time for good things to do—WRNX's list of—well, good things to do. For instance,

. . . It's always a good time to sponsor a meal or a couple of meals at "Not by Bread Alone," a non-profit soup kitchen in Amherst that offers free meals and groceries to those in need. . . .

Children are invited to make and donate ornaments to the children's giving tree at Tower Square in Downtown Springfield For every ornament placed on the tree, Milton Bradley donates a toy or game to one of three local children's charities.

. . . If you want more information on how you can get involved in these good things to do, call WRNX at 493-7755, Extension 170 and we'll give you the low-down. Good things to do—brought to you by the Valley's only quality Rock, 100.9 WRNX.

Source: Advisory from MILTON BRADLEY® & Hasbro, Inc., East Longmeadow, Massachusetts. All rights reserved. Reprinted with permission. Radio script reprinted with permission of WRNX 100.9 FM, Holyoke, Massachusetts.

Note: This illustrates well that no matter how carefully you write a release, once it is out of your hands, you have no control over its presentation in the mass media.

Obviously, the radio station did not attend the event, but Milton Bradley might well have been pleased with the coverage, especially given that the company name figured prominently and that the station chose to include the story in a feature that the public could be expected to pay attention to—that is, "Things to Do."

It makes the point that for better or worse, news releases are uncontrolled in both content and distribution. In Chapter 10, we discuss the use and advantages of controlled media.

✦ Go to www.sagepub.com/treadwell for web exercises, study hints, case studies, and additional examples appropriate to this chapter and chosen or developed to supplement the chapter content.

WRITING WRAP-UP

1. Write a media release for your campus newspaper announcing an event to be held by the campus organization you have worked with since Chapter 3. Write the same release for the local newspaper. How and why will they differ?

2. Refer back to the Phoenix Coyotes FanTrak release shown as Exhibit 9.5. Write a media alert for the media conference held to make this announcement. The release includes the information needed for the alert.

3. Write a pitch letter to persuade the media to write a feature on the FanTrak research system. What angles might appeal? What time of year might be appropriate to pitch the story? Why?

REFERENCE

James, D. (2004, January 14). *Radio: How to get them talking about you.* Paper presented at "Getting Noticed in the 21st Century: A Communications Conference," Western New England College, Wilbraham, MA.

RESOURCES

Style Guides

Goldstein, N. (Ed.). (2004). *The Associated Press stylebook and briefing on media law.* Reading, MA: Addison-Wesley.

Martin, B., Cook, H., and the Editors of UPI. (2004). *UPI stylebook and guide to newswriting* (4th ed.). Sterling, VA: Capital Books.

Science Magazine, online style guide, http://www.sciencemag.org/feature/contribinfo/prep/index.shtml

Release Distribution

Bizwire	www.bizwire.com
eNR	www.enewsrelease.com
PR Newswire	www.prnewswire.com
PRWeb	www.prweb.com

Featured Organizations

10

Under Your Control

Features and Newsletters

KEY PRINCIPLES

1. Feature writing challenges the public relations writer's creativity.

2. Feature writing lends itself to stories without time sensitivity.

3. Most feature stories are *not* published in the mass media.

4. The versatility of newsletters makes them appropriate for multiple audiences, messages, and formats.

5. Newsletters offer precise control over message and distribution.

THE PRINCIPLES IN PRACTICE

1. Feature writing—when you have time to be creative.

2. Newsletters—relationship-building with many publics.

Chapter 9 dealt with newswriting for the press. It focused on uncontrolled print media in which distribution of a message depends on the willingness of the media to publish the message. In that case, the public relations writer has relatively little control over the final treatment and reach of the message.

In contrast, this chapter focuses on newswriting for "controlled media"—methods of disseminating messages in which the writer can exercise much more control over both content and distribution. We look first at how to use controlled media to disseminate the same good news for which you used the press in Chapter 9 and then at a style of writing that for public relations is most often used in controlled media: features. We end by talking about newsletters, a news and feature medium with great potential over which you theoretically have complete control.

Using Controlled Media for News

Except in organizations for which "*a* public" is truly "*the* public" (thereby making the mass media an obvious choice), most communications are sent to usually smaller and always more targeted audiences. Once you eliminate the gatekeeper-controlled mass media, the issues of external control disappear; what you write/design/record/produce/post is what the publics receive. You can send the message you want when you want, and you can, within some limits, send it directly to individual members of the target public.

Why Use Controlled Media for News?

Theoretically, using controlled media for news leaves you with a choice of all media other than mass media, but each medium will be more or less appropriate depending on the message and purpose. Sometimes a medium does not reach the necessary audiences. Although a company's release about a new office would reach the public in the city where the new office is to be located, it would not get the news to employees, clients, affiliates, or government agencies.

In other cases, a news release may not address the concerns of specific publics. Although a media release from a hospital about the purchase of a building for a community fitness center would inform the public, it would not address the concerns of employees about inconvenience during the construction or advise physicians how to refer patients for physical therapy. Sometimes particular audiences (usually employees) should be told before they find out through the media. In all of these situations, you need alternative ways to reach particular publics with messages that address their concerns.

Remember too, that although the news media specialize in the "now," news doesn't necessarily mean immediate. Many news determinants—particularly relevance, proximity, and human interest—make successful news features or newsletter articles. As such they are the mainstay particularly of newsletters that seldom contain "hot" news because they are published at weekly or monthly intervals. News features seldom deal with immediate news because of the time required to research, write, and "polish" the copy.

DISCUSSION   1

Consider the news release samples in Exhibits 9.4, 9.5, and 9.6 in Chapter 9 (Red Cross, Phoenix Coyotes, and Alteon Training). List as many publics as you can for each of these three organizations. Which publics would a news release *not* reach? Why not? What other media would reach these publics? What form would the message take for these media? How would you change the message?

Feature Writing

Although feature writing is often considered part of writing for the news media, this is not where most public relations features are used. That is why we did not discuss feature writing in Chapter 9. Thinking of feature writing separately from the newswriting will help you to see its vast potential for other documents, especially newsletters and annual reports.

This is not to suggest that public relations writers never write features used in the news media. They do. But most of their involvement with news media features is limited to suggesting and "selling" an idea to the media that then write/shoot/produce the piece themselves. In such cases, the public relations writer's talent lies in writing effective pitch letters.

On the other hand, public relations writers *are* responsible for virtually all of the features used in newsletters, organizational videos, annual reports, and corporate web sites. These features range from personal stories and backgrounders to product-in-use stories and research results. Because you can guarantee they will be used, it is worth spending the extra time on them. And you can always send them to the news media if you wish. The fact that features are often considered "soft" rather than "hard" news should not imply that they are less important, only less immediate.

There are a number of advantages to feature writing. For the writer, features typically have the luxury of longer deadlines that allow more research and detail. They may be more satisfying professionally because they offer the opportunity for creative writing with novelty leads or character development. For the reader, features provide human interest, background, and detail that they may not get from a hard-news story. And because features often focus on human interest, readers may identify with the characters, learn new behaviors, or develop an emotional bond with the characters. From a psychological or marketing viewpoint, this bonding is important because it involves the reader with the organization—which is the basis for successful relationships.

What Is a Feature?

For the purpose of public relations writing, feature stories are those that do not necessarily have *immediate* topical relevance, importance, or urgency but that have appeal because they attract reader interest. We would also add stories that entertain, educate, inform, and motivate.

Although feature stories may be news, it is more likely that they will supplement or provide background on a timely news item. They may also present a new aspect of the story, explain how the product/service was developed/should be used/will influence the future, or introduce the employee who developed it. Look at how weekly sports magazines such as *Sports Illustrated* handle any event for which the readers know the results long before the issue appears in print. The writer usually adopts a feature approach, leading with the injury that sidelined a key player, the 10-year rivalry between the finalists, or the drug scandal that nearly kept a key competitor out of the game. The article reviews the results, but the details—even play-by-play details—are chosen with the "theme" in mind.

Similarly, newsweeklies such as *Time* and *Newsweek* adopt feature techniques to make news that may be a week old relevant and topical. This approach is as valid for public relations writers, especially when you need to write a newsletter story several weeks after the event.

In Chapter 9, we looked at the topics that the press might consider news and discussed how the definition of news varies depending on the media's audience(s). Your employer is likely to consider news to be anything the organization wants to promote.

At times like this, it may be helpful to consider that there is no clear-cut line between hard news and soft feature. Rather, there is a continuum in which "hard" news items may have feature appeal and "soft" features may have news value. The *New York Times* approaches feature style in its lengthy, analytical coverage of current events. Its softer profiles on politicians, scientists, and celebrities are written typically because the individuals are newsworthy.

The successful public relations writer should be able to look at a topic and recognize the potential for both hard and soft stories. If the event, person, or project has news value, you will use the newswriting and distribution techniques described in Chapter 9 to write a news release and/or you will alert the media to entice them to cover the news themselves. If the activity does not have immediate news value, look at it again to identify aspects that lend themselves to feature treatment.

This is not an either/or decision. You should also take a second look at hard-news stories to identify features that have the potential for a double hit in the news media and at features to find news that would be suitable for a trade or regional interest publication or certainly for the organization's newsletters.

Feature Subjects

For the public relations writer, there are several starting points for a feature. Like all other projects, the feature subject and its treatment should be determined by the organization's goals and priorities. Following are examples of common feature topics that may or may not fit into your communication plan.

✦ *People features (e.g., employees)* focus on a human interest angle of the subject. People features have the potential to help the public appreciate even complex scientific or medical research or legal processes. They are an especially popular type of story. People features are easily tailored to external or internal audiences and media and can be used to supplement news stories, to entertain, or to support the organization's human resources program, for example.

Exhibit 10.1 is a feature written to highlight a fan of the Phoenix Coyotes hockey team, in this case a fan who does not live locally. We have already seen that fan interest is a key value of the team, so fan interest is a natural subject for the Coyotes' public relations team.

✦ *Case studies or application features* show how a product or service improved someone's life or work, or demonstrate how to use the product or service effectively.

✦ *Case histories* trace the activities of a product or person over a period of time, taking a historical approach to the topic.

✦ *Research findings* often generate stories about how the produce affects everyday life. It is not unusual for the news media to run such a feature to supplement a hard-news story about the research findings.

EXHIBIT 10.1 Fan feature.

FAMILY AFFAIR IN COLORADO

By Damon Markiewicz

When the Phoenix Coyotes played the Colorado Avalanche in a home and home series on March 12 and March 14, for one proud Coyotes fan and sponsor, it was literally a home and home series.

Coyotes supporter Burt Stewart, anytime the Coyotes and Avalanche face each other, has a very strong interest in the outcome for the simple fact that he is currently a resident of Colorado but has developed a strong relationship with the Coyotes organization. Stewart is the vice president of sales for the Patron Spirits Company and dating back to last August, he decided to develop a corporate partnership with the Coyotes. It's a relationship that has blossomed throughout the 2003-04 campaign and because it's so strong, Stewart is now proud to wear his Coyotes jersey when attending games back in Denver at the Pepsi Center.

"I can honestly say that it has been a pleasure to have worked with the Coyotes organization this season," said Stewart, who attended the Coyotes game in Colorado with his wife, daughter and son. "Here I am at the Pepsi Center in Colorado wearing my Coyotes jersey. Everything has gone well starting all the way back to last summer. I have witnessed the opening of the new Glendale Arena and have very quickly become a strong supporter of the Coyotes."

Stewart spends time in the Valley every six weeks and had the chance to attend a Phoenix home game at Glendale Arena on March 12 when the Avalanche was in town. It was a contest that brought Stewart's partnership with the Coyotes full circle due to the fact that he was able to watch his hometown Avalanche square off against his newfound love, the Coyotes.

"It was unique sitting in Glendale Arena watching those two teams play. It was a great game and we had a lot of fun that night," said Stewart. "I thought Phoenix was going to tie the score late in the third period and I was hoping for overtime. Glendale Arena is a fantastic facility, and having a chance to be part of the opening of our new home in Glendale was very memorable because I remember being in the arena before the seats were in. Working with Nathan Berkowitz, Doug Moss and everyone with Aramark has been very enjoyable this year."

Enjoying Coyotes hockey with the entire family isn't just a cliché for Stewart; he makes it one of his top priorities. In fact, Stewart had another moment of a lifetime earlier this season when he brought his son to his very first hockey game. The father and son bond at any sporting event is special, but for two hockey fans it was the perfect setting.

"My son was funny; he sat there and didn't want to leave his seat, not even to go to the restroom," said Stewart. "We had great seats down near the player's bench and he got a kick out of being that close to the action. It was a fun night and I think we have him hooked on the sport forever. He loves watching the games and as long as he is having fun with the sport, it's all worthwhile for me."

When looking into his crystal ball, Stewart views a very bright future of the Coyotes organization. With a brand new arena and a young core of players, Stewart is anticipating watching a Phoenix team next season that will allow him to take advantage of another perk, playoff tickets.

"I am really looking forward to continuing my relationship with the team next year," said Stewart. "My last trip into Phoenix, I started looking at some homes and due to the fact that I am traveling to the Valley quite often, who knows maybe we will have residence in Arizona. The fans in Arizona should be very proud of their home and sooner or later, they will have what they deserve, a team that is competing for the ultimate prize, the Stanley Cup."

Source: Reprinted with permission from the Phoenix Coyotes.

◆ *Background information* may be written feature style, perhaps profiling the founder of the company or its changing technologies. An organization with an interesting history may successfully place feature stories in the news media based largely on historical interest, especially when there is a logical tie-in with an anniversary, a local historical celebration, or industry or sector promotion.

♦ *Educational information* has a good chance of being printed in the news media, especially if it also has an interesting feature-focus. Implicitly, such stories give an organization the image of being the "good guy" acting in the public interest without actually promoting the organization's activities.

The article in Exhibit 10.2 uses a "how to," educational twist to appeal to editors even though it is soft rather than hard news. Bullets, generally taboo in hard-news stories, call attention to important points, and contact numbers are highlighted for further information. This article was sent out by the U.S. Department of Health and Human Services in hard-copy, single-column format, complete with graphics. Because it is not time-sensitive, an editor can easily drop it into available space or as support material for a local story.

If it fits your communications plan, you may find that a stock of educational articles, ready for monthly or quarterly release, will keep your organization in the news and provide topical, regular features for your own publications. Arm & Hammer, Inc., for example, receives considerable press coverage from seasonally topical articles on the uses of baking soda. The company web site translates the releases into a houseful of online hints. All of these promote the company as consumer-friendly and a source of good advice.

These feature approaches—and there are many more—increase the opportunities to reach specialist media, especially magazines, that may not be interested in straight news. They also provide copy for internal publications. If you are going to spend time on a feature story, it is always a good idea to have a solid internal use for it rather than relying on the news media to print it.

Feature Structure

Just as feature writing allows you to write on topics that might never be considered hard news, so too it allows you greater latitude in the choice of approaches and structures than is available in conventionally structured news.

Feature writing relies on the story having an "interest" rather than an immediate "news" value. Unlike newswriting, the feature story lead may not be the most informative part of a story, although it must draw the reader into the story. Feature writers may not reach the main point for several paragraphs, taking time instead to develop a theme, build a premise, and capture the reader's interest. The writer may even hold the message until almost the end and make it the climax of the story. Long articles may oscillate between perhaps mundane information the reader needs and high points designed to grab and sustain the reader's attention.

Feature Style

Perhaps the greatest difference between newswriting and feature writing lies in their styles. Whereas newswriters are restricted by the inverted pyramid and who-what-when-where-why-how story conventions, feature writers have a wide range of approaches, styles, and techniques open to them to attract reader attention and to develop and hold reader interest. This is an important distinction and one that we believe goes further toward differentiating news and feature than does the choice of subjects (which may be appropriate to both genres).

A Healthy Start for Healthy Babies

WASHINGTON—Earn a lifetime of hugs by giving your baby a healthy start even before you give birth.

Healthy Start, a federal initiative promoting healthy behaviors by mothers-to-be and quality health care for newborns, encourages women to see a health care provider as soon as they know they are pregnant and to keep all follow-up appointments.

Other tips for mothers-to-be:

- Eat three healthy meals daily, plus healthy snacks.
- Drink six to eight glasses of water, fruit juice, or milk daily.
- Gain 25 to 35 pounds during pregnancy.
- Exercise regularly—walking in a safe place is a good exercise for mothers-to-be.

Don't smoke cigarettes, or drink liquor, beer, wine, or coolers; don't use over-the-counter medicines such as aspirin, cold remedies, antacids, or other pain relievers or get an X-ray without checking with your health care provider; don't use illegal drugs such as marijuana, heroin, cocaine, or crack. These substances can be harmful to pregnant women and their babies. They can cause babies to have breathing problems, brain damage, and birth defects.

The Healthy Start Initiative encourages pregnant women and their partners to adopt healthy behaviors during pregnancy and to maintain them once their babies are born.

For more information on prenatal care services, tips for a healthy pregnancy, or to find out if there is a Healthy Start program in your community, call toll free, 1-800-311-BABY (2229) (English speakers) or 1-800-504-7081 (Spanish speakers).

Source: Produced by Vanguard Communications, Inc. under U.S. Department of Health and Human Services, Health Resources and Services Administration contract #240–92–0019 for the National Healthy Start Campaign.

Feature writing attracts and holds a reader's interest by creatively presenting a particular aspect of the organization or its business. Following are some of the most common options for feature presentation. Use them as appropriate to the topic, but remember that feature stories lend themselves to exercising your creativity.

✦ *Greater length.* The feature story may be longer than a news story because it has detail, description, explanation, humor, interest, and often, graphics or photographs. Feature stories used in newsletters and other controlled media are likely to be displayed prominently in the publication, often on the front page or centerspread.

✦ *Human interest focus.* Feature stories often focus on people. Even features about financial management, technological advances, or research developments use human interest, rich description, speech, and normal vocabulary to keep the reader interested and to illustrate important points. The inherent reader/viewer interest in "people words" such as real names and "he," "she," or "they" is a major factor in attracting readers. Another way to bring a human interest focus to a story is to use direct quotes, even to the point of setting up a dialogue between two characters.

The fan feature in Exhibit 10.1 is rich with quotes that not only give character to the subject but also convey public relations messages on behalf of the team. The fan's focus on the new arena, the family-friendly atmosphere, and, of course, the prospect of a winning team are all messages that echo the team's own mission. To the extent that you can "lead" a subject, or, with the subject's permission actually write or edit the quotes, you will often use them to send a public relations message on behalf of the organization.

✦ *Descriptive details.* With feature stories, the appeal is partially in the details, especially details that humanize a story or explain a process. Although news stories seldom if ever describe people, feature stories may describe exactly how they dress or talk. Such details make readers believe that they know the person being described. Similarly, details of the office, lab, or factory environment or the scenic location of the new mining operation help the reader understand what the organization does and how it operates.

✦ *Humor.* It is a rare news story that includes humor, but feature stories may lend themselves at least to humorous anecdotes if not to a full comedy approach. Humor is always a delicate and sometimes a contentious issue. What is humorous to one person may not be humorous to another, and sometimes a humorous story may even backfire on the teller. Humor must also be fresh, not borrowed from other sources.

It should be obvious that you must avoid racial, ethnic, religious, or tasteless humor (explicit or implicit), but you should also weigh carefully the snap comment or quip that may be misunderstood. We recall, for example, a young writer reporting for a staff newsletter on an office party (paid for by management) who turned in a story that began, "The head office holiday party was very well-attended . . . where else could you get a free meal on a Wednesday night?" The writer claimed it was intended to be funny, but it wasn't seen so by the editor, who wisely rejected it before management had a chance to see it.

✦ *Question and answer.* For issues that require explanation, such as a new staff insurance plan, a question-and-answer (Q&A) approach is often a good strategy. If you can anticipate your audience's questions, do so—and then answer them. They are the same questions you might use to prepare your CEO for a news conference or that you should also answer on the FAQs (frequently asked questions) page on your web site.

✦ *Compare and contrast.* Compare and contrast is a useful approach if the audience already has a frame of reference for the subject. Examples of compare and contrast approaches include then/now, social status (black/white, rich/poor), or even have/have not.

Remember, compare defines similarities while contrast defines the differences, and you may choose to do either or both in the article. For example, you might explain the provisions of a new law by showing how it differs from a well-understood old law, or make users comfortable with new software by showing its similarities to another old-favorite program. Or you could do both.

Writing approaches such as these also offer many opportunities for design support. Readers may understand comparisons more readily if you present them side-by-side in a two-column layout.

The following sample demonstrates effective use of contrast. Headlined "Wrap Star," the article announced the extension of an exhibit of Egyptian artifacts at a local museum (Lenker, 2003). Note how the author naturally works the name of the sponsoring museum into the second paragraph.

> He's been around for more than 2,500 years, so six months probably would be like the blink of an eye to the mummy Padihershef, if he were still alive.
>
> But for the George Walter Vincent Smith Art Museum at the Quadrangle [in Springfield, Massachusetts], the six-month extension to Padihershef's stay here is the break of a lifetime. (Copyright © 2003 by *The Sunday Republican*. All rights reserved. Reprinted by permission.)

The rest of the article describes the mummy's "serendipitous" journey to Springfield and provides details about the exhibit.

◆ *Description by time (e.g., process descriptions).* Process descriptions start at the beginning and take the reader through a process to the end. For variation, you may be able to lead with the final product and then flash back to the beginning of the process or choose to tell the story of the product, but ultimately it will be a linear, start-to-finish story.

Process descriptions are especially good places to use graphics or photographs. At the most extreme, you may be able to present the whole process in pictures, with the only copy being supporting captions. This is an excellent approach for technologically unsophisticated audiences who might otherwise not read the piece. Save the detailed descriptions for savvy audiences or for the research report or product specification package.

◆ *Description by space.* Similar to the description by time, this method describes a place, top to bottom, north to south, east to west, or front to back. Consider it when your organization moves into new premises or opens a unique new manufacturing facility. It is a written guided tour of the facility.

◆ *Cause and effect.* Employees and other stakeholders need to know about changes in the organization and how these changes affect them. Good feature style cause-and-effect writing can also help publics understand why the changes are taking place.

Feature Leads: Attracting Attention

Unlike hard news, which demands a summary lead that essentially tells the whole story in one or two lines, feature writing allows a diversity of leads to support the diversity of approaches. There are as many types of leads as there are rhetorical devices, and almost all of them are valuable tools for feature stories. Note that we don't recommend rhetorical questions; readers ignore them or answer them and either way they are a distraction from the body of the story. (So why would anyone use them?)

This section includes examples of many types of feature leads, demonstrating the writer's freedom to develop interesting approaches for feature stories. And there are many more.

◆ *Metaphor.* A metaphor explains the vague or complex in terms of the familiar. For example, in the statement "After allowing expenditures to run rampant, the Board of Trustees has decided to rein in the unauthorized acquisition of software," the phrase "rein in" is metaphorical. It evokes the image of a rampaging high-speed expenditure program being brought under control and subject to the direction of the board.

Topical metaphors can help bridge the gap between why you want to write the story and why readers may not see it as relevant. In addition to making even mundane topics memorable, good metaphors give readers a point of reference from which to understand the story and its relevance.

Metaphors are especially powerful figures of speech because we usually accept them (and implicitly the argument being made) without thinking too much about them. For example, the Reagan administration's Strategic Defense Initiative (SDI) to deploy missile interceptors in space is a good example of the use of a metaphor and also of how metaphors can be ambiguous or backfire.

SDI quickly became known as "Star Wars," a metaphor with the high-tech, into-the-future quality that the administration was looking for and that the public could easily relate to. However, for many people, the interpretation of the metaphor was "fantasy" as in "it could never really happen." It was not the ideal metaphor to support a request for congressional funding.

✦ *Narrative leads.* A narrative lead tells a story to open a story. It should take readers to the point where they must continue reading to reach a conclusion, as in the following lead about a young letter-writer sans equal.

> The next time you despair of replying to that mountain of unanswered letters or of starting every note on your Christmas cards with "Sorry I haven't written but . . . ," spare a thought for Kathleen Scott, who ranks second to none when it comes to writing letters. Kathy, a secretary in the Human Resources Division at ABC Industries, corresponds with 26 pen pals, including a New York City cop who befriended Frank Serpico, a cross-country truck driver, a Japanese telephone operator at IBM in Tokyo, and a hotel manager in Alaska, to name but a few.
>
> How does she do it when the rest of the world barely manages to find time for a letter each week to Mom?

✦ *Chronological leads.* Chronological leads are similar to narrative leads except that chronological leads emphasize the passage of time: " . . . at 6:01 . . . at 6:15 . . . at 6:32 . . . ." or "In 1994 . . . five years ago . . . today." For example:

> In 1994, Colin Williams received a husky from a friend who could no longer care for it. Five years ago he bred the dog "Sally" to a malamute with "connections" to the famed Iditarod sled race. Today, Sally is the oldest in a dog team that leads the fit on treks through the northeast wilderness and helps Williams teach people of all ages the principles he holds dear, such as the responsibility of owning an animal and the need to care for the wilderness. Three of Sally's puppies are also in the team.
>
> Williams says his interest in the outdoors was sparked by youthful dreams of adventures in the wild with Jack London and Sergeant Preston.

✦ *Descriptive leads.* Descriptive leads use word pictures to portray an individual or scene.

✦ *Anecdotal leads.* Anecdotal leads tell a mini story that encapsulates the major story. The following lead adapted from an alumnae magazine, for example, tells the story of a young girl's introduction into a foreign language.

Ann Wilson likes to tell the story of her own introduction to foreign language as a six-year-old enrolled in a school in France. "Before I went to school, my mother taught me one word of French, 'non,' and I used it proudly all day, even when they asked my name. The next day she taught me another word, 'oui.' Three months later I had earned class honors. Thinking back on it now I realize my mother had empowered me; she made it possible for me to participate; I didn't have to sit there and say nothing."

Today, as head of languages for Eastern Bay Schools, Ann uses this example to encourage parents, teachers and aides to help immigrant children take their first step into English.

◆ *Teaser leads.* The purpose of teaser leads is simply to entice the reader into the story, to make it virtually impossible for the reader to stop reading. The following teaser is the start of a personal memoir by Thomas Goltz (1997) on getting a shave in Turkey.

It takes a certain amount of faith to let a perfect stranger singe your ears, stick scissors up your nose and run a straight razor around your throat. (Copyright © 1997 by Thomas Goltz. First published in the *New York Times,* Travel Section, November 2, 1997. Reprinted by permission of Ellen Levine Literary Agency.)

After an introductory paragraph like that, it is difficult not to proceed to paragraph two.

As published, the article was a personal recollection, but it isn't a big step to imagine the author turning the same lead into an effective public relations teaser for an article on the pleasures of a travel agent's tour of the Bosporus and Dardanelles.

◆ *News style leads.* From time to time, feature leads may also be a variation on the "5W+H" formula of journalism. Newswriters typically lead with the "what" (happened); the feature writer may find intriguing leads in the who, when, where, why, or how, as in the following lead for a newsletter article on exporting animals.

What looked like a flying Noah's ark left Auckland recently bound for destinations nearly as diverse as its cargo: Hungary, Bulgaria and the United Kingdom.

On board were 85 stud Merino rams, 200 Corriedale ewes, 25 Angora goats, 15 horses and one Hereford bull.

The flight was an export shipment from Wrightson Livestock Export, Inc.

Feature Transitions: Maintaining the Flow of the Story

In Chapter 2, we introduced the importance of transitions for professional writers. They are key to the success of feature stories. The lead entices readers into a story, but transitions keep them reading. Just as a road map makes unfamiliar terrain familiar to a traveler, so transitions ease the reader's route, and in so doing lead the reader through the article.

Let's look at how transitions control the flow of a story. We use for our theme one of the most common of all newsletter features: a retirement profile of a long-serving employee. The raw information for such articles typically comes from the Human Resources Department, from interviews with the retiree, and, if appropriate, from interviews with the retiree's associates.

If you are fortunate, you will find the retiree glib, entertaining, and full of anecdotes he cannot wait to relate. More likely, he will be reluctant to talk about himself and even more so to share any story that doesn't promote the company or that involves anyone "who might not want to be mentioned." Your challenge will be to find the aspect with the greatest interest and to shape the story around it. Even a small anecdote can pave the way into a full and interesting story for a diligent and creative writer.

Fortunately, with feature writing you have as many options as there are stories to tell. The following options demonstrate how transitions help develop a story on the retirement of Marvin Johnson after 35 years as a sales representative.

◆ *Chronological.* The most logical, common (and least interesting) approach to career profiles is chronological, a start-to-finish review of Mr. Johnson's career. The lead is typically something like "XYZ Company will lose its longest-serving employee when Marvin Johnson retires next month," but even this offers multiple options for story flow. It could be developed year-by-year (or more probably decade-by-decade), location-by-location (if he transferred a lot), or in parallel to a review of organization growth and change during the same 35-year period.

Because the structure is obvious, the writing challenge will be to keep the time frames moving, making it easy to follow Johnson's career while avoiding the temptation to begin each section with "In (date) Johnson. . . ." A grasp of transitional phrases that indicate the passage of time will help you chronicle his career without turning it into a list of dates.

Some transitions are obvious: "after this," "soon after," or "by this time." Others convey the passage of time more colorfully, highlighting benchmarks rather than years: "By the time he was ready for college . . ." or "When he returned to work after four years in the Navy. . . ." These techniques and some of the phrases work equally well for process descriptions.

◆ *Human interest: Quotations and attributions.* If Johnson is a senior executive or widely recognized as a "character," you may be able to use quotes and attributions from him or his colleagues as transitions. They will allow you to trace the highlights of Johnson's career while using few, if any, dates.

For example, "Even as a teenager, Johnson was the hardest worker on the production line" clearly introduces a section on his start in the company. "Johnson's natural leadership was as evident in the bowling alley as in the office" presages a section on his leisure activities, or support for company functions. If used consistently to start (or end) sections, the quotes will help make the structure of the article clear.

Clearly, this requires research and time interviewing Johnson's affiliates, but you can reduce the effort by having a clear idea of the topic you want each commentator to speak on. This will allow you to coordinate their interviews and ensure that their comments are pertinent.

◆ *Compare and contrast.* Retirement features can be a wonderful opportunity to use a compare-and-contrast approach if the subject has worked through a period of great change and has a good memory for details.

Such features often turn into interesting history lessons as Johnson remembers how the whole company used to "take the west side tram to the annual picnic at Marshall Lake." Having a good grip on the organization's history will help you ask questions that jog Johnson's memory for funny or interesting anecdotes.

Transitions you will find useful for features that compare and contrast eras or locations include "on the other hand," "things haven't changed much since then," or, obviously, "in contrast." They serve the important purpose of letting the reader know you are switching gears and presenting the opposite viewpoint or alternatively that you are emphasizing a continuation of the previous sentiment.

◆ *News structure.* Feature stories can also follow a basic news structure in which you write from summary/most important to detail/least important. For example, if Johnson was once named "sales person of the year for his tenacity, attention to detail and willingness to go beyond the call of duty in servicing a client," you have a natural lead and also three topics to pursue. If you can find a good example of each of these characteristics, you will not only have a good story but also have one that flows naturally from the characteristics.

And although Johnson may be reluctant to talk about his award, you may find him comfortable giving advice to the "young folk" in the organization. In this case, you could use the same examples as above to support a theme of "what makes a good salesperson."

Creativity is the soul of feature writing and also what makes it so much fun.

EXERCISE 1

Look at the Phoenix Coyotes release shown as Exhibit 9.5 in Chapter 9. The FanTrak system, in which fans record their opinions and answers to survey questions on their Palm Pilots, at kiosks in the arena, or on home computers, provides instant feedback to the team on subjects as diverse as ticket-purchasing habits, fan demographics, quality of amenities, and personnel changes. This clearly has human interest feature potential from many angles. Write the lead paragraphs for three features on the Coyotes' use of the FanTrak system.

Newsletters

Among the options open to organizations to communicate with their publics, newsletters (and now web letters) are among the most popular. Management likes them because they are less expensive and more controlled than other forms of communication. They provide a clean slate on which management can promote its view of the organization. Employees see newsletters as a source of information that may otherwise be unavailable and, except for the very cynical, as an expression of the organization's interest in them.

External audiences, even while recognizing the public relations source, see newsletters as less biased than advertising with its inherent sales or marketing focus. And public relations writers regard newsletters as an opportunity to flex their creative muscles, combining news, feature, and sometimes persuasive writing and design in a format that provides much scope for creativity and approach. It is small wonder that newsletters are an important part of many organizations' communications with employees, clients, and sometimes even the general public.

Understanding Newsletters

Apart from the fact that everyone seems to like a good newsletter, there are many practical reasons why they are such a popular medium. Newsletters are

- ✦ *Adaptable to multiple audiences.* They are flexible and easy to distribute.
- ✦ *Cost-effective.* They can fit any budget.
- ✦ *Implicitly credible.* Because newsletters are regular, it is possible to be subtler with self-promotion and to develop important ideas or positions over a period of time.
- ✦ *Targetable.* Controlling the mailing list and the method of distribution gives you considerable control over who receives the message.
- ✦ *Editorially flexible.* Depending on their purpose, newsletters can accommodate a multitude of styles and approaches. Newsletters that are free generally promote relationships between the organization and its reading (or web-viewing) publics. Such publics implicitly accept a certain degree of promotion for the sponsoring organization. On the other hand, if readers must subscribe or pay for a newsletter, as for many investment guides, the readers expect either unbiased advice or advice that identifies its biases.
  There is always a level beyond which too much or too obvious promotion will hurt a newsletter's credibility, but this varies by organization, by newsletter, and by public.
- ✦ *Effective communications tools.* People expect to find something of value in newsletters.
- ✦ *Formal and tangible.* Formal communications such as newsletters give the organization an opportunity to send common messages to many publics in a consistent, timely, and credible fashion, often counteracting the effects of the office grapevine.

In addition, newsletters provide information in tangible form. Readers can retain the publication and refer back to it or pass it along to additional readers.

The Purpose: What Can Newsletters Help You Do?

Organizational theorists suggest that organizations have three functions: to conduct activities that fulfill the mission of the organization, to cultivate relationships with publics whose attitudes and behavior can affect the organization, and to innovate by adapting and changing as their environments change.

Because they can accommodate articles on every subject, newsletters are ideally suited to helping organizations achieve these aims. Messages about the organization's support for a local charity help fulfill its mission of community responsibility; work-related messages help employees do their jobs better; and messages about a new distribution method might both help employees understand a change in working hours and influence clients to increase their orders.

For newsletters to consistently achieve these goals, they must have their roots in the broader organizational culture and management style. They should also have a clear purpose (preferably written) against which decisions about message, style, and distribution can be measured.

DISCUSSION 2

An organization's mission statement and goals and what you know about the corporate culture and audiences should help you define newsletter goals and functions.

Write a statement of purpose for each of two newsletters, one aimed at your college's or university's employees and the other at alumni.

Internal Versus External Newsletters

Newsletters generally fall into two camps: internal and external. External newsletters directed at customers, clients, government, suppliers, retailers, and indeed the general public usually take a "news" approach. External newsletters exist to cultivate professional relationships. They aim to make the target audience feel good about an organization so that they want to buy its products, use its services, or contribute funds.

Newsletters provide the opportunity for the organization to tell its story without external gatekeepers interfering with the content and/or distribution. Even if the news is bad or complex, a controlled newsletter provides the forum for a spokesperson *of your choosing* to explain and provide evidence that reflects the organization's position.

External newsletters are highly professional, sometimes of magazine quality, and often include photos, color, and graphics to make them stand out and reflect the organization's image.

In contrast, internal newsletters, directed usually at employees, are typically less elaborate and more frequent, even weekly. Regardless of the form, the purpose of employee newsletters is to make employees feel like members of the organizational family. Their tone is usually casual, even conversational, and their contents are a combination of human interest, policy changes, employee accomplishments, and "business" news.

Newsletter Content

Because you know within some limits who will read a newsletter, you can make wise decisions about what will interest them as well as about what the organization wants them to know. You have complete control over content.

This does not mean the principles that govern news should be overlooked. The topic of a press release to the news media would likely be the topic of a story for all of your newsletters if only to ensure that all of your key publics are aware of the activity or understand your employer's full position on the issue.

Similarly, the public's interest in other people does not disappear just because the medium is an organizational newsletter. To the contrary, even for external audiences the idea of focusing on staff with whom they may have contact is a valid approach. Knowing your audience will help you determine whether to feature a research scientist, the head tax accountant, or a new programmer. Whose story will resonate most closely with your audience?

You may be able to use the same articles in multiple publications—many professionals enjoy the challenge of shaping the same material for such different audiences. An article about the organization joining several industry associations might suit both employee and client newsletters. For employees, it will be a minor story showing what sales staff do at trade shows. For a client newsletter, it might have front-page status because it implicitly positions the organization as a committed player in the industry.

News Gathering

To publish a regular newsletter, you have to keep the news coming. Some of the issues involved in newsletter creating are discussed in the "Should You Start a Newsletter?" Planning panel. Many newsletter editors have a team of contributing reporters who are responsible for submitting news from departments and branches. Some of these reporters will enjoy writing and be willing contributors; others will see the responsibility as a chore and provide little if any news. The majority will need encouragement and support. The line "if you just point me (the editor) toward the news, I will be happy to write the story" is often a comfortable compromise.

In other organizations, editors gather news through news referral forms, publishing their e-mail addresses and scheduling monthly meetings with other managers to maximize news-gathering opportunities. And *never* underestimate the value of reading department bulletin boards, listening in the coffee room, getting copies of social club minutes, and generally "being on the grapevine." If you can't do this personally, find an assistant who can. Editors must also communicate effectively with management so that they always know not only what is going on but also what is coming up.

Don't hesitate to solicit news or readers' ideas in the newsletter itself. Space permitting, you can even include a form for submissions. A word of caution is that you require submissions to be signed so you can check details and protect the publication and yourself from misinformation and potential invasion of privacy. (You never know when one employee will submit information another employee considers private.)

Content Ideas

When determining what to write, you have two considerations: What do your audiences want to know, and what does the organization want to tell them? Articles that respond to these questions should also fulfill the objectives you identified for the publication.

Planning

Should You Start a Newsletter?

As many public relations writers have found to their chagrin, intentions alone do not keep newsletters coming. It is far more likely that management enthusiasm will wane and other tasks begin to take priority over the newsletter. A significant percentage of well-intentioned newsletters die before even the third or fourth issue.

So how do you know when to consider recommending a newsletter? You should do so when you want a regular and controlled means of providing information to one or more publics *and* when you are certain that you have the time and content to fill issue after issue. Well before you put pen to proposal, it is critical that you openly and honestly assess where the content will come from and how difficult it will be to gather it.

Try to create the table of contents for as many issues as you can, using activities of the past year as your examples. Identify ongoing topics (such as new personnel, conference news, product releases, or fundraising updates) that you can rely on to fill space issue after issue. You should be able to come up with the contents for at least six monthly issues or a full year of quarterly issues before you feel comfortable starting a newsletter.

And before you plunge ahead, talk with the manager of every department to see what information they will have to contribute, whether they support the idea, who they will assign as your liaison for information, and whether they will make news gathering part of this person's responsibilities.

This will not only help you map out sources of information but also give you a sense of how news-savvy your organization's managers are. Finding out that they have little "news sense" should not in itself deter you from starting a newsletter. But it will give you a realistic picture of how easy it will be to gather material and whether you are likely to need additional staff and/or management support to obtain material.

If you are not sure you can maintain a monthly publication, for example, consider publishing a full issue two or four times a year and a smaller, interim version named "News Flash" or "Late-Breaking News" or "We Couldn't Wait," as news dictates. Many organizations now maintain a regularly updated news column on their web sites so that any user can easily access the most current news about the organization. Controlled access will even allow you to provide information targeted at individual audiences via the Web.

For external newsletters, arguably the audience wants information and the organization wants to cultivate loyalty. Fortunately, it is not difficult to achieve both of these aims if you stick to business concerns that convey an image of professionalism and leadership. Look first to the news releases you have issued. You may want to add quotes on information that is particularly relevant to the newsletter audience such as the new responsibilities of staff members they may know.

Messages from the president, chair, or executive director will be a critical part of each issue. Giving your president a monthly column establishes visibility and credibility. This can be turned to the organization's advantage if you need to explain a downturn or seek client support for legislation or alumni support for a capital

---

EXHIBIT 10.3   Message from the president of a retirement community for a newsletter aimed at the community.

Message From the CEO

What motivates some people to move to retirement communities? There are lots of reasons—lifestyle, security and safety, access to health services, services and amenities, just to name a few. But one of the greatest benefits is an elusive one to explain—and that is the creation of community. Growing social relationships and active resident life make our communities vibrant and exciting places to be.

Residents themselves plan and carry out a variety of activities and programs. They have established book clubs, computer clubs, lecture series, choral groups, concerts, trips, art appreciation classes and gardening activities to name a few. Staff members help to plan and coordinate some of the activities and arrange for transportation, based on residents' preferences. There are exercise and tai chi classes, trips to Tanglewood and the Springfield Symphony, gala social activities and lifetime learning in this vibrant 5-College Area.

The old stereotype of a calendar full of bingo and sing-a-longs has flown out the window (but wait, there's a touch of gambling to bingo, and some folks still love it . . .). Today's residents discover and nurture their talents and passions, living what they love.

Carol Katz

Chief Executive Officer

Source: Reprinted with permission from the Loomis Communities, Holyoke, Massachusetts.

---

fundraising campaign. Such columns also have the benefit of giving even the most distant company a human face.

Exhibit 10.3 is one of the columns written for the public newsletter by the CEO/president of Loomis Communities, a chain of retirement communities. The newsletter is sent quarterly to a mailing list of senior citizens and organizations that reach senior citizens. Its purpose is to familiarize the audience with activities at the residences. The article is informative and upbeat and the message addresses some of the concerns that senior citizens have about moving to a retirement facility, such as loss of independence and leaving one's friends and family. From a public relations viewpoint, the article sends the message that the Loomis organization understands and is responsive to the needs and attitudes of senior citizens. The touch of humor in the "aside" at the end adds warmth to the article, to the writer, and, by implication, to the communities.

Never underestimate the value of helping your readers with their own businesses. You can run a regular business tips column; provide an easy-to-read summary of legal, regulatory, or technological changes; or offer a list of online sources or local numbers for additional health information. It is always good to be seen as a reliable source of information.

If your audience is business or professional, it is wise to keep fillers (material used to fill extra space) to a minimum unless they are obviously helpful. Not only do they waste space, but also you risk being seen as wasting your audience's time. On the other hand, newsletters aimed at the general public often include photos, children's games, or simple topic-related crossword puzzles or contests to attract and involve as many readers as possible.

A Word to the Wise: Good Ideas to Make an Employee Newsletter Writer's Job Easier

Court your human resources staff

Human resources (HR) departments can be valuable allies, both as a source of news and a source of verifying years of service, job titles, formal qualifications, and what information, if any, you can release about employees.

Beware of gossip

Turning the employee newsletter into a branch of the office grapevine is unprofessional. As a strategy, it is sure to backfire. Stick to confirmed events that are approved for public dissemination.

Pay attention to social events and sports teams

Focus on events that you know staff are interested in and that provide variety and fun in a publication.

Try not to play favorites

This applies even if getting news from head office is easier than from any other branch. If you are reporting on one summer picnic, report on them all. Include social notes, for example, births, deaths, marriages, from all branches.

Keep the tone conversational

Don't preach.

Follow up all leads and use them if you can

Failure to act on a lead is a surefire way to discourage the future news tips that are your bread and butter. If you cannot use an article, quietly tell the person who submitted it that it will not run, and why. It will avert that person's (likely vocal) dissatisfaction when the article does not appear.

Set editorial policies and stick to them

It is wise not to create too many editorial policies, but when you do, apply them consistently. How to treat names and nicknames is a policy you might wisely consider, remembering that just because everyone calls the 6'6'' tall accounts clerk "Stick" does not mean he likes the name or that he wants to be referred to by that name in print.

If appropriate, give bylines to branch editors

This is true even if you rewrite the stories they submit. It costs you nothing, gives them a pat on the back, publicizes their role in the newsletter, and, it is hoped, encourages more submissions. If possible, run a list of contributors in every issue.

Internal newsletters, usually directed at employees, are both fun and challenging, if only because they are one of your few opportunities to get immediate, first-hand feedback—and you will. See the "Word to the Wise" box for hints on managing the people and issues critical to internal newsletters.

In contrast to client and public newsletters, internal newsletters are usually "people-heavy." Although employees should be exposed to the same news as external audiences, the focus should be on how the news will affect the employees, especially as it helps them and the organization adapt to change. Whenever possible, bringing staff into the stories is good for morale. Even the president's message can be used to commend good performance as well as to urge better performance. Employee newsletters often have popular columns from the human resources or staff training departments that help employees do their jobs better. Designated "branch office" columns help even the most distant staff feel connected to the organization.

With regard to management participation, although you want to avoid having the publication appear too "top-heavy," recognize that employees want to know how and what the organization is doing. Public relations writers with access to management planning will be able to guide the president in selecting topics that answer staff questions and in presenting them in a way staff will read. It may be the one opportunity for staff to hear from their leader, so it is wise to let the messages reflect the leader's personality and character. A conversational tone and, with caution, a bit of humor are usually appropriate.

Assuming you have a well-liked executive, a good ground rule is to capture the executive's personality. Even routine messages encouraging hard work, cooperation, and focus can be interestingly, even memorably, presented using sports or current events as an analogy, if it is credibly a theme the president would use.

E X E R C I S E   2

Newsletters are fun. They provide opportunities to combine writing and design and to write about many topics. It is likely that your college or university has several newsletter style publications, individually aimed at alumni, students, faculty, and perhaps the community. Make a list of topics that you believe would be appropriate for two such newsletters. Which topics would be regular? Which would lend themselves to feature treatments? Which would you consider "news"?

Newsletter Structure

A look at any newsletter—and you should accumulate many in your personal resource file—will quickly reveal two of the characteristics that make newsletters effective: short articles and a consistent format.

Long Versus Short Articles

Most newsletters have one, perhaps two, main articles accompanied by many articles of three paragraphs or less. The main news article occupies the front page as in a newspaper. Feature articles typically occupy the centerspread where you can showcase them effectively. But even in these positions, main does not mean lengthy. Adopting a practice of not continuing articles to a second page will help you keep text to a length that appeals to the busy reader.

Short articles and columns are the mainstay of newsletters. Most newsletter articles are brief. They let people know what's going on with little elaboration or detail. Short articles are easy to read and very popular. The challenge is to organize them effectively. See Chapter 7 for a discussion of the advantages and disadvantages of common column formats to help you organize newsletter content.

Structural Consistency

Because newsletters have many elements—news articles, graphics, perhaps a feature, and a range of short items—putting them together is sometimes like assembling a jigsaw puzzle. But just as you use the corner pieces to put some boundaries on the puzzle, it is wise to give some elements a consistent and identifiable place where readers can expect to find them.

Knowing where to find the op-ed page, cartoons, or sports section of your daily newspaper gives you a level of comfort with the paper. Doing the same with the president's message, staff promotions, and department reports, for example, will do the same for a newsletter.

Newsletter Style

Knowing the newsletter audience also gives you control over style. You are not bound by the inverted pyramid or the "who, what, when, where, why and how" of media conventions (although you would be wise not to forget them). Instead, you will be identifying and using styles that suit the purpose of the publication, the article, and the audience.

Sending the Public Relations Message

In newsletters as in media releases, you have an obligation to consider the organization's mission and to promote it whenever possible. This means choosing words and framing ideas to create a comfort level with the organization, even in routine articles. For example, writing with a news focus might produce the following lead: "ABC Company has completed a strategic plan that will take us into the next decade"—factual but bland and boring. Writing from a public relations focus will produce copy such as "ABC Company has completed a strategic plan that builds on our reputation for high-quality products and positions us to expand into exciting new ventures in the next decade." The latter reminds the reader of the organization's reputation and its commitment to quality and paints an enthusiastic picture of the future. And it is not false or deceitful.

Similarly, it is logical that you would congratulate sales rep Joe Johnson in both external and internal newsletters for completing his associate's degree. However, you will miss an opportunity to promote the organization as a supportive employer if you do not also mention that Joe took advantage of the company's tuition-reimbursement program, especially in the newsletter to employees.

Ethical Issues

Photo Ethics

Staff photographs are theoretically a newsletter editor's dream. In reality, they are the source of many ethical dilemmas, especially when they are "party photos" sent in by contributing reporters. Where the photographer sees happy staff members toasting their success, the editor sees tables filled with empty glasses, full ashtrays, and fuzzy backgrounds of "enthusiastic dancers" evoking the questions, "Is that Jack, and what is he doing?"

Such photos send a generally positive message about an organization's culture; however, there are many levels of detail that may make them contentious. Are the subjects having "too much fun"? Are you exploiting someone's handicap, even inadvertently? What is in the background? Does it include distracting or inappropriate advertising or signage? Generally, do the photos send the wrong message?

It is wise to have a policy regarding photos of social occasions and to make it clear that you always have the right to use or not use photos in the interests of simple good taste and to protect the subject's dignity, or indeed privacy.

The following well-used tricks may help you deal with such problematic photos.

- ✦ Crop out as much of the food and drink as possible.

- ✦ Overlap or inset photos to hide the glasses or bottles.

- ✦ Crop out anyone doing anything that may embarrass him, her, or the organization.

- ✦ Create a collage of faces, cropped from multiple photos, showing everyone having a good time and no one embarrassing themselves.

As a public relations writer it is your obligation to "think public relations" in everything you write. This even extends to using photographs, as discussed in the "Photo Ethics" Ethical Issues panel.

Tone

Generally speaking, the tone for articles in external newsletters is professional, closer to formal news style than to conversational or persuasive style. You should know or be able to find out how much readers know about the organization and its sector, and to choose appropriate terminology and examples. Hospital newsletters targeted to doctors would likely use medical terminology that the general public would not understand. In contrast, an article on the same subject for the newsletter sent to local residents would require either explaining the medical terms or finding an appropriate analogy.

Even in internal newsletters, organizational news should be taken seriously, so maintaining some formality for such articles is a good idea. Present the news as news. Articles based on staff or social events, however, may take a less formal, more inviting tone. If the news is a staff benefit for which the organization wants to generate enthusiasm, try to get quotes that are encouraging and motivational—or encourage the president to promote the benefit in her monthly column.

For both types of newsletter, the tone of feature articles will be driven by the approach you adopt. But you should still choose it carefully with your audience in mind.

Bylined Columns

One exception to the style you adopt for news articles is the style you write, or allow, for columns. Columns are special interest articles that appear regularly over a byline. Client-oriented newsletters often have regular columns from the sales and customer service departments. Such columns highlight the organization's ability to meet client needs and send subtle public relations messages even while providing information that clients need.

It is likely that you may ghost write many of these columns. If so, you will be challenged to reflect the personality and character of the "writer," so the column is credibly theirs. Even in formal business newsletters, the president's column will have a more personal touch than the rest of the articles. The reader should believe the president is sending a message just to her.

Headlines

As newsletter editor, you have the freedom to write headlines knowing that they will be used, unlike headlines on new releases. The same principle applies, however: Write headlines that will attract readers to the article. Summarize the article, highlight the benefits, or "tease" the reader, but at all costs, attract attention. Following are examples of headlines that work: "Recognition Week Honors 294 Western Health Employees," "How much are your benefits worth?" "Meet John Marshall— New Director of Employee Relations," and "Two Victories for Clean Air in Oregon." What they have in common is their clear appeal. Readers will know immediately whether the article is of interest. They answer the inevitable question: "What's in it for me?"

When writing headlines, be consistent. Readers understand the "language" of headlines: The largest headline is the most important; the next largest is secondary. Do not break the rules of this language lest you confuse the reader. It is wise to use type styles and color as consistently as size in helping readers understand the relative importance of various messages.

Purists would also advise that such consistency extends to headline length, for example, all secondary headlines are four words, or two lines, long. Since reader attention often does not extend to this level of detail, it seems reasonable to sacrifice it if necessary in the interests of providing more white space or fitting in an extra line of copy. Your organizational style manual will provide guidance on this issue.

Bullet Points

It is a fact of public relations life that every message you send competes with other messages. The reality of newsletters is that your messages compete with each other. From the readers' viewpoint, writers are challenged to help them understand what is available and decide what to read. From the organization's viewpoint, writers are challenged to bring the important messages to the readers' attention. Headlines and a clear table of contents are two ways to meet both challenges.

A third way to do this is to remember the bullet points we introduced in Chapter 2. Although inappropriate in a release to the media, bullet points are a valuable tool in newsletter articles. Just by virtue of looking different, they draw attention to the points. Also, because they are usually short, they are inviting.

Bullet points as an organizational strategy. Newsletters often include series of short articles that can either clutter the document or send important public relations messages. For external newsletters, these might be a quick review of relevant new laws or upcoming conferences that demonstrate that the organization has its finger on the industry pulse. For internal newsletters, they include staff moves and the births, deaths, marriages, or other personal news typically called "social news" that promote relationships with staff.

Thinking in terms of bullet points will help you organize these items effectively. (Note that you may not actually use "bullets"; it is the concept that is important.) Instead of scattering short articles as filler throughout the newsletter, bring them together in identifiable segments and write the items with attention to parallel structure. For example, if you are presenting a brief review of new regulations, start each with a three-to-five word subject heading (in bold) such as "nonprofit tax deductions," "changes in Medicare reporting," or "mid-term report on safety regulations." Or make a point of starting all "social notes" with the staff member's name, or with "birth," "sports," "school" notation.

The bullet points approach is useful even for unrelated short news items. Exhibit 10.4 demonstrates this technique for an employee newsletter (left column) and a client newsletter (right column). Note that some of the information is appropriate for both documents, but with different emphases. Other information is appropriate for only one of the newsletters. Part of a public relations writer's responsibility is to develop information for multiple audiences.

The key to using this technique successfully is to group items by theme and to keep the individual highlights parallel for each group. If you lead with "Congratulations to," then begin each bullet with the person or group being congratulated: the Los Angeles sales team, Amy Stearns, IT specialist William Dorn. In contrast, using a "news briefs" heading requires that you present each highlight as if it were a brief, but self-contained, news item.

Note that such sections of employee newsletters often attract immediate attention as staff seek information about themselves or people they know.

EXERCISE 3

The chair of your department has asked every class to provide two lists of highlights about the class. One list, aimed at prospective majors, will be included in a section titled "What makes our courses stand out" on the department web site. The second list will be part of the department's annual report to the administration. It is likely that these lists may include different information and certainly a different style. Write both lists, including the headings. Pay careful attention to parallel structure. Each list should have at least five items.

EXHIBIT 10.4 **Sample highlights column for an employee newsletter (left column) and a client newsletter (right column).**

Congratulations to

The **Los Angeles sales team** who signed 14 contracts in July—a new company record.

Amy Stearns (Atlanta) on being named "Customer Servicer of the Year" by the Greater Atlanta Chamber of Commerce.

IT specialist **William Dorn** (HQ) who has received a Certificate of E-Commerce from Central States Institute of Technology.

Accounts clerk **Norman Butts** (Maryland) who pitched a two-hit shutout in the branch softball team's 6-0 victory in the final of the "Biz-ball" league championship.

New parents, Jerry and **Sandra Smith** (St. Louis) on the birth of their daughter, Alison; Peter and **Caroline Andrews** (California) on the birth of their son, Peter Jr.; and Bonnie and **Ray Samson** (Maryland) on the adoption of twins, Jeremy and Joanne.

July News Briefs

Treadwell Communications signed 22 contracts in July, 14 of them by the California sales office. Welcome to all of our new clients.

Atlanta customer service representative **Amy Stearns** was named "Customer Servicer of the Year" by the Greater Atlanta Chamber of Commerce.

IT specialist **William Dorn** (HQ) was awarded a Certificate of E-Commerce from Central States Institute of Technology. Clients may expect to reap the benefits of William's knowledge in an e-business column to be featured in future newsletters.

Treadwell Communications has signed on to attend the 200X APRA conference to be held September 22-25 in San Diego. We will be taking all of our sales representatives and hope you will join us for our client appreciation lunch on the 24th. Details will follow. Please let us know if you want to meet with your representative.

Pull Quotes

Another technique with both message and design advantages is to use *pull quotes*, that is, lifting strong or important quotations from the text and using them as graphic elements. From a design viewpoint, it provides interest; from a message viewpoint, it is an opportunity to make a key message obvious. Even if it is the only thing a reader notices, the key message will have been sent. In an article on an improved customer service program, for example, why would you *not* take the opportunity to emphasize the organization's "commitment to responding to every inquiry within 24 hours"?

As you write articles, and particularly as you solicit quotes for them, keep the value of pull quotes in mind and try to write or help shape another's words into "print bites" that will help you emphasize important points.

Newsletter Production and Distribution

When planning a publication, you must take into account your budget, reproduction and distribution methods, and your time. These same considerations may be part of your evaluation of existing newsletters and the foundation of changes to better meet the needs of your employer and your audience(s).

Planning

Newsletter Frequency

Timing is everything. The credibility of a publication is inevitably tied to its timeliness. Before launching any newsletter, you should have the answer to one critical question—how often will it come out?

Newsletter frequency will be influenced by the purpose, the availability of content, and the limitations (if any) of the production and distribution methods. Try to set a schedule that is frequent enough that the news is not stale and seldom enough that the issue is not repetitive or obviously made up of filler.

Because a common purpose of employee newsletters is to raise morale, they typically come out at least monthly to reduce the impact of the rumor mill that will operate if official information is not readily available. Web letters or photocopied flyers may allow you to maintain even a weekly schedule with minimal effort.

External newsletters are a different story. They are generally at least four pages long, increasing in multiples of four pages for ease of assembly and mailing. To determine the optimum frequency, identify when you want or need to communicate with your target audience. Is the purpose of the newsletter to report on the past season or to anticipate the new one? Is your audience on vacation during the summer? Should you tie in with the state or federal legislative sessions so you can report on fast-breaking regulations? Questions like these will influence when and how often to publish.

From a practical point of view, it is wise to err on the side of the conservative in both size and frequency when planning a newsletter. It is always a positive step to be able to increase the size or frequency because you have so much information and/or because the publication is so well received by its public. On the other hand, it is embarrassing to miss a stated publication schedule or to produce a publication that is not filled or is smaller than the reader expects.

Budget and Production Methods

Newsletters can be any size that suits your purpose and your budget. At one extreme are single-page newsletters printed from the office computer, reproduced on the photocopier, and distributed by hand to each employee's desk or mailbox. At the other extreme are multipage, full-color publications prepared with sophisticated page layout programs, commercially processed and printed, and distributed by mail.

In between lie most of the newsletters ever prepared. They range from 2 to 16 or 20 pages; most are prepared in house using word processing or desktop publishing software; many are printed in one color—black—but have a multicolored masthead. Growing numbers are taking advantage of the new generations of color printers and photocopiers that make color affordable for small print runs.

Distribution

It is important that a newsletter reaches everyone it is destined for simultaneously and in a timely fashion. Print media are traditional, but difficult to time precisely.

There is nothing worse than to have the news of a major acquisition, promotion, or staff benefit reach only part of your staff on the day intended. Not only will the rumor mill swing into furious action, but also the staff who did not get the information are likely to be angry.

Electronic media have the potential for simultaneous distribution, but there is no guarantee that the information will be read or watched. If you want to limit access to some information, you may choose to set up a special, internal intranet that only employees can access. But even then you may also have to alert staff to log on.

Most external newsletters are distributed by mail and take advantage of U.S. Postal Service bulk rate discounts. It is usually worth the effort to develop mailing lists that can be bar-coded and sorted by zip code/carrier route to receive these discounts.

It is also cost-effective to make the newsletter a self-mailer in which the recipient's name and address are either printed directly on the newsletter or on a label. Remember that self-mailers must be wafer sealed to keep them closed and the space left for the address or label must meet postal standards for size and positioning. It may be wise to talk with a commercial mailing house about handling the mailing on your behalf. Many of them will create and maintain your mailing list as well as processing the mailing.

Employee newsletters may be distributed by the U.S. mail to the employee's home or by internal mail to the employee's mailbox or desk. If mailed to the employee's home, you can expect a substantial pass-along audience as family and friends also read the publication. If distributed internally, the issues may or may not be taken home. Keeping a casual eye on the trash after an issue comes out will give you an informal evaluation about whether the staff read it thoroughly and whether they take it home. Internal distribution may interrupt work time as employees read and discuss the issues as soon as they receive them, but if your aim is to generate interest and interaction, this may be a plus.

Web Letters

Electronic newsletters take many forms:

- ✦ News posted to an organization's web site and available to all visitors
- ✦ Semi-targeted web letters posted to newsgroups and accessible to its members
- ✦ Fully targeted letters sent individually to a mailing list, much as you send e-mail to the names in your address book

Production can be as simple as creating .pdf copies of printed newsletters and uploading them to the site or as complex as creating and programming newsletters especially for the Web. Depending on which you choose, you may or may not be able to control the distribution, audience, or timing although you can control the content.

We will discuss the details of writing for the Web in Chapter 13. In this section, we limit discussion to using the Web as a newsletter strategy.

The first type of web letter—posting the news on a web site—is akin to the mass media; you have a huge potential audience that is primarily unknown and many of whom may not be of particular concern to you. You can develop information that even these casual visitors may find interesting and that may turn them into supporters or investors, or you can target the information to the audiences you know and value, and hope that casual visitors find something interesting.

The second and third types of electronic newsletter—those sent to newsgroups or individual mailing lists—require the same knowledge of audience as printed newsletters. You must select topics that are of interest or of "must-know" importance to the audience, and you must write and present these topics in a style appropriate to that audience.

In either case, topicality is a continuing issue. If the strength of the web letter is its topicality, you must be prepared to update it frequently. On the other hand, web letters that focus on broad, non–time-sensitive issues may attract a wider audience. You may electronically archive these letters so that readers can access back issues.

You will also have to address the issue of hyperlinks that may add value to your web letter but that will require additional strategic decision making. What sites should you link to? What sites do you want to avoid? The web letters of private enterprise organizations are unlikely to link to their competitors even if the competitor has valuable information to offer. On the other hand, if the subject of your CEO's message is the threat of pending legislation, you may want to link not only to the text of the legislation but also to the web sites of sympathetic legislators where users can register their support for your organization's position. All links, of course, should be undertaken with the permission of the owner of the linked site. Remember, too, that links may take visitors out of your web site, so it may be wise to have no links from the web letter.

DISCUSSION 3

Generally, newsletters have a number of distribution options: place of work, mail to home, pick-up points at, for example, cafeterias and building entrances, e-mail distribution, and web sites. Which distribution method(s) will you recommend for a college/university newsletter reaching all employees? What distribution for an alumni newsletter?

Another way of distributing a web newsletter is to ask other organizations to link to your newsletter site. Assuming your college or university has an alumni web site, what institutions or individuals would you request provide a link to it? What organizations or individuals would not want to link to it? Is this censorship?

Evaluation

One test of an effective newsletter is whether it has met the aims of promoting the organization's mission, establishing and cultivating positive relationships, and helping internal and external publics adapt to change. In other words, has it helped the organization's "bottom line?" Has it helped build a positive, credible image or meaning for the organization with its publics? And has it helped smooth any transition to new conditions?

You can obtain answers to these questions by conducting reader surveys as discussed in Chapter 5. Such surveys can be included in issues of the publication, sent to all readers or a random sampling, or put on the organization's web site. You may choose to ask questions about the publication's content (likely to attract opinion from all respondents) and/or about the style, grammar, and presentation (possibly of less general interest, but of particular use to you as the publication creator). Although we do not pretend that reader surveys are easy, they are useful and one of the surest ways to help you monitor the pulse of audiences important to your employer and to help you keep routine publications fresh and interesting—for you as a writer as well as for the public as readers.

ON THE TEXTBOOK WEB SITE

✦ Go to www.sagepub.com/treadwell for web exercises, study hints, case studies, and additional examples appropriate to this chapter and chosen or developed to supplement the chapter content.

WRITING WRAP-UP

1. Your academic department has decided that there are enough activities going on that students should be kept up-to-date with a brief, weekly newsletter. Identify the topics that you will cover regularly, and write and design the first issue. Suggest how you will distribute it. Write a covering letter to the head of your department seeking approval of your recommendations.

REFERENCES

Goltz, T. (1997, November 2). The barefaced pleasure of a shave in Turkey. *New York Times,* Sec. 5, p. 29.

Lenker, G. (2003, September 28). Wrap star. *Sunday Republican,* p. D1.

RESOURCES

Featured Organizations

Loomis Communities .... www.loomiscommunities.org

Phoenix Coyotes .... www.phoenixcoyotes.com

U.S. Department of Health and Human Services .... www.hhs.gov

Let's Hear It

Writing for Broadcast, Scripts, and Speeches

Most public relations writing is meant to be read. However, as communication becomes increasingly electronic this may change. Even the capability of the Web to carry audio and video messages means that writing to be heard will be a more important skill for the public relations writer.

Writing to be heard means writing so that audiences understand the message on first hearing. It is different from writing for print for three reasons.

◆ Listeners typically have only one opportunity to understand speeches and broadcasts. They cannot easily revisit the message as they can with newspapers and other print media.
◆ Writing to be heard means capturing the personality of the speaker as much as the culture of the organization.
◆ Writing to be heard may bend conventional rules of grammar and punctuation. Factors such as alliteration, rhythm, and timing are important. Short sentences are critical. Listeners have to "get it" the first time.

In this chapter, we discuss three types of writing for the ear: newswriting for broadcast, scriptwriting, and speechwriting.

Newswriting for Broadcast Media

What you have learned about news determinants does not change when you switch from print to broadcast media. Timeliness, relevance, proximity, prominence, rarity, and human interest are as important to the broadcast news editor as to the press. They may be even more important given the very limited amount of time broadcast editors have to fill. A typical half-hour local TV news program includes only six to eight stories, not including weather and sports. To get your organization's story aired, it must be very appealing indeed.

The differences between writing news for the press and writing news for radio and television are issues of writing for sound, visuals, and time. Each issue brings with it constraints on style and formatting that are usually not a factor with print media.

For most public relations writers, writing for broadcast is but a small part of their responsibilities. It is limited to writing copy for an occasional radio ad or public service announcement (PSA). Many organizations do not write news releases specifically for broadcast, instead sending the same release to both broadcast and print media. Broadcast media do not automatically reject releases written for the press, so this may be the wisest use of your time unless the release topic is especially appropriate for audio or video.

Media Comparisons

Broadcast media have many advantages over print. First, they are ubiquitous. Radio especially reaches individuals 24 hours a day, at home, at the workplace, and in the car during "drive time." The fact that the phrase "sound bite" has become part of our daily lexicon shows the degree to which television pervades our lives. Sound and movement are attributes of electronic media that newspapers and magazines can seldom match.

On the down side, video news releases (VNRs), the TV counterpart of the news release, may cost thousands of dollars to produce and may still not be aired. But the fact that many organizations are willing to pay tens of thousands of dollars for an A-roll (a VNR ready for broadcast) or B-roll (additional video that local stations can edit or use for background) says that they believe that VNRs can be a good return on investment. If you need motion or action to make a point, video is the medium of choice.

Radio has been called the medium of the imagination. The response to radio is powerful because the mental images from radio are yours, built in your own mind from the foundations that radio feeds you. As comedian Stan Freburg demonstrated so memorably, on radio it is entirely possible to build the world's largest ice cream sundae, complete with giant cherry, in Lake Michigan; try doing it on TV.

Some theories of rhetoric and persuasion suggest that effects on the listener are stronger if the receiver participates in constructing or finishing the message. Because radio makes this demand on listeners, it may have a one-to-one level of engagement that its mass media image and low profile do not suggest. It may have more of a hold on listeners than television, whose explicitness makes it possible for viewers to be passive rather than active participants in the message.

Both radio and television provide the opportunity to use real-life examples to help tell the story. An *actuality* is an audio of the organization, product, or person you are promoting. It is real, live, and first person. Video includes visual footage. Print media's best attempts at this are color stills and quotation marks representing speech—somewhat feeble alternatives.

Broadcast media should be an option for disseminating public relations messages but not at the expense of print. For many situations, print still offers significant and unique advantages. Readers can view the material at their own pace, and start at any point in the message. Furthermore, because print messages can be easily stored and retrieved, readers can repeat their exposure to the message. If a message needs to be revisited by the audience and easily recalled, print (including the Web) wins.

As media converge, new possibilities arise. *Web casts* send live or delayed audio and/or video transmissions across the Internet. Organizations may web cast a news conference instead of or in addition to the live event. CD-ROM and the Web offer interactivity and repeated viewing. Hypertext makes it possible for users to jump from still graphics to video to text along a path of their own choosing rather than following linear videotape or news release structures. A related advantage of CD-ROM and computer-based technology is the opportunity to provide publics with far more information than can ever be contained in conventional print and broadcast news media. Furthermore, it can be stored, downloaded to print, and easily archived and retrieved.

DISCUSSION 1

As a source of news, which of the following media do you prefer and why: newspapers, radio, TV, the Internet? What are the advantages and disadvantages of each as a news medium? What kind of "news" do you expect to get from each medium?

Broadcast Media Selection

In the spirit that most news is local news, it is likely that you will direct broadcast news toward local or regional TV and radio stations. In typical markets, you may have only one or two TV outlets providing local news. Although this appears limited, remember that local news often has 90-minute segments during the dinner hour and sometimes in the early morning. Those 90-minute slots should be your target.

There are many more radio stations targeting many different demographics. Radio stations are not one-size-fits-all entities. Instead, each station appeals to particular ages, interests, and listening preferences. Identifying these demographics will help you find the station or stations that reach your target audience. The success of this is the way NASCAR has embraced country music stations, recognizing that the two very disparate organizations share a large audience.

Newswriting for Broadcast: Content

Audio releases must be easy to read aloud and include instructions for actualities you may send with the release. If you can do these two things well, you will be able to work easily with a production team. If you can do them very well, you may have a career as a scriptwriter.

From a news viewpoint, the public relations message is the same for broadcast as for print media. In practice, however, the content of broadcast releases may be driven by the availability of actualities that will carry some of the message. An actuality is typically an audiotape of an interview or formal statement that the station can play. If you are providing radio stations with an actuality of the CEO's speech to shareholders, then the release may include a summary of the important points but exclude quotes that you might include in a release to the press. The detailed quotes are available on the tape. Remember that the actuality or the release must identify the recorded voice(s) and put them in context.

Similarly, a release to a television station that is accompanied by a video of a state senator cutting the ribbon on a new factory must identify the senator and other people. It must also make it clear what the viewers are seeing on the tape. Even if the station does not use the release as you wrote it, the producers will need such information to generate their own scripts.

Think Live

Statistics indicate that radio listeners especially are fickle, listening intermittently and changing stations whenever the music or chat no longer interests them. Stations are challenged to keep as many listeners as possible for as long as possible. You can use this to your advantage if you consider what you can do to help the station keep its listeners.

Think beyond traditional news: "who, what, when, where, why, and how." With news segments often running less than 5 minutes, stations may not have a way to use your release even if they want to. But if you "think entertainment," you may well find that a station not only covers your story but also becomes an active participant in promoting your cause.

For example, one theater company parlayed a one-time release about a new show into a monthly drive-time promotion. How? Because the public relations manager is willing to appear live to help the studio host conduct contests related to the show of the month. The prize: free tickets, of course. The cost to the theater is minimal but the benefits are huge. And the station gets a contest to help hold listener attention. Think "WIIFTRS": What's in it for the radio station.

Is your guest speaker available for an interview? World Wrestling Entertainment (WWE) routinely sends a wrestler into a region in advance of matches to promote the event on local radio stations. The wrestler is primed for the demographic mix of each station, sending different messages to families, college-age males, and hard rock listeners, for example. The public relations staff for a local peach festival annually shows up at radio stations with the festival queen and her court—and a pie. Radio hosts admit that such tactics get their attention because they are interesting to their audiences.

What this means, of course, is that writing an effective pitch letter may be your best strategy.

Newswriting for Broadcast: Style

Broadcast writing is writing for sound. Nuances of inflection, pronunciation, and pauses on the part of the "talent" will add to or subtract from the message, just as good or bad design adds to or subtracts from a printed document.

Writing for Sound

To understand the need for a broadcast style, consider a news release written for print media. If the release is easy to read, flows smoothly, sounds like normal speech, and lasts only 30 to 60 seconds, you may be a natural at writing for broadcast. More likely, however, the release took considerably longer to read and sounded stilted and unnatural when you read it aloud.

The power of words is such that we persist in using the term broadcast writing style when what we really want to think about is broadcast *talking* style. Think in terms of talking rather than writing. This also applies to scriptwriting, speechwriting, or anything that will be spoken and heard rather than read and seen. The important fact is that you are writing for the ear, not the eye.

Above all, broadcast writing must capture speech and speech patterns so that the copy sounds natural when spoken on air. So, while "writing style" suggests pen, typewriter, or word processor, the best tool for the beginning scriptwriter is actually sound recording equipment. Alternatively, you can always find a friendly but critical ear.

The ultimate test of broadcast writing is this: Tape the message. Play the tape. If it sounds like someone reading, you have written print, not broadcast. If it sounds like someone talking naturally, congratulations—you have mastered broadcast style. Some writers and broadcast journalists wander around the office reading aloud or even worse, semi-audibly. It may not make them a lot of friends, but it's the sound of a professional at work making sure that the final product will be interesting to listen to.

The idea of writing the way you speak poses a problem for many students because it results in copy that may be ungrammatical. It may have sentence fragments, run-ons, omissions, contractions, and a casual style that may horrify your high school English teacher. In other words, it sounds the way you speak. *Some* of the formal rules of grammar may have to take second place to sound and flow (with apologies to grammar purists). This does not mean that "me and the president met on the White House lawn" is ever acceptable, however.

Writing for Time

The other unique requirement for broadcast writing is the ability to write to time. Broadcast media have time constraints just as print media have space constraints. Even with the best will in the world, the producer of a 30-minute program cannot give you more than 30 minutes. So another reason scriptwriters walk the corridors reading aloud is to get a sense of timing. The second most valuable tool after the tape recorder is the stopwatch.

Writing for time is a serious test of your editing skills. How objectively can you look at your own copy, recognize the unnecessary words, and reduce it to just the facts? Remember, newswriting is telling a story so that the listener/viewer understands what happened, to whom, when, where, how, and why. With a 30-second time limit, it is likely you will have to sacrifice at least one of these criteria while making sure that the most important criteria are part of those 30 seconds.

EXERCISE 1

Time yourself while you read aloud one of the media releases shown as Exhibits 9.2, 9.4, 9.5, and 9.6 in Chapter 9. How long did it take? Would a radio station air this full release as written? Why or why not? What recommendations would you make about content and structure to turn it into a release for broadcast?

Writing Styles to Help the Speaker Express What You Mean

Broadcast copy includes cues to help the reader speak the text smoothly and interpret it correctly. The text should include pronunciation guides and special punctuation to help the reader know how to express the words. It must make clear exactly what the reader should say.

Following are some of the commonly accepted broadcast styles with which you should be familiar. If you want to target broadcast media, following these guidelines may make the difference between acceptance and rejection. Many of them also make sense for other writing for speech and presentation.

✦ *Referring to people.* There are three ground rules for handling people's names:

Use the names people know. Use Madonna, Tiger Woods, and P. Diddy, instead of Madonna Ciccone, Eldrick Woods, and Sean Combs. Do not use middle initials unless the person is known by a middle initial—Mary J. Blige, Robert E. Lee, Jubilation T. Cornpone—or you need to differentiate your subject from others with a similar name—West College President Hilary C. Clinton, Senator Hillary Rodham Clinton.

Spell out first names, last names, and titles. The only exceptions are "Mr.," "Mrs.," and "Ms.," whose pronunciation and meaning are commonly accepted.

Write titles before names. The title is usually more important. Attribution (who said it) precedes what was said (e.g., State Commissioner of Education Gladys Spoilrod says that students need more financial aid). To avoid confusion, spell out all titles in full, even if the title is a long one.

✦ *Quotes and attribution.* Broadcast viewers and listeners cannot see the quotation marks (" ") that print media rely on to indicate that someone is speaking. You have two alternatives when writing for broadcast:

> *Use direct attribution* (e.g., Hamilton says that the recall will continue as long as defective units are found).

> *Use actualities* (e.g., an audiotape of Hamilton making the statement).

✦ *Naming organizations.* This is one of the few situations in which abbreviations are allowed in broadcast copy—as long as they meet two conditions:

> The organization and abbreviation must be well known (e.g., NATO, FBI, AFL-CIO, and UN).

> The acronym must be pronounceable as a word (e.g., UNICEF). If it is not, you have two options. If the organization is well known, use hyphens to indicate that the individual letters are to be pronounced (e.g., F-A-A, N-F-L, and N-C-A-A). If the organization is not well known, spell out the full name.

✦ *Presenting in the present.* Radio and television must be topical and current. Broadcasters try to speak in the present and avoid the past tense. Note the stylistic difference between "XYZ auto company *is recalling* 10 models that have been on the market since 1996" (broadcast), and "XYZ auto company *yesterday recalled* 10 models sold since 1996" (press).

✦ *Writing numbers for speech.* Perhaps the biggest style difference between writing for press and writing for speech is how they handle numbers. When reading numbers, we can understand complex figures. Speaking and listening to numbers is a different matter. For example, in speech the word "dollar" typically comes after the amount, so rather than writing $20, you must write "twenty dollars." And if the number is complex, such as $12,345,678.90, for broadcast purposes it is wise to use an approximation such as "more than twelve million dollars."

✦ *Write out numbers from one through nine* and use numerals for numbers from 10 through 999.

✦ *Write words for numerical figures that are long* or complex or that may not be obvious to a speaker. This includes figures such as thousands, millions, fractions, and second, third, fourth.

✦ *Write years as numerals* (e.g., 1999 or 19–99).

There are many broadcast stylebooks available that will help you with the specifics of broadcast style.

Pronunciation and Pronunciation Guides

You may know how the strange words in your script should be pronounced, but typically you are writing copy for someone else to read and the talent may not be familiar with the correct pronunciation. For example, how would you read the following?

On December 5, 1977, His Majesty the King Bhumibol Adulyadej of Thailand bestowed upon his second daughter, the Princess Sirindhorn, the title of Somdech Phra Debaratanarajasuda Chao Fa Maha Chakri Sirindhorn Rathasimagunakornpiyajat Sayamboromrajakumri. (*Long Live Her Royal Highness*, 2002)

The title may have some human interest news value for its length alone, but the story is clearly destined for the print rather than broadcast media. No anchors or newsreaders would risk their reputations for on-air cool by trying to pronounce "Rathasimagunakornpiyajat Sayamboromrajakumri" even though the princess is a prominent figure in the government of Thailand. When the princess visited western Massachusetts in 2004, local TV stations simply referred to her as "Princess Sirindhorn." Although most pronunciation issues are not as extreme, this demonstrates why you should provide the correct pronunciation parenthetically where it is needed.

The style for providing pronunciation guidelines varies. Purists often argue for phonetic spelling, but this makes sense only if the newsreader understands phonetic spelling. The reasonable solution is to use upper- and lowercase to indicate stress and pronunciation, for example, Sri Lanka (Sree LAN kuh) or beta (BAY tuh). Even following this style, it would be difficult to provide guidelines for the Thai princess, assuming you could pronounce her name.

A related issue is the use of contractions (can't, won't, didn't, etc.). Contractions are usually a "don't" in written copy, but broadcast writers generally prefer them because they sound more natural. Remember, however, that listeners may tune into a broadcast at any time. You cannot assume that they have heard the preceding sentences that may help make sense of a contraction. In particular, negative contractions are easily misheard, so it is probably safer to use "cannot" and "will not." You may prefer this anyway to emphasize a negative point.

Punctuation

Punctuation is another area in which the scriptwriter's concern is to help the talent correctly convey the meaning of the copy. Often this may violate rules of written punctuation. For example, in scriptwriting, commas indicate where you expect the reader to take a breath or pause while reading the copy. In print copy, comma placement follows strict rules to separate phrases or other grammatical units.

Newswriting for Broadcast: Formatting

Writing for any electronic medium raises the opportunity to call on all the resources of the broadcast station or production company. Even simple news releases may call for actualities to provide credibility or illustrate parts of the story. This means that unlike print copy, broadcast releases must also contain instructions to talent, directors, or producers. Audio-only scripts will contain instructions about playing tape inserts or sound effects. Video scripts will contain instructions about both audio and visual content. The following formatting conventions will help your copy appear easy to read and use.

- ✦ Broadcast copy is double spaced and must be absolutely clean so the reader does not get confused on air. Do not make corrections on broadcast copy. Instead, retype it.
- ✦ Use paragraph indentations.

✦ Do not *ever* break words or sentences or paragraphs across two pages.
✦ Avoid anything that may cause the reader to pause in mid-delivery.

If you write broadcast copy frequently, we suggest you talk with your local radio or TV stations to determine how you can best present it for their convenience. Doing so will increase the likelihood that an editor will choose to air your story.

Line Length

Conventionally, broadcast copy is typed to a 60-character line. This will give you about 12 words or 5 seconds of copy per line. A line count will give you a rough estimate of the time it will take to read the text (e.g., five lines approximates 25 seconds).

Providing Production Instructions

If you are providing the radio or TV station with sound or video clips, the release must show where the additional material should be played or shown.

There are two ways to indicate actualities in the text. The first is to begin the instruction in the margin so that it stands out. The second is to keep the same margin but to obviously change type style for the instructions. You might, for example, type the tape instructions all UPPERCASE. Either way, it is important that the instructions clearly stand apart from the copy that is to be read by the talent.

The instruction for actualities includes the following:

✦ The instruction "Roll Tape" or "Play Tape" plus the tape ID
✦ The time the tape will run
✦ The last three or four words of the tape so that the producer or reader can recognize the end of the tape

Some writers also provide the first words of the tape so producers can check that they have the correct tape. For a short audio actuality, you might type the entire content.

Exhibit 11.1 is a sample release prepared in an audio layout. We have inserted numbers above the release to show that it uses a 60-character line. Using the formula cited above, the broadcast length of the spot will be about 30 seconds. Note that the release incorporates an actuality into the script and provides information to help the station use the tape.

If the release is for a specific event, you do not want to start the publicity too early or to continue it after the event is over. The release, therefore, has both a start and an end date. The day, date, and time of the event are spelled out specifically. Sloppy uses such as "next Tuesday" or "next week" will confuse the listener. And as with press releases, provide both home and work contact numbers in case the media want to contact you for more information or to arrange for live coverage.

Video News Releases

The key question with regard to television news media is whether you should put time and effort into VNRs aimed at TV. It is clear from even a casual viewing that the majority of stories aired on local television news broadcasts are produced by the station itself. The station's talent usually hosts even public relations stories. Reporters attend the function or stand outside the company, interview subjects, and tell the story in their own words.

EXHIBIT 11.1   Audio release, including instructions for handling an actuality.

```
123456789012345678901234567890123456789012345678901234567890
```

LETTERHEAD and ADDRESS

Date

For Immediate Release - Broadcast - 30 Seconds.

PUBLIC SERVICE ANNOUNCEMENT

Start Date: November 12, 200_

End Date: November 26, 200_

For more information, contact:
(Name)/w 000-0000   h 000-0001

                   MUDVILLE FOOD BANK DRIVE

   Mudville area homeless will benefit from fundraising
organized by Central University students this month.

   Mudville Mayor Deanne (DEE-ANN) Jorgensen will host a
variety show November 26 at 8 P-M at Central's Winger
Auditorium featuring area celebrities and university talent.
All proceeds go to the Mudville Food Bank. Tickets are two
dollars or a canned food item which can be left at the door.

   Professor Siri Onoloke (Si-REE On-oh-LOH-key) of
Central's Theater Department says the event will also provide
valuable experience for the students.

ROLL ONOLOKE TAPE.   15 SECONDS
   " . . . BENEFITS CAMPUS AND COMMUNITY."

   Contact Central University's Theater Department at
123-4567 for tickets and information.
                        ENDS

This does not mean the station initiated the stories or that you as a public relations writer have no role in television news content. To the contrary, it is likely that the stories were initiated by public relations writers doing their job well. They wrote effective pitch letters or media advisories that tempted the station to send a news crew for live coverage. The media alert shown as Exhibit 9.9 in Chapter 9 has clear appeal for both broadcast and print media.

Some TV news stories, however, are produced and provided to the station by organizations or commercial video-distribution services. If you have the time and budget and a story whose uniqueness and potential for great visuals lends itself to TV, you may produce and distribute a VNR.

The first criterion for a successful VNR is that it has some news value. The second is that it meets media criteria for sound and video. The news value is often seasonal or long-term rather than immediate so that producers can use the tape whenever it is convenient. This increases the opportunity to have the VNR aired.

EXERCISE 2

Writing scripts for broadcast is more than just putting pictures to your press release. The copy must be brief and suitable for speaking, and must follow the action or graphics. Count the words of PSAs that you see on TV or that are archived on the Ad Council web site at www.adcouncil.org to see how few words actually are spoken.

Read aloud the audio release in Exhibit 11.1. Time yourself while you read it. How long did it take? Time two or three other students reading the same release. How do the times differ? What does this tell you about speaking styles that accounts for this difference?

Distributing Releases to the Broadcast Media

Distribution to broadcast media differs from distribution to the press in that broadcast media will accept a range of media including script, actuality, and VNR. There are also a number of distribution methods that you can adopt.

Broadcast Distribution Formats

Because of its speed and minimal cost, the most common type of broadcast release is the script. This is simply the text of a release mailed, delivered, faxed, or e-mailed to the station. Because editors are busy and on deadline, they may be predisposed to using releases that are written in the broadcast style described above.

For major broadcast media, if you do not write broadcast style, you should not be surprised when your story does not air. On the other hand, small stations without sophisticated news feed may welcome local news regardless of style or format. We also know television news directors who specifically want to receive press rather than broadcast releases so that they can see exactly what their colleagues and competitors in the print media are getting. Depending on the preferences of your local media, it may not be worth the effort to write to broadcast style.

While actualities make it easier for radio news editors, they are useless if not provided in the format the station can use. Check ahead, but also provide a script and possibly background information and bios to help the editors decide if they should do a follow-up interview. Another option is to send a print release with a phone number or web address from which an audio actuality can be downloaded and recorded.

If yours is a large organization that enjoys regular media coverage, you may produce complete video packages that you hope TV stations will just "plug and play." The complete package (audio plus video) is called the *A-roll*. What editors understandably prefer is the *B-roll*, which is video only, no sound. B-rolls might also contain separate audio and graphics. The advantages of B-rolls are that they can be edited to fit the needs of the station. Voice-overs by the local anchor can be added at the station to make the piece relevant to the local market. The bottom of Exhibit 11.2 is a sample of how to alert media to the availability of A- and B-rolls.

Research indicates that news directors differ on whether they prefer to receive VNRs by tape or satellite download. They are also understandably wary of broadcasting a complete video package from a public relations source. A common criticism they have of VNRs is their lack of a local angle.

You can maximize the chances of getting A- or B-rolls used in a timely fashion by explaining their local relevance. One technique is to combine the VNR with a satellite media tour (SMT) or web cast. Stations are notified of the availability of a VNR and at the same time offered one-on-one interviews with a spokesperson. The VNR is released about a week before the satellite tour so that as many reporters as possible have it before the SMT or web cast starts. VNRs can be made even more locally relevant by providing local contact and other information at the organization's web site.

Your skills as a writer come through in arranging the wire service alert, fax, or even telephone message that will have stations decide to download the VNR. See Exhibit 11.2, a video alert announcing the times and dates of a satellite feed on technology and retail shopping. West Glen Communications, one of many companies that specialize in producing and distributing electronic media releases, released it. You should be aware of such organizations so that you can take advantage of their capabilities and contacts. Note that this alert includes information about the formats available as well as a summary of the item itself and information on how to receive the feed.

Scriptwriting: Writing for Sound and Visuals

Scriptwriting for public relations was once limited to speechwriting, usually putting well-crafted words in your CEO's mouth. As visuals became easier and more cost-effective, scriptwriters found themselves writing to support flip charts, 35-mm slides, overhead transparencies, and now CD, DVD, video, and multiscreen presentations.

Computer capabilities make it possible for organizations to produce their own videos, and many do so for sales and marketing, human relations, and staff training purposes. Collection agencies produce video demands for payment, and home improvement companies provide instructions for assembling furniture. Corporate videos are a common part of shareholder meetings and trade show displays. Staff training videos can be viewed at the employee's convenience and reviewed as necessary to refresh skills.

As electronic media have developed, scriptwriting has become an increasingly large part of the public relations writer's role. Scriptwriting usually focuses on soft news or feature productions in controlled video presentations for special events. The "talent" is often a corporate spokesperson. Once you have developed the concept and at least a rough script, you can easily find a commercial production house to assist you in the filming and actual production.

EXHIBIT 11.2   Video alert. Note how the agency describes the options (e.g., VNR, B-roll, sound bites) available to media that want to receive the VNR.

West
Glen

SATELLITE FEED
WEDNESDAY, NOV. 26th
2:00 pm ET
VNR + B-Roll

**SHOPPERS REJOICE! RETAIL STORES USE NEW TECHNOLOGY TO HELP
YOU WIZ THROUGH YOUR HOLIDAY SHOPPING FASTER THAN EVER!**

*Caught by unemployment lows, many stores can't staff-up as much as they'd like.
New technology is stepping in to help fill a real void.*

What's hot in stores this holiday season is technology — but it's not the kind you buy. Instead it's new retail systems and software that actually make your shopping experience faster and more customer-friendly.

The first thing consumers should be finding this year is that the lines at the cash register will be moving along a lot faster as credit card approvals take less time. **New networking technology, along with higher bandwidths, is helping speed credit authorizations by more than 60% — slashing approval times from 45 seconds down to 15.**

New technology is also making it easier than ever for store personnel to provide more useful information to customers. For example, ever find the perfect gift — only the store doesn't have it in the right size or color? Ever spend hours driving from one mall to another chasing after the item? Not any size or color? Ever spend hours driving from one mall to another chasing after the item? Not any more. With new networked applications, sales associates can now punch in a few buttons in a computer and tell you which stores in the area do have it in stock — or better yet — simply take your address and the item can be shipped directly to you!

Retailers know that the key to keeping customers happy is to offer good service. Increasingly, technology is playing a big role in meeting the needs of the retailer and customer

###

WHAT WE HAVE: VNR and B-roll on how new technology in retail stores is helping make the shopping experience faster and easier. Also sound bites with Jeffrey Siegel, retail industry group manager, 3Com Corp.; plus sound bites from retailers on why they have turned to new technology and how it has given them a competitive edge.

HOW TO RECEIVE: (C-Band)
Weds., Nov. 26, 2:00-2:15 pm ET(1400-1415). Galaxy C4, Transponder 14, audio 6.2/6.8

FOR MORE INFORMATION OR HARD COPY: Carol Varnas 1-800-325-8677

West Glen Communications, Inc.   1430 Broadway   New York, NY10018 212-921-2800 Fax: 212-944-9055

Source: Reprinted with permission of West Glen Communications, Inc., New York, New York.

Scriptwriting: Content

Video content is often based on documents that you have written for other purposes. Training videos usually begin as written training manuals. They may be supplemented by the training manager's notes and by anecdotes and examples to make the presentation more interesting. College recruitment videos start out as the full-color view books that they may someday replace. And a PSA may evolve as a print ad concept developed for the electronic media.

Scriptwriting: Approach

When planning a presentation, it is wise to think back to the approaches discussed for feature writing. Narrative, question and answer, process, or description by time, compare/contrast, humor, or even a combination are all good approaches for presentations. Scriptwriting offers the potential to integrate these approaches with visuals and visual thinking.

Sometimes the approach is obvious and natural, dictated by the purpose or content of the video. For example, the video about a new manufacturing method is likely to be a visual version of a process description. It will answer the question of "how?" This approach might be appropriate for a VNR demonstrating that a state-of-the-art waste disposal system prevents contaminants from reaching the local aquifer. Local media might run the VNR in its entirety if broadcast time allows. Alternatively, or possibly in addition, they may use it later as visual support for a series on local companies that are making environmentally responsible decisions. In either case, your organization "wins" with positive exposure.

A video of the CEO's annual meeting speech prepared for employees around the world might adopt a question-and-answer approach, paying special attention to issues that you know concern employees. Monitoring employee attitudes through surveys, "letters to the editor," and suggestion boxes will reveal their priorities. Just as these might be turned into feature stories or Q&A sections of an employee newsletter, so they can become the basis of a variety of scripts and visual treatments that send the message that the organization cares.

For example, you might produce an audio "topic of the day" that employees can access by voice mail or from an intranet web page. Other possibilities include a monthly video address from senior executives, or a taped question-and-answer session with the CEO. You have the option to fully script the presentation or to provide just an outline so that speakers are free to ad-lib and expand on a general topic if they wish.

Another appeal of video production is the range of graphics, theme music, special effects, and production techniques that you can call on for a fully professional presentation.

The Use of Voices

One advantage of an oral over a written medium is the potential for using multiple voices to add interest, express different opinions, or change the pace of the presentation. Voices that are clearly identifiable as good/bad, history/future, or trainer/tutor can help lead the listener/viewer through a script. This means that writers must be able to script for different voices or to select talent who can speak well without a script.

Especially on radio, multiple voices will help you tell a story without visuals. Note how effectively the voices of eight children build impact in the PSA script on childhood asthma shown as Exhibit 11.3. The words of the last child, "I feel like a fish with no water," are the campaign theme.

The basic decision regarding voices, and one that will shape the script, is the number of voices to use. Will one voice narrate the entire presentation, or will the narrator be supplemented by others (such as managers) explaining special sections? Can you set up a dialogue between the narrator/moderator and the CEO or a panel of experts? A single, identifiable narrator, even if he or she is not seen, acts as a transition in the presentation. It provides continuity and usually controls the flow. When the narrator comes in, listeners and viewers implicitly understand that you will now change subjects or opinions.

At the same time, having multiple voices adds interest. If the voices are articulate and the topic lends itself to ad-lib interviews or comments, it is wise to just let the talent speak rather than scripting every line. You simply provide an outline to keep the script flowing, and edit the recordings afterward to ensure that it does.

Leads

Effective leads are as important for broadcast writing as for press writing. They are as important for the internal training video or sales DVD as for a VNR. An effective

---

Exhibit 11.3   Audio script for 60-second radio spot of the EPA Childhood Asthma Campaign.

Fish: 60 (English)

CHILD 1:	When I have an asthma attack, I feel scared.
CHILD 2:	It's like tiny nails in the air poke my lungs.
CHILD 3:	I start to cough.
CHILD 4:	Sometimes my parents have to take me to the hospital.
VOICE OVER:	Today 1 out of 13 children suffer from some form of asthma, accounting for nearly 1/3 of all emergency room visits.
CHILD 5:	I feel like I'm choking.
CHILD 6:	It's kinda like an elephant is on my chest.
CHILD 7:	A little whistle sound comes out when I breathe.
VOICE OVER:	But while your child may suffer from asthma, asthma doesn't have to make your child suffer.
	There are simple ways you can prevent your child's next attack.
	To learn more call 1-866-NO-ATTACKS, that's 1-866-662-8822, log on to WWW.NOATTACKS.ORG or call your doctor.
	Because even one attack is one too many.
CHILD 8:	I feel like a fish with no water.
VOICE OVER:	Brought to you by the EPA, the Ad Council and this station.

Source: Used with permission of the U.S. Environmental Protection Agency.

lead is always an open door into the rest of the story. It may be serious, comedic, or dramatic as suits the message.

The leads for VNRs, of course, should be terser than for other forms of video because VNRs have a time limit and must get into the story quickly. This does not mean they must be news leads. Humor or teaser leads can be especially effective VNR techniques, but they must quickly resolve themselves into the main message of the VNR. You do not have the luxury of delaying the main idea.

Developing the Story: The Benefits of a Storyboard

The point that you cannot forget when developing a script is that your golden words will share the spotlight with visuals that may well overshadow them. Although it is possible to produce a video that simply puts pictures to the same audio script you used successfully on radio, this does not take advantage of the unique opportunities provided by visual productions. You lose the opportunity to let the visuals tell part of the story.

Many consider scriptwriting as writing to supplement the visuals. The script exists to puts the visuals in context. It fills in the blanks and provides information that the visuals cannot. The visuals are the center of attention. The old adage "a picture is worth 1,000 words" is unquestionably true when you are trying to squeeze 10 years' worth of research into the 30-second television spot you have budgeted for.

This means that planning the visuals should be an integral part of the scripting process. Words and graphics should be planned together from the start. This is where a *storyboard* comes into play. At its most basic, a storyboard is a script with drawings that show what you expect will be on screen as the words are uttered or the music is played.

Exhibit 11.4 is part of the draft storyboard prepared for 30- and 60-second PSAs from the National Science Foundation (NSF). We call it a concept board because it is the type you might use when presenting ideas to a committee or to the team that will produce the video. Even if you cannot draw well, it lets you say, "This is the visual I want with these words." It is a very early version, simply drawn in colored marker that underwent many changes before the final version was released to the media. The final PSA used animations in neon colors on black backgrounds.

This illustrates several features of a good storyboard. It focuses on the story rather than finished visuals. It includes the spoken text (the first line under each frame) as well as simple production instructions and ideas (the second line under each frame). It is a clear start to shaping the technical production.

When starting a script, you should be able to create a similar storyboard, illustrating (or describing) visuals to accompany each element of the script. This will help you see when you do not have enough visuals or enough changes in visuals to support the amount of text, and vice versa. You may be able to resolve the problem by inserting more visuals or by making something happen in the visuals you have. For example, if you must review a page of figures shown on the screen, consider having the relevant ones change color or be circled as you discuss them. This will focus the attention where you want it and help viewers understand the numbers. Most important, it will keep something happening on screen to retain interest.

Remember that visuals must be as professional as the script. Hiring a professional artist, voice, videographer, and multimedia specialist will take a production from good, appropriate, and suitable to great, memorable, and spectacular. It will be money well spent. It is wise to take advantage of the talents of other professionals,

EXHIBIT 11.4   Eleven of the 56 frames of a PSA storyboard.

Previous screens asked and illustrated questions about the world that could be answered by science and technology.

"You'll find ....
/cut to child watering seedlings that grows into enormous stalk

there's lots

to know
/cut to kids at computer

"Exploring ....as...............
/cut to kids outdoors looking at stars + moon

You...............
/cut to kids at aquarium

.... go"
to kids letting balloons go for experiment

"Unlock the world
/cut to world (maybe a key)

from A to Z
Open S

Discover   Science

and

technology......"

Source: Reproduced with permission of the National Science Foundation and Buzzco Associates, Inc., 1988. PSA directed, animated, designed by Candy Kugel and Vincent Cafarelli, music by Lanny Meyers, produced by Buzzco Associates, Inc.—Marilyn Kraemer, Producer.

especially when your time is limited. Your role is *always* to ensure that the organization's message is well presented and goals are met.

Scriptwriting: Style

As with writing for broadcast, scriptwriting is writing primarily for sound, and to a lesser degree, time. The script must be easy for the talent to speak or it will be awkward and difficult to listen to. If you have multiple voices, you must be able to script for each of them. Always read the script aloud to ensure it sounds like speech instead of formal writing. Reading it will also give you an idea of its length so you can edit to fit the time available.

Scriptwriting: Formatting for Production

Production scripts have three parts: the audio (sound and words), the video (visuals), and the instructions (for production). Depending on the purpose of the script,

EXHIBIT 11.5	Script with video commands for NSF TV spot.

TIME: :30

VIDEO	AUDIO
1. Various shots of Arctic Ice Cap	ANNCR V/O: "Imagine. A desert of ice more than 3000 miles wide. What secrets does this land hold to help us unlock the mysteries of our everyday lives, and what creatures can withstand the extreme temperatures of this harsh polar region known as Antarctica?"
2. Penguin walks across ice	SPOKESPERSON V/O: "Join the National Science Foundation and this year's celebration of science and technology with a look at our polar connections."
SUPER National Science & Technology Week April 26 - May 2 1-800-672-2716 National Science Foundation Where America's Discoveries Begin NSF Logo	"Call 1-800-672-2716 today and help your children discover the polar regions and the mysteries they hold."

Source: Reproduced with permission of the National Science Foundation, Arlington, Virginia.

you may or may not have to worry about all three parts. Simple audio scripts may not include production instructions unless an actuality will accompany them. On the other hand, even first-draft video scripts include at least the visual concepts and simple production instructions. Final video scripts include detailed production instructions for cuts, fades, cues to video and audio, the type and length of a camera shot, and special effects and graphics, to name but a few. They ensure that everything happens when it is supposed to happen.

It will pay you to be familiar with some of the technical terms regarding audio and video production. They will help you understand what the production team is talking about as well as enable you to include instructions in the scripts as you write them. Some of these terms are included in the glossary.

At its simplest, a production script is a two-column format with a description of the visual in one column and the script that will accompany it in the adjacent column. Exhibit 11.5, another PSA from the NSF, is an example of such a simple production script. In this case, the visuals for the first two frames are videos, so they are just described briefly. There are two voices, an announcer and an NSF spokesperson, whose words will be voice-overs to the videos. Voice-over is designated as "V/O." The spot ends with a "super" of a print message that is superimposed over the final visuals. It lasts just 30 seconds and the production will all be done behind the scenes with the production house bringing the visuals and audio into a single unit for distribution.

If your visuals consist of just a few illustrations or preexisting tapes or video footage, this script may be all you need to instruct a production team. The more visuals you have, the more production instructions you must include in the script. For complex productions, it may be wise to use a three-column format, one column each for audio, video and detailed instructions.

From DTP to DTV

Not too long ago, desktop publishing (DTP) brought the ability to produce a finished printed product, including copy, illustrations, color, layout, and pagination onto the desk of even the single-person public relations department. Today, desktop video (DTV) and media production software provide similar capability for electronic media. You can produce full, interactive multimedia productions single-handedly if necessary, limited only by the system you are using and your own talent and knowledge. At one extreme is the potential to simply add animation and audio to text. On the other is the potential to produce computer-generated videos. In between lie most of the public relations videos/presentations we have talked about.

Speechwriting

From the beginning of human communication, issues have been settled and audiences swayed by the skill of the orator. Some 23 centuries ago, Aristotle identified three types of speech that have a strong persuasive character: epideictic (praise, used for ceremonial or "honoring" occasions), forensic (what happened?), and deliberative (what should happen?). The potential to inform, persuade, or entertain is no less today. It may even be greater—at least in terms of audience numbers—given the potential of television, radio, the Web, and other media to carry a topical and relevant speech nationwide or worldwide. Despite this change in magnitude, the basic concerns of the orator—"Who is my audience?" and "What is my purpose?"—have not changed.

However, today's speechwriter must recognize that for a successful speech, words alone won't cut it. Television and film have created new generations of visual sophisticates who will not be impressed by a visually substandard performance. Their criteria for a successful speech include not only the speaker's dress, appearance, and body language but also the use of support materials and visuals. In some cases, success may depend on the visuals. Study after study indicate that audience comprehension, persuasion, and retention are all significantly enhanced when speeches are enhanced with appropriate visuals.

The speechwriter's responsibility therefore may extend to mastering presentation as well as writing techniques. You may also find yourself coaching the speaker on likely audience reaction, presentation style, dress, and body language. It is little wonder that speechwriting is a specialized and often well-paid discipline in its own right.

Ethical Issues

Ethical Decisions in Speechmaking

In its many forms, as a formal speech, script, PSA, or conversation, speech has many functions, among them to inform, persuade, or entertain. Public relations writers may work with any of these three as a goal or, more likely, as a means to an end.

The speechwriter or scriptwriter faces many decisions. Should the speech be one sided or two sided? Who should give it? What level of education should it be written for? Should it answer questions an audience will have or promote an agenda the speaker wishes to promote? Every decision is, in a sense, a micro-level ethical decision on how and to what extent an audience will be informed.

The macro-level ethical decision is the nature of the relationship the speechwriter hopes to establish with the audience. Public relations history suggests that three types of relationship are possible: a one-sided, propagandistic relationship; a neutral, informative, relationship; or some form of two-way, reciprocal relationship.

Public relations writing is writing that is designed to initiate, develop, and sustain positive attitudes and behavior. The key concept here is "sustain." A relationship is of little value unless it is sustained.

The basic ethical test of any writing for speech, then, is, what effect will this speech have on *long-term* relationships with the audience? If the speech or script achieves short-term gain at the expense of long-term relationships, for example, it may be ethically inappropriate.

Speechwriting Considerations: Audience and Purpose

Many of the issues that will shape your speechwriting should be familiar. They include the following:

- ◆ *Your employer's mission* and how the speech will contribute to it.
- ◆ *Audience.* You must know whether the audience is on your side or hostile, informed or uninformed about both the subject and the organization. You must understand audience members' level of education as well as their demographic and psychographic attributes. You must also be prepared for the fact that the audience may be a mixture of interest and indifference, support and antagonism. Speeches must frequently address not one public, but rather multiple publics.
- ◆ *Precedent.* What, if anything, has the organization said in previous speeches or media releases on the same subject?
- ◆ *Purpose.* Is this speech expected to reinforce or change the public's attitude or behavior toward the subject, the speaker, or the organization? Is it meant to motivate employees? To defend corporate actions? To persuade voters to change parties? It makes a difference. See the "Ethical Decisions in Speechmaking" Ethical Issues panel for more discussion on this.

◆ *The speaker.* Above all, speeches are verbal communication. If the speech does not reflect the speaker's personality or follow the speaker's natural speech patterns and style, it will be difficult to deliver. To make the speech natural, the writer needs to know the speaker's vocabulary, speech, and breath patterns (e.g., long or short sentences) and write the speech to suit them. You will also need to know whether the speaker's style is folksy and homespun, humorous or formal.

The style and delivery points for broadcast writing are just as valid for speechwriting. If the speaker cannot deliver it naturally, even the best speech in terms of argument and style will lack credibility.

These factors will influence many decisions about a speech including the length and tone, the structure of argument, the nature of supporting evidence, and the type of visual support needed. It will also tell you if making the speech available as a handout or transcript or if also writing it as a news release or newsletter article will increase its impact.

Structure

A generic structure for any speech is to set the stage for the argument, support the argument, and succinctly ensure the audience remembers the argument. The introduction previews the speech, the body provides details, and the summary recapitulates it. This is a useful formula as long as you temper it by what you know about the speech's audience, purpose, and situation.

The chart shown as Exhibit 11.6 provides a basis on which you can construct speeches for most occasions. How you build on this foundation is what separates the professional from the amateur speechwriter and what makes the difference between success and public embarrassment for the speaker. The objective is to keep the audience interested and involved.

Introduction—Getting Their Attention

Generally, a greeting followed by an attention-grabbing statement prefaces most speeches. Its tone will depend on two basic audience attributes: active/passive and hostile/friendly. Active audiences seek information and listen to the speech because they want to. Passive audiences are neutral, disinterested, and may have to be motivated with a "what's in it for me?" opening. It will take less effort to establish rapport with a friendly audience than with a hostile audience. Mixed audiences require a something-for-everyone approach, but not at the expense of losing the two or three most important points.

Ease into the speech with some preliminary comments. If you hit your key point in the first sentence, you may lose an audience that is still tuning in.

Be very careful with standard speech openings, stories, and jokes. Many a speaker has been embarrassed by having to use a joke or introduction the previous speaker just used.

Body—What Is It All About? Why Are We Here?

The intent and structure of the speech must be clear. Listeners do not have the luxury of rereading information they do not understand. If you lose them or if they

EXHIBIT 11.6   The classic speech structure with its implications for strategy.

Section	Purpose	Strategy
Introduction	Get attention.	May be done with humor or anecdotes (but be careful). Personalize the topic to the audience so they understand why it is important. This has the effect of previewing the speech.
Body	State the theme or make the argument.	Stick to one argument or theme. Even speeches as complex as the U.S. president's State of the Union address usually have one underlying theme, e.g., economic stability, social harmony, or technological progress.
	Provide examples or support the argument.	Ensure that the evidence is accurate, timely, and easily understood. Analogies and metaphors are important. One way to understand new or complex issues is in terms of concepts or experiences with which we are familiar. Remember, hearing alone lies far behind sight or sight and hearing together, verbal arguments must be simpler than written ones.
Conclusion	Summarize speech.	Ensure the audience remembers the most important points. Make them memorable.
	Call to action.	If you want the audience to act, tell them; do not expect them to figure it out. Above all, what to do is what they should remember. If possible, leave them with a phrase or slogan that captures the spirit of the argument.

have to figure out what the speaker means, they are unlikely to catch up to the message. On the other hand, if you provide a road map, tell them where you are going (the aim or conclusion) and how you intend to get there (the structure of the argument), they will be able to focus on the message (the trip).

For structuring the body of a speech, you don't have to stray far from the feature-writing structures discussed in Chapter 10. Any of them can form the basis of interesting speeches that hold the audience's attention. For example, any of the ideas for a feature article on the career of retiring employee Marvin Johnson could be an effective speech for his retirement dinner. Just be sure that the speech is written for spoken delivery. Following are occasions for which the other feature structures would be appropriate for speeches.

+ *Chronological order*—the history of the company or career of a retiring employee
+ *Spatial*—describing a new facility
+ *Problem/solution*—announcing new corporate policies

✦ *Compare/contrast*—new product update or incentive speech on marketing the company against its competitors
✦ *Cause/effect*—explaining organizational restructuring or a crisis response
✦ *Question/answer*—providing research results or new plans
✦ *Past/present/future*—introducing a new business venture or long-range plan

For each of these structures, you must select the best supporting evidence. Evidence that can used to support an advocacy position includes statistics, experts, history-precedent, and research. To these we would add personal experience (of the speaker or audience) and anecdotes. Both of these can personalize the argument to the audience.

Speeches also offer the opportunity to use visual evidence. Show the audience how it works (or doesn't), in real life or through videos, audiovisuals, demonstrations, or even static charts and graphs. If written successfully, analogies and metaphors provide "mind's eye" evidence.

Conclusion—Recap the Argument and Leave 'em Ready to Act

It is too much to expect listeners to remember all of the points of even a short speech, so a quick recap of the important points will be necessary. Plus, it allows you to bring together the flow of the argument, reminding the listener of its logic and leading into the conclusion. If you gather appropriate evidence, present it logically, and recap effectively, the listener should be "with you" at the end, and ready to agree with your conclusion.

Try for a memorable conclusion. It can be a call for action, an implicit threat of what will happen if nothing is done, or a great quote. The point is that it should be clear and memorable.

Presidential speechwriters crafting the annual State of the Union address deliberately strive for the quotable phrase that will go down in history, such as the "new deal," "new frontier," or "evil empire," or become a media sound bite. If this can be interpreted as controlling the media or the audience's recollection, so be it. It works.

Techniques for speechwriting vary greatly. Some writers outline the speech, write rough draft, and then flesh it out with detail. Others write a full text and then edit, change, and rewrite. Many writers find it helpful to write the introduction last. Although it comes first, you may not know what would make a great introduction until you have written the speech it is needed for. Over time, you will develop your own style.

Speechwriting: Style

There are some obvious differences between broadcast copy and speeches. Speeches are generally thought to be too long at 20 minutes, whereas broadcasters may consider an actuality too long at 20 seconds. But many principles remain the same. To capture speech style, you must write speech style. Leave out complicated detail. Round off or generalize statistics. Write in active rather than passive voice. Choose colorful images. And speak to the audience.

Draw the audience into the argument. Speeches are dialogues, sort of, and you must imply the audience's part. Many speakers work hard to build solidarity with the audience by deliberately choosing terms that are inclusive: "we," "our," "us," or "my fellow Americans," rather than the more distancing "you" and "your."

The following points should help you get from written to spoken style successfully.

◆ *Keep sentences short.* Not only are long sentences difficult for audiences to follow, they are also difficult for speakers to deliver.

◆ *Use effective transitions.* As in feature writing, transitions such as "on the other hand," "another example," and "this also demonstrates" are valuable road signs for the audience. They help the audience follow your argument.

◆ *Use simple sentence construction.* Limit yourself to one idea per sentence. Anything more may be confusing. For example, which of the following sentences is easier to understand?

> "Johnson's research led to several discoveries, *not the least of which* is the chemical that . . ."

> "Johnson's research led to several discoveries, *the most important of which* is the chemical that . . ."

The phrase "not the least of which" is confusing. The listener may be distracted while trying to understand the phrase or, even worse, hear only the word "least" and miss the point entirely. Perhaps a clearer option is to divide the sentence into two: "Johnson's research led to several discoveries. The most important of these is the chemical that . . ."

◆ *Take advantage of alliteration.* When used well and judiciously, alliteration almost guarantees memorability. Alliteration is one of the few word patterns that work better in spoken than written communication. It is the repetition of sounds, usually the first letter of several words, to create a memorable pattern. Alliteration is why "Better Business Bureau" is a more memorable name than "Association of Businesses." It is why a politician who ends a speech with the promise of "peace, prosperity, and progress" knows that this phrase will likely become tomorrow's sound bite if not headline. Beware that alliteration is an obvious technique, and if it is not used well, it will be annoying.

◆ *Speak (write) the language of the speaker.* There is no substitute for face-to-face meetings with speakers to hear how they speak. You need to hear the length and rhythm of their sentences and the type of words they use. Speakers who are uncomfortable with the pacing of a speech or with the difficulty of the words will not deliver the message effectively.

◆ *Speak (write) the language of the audience.* Effective public relations writers are mediators between the speaker and the audience, responsible for meeting the needs of both. Audiences who cannot identify with the speaker are unlikely to believe or buy into a message. If the speaker cannot convincingly speak the audience's language, you have the wrong speaker.

The benefit of speaking appropriate language can be seen in the politician who gives an eloquent oration on the floor of Congress, citing legislation and presenting sophisticated arguments, and a day later returns to his home district to give a folksy, down-home address that convinces constituents that he is still "the boy next door."

◆ *Think rhythm.* This is closely related to the language of the speaker and the audience, but it also involves listening to what you write. Rhythm is another test of writing to be heard. If your speech sounds like a book chapter, you have written reading style, but not spoken style.

Closely related to rhythm is the use of parallel structure. For example: read the following sentences aloud.

"Tonight we will talk about our environmental audit, plus your questions will be answered, and I will discuss the benefits of the project."

versus

"I am here tonight to explain our environmental audit, answer your questions, and outline the benefits of the project."

Which is easier to read? Which flows better? Which would you rather have as part of a speech? Why? The difference is parallel structure among the parts.

◆ *Write for timing.* Listen to the delivery of some of the masters of public speaking: stand-up comedians. Only part of their success comes from the jokes. The rest is in the timing. Do they plunge straight from opening to punch line or do they strategically pause, or introduce a diversion, to keep the audience anticipating the punch line? The idea that "what you say isn't as important as how you say it" is often true.

◆ *Build to a climax.* Leave the audience with the most important point. Briefly recap the argument. Structure it so the audience reaches the same conclusion as the speaker at the same time as the speaker. Then tell them what to do: help, write letters, donate, vote, or get an inoculation against the flu.

EXERCISE 3

The PBS archive of Great American Speeches at http://www.pbs.org/greatspeeches/timeline/ offers scripts and some audio clips of American political oratory. Find a speech that offers both an audio clip and a script so that you can read and listen to the speech at the same time.

How well do you think the speech

◆ captures the language and interests of the audience?
◆ captures the personality of the speaker?
◆ responds to the time and circumstances of the speech?

How effective do you find the introduction, arguments, evidence and appeals, and conclusion?

As you look at the script, how do you see that writing for the ear differs from writing for the eye?

Listen to What You Have Written

Just as we suggest that you check your newswriting with a readability test and your layouts by viewing them upside down, we advise that you check your speechwriting by reading it aloud. Then have the speaker read it aloud—again and again and again, if necessary. Part of your job may be rehearsing speakers so they give the best possible presentation of your speech.

Planning

A Speech

Speeches are a classic example of language applied to building relationships between two parties for a specific purpose, but the speechwriter's job is not over when the speech is written. Knowing speaker, audience, and purpose will help the writer make decisions about the structure, vocabulary, style, and length of the speech, but the following also need to be considered if the speech is to be presented effectively.

Physical Setting

The size of the venue will dictate the need for a public address system and/or monitors to relay the address. It will also dictate the extent to which the audience can see the visuals and, therefore, whether they will need ancillary handouts. The presence or absence of lighting and blackout controls will dictate whether some visuals can be used effectively.

Technology

Speakers often require lighting, public address systems, video projection, and phone and Internet connections (if the presentation is interactive). It may/should be your responsibility to ensure that (a) all of them work and (b) are compatible. Speakers may travel with their own presentation equipment (typically, a laptop computer running PowerPoint) that they expect to connect to the venue's projector. Under such conditions, you will need to ensure version-to-version software compatibility, Mac to PC platform compatibility, and physical (e.g., USB) connectivity.

Ancillary Materials

Fact sheets, biographies, backgrounders, technical specifications, PowerPoint notes, and sign-up sheets can all be part of a speaker's presentation. If so, you will need to ensure that sufficient copies are available and that their distribution does not detract from the presentation.

Publicity

If you want media coverage, you will need to plan to meet the media's needs, from parking through reserved seating to electricity and satellite connections. After the event, you may continue to publicize it with news releases, arranged interviews with the speaker, perhaps a feature story for an employee magazine or newsletter, and by uploading the speech to a web site to make it available to a wider audience.

Generally, reading a prepared script word for word is a bad idea. At a minimum it is less than exciting and participative for the audience. At worst it is downright boring. Once again, audience and situation will dictate what is appropriate. If the speech is detailed and legally significant, such as testimony before a legislative committee, you will likely prepare a full script and ensure that the CEO follows it exactly. Legal counsel will no doubt endorse this strategy. You should also provide the script in advance to a translator if the text is to be simultaneously translated into sign or a foreign language. But if the speech is to a group of business associates on a subject the CEO knows well, you may have to do little more than provide an outline and rely on camaraderie and expertise to shape a successful speech.

Presentation Support

Speakers may opt for you to provide presentation notes. These range from the full text on paper or cards, a teleprompter script, the key points only, the full text with key points highlighted, or presentation software the speaker can control. Some speakers may choose to memorize the whole thing. Remember too the principles for writing audio scripts: 60-character lines, double spacing, phonetic pronunciations, and simplifying complex concepts and details.

Presentation software, notably PowerPoint, allows output in a variety of formats—visuals and text, text only, or text down one side of the page with the other side blank for notes.

Speeches can be further published in transcript, booklet, CD, web-based actuality, or text formats or as newsletter articles. They may also lead the speaker into follow-up interviews, talk shows, and panels. If it seems likely that these opportunities may arise, you may also want to anticipate questions and prepare a question-and-answer format fact sheet and rehearse your speaker through this as well.

ON THE TEXTBOOK WEB SITE

✦   Go to www.sagepub.com/treadwell for web exercises, study hints, case studies, and additional examples appropriate to this chapter and chosen or developed to supplement the chapter content.

WRITING WRAP-UP

1.   Return to the news release you wrote for a campus organization ("Writing Wrap-Up" in Chapter 9). Rewrite it for use on your campus radio station. Read the release aloud. If it is longer than 30 seconds, rewrite it to that timeframe.

2.   Write a 5-minute speech that you will deliver to your campus's student government to achieve a student government resolution that the campus should close on Election Day to allow students to vote. Do you expect this audience to be positive, neutral, or negative? Will this affect what you say?

3. Write a 5-minute speech that you will deliver to your college's or university's trustees arguing for a change in campus policy to close the campus on Election Day. Do you expect this audience to be positive, neutral, or negative? Will this affect what you say?

REFERENCE

Long live Her Royal Highness Princess Maha Chakri Sirindhorn. (2002). Retrieved June 14, 2003, from http://sunsite.au.ac.th/thailand/special_event/sirindh

RESOURCES

Broadcast Writing

Cameron, G. T., & Blount, D. (1996). VNRs and air checks: A content analysis of the use of video news releases in television broadcasts. *Journalism and Mass Communication Quarterly, 73*(4), 890–905.

Kalbfeld, B. (2001). *Associated Press broadcast news handbook.* New York: McGraw Hill.

MacDonald, R. H. (2002). *A broadcast news manual of style.* New York: Longman.

Papper, R. A. (2002). *Broadcast news writing stylebook.* Boston: Allyn & Bacon.

Simon, D. (1996). VNR/SMT packages are a hot PR tool. *Public Relations Quarterly, 41*(3), 36–38.

Speeches

There's a library of speechwriting texts you can take advantage of, and a library of resources—quotations (online), thesauri, jokes.

Bartlett, John, *Bartlett's Familiar Quotations,* 10th ed. www.bartleby.com/100

Bartlett, J., & Kaplan, J. (2003). *Bartlett's Familiar Quotations,* 17th ed., New York: Little, Brown.

Moncur, Michael, *The Quotations Page* .... www.starlingtech.com

Northwestern University Douglass ....http://douglassarchives.org/ archive of American oratory

PBS Great American Speeches..........................http://www.pbs.org/greatspeeches/timeline/

Vital Speeches of the Day (select "The Quotations Page") .... http://www.votd.com/

Featured Organizations

Ad Council .... www.adcouncil.org

EPA Childhood Asthma Campaign .... www.noattacks.org

National Science Foundation.. www.nsf.gov

West Glen Communications .... www.westglen.com

When the News Isn't Good

Crisis Messages

1. It is possible and ethically responsible to plan for a crisis.

2. Crises in other organizations can affect your organization.

3. Because they know the publics, public relations practitioners should play a key role in crisis planning and response.

4. Crisis writing should be ethically sound, responsive, honest, and timely.

5. You can and should "think public relations" when writing crisis messages.

6. Its immediacy and potential for interactivity make the Web an important medium for crisis communications.

1. Crisis planning—an exercise in understanding publics.

2. Crisis writing—the same message to multiple publics.

Generally, crisis writing implies writing under pressure of time to restore normal relationships with publics. It calls on all of the foundational skills we have emphasized in previous chapters—research, planning, ethics, and prioritizing publics. You will consider the full range of media and methods as you make crisis-writing decisions. In this chapter, we discuss the nature of crises, general crisis response strategies, and the specifics of crisis writing.

What Is a Crisis?

Much literature exists on the subject of what constitutes a crisis and how crisis communication should be defined. The definitions of crisis generally converge on the ideas that a crisis is both a surprise and a threat to the organization.

Smudde (2001) draws a useful distinction between issues and crises, especially as they relate to public relations writing. Issues evolve over time, and their resolution may lie in the hands of external publics. In contrast, crises are characterized by their surprise, magnitude, and threat to the basic functioning of the organization. Crisis control, at least initially, lies with the organization that has the available information. It is likely that the public relations writer will play a key role in this crisis control.

Issues can turn into crises and vice versa. For example, a food poisoning crisis can turn into a long-term issue of food safety. Alternatively, the issue of the future of space exploration suddenly reached crisis status for NASA when faced with the aftermath of the space shuttle *Columbia* (and previously, the *Challenger*) catastrophe.

From an organizational viewpoint, a crisis provides little or no time for decision making. Responses must be immediate because of the negative impact it can have on the organization's financial or operational status. From a public relations viewpoint, a crisis can result in a major change in how publics, including employees, see the organization. Crises also change the organization's self-image. Typically, it takes the organization a long time to recover from a major crisis.

The crises of the early 21st century support this definition: 9/11, the Enron/ Arthur Andersen scandal, anthrax mailings, and outbreaks of mad cow disease, West Nile virus, and SARS all occurred with little or no warning. They affected multiple publics seriously and required immediate responses. They continue as issues long after the crisis has passed.

Crises can result from natural causes such as floods, fires, and blizzards. They may be technology based as when power, computer, and communications systems shut down. Or they can be relationship based as in charges of racial or sexual discrimination or harassment. They may be deliberate as in the case of financial malfeasance, sabotage, and tainted products or accidental as when negligence leads to an industrial disaster. They may come about when publics see organizations as violating contemporary norms and charge them with social irresponsibility.

With today's pervasive and immediate media coverage, there has emerged another category of crisis that frequently requires a response. We call it a reflected crisis. Reflected crises begin with a crisis incurred by a person or organization with which your organization is associated in the public mind. Even though your organization is not involved in the crisis, its shadow threatens to affect your relationships with your publics. It is also likely to bring the media to your door. In such cases, although responding to the crisis itself may be out of your hands, how you respond to your publics and to the media is clearly in your control.

Consider, for example, the plight of the U.S. beef industry when the Canadian beef industry reported a case of mad cow disease (bovine spongiform encephalopathy; BSE) in 2003. Fearing a backlash against U.S. as well as Canadian beef, the U.S. National Cattlemen's Beef Association immediately launched a campaign designed to protect the image of the U.S. industry. The research-based strategy included a web site, a special crisis web site on the subject of BSE, news releases, and letter and fax communications with targeted individuals—all because of a crisis in Canada. The campaign received a 2004 PRSA Silver Anvil Award for crisis communication.

As a footnote, what the industry learned from this crisis stood it in good stead when the U.S. industry faced its own mad cow scare later the same year.

You might also incur a reflected crisis based on the misconduct of the celebrity VIP you have chosen as a spokesperson. In 2003, many charities reconsidered their ties to singer Michael Jackson after he faced allegations of child molestation. Others remained steadfast in their commitment to him on an "innocent until proven guilty" basis. All of them had to determine if the charges compromised his credibility and/or reflected negatively on their programs. Similarly, aircraft manufacturers such as Boeing often have to deal with reflected crises as the result of an airline crash that may well have resulted from weather conditions or pilot error rather than from a manufacturing problem.

The growth of Internet chat rooms, "anti-" web sites, and even blogs increases the potential for an organization to be "tarnished by someone else's brush" and to find itself with a reflected crisis.

From a communications viewpoint, crises can be identified by looking again at the issues of audience, control, and purpose. You have a crisis demanding a communication response if the issue is critically important to your public, if your public needs the information immediately, or if the information needs to come from you.

✦ *Audience*—the issue is critically important to at least one of your publics and you have no choice but to respond. A public crisis usually means one of two things: Either the health, safety, or financial well-being of the general public is threatened, or the negative story has already or is imminently likely to hit the airwaves on its own. This dictates communication with and through the mass media.

On the other hand, the threat may be less widespread but nonetheless important to a smaller group. Employees will be affected by a downsizing and clients will be affected if a fire puts the organization's major plant out of commission. You may still have to respond, but the mass media may not be the communication vehicle you choose.

✦ *Timing*—you must respond immediately. The audience needs information or you are legally obligated to provide it, such as under SEC regulations. In such cases, you cannot afford to have information gatekeepers, that is, media editors, choose to *not* run your story at all, to edit the content, or to run it later. This will dictate buying media space and/or choosing other methods of communication.

✦ *Content*—your purpose is to quell or, you hope, reverse negative attitudes and behavior. It is important that your message be delivered exactly as you wrote it. Sometimes you may want to protect the organization. At other times, you may need to give the audience information or directions that are critical to their health or well-being or to your employer's future. Either way, content control is critical.

DISCUSSION 1

As a public relations specialist, you should be able to identify communication strategies that would help you manage public opinion and reaction to negative events to which an organization may be vulnerable. These may include technology failure, employee actions, policy decisions, financial problems, privacy issues, competitor's actions, industry problems, and natural disasters.

For your college or university, what specific potential crises can you identify under each of the above broad areas? For each, to what audiences would you need to respond and how quickly?

Crisis Management

If crises are defined by their unpredictability and sudden onslaught, how is it possible to plan for them? There are two answers to this question. First, it is possible to anticipate *generally* the type of crises to which an organization may be vulnerable. Second, it is possible to develop plans for a general crisis response. Barton (1993) identifies five crisis stages:

- ✦ *Detection*—watching for warning signs of a crisis
- ✦ *Preparation*—for a proactive or reactive response to the likely crisis
- ✦ *Containment*—limiting the duration and effects of the actual crisis
- ✦ *Recovery*—the return to normal
- ✦ *Learning and evaluation*—to prevent or deal more effectively with future crises

Public relations writers may be closely involved at each of these stages. Writing projects may include research reports, news releases, employee communications, speeches, newsletters, mailings to constituents, and web site updates. You will also act as liaison with the media.

What is generally called crisis management has two parts. The first is managing the crisis itself, which is an operational response. The second is managing how the publics learn about, understand, and respond to the crisis. This is a communication response. Although public relations practitioners may not play a direct role in the operational response, their knowledge of audiences, media options, and communications skills should be the key to an effective communication response—but this is dependent on the role that public relations plays in the organizational hierarchy.

The recognition that public relations should play a "top of the office" role is increasing. Grunig, Grunig, and Dozier (2002) argue that effective public relations departments are represented in the organization's top management team. Their strategic insights will then be a part of a crisis response. Koplan (2003) argues that public health emergencies—such as anthrax attacks, SARS, and West Nile virus—require an "unprecedented degree of top-level attention to communications" (p. 144).

The Institute for Crisis Management maintains a web site, www.crisisexperts.com, on which it analyzes crisis strategies. You may find this site interesting as well as a good reference for communication options.

The Crisis Plan

The extent to which organizations engage in monitoring the environment for potential crises and preparing plans for responding to them varies widely. In 2002, Horsley and Barker found that many state agencies had little proactive communication with the media and that less than half of them had a written crisis plan.

However, it appears that businesses and nonprofits at last are taking an interest in crisis plans. There are two reasons for this change. First, 9/11 was a wake-up call for emergency preparedness generally. Second, even nonprofit and community service organizations are recognizing the potential for litigation and public scrutiny in the face of stories of malfeasance, and racial and sexual harassment.

One of the arguments against such plans is the fear (held by many businesses) that the very existence of a crisis plan may be seen as evidence that the organization is aware of a pending problem. Such businesses may opt to conceal their crisis plans. It may be your job to help frame the plan as a generally proactive, responsible management action.

The arguments in favor of crisis plans are stronger. In particular, crisis plans will help you manage not only public opinion but also media attention on the crisis. They will help you minimize the length of time the media is focused on the crisis and maximize the opportunities to send positive messages.

The canny public relations writer will watch how other organizations, especially competitors, handle negative publicity. This will go a long way toward helping you develop strategies to reach target publics with messages that will aid recovery. In addition, competitors often become colleagues when a crisis or reflected crisis affects an entire sector.

Planning

Crisis Strategies

If by definition you can't predict crises, it may seem illogical to plan for them. But even if you can't plan for specific crises, you can plan for the likelihood of some of them. The public relations practitioner brings to the process an understanding of the environments in which the organization operates. This will be useful in predicting publics to which the organization may be vulnerable and communication options for managing the crisis. The practitioner also brings to the table several approaches that may be useful.

The Journalistic Approach

The journalistic approach asks basic news questions such as the following:

* Who has the potential to hurt or harm the organization?

* What—for better or worse—could they do to us?

* Why would they do it?

* Where in the organization or geographically could they have most impact?

* When might they act?

It is essentially the same thought process used to identify key publics and devise effective communication strategies for dealing with them.

Murphy's Law Approach

A more despondent but useful beginning to crisis planning is Murphy's Law. If something can go wrong it will. "What could possibly go wrong?" is a good basis for generating possible crisis scenarios.

The Public Relations Approach

Crisis planning is best conducted as a cross-disciplinary exercise involving public relations alongside legal and technical experts. This should result in a generic action plan that spells out responsibilities, key publics, and contacts within and outside the organization and identifies resources—information and otherwise—to deal with the crisis.

The Public Elations Approach

Not all crises are negative. "Happy planning" might deal with how to handle an unannounced visit from a VIP or a major donation or award. Planning means being able to cope with the unanticipated good times as well as the bad ones.

The first objective of a crisis plan is to anticipate your vulnerability to as many potential crises as possible. Having done this, you can identify the strategic responses and the talents, resources, and procedures needed to execute the responses. To this end, a crisis plan will identify the following.

◆ *The areas of risk* including violence and terrorism, litigation, ethical lapses, natural disaster, technology failure, or the deaths of key executives. Generally, you should be able to prioritize them in order of the organization's vulnerability to each and their potential impact on the organization.

◆ *Key publics and procedures for reaching them.* Generally, there are three key publics to whom you would expect to pay attention in a crisis:

External constituencies such as existing customers and clients.

The news media through which you hope to reach such constituencies. Especially in crises, it helps to work with reporters who understand the organization and its industry. This is one of the strongest arguments for cultivating positive media relationships.

Employees or other internal audiences such as students in the case of a college or university or patients in the case of a hospital. Internal audiences are perhaps the most important of the three.

The plan should lay out specific procedures for reaching each of them.

Crises also have the potential to catalyze the attention of new publics who suddenly find an area of common interest with the organization—for better or worse. For example, many organizations have little or no contact with their local legislators. But an environmental crisis may suddenly have them on your doorstep seeking information on which to support or oppose stricter emissions standards that could cost millions. The same crisis might find you allied with companies that have experienced a similar crisis but in completely different industries. You may also find your employer in an adversarial position with environmental groups that previously paid you no attention but that are now picketing outside corporate headquarters. They may also be active in cyberspace, vilifying your organization in chat rooms and newsgroups across the Web.

Roles that the public relations writer may play include identifying the key publics and their likely attitudes toward the issue and monitoring public opinion and the response of government and industry. You will also identify the messages and strategies and the media and media contacts that can be used to reach each of the key publics.

◆ *The crisis team.* The crisis plan should identify key executive, public relations, legal, and technical experts and spokespersons and the roles, locations, and contact information for each of them. You may be involved in recommending and training them for media and public contacts.

◆ *Facilities.* From a communication point of view, this addresses the needs of media as well as public relations staff. This includes photocopying, Internet access and web site updates, teleconferencing, and news media parking and conference rooms.

◆ *Background materials.* The crisis plan should identify the information available as background on the organization and perhaps on the issue itself. This material may include fact sheets, technical specifications, biographies, maps, photographs, web pages, and lists of relevant resources. Having such materials ready allows you to release some information when little may be known in the early stages of a crisis.

One of the most important emergencies faced by colleges and universities is the death or injury of a member of the campus community, especially a student. Such an eventuality is a component of most institutional communication plans. Exhibit 12.1 is example of the Emergency Notification Procedures that form part of the Westfield (Massachusetts) State College communication policy.

This communication policy clearly establishes which publics the college believes are most important. In this case, it is the student's family and associates. It then identifies which officers will communicate with these publics. All public information is the responsibility of the director of Marketing and Media, who is the designated college spokesperson. She is already on positive terms with the local media, knows who they are, and understands how to work with them. She also recognizes the implications of privacy and the release of information.

Crises and the Media

If the crisis is truly local or internal, you may be able to handle communications quietly, perhaps with well-targeted personal communications. Sometimes, however, you cannot avoid having the mass media play a part in your crisis communications. This is especially true of crises that affect the public's health or safety, affect the financial status of public companies, or involve celebrity spokespersons. We are all familiar with headlines such as

NASA culture contributes to shuttle crashes

(Name your sport) star faces rape charges

E. coli found in park swimming pools

SWAT team tactics under attack in wake of school shootings

Diocese faces sexual abuse charges

(Name the executive) faces prison term for financial dealings

Suspected anthrax spores found in mailings

Power outage blacks out Northeast

EXHIBIT 12.1   Westfield State College Emergency Notification Procedures, part of the college's policy manual.

Emergency Notification Procedures

PURPOSE: This policy describes the procedures for notifying campus personnel of emergency information, such as the serious injury or sudden death of an employee, student or immediate family members of employees or students.

1. Any College employee in receipt of emergency information shall immediately report it to the Department of Public Safety (with phone number).

2. The Executive Director of Public Safety/designee shall verify the facts reported, if necessary, and notify the college President, appropriate Vice President and the College Chaplain.

3. The college President or designee shall contact the immediate family of the injured or deceased person to extend condolences and/or offer of assistance.

4. The Vice President shall notify the respective personnel in their divisional/departmental areas.

5. Any general information shall be submitted and released by the Director of Marketing and Media.

Source: Reprinted with permission from Westfield State College, Westfield, Massachusetts.

Such events send public relations specialists, the media, and their publics into overdrive as the uncertainties fuel speculation and rumor and as the certainties impact negatively on the health, safety, or economic and psychological security of those affected.

In other situations, the event is a crisis because the media (on behalf of its audience) sees it as such. For example, when International Paper Company announced the closing of its Strathmore Paper plant in Turners Falls, Massachusetts, it issued a release to the local media. The second paragraph of the news release included the number of jobs that would be lost. Remembering the news determinants discussed in Chapter 9, are you surprised that these numbers made the *first* paragraph of the story as printed in the local media? In many cases, it might have been part of the headline. To the small town, it was a crisis and had to be handled as such by the paper company.

In still other cases, what was a quiet internal issue may take on crisis proportions because the media have learned of it and intend to make it public. Think of leaked memos in which tobacco executives reportedly acknowledge the link between tobacco and cancer, or of rumors of a merger for which negotiations have not yet concluded.

These examples have all occurred at the level of catastrophe for large organizations, but they have their counterparts in even the smallest organizations. A drum of weed killer falling off a delivery truck or a college cafeteria closed because of food poisoning constitutes a crisis for a small organization. They require the same problem-solving abilities and pressure of deadlines as their national or international attention-grabbing cousins.

E X E R C I S E   1

A transformer fire on campus means that, effective immediately, two of the largest dorms will be uninhabitable for at least two weeks. Identify three priority audiences that need to be reached, and recommend the best method/s for reaching them.

Crisis Writing

Writing during a crisis is not *significantly* different from writing under normal circumstances. Everything you know about writing for particular audiences still applies. You are writing to audiences you should know using media you should know. And your purpose will be especially clear, that is, providing information while protecting the organization's position and reputation.

The primary difference is that in a crisis both the time available and the timing of messages become much more important. In a crisis, you are always writing under pressure.

The Message

Although it would be nice to have the public as interested in positive news as in negative news, this usually isn't the case. To the contrary, you may find the public and media most interested when the news isn't good.

The information you release during a crisis will be a function of your employer's culture, controlling legislation (e.g., SEC), and your communication policy. If culture and policy allow, you will opt for free and open disclosure. However, if the organization has a closed culture—or if legal counsel prevails—you may focus on containment and release as little information as possible.

If the crisis is not yours, but rather that of an associated organization, you may find yourself trapped into a public stance because the public demands your comment. This demand typically comes via the media. This is one case in which you and the legal counsel may jointly advise your employer to try to "lay low." You hope the crisis abates or public interest wanes before the attention comes your way. This is where a positive relationship between public relations and legal counsel can pay dividends.

Strategies for Crisis Communications

Crises are situational and their seriousness is subject to many factors such as timing, location, organizational finances, and personnel. Accordingly, different publics will in themselves dictate different response strategies. The following are general considerations with regard to communicating during a crisis.

Writing Strategies

♦ *Establish a clear position.* Determine one clear message and stay with it through all messages and all media to all publics. Confirm the problem and state its nature, but do not speculate. You may be able to buy some time by writing a statement that initiates the dialogue on your terms but does not make any claims or projections. This is typically called a *holding statement* because it puts a more detailed response on hold as shown in the accident example that follows.

Although the idea of writing a crisis statement before a crisis may be unnerving, you can at least prepare a template for holding statements. It will provide initial information for the news media and affected parties while giving the organization time to gather further information, as in for example, the following:

An accident potentially involving employee injuries has occurred at the XYZ (location) plant. Fire, ambulance and police services have been summoned. Because XYZ's policy is to first ensure the safety of employees and neighbors, the site is not currently accessible to the news media.

XYZ has procedures in place to handle such emergencies. Our first priority is to care for any employees who may be injured and to obtain information about the situation. The company is now doing this and will provide further information as it becomes available.

Such a statement could also provide contact information and, as appropriate, details about the location of briefing rooms, parking, and the need for identification.

♦ *Be honest*—and be seen to be honest. Especially in today's media-centric world, the truth, as they say, "will out," so lying is never a wise strategy. But even if the truth was unlikely to be told, you still have obligations to yourself, your organization, your publics, and the public relations industry to provide true *and accurate* information to support the free flow of information and informed decision making.

Ethical Issues

The Ethics of Crisis Strategy

There are many ways of responding publicly to crises, especially when it comes to having to deal publicly with the issue of guilt. Hearit (2002) identifies five basic message strategies that an organization may adopt as it seeks to clear its name.

✦ *Denial.* A public position of denying guilt may be taken because the organization truly is not guilty, is guilty but unintentionally so, or is guilty but not legally so until proven in a court of law.

✦ *Counterattack.* To counterattack is not only to deny but also to go one step further and suggest that one's critics are ethically suspect for having leveled false charges. The goal of a counterattack is to place critics on the defensive. Typical counterattacks on the media include charges of unfair reporting, media bias, and ratings-driven media hype.

✦ *Differentiation.* Differentiation is a strategy used when the organization cannot escape at least some blame. Under such conditions, it will differentiate itself from a "more guilty" individual or group. The organization may find scapegoats in disaffected employees, unions, or its advisors. Scapegoats are rarely in management. The basic position is, "*They* did it; *we* are innocent."

✦ *Apology.* Apologies happen when the company is genuinely apologetic or has no other choice but to apologize. Generally, it is not a full apology. Messages will refer to an "isolated incident" or "the actions of a few." Apologies may come in the form of a personal apology from the CEO rather than a corporate apology.

✦ *Legal.* Of course, a corporation may also adopt an essentially legal position of saying little or nothing but never admitting blame.

The Ethics of Crisis Response

One way to decide on an appropriate response is to consider the effects of a strategy on key publics. Scapegoating or blaming employees may appeal to stockholders, but it will alienate employees—the very group the organization needs most as it attempts to recover from a crisis.

A second way is to consider both the long-term and the short-term effects of each strategy. A full and open apology may be difficult in the short term but desirable in the long term if the crisis has been truly dealt with and the confidence of publics restored. Counterattacking the news media may be effective in the short term by drawing attention away from the crisis itself but not a good decision in the long run when you will be looking for media cooperation.

Third, of course, is the PRSA Code of Ethics, which emphasizes truth and accuracy and full disclosure in the public interest.

✦ *Be concise.* Provide necessary information and explanations, but do so as briefly as possible. The less elaboration you provide, the less opportunity there will be for misunderstanding or misinterpretation.

✦ *Look forward.* When possible, focus on solutions rather than the problem. Discuss what is being done now and will be done in the future rather than what happened in the past.

♦ *Do not assign blame.* It is best to follow legal counsel's advice and not discuss blame. Acknowledging and accepting blame may open legal doors that legal counsel wants to remain closed. The most you may do is honestly and sincerely "regret the incident," "offer sympathy or condolences," or "set out a plan to avert a recurrence."

♦ *Take advantage of your employer's good reputation.* If this is the first time you have had such a problem or that you have the resources in place to deal with it, say so. But do not expect this alone to restore public confidence.

The Westfield State College crisis response policy shown as Exhibit 12.1 was put to the test when an off-campus apartment fire claimed the life of one student and injured several others. Exhibit 12.2 is the text of the release issued by the college after the victims had been identified. Note that it is limited strictly to the facts. It is brief, to the point, and professional. It avoids speculation or blame and positions the college as actively helping people deal with the tragedy.

All staff and members of the college community wish this event had not occurred and that the Emergency Notification Policy had never been tested. But the fact is that when tested, it worked. All publics received the attention they deserved in the priority they deserved it. Family and friends were notified first. The Public Affairs staff managed external communications and subsequent follow-up questions from the media.

News media coverage of a crisis may never be positive, but the above steps can build the credibility you may need to manage the storm. They may move a story that may have been 90% negative to one that is only 60% negative.

Media Strategies

If the crisis affects more than just internal audiences, the media will be interested, and you will have to deal with them. But there are strategies you can adopt to ensure neutral rather than negative coverage and to maximize the opportunity for the organization's message to be printed or aired.

♦ *Centralize communication in one office or spokesperson.* This lets you control what is said about the event. Issue all information in writing. Spokespersons should speak from prepared statements with written copies available. Spokespersons should be trained and aware of the policy and strategy. Keep a log of these statements and all media contacts.

♦ *Cooperate with the media.* If you can't do this fully, at least be seen as *trying* to cooperate. This is especially important if the organization chooses not to comment. Avoid the phrase "no comment," substituting instead "we cannot answer that right now" or "we can't answer that until we receive the results of XYZ test," or "until our attorneys have reviewed the situation," or "until all employees or affiliates are notified." "We prefer not to speculate on the cause" is also useful. The point is to be seen as cooperative while at the same time not releasing information you do not choose to release.

This tactic will only go so far, so even while you are deferring comment, you should be working to identify what you *can* say. If necessary, you should be

---

EXHIBIT 12.2   Media release issued during crisis. Note especially its brevity.

Westfield State College Public Relations Crisis Release

Sept. 5, 1997

The Westfield State College community is saddened by the death of one student and the injury of five other students in a fire at an off-campus apartment house in Westfield at 3:40 a.m. Friday.

(Name), a junior from Attleboro, Mass., who majored in geography and regional planning, was transported from a building at 11 Lincoln Street to Noble Hospital where he was pronounced dead, according to hospital officials.

Two students were hospitalized and released. They are (Name) of North Easton, Mass., and (Name) of Brighton, Mass. The three students who remain hospitalized for treatment of injuries resulting from the fire are (Name) of Westford, (Name) of Grafton, and (Name) of Chicopee.

"Our campus is saddened by this tragedy and all of us feel deep sympathy for the families of the students involved," said Jeanne Julian, college spokesperson. "They have many friends and concerned mentors at the college. Our staff is working to inform our community and to offer counseling to anyone affected by the pain and loss resulting from this accident."

The cause of the fire is under investigation by the state fire marshall.

-30-

Source: Reproduced with permission of Westfield State College, Westfield, Massachusetts.

---

persuading management and legal counsel that open disclosure is the wisest tactic in the long term.

◆ *Work with media you know.* Cultivating positive relationships with the media reaps the greatest rewards during times of crisis. If wide publicity is necessary or appropriate, your best ally may be a friendly reporter or editor who understands the organization and its industry. At best this may ensure the placement of a story *you* write. At least it may ensure that original coverage is neutral if not sympathetic.

◆ *Remember your newswriting skills.* Write crisis media releases in the same style and format as "good news" releases. This makes it easy for editors to review the story. The less an editor has to do to shape the story to news conventions, the more likely it is that the printed story will resemble yours.

◆ *Make collateral materials readily available.* Bring out fact sheets, backgrounders, and educational materials that support the organization's position, reinforce its reputation, and promote its positive qualities. If the crisis is technological and requires explanation, then photographs, video, diagrams, and other visual content may also be helpful. Also consider media conferences, toll-free numbers with actualities, satellite feeds, fax distribution of updates, and web updates. These are especially useful for providing details and clarifying your position.

Think Public Relations

There is something about a crisis that implicitly leads a questioning public to assume it is the fault of the organization. Even in off-campus fires, there is an assumption that the institution was somehow negligent in its management of student housing.

This should indicate the need to choose your words carefully and to accentuate any positive messages you can find. You must pay attention to the organization's image even while responding to the public's need or desire to know.

Skilled writers can send valuable public relations messages even while being up front about negative news. Ensuring that the organization is presented positively as well as truthfully is part of your obligation to the organization.

Proven tactics for doing this include focusing on the future rather than the past and on the positive rather than the negative. Describing the actions the organization has taken positions the organization as responsible. Presenting the plans for the future puts the emphasis on the solution rather than the problem.

Exhibit 12.3 is a release issued by Amtrak announcing the cancellation of service on its premier high-speed Acela Express service after cracks had been found in some carriages. This is clearly not a subject that Amtrak would have chosen to write about, but it is news, it relates to public safety, and it will affect public opinion. While perhaps not of crisis proportions (although it could have been had the cracks not been discovered), it demonstrates many of the principles of good crisis communication. Although Amtrak had to deal with the negative news, the writer's attention to public relations makes the best of a bad situation.

Note how the careful choice of words positions Amtrak as proactive, responsible, and concerned for the public. The facts are true and accurate, but the message is positive and forward-looking. It focuses on what Amtrak has done and will do, rather than on what went wrong. Phrases such as "inspections ordered by Amtrak," "during a periodic maintenance inspection," and "Amtrak immediately directed" are especially public relations–friendly. While it was not possible or advisable for the company not to alert the public to these cancellations and to admit the reason, the writer's careful word choice nevertheless sent an important public relations message on behalf of the railroad.

Even the Westfield State College apartment fire release carefully positioned the college as concerned and actively trying to help. The writers know how to "think public relations."

Think Beyond External Publics

While the general public is often the first audience of concern in a crisis, there may be many other publics with which you must also communicate. Chief among these are employees or other internal audiences.

In times of crisis, employee communication is critical for two reasons. First, it seems ethically suspect to have employees get the news about the crisis from the evening broadcast or the morning newspaper. Second, employees who are well informed in advance can be effective spokespersons. They provide a valuable "multiplier effect" for the organization's position.

EXHIBIT 12.3   Amtrak media release.

National Railroad Passenger Corporation
60 Massachusetts Avenue, NE
Washington, DC 20002
www.amtrak.com

FOR IMMEDIATE RELEASE
Contact: Media Relations, 202 906-3860
ATK-02-112
August 13, 2002

WASHINGTON — Most Acela Express service will be cancelled today to accommodate inspections ordered by Amtrak, but other trains operating in the northeast will be unaffected by the inspections. During the busiest times of the day, morning and mid-afternoon, a schedule of at least hourly departures from Boston, New York and Washington will be maintained.

During a periodic maintenance inspection yesterday of an Acela Express trainset, a crack in the yaw damper bracket of the power car, or locomotive, was observed by maintenance engineers. (The yaw damper is a type of shock absorber that reduces lateral motion. There are four dampers on each power car.)

Amtrak immediately directed the trainset's manufacturing consortium, Bombardier-Alstom and its subsidiary maintenance company, to begin inspections of all brackets to ensure their structural integrity. These inspections resulted in the discovery of similar cracks in the brackets of two trainsets by 11:00 p.m. yesterday.

Consequently, a decision has been made by Amtrak not to place into service any Acela Express trainsets found to be defective by these inspections. However, several trainsets, which have been inspected and found not to have the defect, are being returned to service today under an enhanced inspection regime.

While the Acela Express trainsets will operate under a reduced schedule, other train services such as Acela Regional and Metroliner are unaffected by these inspections. In cases where passengers holding Acela Express tickets instead travel on Acela Regional or Metroliner service, they will be credited with the difference between the fares. Amtrak passengers are encouraged to check departures by contacting Amtrak at www.amtrak.com or (800) USA-RAIL.

Source: Reprinted with permission of Amtrak.

Journalists covering the story as it breaks may turn first to their employee contacts—and they *will* have them—for information. It is in the organization's interest to have informed and up-to-date employees. Of course, if the crisis is an employee strike, a different set of rules will apply.

If you expect the media to approach employees for information, it may be wise to formalize policies regarding such communication. Such policies set out both what to do and what not to do. You do want employees to report to public relations staff the names and numbers of all reporters inquiring about the organization. You do not want them to provide any information to reporters without authorization. Talking to the media is your job.

Such policies are often part of employment contracts and personnel manuals. You might remind employees of the policy when you provide them with information about the crisis.

Other publics will be more or less important depending on their relationship to the issue, and this will determine especially the timing and urgency of your communications. College alumni, for example, should be told about issues facing the institution, but an article in the next alumni newsletter may suffice. Compare this with the need to personally call members of the board of trustees if the college president dies.

E X E R C I S E   2

In the previous exercise, you identified three publics that must be notified about the transformer fire that has closed two dorms on your campus for two weeks. Now write the message that each of these audiences is to receive.

Media Decisions in a Crisis

Crisis communications requires that you understand all possible ways to reach all necessary publics—and the benefits and drawbacks of each. Although the mass media allow quick dissemination to large audiences, you will lose critical control over content and timing. Faxes, meetings, or personal explanations from supervisors may work for groups of employees, but they will not reach large audiences. Newsletters will reach a target audience, but not immediately.

The purpose of crisis communications may be to provide information, but more often it will be to support or protect the organization's relationships, to make the publics feel important, and to reassure them that their opinions and support are important to the organization. Accordingly, for reasons of reach, purpose, and control, you may well look for dissemination methods other than the news media.

Management should rely on your knowledge of publics and your recommendations on how to reach them. Depending on the size of the public, you might consider individual phone calls, faxes, bulk faxes, or e-mail for urgent messages. If the message is important but not urgent, courtesy letters, special newsletters, or other informational communications can be tailored for small groups. Such publics might include clients not affected by a midlevel computer problem or staff who are not being downsized. Nike's use of letters to plead its case regarding child labor to coaches and others involved in college athletics landed it in court is an example of this strategy. Although, as described in Chapter 6, Nike landed in court over the letters, it is nevertheless a valid strategy for reaching target publics for whom the mass media are unnecessary and/or inappropriate.

If the message is not time-sensitive, you may be able to publish it in the next issue of a newsletter. This is a routine way of keeping employees up-to-date on events that affect the organization but that do not require urgent communication.

To take advantage of the benefits of the mass media while avoiding the loss of control, you may choose to pay for an op-ed article or an issues ad that is scheduled when you want it and that is guaranteed to send the message you want. Ford Motor Company used extensive newspaper advertising during the recall of Firestone tires in 2002.

Messages that require frequent updating can be posted to an intranet for employees or a web site for public and news media use. The Ford advertising mentioned above referred readers to the company's web site for additional information on the product recall.

The Web in a Crisis

Generally, organizations that handle public relations crises successfully are proactive in dealing with the problem. They listen to their publics, especially activist publics, and use a variety of methods to reach them. This means almost inevitably that they have mastered the use of the Internet. No other medium offers such opportunity to both talk with and listen to key publics. It allows you to target individuals and organizations and to take advantage of speech, text, audio, and visuals. The Internet provides immediacy, responsiveness, and a level of relationship building through traditional media.

At the beginning of the 21st century, the potential of the Web as a crisis communication/management tool was really just that: a potential. Airlines had begun to explore its benefits, but many companies did not have web sites capable of handling instantly changing messages to multiple publics.

On September 11, 2001, the potential turned to reality when the United States was attacked by terrorists, and the Web came into its own as a crisis tool. Web writers and web managers turned from technicians to essential members of the crisis management team.

While traditional mass media carried the news to the world at large, the Web carried the news to specific publics. Within hours of the tragedy, companies and organizations began to post on their web sites messages aimed specifically at employees, employees' families, investors, and customers as well as at the general public.

In addition to updates, the messages typically included instructions, phone numbers, links to support services, and, often, private pages where families could get information and assistance. Because its London office could seamlessly assume responsibility for communications thanks to the Web, even Cantor-Fitzgerald, the brokerage company hit hardest by the tragedy, was able to begin communicating with employees and their families within hours.

Although many who used the Web during this time were organizations with offices in or near the World Trade Center, many were not. Organizations worldwide went online to express their outrage, sympathy, and offers of help. The Web also facilitated the collection of millions of dollars to aid the victims, and the recruiting and deployment of thousands of volunteers. The Web unquestionably came of age as a crisis tool during this disaster, and its use during crises since then is usually based on our 9/11 experiences.

For example, the September 2003 blackout that affected the northeastern United States saw organizations again take to cyberspace to get information to target publics quickly. During the 2004 tsunami disaster, the Web was an important vehicle for charity appeals and for those seeking and providing information about possible victims.

Beleaguered style diva Martha Stewart, found guilty in March 2004 of lying to SEC investigators and covered at length by traditional news media over which she had little control, took to the Web to tell her side of the story. She launched a web site, marthatalks.com, to serve as a forum through which she could "set the record straight." The site included regular updates on the judicial process, statements from Stewart, favorable media articles, and letters and notes from supporters. In October 2004, she began posting news from inside prison on the web site.

DISCUSSION 2

Martha Stewart's www.marthatalks.com has been described as an end run around press coverage and the story put out by prosecutors who can use press conferences and court papers to tell their version of the story. What do you think of this site as a communication strategy? Is it ethical for her to do this? Why or why not? What publics do you think it is aimed at? Why?

Poland Spring, which delivers its brand of natural spring water to homes and offices, developed a similar web site in response to a lawsuit challenging the validity of its advertising claims. It is likely that more such web sites will appear as organizations respond to future crises.

Companies under fire for questionable financial, environmental, or employment practices, including Nike, McDonald's, Shell Oil, and Enron, have adapted Internet strategies of their own. They monitor the Web for all mentions of the company name, respond to e-mail, and maintain "social responsibility" pages on their web sites. The strategies are responses to the net activists who have put the hiring, business, and environmental practice of such multinationals under a global spotlight.

Such companies have learned the hard way that a multinational presence and a matching communications budget are no match against activist groups. Even aggrieved individuals can publicize their grievances at such web sites as Baddealings.com or company-specific "anti-" sites. Using the above-mentioned techniques, companies are meeting activists and the disaffected on a new middle ground called cyberspace. A number of companies are buying the domain names of potential anti-sites. If you can't join them, beat them.

The Internet's immediacy makes it both a blessing and a curse as organizations respond to negative events. In addition to allowing misinformation to be disseminated quickly to unlimited numbers of people, it also removes the gatekeepers who, in traditional media, at least examine both sides of the story or issue. Rapaport (1997) says that the Internet provides a "through-the-looking-glass distortion that can make a single person on an Internet newsgroup more potent than the entire public relations department of a major corporation." The best response mechanism may be the Web, partly to respond in the same forum as the attack and partly because the Web can bypass traditional media to reach affected publics directly.

Using the Web for a Preemptive Strike

In this vein, the potential for using the Web in a crisis is not limited to external publics or for after-the-crisis strikes. If anything, it is even more useful for reaching that all-important public—your employees—and for preparing them before the crisis. You can educate employees to expect information on the Web. They will become accustomed to seeking it there. This means that your messages stand a good chance of being seen.

Second, you can keep them up-to-date with news about the industry as well as the organization. This gives them the background to make informed assessments about the organization.

Third, keeping employees informed is an excellent relationship-building strategy. It makes them feel valued and worthy. A committed body of loyal employees can play a key role in defusing some crises. Call the strategy a pre-emptive strike.

This strategy has been used by the U.S. Postal Service (USPS) to raise morale and help employees deal with the jibes they often hear about the organization. After hearing what he called a TV network "hatchet job" about the Postal Service, USPS vice president of public affairs and communications Azeezaly Jaffer initiated a link on the USPS web site called "Setting the Record Straight" ("Rumors, Accusations," 2003). This link contains all of the advocacy documents that the service writes in defense of its services, and particularly its employees. "Our employees take criticism to heart . . . especially if it's unfair" notes Jaffer ("U.S. Postal Service Uses," 2003). "If I got the employees fired up, maybe the rest of the world will know that we're not going to sit back and let people take potshots at this organization" ("Rumors, Accusations," 2003).

The response to the web site was excellent. "Overwhelmingly, employees continue to react favorably, give us feedback and to refer articles to me that they believe have not been fair to the Postal Service," Jaffer says. "I know there are those who regularly look at the site to see the latest STRS [Setting the Record Straight] because they let us know" ("U.S. Postal Service Uses," 2003).

When you persuade employees to participate in defending your organization, you know you have done something right.

Jaffer continued to defend his organization through letters to the editor and other public statements.

Think Global

This all reinforces the idea that public relations writing serves to strengthen and restore relationships. The writer is not a simple bridge between organization and publics. Rather, he or she works within a network of values and responses to organizational behavior. Even while managing your own outward crisis communications, you should also monitor online mailing lists and newsgroups and any anti-sites to see what the critics are saying, to help you gauge support and determine communication strategies. Listening is as important as writing.

Organizations that now face the possibility of managing a crisis in front of a global audience must be prepared at a global level. The Internet permits this. When Swissair Flight 111 crashed off the coast of Canada in 1998, killing more than 200 people, the company was prepared with a "ghost page" of contact information linked to the corporate web site. After the crash, the company was able to insert information about the crash, activate the ghost page, and link it to the home page so that thousands of people could quickly get information. Managers believe that this reduced the number of phone calls from the media, thereby allowing the company to deal more effectively with calls from relatives of the victims (Helperin, 2001).

Postcrisis: Follow-Up and Evaluation

Unfortunately, the only true test of a crisis communication plan is to see how it works in a crisis. Occasionally, it may be possible to test out a crisis communication plan to verify that you do indeed know how to reach your audiences. For example, an elaborate, real-time simulation of a fatal accident between a train and a van full of teenagers in Chicopee, Massachusetts, was designed to test the emergency response units of fire and police departments and area hospitals. As an unforeseen benefit, it also tested the crisis plans of the associated public relations departments. They experienced first-hand the challenges of meeting the needs of the media— what information they wanted, when it was needed, and from whom. The simulation itself became a media event when local television chose to air it during prime time as the drama unfolded. The newspaper reported it in depth the following day. This may be a rare opportunity, but if it occurs, take advantage of it.

In most cases, this does not happen. The test comes when the crisis happens. After the crisis is over, there may be a period of adjustment as the organization deals with continuing questions about the crisis itself as well as questions that the crisis raises. For example, after high-profile passenger train derailments, Amtrak has had to deal with questions about track safety even though Amtrak does not own or control any tracks.

Consider too the public criticism of airlines based on their handling of information about air crashes. Not only must the public relations staff respond to the crash itself, but they commonly must also deal with ongoing public reaction to that response. Is it better to release a passenger list with names of people who may not have been on the plane or to delay the list until the actual passengers have been confirmed and relatives notified (and endure criticism as being slow and uncooperative)? Is there an absolute "right" or "wrong" to what the airlines do?

The apartment fire that resulted in death and injury of college students living off campus continued to raise questions regarding the living conditions, safety standards, and housing codes of student apartments. Many local residents called a response line to express concern about these issues and to question the responses of the city and the college. Eventually, the college president issued a public relations statement clarifying the institution's policies regarding off-campus housing and student conduct and pledging cooperation with local authorities in resolving neighborhood issues.

Follow-up is a process both of recovery and of learning and evaluation. The recovery may involve restoring not only the organization but also its reputation and relationships with publics. For the writer, it may mean reaching out to new publics as well as normalizing communication with traditional publics.

Evaluation focuses on both process and outcome during the precrisis planning, the handling of the crisis, and the outcome of the crisis handling.

The end of a crisis will reveal the strengths and weaknesses of the crisis plan and point to directions in which the plan should be revised. Crisis evaluation will reveal the importance of up-to-date backgrounders, fact sheets, and biographies. One tragic but common crisis is the loss of a senior executive or CEO in a transport crash. Routine information such as a biography cannot be brought up-to-date if the subject is dead, and you can be certain you will need this information if the tragedy happens.

EXHIBIT 12.4   **Checklist to help you evaluate crisis preparation and response.**

Precrisis preparedness

Potential employer crises identified _____

Contingency plans prepared:	Liaison with legal counsel	_____
	Media contact list	_____
	Liaison with technical specialists	_____
	Media facilities	_____
	Designated spokesperson	_____

| Background materials available: | Bios of key personnel | _____ |
| | Technical specifications | _____ |

Postcrisis process evaluations

Management, legal, pr, technical _____
    coordination

Media relations effective _____

Key publics informed successfully _____

Crisis logs maintained _____

Public opinion monitoring effective _____

Outcome evaluations

Opinion of key publics	Positive _____	Neutral _____	Negative _____
Media coverage	Localized _____	Widespread _____	
	Positive _____	Neutral _____	Negative _____
	Accurate _____	Neutral _____	Inaccurate _____
Further communication efforts required	Yes _____	No _____	
Different/new messages required	Yes _____	No _____	
Review of crisis logs shows need to change crisis plans	Yes _____	No _____	
Recommendation made to management for new/revised plans	_____		

Outcomes can be measured in terms of the content and volume of media coverage during the crisis. Alternatively, you may measure the effect of your communications on relevant decision makers and publics or on how shareholder confidence or employee confidence changed.

Evaluation implies the assessment of almost all aspects of the organization's operations, but from a writing perspective we might consider the topics listed in Exhibit 12.4.

ON THE TEXTBOOK WEB SITE

✦ Go to www.sagepub.com/treadwell for web exercises, study hints, case studies, and additional examples appropriate to this chapter and chosen or developed to supplement the chapter content.

WRITING WRAP-UP

1. Several campus athletes who live in a so-called jock house off campus have been arrested by local police and charged with offenses including assault, rape, and possession of drugs. They have been identified in the media as students at your institution, and the jock house has a history of such events. Local reporters have called you for a response. What is your response?

2. State police have informed you that a number of students and faculty—individuals not yet identified—have been killed in a bus crash on an out-of-state field trip. Several others have been injured. Write the crisis response plan for such an event and the messages needed for the priority audiences you identify.

REFERENCES

Barton, L. (1993). *Crisis in organizations: Managing and communicating in the heat of chaos.* Cincinnati, OH: Southwestern.

Grunig, L. A., Grunig, J. E., & Dozier, D. M. (2002). *Excellent public relations and effective organizations: A study of communication management in three countries.* Mahwah, NJ: Lawrence Erlbaum.

Hearit, K. M. (2002). Corporate apologia: When an organization speaks in defense of itself. In R. L. Heath (Ed.), *Handbook of public relations* (pp. 501–512). Thousand Oaks, CA: Sage.

Helperin, J. R. (2001, July 10). Uh-oh. *Business 2.0.*, pp. 32–33.0.

Horsley, J. S., & Barker, R. T. (2002, October). Toward a synthesis model for crisis communication in the public sector: An initial investigation. *Journal of Business and Technical Communication*, pp. 406–441. Retrieved March 2, 2004, from EBSCO Communication and Mass Media Complete database

Koplan, J. D. (2003). Communication during public health emergencies. *Journal of Health Communication, 8*, 144–145. Retrieved March 2, 2004, from EBSCO Communication and Mass Media Complete database

Rapaport, R. (1997, October 6). PR finds a cool new tool. *Forbes ASAP*. Retrieved December 12, 1998, from www.forbes.com/ASAP/97/1006/100/htm

Rumors, accusations on Internet lead to corporate truth sites. (2003, August 12). From *PR News* via NewsEdge Corporation. Retrieved March 18, 2004, from U.S. Postal Service web site: http://www.usps.com/communications/news/strs/strs_article1_print.htm

Smudde, P. (2001). Issue or crisis: A rose by any other name. *Public Relations Quarterly, 46*(4), 434–437. Retrieved March 12, 2004, from EBSCO Communication and Mass Media Complete database

U.S. Postal Service uses the Web to deliver truth to employees. (2003, September 1). In *The Ragan report.* Retrieved March 18, 2004, from U.S. Postal Service web site: http://www.usps.com/communications/news/strs/strs_article2_print.htm

RESOURCES

Institute for Crisis Management .... www.crisisexperts.com

Institute for Public Relations .... http://www.instituteforpr.com/crisis.phtml

PRSA, Tips and .... http://www.prsa.org/_Resources/resources/crisis.asp?ident=rsrc3
     Techniques: Crisis Management

The Multipurpose Medium

Writing for the Web

1. No other medium offers the Web's combination of immediacy, multimedia capability, and interactivity or the potential for developing two-way relationships with multiple publics.

2. All public relations writing can be used on the Web.

3. The most important web publics may be those who seek and provide information through chat rooms, newsgroups, and blogging sites.

4. Writing for the Web involves targeting both groups and individuals.

5. The Web challenges the writer's ability to organize information and to write with brevity and relevance to multiple audiences.

6. Web writing and web design go hand in hand.

1. Writing for chat rooms and newsgroups—targeted responses.

2. Writing for web sites—writing for global audiences.

As technology lowers the cost and raises the speed and level of sophistication with which we can reach audiences around the globe, it is critical that public relations writers master the medium that brings organizations and publics together with dramatic speed—the World Wide Web.

The Web and Communication Thinking

The World Wide Web provides a unique combination of benefits for public relations, including global reach, instant communication, feedback potential, interactivity, and the opportunity to use text, visual, and audio modalities. It is the only medium that allows you to easily reach both mass audiences *and* individuals, sometimes simultaneously. You can execute both rifle and shotgun strategies at the same time.

Because of this, the Web poses a dramatic challenge to traditional, telecommunications-based, linear models of communication. Unlike traditional media, the Web is characterized by its potential for interactivity and especially as being a site of multiple voices—pro-, anti-, and indifferent to your client.

The Prospect of Multiway Communications

Public relations thinking has shifted from the notion of one-way propagandistic messages to the idea of two-way relationships. Of all public relations media, the Web offers the greatest opportunity for achieving such two-way symmetrical dialogues. Organizations and their publics can develop relationships based on shared information. Immediate feedback from consumers, shareholders, alumni, donors, and employees can be used to shape organizational policy that meets the interests of these publics.

Your organization's publics will receive information from intermediaries you may not even know about. And you may receive feedback and messages from fleeting coalitions that may cease to exist after an issue is resolved. The potential for newsgroups to take an issue, shape it, and develop a response is vast and immediate. The Web also allows publics to talk to each other. Never have so few had the opportunity to reach so many so easily. And never have so many had the opportunity to represent (or misrepresent) themselves and others to the world.

Organizations that are sensitive to public opinion are obligated to monitor web communication in all its forms. They must also establish response mechanisms to communicate with the influential web groups who serve as alternative sources of information about the organization. The opportunity afforded by the Web for two-way communication also forces writers to consider the nature and purpose of writing for the Web.

Web Cosmology and Anti-information

Just as cosmologists infer the presence of antimatter and parallel universes, corporate, official web sites may have "anti-" sites and hostile discussion groups that parallel the organization. Their purpose is to expose an organization's ineptitude and shortcomings. McDonald's, America Online (AOL), Nike, Clear Channel, and ADT are just a few of the corporations that have been the targets of anti-sites. Monitoring such anti-sites is part of understanding your publics and the environment in which the organization operates.

The cosmological analogy only goes so far. Official sites and their anti-sites do not annihilate each other when they collide in cyberspace. Rather, they provide web users with a multitude of resources and a diversity of information and viewpoints on an organization. Anti-sites and newsgroups about Company X dramatically increase the likelihood that web users may bypass the company as a source of information. You cannot assume that your web site is an automatic source of information about the organization.

This makes a compelling argument for systematic and professional web monitoring. It also points to the need for web content to be professional, accurate, timely, and credible. If users cannot find the information they need at your site, they may often resort to the misinformation available from anti-sites or discussion groups.

Control of Distribution, Content, and Timing

Web publics are hard to define. The potential audience is limited only by the user's need to be web-literate and to have access to necessary hardware and software. Whether or not you intend it or like it, your audiences will be global and constantly changing. You may not even be aware of many of them. Perhaps more important, the Web allows individuals to be publics. One individual with web access theoretically has as much potential to sway global opinion as a multinational corporation.

Theoretically, you have complete control over web content. What you post is what the user sees. But the Web increases in a quantum fashion the extent to which publics can also compile their own content. They can individualize searches to meet their specific needs. Because search engines may take visitors into the middle of a web site, they may never see the introduction you have written. "Pull" technologies make it possible for them to request information at random or on a predetermined schedule. Even pushing information does not guarantee that the user will open it or when.

The Web also raises a new level of control in which users serve as their own gatekeepers. You must persuade users to visit and stay in your web site in the same way that you persuade news editors to print or air your news release.

All of this should not in itself deter you from using the Web as a medium for sending public relations messages. It is simply a caution that you have very little control over exactly who receives web messages, when they are read, and how they are used.

D I S C U S S I O N   1

Rapaport (1997) said that the Internet provides a "through-the-looking-glass distortion that can make a single person on an Internet newsgroup more potent than the entire public relations department of a major corporation." What do you think? What evidence do you have for your opinion?

Public Relations on the Web

With the shifting Internet population, it is difficult to provide statistics that have any stability, and the statistics and estimates that are available vary considerably in focus and findings. One ongoing research program, the Pew Internet & American Life Project, is starting to paint a picture of what the Internet means in American life. Sponsored by the Pew Charitable Trust, the project researches and publishes frequent reports on Internet publics and how they use the Web. These reports are available for public use.

Following is a snapshot of the Internet as of June 2004 obtained from Pew research and other web-monitoring sources. This will change over time, but it gives an indication of trends that will affect your thinking about Internet use.

✦ Globally, the overall growth is dramatic. Internet users grew from 254 million at the turn of the century to more than 605 million in September 2002 (Nua Internet Surveys, 2003).

Internet use in the United States has flattened since 2001, stabilizing at 60%–65% of the U.S. adult population (Pew Charitable Trust, 2003a). However, even many nonusers have access through family, friends, or local libraries (Pew Charitable Trust, 2003b, pp. 3–4).

Access to the Internet in the United States reflects differences in the following:

Age—74% of 18- to 29-year-olds are online compared to 18% of those over 65.

Income—38% of households with income less than $30,000 are online compared to 86% of households over $75,000.

Education—only 23% of those who did not graduate from high school are online compared to 82% who have graduated from college (Pew Charitable Trust, 2003b, p. 8).

These and other results from the study give the public relations writer valuable clues regarding whether a target public is likely to be online, the type of information it wants (e.g., information, news, entertainment), and the level at which you should write.

✦ An increasing number of web users generate web content. Forty-four percent of adult Internet users have posted photos, video, audio, commentary, or other content on a web site or to a newsgroup (Pew Charitable Trust, 2004, p. 1). As many as 9 million Americans may have created online diaries called blogs, and many more read them (p. 6). Insofar as they have the potential to draw attention to situations involving your organization, you may need to add blog-monitoring to your media research.

✦ Only 36% of the online population is online in the English language. Over 63% work in a language other than English (Global Reach, 2003). This is a key statistic for organizations that have any interest in cultivating a multicultural web presence.

✦ The Web clearly competes with the traditional media of print, television, and radio for users' attention.

EXERCISE 1

The statistics on Internet use reported above change on a daily basis. Refer to the web site for the Pew Internet & American Life Project, www.pewinternet.org, to find updates and/or new trends that will influence your public relations writing.

This all raises the question of how the Internet is used in public relations. A casual review of web sites and newsgroups shows that public relations practitioners use the Internet for three types of activity: for communicating with their organization's publics, for research, and for their own personal and professional development. Detail is provided in Exhibit 13.1.

Exhibit 13.1	Ways in which public relations practitioners use the Internet.	
Communication with publics	*Research*	*Personal and professional development*
Service clients at a distance that would normally preclude a relationship.	Track public opinion.	Access software and specialist services such as web page design.
Make information readily available to clients.	Monitor visitors to the web site to identify user demographics to improve the site.	Maintain contact with and exchange ideas with other practitioners.
Answer frequently asked questions (FAQs).	"Clip" published articles about your employer.	Maintain contact with professional groups.
Distribute news and information to the media electronically.	Provide job costing, contract details, and legal issues related to your employer.	Participate in formal or informal conferences.
Develop mailing lists.	Monitor the competition.	Link with colleagues in an international public relations network.
Recruit personnel.	Identify demographics and data on key publics and industry sectors.	Engage in collaborative writing with colleagues in another location.

A 2001 report by the Institute for Public Relations examined the role of the Internet in the creation and dissemination of news. The study found that journalists rely on the Internet for story research (Wright, 2001). If nothing else, this should give you reason to keep your organizational web site up-to-date and to ensure that the content presents the organization's position on current issues as well as information that will help journalists "add depth and breadth to the news stories they write" (Wright, 2001, p. 19).

DISCUSSION 2

Your college or university undoubtedly has a web site through which it communicates with key publics. Who are the target publics for the site? What other publics might be casual visitors? What publics cannot be reached through the Web. What does the institution hope to achieve with each of these publics? How does a web site help achieve these aims?

The Web Audience

The issue of audience is no less important when writing for the Web than when writing for more traditional media. You will find it useful to understand who the Internet public is and, as important, how this audience uses the Internet.

Who Is the Web Audience as a Whole?

Theoretically, the web audience is anyone who can access the Web. Because this is too broad a definition to be practical, research focuses on defining characteristics that web users have in common as well as the attributes of specific user groups. Research shows that web publics have the following characteristics:

♦ They have broadcast television and in many cases sophisticated computer software as their standard of presentation.
♦ They are comfortable with screen presentations, and sophisticated with respect to design and presentation.
♦ They are comfortable handling sound, sight, and motion simultaneously.
♦ They are accustomed to nonlinear research, information processing, and presentation.
♦ They do not read in detail. Rather, they browse or scan. This especially has tremendous implications for you as a writer.

Some members of this audience are enthused and motivated and will stay at your site until they find the information they need. Others will be casual browsers with no initial reason or motivation to either visit or stay at your web site. Writing for the first group is relatively easy. The second group provides a greater challenge. If you want to influence the opinion of these users, you must provide reasons for them first to visit your site and then to stay with it.

Who Is *Your* Web Audience, and What Does This Mean?

Having acknowledged that public relations writers conceptually deal with a huge and largely uninterested-except-in-a-crisis, global audience, we look at three categories of the web public on which writers focus attention: critical commentators, committed visitors, and casual browsers.

♦ *Critical commentators* belong to newsgroups and discussion groups that usually operate apart from the organization. Whether they actively participate in the debate or just listen from the sidelines, these users are a public that an organization should be aware of. Increasingly, *bloggers* who attract a following are another public that should be on your audience radar. You may or may not target messages to these publics.

Although they may visit your web site for new information, commentators also express their opinions and conduct dialogues external to the web site. In extreme cases, critical commentators may establish anti-sites whose purpose is to disseminate negative information. They do so with or without your participation and sometimes with little concern for accuracy. They should not do so without your knowledge. This is a clear case for careful and thorough web monitoring.

♦ *Committed visitors* deliberately visit your employer's web site for specific information. They pull updates and new data as they are posted to the site. Committed visitors include traditional publics that currently use the Web to follow the organization's activities. What you already know about their interests and preferences is a good baseline for determining the information they will be seeking, the level of detail they will require, and in the order in which they will seek it. These publics will be a primary concern.

✦ *Casual browsers* visit the site while searching for general information. If the site is well organized and includes both general and specific information, you should be able to satisfy the casual browser with no additional effort as you provide detail for the committed visitor.

Any or all of these categories may include employees.

To the extent that commentators and bloggers have a following and may influence thousands of people, many experts regard them as the most important web public. They want and often seek information about the organization or about topics on which the organization is knowledgeable. You may put considerable effort into establishing relationships with them.

But casual browsers and committed visitors also have the ability to become powerful web-voices. Consider, for example, how U.S. Postal Service employees turned into vocal advocates for the organization as the result of information posted on their web site (see Chapter 12). Prioritizing all of these publics comes back to deciding which can have the greatest effect on your organization and which are most accessible and persuadable.

Reaching Your Web Audience

The question of how to reach these three types of audience returns us squarely to the issue of control. Are you content to have audiences simply access the information as they want or need it, or do you want/need to push information to them?

Web sites generally include information for general public access, and the distribution method is simple. You post the information and the public visits the site to access it. The content is selected for the web public at large.

Distributing information to *selected* publics is another matter. In this case, you may take advantage of the web's ability to reach audiences as groups or as individuals. Pushing information to target audiences helps you regain some of the control over distribution, timing, and audience that you lose by simply posting messages on a web site.

The potential of the Web for interactivity opens another avenue of communicating with perhaps new, target publics including newsgroups and mailing lists.

✦ *Newsgroups.* Internet discussion boards or newsgroups give you direct or indirect access to a potentially huge number of web users to whom you can send messages via the newsgroup or mailing list. Generally, they are large bulletin boards on which members (or sometimes anyone) can post and retrieve messages sent to members of the group. *Chat rooms* are real-time bulletin boards.

Newsgroups are organized by interest. Their members are a self-selecting group with a common interest, potentially in an organization and/of its industry or sector. Many Internet service providers (ISPs) offer access to newsgroups as part of their service to subscribers. You can also identify relevant newsgroups through web searches.

Depending on your industry, these groups should be taken very seriously, and communicating with them will be part of your communication strategy. Public relations strategists in the 21st century will select appropriate newsgroups and mailing lists just as 20th-century practitioners selected newspapers and radio stations.

Ethical Issues

Ethics and the Web

The ethics of web design are essentially the ethics of copyright, misrepresentation, and research.

Copyright

Web content is commonly constructed from the work of others, often appropriately so. Organizations with a product safety crisis may link to federal agencies such as the FDA or USDA so that visitors to the site may obtain credible information on *e. coli* or mad cow disease (BSE).

You cross an ethical boundary, however, when the pages of other agencies are passed off or seen as the work of your organization. In the framework of academia, this is plagiarism; in the framework of the law, it may be seen as a violation of copyright.

Misrepresentation

Linking and (especially) framing information from other sites on your own site not only calls your authorship into question but also raises the possibility of misinforming your audience. Even when there are no legal or ethical issues with using others' material, problems arise when using only part of those materials or using them in a context that might have visitors misread them as your own or misinterpret their content.

Information from federal government sites, for example, cannot be used for commercial purposes, to imply government endorsement. Extracts may not be used in such a way that the original document is misrepresented.

Research

The ultimate purpose of public relations writing is to facilitate relationships. To understand visitors to your web site, you will want to track their behavior at your web site or post to your web site questions that you would like visitors to answer.

The ethical questions are essentially those of disclosure and privacy. Are you monitoring the activities of visitors to your web site? If so, do visitors know this? What practices do you have in place to handle information they provide? For example, will you keep information for your own purposes or sell it?

Ethical organizations make their privacy policies obvious.

When selecting newsgroups, consider the group's interest, whether it is moderated, and whether it is public or private. Moderated groups may restrict both membership and message content. At best, messages must be issue oriented rather than promotional. At worst, companies and organizations will be prohibited from posting messages altogether.

Newsgroups are useful sources of feedback on an organization and its sector. Generally speaking, if you can find a discussion group that is talking about topics relevant to your organization, you will have also found a group likely to be interested in what you have to say. Recognizing the potential of such audiences, many organizations host relevant discussions on their own web sites.

✦ *Mailing lists.* Check the Web for sites that will let you access and/or purchase mailing lists for particular interest groups. These are similar to the mailing lists you purchase for direct mail. You can also build a list online at sites such as groups.yahoo.com that allow you to start and manage new mailing lists, subscribe to existing lists, and view archives of old list messages.

Pros and Cons of the Web as a Public Relations Medium

From the public relations writing perspective, every medium has its strengths and limitations. The press reaches large numbers of people, but you first have to pass the review of editors and reporters. Radio isn't visual. TV has limited airtime for news. Newsletters have long deadlines. Faxes lack sophistication and class. The public relations writer must find ways to overcome or write around these limitations to capitalize on the strengths of the medium.

The same is true of the Internet. Following are some of the issues that will affect particularly how the public relations writer thinks about and structures web messages.

Screen Limitations

Lengthy documents that require scrolling do not meet expectations of user friendliness. Choose typefaces, type size, line spacing, and color to reduce eyestrain and maximize legibility.

Page Length

Opinion differs on the issue of page length, and it has changed as users have grown accustomed to navigating web pages. On one hand are recommendations to limit pages to one screen, starting a new page whenever the information exceeds this length. On the other are cautions about multiple pages and long download time. Many people regard horizontal scrolling as more irritating than vertical scrolling.

It may be wise to provide hypertext links at the beginning of long articles so that viewers can go directly to relevant sections. The point is to make it easy and fast to navigate the web site. As not everyone has the latest and fastest browser or operating system, think in terms of small files rather than large to give the visitor information as quickly as possible.

Navigation Cues

Relative to other public relations media, navigation on the Web poses a unique opportunity for writers. Other media have a single, fixed order of presentation. The writer decides, for example, on a chronological or compare/contrast structure, and the reader must live with it. In contrast, web users determine their own paths through the site, and multiple structures are simultaneously possible. Links further increase the potential for different routes to the information the user requires. Good web writing is writing that makes it easy for visitors to *find* as well as to read information.

This does not mean that a web page or web site should be an unstructured morass of hypertext links. Instead, effective web design demands that you make it clear where users can find the information they want. Tables of contents, site maps, and navigation cues all answer the questions, "Where am I?" and "How do I access the information I want?"

These navigation cues should be clearly presented throughout the web site beginning with the home page. See, for example, Exhibit 13.2, the home page for a public service web site on childhood asthma sponsored by the U.S. Environmental Protection Agency (EPA). The links at left appear on every page. Copy is brief and titles are clear. These cues allow visitors to easily find information in any order they wish.

Links: A Blessing and a Curse

The Web is about connections. Nowhere is this more obvious than in the issue of links. Internal hyperlinks make it possible for users to move to other parts of the text or to another page on site. Other links take the user to external web sites for additional information.

Use links to expand the amount of information you are able to provide from your site. For example, when a case of mad cow disease was found in the United States in December 2003, the National Cattlemen's Beef Association (NCBA) linked its web site to BSEinfo.org, a site dedicated to providing information on bovine spongiform encephalopathy, or BSE. Links from this site included the U.S. Department of Agriculture, the World Health Organization, and the Centers for Disease Control and Prevention. These links not only provided a service but also gave implicit credibility to the original site.

You can provide too many links and confuse the visitor with too much information. The number you use will be a function of the credibility and relevance of the linked sites, the need to maintain effective page design in your own site, and the legal constraints on linking and the related issue of frames, as discussed in Chapter 6.

Remember too that although you can select the web sites you choose to link to, you have no control over who links their site to yours. It is possible to find your site linked to sites you do not want to be associated with and to be tarnished by those associations. Most search engines make it possible to determine who has linked to your site.

Multimedia Possibilities

The term *multimedia presentation* once meant providing multiple media. This generally meant print plus photos plus audiotape or VCRs, with the occasional display, video, or sound-slide presentation. The Web allows the seamless integration of all media—text, visuals, audio, motion, and animation—into one package.

This requires the public relations writer to consider the relevance not only of text but also of text versus other formats. Why should you print your CEO's speech as text when you can make it possible for visitors to hear it? Why describe a new software package when visitors could try it out online or download a demonstration copy? Why show new vehicle or house designs when VRML (virtual reality modeling language) makes it possible for visitors to take a test drive or a walk through?

One strategy is to provide all possible media so that visitors can access it as they need and as their computer systems allow. Offer "reader" programs such as Acrobat Reader, PowerPoint Reader, Real Player, and Flash so that viewers without such software can access the features. You can link to free downloads of basic versions for most of these programs.

At the other extreme is a plain-vanilla web site with a high-text/low-graphic content. This allows as many people as possible to access the site unhindered by the limitations of their computers. Many advocates counsel against sophisticated visual presentations with large files that visitors may have difficulty downloading because it makes the site less accessible. As a compromise, it is always a good idea to offer a text-only option for users without the capability or time to deal with complex graphics.

Writing for the Web

While writing is a primary skill for the public relations professional, the Web clearly places writing in context. It is *an* option, not necessarily *the* option. Technology, turf issues, and training are rapidly influencing a new definition of "writer." Are web designers and web writers the same?

Writing for the Web demands that the writer be conscious of the graphic capability of the Web and of the routes that reader/viewers will navigate. This will increasingly describe a team approach to web writing, with team members bringing to the project specialized skills such as content development, presentation, production, researching and testing, and, of course, writing.

Writing for Newsgroups

Writing for newsgroups is essentially e-mail posted to a group. It is usually conversational and friendly. But as anyone who has spent more than a few minutes on a web forum knows, it has the potential to be tedious and overwhelming, and sometimes to "flame" uncontrollably when a contentious issue arises. Following some conventions will help you be seen as a valuable and contributing member.

Writing for Newsgroups: Content

Generally, newsgroup messages must be relevant and issue oriented, factual, and *brief*. You may provide information, refer members to other sources, or even refute an argument as long as the message contributes to the discussion.

Take a leaf from your advocacy and newswriting experience. Just as you cannot and should not in a letter to the editor present every benefit of your program or refute every opposition argument, so you cannot and should not try to do this on the Web. If anything, you should be even more concise on the Web. The most effective message you contribute may be one sentence drawing the group's attention to a web site address (Uniform Resource Locator, or URL) that they should know about.

Possibly because of the academic origins of the Web, many discussion groups have a residual suspicion of commercial messages. Promotional messages may get a hostile reaction from group members. Blatantly promoting your organization or its services may meet with massive retaliation, or "flaming." Limit promotion to directing the newsgroup members to the organization's web site.

You can also use a modified boilerplate paragraph or short slogan in your own signature line. Organizations may gain significant long-term benefits from being seen as a credible source of information, even at the expense of immediate publicity.

Thinking back to your newswriting experience, lead with the most important points and evidence and work toward the least important. You may have even less time to attract attention on the Web than in print, so the only thing your audience may see is the first paragraph of your message. Make it count.

Remember, if the group has a negative view toward your organization, the most you may be able to achieve is to move them to a neutral or quiet stance. This would be a real achievement.

Writing for Newsgroups and Online Discussions: Style

The first rule of writing for online discussions is to observe the courtesies (often called "netiquette") of the group. The site operator, the posted FAQs, and feedback from members will guide you on the group protocols. Generally, the basic courtesy is to be brief and to the point. If you have a lengthy submission (as you may if your employer is offering educational material of interest to group members), it may be more appropriate to summarize the document in your message and make the full text available on your employer's web site rather than posting the whole document.

Professionalism Is Important

You are acting on behalf of your employer (and you should be open about this). This means you must be especially careful not to be inflammatory. Do not get into an adversarial position on the Web, especially with a committed opponent whose aim is to provoke you. "Arguing" on the Web is the equivalent of having an argument in front of the world. Even if you win, you lose. Maintain a professional style that presents your organization as a credible source of accurate and reliable information.

DISCUSSION 3

Assume that your college or university has announced an increase in tuition, housing fees, or other fees for the next academic year. As public relations practitioner for the institution, you become aware of a web discussion group on which current students are denouncing the increase and claiming that it is unnecessary and that it will hinder their ability to get an education. Members of the discussion group also include high school students seeking information about colleges they may attend.

Should you respond to the charges made on this web site? Why or why not? To whom would you choose to respond? Why? What arguments would you use to address these issues? What evidence could you use?

Writing for Web Sites

Organizational demands for visibility and a web presence usually mean that web content is initiated by the organization. It is supply driven. At the same time, as users search for what they need, their use of the Web is demand driven. It is the public relations writer's role to reconcile these two positions to develop and support positive relationships between the organization and its web publics.

If your site does not tell users what they want, they will search for and probably find it at another site whose information may or may not be credible, timely, or accurate. It behooves the web writer to design content that provides one-stop shopping for information, with links that you anticipate users will need and that will reflect credibly on your site. Think of your home page as a sales catalog that announces all of the specials (contents) on the front page and directs shoppers (visitors) to the department (page) where they can obtain (read) the goods (information).

Web Site Content

Except for refereed electronic journals, basically there are only three constraints on web content: your own sense of ethics and professionalism, the legions of web activists who can instantly and massively rebut your assertions if they so choose, and the legal remedies available to those who decide that you have libeled them or violated their copyright. Within these constraints, web site content will be determined by the organization's purpose in hosting the site and what you know about the audiences you expect will visit it.

When developing a web site, there are four important communication issues: the need to make information manageable, the need to provide directions through the site, decisions on the topics to be covered, and decisions on the links you provide for additional information.

Make information manageable. One of the aims of good text is to make the readers comfortable with where they are and where they are going. The same is true of "text" for the web. It must keep web visitors comfortable with the information they can access and the path they should take to access it. This suggests that you should do the following:

♦ *Keep it brief.* Present information in small bites, no more than two screens long. Use links to give the reader the option to access further information if he or she wants it.

♦ *Label pages, sections, and links clearly.* The user should never have to ask, "Where am I?" even if he or she enters the web site in the middle. See, for example, how simply and logically the Childhood Asthma Campaign web site (Exhibit 13.2) is organized. Each page is only one screen long, but there are clearly labeled links for the next level of detail.

Provide directions. Although the format and location of navigational buttons may be seen as part of the site design, it will probably be the writer's responsibility to ensure that the topics are selected with the user in mind and that they provide the broad range of options that your publics will demand. In this context, your job as a web writer is twofold. You must help users retrieve the information they want as quickly and efficiently as possible. And you must bring to their attention the messages your employer wants them to see. This is the same lesson we presented when talking about newsletters. It also relates to direct mail and brochures.

This balancing act begins on the home page, the first page a visitor sees when entering your site through the URL or domain name. Remember, of course, that searches may lead some visitors to enter the site in the middle. Graphically and topically, the home page sets the tone for the rest of the site. Its purposes are to introduce the site, to entice users to stay in the site, and to act as a table of contents/map/guidebook to the rest of the site. It should make visitors feel comfortable, confident that they can access the information they want.

The home page also provides basic links to the rest of the site. The effective web writer chooses words carefully to describe the link content so that people know what they're linking to. Words such as "here," "click here," "forward," "back," and "next" tell a visitor nothing. Instead, labels such as "home page," "press releases," and "The Beginner's Guide to . . ." provide a clear launch pad for more detailed searches.

Exhibit 13.2 is the home page of the web site for the Childhood Asthma Campaign, www.noattacks.org, sponsored by the EPA and designed under the sponsorship of the Ad Council. The image of the fish gasping for air is the campaign theme. As demonstrated throughout this text, it is adaptable across many media. Note the simple but clearly labeled links.

Although very simple, the site provides valuable information, especially for the parents of children afflicted by asthma. It recognizes the questions that users will have and is structured around answering them. The only page that is longer than one screen is "Triggers in Your Home," a link from the "Preventing Attacks" page. Even at two screens, it clearly presents a range of problems followed by succinct solutions. All primary pages listed on the home page are accessible from all other pages. Subpages are accessible as appropriate.

Web site topics. Typical subjects include the following, each of which may be further divided into subsections or additional pages.

◆ *Official material.* An organization's official material is both critical and easily overlooked. It includes, as appropriate: the name and address of the organization, the site creator, the date the site was created, and the date of the last update and copyright or other restrictions. Public relations writers especially should appreciate the importance of such information.

◆ *Summary information or teaser.* Organizations that want to appeal to a large browsing audience may design features to satisfy their interests. Easily accessible "News," "Top Ten . . . ," "Preventing Attacks," or "For Kids" sections provide a quick point of reference for more committed audiences.

◆ *About the organization.* This will challenge you to identify the needs and wants of visitors and to balance this with what the organization wants to tell them. Although your employer may be especially proud of its 12 factories and distribution centers in every state, the exact locations may mean little to visitors. A simple map will convey the impression of size without unnecessary detail.

EXHIBIT 13.2   **Home page for the EPA Childhood Asthma Campaign.**

ATTACK ASTHMA. LEARN MORE.

Did you know that things on shower curtains, blankets, or teddy bears can trigger an asthma attack?

- Mold and dust mites trigger asthma.
- Mold grows on shower curtains.
- Dust mites live in blankets and teddy bears.

Learn more about other triggers that may be found in your home

HOME
ABOUT ASTHMA
PREVENTING ATTACKS
ASTHMA ACTION PLAN
ASTHMA HOTLINE
VIEW ADS
FOR KIDS

En Español

Subscribe to Our Newsletter   Privacy Policy

1-866-NO-ATTACKS

EPA   Ad Council

© The Ad Council

Source: Reproduced with permission from the U.S. Environmental Protection Agency.

"About . . ." information may include memberships in industry organizations and a brief history as well as descriptions of divisions, operations, and offices. Sections with a particularly public relations focus include media centers, newsrooms, and social responsibility pages.

◆ *Public education.* The Web is increasingly used as a research medium. Educational topics range from the "How to . . ." pages of Arm & Hammer to the IRS annual warning of consumer tax scams and the Department of Homeland Security release on getting through airport security checks easily. Consider what information your organization has that will help people—and make it obvious. Being seen as a source of information is a smart public relations strategy.

◆ *Online help.* Online help capabilities earmark the web site host as user-friendly and responsive to the information needs of its visitors. Identify whom

EXHIBIT 13.3   **Former home page for the Internal Revenue Service, featuring "The Digital Daily," www.irs.gov**

to contact for what information, including alternate methods of contact such as phone and fax numbers and mailing addresses.

✦ *XYZ people.* Web sites are another place you can use those bios you wrote. Include links to e-mail addresses.

✦ *Online newsletter.* This can be password controlled if you wish to restrict it to employees or paid subscribers. Regardless of whether it is open access or restricted, it must be updated frequently to remain credible. If you archive the publications, visitors can access all issues long after they have discarded print versions.

✦ *News.* Usually composed of the organization's media releases, the "News" section is often catalogued by date and topic and separated into "current" and "archived" options. Organizations with frequent media contact may provide reporters with restricted access to special information such as audio or video links.

✦ *Crisis information.* Web sites make it possible to provide, as appropriate, up-to-the-minute information and directions to emergency, medical, and technical services; consumer instructions; and links to relevant related information.

✦ *Financial information.* This is especially relevant for public companies. Full financial statements are more detailed than most people want or expect from a web site. A better use of web capabilities might be to present summarized financials, possibly illustrated by charts and graphs. You can always make the comprehensive financial statements or annual report available for download.

✦ *Feature stories.* Some organizations capitalize on the appeal of features to attract attention. For example, in the late 1990s when the IRS wanted to rid itself of its "big brother" image, it launched a web site called "The Digital Daily." It was designed to look like the front page of a newspaper, and it was updated every day—how's that for user-friendly? The daily lead was a short human interest feature, an effort to humanize the agency's image. One of the daily versions is shown as Exhibit 13.3.

The page also included expected links to tax forms, regulations, and consumer, business, and taxpayer concerns. At the bottom of the home page it also offered an opportunity to "Meet the Commissioner," a variation on introducing the CEO.

◆ *Research reports.* As with financial information, it is wise to provide a summary as well as the full report so users can access the level of detail they need.

◆ *Links.* No matter how much information you provide, it is unlikely to be all of the information available on a subject. Linking to external sites provides visitors the opportunity to obtain more detailed information as the NCBA did under the mad cow scare.

When linking to outside sites, provide a description or context of what the user can expect. What information does it provide? Anyone can compile a list of links. What makes *your* list valuable is that you have read, understood, and can recommend the links. Give readers the benefit of this knowledge and gain some credibility in the process.

◆ *Contact information.* Link contact information to an e-mail screen to encourage immediate response.

◆ *Comments.* These can be worded as "Sign our guest book," "Tell us what you think," or "Sign up for automatic, online updates." Ask visitors for their names and e-mail addresses so you can provide further information.

◆ *Date.* "Currency" is important for web site credibility. You should have a "Page last updated" notation on every page, or at least a "Site last updated" notation on the home page. And keep it current.

◆ *Privacy policy.* Privacy statements provide the public with your policies regarding the collection of data and its use. Whether or not you are legally required to provide them, it makes good public relations sense to do so.

E X E R C I S E   2

Conduct a web search of the web sites of companies, nonprofits, and even your college or university. Which of the above sections can you find on them? Which are rare? Which sites are especially difficult to navigate? Which are easy? Why? What other features do you especially like or dislike?

Web Site Plan

After you have determined the topics for the web site, you must identify how they will relate to each other. What will appear on the home page or primary pages versus which are essentially subcategories? This is also when you will determine whether you will present information as single long stories or broken into separate pages.

The easiest way to plan the web site is to create a simple flow chart starting with the home page. Remember that web sites are actually mini-networks of information that make it possible for the visitor to move in any direction.

Exhibit 13.4 maps the structure of the childhood asthma web site discussed throughout this chapter. The home page (shown as Exhibit 13.2) connects directly to six primary pages, each of which can be accessed directly from menus on all of the pages. The map shows that pages labeled "Triggers" in your home and outdoors

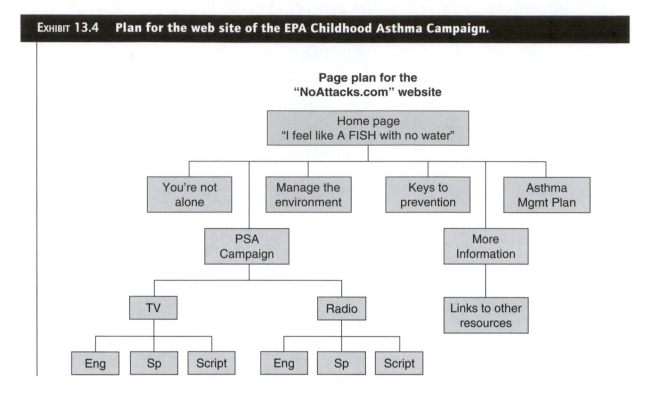

EXHIBIT 13.4   Plan for the web site of the EPA Childhood Asthma Campaign.

are subpages to the "Preventing Attacks" page with links to other pages. The map also shows that both the "View Ads" and "Action Hotline" pages provide links, the former to the electronic media used in the campaign and the latter to external resources about asthma and its treatment.

This structure bears more than a little resemblance to a corporate organization chart and to the inverted pyramid of news stories, working from the most general information on the home page to consistently greater levels of detail.

Most web sites have more pages than this one. Some have hundreds. But all of them begin with a basic plan that lays out the relationships among the pages.

Web Writing Style

Effective writing for the Web is built on effective writing for other media. In particular, it bears close resemblance to the principles of good brochure copy presented in Chapter 15. Web sites and brochures share the need to attract and hold the attention of unknown audiences as well as target audiences that may or may not be aware of their interest in the topic or organization. Compare the information and style of the Childhood Asthma Campaign web site (Exhibit 13.2) with the campaign brochure (Exhibit 15.4).

You already know many of the guidelines such as keep it simple, edit-edit-edit, use headings and layout to support the content, and provide an obvious structure.

Writing effectively for the Web is not difficult if you understand what makes effective newswriting, advocacy writing, or multimedia presentations. These media and the Web share the following writing requirements:

+ The main idea and purpose must be clear.
+ The underlying structure must be obvious so that the piece is easily navigated.
+ Content must meet a visitor's need or interest.
+ Content must be at the visitor's level of education or vocabulary.
+ Content must direct visitors to where they can access further information or to how they can implement the behavior you may be advocating.
+ Key ideas must be presented within the viewer's attention span.

In 1997, Morkes and Nielsen suggested that writing for people who scan—as opposed to read—means that you must present your message clearly, concisely, and quickly. You should make it easy as possible for the scanner to grasp the overall message and to identify and execute the options for further information.

Nothing has changed. Research shows that concise editing, simple layout, a clear message, and an obvious structure lead to a significantly increased ability to find information efficiently (Morkes & Nielsen, 1998). Since there is no conflict among being concise, scannable, and objective, web writers can use all three techniques to improve the quality of copy for users.

+ *Concise.* Some would argue that bare-bones text is required for web sites. Web guru Jakob Nielsen (1997) suggests 50% of the word count of conventional writing as a guide. This is valid if your purpose is simply to convey a message—the shorter the better.

On the other hand, if your aim is also to convey a sense of the organization's culture and to provide a foundation for building relationships, then we suggest that you stop short of editing down to bare bones. Retain some of the "color" that expresses what the organization is and what it stands for. Either way, make detail available through links to other pages in your web site or to external sites.

A useful guideline is to approach both the web site as a whole and pages individually as you would a news story. "Think inverted pyramid," and start with a summary (the home page). Provide additional information in increasing levels of detail, first through additional pages and ultimately through links and hyperlinks.

+ *Scannable.* Make it easy for visitors to scan the information on every page. Bullet points, subheads, outlines, and short paragraphs turn even lengthy documents into manageable messages whose important points are obvious on the briefest scan.

+ *Objective.* Research suggests that people do not like extravagant sales pitches on the Web. Designing a site that concisely provides the information they need to make a decision should take priority over flowery sales hype. This is also a useful guideline for writing for newsgroups.

To these three qualities, we add a fourth:

+ *"Navigability."* Many web sites are not easily navigated. Accordingly, we reemphasize the importance of easy navigation. Keep in mind the visitors' need to know where they are and what their options are for going elsewhere in the web site or to external links.

For the Web

There are three planning issues unique to the Web.

The Unknown Audience

Far more than any other medium, the web has a vast unknown audience, linguistically, culturally, and geographically. You can decide that your organization's web site is designed only for defined audiences, or you can plan it to build relationships with the many unknown visitors who visit you in the course of browsing.

Multimedia Capability

Web design software easily allows you to produce messages in print, audio, graphic, and movie formats. Planning even a news release therefore requires more careful thinking about what format the information will take. Because graphics and audio, for example, can easily be made available, the classic text-only press release is no longer an automatic first choice.

Integration With Other Systems

The writer as manager must be able to link effectively to other web-based systems. For example, can a human resources manager automatically post information about new employees to your office? Do you e-mail news releases to your legal office before release? Are releases posted to the "Newsroom" section of your web site also posted automatically to employees? Planning for the broader benefits of electronic communication will make your job easier as well as help you be more effective.

Using the Web for Specific PR Aims

Online News Releases

Electronic news distribution services such as PR Newswire, eNewsRelease, and Business Wire simplify the process of disseminating news releases to thousands of media outlets. For many companies, the most valuable feature of newswires is the one-stop access they provide to regional and trade publications.

If you can access a newsgroup whose purpose is to disseminate organizational information or if you have developed your own mailing list, you may be able to get public relations mileage from posting news releases directly on the Web. Most e-mail releases are no longer than four paragraphs, and they strictly follow the inverted pyramid style.

What may be even more acceptable is a simple announcement. Send a short, routine e-mail directly to a mailing list including a pitch that you hope will attract recipients. Its purpose is primarily to direct them to a site where the full information is available.

Archive these announcements and releases in a news file, highlight the most recent on the home page, and make the rest available through hyperlinks.

Online Newsletters

Web letters (or e-letters) range from general news posted to an organization's web site to fully targeted letters sent individually to a special mailing list. In between are semi-targeted web letters posted to newsgroups. Newsletters may be password protected for restricted access. This provides the opportunity for you to post information that is not relevant to the general public. It is often used for employee newsletters. A valuable ground rule is: If you don't want it public, don't post it at all.

Unlike printed newsletters, however, you cannot rely on all of the audience receiving web letters in the form you created. You will have to anticipate and contend with the limitations of the visitors' computer systems. You may have to provide two versions—a text-only model for those with text-only browsers, and a more sophisticated HTML version with links that allow "cybernauts" to take advantage of web formatting, hyperlinks, graphics, and Java technology. Many organizations provide files in .pdf format so that visitors can download and print documents that will be fully and properly formatted. This is as common for forms and survey questionnaires as for newsletters.

Targeting electronic newsletters through "push" technology has two advantages over simply posting them on a web site. First, it pushes information to the readers rather than depending on them to come to the site. Second, you can control the distribution list.

Using the Web for Advocacy

The 2001 "Magic Communication Machine" report of the Institute for Public Relations (Wright, 2001) suggested that the Internet was being used most effectively by special interest groups—those whose primary purpose is advocacy. A web search for "advocacy" or "causes" indicates that little has changed. Hundreds, maybe thousands, of organizations are conducting full-fledged advocacy campaigns on the Web. Strategies include the following:

✦ Targeted e-mail to users who have asked to be included on an e-mailing list.
✦ Online postings of media releases, reports, and backgrounders.
✦ Assistance for individuals or groups wanting to mount local campaigns with contact information for local media and legislators.
✦ Interactive capability for accepting contributions online.
✦ Interactive capability for supporting the campaign with messages to legislators. Options include ordering postcards preprinted with the advocacy message, downloading a sample letter, or submitting an online form directly to the target audience. Regardless of the format, such messages will be consistent with those you are sending through other media. The difference is the potential for the user to take action immediately.

Online Annual Reports

The World Wide Web has the potential to turn "annual" reports into "current" reports. This will require the public relations writer to keep the narrative as up-to-date as the financial information. Rather than just reviewing the past year, online annual reports will likely approach a newsletter in purpose. They will keep audiences current with happenings in the organization and strengthen its relationships with investor publics.

Public companies are already required to file SEC reports online, so posting them on the Web may not be a major project. The challenge for the writer will be to maintain the high level of credibility required in an annual report while still promoting the organization's interests.

The Web as a Crisis Medium

The ability of the Web to help organizations develop and maintain relationships also makes it a critical part of 21st-century crisis management plans. For the organization, the immediacy of the Web makes it possible to take a proactive stance, to counter the charges of critics, and, most important, to respond to its publics' various needs for information. For the general public, the Web fills a desire for information. For stakeholders, it provides an immediate link to answers, solace and advice, and interactive capability that cannot be matched by any other medium.

The Web and Cross-Cultural Communication

Depending on the products, services, or message you are promoting, the Web has the potential to cost-effectively reach a widespread audience. This is likely to increase as more and more of the world becomes wired. Already 64% of web users sign on in a language other than English (Global Reach, 2003), even though as recently as 2001 over 70% of web sites had content predominantly in English ("Trends in the Evolution," 2003). And a University of California, Los Angeles, study found that Latinos were the fastest-growing population of Internet users, recording 25% growth since 2000 (UCLA Center for Communication Policy, 2003).

You may want to allow visitors to browse in the language of their choice. It is also possible to create a parallel-track web site that replicates yours in another language. This is a courteous gesture and has great benefit for organizations with an international focus. Ensure that *all* translations are done by qualified professionals who understand not only the grammar and message but also the cultural conventions that will affect how your message and organization are perceived.

Publicizing the Web Site

Advertising, browsing, and good old "word of mouth" are all sources of information about web sites. However, most people find sites through the many search engines that are publicly or commercially available. Some of these, called meta-searches, search other search engines. Some make basic decisions regarding the search results to present the user only with those that are most appropriate. This refinement will continue.

This means that simply posting a site on the Web is not the end of the process. If no one knows the site exists, or its address, you cannot expect publics to visit it. It is important to publicize the web site or in some cases to "advertise the advertising."

Publicizing a web site begins with the choice of domain name, especially if the organization's name or initials have already been taken. Some of the problems with this issue relate to trademark infringement, but in many cases a domain name or especially initials may legitimately be claimed by more than one organization. If your corporate name or organizational initials have already been taken, the challenge becomes finding an easily recognizable and appropriate alternative.

One option is to register with another extension. Although .com is the most common domain name extension, if .com is taken, the same name with .biz, .net, or .org or other appropriate extension may be available. The .biz extension is popular with small businesses and .org is the extension of choice for nonprofits. New extensions are available from entrepreneurs who see the opportunity to capitalize on groups that want a common Internet bond. For example, the extension .md has been made available to physicians by an organization that procured the rights from its legal holder, the country of Moldavia (Moldova). It is a logical extension for the medical community and is a sign of the importance of addressing Internet marketing.

When registering a domain name as a URL, also register the site with Internet directories and search engines so that search engines will find it. Select keywords that will bring your organization to the top of a search. Your ISP should be able to assist you in this. You can submit them to each service individually, or you can use a service that will register with all services on your behalf. Then monitor hits to the web site to determine which keywords yield the greatest number of visits.

Another way to attract visitors to your site is to link it with sites that interest the organization's publics. You can also ask other relevant sites to link to yours. Be prepared to execute reciprocal links.

Other ways to promote your web site are through e-mail notices to discussion groups and mailing lists, traditional media such as news releases, and business cards, client and employee newsletters, and annual reports. You can also hire commercial Internet publicity services to do the promotion for you.

EXERCISE 3

When the American Gas Association (AGA, 2004) launched a new web site, it issued a media release via PR Newswire to introduce the features of the site to its many audiences. You can find this release in the news section of the AGA web site, www.aga.org. What audiences do you think the AGA wanted to reach? What media do you think would run the story? Why did the AGA also post it on the AGA web site? What PR messages did the AGA send in the story? Identify specific words and phrases that send these messages.

Research and Evaluation

In Chapter 5, we touched on the Web as a research tool and will not revisit research methods here. Instead, we will limit our discussion to the use of newsgroups and web sites to gather data about your employer and its industry. Clearly, public relations practitioners will have to pay more attention to assessing the impact and uses of the Web.

At one extreme, Web research is as simple as a hypertext link to a "tell us what you think of this web site" screen. At the other extreme, it is a complex, full-fledged survey conducted on your web site.

Although "comments" screens capture informal opinions and perhaps some demographic data, the people who respond are unlikely to represent the overall visiting public. Comments screens may be most useful as a guide to questions you should be asking and as an alert to possible negative information surfacing about the organization. They merit special attention because the visitors were interested or concerned enough to spend the time sending them.

The host server can capture visitor data in a more structured, quantitative way. It can tell you when visitors enter your site, how long they spend, what pages they visit, and for how long and in what order. Such information can help you make assumptions about the effectiveness of the web site and direct you to further research.

"Cookies" are ways of identifying information delivered directly to the hard drives of web visitors by the web sites they visit. They are a classic example of unobtrusive research used to capture information about users' web behavior. Hailed by proponents as providing valuable data that will help improve web services, and reviled by opponents as unethical snooping without the visitor's informed consent, cookies continue in use with many users unaware of their existence. Such research is at the heart of web privacy debates. Be conscious of the problem, the ramifications, and the likely constraints on it.

You can, of course, post a brief questionnaire on the web site and ask visitors to complete it. If you keep it to the point, ask for only basic demographic information, and give the visitor a reason to complete it, you may get a reasonable response.

The EPA Childhood Asthma Campaign includes a user-response survey on its www.noattacks.org web site. Shown as Exhibit 13.5, the survey seeks information about users' reasons for visiting the site, their relationship to asthma, and their reaction to the site. This will provide information on which to base future campaigns and modifications to the web site.

EXERCISE 4

Other web surveys are much more complex than the EPA survey in Exhibit 13.5. Compare the EPA asthma survey with the one used by the U.S. Department of Education. It can be found at http://www.ed.gov/help/support/survey/index.html. What are the advantages of each? What are the disadvantages?

EXHIBIT 13.5   Online survey conducted with visitors to the web site of the EPA Childhood Asthma Campaign, www.noattacks.org

1. How did you find or hear of this Web site? *(Check all that apply.)*
    - ⊙ Link from another site
    - ⊙ Internet search engine
    - ⊙ TV ad
    - ⊙ TV news story or program
    - ⊙ Radio ad
    - ⊙ Radio news story or program
    - ⊙ Newspaper or magazine story or article
    - ⊙ Billboards or posters
    - ⊙ From a doctor or other medical professional
    - ⊙ Acquaintance/word of mouth
    - ⊙ Other - Specify:
    - ⊙ Not sure

2. Why did you come to this site? *(Check all that apply.)*
    - ⊙ To learn about my child's asthma
    - ⊙ To learn about asthma triggers
    - ⊙ To learn about new medications
    - ⊙ To learn about my own asthma
    - ⊙ To learn how to prevent attacks
    - ⊙ To learn how to treat attacks
    - ⊙ To find doctors
    - ⊙ I work in the field
    - ⊙ Happened to arrive at the site via Internet browsing
    - ⊙ Other - Specify:
    - ⊙ Not sure

3.

	Strongly Agree	Agree	Neutral	Disagree	Strongly Disagree
Easy to Navigate	⊙	⊙	⊙	⊙	⊙
Useful	⊙	⊙	⊙	⊙	⊙

4. How likely are you to return to this website?
    - ⊙ Definitely will return
    - ⊙ Probably will return
    - ⊙ Might or might not return
    - ⊙ Probably will not return
    - ⊙ Definitely will not return

5. What is the age of the child in your household who has asthma? *(Check all that apply.)*
    - ⊙ Under 2
    - ⊙ 2-6
    - ⊙ 7-12
    - ⊙ 13-18
    - ⊙ No children in my household have asthma

6. Which things trigger your child's asthma? *(Check all that apply.)*
    - ⊙ Dust
    - ⊙ Pet dander/pets
    - ⊙ Pollen
    - ⊙ Mold
    - ⊙ Cockroach/pest
    - ⊙ Tobacco/cigarette smoke
    - ⊙ Exercise
    - ⊙ Weather
    - ⊙ Scents/sprays/perfume
    - ⊙ Don't know
    - ⊙ No cause, it just happens

7. How often do you take your child to the Emergency Room because of an asthma attack?
    - ⊙ Once a year or less
    - ⊙ Once every few months
    - ⊙ About once a month
    - ⊙ 2-3 times per month
    - ⊙ Once a week or more

Followed by six demographic questions on age, sex, ethnicity, state of residence and whether you allow smoking in your home. For statistical purposes only,

13. Do you have any suggestions on how to improve the web site and/or on additional content you would like to see?

14. Email Address

Thank you very much for your time.

Source: Reprinted with permission from the U.S. Environmental Protection Agency.

ON THE TEXTBOOK WEB SITE

✦ Go to www.sagepub.com/treadwell for web exercises, study hints, case studies, and additional examples appropriate to this chapter and chosen or developed to supplement the chapter content.

WRITING WRAP-UP

1. Write a brief objective for a web site to be developed for a campus club or organization. Write the copy for the home page and show the basic design of the site, including any graphics you would recommend.

2. Assuming your intermediate-term objective is to be hired at a handsome salary as a public relations writer, write and design your own home page. If you already have one, how should it be reworked in light of the above objective?

REFERENCES

American Gas Association. (2004, March 11). *American Gas Association launches redesigned website* [Press release]. Retrieved March 12, 2004, from www.aga.org

Global Reach. (2003, September). *Global Internet statistics (by language)*. Retrieved October 7, 2003, from www.global-reach.biz/globstats/index.php3 and http://www.global-reach.biz/globstats/index.php3

Morkes, J., & Nielsen, J. (1997). *Concise, scannable and objective: How to write for the Web*. Retrieved October 7, 1998, from www.uneit.com/papers/webwriting/writing.html

Morkes, J., & Nielsen, J. (1998). *Applying writing guidelines to web pages*. Retrieved July 23, 1998, from www.useit.com/papers/webwriting/rewriting.html

Nielsen, J. (1997, March 15). *Be succinct!* (Writing for the Web). Retrieved September 19, 1998, from.http://www.useit.com/alertbox/9703b.html

Nua Internet Surveys. (2003). *How many online?* Retrieved June 14, 2004, from www.nua.com/surveys/how_many_on15

Pew Charitable Trust. (2003a, December 22). *America's online pursuits*. Research report, Pew Internet & American Life Project. Retrieved March 14, 2004, from www.pewinternet.org/reports.asp

Pew Charitable Trust. (2003b, June 16). *The ever-shifting Internet population: A new look at Internet access and the digital divide*. Report, Pew Internet & American Life Project. Retrieved June 14, 2004, from www.pewinternet.org/reports.asp

Pew Charitable Trust. (2004, February 29). *Content creation online*. Research report, Pew Internet & American Life Project. Retrieved March 15, 2004, from www.pewinternet.org

Rapaport, R. (1997, October 6). PR finds a cool new tool. *Forbes ASAP*. Retrieved December 12, 1998, from www.forbes.com/ASAP/97/1006/100/htm

Trends in the evolution of the public web 1998–2002. (2003, April). *D-Lib Magazine* Online Computer Library Center. Retrieved October 13, 2003, from wcp.oclc.org

UCLA Center for Communication Policy. (2003, August 4). *Latinos are fastest growing Internet users*. Retrieved September 17, 2003, from www.hispanicbusiness.com/news/newsbyid.asp?id=11897

Wright, D. K. (2001). *The magic communication machine: Examining the Internet's impact on public relations, journalism, and the public*. Research report, Institute for Public Relations. Retrieved January 2, 2004, from http://www.instituteforpr.com/internet_ _new_technology.phtml?article_id=2001_worldcom

RESOURCES

Following is a list of the web resource sites relevant to topics in this chapter. In some cases, we have provided a series of steps to direct you to specific pages of a web site; in other cases, we have listed just the URL because the information is obvious or because the site includes much information you may want to review. Caution: Some of the sites are commercial sites and you may be unable to use them fully without subscribing or becoming a member.

Public Relations

Institute for Public Relations.. www.instituteforpr.com

PR Central .... www.prcentral.com

PR Place .... www.prplace.com

Public Relations News and Discussion Groups

Note that PRForum is not a web site; it is the address for a mailing list. Consult with your tutor or computer center on using e-mail commands to access mailing lists from your campus.

PRForum... www.prcentral.org/lists/prforum

PRQuorum... groups.yahoo.com

Web Statistics, Use, and Publics

ClickZ Stats (formerly CyberAtlas: The .... www.clickz.com/stats/
    Web Marketer's Guide to On-line Facts)

Institute for Public Relations .... www.instituteforpr.com

eMarketer .... www.emarketer.com

Georgia Tech's GVU WWW User Survey .... www.gvu.gatech.edu/user_surveys

Nielsen//NetRatings .... www.nielsen-netratings.com

SearchLogic .... www.searchlogic.com

Whatis (definitions of Internet.. www.whatis.com
and computer terms from @ to z-modem)

World Wide Web Consortium "W3" www.w3.org

Yahoo! Stats (select "Computers and Internet")...................................... www.yahoo.com

Legal Issues

U.S. government privacy policy www.whitehouse.gov/omb/memoranda/m00-13.html

Web Writing and Style

Jakob Nielsen's web site .... www.useit.com

Finding Links and Newsgroups

Google Groups (select "groups" from home page) .... www.google.com

Landfield Group .... www.landfield.com

Yahoo! Groups (select "Groups") .... www.yahoo.com

Domain Name Registration and Listing Your URL

Interland .... www.interland.com/

Internet Corporation for Assigned Names and Numbers (ICANN) .... www.icann.org

InterNIC .... www.InterNIC.net

Microsoft bCentral .... www.submit-it.com

Network Solutions (NetSol) .... www.networksolutions.com

Featured Organizations

American Gas Association .... www.aga.org

EPA Childhood Asthma Campaign .... www.noattacks.org

Pew Internet & American Life Project .... www.pewinternet.org

Project Bread.. www.projectbread.org

14

Persuasion for Mass Action

Advocacy Campaigns, Op-Eds, and PSAs

KEY PRINCIPLES

1. The classic appeals of ethos, pathos, and logos still work today.

2. Credibility is the public relations writer's greatest asset.

3. Advocacy is a two-way process based on understanding publics.

4. Image public relations positions the organization in society.

5. Advocacy public relations promotes the organization's positions on issues or causes.

6. Advocacy may tread the fine line between commercial speech and free speech.

THE PRINCIPLES IN PRACTICE

1. Image ads and campaigns—to establish an organization's visibility and personality.

2. Advocacy ads—to gain public support for your position.

3. Letters to the editor and op-eds—to tell your side of the story.

4. PSAs—to serve the public interest.

Contemporary views of public relations recognize that the basis of public relations is building relationships on an ethical foundation. Communication practice involves recognizing the following:

✦ A message may have multiple publics. These publics may be intended or unintended.
✦ There is a need for truth and accuracy in message design.

✦ Taking responsibility for the social outcomes of a message needs to be considered.
✦ Effective communication involves listening to publics through formal and informal research.
✦ Advocacy is a dialogue or conversation with one's publics.

Effective advocacy therefore is based on the values of key publics and focuses on building ethically sound relationships with them. Studies show that it can work. Recent studies show that over 28% of the adult U.S. population performed some regular volunteer work (U.S. Department of Labor, 2003). Seventy percent of households made some charitable contribution (Independent Sector, 2001). Clearly, they all responded to a persuasive message. No wonder the ability to write a persuasive message ranks so high among the skills employers look for in the writers they hire (Treadwell & Treadwell, 1999).

This is not to say that we believe—or even read or watch—the majority of persuasive messages we receive. In fact, the persuasive message is at the heart of public suspicion of the public relations industry. Rightly or wrongly, persuasion conjures up images of politicians, salesmen (usually for insurance or used cars), and the plethora of direct mail pieces we find in our mailboxes on almost a daily basis. It is little wonder that, as a public relations writer, you may find your work labeled as propaganda, brainwashing, empty rhetoric, or one sided.

On the plus side, persuasive messages raise hundreds of millions of dollars for charity every year. Colleges, universities, and even summer camps solicit their alumni for support. Hospitals ask local citizens to fund new facilities that will benefit the community. And health and medical research organizations ask for help in "finding the cure."

Techniques range from celebrity testimonials to promises of financial gain to self-improvement. The multi-million-dollar direct mail industry is built on finding the right combination of appeal, technique, spokesperson, and message that will persuade targeted message recipients to act as the sender wants them to act.

Does this mean that some persuasive messages work? Yes. The question is, "What makes them work?"

Foundations of Motivation and Message

There is an exhaustive if not exhausting literature on persuasion. Experimental studies try to determine what maximizes the effects of a persuasive message. Rhetorical studies focus on message strategies and techniques. Ethical studies look at the conditions under which persuasive communication can appropriately occur.

There are hundreds, maybe thousands, of studies dealing with persuasion. All of them aim to answer the question, "What makes people change their behavior or attitudes?" This translates into "What makes a persuasive message work?" or ideally, "What is the perfect persuasive message?" The study of persuasion spans disciplines from advertising to sociology and covers settings from the individual and small groups to organizations and the mass media.

In Chapter 1, we discussed many theories of behavior and attitude change. Most of them are related to persuasion. We introduced them at the beginning of the text to make the point that all public relations writing has a persuasive foundation. Even the most informative communication has the long-term goal of positioning the organization as valuable, credible, and honest. It promotes qualities that help set the stage for building relationships and ultimately attitude change and behavioral change (K-A-B).

Writers must also establish in a public's mind that their organization is uniquely worth supporting. They will have scored only a partial success if they persuade people to support charitable organizations in general. Their real goal is to convince publics to specifically support, for example, the United Way, Red Cross, or a local homeless shelter.

It will help to understand theories of motivation and message appeal. Some of these theories are outlined below.

Motivation

Understanding the basis of public relations advocacy requires that you first understand what motivates people to act. Every public relations writer wants to believe his or her writing is the "magic bullet" that inspired the reader to contribute, buy, vote, or otherwise act as the writer hoped.

In practice, a message is just one of many factors that affect a person's behavior at a given time. Some of these factors increase the likelihood that you will adopt the desired behavior. A family that wants you to quit smoking reinforces the antismoking messages you receive. If your family doesn't care, or if they all smoke, you may be influenced against the antismoking message.

Writers must be alert to factors in people's lives that may prevent them from acting on a message. You can then provide solutions that negate or circumvent the effect of these factors. For example, writers might do a brilliant job of persuading parents to have their children immunized. But unless the parents have access to health services and believe they can afford the services, the immunizations probably won't happen. The communication may result in persuasion, but it will not necessarily result in action. In such a case, it is the writer's job not only to persuade parents of the merits of immunization but also, perhaps, to educate them on the availability of free immunization services.

The law also influences behavior. Regardless of their attitude toward seat belts, most people wear them because they are legally required to do so. The force of law is also why shop owners refuse to sell alcohol or cigarettes to minors even if they sympathize with the alcohol and tobacco companies.

Individual characteristics beyond the control of the writer can also prevent or facilitate behavior. Income clearly influences purchasing decisions. Religion may influence dietary practices. Age typically predicts media and music preferences. And language ability may affect acceptance in a group or culture.

If environmental or personal factors make it difficult for people to adopt the behavior, it is likely they will not do so. In such cases, the problem has to be addressed at other levels, such as by providing access to services or by effecting statutory changes. This is why public relations professionals insist that public relations is a management function. It is also why organizations increasingly speak of marketing communication or integrated marketing communication rather than of advertising, publicity, and marketing as if they were all separate functions.

Many behaviors can be seen as a product of the three Es: education (communication), engineering (changing factors in the environment), and enforcement (the law). Public relations writers may have to address all three. It is clear that persuasive messages will not succeed without a two-way relationship with publics that will give you such information about your publics.

Appeals

Topics and issues that appeal to people are well known at a general level. Research into news values tells us that people are interested in topics that are new, close to home, relevant, and unusual or bizarre or that deal with human interest, "people being people" concerns. They are often the day-to-day dramas of people relating to each other or to issues, products, organizations, and lifestyles. If they sound familiar, it is because they are the "news determinants" discussed in Chapter 9. Interests do not change just because you change writing or document formats.

Maslow and the Public Relations Writer

Many persuasive appeals are based on Maslow's (1954, 1962) hierarchy of needs. As Exhibit 14.1 shows, Maslow's hierarchy looks at motivation from the perspective of human needs. It divides these needs into five levels from basic survival (physiological) to personal fulfillment (self-actualization). Maslow's premise is that we must meet our most basic needs before we will pay attention to higher-level needs.

Although not without its critics, the Maslow hierarchy remains a staple of many advertising, marketing, and public relations texts. We see two reasons for this. First, it provides guidance for persuasive communications. There is little point in using higher-level persuasive appeals such as self-improvement when readers are concerned with more pragmatic issues at a lower level of the hierarchy. For example, self-improvement is an obvious benefit of higher education. In a tight economy, however, colleges that use this as a recruiting approach may find that it doesn't appeal to individuals for whom every dollar spent on higher education means less money for home and family. In this case, an appeal based on the likelihood of a higher-paying job after completing a course might have more relevance.

Maslow's hierarchy also serves as a checklist of appeals on which message content or arguments can be based. A software developer pitching an educational product might appeal to the higher levels of intellectual stimulation or curiosity. A coalition of counseling services attempting to develop support groups might emphasize the social benefits of belonging to a group. Using Maslow's hierarchy will help you decide

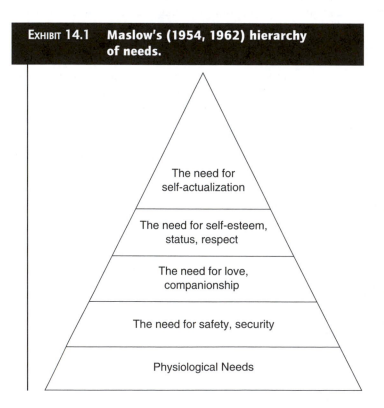

EXHIBIT 14.1   Maslow's (1954, 1962) hierarchy of needs.

- The need for self-actualization
- The need for self-esteem, status, respect
- The need for love, companionship
- The need for safety, security
- Physiological Needs

between an appeal based on social links to good ol' Central U and one based on the higher-level self-actualization to be achieved by supporting higher education.

A cursory scan of advertising messages reveals the influence of Maslow's hierarchy at work on consumers. Social appeals, sex appeals, ego appeals, and safety appeals all have a basis in Maslow's hierarchy. Many power drinks and vitamin supplements base their messages on meeting the physiological needs of the athlete. Colleges recognize that safety issues need to be communicated to parents as crime on campus increases and families want to know that their students are safe. The social and ego needs of love, friendship, and sex sell consumer products based on the classic "bandwagon" appeal of "everybody's doing it."

Appeals based on the respect of others promote everything from up-market vehicles to the latest software. Self-actualization needs appeal to our potential for growth, improvement, and success. Used notably by the U.S. Army in its "Be all that you can be" advertising, self-actualization appeals effectively sell educational services, products, and lifestyles.

DISCUSSION   1

What are current or classic "hot words" that you might put on an envelope to grab readers' attention and entice them to open it?

In Chapter 15, you will be asked to develop envelope copy driven by the needs of a direct mail client. For now, consider envelope copy driven by one specific theorist—Maslow. Write five one-sentence messages you could put on an envelope to persuade readers to open it. Each message should use a different level of appeal from Maslow's hierarchy. The client is a nonprofit agency of your choice seeking to raise funds.

Theories of behavior and information processing tell us that before making decisions about message content or format you must understand your public(s). Maslow would also argue that you must understand the levels at which they can be influenced.

Knowing this information will not guarantee success, but it will greatly increase the likelihood that you will adopt a spokesperson (source), select an appeal (approach), develop content (message), and choose a medium (channel) that will effectively influence your public.

Developing Persuasive Messages

The issues of source and appeal are the point at which persuasion theory most closely influences message development. It is but a short step from Aristotle's ideas about message content and persuasion to our discussions of source credibility (ethos) and appeals of logic (logos) and emotion (pathos). The first step in determining an appropriate appeal requires understanding the strengths of logic, source, and emotion.

Logos: The Importance of Message Content and Structure

Although emotion is often part of a public relations appeal, it is possible to build successful persuasive messages on evidence and logic alone. This occurs most often in newspaper editorials.

Planning

Advocacy Communications

When it comes to planning advocacy communications, there are two overriding things you need to know about your target publics: What is their attitude toward the issue—are they negative, neutral, or positive? Why?

The answer to these questions will influence both strategy and tactics of your writing, beginning with your aims. Persuasion seldom happens in one big leap. Rather, publics change attitudes and behavior in small steps. Accordingly, the most realistic goal you might hope for with regard to a negative public is to move them toward a neutral stance or perhaps to reduce their level of antipathy. At the other extreme is the potential to motivate an already positive public toward advocacy on your behalf. In between are neutral publics that you want to introduce to the organization or move toward a positive position.

These differing goals point toward very different advocacy strategies and messages. For example, recognizing that negative publics hold their views for a reason, you will need to rebut these reasons as well as provide evidence that your position is superior. Neutral publics may not be aware of either the issue or your position, leading you to focus on informative rather than persuasive messages. If you believe they are aware of the issue, then you will need to provide reasons they should care about it. Positive publics need clear messages that rally them to the cause, telling them what they can do to help. All of these strategies come from just the knowledge of whether the public's attitude is pro, neutral, or con.

Knowing the "why" behind an attitude is a further help. Publics may share an attitude toward a cause, corporation, or political candidate but with different beliefs. For example, publics may be equally opposed to Corporation X, some because of its hiring policies while others because of its environmental practices. Knowing the beliefs behind the attitudes will help you target the issues that are actually relevant to audiences. You can see this strategy in practice in most political campaigns.

The structure of logical persuasion should always be clear and in itself logical. It should flow from beginning to end, claim to proof to restatement of claim, question to answer, or premise to conclusion. If the reader understands your argument and agrees at each step, it will be difficult for him or her to reject your final position.

Supporting evidence. Supporting evidence is critical to logical appeals. The evidence typically will be statistical, historical, the results of surveys and polls, or endorsements from authorities in the field. Often it will be complex.

It will be your task to select the evidence that best supports your persuasive case and to present it succinctly and clearly. This means that you must understand the material yourself or be willing to ask questions until you do understand it. If financial or statistical reporting is a large part of your job, you may find it useful to take courses in accounting and statistics to improve your ability to interpret such information.

Most important, you must make the evidence relevant and understandable to the public. Determine what the public wants and needs to know about the topic. Then provide answers that help the public understand the facts. Spending part of your budget on graphs or artwork may be wise if it quickly gets across a message that would otherwise take several paragraphs to explain.

At other times, making evidence relevant means expressing numbers or statistics in terms the public can understand. The writer for a fact sheet produced by the Westover Air Reserve base memorably made the size of the C-5A transport meaningful to the general public by stating it could hold 48 Cadillacs or 108 Volkswagen Beetles. Similarly, distance is often described in terms of the length of football fields.

Fairness and objectivity. Offering both sides of the argument is generally the most credible approach for an audience with mixed feelings. A completely one-sided, card-stacking story will be seen to be biased and may raise questions about your honesty and integrity. On the other hand, raising the opposing point of view allows you to be seen as fair. It actually adds to the credibility of *your* message. And, as debaters learn early, dealing with negative issues preemptively may be more effective in the long term than allowing others to raise them, especially if they relate to a crisis that you can anticipate.

Generally, you will present your position before the opposing position because you want your audience to know what you are talking about. Plus, if your position represents good news for the audience, basic news structure suggests leading with it. Writers may choose a similar approach for advocacy ads or op-eds.

DISCUSSION 2

Organizations don't just promote products. Many use letters to the editor and paid advertising to promote positions on, for example, raising or lowering the speed limit, strengthening or relaxing local regulations on handgun control, or increasing or decreasing sales taxes.

For each of the above issues, which techniques of persuasion would you expect to be most effective: statistics, research results, expert opinion, public opinion survey results, case studies, personal experience stories, or celebrity endorsements? What others might you recommend for each topic?

Ethos: The Importance of Source Credibility

Finding relevant sources is a vital part of thinking about public relations writing and how to make it credible, especially since source credibility is an aspect of presentation that you can usually control. For example, your university or college is seeking donors to fund construction of a state-of-the-art student center. Who should sign the fundraising letter—the president? head of student affairs? a student? president of the alumni association? board of trustees? Depending on the donor list, it might be any of the above. The challenge is to find the source with the greatest credibility *for the target audience.*

In contemporary theory, Aristotle's *ethos* (the expression of character in discourse) has become the issue of source credibility. Research has identified three main components of source credibility: expertise, dynamism or charisma, and sincerity. No message can be effective if it is seen to come from a source that is not deemed credible. Audiences are more receptive to sources who demonstrably know what they are talking about. They should also have appealing personal qualities and be sincere in their beliefs.

Depending on the message, audience, and medium, you can choose sources for their expertise, charisma, or sincerity. Of course, expertise, charisma, and sincerity are not fixed attributes of any source. Rather, they are attributes that audience ascribes to the source. You must determine which type of credibility is most important to your target public and then identify a spokesperson who carries such credibility. Although it would seem that physicians would be the most credible spokespersons on health topics, pain reliever ads often feature "regular people" who admit they know nothing about chemical formulas—they only know that Painkiller X works. Presumably, the manufacturers have evidence that sincerity is a stronger appeal than expertise to audiences who are already saturated with medical details they may not understand.

In many cases, spokespersons will be internal, generally the public relations practitioner or organization's chief executive. In times of crisis, it may well be the legal counsel. As a spokesperson, you will likely liaise with the media and field questions from interested publics. Public relations professional James Lukaszewski (2000) defines clear roles for responsible spokespersons. These roles include ensuring that audiences (including the news media) get accurate information and that messages are crafted and delivered with attention to the "organization's important messages, [while being] responsive to news media inquiries and the concerns of audiences."

This should sound familiar on several levels. First, Lukaszewski reflects the PRSA Code of Ethics for honesty, loyalty, and acting in the public interest. It should also sound like our advice that you should think in terms of the organization's relationships and public relations messages in all of your communications. Attention to nuances at word and phrase levels can mean the difference between positive and negative coverage, or between accurate statements and misquotes, especially in crisis situations.

When the source is internal, the appeal will likely be based on expertise and sincerity, both of which should be apparent. If you can also find an internal spokesperson with charisma, you will have a bonus.

Celebrity "sources." In today's media-driven society, you may also have to consider the use of outside spokespersons who have the ability to draw attention to your campaign just by virtue of their fame. In such cases, "source" equals celebrity, and charisma and expertise go hand in hand. Consider the high-profile "sneaker wars" in which a new battle starts every time a high school phenom enters the professional ranks. In this situation, charisma and name recognition are clearly the most important sources of credibility. Does the public buy LeBron James's basketball shoes or Serena Williams's tennis clothing because products with a Nike "swoosh" are actually superior? Or do they buy it for the prestige of owning the signature garment? As a marketing theme for many products aimed at teenagers especially, the attributes of a product often run a distant second to the appeal of the celebrity spokesperson, even if (as with soccer star Freddy Adu) he signed the contract at age 14.

This spin-off of celebrity spokespersons is not restricted to national campaigns or to product advertising. After his angioplasty, talk show host Larry King fronted a public relations campaign for New York Hospital–Cornell Medical Center under the theme "Larry King. Alive." Local charity fundraisers (or even the Jerry Lewis Telethon for Muscular Dystrophy) are nominally headed by local media personalities whose names have local credibility. And colleges seek prominent alumni/ae to sign fund appeal letters to other alums.

Celebrity "names" may raise as many problems as they solve. For example, other clients or campaigns that the person is also committed to may have a "shadow" effect on your cause. On a local level, it is common for charities to use regional media personalities such as news anchors as their spokespersons. While this will surely gain you attention on that person's station or channel, other media outlets in the region will likely ignore you because of that spokesperson. There is even, in some regions, an intrinsic competition between the press, radio, and television that you should be aware of.

It is also possible that the celebrity will overshadow the company or product. If your audience remembers the celebrity and not the message, you have chosen unwisely, not written the copy well, or both.

And, as many organizations have learned to their chagrin, even the most esteemed celebrities may lose their role model status. Even the suggestion of malfeasance has been enough for companies to cancel the multi-million-dollar contracts of their star spokespersons, as LA Lakers superstar Kobe Bryant learned after he was accused of sexual assault and one-time mega star Michael Jackson after his indictment for child molestation. Even if the celebrity is later acquitted, you must ask yourself, "What message does this person now send?"

Ethical Issues

Ethics and Celebrity Endorsements

Should you pay for celebrity endorsements? Is a paid spokesperson the equivalent of false advertising? Although broadcast stations are not averse to running PSAs or ads that use paid celebrities, the endorsement of a paid spokesperson may not be seen as genuine and the name alone may not be enough. Although paid spokespersons may effectively speak on your behalf, generally their word is not as credible as that of a spokesperson who actually supports your cause or uses your product. Even celebrities need expertise, sincerity, and demonstrable commitment to go along with their charisma.

UNICEF has taken advantage of this for more than 50 years, annually appointing celebrity "goodwill ambassadors" who participate in advocacy programs throughout the world at the same time as they speak out on children's issues. The visible commitment of celebrities such as 2003 appointees Shakira, Liv Tyler, and Angela Bassett gives credibility to their words.

The strength of personal involvement is behind the choice of celebrity spokespersons for many public service campaigns ranging from literacy (Oprah Winfrey) to feeding the hungry (Harrison Ford) to autism (Doug Flutie), cystic fibrosis (Boomer Esiason), and HIV (Earvin "Magic" Johnson).

Liability issues may also affect your use of celebrity spokespersons. FTC liability regulations take the position that businesses and individuals may be held liable for unfair or deceptive acts committed by other parties if the business or individual "should have known" about the violation. Implicit in this is that celebrities—and advertising and public relations agencies and practitioners—should be held accountable for the claims they are asked to make in their endorsements or their campaigns. That this liability may include you as a writer is reason enough to make sure you fully understand the truth of everything you write and the appropriateness of any celebrity you may recommend as a spokesperson.

It may be wiser to find a less expensive but not necessarily less convincing, "no-name" spokesperson—or to create your own "spokes-dog" or cartoon character—over which you have control.

Pathos: The Importance of the Audience

Aristotle's third appeal, *pathos,* focuses on the appeal of emotion to the audience. Appeals based on emotion are grounded in what you know about the audience. This will help you determine which of Maslow's levels is appropriate. Should a charity appeal focus on the safety and security your donation may provide or on the feeling that you will get from belonging to a like-minded group of people? Or will the public relate to the personal satisfaction of becoming a better person as a result of donating?

Perhaps more than any other type of writing except poetry, persuasive appeals depend on language, or more accurately, on your mastery of it. What you know about the audience will help you identify micro-level writing strategies that will make your messages more effective. Some of the most effective strategies are dramatization, labeling, and word choice.

Dramatization. Many of the techniques and approaches used in feature writing also support emotional appeals. Dramatizing an issue by detailing the experiences of a single named individual has more impact than writing in the abstract about thousands who are similarly affected. Health services frequently present new medical technology by describing the experience of one patient. They use photos, quotes, and rich description to convey how the technology could also help you, the reader. Testimonials from patients have a similar effect. Testimonials from celebrity patients may be even better.

Ripley and Lichtey (1970) suggest that broadcast audiences (at least) are more interested in situations that involve conflict than in situations that simply provide information. Note that conflict does not have to be serious. A well-known beer brand has parlayed the theme of a "battle" of appeals—"tastes great, less filling," regular versus "lite"—into decades of popular consumer ads.

Labeling. The notion of semantic tyranny discussed in Chapter 1 suggests that getting the right label on an issue is as important as getting the right label on a product. Most people are not enthused about, even recoil from, eating squid but that doesn't deter them from eating calamari. Pork has been repositioned as "the other white meat." With one carefully chosen phrase, the Pork Industry Council distanced pork from beef at the same time as it positioned it closer to lower-fat poultry.

In a classic propaganda approach, labeling may also be used to generate emotional stereotypes that further or refute an argument. When applied to an opponent, the word *fascist* still conveys a strong negative image even if readers or listeners do not fully understand what a fascist is. A "grandmother" label usually evokes ideas of love, nurturing, and good home cooking. The "plain folks" label (e.g., "I'm just like you," "I understand your problem," "I share your grief") attempts to establish a common bond with the audience. Such self-labeling is especially popular in political campaigns as candidates try to establish rapport with every voter and/or discredit their opponents.

Power words. In some ways, power words and power phrases are predictable. The right power words can make even a "non-offer" sound irresistible. The familiar ring of the letter shown as Exhibit 15.1 in Chapter 15 comes from the power words and phrases that we are accustomed to seeing again and again particularly in direct mail communications. *Free, Now, Special Offer,* and *Pre-approved* are but a few of these power phrases. Others include *Save, Lite!* and that most intriguing of all words: *You.*

Nostalgia words are also powerful motivators, increasingly so as the audience ages. Generally, "the good old days" evoke good feelings of times when life was happier, simpler, cheaper, and less stressful. Depending on the generation, *Glenn Miller, peace, Woodstock, punk,* or *cyber* may be power words. Products aimed at baby boomers often use 1960s rock music as the score. If nostalgia were not a powerful appeal, it is unlikely that Volkswagen would have spent time and money launching a 1990s version of the popular Beetle or that BMW would have resurrected the Mini Cooper.

Relevant vocabulary. When writing for professional audiences, relevant rather than topical vocabulary is a key approach. Every occupational or demographic group has an expectation that it will be spoken to in its own language. This means that public relations writers must repeatedly prepare the same message for multiple audiences. Communications must be adapted to the education level, occupation or specialization, interests, and motivation of each audience.

Persuasive communicators especially face a constant challenge of ensuring that *cool, grunge,* and *extreme* are relevant terms for the youth market. At the same time, they face the task of researching what the (inevitable) replacement phrases are going to be. Similar problems exist as we address other culturally distinct groups that define themselves by language rooted in the worlds of technology, music, sports, or social or environmental cause. The Random House dictionary has already added *webmaster, magalog, zip* (as a file format), and *petabyte* and *exabyte.* And Merriam-Webster added *blog* in 2004. Can you predict what might be next?

Persuasion in Practice

The theories of human behavior and personal motivation and the strategies of message design discussed above and in Chapter 1 suggest that persuasive messages will be successful if you have considered and can answer "yes" to the following questions:

- ✦ Is the behavior you wish to see feasible, that is, not prohibited by cost, access, or personal constraints on the receiver's behavior?
- ✦ Do you understand the beliefs of publics and how important those beliefs are to the public?
- ✦ Can you show people that a significant number of the people whose opinions are important to them believe in the behaviors you are advocating?
- ✦ Do people feel confident that they can carry out the behaviors you are advocating?
- ✦ Have you demonstrated the behavior you are seeking?
- ✦ Are your messages attention grabbing, comprehensible, persuasive, and memorable?

✦ Do the media you have selected reach your target audience?
✦ Is the message relevant to your public(s)?
✦ Have you ensured that people cannot misinterpret or disregard the message?
✦ Do you know how people might use the information you present?
✦ Are the length, level, detail, structure, logic, and appeal appropriate for the message, the medium, and the target audience?

The following sections of this chapter look at how persuasion and message theories and your knowledge of your organization's publics relate to several common types of persuasive communications. These communications aim at developing an organization's image, advocating for change, promoting ideas, and generally strengthening relationships with publics.

Image Communications

Goldhaber (1993) argues that "positioning products and organizations may be the most important element in successful marketing today" (p. 299). He suggests two reasons for the increasing concern many organizations have with such positioning. First, as businesses respond to calls for greater social responsibility, it becomes increasingly important that they establish visibility and a personality in the public mind. Second, as the number of brand names and logos increase, it is increasingly difficult for organizations to stand out from the crowd.

Thus, design consultants may be called on to create a unique name and a visual identity (e.g., logo, colors, typeface). Consider the mileage that the delivery service UPS has gotten simply from leveraging the color brown. Writers will be asked to produce slogans (see Exhibit 14.2) and write copy that will establish and maintain an image that is unique, positive, and memorable in the public mind. This may involve purchasing paid advertising space or time (called image advertisements) to promote the organization's name and mission. The copy may or may not directly relate to messages used in paid product or service advertising, but image and product messages should present complementary (and complimentary) images of the organization.

Organizational image is an emotional issue for many organizations. Even a superficial change of logo may generate as much passion as a pay cut. Organizations that attempt to examine their activities with a view to redefining mission and image may find themselves caught in impassioned and perhaps rancorous debate. Factions may lock horns on the nature of the organization and how it should be presented to the public. Such free and open debate usually leads to a superior result, but the process is likely to be long and onerous.

It is useful to make a distinction between image and identity. Generally, image is how publics see the organization. An organization may have many images to many publics. Identity is how the organization sees itself or wants to be seen. Identity is the organizational ideal encapsulated in mission statements and vision statements. Identity drives the messages that build an image in the public's mind.

In an ideal world, an organization hopes that its public images converge toward its defined identity. In many cases, this model is oversimplistic because both the desired and actual images vary from public to public (Treadwell & Harrison, 1994).

EXHIBIT 14.2   Positioning slogans for public utilities.

Among the most visible expressions of corporate identity pointing the way toward public image is the corporate slogan. Slogans are carefully chosen to establish a desired image in the minds of relevant publics. In the late 1990s, deregulation among public utilities resulted in many new identities and image campaigns as the companies positioned themselves in a now-competitive market. Following are some of the slogans that arose from this effort.

ConEdison... The Company You Know. The People You Trust

ConEdisonSolutions .... A New Company. An Old Friend

PP&L Energy Plus™.. Delivering on Our Promises

PG&E... People with Energy

Westfield Gas & Electric .... We Are Driven by Your Best Interests

BayState Gas... The Energy to Do More!

Massachusetts Electric .... Always Been There; Always Will

Western Mass. Electric .... The Energy of Massachusetts

An example is health care where a provider might strive for an image of caring and accessibility with clients and patients and for an image of efficiency and fiscal responsibility with shareholders and directors.

The public relations writer therefore works with the multiple images held by internal groups and the many more held by external publics. Note that in the ongoing work of bringing disparate images into alignment, the public relations writer has a powerful voice in the form of employees who, if fully informed about a new image, can act as informed spokespersons for it.

D I S C U S S I O N   3

Refer to Exhibit 14.2. What do these slogans have in common? Which slogan appeals the most? Which the least? Why? Based on the slogans, what is your image of these companies? Which company do you expect to be the most progressive? The most conservative? What leads you to this impression?

Issues and Advocacy

Advocacy communications arise from public issues that confront an organization. Often these issues are or will be the subject of legislation or regulation. They may result from outside forces threatening the organization or from organizational pressures to change the outside environment. They range from influencing a city council to change zoning restrictions to lobbying for tax incentives so that the company can build a new manufacturing plant. Issues management, as it is called, is a specialized area of business and public relations management.

Some organizations use advocacy messages as a part of their routine public relations strategy. One such organization is (now) ExxonMobil Corporation, which "takes positions on issues critical to our business and to the communities we are associated with. Few things provide greater insight into the character of a company than its editorials and the news it makes" (Mobil Corporation, 1998).

Post (1978) argues that the way an organization responds to criticism is a function of its stake in maintaining the status quo and of whether it sees its critics' complaints as legitimate. If there is a communication response, the strategy may take several forms. The organization may make no response (avoiding the issue) or collaborate with critics. It may undertake aggressive argumentation for the organization's position.

Public relations writers may be called on to support management with reports to clients, proposals for dealing with the issue, and external communications. Target audiences may include consumers, policy makers, the media, and government agencies. It is no accident that advocacy messages bear a close resemblance to crisis communications.

Advocacy Campaigns

Advocacy campaigns are elaborate, often expensive efforts to influence the opinion of key publics on a particular issue or toward a particular cause. Advocacy campaigns typically evolve over time. They usually involve the press, and often TV and radio, direct mail, and certainly the Web. Strategies typically include advertising (paid or public service), letters (to the editor, legislators, or other decision makers), op-ed articles, and support for community and other groups that are also in favor of the cause.

Although some advocacy campaigns are large, national, and expensive, many more are modest, local, and targeted. They seek support for projects that affect a small but identifiable audience. Because of their intense local relevance, they may spawn as much interest, public awareness, and controversy in a small area as do national campaigns.

Look, for example, at the advocacy campaign conducted by Cornell University to gain approval to build a heat exchange facility on the shores of Cayuga Lake in upstate New York. The facility was at the core of the university's proposed Lake Source Cooling (LSC) project to cool campus equipment and buildings. The process takes cool water from the lake depths and passes it through a heat exchanger to cool the warm water piped from Cornell. The warmed lake water is returned to the lake while the newly chilled water is pumped back to cool the university. The project represented significant cost savings to the university.

At issue was the university's need to gain local and state approval for a project that involved a large public lake and the disruption of miles of city streets. Despite benefits to the community, the project was not without critics who represented both environmental concerns and the "town-gown" clash common in many university locales. To gain support and quell opposition, the university undertook an advocacy campaign that was explained as follows by the communications team that developed the program (E. Hershey, director, Communication and Marketing Services, Cornell University, personal communication, November 30, 1998, and personal interview, April 28, 2001).

The Audience(s)

At the start of the project, the university identified several audiences to whom messages should be directed. Four of the key audiences were the Ithaca community, especially residents along the proposed route of the pipes; government and civic leaders expected to lead public opinion on both sides of the issue; environmental and recreational groups with special interests in the lake; and local and state government agencies that would approve the project.

The Plan

The goal of the public relations plan was to "alert, inform and involve the community on an unprecedented scale" (Lake Source Cooling at Cornell, 1997). Transparency and accessibility were hallmarks of the strategy. The community was consulted regularly and provided with all survey results and environmental assessments. Cornell project managers were available for public meetings and presentations. Written support materials ranging from an introductory booklet, brochures, fact sheets, and newsletters to a newspaper ad campaign, letters to the editor and op-ed pieces, and a special LSC web site kept all publics well informed.

The writing strategy: Focus on the publics' concerns. The public relations documents focused on addressing the community's concerns and answering the questions that surveys showed the community was asking. This focus allowed Cornell to achieve many aims. Answering questions such as "What is LSC?" and "Will it harm the lake?" provided the information the public needed to make informed decisions on the project. Answering questions such as "How will Cornell be monitored?" and "What if something goes wrong?" responded to concerns raised by the LSC critics and underscored the university's willingness to be open and honest. And answering questions about how the public would benefit gave the university the opportunity to argue persuasively.

A question of particular concern was, "Does the university have the right to use the lake for cooling?" No doubt to many readers' surprise, the answer was "no." Raising the issue gave Cornell the opportunity to point out that, rather than receiving special treatment, it was following all legal procedures regarding the project. Preempting the opposition (as this did) is a key strategy in formal persuasion. From a public relations writing viewpoint, it is a lesson in the importance of understanding your message and your audience.

The writing strategy: Send consistent messages. The university adopted two key messages and used them consistently. First, the project will be good for the community. Ithaca schools will receive free cooling, land will be donated for a town park, Cornell will resurface streets along the pipeline, jobs will be created, and $22 million will flow into the area from the project. Second, the project will be environmentally safe (with scientific evidence).

These themes formed the basis of all communications throughout the campaign. Text and graphics supported these themes in both informative and persuasive documents.

The Results

The LSC project met all requirements for feasibility and environmental compliance. It was completed in 2000 and has since won many awards from engineering, environmental, and energy associations. It received the 2001 New York State Governor's

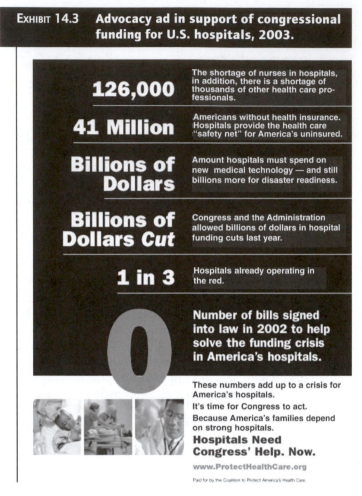

EXHIBIT 14.3   Advocacy ad in support of congressional funding for U.S. hospitals, 2003.

Source: Reprinted with permission from the Coalition to Protect America's Health Care.

Award for Pollution Prevention. The city and schools of Ithaca received an estimated $2 million value in infrastructure improvements. The vocal opposition to the project continues to monitor the lake, but the adverse effects the group predicted have, to date, not materialized (Lake Source Cooling at Cornell, 2002).

Advocacy Advertising

The most common public advocacy documents are advocacy ads. They are typically print-media ads (often full page) that argue an organization's position on a policy issue, referendum, or other issue. The aim of advocacy ads is to influence public opinion, legislation, and policy. Essentially, advocacy ads are a lobbying technique.

Many advocacy ads are situational. They call for an immediate response to, for example, an upcoming debate on a bill in Congress. Exhibits 14.3 and 14.4 are examples of two such ads produced as part of the lobbying effort for federal legislation on health spending by the Coalition to Protect America's Health Care. Exhibit 14.3 focuses on numbers in an attempt to highlight the disparity between the funding needs of U.S. hospitals and the level of support provided by Congress to meet these needs. The ad ends with a plea for congressional help. Exhibit 14.4 has the same aim, but uses the analogy of a hospital emergency room to convey the message of urgency. The text is carefully structured around the medical emergency terms that have become household words thanks to television medical dramas. This time, the ad finishes with a direct plea to the reader to help send the message to Congress.

These and most other advocacy ads are part of an organization's strategy to influence legislative or public affairs issues. Kathleen Jamieson, an expert on media campaigns, argues that the goal of such campaigns is not to change attitudes on the part of the public but rather "to persuade the legislative body that you are a player" (Cushman, 1997, p. 28).

Many advocacy ads take the form of open letters addressed to the president of the United States, members of Congress, or other decision makers. It is also common for the ads to be "signed" by a list of well-known supporters. This broadens the appeal to their supporters as well.

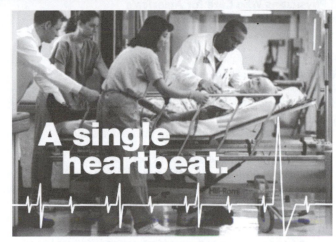

EXHIBIT 14.4   Advocacy ad in support of legislation to fund U.S. hospitals, 2002.

A single heartbeat.

All your hospital's resources matter ... *in that heartbeat.*

In a Code Blue, a patient's life hangs in the balance ... of a *single* heartbeat.

Today, there is a "Code Blue" for America's hospitals.

Our hospitals:
- face a critical shortage of workers;
- continue to provide the "health care safety net" for America's 39 million uninsured;
- must invest billions in the latest medical technology and may spend billions more on disaster readiness.

Hospitals are under intense pressure to make ends meet. Many hospitals are eliminating vital services. Some have even closed.

Today, more than one-third of all hospitals are already losing money . . . and on October 1st, hospitals face billions of dollars in new cuts.

**Tell your Senators to help our hospitals ... now.
Because in a heartbeat ... that could make all the difference.**

Call 1-866-456-CARE.   www.ProtectHealthCare.org

A message from the Coalition to Protect America's health care.

Source: Reprinted with permission from the Coalition to Protect America's Health Care.

In an ad targeted at the same 2003 legislative calendar as Exhibit 14.3, the American Hospital Association (AHA) purchased double-page spreads in major national newspapers under the heading "Hospitals and Physicians Who Care for America's Families Put Their Names on the Line." It advocated for increased funding for Medicare. The text of the ad was an open letter to Congress. It is shown as Exhibit 14.5. The letter was signed by more than 1,000 physicians and hospital representatives. Shaded behind the signatures were the words "Committed to the patients and communities we serve."

Advocacy Ad Writing Strategy

Note in particular the similarity between the letter to Congress shown as Exhibit 14.5 and the letters to the editor we discuss below. The same principles apply.

Insofar as advocacy ads target government officials, the message must convey the credibility of the source, the importance of the issue (especially to their constituents), and what you want them to do. Insofar as they target the constituents of these officials (seeking their support), the message must establish a rapport with the audience and give them reason to act.

Exhibit 14.5 demonstrates many strategies of advocacy persuasion. Note how the writer establishes credibility in the very first line, "On behalf of institutions and physicians dedicated to patient care . . . ," and continues this emphasis throughout. The message consistently frames the AHA argument in terms of concern (evoking images of seniors and the disabled) and the quality of patient care. Unlike issues of health care management (perhaps), these are positions the AHA shares with Congress (and implicitly with voters). The writer has found common ground that puts the AHA and Congress on the same side of the issue. This is a time-honored persuasive strategy for moving an audience from an adversarial to a compromise position. "Keeping the promise" of Medicare frames the issue as (just) another step in a continuing program of caring rather than as a bold step that some members of Congress might be loath to take.

The emphasis on the need for help in serving the needs of Medicare beneficiaries is likely to strike a chord with the public as well. There is a strong public relations

EXHIBIT 14.5   **Text from an open letter to Congress.**

Hospitals and Physicians Who Care for America's Families Put Their Names on the Line

Dear Member of Congress:

On behalf of institutions and physicians dedicated to patient care, we must voice our grave concern that Congress has not yet addressed new and impending Medicare and Medicaid cuts for America's hospitals and physicians. Both doctors and hospitals are absorbing payment cuts—and that situation will worsen unless Congress halts implementation of hospital and physician cuts in FY 2003. We believe Congress should provide additional Medicare funding to adequately compensate those who care for America's elderly, poor and disabled.

Because physicians and hospitals rely on Medicare payments to help cover the costs of patient care, we urge Congress to take immediate action to help both doctors and hospitals. Hospitals and physicians are inextricably linked in their commitment and their collaboration to ensure that Medicare beneficiaries receive the care they need and deserve. Keeping Medicare's promise to America's seniors and disabled means ensuring that those who take care of them have the resources to do the job. We look forward to working with you to maintain that commitment.

America's hospital and physician leaders call on Congress to act to protect Medicare and Medicaid beneficiaries immediately.

Signed by more than 1,100 physicians and medical institutions.

Source: Reprinted with permission from the American Hospital Association.

strategy behind including the words "who care for America's families" in the headline. This message is reinforced by more than 1,000 signatures representing a community that we know and trust. If the public is going to respond to this message, it will likely be on the side of these trusted advisers, and therefore on the side of the AHA. Elements of this strategy will feel very familiar when we discuss letters to the editor below. The same principles apply.

E X E R C I S E   1

An important but often overlooked advocacy document is the humble bumper sticker. With the potential to be seen by thousands without regard to location or time of day, they are good exposure. Which of us hasn't read them (and laughed or groaned) as we sat in traffic? If you can devise such a message, it will likely be the basis of the rest of your campaign. Think "I Love NY" or "Friends Don't Let Friends Drive Drunk."

Writing a bumper sticker message with impact (and taste) is a good exercise in concise persuasive writing. Try to write the text of a bumper sticker taking an advocacy position on one of the following: reducing college tuition, date rape, or campus violence. To be readable "on the road," it should be readable in 3 seconds or less—that's about 10 words.

Public Service Announcements: The PSA

Arguably, a better-known form of advocacy ad is the public service announcement, or PSA. Although the line is a fine one, if true advocacy ads argue a position, then PSAs argue a cause. If advocacy ads attempt to influence policy and legislation, then PSAs attempt to influence public behavior. PSAs serve the public interest or promote behaviors considered to benefit society generally.

PSAs once were clearly defined as ads produced by nonprofit organizations and aired or printed free of charge as a community service by the broadcast media. Today, however, the definition of a PSA is far less clear. The issue has been clouded by several important events and trends.

♦ Deregulation of the broadcast industry removed the requirement that broadcast media had to air social or community-oriented material as a percentage of their programming. Many stations used PSAs to fill this obligation, albeit often in the least desirable time slots.

♦ Nonprofit organizations began teaming up with corporate benefactors willing to fund the cost of ads and ad space. Think, for example, of Avon's sponsorship of the "Race for the Cure."

♦ Corporate interest in social responsibility has led to many "causes" being espoused by companies that are willing and able to pay for the space to promote their causes.

♦ The "tobacco settlement" required that tobacco companies sponsor ads warning children against smoking. These ads are similar in tone and message to those produced by nonprofit antismoking coalitions and have added to the confusion about what is a PSA.

♦ Thanks to the stewardship of the Ad Council, the once-humble, low-budget PSA now competes favorably for airtime and public attention with major commercial ad campaigns. The Ad Council is the nonprofit organization that coordinates PSAs on a national scale. It links worthy nonprofit and government organizations with the best and brightest of the advertising and public relations worlds, who produce professional, high-quality campaigns on a pro bono basis.

♦ Such well-known public symbols as Smokey Bear, Rosie the Riveter, McGruff® the Crime Dog, and the Crash Test Dummies all resulted from Ad Council campaigns. The Ad Council secured more than $1.3 billion worth of donated media placements in 2003 for PSAs produced by its members. This made it the seventh largest advertiser in the United States (Ad Council, 2004a).

Together these events and trends have led to a looser definition in which PSA generally refers to ads that promote causes that benefit society. Accordingly, the subject of PSAs varies widely. Examples include campaigns related to health behavior (prevention, detection, treatment); campaigns related to education, literacy, the arts, the environment, historic place preservation; and issues ranging from terrorism preparedness to religious tolerance.

Most national campaigns aim at changing attitudes and behavior, and, of course, at raising funds. Many local PSAs are events oriented, announcing a fundraising event for local health, education, or social service agencies. The objective is usually not to change people's attitudes but to encourage participation in an event or contributions to a fundraising campaign.

To be sure, the traditional PSA does still exist. Although deregulation removed the mandate for broadcasting PSAs, media outlets still recognize that supporting noncontroversial community causes is good for their image and good for their relationships with their local communities. A 2003 survey of TV directors showed that not only do radio and TV stations still run PSAs enthusiastically, but also they increasingly do so in the desirable TV prime-time and radio drive-time slots (West Glen Communications, 2003). Even so, nonprofit agencies may choose to pay for commercial placements to guarantee exposure at a time they can control.

Local stations may also support community groups and activities by promoting their activities on local news or community calendars. Some offer additional, free advertising for agencies that buy an advertising package at full price. Print media tend to make PSA space available as advertising load permits. They place PSAs in unsold advertising space.

Ad Council surveys and campaign monitoring show that PSAs are effective means of communication and education. Over time, Ad Council research has measured recall rates for characters such as McGruff, hits on the Department of Homeland Security web site, and behavioral changes on the part of gun owners to validate the success of public service campaigns (Ad Council, 2004b).

PSA Writing Strategy

♦ *Attract attention* with headlines and visuals, but keep it simple. Most PSAs succeed with one strong visual. Think of the frying egg used in the "This is your brain on drugs" ad or with one simple headline such as "Friends don't let friends drive drunk."

EXHIBIT 14.6   Print ad from the EPA public service Childhood Asthma Campaign.

"WHEN I HAVE AN ASTHMA ATTACK I FEEL LIKE A FISH WITH NO WATER."

–JESSE, AGE 5

ATTACK ASTHMA. ACT NOW.
1-866-NO-ATTACKS   ♻EPA
WWW.NOATTACKS.ORG

Ad Council

T2-716-FC-7

Bus Shelter   AD-CCA-021671-FC
Mechanical Size:
Bleed: 17-1/4" H x 12" W
Live: 16-3/4" H x 11-1/2" W

the kaplan thaler group, ltd.

Source: Reproduced with permission from the U.S. Environmental Protection Agency.

In 2001, the U.S. Environmental Protection Agency (EPA) undertook a public service campaign to help combat childhood asthma. The campaign, which was produced with Ad Council support, included radio, TV, and print ads as well as a brochure and web site. The campaign theme used the common analogy of a fish out of water to help readers and viewers understand what it was like to experience an asthma attack. Although documents have been updated over time, this theme remains central to the campaign.

Exhibit 14.6 is the print ad from this campaign. The simplicity of the ad takes advantage of two powerful elements: the child's quote "I feel like A FISH with no water," and the flopping fish. The rest of the ad directs readers to the campaign web site for additional information.

If you can identify a powerful headline and/or a powerful image that will reproduce effectively across multiple media—such as the gasping fish—take advantage of them. They will save you many words. The radio script shown as Exhibit 11.3 (in Chapter 11) demonstrated how this theme works even without visuals. The campaign web site was shown as Exhibit 13.2 (in Chapter 13).

◆ *Involve the reader.* Ask a question. Tell a story.

◆ *Simple style.* Exhibit 14.7 shows two print ads from a national lead awareness campaign sponsored by the U.S. Department of Housing and Urban Development (HUD) to increase knowledge about the dangers of lead paint and its effects on children. Note how the common message of keeping children safe is developed for families (left) and for contractors (right). Other ads in the series focused on landlords and renters, and developed the family theme for African American and Hispanic audiences, the latter in Spanish as well as English.

The language of the campaign is very simple and the sentences are short. The agency understood that the campaign audience varied widely and represented all levels of education and reading skills. So the copy is written at a level that adults can easily understand.

◆ *Single concept.* Work with only one topic.

◆ *Action oriented.* Tell the reader/viewer/listener what to do, such as the simple solution "Call 1–800–424LEAD for more information."

◆ *Send a positive message.* In *The Art of Cause Marketing,* PSA guru Richard Earle (2000) makes a strong case for positive rather than negative messages. He says that people are prone to reject messages telling them *not* to do something. Instead, find ways to send messages that they believe they can follow. This is closely related to Bandura's (1986) theory of self-efficacy.

Earle cites as examples the differences between "anti-abortion" (negative) and "pro-life" (positive), between "pro-abortion" (negative image) and "pro-choice" (positive), and between "anti-litter campaign" (negative) and "Keep America Beautiful" (positive) (p. 59). In the lead awareness campaign, "HUD wants every child to have a lead-safe home" is a positive message. You can find many other examples.

EXHIBIT 14.7   **Print ads from the Campaign for a Lead-Safe America, for families (left) and for contractors (right)**

We thought our home was a safe place for our children.

We didn't imagine they were being poisoned by lead.

Most children are poisoned by lead in their own homes. If your home was built before 1978, make sure that peeling or damaged paint is repaired promptly and safely.

Call 1-800-424-LEAD for more information.

HUD wants every child to have a lead-safe home.

 Sponsored by the U.S. Department of Housing and Urban Development

They didn't know dust from lead paint could poison their child.

Good thing their contractor did.

Protect your clients by keeping lead dust away from people and cleaning up thoroughly at the end of each day.

Call 1-800-424-LEAD for more information.

HUD wants every child to have a lead-safe home.

 Sponsored by the U.S. Department of Housing and Urban Development

Source: Produced by Vanguard Communications of Falls Church, Inc., under U.S. Department of Housing and Urban Development Grant #DCLHR0049–98 for the Campaign for a Lead-Safe America.

◆ *Emphasize what's important.* The sponsor of a PSA is never as important as the message, and in all of the examples, the sponsor's name is small.

These principles do not differ from the principles of good advertising copy in general.

◆ *"Think news."* Remembering the news determinants discussed in Chapter 9 and the importance of working with the media will also help increase the probability of exposure for PSAs.

◆ *Localize it.* Survey results show that both TV and radio directors considered local relevance to be the most important determinant on whether to air a PSA. Receiving PSAs that were not locally relevant were the news directors' "top pet peeve" (West Glen Communications, 2003).

If the Ad Council accepts your organization as a client, your chances of exposure are increased because the ads will be professionally produced and distributed. But you must still ensure that local media understand the local relevance of the campaign. It is also a good idea to make local spokespersons available.

◆ *Localize it.* If you do not have Ad Council support, the same principle applies. Use your writing skills to explain the relevance and timeliness of the PSA to local media.

◆ *Work to the media's requirements and deadlines.* Find out the preferred length of time or space available for a PSA. Sixty-second PSAs exist but most TV stations prefer 30-second spots. Radio spots range from 10 to 60 seconds, preferably in CD rather than cassette, script, or reel-to-reel format.

Writing for Op-Ed Pages or Broadcast Editorials

Closely related to advocacy ads are letters to the editor and columns that appear on the opinion-editorial (op-ed) pages of daily newspapers. Always controversial and sometimes entertaining, op-ed pages allow individuals and organizations to express opinions on issues in the news. TV stations that air editorials also may make limited time available for responses to them.

Letters to the editor provide the opportunity for organizations to give their side of a story outside of the constraints of the news release. The downside is, of course, that just as with news releases, media gatekeepers ultimately determine if, when, and in what form the letters will be used. If you want to express an opinion without change, then you will have to pay for advertising space for an open letter or an op-ed.

Advocacy Letters: To the Editor, to Legislators, and to the Public

Typically referred to as "letters to the editor" (or other official), advocacy letters respond to particular situations. When written as letters to the editor, they respond to an article or editorial that the media has printed or broadcast previously. When written to Congress or other decision makers or as "open letters to . . . ," they respond to impending legislation or other immediate issues (much like advocacy ads). Although no one expects them to be unbiased, you must be careful to stick to the issue and ensure that you only respond to issues that are public issues.

Content and format. Letters to the editor (and op-ed articles) usually take advantage of the appeal of logic and the use of logical structure in a persuasive message. They are based on the techniques and structure of formal debate:

◆ Describe your position (i.e., state your claim).
◆ Provide supporting evidence.
◆ Raise the opposing point of view.
◆ Refute the opposing point of view.
◆ Restate your position.

Generally, there are several good reasons to present your position on an issue before your opposition's position. First, you want your audience to know what you are talking about. Second, readers may not read the full article, and yours is the position you want them to remember. This is borne out by basic news structure: If your story represents good news for the public, lead with it. Third, it lets you define the terms of the argument.

In addition to the points we made previously about supporting evidence, we add that it is wise to limit yourself to two, perhaps three, key points, rather than referring to everything ever written on the subject. Keep it simple and clear.

While it may seem logical to avoid the opposing viewpoint at all costs, in fact raising it is a particularly effective tactic. Not only does it identify you as knowledgeable about the complete situation, but it also positions you as fair and committed to the public interest. Both of these contribute to your credibility.

Once you have identified the opposing point of view, the principles of argument provide guidelines for responding:

◆ You can cite evidence to discredit the opposing argument (or source).
◆ You can rebut it, showing why it is false.
◆ You can acknowledge its validity while pointing out the superiority of your own position.

All three strategies are actually opportunities to present your own persuasive argument. A "first strike" is often more effective in the long term than ignoring a problem issue until such time as others raise it. Think proactive rather than reactive. This is especially true if you can anticipate a crisis.

Exhibit 14.8 is a letter to the editor written to the weekly Washington, D.C., publication *The Hill,* "a self-described newspaper for and about the US Congress." In the letter, the president of the National Federation of Independent Business (NFIB) responds to an article that *The Hill* had published about small-business health care, a matter of particular concern to the NFIB's members. The letter does many things well. It clearly states the situation and references the original article. It takes a clear stand and provides evidence for its position. It acknowledges an opposition campaign and turns immediately to evidence refuting it. And it is brief.

From a public relations viewpoint, it is also important to note the publication in which the letter appeared. Issues of concern to an organization are often discussed in publications with a focus on an industry or special interest rather than in the daily news. Publications grounded in an industry or business specialization are collectively referred to as the *trade* press. Responding to an article in a publication with a focus on political issues would have been a clear choice for the NFIB, although it might not have responded to the same article in a publication less likely to be read by its target audience for this issue, that is, Congress. Public relations writers should monitor such publications and recommend and write responses when the issue and target audience are appropriate.

Style. Although letters to the editor are by definition biased on one side of an issue, it does not mean you can spend the space in organizational self-promotion. Rather, the organization's involvement and especially its self-interest should be

EXHIBIT 14.8   Letter to the editor.

Small Businesses Support Association Health Plans

From Jack Faris, president, National Federation of Independent Business

In his April 14 article, "White House looks to roll key senators," Bob Cusack discusses the Bush administration efforts to pass small-business health plan (also known as association health plan, or AHP) legislation.

The NFIB applauds the commitment this administration has shown in working with NFIB's 600,000 members to provide health insurance to their employees. More than 60 percent of the nation's uninsured work for small businesses with less than 100 employees, and they would benefit greatly from Senate action on the Small-Business Health Fairness Act (S. 545).

Despite a well-funded misinformation campaign, this legislation would give small businesses the same bargaining and buying power as big government, big labor and big business. Small-business health plans would extend health insurance to the working uninsured and would do so at savings of 13 to 25 percent on premiums, according to the Congressional Budget Office.

On April 1, NFIB members launched a petition drive to mobilize the Senate to pass this legislation. NFIB is hopeful this will illustrate to the Senate that small-business health plans are critical to addressing the problem of the uninsured.

There's a reason this legislation has the support of more than 160 organizations, representing more than 12 million employers and 80 million American workers—it brings fairness and choice to the marketplace! We're counting on the Senate to deliver this year.

Washington, D.C.

Source: Reprinted with permission from *The Hill.*

secondary to the public interest. The city council's refusal to rezone an area so that your company can build a new plant will undoubtedly affect your profits. To the community, however, the important issue is the layoffs that will result if the company cannot expand. What you know about your publics and their values, interests, and needs will help you choose arguments that will cultivate positive relationships and contribute to informed decision making.

Letters to the editor should be written simply and directly, avoiding exaggerated claims, inflammatory phrasing, and adjectives. Let the argument and logic lead the reader to your conclusion. In terms of phrasing, think news rather than direct mail. Remember that there is an editor making decisions on whether the letter will be printed.

It is also worth mentioning bullet points, which are not part of normal media style. They may be used effectively, however, in letters to the editor. When used, they have very tight parallel structure that likely makes it difficult for editors to rewrite them. Since bullet points are an effective way to call attention to key arguments, this is a point worth noting.

A word to the wise. To persuasively express your organization's position, it is critical that you understand your opponent's position. Public relations writers should be able to write to both sides of many issues, although their employer's position will be what they publicly present. This is not to imply that they break any rules of ethics. Rather, it recognizes that if you can predict the argument that will support your opponent's position, you will have an edge in formulating effective rebuttals. And remember, no matter how ardent you are in supporting your current employer, in your next job you may find yourself arguing the opposite side. The more you know about an issue, the more you become an expert in the field and the more likely it is that you will be sought after by other organizations.

Remember too, the relationship between source and credibility. Sending the letter over the signature of an executive or expert with public credibility will increase the likelihood that it will be used and that readers will pay attention and be predisposed to accept your argument.

Op-Ed Articles

Although similar in purpose, style, and content, there are significant differences between letters to the editor and op-ed articles (op-eds). Whereas letters to the editor typically respond to previous editorials, the subject of op-eds may be any issue the organization considers important. Whereas letters to the editor are run free of charge in a designated section of the paper, op-eds are typically paid advertising space. And whereas letters to the editor are subject to the discretion of the media, op-eds will be run as written.

Exhibit 14.9 is an op-ed column on a subject of particular interest to public relations practitioners: the relevance of public relations in the 21st century. Written by the president of the PRSA, the op-ed was run in *PRWeek* and addresses questions commonly posed by both public relations practitioners and their critics: Is public relations relevant? What is its role in society?

Paid op-ed articles are part of the routine public relations strategy of many organizations. Mobil (now ExxonMobil) launched its first advocacy program in 1971 with a campaign to warn the public of an impending crisis in energy supplies. Three decades later, it continues with editorials and op-ed advertising to keep the company's position on energy, conservation, trade, and technology issues before the public. One example was shown as Exhibit 4.3 in Chapter 4. Microsoft has a similar program.

Even without media gatekeeping, there are conventions that you should follow when writing effective op-ed articles. These conventions are generally those found in the Pulitzer Prize criteria for op-ed awards: "clearness of style, moral purpose, sound reason, and power to influence public opinion in what the writer conceives to be the right direction" (Pulitzer Prizes, 2003).

Look at Exhibit 14.9 in light of these criteria. Remembering that an op-ed is a type of feature article and that it must attract the reader's attention, the author leads with a relevant, brief anecdote and links the story to a much broader but analogous problem, that is, the role of public relations.

It is clear, direct, and interesting, and the examples are ones with which we can all identify. The author takes a strong stand regarding the value of public relations, presenting it as a solution rather than, as many charge, the cause or symptom of the problems. He presents a rational argument demonstrating

EXHIBIT 14.9   Op-ed article. Printed March 15, 2004.

In Today's Absence of Trust and Truth, PR Is Paramount

Written by Del Galloway
Published on March 15, 2004

There's an old story about two gangsters trying to get one of their accomplices to reveal where he'd buried their stolen loot. The first, one of your sensitive, new-wave gangsters, spoke softly of the importance of team play; he cajoled and pleaded to no avail. Finally the older gangster leaned in and said, "Tell us where the money is or I'll kill you." The man immediately told. "Why wouldn't you tell me?" the kinder, gentler gangster asked. "Well," said the man, "you didn't explain it as well as he did."

Today, more than ever, we need blunt, frank, and open communications. Look around at the problems of the world, and more than likely you'll find at the root a breakdown somewhere in basic communications. A new film by Mel Gibson threatens to launch a new era of divisiveness. Presidential candidates say one thing one day and back-pedal the next, or they alienate voters because they won't provide direct answers to simple questions. People throughout the world say they love Americans, but hate America. We all subscribe to the old adage, "I may disagree with what you say, but I will defend to the death your right to say it." Yet, when you say something I don't like, I organize a boycott to silence you by trying to put you out of business.

We abhor censorship, yet more than 8,000 words are banned from textbooks used in schools and colleges because they've been deemed offensive by one "language police" group or another.

As the media worldwide become more professional and more skilled at reporting news, public confidence in the media erodes more rapidly. Influenza. SARS, mad cow disease, criminal prosecutions — and even imprisonment, in some cases — of corporate executives, breakdowns in trust between nations, these stories that demand the essence of candor often fall victim to blame-placing or just pure, old-fashioned spin. As the world grows smaller, many of its people seem to grow further apart.

"Trust is like the air we breathe," Warren Buffett said once. "When it's present, nobody really notices. But when it's absent, everybody notices."

Trust and understanding is what PR is all about. In this complex world, communications become technologically easier by the minute, but the actual communications process seems to get more difficult.

We have lost confidence in the power of open, truthful, candid communications. What that means to you, me, and our organizations is that PR is more relevant now than ever before — not just "good" PR, but "great" PR in every aspect of our lives.

The PR profession helps our complex, pluralistic society to reach decisions and to function more effectively by contributing to mutual understanding among groups and institutions. It serves to bring private and public policies into harmony.

Truly, the PR profession, like many others, has evolved significantly from its origins. Just as lawyers, sales professionals, scientists, engineers, and other professionals have expanded their basic skill sets to find a place at the decision-making table in corporations and other organizations, PR professionals show their acumen and worth in that setting, as well.

Source: Reprinted with permission of *PRWeek and* the Public Relations Society of America.

the need for public relations and justifying its ability to respond effectively to this need.

The diversity of formats we have discussed in this chapter have one common purpose: to effectively argue an organization's case in order to achieve a specific result in the court of public opinion. There are close parallels to attorneys arguing their client's case in a court of law. First, vigorous advocacy must be tempered by respect for the law and for relevant ethical standards. Second, effective advocacy is based on listening. You must understand both the situation and any opposing arguments to be effective. The difference between the two "courts" lies in the question of relationships. Whereas many legal actions may shatter relationships, public relations writers remain conscious of the need to cultivate positive relationships wherever possible. They recognize that today's adversary may be tomorrow's ally.

ON THE TEXTBOOK WEB SITE

✦ Go to www.sagepub.com/treadwell for web exercises, study hints, case studies, and additional examples appropriate to this chapter and chosen or developed to supplement the chapter content.

WRITING WRAP-UP

1. Your campus newspaper recently printed a letter to the editor written by senior communication major Julie Smith. In the letter, Julie charges that students on your campus are not serious about their education. She cites as evidence the facts that students try to get 10-page papers reduced to 5 pages, 5-page papers reduced to 3 pages (double-spaced, of course), and still typically write only the minimum number of pages. She claims they whine for multiple-choice rather than essay exams, avoid the library by doing as much research as possible on the Web, and usually use the first sources they find regardless of whether they are good sources or not.

    Write a one-page letter to the editor supporting or rebutting Julie's position. Observe the conventions of letters to the editor when writing the message.

2. You recognize that Julie is not alone in her feelings and that many people believe students treat college as a glorified high school. With debates about to start in your state legislature on the issue of tax deferments for tuition payments, you recognize that public support for students is critical. Your student government association has agreed to pay for op-ed placements in the local newspapers of key legislators. Write an op-ed from your student government association presenting the students' side of the story. Present it exactly as you want it to look in the paper.

3. You have been asked by your college or university administration to develop a campus public service campaign on the subject of plagiarism. The campaign must include a poster or ad for the campus newspaper, a 30-second radio spot, and a letter to the editor.

References

Ad Council. (2004a, May 6). *Ad Council announces $1.3 billion in donated media support in 2003 and $250 million in upfront media commitments secured for 2004* [Press release]. Retrieved June 15, 2004, from http://www.adcouncil.org/about/news_050604/

Ad Council. (2004b). *Impact of public relations campaigns*. Retrieved June 16, 2004, from www.adcouncil.org/fr_research_impact.html

Bandura, A. (1986). *Social foundations of thought and action*. Englewood Cliffs, NJ: Prentice Hall.

Cushman, J. H., Jr. (1997, December 7). Intense lobbying against global warming treaty. *New York Times*, p. 28.

Earle, R. (2000). *The art of cause marketing: How to use advertising to change personal behavior and public policy*. New York: McGraw-Hill.

Goldhaber, G. M. (1993). *Organizational communication* (6th ed.). Madison, WI: Brown and Benchmark.

Independent Sector. (2001). *Giving and volunteering in the United States*. Retrieved September 15, 2003, from http://www.independentsector.org/

Lake Source Cooling at Cornell. (1997). *Lake Source Cooling at Cornell: An idea whose time has come* [Media kit]. Ithaca, NY: Cornell University Offices of Communication Strategies and Publications Services.

Lake Source Cooling at Cornell. (2002). [Project web site]. Retrieved October 16, 2003, from http://www.utilities.cornell.edu/LSC/default.htm

Lukaszewski, J. (2000). *Speaking for others: Current practices and issues*. Professional Standards & Business Practices Committee of the Counselors Academy of the Public Relations Society of America. Retrieved March 2, 2004, from http://www.e911.com/monos/A005.htm

Maslow, A. H. (1954). *Motivation and personality*. New York: Harper and Row.

Maslow, A. H. (1962). *Toward a psychology of being*. New York: Van Nostrand.

Mobil Corporation. (1998). Retrieved December 2, 1998, from www.mobil.com/world and www.mobil.com/this/history/mobilhist/briefhist.html

Post, J. E. (1978). *Corporate response and social change*. Reston, VA: Reston.

Pulitzer Prizes. (2003). *The Pulitzer Prizes plan of award*. Retrieved March 6, 2004, from http://www.pulitzer.org/Entry_Forms/entry_forms.html

Ripley, J. M., & Lichtey, L. W. (1970). *American broadcasting: Introduction and analysis readings* (2nd ed.). Madison, WI: College Printing and Publishing.

Treadwell, D. F., & Harrison, T. M. (1994). Conceptualizing and assessing organizational image: Model images, commitment and communication. *Communication Monographs, 61*(1), 63–85.

Treadwell, D. F., & Treadwell, J. B. (1999). Employer expectations of newly-hired communication graduates. *Journal of the Association for Communication Administration, 28*(2), 87–99.

U.S. Department of Labor. (2003). *Volunteering in the United States*. U.S. Bureau of Labor Statistics. Retrieved March 3, 2004, from http://www.bls.gov/CPS

West Glen Communications, Inc. (2003). *2003 television, radio & print survey*. Retrieved October 6, 2003, from www.westglen.com/pr_news/pr_news_survey.html

RESOURCES

The *U.S. Congress Handbook* and the *U.S. Congress New Member Handbook* include contact information for all members of Congress and tips on writing to members. Published for each Congress. (McLean, VA: Pullen.).

Claritas.. www.claritas.com

Causemarketer (Richard Earle).. www.causemarketer.com

Independent Sector (research on.. www.independentsector.org
nonprofit giving and volunteering)

West Glen Communications .... www.westglen.com

Featured Organizations

Ad Council .... www.adcouncil.org

American Hospital Association .... http://www.hospitalconnect.com/aha/about/

Cayuga Lake Defense Fund..www.cldf.org

Coalition to .... http://www.protecthealthcare.org/protecthealth care/about/index.html
Protect America's Health Care

Cornell University Lake Source Cooling .... www.utilities.cornell.edu/LSC

EPA Childhood Asthma Campaign .... www.noattacks.org

National Federation of Independent Business......... http://www.nfib.com/page/home.html

U.S. Postal Service... www.usps.gov

U.S. Department of Housing and Urban Development... www.hud.gov

15

Persuasion for Individual Action

Direct Mail, Brochures, and Proposals

There is a fine line, admittedly, between the topics discussed in Chapter 14 and those in this chapter. All of them are exercises in persuasion to a degree not seen in fact sheets, newswriting, newsletters, or VNRs.

However, the advocacy umbrella, under which advocacy ads, letters to the editor, and PSAs lie, essentially relates to issues. Advocacy documents address ideas or causes that have an implication of social or political rather than corporate good. Advocacy documents are usually "mass documents." They are printed or aired on the mass media.

But there are also persuasive documents that have commercial or organizational as well as public interests at their heart. Direct mail—and to a lesser extent brochures—fall into this category. They have the advantage of being targetable, even while sending mass messages. Response and evaluation measures can be part of the message. Because they are grounded in marketing, direct mail has the reputation for promoting products rather than ideas. But that is no longer the case. Note that the same "targetability" and measurability that make them staples of marketing also make them appropriate for some charitable and educational purposes. Hence the fine line between, for example, PSAs and direct mail.

Direct Mail

The U.S. Postal Service (2004) delivers more than 2 billion letters per year, averaging five pieces of mail to every address in the United States every day. And as we all know from daily experience, a significant portion (nearing 50% although it often feels like more) is direct mail.

In its broadest sense, *direct mail* is any communication that is mass produced and sent by mail (or fax or even e-mail or CD) to a large number of people. Theoretically, direct mail can reach every household in the nation. It is a mass medium in its own right.

However, direct mail also has the potential to be targeted, individualized, personal, and intimate. Thanks to mail merge and computerized mailing lists, the days of "Dear occupant" are long gone. What you know about your audience can be applied even to mailings involving thousands of pieces.

Direct mail includes special offers in magazines (*blow-ins*), catalogs, and price lists. Even the demand letter that collection agencies send to debtors is a form of direct mail. The letter is essentially a form; only the details change. *E-commerce*, the selling of goods and services over the Internet, is a close relative of direct mail.

The Universal Postal Union (2004), that body that links postal services throughout the world, reports a significant increase in direct mail on a global scale. It is expected to soon exceed 50% of U.S. mail. The number of products and services available by mail and the explosion of e-commerce indicate that direct mail will play a strong role in 21st-century business.

In spite of the junk mail aura that surrounds the medium, the reality of direct mail does not match the negative rhetoric. A study by the Direct Marketing Association (DMA, 2003) reported that the industries most likely to use direct and interactive marketing approaches to reach their publics were (in order) nonprofit fundraisers, retail stores, business suppliers, manufacturers, personal and repair services, travel, computer and electronic products, and packaged goods. The study also showed that response rates differed greatly among the industries depending on the medium used. Nonprofits and educational institutions far exceeded all other industries in positive responses to telephone appeals, recording a whopping 19% and 12%, respectively. Packaged goods and store retailers had the highest response rates for direct mail. Companies in the "business to business" market had the highest response rates for e-mail appeals (DMA, 2003).

Direct mail is designed to elicit a measurable response from the reader. It takes talent and care to realize this potential, but it is there.

As you no doubt recognize, the letter sample in Exhibit 15.1 is a loose interpretation of all that is obvious about direct mail. It is typical of the flood of

EXHIBIT 15.1   Letter demonstrating many of the principles of direct mail.

Dear Aspiring Public Relations Persuader,

CONGRATULATIONS! You have been **PRE-APPROVED** to move to the next level of public relations writing — persuasion. That's right: Persuasion, the driving force behind political campaigns, fundraising, public service advertising *and* your own self-promotion is the subject of this never-to-be-repeated chapter on persuasion from the same people who brought you chapters on planning, research and news writing.

Like the previous chapters, this one comes complete with fresh, topical examples and exercises to help you understand how even the most complex theories apply to day-to-day persuasive writing. As a special bonus, it has been sequentially paginated by skilled editors for your reading pleasure.

No experience necessary! The authors take you from start to finish in the why and how of effective, persuasive messages. Read what the experts have to say about why people act as they do and learn how using the right appeal will improve your chances of having them behave as you want. Learn to use their theories to command attention, interest and action.

Just look at the thrills that await you in this chapter:

- ■   Theories of behavior: What do they mean to the public relations writer?
- ■   Themes and strategies for appeal and action.
- ■   Persuasion in action: PSAs, advocacy messages, brochures and proposals.
- ■   And everyone's favorite: direct mail.

You, too, can write some of the thousands of persuasive messages distributed every day on radio, TV and the Internet, in the newspaper, through the mail, and yes, on bumper stickers and t-shirts — the messages that urge us to buy, donate, volunteer and vote.

Think of the **REWARDS** that knowing how to write effective persuasive messages may bring. Power, prestige, popularity and money — perhaps even lots of money — are but a few of the potential benefits of being the strategic and creative source behind the persuasive message that gets the results your employer wants.

And best of all, it's all **FREE** with the purchase of this book! There is **NO MONEY DOWN** and **NO MONTHLY PAYMENTS.** The only cost is your time and attention.

DO NOT WAIT! Act now before the deadline for this chapter's assignments passes and the only remaining opportunity to demonstrate your persuasive abilities is to persuade your professor to grant an extension. Turn this page now for exciting details, presented in easy, one-page-at-a-time installments.

Sincerely,

The Authors

P.S. If you choose not to take advantage of this once-in-a-semester opportunity, you may still be able to write news stories, but when your employer's future hangs on public or political opinion, you'll wish you knew more about writing to persuade.

direct mail pieces every U.S. consumer receives daily from advertisers, charities, and nonprofit institutions. If it seems familiar, it is because you have no doubt read similar copy again and again.

You may recognize it from the pledge drives for your local Public Broadcasting Station or the annual Jerry Lewis Labor Day Telethon for Muscular Dystrophy. Or from PSAs in which professional athletes urge you to stay in school. Or from magazine ads for commemorative 9/11 coins (with some proceeds to the 9/11 families charities). Or . . . add your own no doubt innumerable examples here. The appeals used in telethon fundraising are often the appeals used in direct mail, for good reason. The advantage that direct mail provides is that it allows messages to be specifically targeted to individuals.

Direct mail is ubiquitous and often predictable. The media, spokespersons, appeals, and organizations may differ, but the aim is to get you to act in a particular way. The sender wants you to buy/give money/stay in school/volunteer/vote/stop drinking-smoking-taking drugs or abusing your spouse/children. These aims illustrate the close relationship between direct mail and advocacy documents, and indeed they are often parts of a single campaign. Taken to the extreme, one might argue that every message written by a public relations writer has some persuasive component.

Even while making exaggerated claims, Exhibit 15.1 illustrates many persuasive techniques, appeals, and principles. It talks directly to the reader, involving him or her with congratulations and directions to "think of the rewards" and "turn the page." Subheads attract attention and are made obvious with the choice of type and positioning. These techniques increase the amount of time the reader spends with the letter and the amount of time the writer has to present the persuasive message.

Although such copy is hardly the noblest or even most common form of persuasion, it illustrates the importance of every word in the copy and the benefit of understanding the format.

Direct mail campaigns can be expensive. They involve producing and printing the mailing, probably designing special envelopes, and the cost of mailing. It is necessary therefore that you target at least three ways: the audience, the mailing, and the individual.

◆ *Target the audience.* What demographic categories are you trying to reach—voters? women voters? Republican women voters? Republican women voters with children? Based on demographic data, you can either select a category to learn how many copies to produce or keep narrowing the category until you reach the number of copies you can afford.

◆ *Target the mailing to the audience.* Develop a theme that makes your message relevant to the audience. How does your mailing relate to that demographic group? What do you want them to do? Common reasons for sending direct mail include the following:

Raising funds or moving donors to a higher giving level.

Increasing membership or recruiting volunteers.

Moving people to action, such as voting or writing to their elected representatives. "We need your support" is a common theme.

Selling products or services.

Promoting events, for example, "We'll be in Booth 309 at the Orlando Conference; stop by for a snack and a prize." Asking recipients to fill out their name and address and return the card to the booth to qualify for a prize will give you the start of a mailing list.

◆ *Target the mailing to individual recipients.* Direct mail success depends on getting the recipient to open the mail, read it, and then respond to it. Good direct mail writers have mastered the ability to make the reader believe that the letter/brochure/offer is directed especially to him or her—even while he or she knows that 100,000 other people received the same offer.

Making the reader feel special is why so much money is spent developing lists of names. Your budget may be better spent on purchasing a reliable, targeted mailing list than on developing a full-color presentation.

Direct Mail Formats

Letters are the staple of the direct mail industry. This is why Exhibit 15.1 seemed so familiar. Letters give you the opportunity to explain your position in greater detail than in an ad.

Ideally, direct mail letters follow the same principles as the cover letter for a job application described in Chapter 2. This includes the idea that brief should be better. Try to keep letters to one page. If you cannot do so, remember that many people will read only the first paragraph, the headings, and the postscript (P.S.). Pay particular attention to these sections.

Perhaps recognizing that except for already committed publics, people do not read long direct mail letters, many organizations resort to postcard mailers. These have benefits in reduced postage costs as well as being instantly visible. It is almost impossible not to see the whole message. For the writer, this presents the challenge of conveying the important messages concisely. The fact that you cannot enclose a pledge card or envelope may be a disadvantage.

E-mail too is a viable direct "mail" medium, provided that it doesn't look like spam. Its advantage is that readers can respond immediately by purchasing or donating online. Its disadvantage is that it is e-mail from someone the recipient may not recognize. This should tell you that the "subject" line of an e-mail is as critical as the headline of a news release. If it doesn't attract the reader's attention, the message may well be trashed unread.

Writing Direct Mail Copy

The Content or Message

Direct mail always has action as its aim, even if it is not obvious. Information pieces that purport to educate you about the threat to the environment or your children's future or about a candidate's voting record are generally "infomercials." At the end, you will be offered an "opportunity" to donate, subscribe, purchase, or vote. Surveys such as those conducted by the League of Women Voters have a similar aim.

In a print medium, it would seem that you have a limit on space. With direct mail you actually have a limit on time. The reader will give you only a certain amount of time before he or she decides not to read further. This is the point at which direct mail becomes junk mail. Therefore, you must get to the point quickly—a strong argument for the increasingly popular use of postcards as a direct mail medium.

Use a direct appeal, quote, statement, or question to grab the reader, and immediately involve him or her in the message. The more involved a reader becomes, the more opportunity (and time) you have to persuade him or her to act.

Even a casual analysis of the direct mail that comes to your residence will quickly show that there are only two questions that the writer must answer to effect action.

✦ *What's in it for me?* Make the reader an offer he or she cannot resist. The offer does not have to be tangible. Charitable appeals raise millions of dollars by offering self-esteem and the personal satisfaction that comes from helping others. Note how the Red Cross mailer shown as Exhibit 15.2 uses phrases such as "friend" and "compassionate people like you" to draw the reader into a community of people who care.

✦ *Why should I care?* Even altruists want an answer to this question. Involve the reader by presenting situations or asking questions that have relevance to the reader and that draw him or her into the message. The Red Cross mailer reminds readers of situations in which the organization has provided assistance and also that they may need the organization's assistance themselves.

If you can answer these two questions to the reader's satisfaction, you will have a good chance of getting the desired action. How you answer them is where your creativity will be tested.

Andrews (1985) describes the basics of a fundraising letter as the big "IDEA":

✦ *Interest*—Why should the reader care about your message?
✦ *Desire*—Make the reader want to help or to take advantage of the offer. Even making the reader want more information is a step in the right direction.
✦ *Explanation*—Reinforce the reader's disposition to act as you want him or her to act.
✦ *Action*—Tell the reader what to do. How can the reader help? How can he or she take advantage of the opportunity?

These points apply equally well to all types of direct mail messages and to all types of appeals. In Chapter 14, we discussed types of persuasive appeals. Any and all of them can be successfully applied to direct mail.

The almost unlimited options for approach and style are part of what makes direct mail such a challenge and so much fun. For example, will you appeal with cold, hard statistics? Social responsibility? Celebrity endorsement? Guilt? Altruism? Can you take advantage of personal testimony? Will a bandwagon "everyone's doing it" appeal work? What about creating selectivity ("only a few special people will be getting this offer") or urgency ("the offer expires now!")? What you know about

EXHIBIT 15.2   Direct mail letter soliciting funds for the American Red Cross (top) and its envelope (bottom).

American Red Cross

FREE

Dear Friend,

There's one thing the American Red Cross never does.

When a family's home burns to ashes over the holidays . . . and we rush to provide emergency shelter, food and clothing . . . we don't send a bill for our services. Ever!

No matter how costly, how long we must stay on the scene of a disaster, we don't charge the people we help. Not a thin dime.

It's true. The best things in life—like a helping hand in time of dire need—really are free. And yet someone must pay.

Who? The Red Cross is not a government agency. We look to compassionate people like you who have a few dollars to spare. People with a heart to help those less fortunate than themselves. People who realize they may someday need our assistance.

In fact, it's a time-honored tradition as American as apple pie: an annual gift to help the Red Cross serves people in need, with no strings attached.

We hope we can count on you to make a contribution to the Red Cross this year. Could you spend $15, $35 or $50 so we can respond swiftly in time of tragedy, crisis or disaster? So we'll be there when Help Can't Wait!

You can give with confidence. Top financial magazines such as *Kiplinger's Personal Finance* and *Money* have consistently rated the Red Cross as one of the top U.S. charities in their annual reviews.

Please mail your $15, $35 or $50 gift today so we can help people in need, free.

From the Envelope:

The outpouring of support by the American people during the September 11 terrorist attacks is greatly appreciated. The American Red Cross will continue to be there providing help as long as it is needed.

In this time of national crisis, the important work of our local Red Cross chapter must go on. In addition to providing emergency relief, CPR, first aid and disaster preparedness, our local chapter also operates an Armed Forces Emergency Communications Service on behalf of families in our community with loved ones serving in the U.S. military overseas. Please support your local Red Cross today. Thank you!

Source: American Red Cross.

your audience will go a long way toward determining which appeal is likely to have the greatest effect.

For example, the Red Cross mailer uses as its theme a common misconception about the organization's services, that is, that disaster victims have to pay for assistance. In addressing this question, the Red Cross demonstrates sound persuasive strategy; raising the opposing viewpoint provides the opportunity to rebut it. It also provides the opportunity to remind the reader about the organization's services and to tug at a few heartstrings.

Timing is equally important to the success of your campaign. Andrews (1985), for example, argues that medical research is a "magic" appeal, but even diseases have their own image and timing issues with which the writer must contend. Asking for funds to combat heart disease is generally credible. In contrast, researching the common cold is not—unless the common cold appeal follows shortly after the death of a celebrity from complications of a cold.

Sweepstakes appeals traditionally guarantee a high response. However, they have received bad press from recipients who took the "Congratulations! You are a winner!" message literally and attempted to collect their prizes only to be disappointed when directed to the fine print that says, *"if* you hold the winning ticket." In light of this and the public's tendency to regard such appeals with skepticism, you must consider whether a sweepstakes approach fits your organization's image before recommending it as a communication strategy.

DISCUSSION 1

Look at the Red Cross mailer in Exhibit 15.2 in light of Andrews's (1985) "IDEA": interest, desire, explanation, action. Does the mailer follow these guidelines? Identify sections that demonstrate each of the points.

Ethical Issues

Ethics and Direct Mail—Not an Oxymoron

Just as the PRSA provides guidelines for the ethical practice of public relations, so does the Direct Marketing Association (DMA) provide such guidelines for the ethical practice of direct marketing.

Among the DMA guidelines are many that relate directly to the writers of direct marketing materials. They are equally appropriate to public relations direct mail. The DMA guidelines call for the following:

✦ *Honesty and accuracy* in text and visuals, in the presentation of test or survey data, and in the use of testimonials

✦ *Clarity* in the wording, size, placement, and duration of messages

✦ *Open disclosure* of sponsorship and purpose of messages

✦ *Avoiding deception* such as by creating documents that look like bills, invoices, or notices from official agencies

The principles also set standards for the use of words such as *free* and *guaranteed*, and for the collection and use of consumer information and mailing lists. It also defines standards for ethical fundraising.

Public relations writers for educational and nonprofit organizations especially are often responsible for writing direct mail solicitations. They should be especially aware of the DMA as well as PRSA guidelines.

The Source/Spokesperson

Remember the importance of source credibility for advocacy campaigns? The same is true for direct mail. Determining who will sign the letter and whose testimony will appear in the body can affect the success of a campaign. If you are fortunate, you will be able to find an appropriate celebrity voice to endorse your message. For example, the Muscular Dystrophy Foundation and Habitat for Humanity have long benefited from the very public support of comedian Jerry Lewis and former U.S. president Jimmy Carter (and Rosalynn Carter), respectively.

On a more common level, finding a source may mean identifying an influential alumna to sign this year's annual fund appeal to her classmates. The issues for choosing direct mail spokespersons are the same as those we discussed for advocacy campaigns. Your choice must be credible and be seen to be credible. It helps if he or she has charisma. Note how the Red Cross references credible financial sources to support the theme of fiscal responsibility.

If you have an organizational name or letterhead that is well known or that explains your purpose (e.g., Cancer Research Foundation), you may already have implicit source credibility. This is especially true of agencies associated with religious denominations. Regardless of who is quoted in the copy, readers may be predisposed to an appeal sent under the letterhead of the United Jewish Appeal or alternatively the Nation of Islam. It will be difficult for either of these organizations to convince potential donors that they are "denomination blind." People's responses will be governed more by their prior attitudes to the organization than to the worthiness of the cause or persuasiveness of the appeal.

Style

Generally, direct mail is the most overtly persuasive copy you may ever write. It leaves little doubt about its persuasive intent and it unashamedly pursues this end. However, even while being conscious of the power words and emotional appeals that we discussed in Chapter 14, direct mail must be grounded in fact and honest intentions.

The primary stylistic guide for direct mail is brevity. You have a limited amount of time to get your message across, even with a committed audience. Brief is always better.

The use of adjectives is closely related to this. The USPS has determined that adjectives are a primary difference between commercial and noncommercial mail. The USPS assesses the use of adjectives such as "fantastic," "rewarding," or "great" to distinguish mailings that are substantially related to nonprofit purposes from mailings that are primarily commercial. Adjectives and phrases such as "low-cost," "very competitive," "no annual fee," or "designed with members' needs in mind" may be sanctioned as long as the description makes up no more than 50% of the mailing piece (Campanelli, 1998). This will significantly affect your writing for nonprofit organizations.

In the same interest, remember the value of headlines, bullet points, and short paragraphs that lead the reader through the letter. At a minimum they give reader—who may scan rather than read every word—a summary of the important points.

One strength of direct mail is its ability to be targeted. You can appeal to individuals even while sending out thousands of letters. Following are but few examples of this technique. We have underscored information that could come from a mail merge database.

+ As a member of the class of <u>2006</u>, we invite you to …
+ <u>David</u>, please take a moment …
+ All of your neighbors near <u>123 Smith Street</u> …
+ As a resident of <u>Smithville</u> …

Direct mail *always* ends with a call to action. Effecting action is your purpose in writing, and all but the most naïve recipients will expect it. Examples include the following:

+ Volunteer to …
+ Join us for …
+ Ask your senator to …
+ Please return this coupon by …
+ Send your check in the enclosed postage-paid envelope.

Unlike other documents, with direct mail you also have the opportunity to effect a response. Maximize the reader's opportunity to reply by providing response information and mechanisms: return address, 800-numbers, contact information, postage-paid envelopes. The web sites of many nonprofit organizations provide the opportunity for instant reply using credit card or debit card information provided over secure connections. This benefits the organization because the money is instantly available. However, because potential donors may be wary of transmitting financial data online, you must reach them through media they use and trust.

P.S. Don't forget the all-important postscript, P.S. After the first paragraph, it's the most often read part of direct mail letters. Research shows that a P.S. works.

Design

Given the limited amount of space and time in which to deliver your message and persuade the reader to act, direct mail writing and design must work closely together. Typically, copy (what you want to say) drives design (how you present it). But visual impact attracts readers to the copy, which means that you should be prepared to edit copy to make a layout work. You may have to write additional subheads to break up the text or produce an extra copy to fill unanticipated blank space.

Once again, headings and subheadings, bold type, and bullet points help the reader understand the message. They also help you draw attention to key points. Thinking design and emphasis as you write may save you time and words.

The Red Cross mailer was printed on both sides of a 4.5″ × 8″ sheet with an attached reply envelope. At the top of the message was the word "FREE." This took advantage of that tried-and-true appeal while leading naturally into the message theme. Although the appeal message was a national theme, the text on the envelope developed a local theme to further target individual interests.

Evaluation

One of the great advantages of direct mail is the ability to continually assess results. It presents unique possibilities for testing, and it offers specific measurable results: Readers either respond or they don't. You can assess different appeals, sources, and copy by testing two versions and seeing which gets the best return. Similarly, you can test the effectiveness of time of year, envelope and letter design, offers, and premiums.

When you cannot or do not solicit a direct response, you may have to conduct a parallel research program. For example, you may conduct a telephone campaign to determine whether people received the mailing, remember the mailing, or intend to act on the mailing.

How Did They Get Your Name?

Direct mail companies get their mailing lists from compilations and response lists. Compilations are lists built from directories such as the Yellow Pages, professional organizations, town records, and newspaper reports of births, deaths, and marriages. States and municipalities may provide information from driver's licenses, vehicle registration, and town directories. Response lists include people who have responded to a phone, catalog, direct mail, or Internet solicitation. If you have entered a sweepstakes, returned a warranty card or questionnaire, or donated to a fundraiser, you will be on a mailing list somewhere. Magazine subscription lists also are an important source of response mailing lists because they so accurately reflect the subscribers' interests.

Obviously, response lists are likely to be productive because they list people who are predisposed to respond to mail or phone offers or to the topic of the direct mail piece. In Chapter 5, we discussed some of the techniques (e.g., PRIZM®) used to identify demographic groups from census data and zip codes. To a direct mail company, every demographic group is a potential mailing list.

An entire industry has been built around developing and providing mailing lists to clients seeking to target their mailings. Look for advertisements for list companies in the classified section of business magazines. In addition, the DMA includes many list marketing companies among its membership. Many of them advertise in the monthly *DM News* magazine and its online edition.

Envelopes: A Look at Direct Mail From the Outside

Generally speaking, you have only one chance to make a good impression. Research shows this to be true for employers looking at résumés, and it is no less true for consumers looking at direct mail. Remember, in the average household your mailing is competing with 30 other pieces of mail each week. How can yours stand out?

The DMA (1995, pp. 3–6) reports that, in decreasing order, people are likely to open the following:

✦ An envelope that looks like a bill
✦ A teaser package indicating a free sample or special offer
✦ A handwritten envelope

- ✦ A window envelope
- ✦ An official-looking envelope
- ✦ A colored envelope
- ✦ An envelope indicating a sweepstakes

Clearly, the packaging or appearance makes a difference, and direct mail designers are quick to capitalize on this difference. Design helps persuade readers to open the envelope. If they don't open it, then your most creative copy is wasted.

Pay attention to the direct mail that comes to your home. How many envelopes have teaser messages or are addressed in a personalized script typeface? How many are especially large or small? How many are textured or colored? How many have messages that pique your curiosity? How many feel like they have something special in them? How many are interactive? The first challenge is to get you to notice the mailer and open the envelope.

A June 2004 mailer from the Office of Institutional Advancement at Wagner College met all of these criteria. It was oversized; it was peculiarly heavy; the envelope announced, "Your Wagner College Trivia Exam is enclosed." Inside was a standard examination "blue book," familiar to students and alumni alike. The book included 26 multiple-choice trivia questions and room for one essay on the subject "describe your favorite Wagner College memory." The booklet, of course, provided the answers and a brief message from the director of development leading to a request for money.

This mailer achieved the important principle of persuasion, "get the reader involved," in several ways. Alumni recipients would have been intrigued by the envelope, amused by the sight of the blue book, and challenged by the questions. It is likely that they willingly participated in remembering their days at the college and they almost certainly reached the final message. The college hoped they also reached for their checkbooks.

There is a fine line between enticing and deceiving the reader. You may make the envelope look official, but if it "deceptively emulates official government notices," it will be subject to the restrictions and penalties of the 1990 Deceptive Mailings Prevention Act. In addition, the public is becoming inured to pseudo-official documents. One direct mail piece the authors received began with a seal certifying that the document was an "Executory Writ of Authorization." It looked official. It sounds official. But it doesn't mean anything. As far as we can tell, the document certifies that we are "registered" holders of the document. We think it means that we have been approved to open the mail that is addressed to us.

E X E R C I S E   1

The brevity needed for an envelope makes it a good exercise in concise persuasive writing. One sentence is the practical limit. Practice by writing envelope copy for a college fundraising envelope sent to alumni. Write one with a factual approach. Write one as a teaser. Write one as overt persuasion. If this sounds like the lead for feature stories, it should. They are similarly creative.

Planning

The U.S. Postal Service and Direct Mail

Just because an envelope is creative and clever does not obligate the post office to accept it. This is especially true if you want to take advantage of the automation and reduced mailing rates so critical to direct mail budgets. Automated mailing services allow addresses to be scanned and sorted automatically. Since introducing these services, the U.S. Postal Service (USPS) has tightened controls on what can be printed on an envelope and where. It also has limits on the typefaces and sizes acceptable for automated processing.

It is wise to talk with your local post office *before* you finalize a design. You would not be the first to find out when you take the mailing to the post office that you must purchase a special, expensive envelope for the mailing to be accepted. It will help your budgeting and your image as a professional if you find this out in advance. Then you can "sell" the special envelope as part of the total package.

Following are some of the USPS guidelines for positioning addresses so that they can be scanned by the optical character recognition (OCR) software that facilitates electronic mail processing.

In order to ensure that the OCR reads the mailing address and not the return address (or information not pertaining to the address), an OCR read area has been identified. All characters on the last line of the address—the post office, state and/or ZIP+4 code—must be located within the OCR read area, the boundaries of which are indicated below. (It is preferred that the other lines of the address be in the OCR read areas as well.) The OCR read area is a rectangle:

Top of rectangle:	2.25″ from bottom edge of the envelope.
Sides of rectangle:	1 inch from the left and right edges of the envelope.
Bottom of rectangle:	5/8″ from the bottom edge of the envelope (This area is reserved for bar-codes.)

Other printing or marks of any kind should not appear within the OCR read area below the delivery address line (the line containing the street address, PO Box, or route number). This includes attention lines, account numbers, underlines, boxes, computer punch holes, colored borders and similar information. If such information must be part of the address block, it should be placed on the line directly above or below the name of the recipient. Otherwise, it should be relocated to other areas of the mail piece not designated as OCR read areas or bar code read area. (USPS, 1985)

USPS regulations are available in pamphlet form or by downloading them from the USPS web site.

Labels

The issue of labels is another concern for public relations writers who appreciate that what the product looks like affects the public response. Until recently, most direct mailings were sent out with address labels. Their advantages were that they could be produced quickly and in quantity. The disadvantages still are that they scream "direct mail" and generally look unprofessional, especially if they are not applied straight. In the worst case, they actually hide part of your carefully crafted envelope message.

Fortunately, printers and mailing houses can now print an address on an envelope or the mailer itself (for a *self-mailer*). These look more professional and are usually straight and neat. Work with your printer, mail house, or internal mail department to ensure that you have the necessary postage permits in place before you need them. If you are serious about a personalized look, you will probably want to have the envelopes stamped with a real stamp rather than a bulk rate panel (called an *indicia*).

The Package

The typical direct mail package consists of one or more of the following:

- *Outer envelope*, usually with a teaser message.
- *Letter.*
- *Brochure*, for additional information.
- *"Lift note*," essentially a letter or note signed by a second person that increases or "lifts" the response rate. You might, for example, use a lift note signed by a celebrity introducing your organization's services as "the best ever" and recommending that the recipient read the direct mail message for "details that could change your life." Sometimes lift notes are printed on self-sticking notes or stationery that looks like a memo.
- *"Buckslip*," an insert the size of a dollar that details a special offer or premium.
- *Reply card*, which makes it easy for the reader to respond. Reply cards briefly reinforce the action message or quickly deliver it to those who only scan the package.
- *Business reply envelope (BRE)*; if you want a reply, this is a must.

Catalogs and Price Lists

As you become experienced, you will likely begin to see every document as a public relations opportunity. Even catalogs—important direct mail documents for many organizations—can deliver an effective public relations message in the hands of a skilled writer.

There was a time when catalogs and price lists were just that, descriptions of the item for sale and a list of the relevant prices. Today, so many marketers use them for promoting the organization's image that they are being referred to as "mag-alogs" reflecting both their magazine and catalog origins.

Humor, "how-tos," and testimonials are all part of the modern catalog. Cooking equipment marketer Williams-Sonoma, Inc., sometimes prints recipes from famous chefs in its direct mail catalogs. *The Baker's Catalog* sent by King Arthur Flour uses the same technique, except that the recipes are family favorites from the company's staff. In both cases, the recipes use the products advertised in the catalog. Just as important is the implicit endorsement of the products by the chefs or the positioning of the company as a friendly neighbor willing to share family recipes over the back fence. Similarly, a distributor of industrial fasteners designs how-to panels into its product catalog in an effort to position itself as a knowledgeable resource for its commercial clients.

DISCUSSION 2

What does the recipe source (celebrity chef or family cook) in the Williams-Sonoma and King Arthur Flour catalogs tell you about the companies and especially their corporate cultures? What does it tell you about their audiences? How might this be reflected in other documents the companies produce? Test your assumptions by comparing the recipe sections of the companies' web sites at www.williams-sonoma.com and www.kingarthurflour.com.

In the hands of writers who "think public relations," even the humble price list has potential for both sales and public relations messages. Catalogs and price lists are at the point where sales information meets public relations messages that convey favorable images about the organization. This approach is increasingly referred to as integrated communication (IC) or integrated marketing communication (IMC).

Brochures

It is no accident that this section, on brochures, follows immediately after the direct mail section; they are closely related. Brochures are conceptually similar to direct mail but they are seldom mailed or individualized. They also have a much higher presentation element. Brochures pay as much attention to design as to text and are distributed by a variety of methods besides mail.

Brochures come in all shapes, sizes, and colors. They are produced for sales and marketing, solicitation, advocacy, and education. They range from simple, one-color, text-only pamphlets to glossy, full-color, multipage corporate image books. Some fit neatly in a pocket or standard #10 business envelope; others are mailed in special envelopes. And although not yet widespread, a growing number of organizations are following the lead of web pioneers such as Nielsen/NetRatings in posting downloadable brochures on their sites.

Some brochures are stand-alone pieces, designed to be picked up from unattended display racks or exhibit booths and read sometime later. Others are support pieces designed for media or information packages or as part of a series of brochures that together tell a complete story. In many cases, budget dictates that one brochure may have to fill all of these roles. This presents a special challenge to the writer and designer to meet the needs of multiple audiences.

We include in our discussion of brochures the documents commonly termed flyers, pamphlets, leaflets, handouts, and short sheets. There is little agreement on what exactly these terms mean, so you should clarify with your printer that you are talking about the same document.

Generally, flyers are single sheets, unfolded. Brochures are most commonly a single sheet with a range of folds that bring the final product somewhere between approximately 4″ × 8.5″ (to fit in a #10 business envelope) and 8.5″ × 11″ (to fit in a full-page envelope). In fact, the size of a brochure is limited only by your budget and distribution method. At the point where pages are collated and held together with staples, it becomes a booklet. (See Chapter 7 for more information on brochures and booklets.)

Portable document format (PDF) technology has also made it possible to distribute brochures on the web. Users can access and download the file to view on screen or print.

Brochure Themes

Brochures usually deliver a single message. They introduce an organization, product, or product range. They educate readers about a subject or ask for action. Organizations with multiple messages may group them under one theme or produce multiple brochures so that audiences can select those that interest them. Hospitals often produce educational brochures on preventing heart disease, cancer, children's diseases, respiratory diseases, and home accidents as part of an overall public health promotion. The brochures are designed with a similar theme or visual signature to capitalize on the opportunity to convey the scope of the hospital's services, but different colors or cover photos make each one stand out on its own.

This should bring to mind the concept that we have repeated often throughout this text: The needs of the audience will influence both writing and design decisions. What does the audience know about the subject of the brochure? What does the audience *want* or *need* to know? How *much* information does the organization want or need to tell them? Does the audience expect a high-quality, high-cost production, or should it reflect a concern for fiscal responsibility?

As you plan the verbal theme of a brochure, you should also consider the visual and design techniques that will support this theme. Sometimes simply being creative with papers, colors and special effects can reinforce the message and increase its memorability. Exhibit 15.3 shows a brochure used by a printer to promote a new mailing service. The brochure was printed, die-cut to the shape of a business envelope, folded to the envelope shape, closed with a special "stamp," and addressed using the new mailing program. The brochure itself was an example of the service.

This only works when you can think of a simple effect that carries out the theme, but the possibilities are worth exploring when time, budget, and the message permit. Be certain that the special treatment suits the message and that the message suits the audience. Clever for the sake of being clever seldom achieves the end you are seeking.

Brochure Content

Because of the wide range of uses and topics for which brochures may be produced, it is difficult to discuss specific brochure content. The following general rules will help you make decisions regardless of the subject.

♦ *Focus on the audience's needs.* What are their needs and wants?

♦ *Make sure readers know what the brochure is about.* Why should they be interested? Quickly and clearly answer the question, "What's in it for me?"

Remember the "teaser" headlines of feature stories. Many brochures use this technique to attract attention and entice the reader into the text. Beware of being too clever or obscure, however. If the reader can answer the teaser with "I don't care," your efforts will be wasted.

EXHIBIT 15.3   Mailer die-cut in the shape of an envelope used to promote a printer's mailing services.

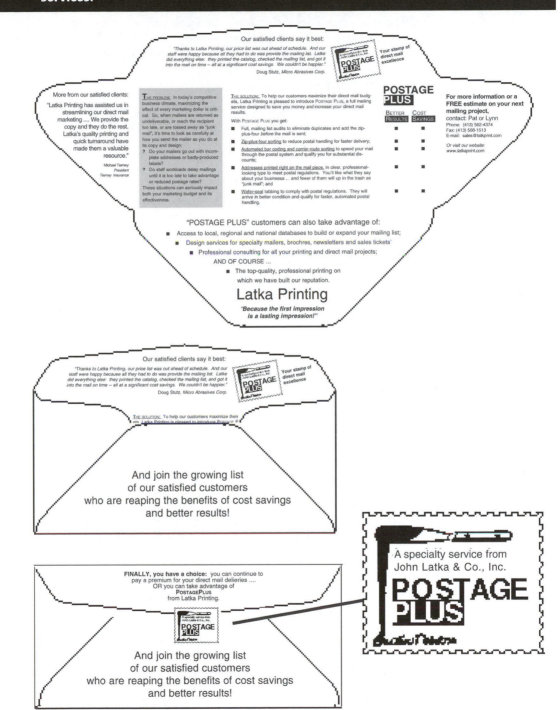

Source: Reproduced with permission from Latka Print, Westfield, Massachusetts.

◆ *Choose an appropriate appeal.* Depending on the purpose and audience, direct mail appeals have as much validity for brochures as in direct mail letters. Many brochures spur the reader to action even while seeming to be educational. There is a fine line, for example, between educating the public about a famine in Ethiopia and supporting a plea for funds for UNICEF, or between educating voters on the issues in a referendum and seeking their votes. Similarly, businesses sell products by designing brochures around a problem-solution theme using the real-life experiences of current users as examples.

◆ *Keep it brief and clear.* Generally, brochures are optional communications. Readers can ignore them with little or no consequence. This means that you have limited time in which to attract their attention and deliver your message. Don't waste it. Keep text brief, clear, and obvious.

◆ *Help the reader scan the content.* Subheads and bullet points help you organize the text and bring attention to important points. If you must present detailed information, as in a technical brochure, break it up with summaries, highlights, or "features at a glance." This will make the brochure as useful to the browser as to the committed reader. We discussed this idea of browser versus committed audience when we discussed writing for the Web in Chapter 13.

◆ *Use color wisely.* It can help the reader understand what is important and what isn't. Put supplementary information in screened boxes so it doesn't interrupt the flow of the argument.

◆ *Use graphics in place of words.* Limit charts and graphs to the important information, and write captions that reiterate the point you want to make. Even if readers only look at the graphics or read the captions, as is often the case, they will get the message.

◆ *Tell the reader who is sponsoring or producing the brochure.* You may know generally who is likely to pick it up, but that is the extent of your knowledge. And it doesn't mean they know who you are. Even brochures mailed to target audiences may have a large, unknown, pass-along readership. This may be a good opportunity to use a version of the boilerplate paragraph.

◆ *Tell the audience what you want them to do.* If you want a contribution, say so, and include instructions and perhaps a tear-off form for the contribution. If you want to sell a product or service, provide a list of the nearest distributors or sales representatives or the URL of a web site that has such a list.

◆ *Provide contact information.* Every brochure should have at least a phone number at which the reader can contact the organization. Most brochures now also include fax numbers, e-mail addresses, and web site URLs. If you expect readers to respond by mail, then a full street address is also a must.

This raises an oft-debated issue of whether to include personal contact details, such as sales representatives' names. Frankly, we've learned the hard way and vote "no" on the issue. The danger of having the named representative leave the organization or change positions within months of printing thousands of brochures is greater than you think. Consider one of the following options so all of your hard work and the organization's money is not wasted:

Print only a head office number and e-mail addresses for sales, customer service department, or development offices.

Have slots die-cut into the brochure to hold personalized business cards.

Print some brochures with no contacts to use as a back up for new representatives, changed addresses, or new phone numbers.

Print all brochures with no contacts and have stamps or labels made for each office. This is not a particularly classy solution, but for brochures distributed from many offices, it is practical. The point is to keep brochures current as long as they are relevant.

♦ *Consider format and folds as you plan the copy.* If you have a three-panel layout, do not set the text in two columns. It is distracting to have text printed across a fold. Use the folds as gutters between columns even if you create design areas that span more than one column.

♦ *Think of the brochure as multiple levels of layout.* The design should be balanced at each level. Is the front panel a good layout? What about the back panel? Each is likely to be viewed on its own.

Now open the brochure—what does the viewer see? In the case of two-fold, six-panel brochures, it will be the left inside panel and the flap. In the case of a gate-fold, it will be the two gate panels. What does this look like as a layout? It should be balanced and the relationship between the panels should be clear.

Now open the brochure completely. Again, how does it look? Do the panels relate to each other? Do viewers know where they are? Can they find the information quickly and easily?

Exhibit 15.4 is the brochure for the EPA Childhood Asthma Campaign we discussed in Chapter 13. It illustrates many of the brochure content principles described above. It also illustrates the close relationship between writing for

EXHIBIT 15.4   Brochure from the EPA Childhood Asthma Campaign.

"I FEEL LIKE **A FISH** WITH NO WATER."

–JACOB, AGE 5
DESCRIBING ASTHMA

You know how to react to their asthma attacks. Here's how to prevent them.

EVEN ONE ATTACK IS ONE TOO MANY.

EXHIBIT 15.4 (Continued)

 IF YOU HAVE A CHILD WITH ASTHMA, YOU'RE NOT ALONE.

Asthma is a chronic disease which causes ongoing swelling of the airways. When certain "triggers" such as dust, smog, pet dander or secondhand smoke enter the airways, they may become irritated and constricted. This makes it difficult to breathe. If you have a child with asthma, you're not alone. More than 17 million people in the U.S. have asthma and the number is growing, especially among children. However, there's good news. You can help manage your child's asthma and help prevent their attacks before they happen.

HOW TO MANAGE YOUR CHILD'S INDOOR ENVIRONMENT

Americans spend about 90% of their time indoors. So, managing your child's indoor environment is an important step in reducing exposure to the things that can trigger asthma attacks. Asthma triggers vary from person to person. You and your doctor should determine a plan to reduce the triggers that most affect your child. Listed below are several common indoor environmental triggers and some actions you can take to reduce your child's exposure.

SECONDHAND SMOKE

Asthma can be triggered by the smoke from the burning end of a cigarette, pipe, or cigar, or the smoke breathed out by a smoker.

WHAT YOU CAN DO: Choose not to smoke in your home or car, and do not allow others to do so either.

PETS

Your pet's skin flakes, urine, and saliva can be asthma triggers.

WHAT YOU CAN DO: Consider keeping pets outdoors or even finding a new home for your pets, if necessary. Keep pets out of the bedroom and other sleeping areas at all times, and keep the door closed. Keep pets away from fabric-covered furniture, carpets and stuffed toys.

DUST MITES

Dust mites are too small to be seen, but are found in every home. They live in mattresses, pillows, carpets, fabric-covered furniture, bedcovers, clothes, and stuffed toys.

WHAT YOU CAN DO: Wash sheets and blankets once a week in hot water. Choose washable stuffed toys, wash them often in hot water, and dry thoroughly. Keep stuffed toys off beds. Cover mattresses and pillows in dust-proof (allergen-impermeable) zippered covers.

PESTS

Droppings or body parts of pests such as cockroaches or rodents can be asthma triggers.

WHAT YOU CAN DO: Do not leave food or garbage out. Store food in airtight containers. Clean all food crumbs or spilled liquids right away. Try using poison baits, boric acid (for cockroaches), or traps first before using pesticide sprays. If sprays are used, limit the spray to the infested area. Carefully follow instructions on the label. Make sure there is plenty of fresh air when you spray, and keep the person with asthma out of the room.

MOLDS

Molds grow on damp materials. The key to mold control is moisture control. If mold is a problem in your home, clean up the mold and get rid of excess water or moisture. Lowering the moisture also helps reduce other triggers, such as dust mites and cockroaches.

WHAT YOU CAN DO: Wash mold off hard surfaces and dry completely. Absorbent materials with mold, such as ceiling tiles and carpet, may need to be replaced. Fix leaky plumbing or other sources of water. Use exhaust fans or open windows in kitchens and bathrooms when showering, cooking, or using the dishwasher. Vent clothes dryers to the outside. Maintain low indoor humidity, ideally between 30-50%.

TO SPEAK WITH AN INFORMATION SPECIALIST ABOUT ASTHMA AND ENVIRONMENTAL TRIGGERS, PLEASE CALL 1-800-315-8056.

For more information, contact one of the organizations below:

U.S. Environmental Protection Agency
Indoor Air Quality Information Clearinghouse
(800) 438-4318
www.epa.gov/iaq/asthma

American Academy of Allergy, Asthma and Immunology
(800) 822-2762
www.aaaai.org

Allergy and Asthma Network/Mothers of Asthmatics, Inc.
(800) 878-4403
www.aanma.org

American Lung Association
(800) LUNG-USA
www.lungusa.org

Asthma and Allergy Foundation of America
(800) 7ASTHMA
www.aafa.org

National Asthma Education and Prevention Program
Guidelines for the Diagnosis and Management of Asthma, 1997
(301) 592-8573

This publication was developed under a cooperative agreement with the U.S. Environmental Protection Agency.

EVEN ONE ATTACK IS ONE TOO MANY | I-866-NO-ATTACKS | WWW.NOATTACKS.ORG

EXHIBIT 15.4 (Continued)

KEYS TO PREVENTING YOUR CHILD'S ATTACK

- Work with a doctor to develop a written *Asthma Management Plan* that's right for you and your child.

- Learn what triggers your child's asthma and eliminate or reduce your child's exposure to those allergens and irritants.

- Make sure your child takes medications as prescribed and tell your doctor if there are any problems.

- Keep a daily symptom diary and use a peak flow meter every day to monitor your child's progress.

WHAT IS AN ASTHMA MANAGEMENT PLAN?

Written details by your physician should include:

- A list of your child's asthma triggers

- Instructions for using asthma medication(s)

- Instructions for using a daily symptom diary and peak flow meter

- Details about how to stop an asthma attack or episode in progress

- Instructions for when to call the doctor

Source: Reproduced with permission from the U.S. Department of Environmental Protection.

brochures and writing for the Web, both of which require brevity, clear headlines, and attention to bullets or other graphic "road signs" to guide even casual browsers through the information. See Exhibit 13.2 for comparison.

Signs

Traditional print media are not the only way to bring an organization's position to the attention of your target audience. Consider as alternatives the signs and billboards that appear on lawns, telephone poles, and along major highways before referenda or elections in which social issues are at stake. And remember the lowly bumper sticker that not only spreads your message but also, by virtue of being on someone's car, implicitly expresses the owner's support for your position.

Regardless of the size, signs are meant to be read "on the fly," perhaps in as little as 3 seconds. This dictates *simplicity*. Often just the campaign theme with a recognizable graphic or color scheme is sufficient. Signs are discussed in detail in Chapter 16.

Proposals and Grants

For many organizations, formal written proposals and grants or case statements are an important means of soliciting new business or funding. Nonprofit organizations in particular rely on funds distributed by government agencies, corporations, and private foundations. For them, grant writing is a critical public relations task. Experienced grant writers with a proven track record of success are highly sought after.

The commercial equivalent of grant writing is proposal writing. Proposals are a common and often necessary way of presenting an organization's expertise to prospective clients. The proposal must demonstrate that your organization is more experienced or better suited to provide products, services, or support than any of the other organizations that have submitted their own proposals.

Grants and proposals are, by definition, competitive documents. Because they target major new contracts or funds that directly affect the future of the organization, they are highly persuasive. At the same time, the persuasion must be tightly controlled and often subtle.

Proposals and grants are generally part of a formal, competitive process in which an organization seeking contractors or a foundation seeking projects to fund issues a document that lists the requirements and asks interested organizations to respond. In the commercial and government worlds, these documents are known as requests for proposal (RFPs) or invitations to bid (ITBs). In the funding world, they are grant applications.

In either case, the response must be written to the specifications set out by the organization asking for the proposal. You might think of these as "audience driven"; the audience tells you what it wants to know, when it wants to know it, and sometimes the format in which it wants the answers. Some even limit the number of pages. As long as all proposals are subject to the same conditions, the details should not matter.

Proposals

In theory, most business proposals are strictly objective. They are evaluated according to published evaluation points and the "winner" is the proposal that accumulates the most points. In practice, there is usually room for a subjective level of persuasion. Learning to develop proposal strategy to maximize points on an evaluation will be part of a new writer's learning curve about accepted practices in the industry. You will learn to tread a fine line between strictly presenting facts and finding ways to subtly weave a persuasive message through those facts.

The most important part of responding to an RFP is just that: *respond* to the agency's requirements and make it clear that you are being responsive. When in doubt, make reference to the RFP section you are answering. Instead of lengthy explanations, use subheads and bullet points to emphasize your organization's capabilities.

RFPs for goods and services clearly differ, but both center on what you, the respondent, can do for the issuing organization. Common topics include the following:

✦ *Introduction/executive summary.* Because it is the first impression, this may be the most important part of a proposal. It prepares the evaluation team to expect that your proposal will meet their needs (or alternatively that it will not). Think bullet points and strong verbs to bring to the fore what the organization can do. Work examples of success (as brief teasers) into the summary and include details in the relevant part of the proposal.

✦ *Personnel expertise (especially for service programs).* This can be management only, all employees, or specific named positions. Discussion may range from recruiting and hiring practices and staff training to the company's safety record. This is a good use for that stack of bios you have on the shelf.

◆ *Organizational experience and expertise.* These are usually a review of the organization's relevant contracts and achievements and a list of references who will likely be contacted to verify your claims.

◆ *Technical proposal.* The technical proposal is the meat of a business proposal. It focuses on how you will fulfill the terms of the contract under offer. It tells the reader what you can do and what benefits the reader will get for his or her money.

Your most important tasks as a writer will be to determine how much detail is appropriate and how to pack the proposal with relevant proof that your organization is the most capable of all the competitors. Think specifics. Don't just say your employer can do it; tell how. Better yet, tell how you have done it before—better, faster, and more successfully. This is similar to the techniques for writing a successful letter of application.

◆ *Cost proposal.* This is sometimes one or two lines, sometimes many pages. It tells the reader what your product or program will cost. Typically, this weighs heavily in the evaluation.

Cost proposals may be subject to strict limitations on the inclusion of any persuasive text. Even if you can, it is wise to keep it to a minimum because of the danger it will be seen as public relations hype rather than legitimate argument. In all cases, the proposal content must demonstrate that the services/products proposed are well worth the proposed price.

Nonprofit Grants

Grants and case statements are a special form of audience-driven proposals. They are used by nonprofit organizations to apply for funds from the thousands of private, corporate, and community agencies that give out billions of dollars in grants every year. The key to winning a grant is to demonstrate that your project will achieve a worthwhile aim (that is also supported by the granting agency). You must also show that your organization is capable of administering the funds to achieve that aim.

Let's look at the situation from the viewpoint of a charitable foundation. Such foundations have a mission to support specific types of programs such as health, community development, or education. As long as a project falls under that mission, the foundation does not care who is awarded a grant. Its concern is funding programs that are needed and that have a realistic chance of success.

This is a clue for you as a grant writer. Focus first on the program. Discussion of the organization should be limited to its experience and ability to administer that program. Taking a leaf from the cover letter for a job application we discussed in Chapter 2, don't just claim to be knowledgeable and capable—prove it through hard evidence and well thought out examples and research. Leave the foundation with no doubt that your organization knows what it is doing and has fairly evaluated the project before asking for funds.

The Foundation Center (2004) suggests a six-part format that will suffice for many grants. It resembles the report formats discussed in Chapter 8.

✦ *Executive summary.* Summarize the proposal.

✦ *Statement of need.* Explain the needs your program will meet or the problems it will address. Be specific and realistic. Granting agencies are unlikely to fund a project for "eliminating poverty in an area of a city." They may look favorably, however, on funding free day care for mothers on welfare while they are enrolled in the local job corps training program. While eliminating poverty may be the objective of both programs, the second is realistic and achievable. It shows that your organization understands not only the benefits but also the pitfalls and difficulties of the program. This is an important public relations message.

✦ *Project description.* Include goals, methods, and evaluation. Clear goals demonstrate your understanding of the issue and what you believe you can achieve. Be sure they are realistic and manageable. How will the program work? What resources will you need? Defining how you will evaluate success demonstrates professionalism and understanding of the project.

✦ *Budget.* How will the grant money be spent?

✦ *Organization information.* What is your organization (be brief)? Why is it qualified to manage the program for which you are seeking a grant? This question is critical. Your aim is to establish credibility, so if the organization has a track record of successful project management, say so.

✦ *Conclusion.* Recap the proposal's main points.

These are guidelines only. Most foundations provide a guide to what they require, sort of a nonprofit RFP, and some use a form for both content and budget. The Foundation Center web site is an excellent source of information on available grants and grant writing.

Source-Driven or Organization-Driven Proposals

In addition to audience-driven proposals produced in response to an RFP or grant application, some proposals are initiated by the organization and used as a routine part of the normal marketing or fundraising process. They are stand-alone documents sent when a hot prospect says, "Do you have anything in writing on that?" or "Send more information about your services." With some individualized content, they are also used as follow-ups to sales calls.

Some industries thrive on such proposals. They have a standard proposal that can be sent as a generic document or personalized to individual target audiences. Advances in word processing software make it easy to completely tailor a proposal template to a prospect's interests. You compile the document from a library of stock paragraphs, chapters, subjects, and graphics.

Standard proposals are a double-edged sword. On one hand, they offer the opportunity to provide interested readers with a high level of detail about the organization and its services. On the other hand, if they do not quickly answer the questions, "What's in this for me? and "Where can I find the information I really want?" they quickly become overkill, even for the committed reader.

Standard proposals generally take their format from reports. They start with an executive summary that provides the relevant facts in one or two pages (maximum). Details follow in clearly marked sections that readers can read or pass over, depending on their interest. Graphics attract attention to important messages and explain relevant but complex ideas, processes, or relationships.

A common dilemma for proposal writers is where to draw the line between generalizations and detail. If the audience is not technologically savvy, then the effort you put into explaining a new computer system will be wasted. You would be better served by a brief explanation of what the new system will mean to the audience with the specifications presented in an appendix. This resolves the dilemma of how much detail is too much and allows your employer's capabilities to be fairly evaluated by readers who will appreciate the technical detail as well as those who simply want to know what the system does. This is yet another example of the benefit of knowing your audiences and writing to their level of experience and education.

Before you invest time and money in a sophisticated standard proposal, however, consider whether this is the most effective medium for the message. Many organizations produce videos or short computer– or CD-ROM–based presentations that the audience can plug and play in far less time than it would take to read a multipage document. You will be able to take prospects on a tour of the plant or demonstrate the effectiveness of new product innovations. Improvements in technology will soon allow you to tailor these presentations to individual audiences just as word processing currently allows the production of individually targeted written documents.

ON THE TEXTBOOK WEB SITE

✦ Go to www.sagepub.com/treadwell for web exercises, study hints, case studies, and additional examples appropriate to this chapter and chosen or developed to supplement the chapter content.

WRITING WRAP-UP

1. The campus club or organization you identified as a client in the "Writing Wrap-Up" in Chapter 3 is beginning a drive for new members. Using the information you have already gathered on this organization, write the following:

   ✦ A direct mail piece to prospective members soliciting involvement in the organization.
   ✦ A brochure that introduces the organization.

REFERENCES

Andrews, F. S. (1985). *Billions by mail . . . Fund raising in the computer age.* Lincoln, MA: TaborOaks.

Campanelli, M. (1998, January 5). Nonprofits expect simplified rules, *DM News,* p. 3.

Direct Marketing Association. (1995). *1994–95 statistical fact book.* New York: Direct Marketing Association.

Direct Marketing Association. (2003, October 12). *Landmark study finds nonprofit fundraisers and retail stores report top direct & interactive marketing response rates* [News release]. Retrieved March 18, 2004, from http://www.the-dma.org/cgi/disppressrelease?article=520

Foundation Center. (2004). *Proposal writing short course.* Retrieved March 27, 2004, from www.foundationcenter.org

U.S. Postal Service. (1985, May). Addressing for automation, Notice 221. See also "C830 OCR Standards." Retrieved January 6, 1999, from http://pe.usps.gov

U.S. Postal Service. (2004, January). *Postal facts.* Retrieved March 18, 2004, from http://www.usps.com/communications/organization/postalfacts.htm

Universal Postal Union. (2004). *What we do: Direct mail.* Site updated January 2004. Retrieved March 23, 2004, from http://www.upu.int/direct_mail/en/index.shtml

RESOURCES

Direct Mail

Direct Marketing Association .... www.the-dma.org

U.S. Postal Service .... www.usps.gov

Proposals and Grants

Foundation Center .... www.foundationcenter.org

GovCon Marketplace (for government contractors) .... www.govcon.com

Independent Sector (research on .... www.independentsector.org
nonprofit giving and volunteering)

U.S. Department of Commerce's .... cbdnet.access.gpo.gov
Commerce Business Daily

Featured Organizations

American Red Cross .... www.redcross.org

EPA Childhood Asthma Campaign .... www.noattacks.org

Foundation Center .... www.foundationcenter.org

16

High-Profile Projects

Annual Reports, Events, and Exhibitions

1. **Annual reports, events, and exhibitions are high-profile projects that attract public attention.**

2. **Annual reports, events, and exhibitions require extreme amounts of organization, coordination, and planning.**

3. **Corporate annual reports are legal and public relations documents.**

4. **You can and should "think public relations" when writing annual reports.**

5. **Events require public relations writing before, during, and after.**

6. **Design for conferences.**

1. **Annual reports—meeting financial disclosure obligations.**

2. **Annual reports—sending public relations messages to investors and donors.**

3. **Writing for events—taking advantage of the opportunities in invitations, speeches, and information kits.**

4. **Writing for trade shows and exhibitions—uniting advertising, display, and personal communications.**

If you look at public relations writing as a means of helping organizations establish and maintain relationships with publics, then all of your writing is important. Even the lowly "social notes" column of the employee newsletter plays a role in the organization's relationships with its internal "family."

There are, however, some projects that stand out as special by virtue of their size, their cost, the time they take, or their potential to impact the organization. Some may be one-time projects such as a capital campaign to raise funds for a new building or the celebration of a significant anniversary. Others, including annual reports, trade shows, and staff recognition ceremonies, may repeat but less frequently than, for example, newsletters.

Special projects are deadline driven, high cost, and important. They have the ability to impact both the organization and your career. They will challenge your best abilities to organize, strategize, and write. Completing them successfully is very satisfying.

Because of their size, it is likely that you will work on such projects as part of a team until you have the experience in the organization and the industry to manage them yourself. Managing such projects will mark your coming of age as a professional public relations writer.

Planning

A Special Project

One way in which the magnitude of special projects differs from media releases, newsletters, brochures, and speeches is in the level of planning required to pull them together. Annual reports, conference participation, and trade shows typically involve many people. You need them to provide ideas, information, graphic skills, display skills, and yes, funding.

This planning demands that you manage not only *your* time and resources but also the time and talents of others on whose input you depend. This may include public relations staff, freelance writers, designers, display companies, accountants, web managers, and colleagues in advertising, sales, or marketing, to name but a few.

Although simple "to do" lists and project checklists may help you manage routine communications, planning special projects requires a more comprehensive process. You need a system capable of tracking multiple documents and changing schedules and deadlines.

A simple web search will identify many products and services to help you manage large projects. You can even use spreadsheet programs such as Excel to produce some of them.

This chapter discusses three of the most common special projects that a public relations writer may become involved in. They are the annual report, a special event such as a grand opening, and support for a trade show, exhibition, or convention.

Annual Reports

Annual reports are statements of an organization's activities for a 12-month accounting period—its financial, or fiscal, year. They are mandated for public companies by the SEC and are a staple for most nonprofit organizations that want to demonstrate their fiscal responsibility. Annual reports are typically a big deal. Even for cost-conscious nonprofit organizations, annual reports are special. For public companies, they may be the most elaborate documents of the year.

Annual reports typically have two sections: a narrative that describes the organization's activities during the reporting year, and a financial section of audited financial accounts. For nonprofit organizations, the reported financials may only include balance sheets and statements of income, but for public companies they include the full auditor's report.

An *American Demographics* study (Fulkerson, 1996) found that two-thirds of portfolio managers and over 50% of security analysts believe that annual reports are the most important document a public company can produce. Eight of 10 portfolio managers and 75% of security analysts say they use annual reports when making investment decisions. Clearly, a great deal is resting on at least corporate annual reports.

Annual Reports as Financial Documents

The primary purpose of an annual report is to report on the organization's fiscal management and financial condition. For public companies, the audience is shareholders. For nonprofit organizations, it is donors.

For public companies, the SEC mandates much of the report content as well as the audience and timing. Although it would seem that the "annual" in annual reports would remove any concern about control over timing, for public companies it indicates an even greater concern. Annual reports are so-called because of their relation to the annual meetings and elections of directors that are mandated by the SEC. The timing of the report is similarly mandated, and you must be careful to meet it.

Annual Reports as Public Relations Documents

Once you have met statutory requirements and provided financial information for shareholders, annual reports have the potential to become public relations documents. Insofar as organizations see audiences for their reports beyond those defined by the SEC, you may be challenged to produce reports that combine advertising, marketing, and public relations messages. As part of their employee communication programs, many organizations now produce annual reports aimed specifically at employees.

Historically, companies viewed annual reports only as a financial obligation. They either failed to recognize or denied their public relations value. Many concurred with the sentiments of mail-order company Great Universal Stores (GUS) executive Paul Cooper, who said, "We simply don't see the annual report as a great exercise in corporate communications. . . . Ours comply with statutory requirements and that's as far as it goes. Our selling documents are our . . . catalogues" ("It's the Results," 1996, p. 12).

Annual Reports as Social Responsibility Documents

By the end of the 20th century, attitudes toward annual reports had changed dramatically. Today, publics demand greater accountability. Legislation such as the Sarbanes-Oxley Act puts the onus on executives to sign off on the accuracy of report content. And movements toward social responsibility influence both corporate actions and reporting.

These developments are reflected in annual report narratives that act as a forum for the organization's views on social issues such as diversity, product safety, and the environment. Financial information is downplayed in the narrative in favor of addressing publics' interests in social, environmental, human rights, and ethical performance. Many companies, General Motors among them, produce separate social responsibility reports in addition to their annual reports.

Recognizing the growing importance of such corporate citizenship reporting (and the need to ensure that it remained as honest and credible as its aim), the United Nations Environment Programme launched the Global Reporting Initiative (GRI) in 2001. GRI has developed and encourages the use of standard guidelines for preparing sustainability, social, or environmental reports. The program encourages the reporting of "relevant and credible corporate environmental, social and economic performance information to enhance responsible decision-making" on an international scale (GRI, 2003b).

Among the more than 300 companies that have already cited use of the GRI guidelines in their reporting are U.S. corporate giants Hewlett Packard, General Motors, Johnson & Johnson, Nike, and 3M (GRI, 2003a). Public relations writers will want to be aware of and to heed such guidelines to help their organizations meet growing demands for social accountability from their global publics.

Organizations that choose to issue multiple reports must ensure that the message is consistent across all reports.

D I S C U S S I O N   1

How would you expect the annual reports of General Motors, your college or university, your local United Way, and Apple Computer to differ with respect to

✦ audience
✦ style
✦ content

Annual Reports for Public Companies

Financial Reporting Under SEC Regulations

For a publicly traded company, the annual report is a legal document. It must provide content that the SEC has determined must appear, sometimes in a precisely defined way. Producing the annual report for such a company requires coordination among the legal, financial, management, and public relations sectors of the organization.

Specific SEC requirements can be found in what are commonly known as "10-K" regulations (17 CFR §240.14a, "Information to be furnished to security holders"). These requirements include (but are not limited to) the following.

✦ Audited balance sheets, statements of income, and cash flows
✦ An opinion from the auditing firm and discussion of changes and disagreements
✦ Analysis by management of the company's financial condition and operations
✦ Disclosures about market risk
✦ Names and descriptions of all subsidiaries
✦ Name, occupation, and employment of each director and executive officer
✦ Information about the company's common equity securities

These requirements dictate how the organization's accounting is audited and reported. Generally, you will rely on the organization's auditors to ensure compliance with the financial regulations. However, you may find yourself the "expert" on the provisions regarding type style, size, and leading and on using tables, charts, and illustrations. You should also be familiar with sections mandating whom the report must be sent to.

You may also be enlisted to ensure that the reporting meets the SEC initiative for "plain English." Since August 1998, the SEC publication "A Plain English Handbook on How to Create Clear SEC Disclosure Documents" has been available on the SEC web site. This document is the result of the call by SEC chairman Arthur Levitt for the elimination of "gobbledygook." To keep up-to-date with issues regarding annual reports, you may want to monitor the web sites of the SEC and individual stock exchanges.

Companies not subject to SEC disclosure requirements may or may not choose to publish annual reports. This includes all privately held companies—those not listed on the stock exchanges. Most of them do not produce such reports.

The financial review and analysis are typically printed at the end of the narrative, often distinguished by different paper stock or color ink. Sometimes the financial information is bound separately and inserted in a pocket in the back of the narrative report. This allows the narrative to be used independently as a public relations piece.

The Narrative

The SEC also has a concern for annual report narrative. Its interest is that the financial information including the interpretation that you provide to the public is the same as that reported to the SEC. You must also ensure that the narrative, photos, and graphs are not misleading or deceptive. The SEC has the same concern with media releases or other documents that can influence an organization's stock price.

Outside of the financial documentation, annual reports are carefully constructed combinations of narrative and visuals that relate the organization's performance to its key publics. You will be responsible for seeing that the narrative fulfills the organization's purpose. This may include positioning the company as an attractive investment and/or as a leader in social responsibility. Either way, you will have to develop a theme and style that have credibility and instill confidence in the audience.

Some annual reports are highly theme oriented. The narrative and possibly the CEO's message focus on a theme related to an industry, societal, or environmental issue. More commonly, they use a theme of growth, success, or achievement.

Your personal resource file should include annual reports to provide ideas on what other organizations are saying and how they handle issues that may affect your organization. There are also many web sources through which you can order annual reports, and many public companies post and archive their annual reports on their web sites.

It stands to reason that if the annual report is the most important document your employer will produce, then it merits your best writing. Attention to writing should guide all of the report narrative.

Annual report narratives typically include the following:

- A letter from the chairman, president, or CEO.
- A description of the organization and summary of operations.
- Personnel or operational features and highlights, reports from other managers, new products or services, historical facts or advocacy or public interest messages. Some organizations even include advertising for their divisions and products.
- Photos, artwork, and charts.

The Chairman's Message

Whether you or your chairman/CEO/president actually writes the message will be a function of your corporate culture as well as how well your CEO writes and how much time he or she has. If you write it, it must reflect the CEO's style and he or she must approve it. It should express the CEO's ideas and ideally his or her personality. It should also use the title that he or she prefers, which may be legally required, and that reflects organizational culture, for example, chairman or chairperson.

CEO messages discuss the organization's performance over the reporting period and provide an outlook on the future. The message reflects, or introduces, the theme of the report if there is one. Occasionally, the CEO serves as spokesperson for an advocacy issue of concern to the organization. If the CEO chooses to address such issues, it should not be at the expense of reporting on performance in compliance with SEC guidelines.

Regardless of who writes the message, it should be direct, open, and honest. If the organization has a policy of open disclosure, the CEO message will set the stage for it. CEO messages may have to overcome an inherent skepticism on the part of the readers. This skepticism makes them doubt the truth of positive messages as well as the whole truth of negative ones.

Annual reports offer a number of positioning options. The CEO letter is an opportunity to stroke management egos or give readers reasons to stay or become involved with the organization. And insofar as there is an internal constituency of readers, the report may also become part of a political balancing act as divisions or departments fight to interpret the message.

Annual Report Features

Features are optional. They are most common when annual reports have a theme. However, even without a theme, features support the organization's achievements and success. They inspire confidence in and loyalty to the organization.

Annual report features may take any of the forms discussed in the "Feature Writing" section of Chapter 10, although we caution that humor is a seldom-used approach. They appeal to readers who may not be interested in financial details or even in what the CEO has to say. They do, however, present a message consistent with the rest of the report. They may be the basis on which readers with a peripheral interest decide to invest in or contribute to the organization.

Highlights

Annual report studies show that most readers do not read the report cover to cover. Accordingly, the writer faces the challenge of bringing the important messages to the reader's attention. One way to do this is through highlights, another version of the bullet points we have discussed throughout this text. For annual reports, highlights are a series of short facts that individually describe specific activities or results and together paint a picture of success and achievement. Even if the reader sees only these highlights, he or she will get the message of success.

What you select as highlights depends, of course, on the organization's industry and what happened during the year. Examples include the following:

✦ Records (e.g., revenue, profit, contributions, or patients served)
✦ The "new" (e.g., premises, products, types of business, or programs)

◆ Milestones (e.g., anniversaries, number of loans recovered, or patients X-rayed)

◆ Industry achievements (e.g., awards or recognitions)

Highlights should be positive, interesting to your audiences, and recognizable as important.

Exhibit 16.1 is a section of highlights from the 2002 Pfizer Annual Report. The topics are 12 months of honors, awards, and recognitions. Although not every organization can fill a highlights panel with such success, if you have the opportunity, seize it.

In particular, look carefully at the technique used by the Pfizer writers in presenting the highlights. Rather than just listing the honors (which might appear self-serving), they chose to quote the people and organizations that bestowed the honors. This adds third-party credibility to the accomplishments. It is good "public relations thinking."

EXHIBIT 16.1   Excerpts from the highlights of the Pfizer 2002 Annual Report.

A YEAR OF ACCOMPLISHMENT

IN 2001, PFIZER ESTABLISHED A NEW MISSION: TO BECOME THE WORLD'S MOST VALUED COMPANY TO PATIENTS, CUSTOMERS, COLLEAGUES, INVESTORS, BUSINESS PARTNERS AND THE COMMUNITIES WHERE WE WORK AND LIVE. IN 2002, WE MADE SIGNIFICANT PROGRESS WITH EACH OF THESE STAKEHOLDERS.

JANUARY	Pfizer is named by *Fortune* magazine as one of the 100 best companies to work for in America. Two-thirds of the score is based on employee surveys.
MARCH	Pfizer Chairman and CEO Hank McKinnell is named one of 25 appointees to the Presidential Advisory Council on HIV/AIDS, which provides recommendations on ways to ensure the highest-quality research, prevention and treatment for this terrible disease.
MAY	Pfizer dedicates a new research and development campus in La Jolla, California, bolstering its commitment to R&D on the West Coast. California Governor Gray Davis says, "This new facility is an economic crown jewel and a crucible of creativity. Lives will be saved because of the people at this site."
JULY	Pfizer is ranked as the world's most generous company by *The Chronicle of Philanthropy*, a leading newspaper for foundations and nonprofit organizations.
SEPTEMBER	*Med Ad News*, a leading pharmaceutical trade publication, names Pfizer its "company of the year," citing our consistent financial growth, the depth and breadth of our pipeline, and the strength of our current product portfolio.
NOVEMBER	Listerine PocketPaks are named by *Time* magazine as one of the best inventions of 2002.
ALREADY IN 2003	Hank McKinnell is named the top CEO in the pharmaceutical industry by *Institutional Investor* magazine. • Pfizer launches the Global Health Fellows program, which will enable 20 colleagues to use their skills to assist nongovernmental organizations in the fight against HIV/AIDS and other diseases that plague the developing world. Fellows will continue to receive their full pay and benefits, and Pfizer also will cover all costs associated with their assignments.

Source: Reproduced with permission from Pfizer, Inc.

Writing Highlights for Annual Reports

Regardless of the highlight topic, you must remember the rules of parallel structure and write them so they flow as a group. It might help to read them aloud so you can hear when one or more of them do not fit with the rest.

For example, the following list might be the notes you make when considering what to highlight. These are all achievements worthy of special mention, but they have no unity. They do not all follow naturally from a single headline and they have no impact.

- ✦ Sold 4 million units.
- ✦ We earned $12 million profit.
- ✦ New office opened.
- ✦ 32 new clients signed contracts.
- ✦ 25th anniversary.
- ✦ Won United Way trophy for greatest percentage of donations for third year.

The following examples demonstrate how the achievements listed above can be expressed to support different headlines and how different details support different highlights. Each highlight individually completes the underlined headline.

"During the past year we ..." (This heading requires a past-tense verb to start all highlights.)

- ✦ Sold 4 million units—1 million more than last year.
- ✦ Earned $12 million profit—a new record.
- ✦ Opened a new office in Morrisville—to serve our NS clients.
- ✦ Signed 32 new clients to contracts—worth $5 million.
- ✦ Celebrated our 25th anniversary—with parties at all company offices.
- ✦ Won the United Way trophy—for the highest percentage of staff participating among all Mansfield Chamber of Commerce members.

"During the past year our achievements included..." (To achieve parallel structure with this heading, begin each highlight with a gerund, i.e., a verb used as a noun such as "selling" or "signing.")

- ✦ Selling 4 million units.
- ✦ Earning a $12 million profit.
- ✦ Opening a new office in Morrisville.
- ✦ Signing 32 new clients.
- ✦ Celebrating our 25th anniversary.
- ✦ Winning the United Way trophy for highest percentage participation.

"The numbers tell the story of our year's success..." (Begin each highlight with a number, preferably listing them in increasing or decreasing order to give them direction and meaning.)

- ✦ 32 new clients.
- ✦ 25 proud years in business.
- ✦ $12 million profit.
- ✦ 4 million units sold.
- ✦ 3 years of United Way leadership.
- ✦ 1 new office.

Choose highlights to coincide with audience interests and write them to send a public relations message. Look for strong verbs that actively express what happened in the most positive way. Strong verbs involve the reader. They help the reader understand and identify with what happened. Readers who understand are also inclined to support the organization. Keep the points parallel to lead the reader through them.

Financial Information: The Writer's Challenge

Although the financial reporting is the responsibility of accountants and auditors, you may well have the task of translating the numbers into terms and references that lay audiences can understand quickly and easily.

In most cases, "translating" financial data means creating charts or graphs that summarize pages of numbers into easily understood verbal concepts or visuals. Although the detail is gone, the concept remains. For example, few readers may care that the company spent $1,250,362 on facilities and $5,001,448 on salaries. However, they may find it interesting that the organization spent four times as much on salaries as on facilities. This can be expressed in words or graphics. Either way, it is a more understandable and useful expression of the numbers than the numbers themselves.

Interpreting "the numbers" is a particularly contentious issue. In the aftermath of SEC investigations and many companies having to "restate their earnings," it is an issue at the core of public suspicion of corporate reporting. Public relations writers who must deal often with financial reporting may find it useful to take a course in public accounting. It will familiarize you with accounting terminology and help you recognize information that should be interpreted for one or more publics. See the glossary for a review of a few of the terms you should know.

Graphics in Annual Reports

An important part of the creative process for most annual reports is selecting visuals to support the text, and particularly the numbers. Depending on the information to be presented, you may find line graphs (to show growth), bar graphs (to illustrate comparisons), or pie charts (to illustrate relationships between the numbers) to be appropriate. Refer to Chapter 7 for a discussion of charts and graphs.

The purpose of graphics is to help readers understand the organization's performance; they should not be used, as can happen, to distort that performance. For public companies, the SEC takes a keen interest in messages sent through graphics.

Ensure that graphics do not send the wrong message, even inadvertently. One UK study found that many annual report graphs were inaccurate and possibly manipulated, generally to show more favorable performance. The study concluded that, instead of enhancing communication, graphs often undermine the neutrality of financial reporting. The study recommended that they should be audited along with regular financial data (Beattie & Jones, 1992).

The same authors found that for charities, many graphs did not conform to recommended principles of construction. For example, they used ellipses instead of circles in pie charts, which distorts the area of segments (Beattie & Jones, 1994).

EXERCISE 1

Effective charts and graphs are an important part of almost every annual report. One way to learn to create them is to work in reverse, from the chart to the concept. This will help you understand the type of relationships you should seek in the financial statements of your organization.

Find two or three charts or graphs that you think are effective. Try to find examples that do not succeed as well as those that do. Write a brief analysis of each. What does it look like? What is it trying to do? What public relations message does it send? Is the format (bar, line, pie, etc.) appropriate to the purpose? Why or why not? What visual techniques help it achieve its aims? Is it effective? Why or why not?

Corporate Reports in a "Bad Year"

Sometimes the news is not good, and if your employer is a publicly traded company, you will have no choice but to discuss it. The documentation of the problem may be obvious in the financial data anyway.

In this case, the issue is *how* rather than *whether* you will discuss it. This is likely to be a hotly debated topic involving the organization's legal and financial counsels as well as public relations. It is a fact of human nature that some managers who gladly take credit for the organization's positive performance will want to attribute negative performance to environmental factors beyond their control.

Your employer's culture and the seriousness of the loss or problem will influence what you say and how you say it. But there are several principles that may help you. First, recognize that the consequences of not coming clean about the issue may be more severe than the issue itself. Second, the same principles that govern the handling of crisis information to the media apply here, especially the need to be brief, direct, honest, and positive. You may also choose to introduce bad news early in the report so the report ends on a more positive note to leave the reader with a more positive impression.

Although you will not be able to deny a problem that the media has publicized widely or the loss that a balance sheet shows so obviously, consider this an opportunity to explain it succinctly and honestly.

If the CEO has a reputation for credibility with your publics, let him or her address a negative issue. Although few CEOs may be willing to be as forthright as Ford Chairman and CEO Bill Ford, who introduced his 2001 message to shareholders with the statement, "Our results in 2001 were unacceptable" (Ford, 2001, p. 2), admitting the problem so bluntly gave credibility to the steps he subsequently laid out to solve it. And it had residual credibility as he reported on the success of the recovery over the next several years.

Annual Reports for Nonprofit Organizations

Although nonprofit, charitable organizations do not fall under SEC regulations, they have auditing and reporting requirements under the same IRS and state regulations that allow them to accept tax-deductible contributions. Generally, they do not require formal reports to the public. Increasingly, however, nonprofit organizations are seizing on the annual report as a valuable public relations document, especially for their all-important donor publics. It is a way to position the organization as a worthy charity. Financial reports answer the question most often posed by donors and would-be donors: "How did you spend my donation?"

Annual Reports as Fundraising Tools

For many nonprofit organizations, annual reports are also an important part of their development/fundraising strategy. They use the report to promote the sense of community that is the basis of their fundraising campaigns. For example, the annual report of the Aloha Foundation (which supports not-for-profit summer camps and outdoor programs) typically includes reports from each camp/program director, dozens of photos of campers in action, and lists and photos of "alumni" donors and volunteers. It is designed to bring back fond memories for the majority of foundation donors and supports the foundation's repeated message theme of the Aloha "family."

Nonprofit Reports: Content

Annual reports for nonprofit organizations typically have five sections:

- ✦ Messages from the board chairperson and executive directors
- ✦ Narrative on the organization's programs and achievements
- ✦ A list of donors and volunteers
- ✦ Audited financial statements—often including, at most, an audited balance sheet and statement of income and expenses, an opinion from the auditor, and perhaps footnotes
- ✦ Names of directors, trustees, and executives

The financial statements demonstrate fiscal responsibility (even in a bad year). They provide evidence that the organization accounts for donations and uses them wisely.

Donor lists—often the first thing people turn to—serve as a public "thank you" to those who supported the organization. They are a morale-building technique, and judging by the very small percentage of donors who ask not to be named, it is effective. Generally speaking, the more ways you can find to acknowledge people's support, the more likely they are to feel like a member of your nonprofit family. That is why many nonprofit annual reports also include lists of volunteers.

In nonprofit annual reports, the narrative is generally less formal than in corporate reports. The narrative may review the activities of all programs or feature one or two of them. You might also choose to write or reprint an article on the philosophy of charitable giving or responses to recent crises—actual or reflected. Organizations focusing on children may print quotes from the children talking about how much they learn or benefit from the programs or equipment that "your" donation made possible. Of course, such reports are also filled with photos of the happy children.

The board chair and executive directors will likely focus on the year's successes, but they may also develop a theme. Their reports put a face to the "thank you" that donors want and deserve. Exhibit 16.2 is the president's message of the 2004 Annual

EXHIBIT 16.2   **Annual report message from the president of a retirement community.**

Report From the CEO

As I write this report, I mark my fifteenth anniversary with the Loomis Communities. Each year as I reflect back on the achievements of the past year and look ahead to the challenges and opportunities that face us, I am amazed at all that our organization has accomplished and I am proud of the residents, volunteer leaders, and staff that have made it all possible.

One of the outstanding achievements of the Loomis Communities has been the success of our Extended Care Career Ladder Initiative (ECCLI) with its emphasis on changing the culture of long term care. During the past year, Loomis House has received regional and national attention for its "culture change" efforts. We have been published in national magazines and on the front page of the *Boston Globe*, have been featured at national and regional conferences, and are recognized as a leader in our field.

Residents and staff both benefit immensely from living and working in an environment that changes an institutional model of care into a residential, resident-centered one. We have just received further ECCLI funding to continue our culture change efforts and our career ladders, including a program to advance Certified Nursing Assistants to become Licensed Practical Nurses.

Across the river in South Hadley, Loomis Village is in the final stages of its major expansion. During this past year, we have welcomed new residents to more than 50 of our 70 new cottages and apartments, and these residents have added their vitality and enthusiasm to the Village. Wellness programming has been expanded to use the new swimming pool and fitness center to their best advantage, and we have extended these programs to include residents at Loomis House and Applewood as well. With the opening of Phylly's—a generous gift by resident [NAME] in memory of her husband Walter—our residents now enjoy a casual dining option in addition to our very popular formal dining program.

Applewood continues to be a premiere independent living community in the Pioneer Valley, with a vibrant resident population, a solid waiting list, and a beautiful setting among the apple orchards of South Amherst. An Applewood resident serves on our Board of Directors, and Applewood residents are represented on the Finance, Development, and Investment Committees as well—a testimony to the growing integration of our organizations since Applewood's entry into the Loomis Communities in 1999.

We face a rapidly changing environment, and will work hard during this coming year to assure that our three communities remain positioned strongly as premiere continuing care retirement communities in the Pioneer Valley. I am grateful to a dedicated and committed Board of Directors; an outstanding and talented staff; and most of all, to our wonderful residents who make the Loomis Communities their home.

Carol Katz
President and CEO
The Loomis Communities

Source: Reproduced with permission of the Loomis Communities, Holyoke, Massachusetts.

Report of the Loomis Communities. In addition to reporting on the important events of each of the organization's residences—such as the opening of 70 new units at Loomis Village—the president pays tribute to employees, positions the year's results in the economic climate, and sets the stage for the commitment and challenges of the new year. These are typical topics for both commercial and non-profit annual report messages.

DISCUSSION 2

Compare Exhibit 16.2 with Exhibit 10.3 in Chapter 10, a newsletter column also written by the president of the Loomis Communities. What do the two messages have in common? What themes does the president use? What phrasing does she use to send a public relations message on behalf of the communities? How do the messages target their individual audiences: the local senior population (for the newsletter), and Loomis donors and supporters (for the annual report)?

Remember that although the report is part of your fundraising efforts, it is first and foremost a report on the previous year. It is typically upbeat and informative.

Nonprofit Reports: Style

If you write for a nonprofit organization, you will have likely developed a casual, conversational writing style that will work for the annual report. Since donor publics consider themselves members of the organizational family, it is important to treat them as such. Use inclusive words such as *we*, *our*, and *partners*. Send the message that every contribution counts.

Annual Reports to Employees

In the same vein, organizations that produce annual reports for employees send a clear message that employees are a valuable public. Employee reports are likely to differ from their public cousins to reflect employees' special interests and concerns. The purpose of an employee report is as much to raise morale as to provide information.

Employee Reports: Content

Employees obviously are interested in the effect of market influences, new technology, and competition on the organization, but their primary concern is, "What's in it for me?" They will appreciate, and often look for, evidence that the organization recognizes their contributions.

Although you will be able to use some of the content from the public report, what you know about the organization's staff will point toward a different approach. Employee reports are an opportunity to raise morale, cultivate an image of the company, answer questions, and improve the ability of employees to become spokespersons for the company. They also provide a welcome opportunity for the CEO to address employees directly.

You can take advantage of these opportunities with approaches such as the following:

- *Review the year through the accomplishments of departments*, divisions, or locations to highlight as many staff as possible.
- *Interpret the publicly reported financial information* in terms that reflect employees' special interests. Answer the questions, "How did my division contribute to the profits?" and "How did we spend what we earned?"
- *Include financial information of special interest to employees* such as the growth of the pension fund or participation in the staff share purchase program.
- *Describe the organization's commitment to projects in which staff are interested.*

Employee Reports: Style and Format

If you produce an employee newsletter or maintain an employee web site, you will already have mastered a style that is appropriate to your audience. It will be appropriate for an annual report, minus, of course, the chatty social news.

Employee reports can be distributed through internal mail but are more typically sent to the employees' homes or included as a special insert in the employee newsletter. Some organizations produce video annual reports that can be shown at employee gatherings at each location. It is the next best thing to a personal visit from the CEO.

Annual Reports and the Internet

There is an argument that the traditional printed annual report is being displaced by instant, up-to-the-minute electronic sources. This argument is fueled by the fact that public companies already file financial reports with the SEC electronically.

Although most web reports are still simply .html or .pdf files of the printed report posted for downloading, the benefits of the Web make it ideal for more sophisticated treatments. These benefits include real-time reporting and search capabilities that allow users to essentially create their own reports from the information provided online. Furthermore, because web use can be monitored, the organization can track what information is most sought after and by whom and better customize its site to the needs of users. This need for customization will challenge both the public relations writer and the nature of the annual report.

Special Events

One of our aims in structuring this book has been to demonstrate that public relations writing does not happen in isolation. Rather, it is an ongoing process of building on what you have written before. You can use relevant parts of a press release for a newsletter, adapt an annual report chart for a brochure, or work the theme of an advocacy ad into a speech.

Over time, you will find that improvements in your public relations writing will rest on two foundations. The first is the continuous revision of organizational materials as you become more familiar with them. The second is the ongoing internal and external relationships that help you assess more accurately the communication needs of the organization and its publics.

The following sections of this chapter deal with the occasions when organization-driven and public(s)-driven writing come together in a highly public fashion: special events. Whether it is a product launch, the celebration of the organization's 50th year in business, or your participation at an annual conference, all of your writing skills must come together in a way that has maximum impact both during the event and after. The message must be presented consistently across a variety of media, often to meet the needs of multiple publics and under circumstances that require your materials to stand out from those of competing organizations.

Events attract publics that may or may not be interested in your organization. They are also one of the few occasions outside of a research setting where you may observe firsthand the reaction of your publics to the materials you have produced for them.

The rest of this chapter introduces two opportunities that will test many of your writing skills. They require you to demonstrate understanding of the organization and the available media and allow you to make use of projects you have already completed. These opportunities are special events hosted by your organization and conferences or trade shows in which the organization will participate.

Celebrations, Grand Openings, and Annual Meetings

Most events take place on a smaller scale than the year-long Hasbro Trivial Pursuit® anniversary event (see the "Trivial Pursuit 20th Anniversary" box), but for the organization they will be no less important, and for the public relations writer they will require no less diligence.

TRIVIAL PURSUIT 20TH ANNIVERSARY

A Celebration of All Things Trivial

What famous game celebrated its 20th anniversary in 2002? If you answered, "Trivial Pursuit," you would be right. You would also be describing the focus of a yearlong "event" that required planning on both small and grand scales.

Faced with the challenge of celebrating the anniversary, Hasbro launched a 20th-anniversary edition of the popular game (TP20) and developed a multimedia advertising and public relations strategy to make "Trivial Pursuit's 20th Anniversary the most successful game introduction in 2002."

The public relations component of the plan focused on three events held throughout the year:

✦ At a February Toy Fair, the game was introduced with a "Be in the Trivial Pursuit Game" contest. The public entered the contest via a web site and the prize was to be a question in the 20th-anniversary edition.
✦ At a June launch of the game, it reached retail stores and Hasbro announced the winner of the contest. Publicity about the winner appeared on more than 100 news broadcasts culminating with the winner's appearance on the *Today Show*.
✦ At a late-September press event, the TV advertising debuted. The event was held at Toys R Us Times Square where former New York mayor Rudy Giuliani served as emcee asking the crowd three questions from the Trivial Pursuit 20th Anniversary game. Special guests, representing each of the answers, burst through the backdrop of the stage after each question. Participants included the former Pets.com sock puppet (representing the dot-com bubble burst of the 1990s), soccer star Mia Hamm, and the Village People (whose song YMCA is performed by the New York Yankees' grounds crew while raking the infield). At the same time, billboard ads, the NBC Jumbotron, and vendor carts in the Times Square area reinforced the Trivial Pursuit 20th Anniversary message.

Results

The excitement generated by the publicity and advertising efforts combined to make Trivial Pursuit the best-selling non-video game of the year. In December, *USA TODAY* said, "The game was one of few bright spots for retailers in the first weeks of holiday shopping." By the end of 2002, Trivial Pursuit was the top-selling board game and ranked number four among all toys in the industry.

Hasbro "won" again in 2004 when the campaign won the prestigious gold EFFIE Award recognizing creative achievement in meeting advertising objectives. The awards are hosted by the New York American Marketing Association.

The contest winner was a Michigan man whose claim to fame is "drubbling"—juggling and dribbling basketballs while running marathons.

Source: M. Morris, Public Relations Director, Games, Hasbro, Inc. Trivial Pursuit 20th Anniversary, personal e-mail, January 15 and June 20, 2004.

Like the Hasbro press event, most events are "by invitation only" and have the same advantage as controlled media. Within some limitations, you know and control who will attend. You will issue invitations or press alerts and thereby have a controlled guest list. The information you produce will likely be the sole source of information during the event.

Although events may include food, music, demonstrations, and entertainment, all of which have a public relations component insofar as they send a message about the organization's knowledge of and relationship to its publics, we will limit ourselves to the roles that a public relations writer may expect to play. These include producing invitations, writing speeches, developing displays and collateral material, and preparing information kits.

Given the absolute deadlines for these projects, we suggest you plan in detail to ensure that you meet printer and other production deadlines. The Planning panel in this chapter will help you.

Invitations

As an expert on the organization's publics, a public relations writer may well be involved in developing the guest list—which will be determined by the purpose of the function, the budget, and available space. It may also include people the CEO wants to meet, impress, be seen with, persuade, or lobby. Typical categories of guests include the following:

- The organization's board of directors and senior executives
- Government officials and legislators—Special events provide an excellent reason to bring such officials to your location to hear your story
- Business associates—Clients, vendors, suppliers, distributors
- Members of the organization's "family"—Members, donors, alumni
- Local business leaders
- Employees
- Personal associates of the president/CEO
- Local media—Even if you send a pitch letter for the event, accompany it with a personal letter inviting the media to attend. Don't forget to follow up personally and send a reminder two or three days before the event.

Also consider inviting celebrities who attract the media and other guests. To keep their focus on your organization, ask them to participate as honoree, guest speaker, or emcee.

Experience says that the invitation itself may be a source of debate. Should it be formal or casual, traditional or imaginative, conservative or daring? It must protect and promote the image the organization has worked to achieve. Even if the invitations are embossed or engraved, you have ample latitude for reflecting the organizational image in layout, type style, color, and choice of paper.

Invitation Content

The invitation must answer some of the questions discussed earlier in the context of news releases: who, what, when, where, and possibly, why:

- ✦ *Who* is hosting the event? is invited? is the guest speaker? is being honored?
- ✦ *What* is the event for? grand opening, retirement, honor, product launch? What will happen? Does it include a reception, dinner, or tour of a new facility? What should the guests wear? This is more important than it would seem and is likely to be the subject of many questions if you do not provide guidance. White tie, black tie, formal, and semiformal are traditional distinctions, but "casual" is truly open to interpretation. "Business attire" may be clearer for men, but what about for women?
- ✦ *When* will the event take place? Be sure to include both the date and time. Naming the day (e.g., Tuesday, January 3) will help to plant it in the reader's mind. And remember that for international audiences you must also spell out the month; you cannot rely on 4/3/05, for example, which could mean April 3rd or March 4th, depending on the culture.
- ✦ *Where* will the event take place? You may want to also provide directions, but we suggest you do this separately.
- ✦ *Why* should the guests attend? This is difficult to do with formal invitations, but more casual ones may include brief persuasive messages, such as "your opportunity to congratulate Jim Marshall on his national award" or "be one of the founding supporters of the children's athletic program."

Don't forget to ask for a response if you need one. Although "RSVP" (*répondez s'il vous plaît*, or please respond) does not guarantee a response, it will save some follow-up phone calls.

Invitation Style

Style will be dictated by the occasion. A direct, business style is appropriate for most occasions. The keywords are "simple and polite." "XYZ Company invites you to the opening of . . ." Or "ABC Foundation is proud to announce the end of our $50 million capital campaign. Please join us for this historic event." Reserve traditional formal invitation style, "XYZ Corporation requests the pleasure of your company at (event)," for white- or black-tie receptions.

Formal invitations are usually engraved or printed commercially. They are usually centered, both horizontally and vertically.

Many organizations have stocks of cards or note-size paper, perhaps preprinted with the organization logo or name, on which small quantities of invitations can be laser printed for less formal occasions. This does not mean that you should spend less time or take less care with the design or wording.

If the event has a theme, the invitation will likely unveil it. Such was the case when the Six Flags New England theme park opened an expanded Water Park "Hurricane Harbor." The invitation for the media was billed as a "sneak preview." When it was opened, recipients heard a hurricane emergency warning on an audio chip followed by the voiceover saying, "The warning is over. The hurricane hits May 23rd." The text was a simple who, what, when, and how (to get further information).

Speeches

It is likely that someone, usually the president or CEO, will formally address the crowd during an event. Speeches on these occasions may welcome guests, introduce keynote speakers, or declare the new facility open, the campaign ended, or the games about to begin.

It is equally likely that you will draft the speech. Refer to Chapter 11 for guidelines on writing to be heard.

Information Kits: Media, Sales, Educational, and Public

Information kits can provide general information for a general audience or targeted information for a specific purpose. They may be produced en masse for product launches or individually for groups of legislators touring your facility. Information kits offer portability, customization, souvenir quality, and the impact that only a first-class personalized presentation can provide. They are a close relative of the press or media kits discussed in Chapter 9.

The purpose and audience influence the contents of information kits. Sales and marketing kits typically include details about products and services that may just be listed in a general purpose kit. Educational kits for consumers may include how-to brochures and contact information for the nearest sales office or service center. If your organization receives many requests from schoolchildren, then you might even prepare a special kit with topical coloring books and stickers as well as information written to their reading level. Kits for adults might include a CD so people can take a test drive, evaluate software, calculate their need for life insurance, or listen to a music sample.

Insofar as you can predict the public's needs for information, you will be able to prepare the information in advance. Fact sheets, backgrounders, and bios can be written and ready for a range of information kits. Information specific to an event must be built into the event planning.

Industry Conferences, Exhibitions, Conventions, and Trade Shows

It's that time of year again—the annual industry conference or community trade show is at hand and your organization wants to make a splash. How do you handle it? If the conference really is at hand, it is too late to be planning for it. Any splash you make is likely to be a belly flop. On the other hand, if your participation has been budgeted and you have several months to execute a planned strategy, then success is well within your grasp.

Why Attend an Exhibition or Trade Show?

Generally, you attend commercial exhibitions and trade shows to display products and services. They are sales events. Conferences are organized for another purpose such as education, motivation, or the discussion of common interests among registered participants. Exhibitions may be part of the program, but they are not the focus of the event. Public "trade shows" usually have a theme, such as health, employment, or local enterprise. Their aim is to bring together suppliers and vendors within a sector, and they often have an educational component as well as a commercial incentive. Because our focus in this section is on developing an effective exhibit presence, we shall refer to all of these events as exhibitions.

Generally speaking, there is only one reason to attend an exhibition: exposure. You will attend an exhibition if it presents the opportunity to reach a key public with a key message.

Exhibitions can be used to promote services or programs, sell products, educate, and generally be seen. Less obvious but no less important purposes include networking, lobbying, and conducting audience research. They are especially valuable for building prospect and mailing lists and establishing face-to-face contact with prospects. It is possible to achieve all of these aims at a single exhibition, but it takes research, planning, careful execution, and effective follow-up.

Exhibitions offer a range of opportunities for publicity and promotion. Take advantage of them; they are challenging, rewarding, and fun.

Preparing for an Exhibition or Trade Show

The Theme

Successful exhibits often focus on a single theme. All communications focus on making this message memorable. Some exhibitions have themes of their own and invite participants to tie in with it for their own exhibits and publicity. Doing so can give you a topical, usually fun, focus, but your own goals should be your first consideration.

Research shows that people visit exhibitions seeking information. A study sponsored by the Exhibit Industry Education Foundation shows that exhibitions are often attended by what they call "hidden buyers." These are people who may not be the target of sales calls but who nevertheless influence and/or make buying decisions (Tanner, 1997). They attend exhibitions seeking solutions to specific problems. To the writer, this should suggest that the exhibit theme should focus on problems and how the organization can solve them.

When choosing a theme, consider all of the media that will be used to deliver it including mailers, brochures, signs, ads, giveaways, and perhaps even the clothing of the people who will staff the exhibit. Think brief, bold, and simple. Beware that a catchy theme does not overwhelm your real message. It is very easy to get caught up in a clever idea and lose sight of the real message.

Our discussion in this section will follow the way Unger and Associates, Inc. (UAI), a student loan collection agency, used the location of an industry conference in Honolulu as the theme to promote its GOLD-Plus default prevention program. The default prevention program was designed to relieve institutions of the administrative burden of tracking and contacting defaulters (i.e., the process of managing what was called their cohort rates). At the time of the conference, stringent regulatory controls and penalties surrounding these cohort rates threatened many of the country's several thousand technical and trade colleges.

The conference was sponsored by the Career College Association (CCA) and attended by the presidents and financial aid directors of many of the threatened schools. The message was expressed in a "reduce your stress" theme. It evolved smoothly from the stress-reduction image of a holiday in Hawaii to the stress-reduction potential of the company's program. The company developed this theme in pre-exhibition publicity and in the display, literature, and collaterals at the exhibition. Look for the following elements in all of the samples: the graphic treatment of the word *stress,* the centered headlines, the flush-left body copy, and a "you have a problem; we have the solution" emphasis. The brochures, mailers, and signs were all printed economically in two colors, black and red. The ads were black and white.

EXHIBIT 16.3   **Preconference mailer used to promote a company booth at a national trade show held in Hawaii. This mailer introduced the company's visual and verbal theme for the conference.**

Are you suffering from

Cohort

STRESS?

Stop by Booth 409 at the CCA convention in Honolulu and let us test your Cohort STRESS. We'd also like to talk with you about our UAI GOLD-Plus remedy.

Even if we can't meet in Hawaii, we'd still like to introduce you to our GOLD and GOLD-Plus programs. For more information, call: Roger Williams, (714) xxx-xxxx, or Tom Guevera, (800) xxx-xxxx

Unger and Associates, Inc.

Source: Reproduced with permission from Unger and Associates, Inc.

Pre-exhibition Publicity

Some exhibitions make it possible for you to begin publicity before the event opens, hoping perhaps that the exhibitors will help generate attendance. Pre-exhibition publicity has four aims:

✦ To alert target audiences to the fact that your organization will be at the exhibition
✦ To tell them where to find your exhibit
✦ To entice them to stop by the exhibit
✦ To attract the attention of prospects by identifying the problem(s) that your exhibit will help them solve

Exhibit 16.3 is the front of a postcard mailer sent to registered participants three weeks before the CCA conference. Although simple, the mailer accomplishes several goals. It introduces the stress theme and the special typographic treatment of the word *stress*. The screened palm tree evokes the laid-back image of Hawaii and the theme of the message. The text clearly directs the reader where to find the exhibit and provides two incentives for stopping by—the teaser "let us test your Cohort STRESS" and a pitch for the GOLD-Plus program. It also provides the names and office contact numbers for sales representatives—a must with every marketing piece.

Another strategy that is effective, but requires careful planning, is to include a code number, colored puzzle piece, or other enticement on or in pre-exhibition mailers. Ask recipients to bring the card to the exhibit to be eligible for a prize drawing or to receive an instant prize. Some companies send out half of a gift (such as the jewel case for a CD or DVD) and ask the recipients to stop by the booth to receive the other half.

Because the purpose of these efforts is to build a mailing list, the attendee's address must be the "ticket" for entry into the contest or the "purchase price" of the prize. This is a useful strategy if the prize is good enough. Otherwise it is likely to be ignored. You must also provide entry forms at the exhibit for those who do not bring the mailer or carry business cards.

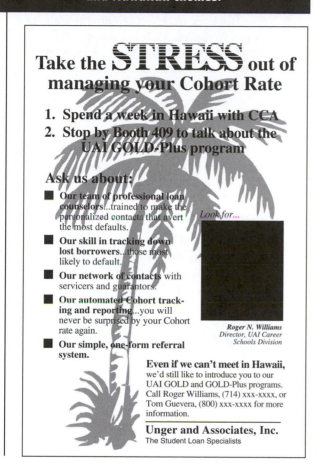

Source: Reproduced with permission from Unger and Associates, Inc.

Exhibit 16.4 is the ad that the company purchased in the conference issue of the CCA magazine. While echoing the mailer's *stress* theme and art, it also acknowledges that the ad will be seen by readers who may not attend the exhibition but who are, nevertheless, prospective clients. It emphasizes features of the GOLD-Plus program under the heading "Ask us about:" and again provides contact names and numbers.

The ad included a photo of the sales manager at the exhibition (shown as a box in the sample). This photo was also printed on the reverse of the mailing panel discussed above, with the text "Look for (name) at CCA. He'll be there to solve your default prevention worries." This echoes the "we have the solution" strategy.

Mail, e-mail, direct mail, flyers, web-based alerts, news releases, and your client newsletter are other writing formats that can be used to publicize your participation at an exhibition.

Publicity During the Exhibition

Most exhibitions print a program, including the booth location, names, business addresses, and representatives of the participating vendors or booth-holders. This may be a good place for the boilerplate paragraph you wrote in Chapter 8. Alternatively, you may write a special paragraph supporting your exhibition theme. Either way, it must be brief.

Booths and Displays

Research by the Center for Exhibition Industry Research (CEIR, 1997) has identified nine factors that strongly influence an exhibit's memorability: size, demonstrations, interest in product, literature, exhibit design, color, booth personnel, the company's name recognition, and giveaways. This should tell you that keeping the organization's name prominent, taking advantage of the opportunities for action, and presenting a common message through exhibit design, documents, and giveaways will influence the exhibit's success.

The driving force behind an exhibit is building relationships, that is, to persuade visitors to involve themselves with your organization. The exhibit should attract their attention and persuade them at least to pick up the literature and leave their business cards and at best to talk with your representatives. Because most exhibits are static, you can gain an immediate advantage with action. Don't just show the product, demonstrate it; action always attracts an audience. Provide opportunities for visitors to test or sample the product.

Ethical Issues

Ethics and Exhibitions: Prizes or Inducements?

Prizes and giveaways are a common and generally accepted part of conferences and exhibitions. Arguably, that is why some people attend.

But these same popular attractions are also the subject of a serious ethical question: Is it ethical for vendors to offer giveaways and prizes and for conference-goers to accept them?

For government employees, there are strict regulations governing gifts in any form. Implicitly, vendors are wrong to offer such items, even if they are not direct inducements. Some companies and other organizations have similar clauses in their employment agreements or ethical codes.

The issue is less clear with other attendees. Small giveaways that everyone has the opportunity to pick up are generally no problem. They are unlikely to induce anyone to do anything except, perhaps, call for further information. Their purpose and use is as a memory aid.

However, once you get into the realm of "big ticket" items such as appliances, trips, cars, sports tickets, and the like, there is a significant chance that any relationship between the company and recipient may be compromised by the prize. If something goes wrong, it will certainly be scrutinized. Once again, it is not what you do (or intend); it is what you are seen to do. Of course, tempting though it may be to ensure that your top prospect goes home with the TV, *any* hint that a prize drawing may not have been honest will clearly damage your organization's reputation.

Again the PRSA Code of Ethics offers some guidance. The core principle "Free Flow of Information" has as its basis maintaining the integrity of relationships. Ensuring that gifts are "nominal, legal, and infrequent" covers the issue of gift value (nominal), government employees (legal), and, for example, season tickets (infrequent).

Using Your Booth for Exhibition Research

By inviting attendees to participate in an opinion survey or research study, you can collect data about issues such as consumer buying habits or other topics of interest to your organization. You can also collect demographic data about exhibition visitors or measure the impact of conference publicity by asking if and how the respondent knew about your exhibit. Such studies can easily be computerized. Because visitors are unlikely to participate in a survey that takes more than a minute to complete, keep it simple and direct.

Signs and Posters

As a public relations writer, you will have responsibility for what goes on the display, that is, the signs and posters that will be attached to the backdrop. There are four primary rules for exhibition signs—indeed for any signs from bumper stickers to billboards.

♦ *Signs must attract attention.* In just a few seconds, signs must answer the questions: "What are you selling or promoting?" "What's in it for me (the viewer)?" and "Whose booth is this?"

Think visual. Photos and charts are certain attention-getters and an effective way to present statistics and technical information, but they must be simple and clear.

Think movement and direction. Use arrows, colors, and bullets to direct the viewer quickly through the message; actual movement is even better. Demonstrate the product, or if you have a video, show it big and elevated, right on the backdrop.

◆ *Signs must be simple.* They must stand out amid hundreds of distractions. Choose a message and repeat it often. When designing an exhibition sign:

Think headlines and bullet points. Save the "copy" for brochures.

Think marketing. Use proven attention-getters such as "New" and, of course, "Free." If your organization is seeking support for a charitable initiative, phrases such as "Help" and "Call to action" have an urgency that attracts attention.

Think visual sound bites. Testimonials from satisfied users or celebrities who support the message are another effective technique. Quotes attract attention and add credibility. Just keep them brief.

Think poster. Big, bright, bold, and obvious are important. This is neither the time nor the place for subtlety.

◆ *Signs must be readable at a distance.* Three types of people attend a convention: those who will seek you out, those who will approach a booth and talk if invited, and those who will only look from a distance or perhaps pick up a brochure. If your signs cannot be read from at least 15 feet, they stand no chance of delivering the organization's message, especially to this third audience.

Think large and clear. Look at the sign at the maximum distance it will be viewed.

Think readable. Choose colors to maximize readability as discussed in Chapter 7.

Choose colors to support the message. Color can have both physiological and psychological effects on the viewer. Blue is calming, red is emotionally charged, yellow (on black or blue) is the best attention-getter, green is positive and calming, black represents power, gold and silver symbol ze premium, and white denotes honesty and purity. Understanding these effects can help you use color to your advantage (or disadvantage) in exhibit design. Remember, however, that these effects may be bound in culture.

◆ *Signs must be visible above the crowd.* If your pre-exhibition mailers and program ads do their job, exhibition-goers may surround your booth. It is equally likely that they will come for your giveaways. Either way, signs below 6 feet high and information on tables may not be seen by anyone outside the immediate booth area.

Collaterals

Even given successful signs and personable staff, exhibitions require hard-copy messages that visitors can take away to remind visitors of your message after the exhibition is over. These messages fall into two categories: brochures and giveaways. Collectively, they are referred to as *collaterals*.

Brochures. In Chapters 7 and 15, we discussed the writing and design of brochures and the principles discussed there still apply. Whether you use brochures that you have on hand or develop new ones unique to the exhibition, they should complement the theme expressed in signs and preconference publicity. If not, you will lose the impact of that theme *and* confuse the reader.

Exhibit 16.5 is the brochure used by UAI at the CCA conference. It continues the *stress* theme, repeats the seven-question test, and directs the reader to open the brochure to learn about the company's remedy for the problem. Inside are seven stress-reduction features of the program. The back panel was the company's boiler-plate paragraph—after all, not everyone will know who you are.

- ◆ *How big?* The size of brochures (and giveaways) is always an issue at conferences when attendees may not want or have the means to carry large or heavy documents. You are always safe with brochures that fit into a #10 envelope. They also fit easily into a purse, briefcase, conference tote bag, or suit pocket.
- ◆ *How elaborate?* That depends on your budget, what the competition will be handing out, and the audience's expectations. Because you should regard most conference brochures as "throwaways," you may want to reserve the full-color, multipage presentations for targeted follow-up mailings.

Giveaways. CEIR research (1997) shows that giveaways increase memorability. There are no hard-and-fast rules about what giveaway to select, however.

Popular giveaways follow trends. When only one vendor gives away coffee mugs or plastic drink bottles, they are popular. When everyone does it, it is stale. Pens and pencils are routinely scorned, even by the hundreds of thousands of conference-goers who eagerly pick them up.

Web searches under "gifts," "trade shows," or "exhibitions" will identify hundreds of gift possibilities, and you can easily get on the mailing lists for novelty or specialty houses. Your local printer will also be able to help.

When selecting giveaways, aim for an item that does the following:

- ◆ *Has room for contact information.* The organization's name and phone number are musts. The company logo and the full exhibit slogan or message are pluses.

    You must also consider the shape of the space to be filled and the use the item will have. How much can you print on a golf ball? What information is appropriate on a baseball cap? Shaping a message to fit on a pencil or pen may be the biggest test of concise writing you will ever have.

EXHIBIT 16.5   The cover and inside panels of the UAI brochure given away at the CCA conference.

How do you score on UAI's Cohort STRESS Test?

YES	NO	
☐	☐	Can you afford to dedicate full-time staff to managing your default rate?
☐	☐	Does your staff enjoy calling borrowers (whom they often know) to ask why they haven't paid their loans? Are they good at it?
☐	☐	Does your default prevention staff *really* understand the Cohort system? Do you?
☐	☐	Do you have the resources to locate borrowers nationwide?
☐	☐	Can you estimate your '92 Cohort rate? How about '93?
☐	☐	If your default prevention specialist leaves, do you have a replacement trained to take over with no costly lapse in accountability?
☐	☐	Do you personally monitor your default prevention program? Can you measure its effectiveness?

If you answered **NO** to any of these questions, you're a prime candidate for Cohort stress. See inside for UAI's simple GOLD-Plus remedy...

GOLD-Plus stress-reduction features:

1 Professional Loan Counselors

The only job of our GOLD-Plus staff is to help you manage your Cohort rate. It's like having a whole team of experienced, full-time default prevention specialists on your own staff.

GOLD-Plus loan counselors are selected for their ability to communicate effectively — the foundation of effective default prevention. Then we train them to persuade borrowers to bring their accounts current. They know how to answer questions, rebut objections and, when necessary, help borrowers obtain deferments or forbearances to keep them from default.

Their approach is concerned, knowledgeable and professional — just the image you want projected for your school.

2 Cohort Understanding

Have you lost track of when an SLS loan enters repayment? Do you know when a Stafford borrower can no longer affect your Cohort rate? Our business is to keep track of these changes and see that your default management program complies with them.

Our system automatically assigns loans to the correct Cohort year and tracks them for as long as they can affect your Cohort rate.

3 Nationwide Skiptracing

We provide our GOLD-Plus specialists with the same state-of-the art skiptracing resources that have made UAI's full-service collection program such a success. We maintain on-line access to national credit bureaus and consumer databases for locating borrowers nationwide. Our skiptracing focuses on identifying new phone numbers to facilitate the personal contacts that avert defaults most effectively.

4 One-Step Account Referral

UAI's one-form system makes referring accounts as simple as possible. Updating our files is just as easy. Plus, we take care of monitoring your PCA reports and contacting delinquent borrowers.

5 Monthly Cohort Rate Updates

With GOLD-Plus, you don't have to wait months to see if your default prevention program is working. UAI tracks all borrowers through our automated system, so we can tell you where your Cohort rate stands at any time. You never have to be surprised at your Cohort rate again.

6 A Proven Track Record

GOLD-Plus has been developed in conjunction with career schools nationwide. It has been tested and proven effective not only in reducing default rates, but also in relieving schools like yours of the stress and cost of implementing, managing and monitoring a program in-house.

7 Full Time Commitment

With GOLD-Plus, it's our responsibility to see that the job gets done. We employ client services staff specifically to help you provide the correct information and keep us informed. They monitor your referrals and take the worry out of missed deadlines.

Furthermore, at UAI your default prevention program doesn't get put aside to accommodate enrolment, or graduation, or loss of staff. It is always our first priority.

◆ *Supports the exhibit theme.* At the CCA conference, UAI gave away small plastic "stress monitors" that quickly became a hit. The following text was printed on each monitor: "UAI GOLD-Plus takes the STRESS out of managing your Cohort Rate. Call (XXX) XXX-XXXX for more information."

Conference-goers enjoyed "testing" each other's stress. They also implicitly turned into agents for the company's message as they referred their friends to the UAI booth to obtain a monitor. The challenge for UAI staff was to see to it that each person also took away a brochure and left a business card.

◆ *Is cost-effective* for the number of visitors you expect.

◆ *Meets your postexhibition aims.* If the aim is to have your organization's name on an executive's desk every day, then plastic cups are a bad choice. On the other hand, executive toys, tasteful desk accessories, and even the humble pen, if it is a good one, are popular choices and will stay with the executive. If your audience is the family, then sippy cups or refrigerator magnets are logical. Furthermore, they will end up in the home, exactly where you want them.

◆ *Is convenient.* Coffee mugs are cumbersome as are note cubes, sports drink bottles, and anything else that won't fit in a briefcase.

◆ *Is appealing.* Fun is a plus as long as it is in good taste and related to the message. Nearly everyone likes things they can play with.

The UAI stress monitors fulfilled all of these aims.

Evaluation and Follow-Up

Given the expense of mounting many exhibits, it is likely that management will want an evaluation of the exhibit's success. This is reason enough to establish in advance both your goals for the exhibit and the ways you will measure success.

If your goals are long term, such as an increase in membership, sales, revenue, or customers, it may be months before you will have the numbers to assess them. Even then it may be difficult to attribute the increases to the exhibit. For immediate evaluation, you must also identify the data that you can capture at the exhibit and determine how it will be useful. Most exhibit research is simple, but telling.

◆ Count the visitors to your booth, usually by sign-ups or business cards
◆ Count the number of brochures and giveaways distributed
◆ Measure audience interests by tracking the relative appeal of different products or messages
◆ Mingle with the crowd to get informal comments and evaluations
◆ Ask exhibit representatives for their opinions
◆ Observe traffic patterns to determine if your exhibit was in a good location

Although it is likely that management may still want a long-term assessment after the numbers are in, having statistics from the exhibit will usually provide immediate answers to the question, "Was the exhibit a success?"

Now that you have your mailing list, take advantage of it. While sales representatives may prioritize the contacts made at the exhibit for immediate/later, strong/casual follow-up, public relations writers often produce at least one follow-up letter for mass distribution within a week of the exhibition. Such letters lead with a "glad we had the opportunity to meet you" message and follow with a reminder of how your organization may be of service.

If you can reliably determine which attendees did not visit your exhibit, you may also send "sorry we missed the opportunity to see you but . . ." letters. Such letters must include the pitch they missed at the exhibit. Include the brochure and giveaway if it is mailable, or suggest that the reader call to request the giveaway.

Be sure to make successful exhibitions the focus of employee newsletters, to thank the participants for their hard work, and public newsletters, to continue the promotional theme with clients. Capitalizing on your exhibition success is good public relations.

ON THE TEXTBOOK WEB SITE

◆ Go to www.sagepub.com/treadwell for web exercises, study hints, case studies, and additional examples appropriate to this chapter and chosen or developed to supplement the chapter content.

WRITING WRAP-UP

1. For the club or organization that has been your campus client since Chapter 3, plan and write all the materials you will need for a low-budget exhibit at an event designed to recruit new members.

REFERENCES

Beattie, V., & Jones, M. J. (1992). The use and abuse of graphs in annual reports: Theoretical framework and empirical study. *Accounting and Business Research, 22*(8), 291–303.

Beattie, V., & Jones, M. J. (1994). An empirical study of graphical format choices in charity annual reports. *Financial Accountability & Management, 19*(3), 215–236.

Center for Exhibition Industry Research. (1997). *Most remembered exhibits: Analysis of the factors affecting exhibit recall* (Report MCRR 5040). Bethesda, MD: Center for Exhibition Industry Research. Retrieved September 28, 1998, from www.ceir.org

Ford, W. C., Jr. (2001). *Building our future.* Chairman's message. Ford Motor Company 2001 annual report. Dearborn, MI: Ford Motor Company.

Fulkerson, J. (1996). How investors use annual reports. *American Demographics, 18*(5), 16–20.

Global Reporting Initiative. (2003a, September 29). *Organizations using the guidelines.* . Retrieved October 14, 2003, from www.globalreporting.org

Global Reporting Initiative. (2003b). *Vision and mission statements: A common framework for sustainability reporting.* Retrieved October 14, 2003, from www.globalreporting.org

It's the results that count. (1996, May). *Management Today,* p. 12.

Tanner, J. (1997). Using trade shows to attract "hidden" buyers. In *Attracting hidden buyers.* Springfield, VA: Exhibit Industry Education Foundation and Trade Show Exhibitors Association. Retrieved September 28, 1998, from www.tsea.org

RESOURCES

Annual Reports

American Stock Exchange (Amex)	www.amex.com
Annual Reports Library	www.zpub.com/sf/arl
Investor Communications Business, Inc. (links to multiple annual report services)	www.wilink.com
NASDAQ	www.nasdaq.com
New York Stock Exchange	www.nyse.com
SEC	www.sec.gov

How to Create Clear SEC .... www.sec.gov/news/extra/handbook.htm
   Disclosure Documents

Sid Cato's Official Annual Report Website® .... www.sidcato.com

Wall Street Journal Annual Reports Service .... http://wsj.ar.wilink.com

Social Responsibility Reporting

CSRWire (Corporate Social Responsibility Newswire Service) .... www.csrwire.com

Global Reporting Initiative .... www.globalreporting.org

Planning Exhibits

Center for Exhibition Industry Research (CEIR) .... www.ceir.org

Trade Show Exhibitors Association (TSEA) .... www.tsea.org

Identifying Exhibitions

Chase's Calendar of Events; The Day-by-Day Directory to Special Days, Weeks & Months.
   New York: McGraw-Hill. Published annually.

Exhibitions 'Round the World .... www.exhibitions-world.com

Appendix A

The Value of Editing

There are few pieces of writing that will not benefit from a prudent editing, usually to express a thought more concisely and sometimes to clarify its meaning, and few readers who will not appreciate the editing effort. For example, there are 37 words in the previous sentence. The same thought could be expressed as "Readers appreciate the clear, concise ideas that result from careful editing"—only 11 words.

One way to learn to recognize unnecessary words and phrases and to understand why extra words add or subtract from the overall message is to write a précis (pronounced PRAY-see) of the document. Writing a précis is distilling copy into its simplest message. It focuses on what you want to say rather than on how you say it. Usually, the précis process occurs in stages; you successively reduce the copy by halves until you have just one paragraph or sentence that conveys the entire message.

For example, in Chapter 2 we looked at the opening phrases of Abraham Lincoln's Gettysburg Address: "Four score and seven years ago, our fathers brought forth upon this continent. . . ." Effectively we wrote a précis beginning "Eighty-seven years ago, our ancestors founded a country. . . ." At the second stage, we might distill that to "In 1789, our ancestors founded the United States. . . ." As a summary of the facts it is accurate and brief, but it lacks the color, charm, and memorability of the original.

As an effective writer, you should be able to see your own writing from both points of view. You should be able to reduce it to its most basic message and to eliminate words and phrases that interfere with the direct delivery of that message. At the same time, you should be able to recognize those words and phrases that give the message character or attitude or memorability.

DISCUSSION 1

Try your hand at précis writing by working on the following three-paragraph article about industrial robots. You should be able to capture the sense of the article in two or three sentences. Does this capture the tone as well? What does the tone add to the article?

The rapid progress in the production and use of industrial robots in recent years has been widely publicized, most often emphasizing the sophistication of the technology employed or the state of development of humanlike capabilities such as vision or tactile sensing. As a result, what is basically an industrial tool, albeit a sophisticated one, has become inescapably identified with science-fiction-inspired persona, usually with human characteristics.

In reality, however, robots that exhibit humanlike behavior are far removed from those actually employed in industry today. In fact, even the high technology systems of the immediate future, complete with sophisticated sensory capabilities, will lack the glamour that the word robot conjures up. In practical terms, the industrial robot is a workhorse whose benefits lie in its functional capacities.

One of the problems of searching for human qualities in industrial robots is that much effort has been put into the development of very high technology systems that do show such qualities. This has been at the expense of systems that are less complex but in many cases more suited to particular industrial applications and that can prove far more cost-efficient for these applications. In short, many manufacturers are being pressured into accepting systems that are over-engineered for their particular requirements and that do not represent value for money, especially for small and medium-size businesses.

You will find the précis exercises useful when it comes time to write for the Web, where space is at a premium and viewers want to receive information quickly and succinctly.

Editing Conventions

Although individual styles may differ across media, there is a single, uniform set of conventions, including copyediting marks (also called proofreading marks) to designate changes in, for example, punctuation, capitalization, and word/letter order. These are the marks that faculty will likely use in commenting on papers. Learn to use them when editing your own first drafts of the assignments in this class.

Editing marks consist of two parts: a symbol in the margin designating what edit should be made and (sometimes) a mark on the manuscript showing where the edit should be made. Exhibit A.1 is a chart of the most common editing marks, showing the edit, an explanation, and a sample for each. Exhibit A.2 shows how these marks are used to note errors in copy and what the edited copy looks like.

Copyediting and proofreading diverge on purpose but converge on method. Copy editors check for accuracy, consistency, and economy of style. You should become adept at copyediting your own material, reading it and rereading it, trying to tighten it, strengthen it, and deliver your message as effectively as possible. Copyediting is generally a less formal procedure than proofreading, with editing marks written between lines as well as in the margins. This is one reason that media releases should be double spaced—that is, to give the editor room to make necessary copyediting marks.

Proofreaders, on the other hand, search for errors when the copy has reached "proof" stage, that is, after it has been typeset but prior to production. Proofreaders look for typesetting errors or inconsistencies. Copy editors and proofreaders use the same set of marks; what the marks are called depends on what you are doing.

Writing Tools

There are a number of writing tools that can help you prepare your writing to a professional standard, whether it is for a media release, brochure, annual report, or

EXHIBIT A.1 Standard copyediting/proofreading marks.

Copyediting marks

Explanation	Marks	Example
Delete marked copy	Del ℓ	Delete the extra extra word.
Insert word(s) written in margin	missing /	Insert the word.
Insert indicated copy	Ⓐ /	Paragraph A was omitted. Insert it here. ⌃
Insert space	# /	These words should not runtogether. ⌃
Close up extra space(s)	⌒	Delete the extra space between these ⌒words
Delete and close up	⌒ ℓ	Sometimes there are two errors to ⌒ccorrect.
Do not make marked change	⋯STET	Oops, this word should not be deleted.
Insert period	⊙	Copyediting ensures better copy ⌃
Insert comma	⌃	Good copy is short concise and accurate ⌃
Insert colon	⌃	The time is 2 45 p.m. ⌃
Insert apostrophe	⌄	The readability software is on Jacks computer. ⌄
Spell out	ⓈⓅ	To avoid confusion, spell out titles like Comm.
Transpose letters	TR	It is easy ot change letters that are out of orde
Transpose words	⌣	It is easy to words change that are out or orde
Start new line	⌐	Sometimes starting a new line may help a-void awkward word breaks.
Set in capital (uppercase) letters	CAPS	e.g., for magazines, like time
Set in lowercase letters (not capitals)	l.c.	e.g., for Magazines, like TIME
Set in roman type (not italic)	ROM	e.g., for magazines like TIME.
Set in italic type (slanted)	ITAL	e.g., for magazines, like TIME
Set in bold type (bold)	BF	Use boldface copy for emphasis.
Start new paragraph	¶	... last sentence in paragraph. New senten
No paragraph, run in (run on)	RUNIN	This is the last line of a paragraph. This should flow from the previous line.
No indentation, set farther to left	MOVELEFT	This line should be aligned left.
Set farther to right	MOVE RIGHT	This line should be moved to the right.

EXHIBIT A.2   Sample of the use of copyediting/proofreading marks.

	Copy with edit marks	**Copy after edits have been made**
RIGHT /CAP/tr	⌐though most newsrooms use video display	Though most newsrooms use video
c/s/ℓ/t	terminals these day, it is still important for	display terminals these days, it is still
i/CAP	writers to be able to edit copy on paper. a	important for writers to be able to edit
u/lc/tr/#	number of symbols have bene designedto	copy on paper. A number of symbols
l/	hep you communicate to the printer what	have been designed to help you commu-
⊙	you want to do	nicate to the printer what you want to do.

memo to your boss. Our review is not exhaustive, but the following are representative of these tools.

- ✦ Web sites
- ✦ Stylebooks
- ✦ Spell check
- ✦ Grammar check
- ✦ Dictionary
- ✦ Save as HTML
- ✦ Readability check
- ✦ A good proofreader is also a must
- ✦ Document templates
- ✦ Mail merge
- ✦ Thesaurus

Web Sites

Some publishers and style manuals make their resources available on the Internet. Some are "old standards" such as common dictionaries or William Strunk's famed *Elements of Style*. Others take advantage of the Internet's interactive capabilities. Some have a cost attached; others are free. Some specialize in, for example, writing for the media, or for publication.

Stylebooks

Without question, you should own *The Associated Press Stylebook and Briefing on Media Law*. Apart from being a standard problem-solving tool on questions of style, it is just plain informative. For example, did you know that attorneys are not necessarily the same as lawyers or that Pikes Peak (no apostrophe) was named after Zebulon Montgomery Pike? The *AP Stylebook* also contains a useful explanation of libel law, which every media writer should have for ready reference. If your employer uses the *New York Times* style, you will need a copy of that too.

The AP also publishes a broadcast manual of style, as do other news organizations and individuals. If writing for broadcast is a large part of your job, it would be wise and media-friendly to have one of these as a reference.

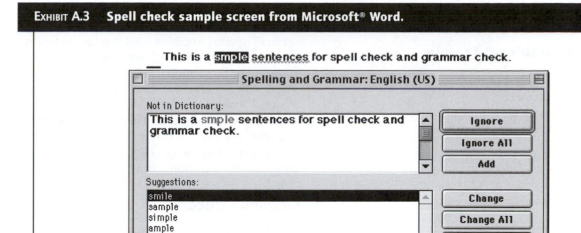

Spell Check

Spell check is a standard component of word processing and desktop publishing software. Spell check programs have two advantages: They find truly bad spelling mistakes, and most allow you to build a custom dictionary so that your employer's name, industry terminology, or abbreviations that you use frequently are not flagged as mistakes every time you run spell check.

The major downfall of spell check is that it accepts any correct spelling, even if the word is wrong. For example, *tan, ten, tin, ton,* and *tun* will all pass spell check; which one did you mean? Perhaps worse, it will not identify some of the most common errors such as *there/their/they're* or *for/fore/four.*

Exhibit A.3 illustrates spell check used on the following sentence:

This is a smple sentences for spell check and grammar check.

Spell check recognized that *smple* was not the correct spelling. It suggests an alternative in the "Suggestions" box. The alternative is based on the first letters you entered, in this case *sm,* which led to the suggestion *smile.* If you accept this, it replaces *smple* with *smile.* Otherwise you may select an alternative—in this case *sample*—or type in the correct word yourself. In the test sentence above, spell check would have accepted either *simple* or *sample.* Both of them make sense, but only one is what you mean. Note that spell check did not find the problem with the word *sentences* because it is spelled correctly.

There is a worst-case scenario. Most spell check programs propose alternatives to any word they identify as suspect. If you blindly accept all of the alternatives (which is

EXHIBIT A.4   Candidate for a Pullet Surprise.

Candidate for a Pullet Surprise

I have a spelling checker;
It came with my PC
It plane lee marks for my revue,
miss steaks aye can knot sea.

Eye ran this poem threw it,
your sure reel glad two no.
Its vary polished in it's weigh;
my checker tolled me sew.

A checker is a bless sing;
it freeze yew lodes of thyme.
It helps me right awl stiles two reed,
and aides me when aye rime.

Each frays come posed up on my screen
eye trussed too bee a joule.
The checker pours o'er every word;
To cheque sum spelling rule.

Be fore a veiling checkers
hour spelling mite decline,
And if we're lacks, oar have a laps,
we wood be maid to wine.

Butt now bee cause my spelling
is checked with such grate flare,
Their are know faults' with in my cite;
of nun eye am a wear.

Now spelling does knot phase me;
it does knot bring a tier.
My pay purrs awl due glad den,
with wrapped words fare as hear.

To rite with care is quite a feet,
of witch won should bee proud.
And wee mussed dew the best wee can,
sew flaw's are knot aloud.

Sow ewe can sea why aye dew prays
such soft ware four pea seas,
And why I brake in two averse
Buy righting want too pleas.

—Jerry Zar

Source: Reprinted with permission from the *Journal of Irreproducible Results.*

tempting to do when you are pressed for time or distracted by a phone call), you may change correctly spelled words as well, thereby ending up with some very unusual sentences. The poem "Candidate for a Pullet Surprise" (Exhibit A.4) shows with a humor that hits home for most professional writers that you can be horribly wrong and still pass a spell check. The fundamental problem with spell check is that it can build a false sense of security. Don't ever rely on it, especially for cross-cultural communication.

Grammar Check

Grammar check needs a similar caution. Most grammar check programs can catch obvious problems such as mismatched verbs and subjects. It is instructive to run a grammar check periodically as a grammar checkup.

The problem with grammar checks is that they also flag creative, but generally acceptable, usages as mistakes. For example: A grammar check on the last sentence flagged the word *creative*, suggesting that we consider an adverb instead of an adjective. Because of its proximity to the verb *flag*, the grammar check assumes creative modifies the verb rather than the noun. Grammar checks can be instructive but tedious.

After completing the spell check on the test sentence, "This is a smple sentences for spell check and grammar check," and changing *smple* to *sample*, the program conducted the grammar check shown in Exhibit A.5. It identified one problem: the number agreement between the singular subject *This is* and the plural object *sentences* and suggested correctly that the word *sentences* be made singular. The resulting sentence "This is a sample sentence for spell check and grammar check" is correct.

Readability Check

A somewhat more useful tool for the public relations writer is one or more of the readability check programs available with word processing software. Generally, readability checks work on formulae involving the number of words, characters, sentences, and paragraphs in the document as well as the average number of characters/word, words/sentence, and sentences/paragraph. A related

EXHIBIT A.5   Grammar check sample screen from Microsoft® Word. It is based on the sentence from the spell check example, Exhibit A.3.

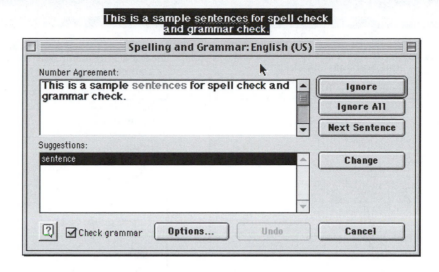

Source: Screen shots reprinted by permission from Microsoft Corporation.

measure—human interest—is based on the use of "people words" such as pronouns and quotes (" ") that indicate people talking.

Readability programs compute the readability level of the document. Most of them report the results across several scales. Two of the most common scales are the Flesch scale and the Flesch-Kincaid scale. The former reports results on a formula in which the lower the number, the more difficult the text. The latter reports results as the grade level at which an average reader would be able to understand the copy (e.g., a score of 5.24 is just over fifth-grade level). Readability check software may report results on one or both of these scales.

You can often make copy more readable just by making long sentences shorter, by dividing them into two or more sentences or by editing them to take out the unnecessary words. For example, the readability of the previous sentence using the Flesch readability scale is 44.3. The Flesh-Kincaid scale reports it at a reading level of Grade 12, the highest level reported. Rewriting the sentence as "You can simplify your copy by making long sentences shorter. Divide them into two sentences or edit them to remove the unnecessary words" takes the score to 61.3 on the Flesh scale and reduces the grade level to 7.1 on the Flesch-Kincaid scale. Rewriting it completely to "Divide or edit long sentences to make them more readable" does exactly that. These changes take the reading level of the sentence from "difficult" (academic/scholarly) to "standard" (e.g., *Time* magazine).

Exhibit A.6 illustrates a readability check on the test sentence used for the spell and grammar checks (left panel) and on the same sentence written with longer

EXHIBIT A.6   **Examples of readability checks from Microsoft® Word. The results in the left panel are based on the sentence used in the spell and grammar check examples. The results in the right panel are based on a version of that sentence with longer words and a more complex structure. Note both the Flesch and Flesch-Kincaid scores.**

This is a sample sentence for spell check and grammar check.

[This sequence of words is provided as an uncomplicated example for the purpose of employing a common computer facility known as spell check.

Readability Statistics

Counts	
Words	11
Characters	50
Paragraphs	1
Sentences	1

Averages	
Sentences per Paragraph	1.0
Words per Sentence	11.0
Characters per Word	4.4

Readability	
Passive Sentences	0%
Flesch Reading Ease	87.9
Flesch-Kincaid Grade Level	3.7

OK

Readability Statistics

Counts	
Words	23
Characters	118
Paragraphs	1
Sentences	1

Averages	
Sentences per Paragraph	1.0
Words per Sentence	23.0
Characters per Word	5.0

Readability	
Passive Sentences	100%
Flesch Reading Ease	32.6
Flesch-Kincaid Grade Level	12.0

OK

Source: Screen shots reprinted by permission from Microsoft Corporation.

words and a more complex structure (right panel). Note how the Flesch score decreases with difficulty while the grade level increases. This illustrates one of the primary difficulties with readability scales: You must refer to other sources to interpret them.

There is considerable debate over what readability scores actually measure and whether any score actually measures readability as the reader might understand it. There are many readability scores, each with its adherents. The one that is popular in your organization may or may not be available as part of a software package.

The problem with such scores is that they assume that we have only one public and that all its members are at the same educational level. One way to resolve this dilemma is through media choices. Although news media generally operate at an average level, your audiences will choose the media that best suits their interests and level of comprehension. It is your job to know what those media are and to write at an appropriate level.

Many companies whose business is technical documentation require that all documents pass a readability test as a matter of routine. You may have to run a readability test as automatically as you would run a spell check. You should be familiar with the concept of readability formulae and what they attempt to measure.

A Good Proofreader

When you have finished putting your copy through spell check, grammar check, and readability check, the final check should be to have it read by another person, preferably someone who has never read it before and who knows little about the subject. It should certainly be someone with a good knowledge of your employer's personnel and structure to catch wrong names and titles (a cardinal sin), factual errors, and the vital, but easily overlooked, misplaced decimal point.

Sometimes you cannot have enough checks. For example, the following piece of copy about a staff member who was a renowned judge of thoroughbred horses actually passed the scrutiny of four readers before the final-check secretary noticed the problem. Fortunately, she quickly altered the line "Ann Martin was selected the 'Horse of the Year'" to correctly read, "Ann Martin has selected the 'Horse of the Year.'"

Writers' heads have rolled for errors less serious than this. The most egregious sins involve financial information and people, especially people's names, and you cannot be too careful.

Document Templates

Many word processing packages also provide templates to help you create documents with a professional look, even if design is not your strong suit, and to ensure consistency in document design, such as for newsletters. Templates are preformatted documents that prompt you for the copy needed at a certain page position. They save you from having to decide how a letter, report, or press release should look. Professional communicators, especially those in large organizations, seldom use such templates either because they prefer to design their own or because the organization already has a defined style. But it is useful to know they are there. Exploring them may give you some ideas for your own publications.

Mail Merge

A template that may have greater value for the public relations writer is the mail merge template for envelopes and labels. Mail merge software makes it easy to customize material for multiple audiences. It is used when you want to tailor a generic message to target a specific group or individual. Typical uses include direct mail and routine media releases.

Mail merge has two components: a master template or generic document and a database of the information that is read into that document. The master template includes a command to insert data from the database in specific fields (such as "name"). The database contains the information that will change according to the media outlet. When you merge the two, the result is a document (or documents) containing individualized information taken from the database.

For example, suppose 12 students from your school have won awards for scholastic excellence. Your campus is understandably enthused and wishes to announce their success in news releases sent to the students' hometown media, but you know that any given paper will not print a release including all 12 students if 11 of them do not live in the area covered by that paper. The top portion of Exhibit A.7 is the master of a basic brief release that college public information staff might use for such occasions.

Mail merge sample

‹‹DATE››

‹‹CITY›› Resident Cited for Academic Excellence

Northfield, MA.   ‹‹CITY›› resident ‹‹FSTNAME›› ‹‹LASTNAME›› has been recognized for outstanding scholastic performance at Northfield College, Massachusetts. ‹‹LASTNAME››, majoring in ‹‹MAJOR››, is recognized in this semester's academic awards list as an outstanding college scholar. Northfield's Director of Academic Evaluation, Dr. Schleswig Holstein, says that only students with a perfect academic record receive such recognition. ‹‹LASTNAME›› is one of only twelve students qualifying for outstanding scholar this semester.

# # #

Database for mail merge sample

LASTNAME	FSTNAME	CITY	MAJOR	HIGH
Anderson	Alan	Glen Rock	Biology	South HIgh
James	Sally	Monroe	Communication	North Academy
Martin	George	Mansfield	Mathematics	Marshall

The bottom portion of Exhibit A.7 is a sample of a data file that could be used to fill in the blanks for this release. Typically, such information is held in a student information file that includes much more information than this, including the names of local media that the student has nominated to receive releases. For ease of explanation, we show in the data file only those pieces of information required by the release. Gathering this information when the student enrolls or an employee starts work will help the public relations writer target a release to the media in which it is most likely to be used.

Save as HTML

Word processing and other programs also allow you to save files as HTML (hypertext markup language), the language of the Internet. This makes it possible to upload the files directly for use in a web site.

RESOURCES

Goldstein, N. (Ed.). (2004). *The Associated Press stylebook and briefing on media law.* Reading, MA: Addison-Wesley.

Strunk, W., & White, E. B. (2000). *Elements of style* (4th ed). Needham Heights, MA: Longman.

Appendix B

*Public Relations Society of America
(PRSA) Code of Ethics*

The PRSA Assembly adopted this Code of Ethics in 2000. It replaces the Code of Professional Standards (previously referred to as the Code of Ethics) that was last revised in 1988. For further information on the code, please contact the chair of the Board of Ethics through PRSA headquarters.

Preamble

Public Relations Society of America Member Code of Ethics 2000

Professional Values

Principles of Conduct

Commitment and Compliance

This Code applies to PRSA members. The Code is designed to be a useful guide for PRSA members as they carry out their ethical responsibilities. This document is designed to anticipate and accommodate, by precedent, ethical challenges that may arise. The scenarios outlined in the Code provision are actual examples of misconduct. More will be added as experience with the Code occurs.

The Public Relations Society of America (PRSA) is committed to ethical practices. The level of public trust PRSA members seek, as we serve the public good, means we have taken on a special obligation to operate ethically.

The value of member reputation depends upon the ethical conduct of everyone affiliated with the Public Relations Society of America. Each of us sets an example for each other—as well as other professionals—by our pursuit of excellence with powerful standards of performance, professionalism, and ethical conduct.

Emphasis on enforcement of the Code has been eliminated. But, the PRSA Board of Directors retains the right to bar from membership or expel from the Society any individual who has been or is sanctioned by a government agency or convicted in a court of law of an action that is in violation of this Code.

Ethical practice is the most important obligation of a PRSA member. We view the Member Code of Ethics as a model for other professions, organizations, and professionals.

PRSA Member Statement of Professional Values

This statement presents the core values of PRSA members and, more broadly, of the public relations profession. These values provide the foundation for the Member Code of Ethics and set the industry standard for the professional practice of public relations. These values are the fundamental beliefs that guide our behaviors and decision-making process. We believe our professional values are vital to the integrity of the profession as a whole.

ADVOCACY

- We serve the public interest by acting as responsible advocates for those we represent.
- We provide a voice in the marketplace of ideas, facts, and viewpoints to aid informed public debate.

HONESTY

- We adhere to the highest standards of accuracy and truth in advancing the interests of those we represent and in communicating with the public.

EXPERTISE

- We acquire and responsibly use specialized knowledge and experience.
- We advance the profession through continued professional development, research, and education.
- We build mutual understanding, credibility, and relationships among a wide array of institutions and audiences.

INDEPENDENCE

- We provide objective counsel to those we represent.
- We are accountable for our actions.

LOYALTY

- We are faithful to those we represent, while honoring our obligation to serve the public interest.

FAIRNESS

- We deal fairly with clients, employers, competitors, peers, vendors, the media, and the general public.
- We respect all opinions and support the right of free expression.

PRSA Code Provisions

The PRSA Code specifically addresses six areas in which public relations practitioners may make decisions with ethical implications. They are: Free Flow of

Information, Competition, Disclosure of Information, Safeguarding Confidences, Conflicts of Interest, and Enhancing the Profession.

FREE FLOW OF INFORMATION

Core Principle

+ Protecting and advancing the free flow of accurate and truthful information is essential to serving the public interest and contributing to informed decision making in a democratic society.

Intent

+ To maintain the integrity of relationships with the media, government officials, and the public.
+ To aid informed decision-making.

Guidelines—A member shall:

+ Preserve the integrity of the process of communication.
+ Be honest and accurate in all communications.
+ Act promptly to correct erroneous communications for which the practitioner is responsible.
+ Preserve the free flow of unprejudiced information when giving or receiving gifts by ensuring that gifts are nominal, legal, and infrequent.

Examples of Improper Conduct Under this Provision:

+ A member representing a ski manufacturer gives a pair of expensive racing skis to a sports magazine columnist, to influence the columnist to write favorable articles about the product.
+ A member entertains a government official beyond legal limits and/or in violation of government reporting requirements.

COMPETITION

Core Principle

+ Promoting healthy and fair competition among professionals preserves an ethical climate while fostering a robust business environment.

Intent

+ To promote respect and fair competition among public relations professionals.
+ To serve the public interest by providing the widest choice of practitioner options.

Guidelines—A member shall:

+ Follow ethical hiring practices designed to respect free and open competition without deliberately undermining a competitor.
+ Preserve intellectual property rights in the marketplace.

Examples of Improper Conduct Under This Provision:

- ✦ A member employed by a "client organization" shares helpful information with a counseling firm that is competing with others for the organization's business.
- ✦ A member spreads malicious and unfounded rumors about a competitor in order to alienate the competitor's clients and employees in a ploy to recruit people and business.

DISCLOSURE OF INFORMATION

Core Principle

- ✦ Open communication fosters informed decision making in a democratic society.

Intent

- ✦ To build trust with the public by revealing all information needed for responsible decision-making.

Guidelines—A member shall:

- ✦ Be honest and accurate in all communications.
- ✦ Act promptly to correct erroneous communications for which the member is responsible.
- ✦ Investigate the truthfulness and accuracy of information released on behalf of those represented.
- ✦ Reveal the sponsors for causes and interests represented.
- ✦ Disclose financial interest (such as stock ownership) in a client's organization.
- ✦ Avoid deceptive practices.

Examples of Improper Conduct Under this Provision:

- ✦ Front groups: A member implements "grass roots" campaigns or letter-writing campaigns to legislators on behalf of undisclosed interest groups.
- ✦ Lying by omission: A practitioner for a corporation knowingly fails to release financial information, giving a misleading impression of the corporation's performance.
- ✦ A member discovers inaccurate information disseminated via a Web site or media kit and does not correct the information.
- ✦ A member deceives the public by employing people to pose as volunteers to speak at public hearings and participate in "grass roots" campaigns.

SAFEGUARDING CONFIDENCES

Core Principle

- ✦ Client trust requires appropriate protection of confidential and private information.

Intent

+ To protect the privacy rights of clients, organizations, and individuals by safeguarding confidential information.

Guidelines—A member shall:

+ Safeguard the confidences and privacy rights of present, former, and prospective clients and employees.
+ Protect privileged, confidential, or insider information gained from a client or organization.
+ Immediately advise an appropriate authority if a member discovers that confidential information is being divulged by an employee of a client company or organization.

Examples of Improper Conduct Under This Provision:

+ A member changes jobs, takes confidential information, and uses that information in the new position to the detriment of the former employer.
+ A member intentionally leaks proprietary information to the detriment of some other party.

CONFLICTS OF INTEREST

Core Principle

+ Avoiding real, potential or perceived conflicts of interest builds the trust of clients, employers, and the publics.

Intent

+ To earn trust and mutual respect with clients or employers.
+ To build trust with the public by avoiding or ending situations that put one's personal or professional interests in conflict with society's interests.

Guidelines—A member shall:

+ Act in the best interests of the client or employer, even subordinating the member's personal interests.
+ Avoid actions and circumstances that may appear to compromise good business judgment or create a conflict between personal and professional interests.
+ Disclose promptly any existing or potential conflict of interest to affected clients or organizations.
+ Encourage clients and customers to determine if a conflict exists after notifying all affected parties.

Examples of Improper Conduct Under This Provision

+ The member fails to disclose that he or she has a strong financial interest in a client's chief competitor.
+ The member represents a "competitor company" or a "conflicting interest" without informing a prospective client.

ENHANCING THE PROFESSION

Core Principle

+ Public relations professionals work constantly to strengthen the public's trust in the profession.

Intent

+ To build respect and credibility with the public for the profession of public relations.
+ To improve, adapt and expand professional practices.

Guidelines—A member shall:

+ Acknowledge that there is an obligation to protect and enhance the profession.
+ Keep informed and educated about practices in the profession to ensure ethical conduct.
+ Actively pursue personal professional development.
+ Decline representation of clients or organizations that urge or require actions contrary to this Code.
+ Accurately define what public relations activities can accomplish.
+ Counsel subordinates in proper ethical decision-making.
+ Require that subordinates adhere to the ethical requirements of the Code.
+ Report ethical violations, whether committed by PRSA members or not, to the appropriate authority.

Examples of Improper Conduct Under This Provision:

+ A PRSA member declares publicly that a product the client sells is safe, without disclosing evidence to the contrary.
+ A member initially assigns some questionable client work to a non-member practitioner to avoid the ethical obligation of PRSA membership.

PRSA Member Code of Ethics Pledge

I pledge:

To conduct myself professionally, with truth, accuracy, fairness, and responsibility to the public; To improve my individual competence and advance the knowledge and proficiency of the profession through continuing research and education; And to adhere to the articles of the Member Code of Ethics 2000 for the practice of public relations as adopted by the governing Assembly of the Public Relations Society of America.

I understand and accept that there is a consequence for misconduct, up to and including membership revocation.

And, I understand that those who have been or are sanctioned by a government agency or convicted in a court of law of an action that is in violation of this Code may be barred from membership or expelled from the Society.

Signature _____ Date _____

Source: PRSA web site, http://www.prsa.org.

Appendix C

Research Methods for Public Relations Writing

Following is a brief review of the methods you will likely consider when researching your employer's publics. You may want to refer to this as you need information to complete assignments in this text.

Generally, information about knowledge, attitude, and self-reported behaviors is captured using structured or formatted questions in a survey that uses phone, mail, the Internet, or personal interviews to deliver the questions to publics, or members of publics whom we have identified as research participants.

In passing, it is interesting to note how word choice influences the way we think of our publics. Researchers typically referred to *subjects* until the term came to suggest overtones of power, that is, the mighty researcher subjecting her subjects to questionnaires or medical experiments. The term *respondents* is more neutral, that is, people who respond to a questionnaire or research request. In human subjects research, where the rights of individuals are spelled out more clearly and where it is recognized that research cannot proceed without people's willing and informed participation, subjects/respondents are often referred to as *participants*.

Survey and Survey Methods

Before putting pen to paper, or fingers to keyboard, to design research questions, it is important to know how you will conduct the research. This will affect question content, tone, and, most of all, format options. Possible research options include phone, mail, interviews, and the Internet. Exhibit C.1 is a brief survey of these methods.

Telephone Surveys

On a cost-per-respondent basis, telephone surveys are relatively inexpensive and fast. For example, a broadcast network could commission a phone survey to be run one evening and report the results on the evening news the following night. You can get rapid national, even international, coverage.

Computer-based telephone technology makes possible a range of automated dialing options ranging from completely random auto-dialing to predictive dialing

EXHIBIT C.1   Survey methods for public relations research.

Survey type	Explanation/ examples	Advantages	Disadvantages
Telephone surveys	"Shotgun or rifle": random mass survey of general public or targeted survey of specific users.	Inexpensive, fast.	Questions are spoken; they must be simple; you are at the mercy of the respondent's time.
Mail surveys	Preprinted questionnaires sent with a cover letter and postage-paid envelope.	People complete them in their own time. Allows more questions than other survey.	Return rates are typically very low; no control over who responds.
Personal interviews	Interviewer conducts one-on-one interview with subject.	Allows detailed answers with follow-up opportunities.	Limited numbers of respondents and there are problems of access.
Focus groups	6–12 people plus moderator who discuss a topic.	Answers "why" people do/do not feel as they do and provides new ideas.	Cannot generalize findings to the general public.
Web surveys— general	Included as part of your client's web site for visitors to respond to.	You know the respondents are interested in your client.	Limited to people who access your site.
E-mail surveys— targeted	Distributed by e-mail.	Rapid delivery to large numbers of people.	Respondents get hundreds of e-mail messages and may not respond.

in which the dialer calls all of a list of numbers selected according to criteria you have provided. The difference, once again, lies in the aims of your survey.

For example, a hospital might survey a random selection of all the households in its area code to assess recognition of the hospital name and how local residents learn about the hospital. The same hospital might use a "predictive" survey of patients discharged within the past three months to determine what the patients thought of the admissions and exit processes. This survey could include all patients who meet the discharge criteria or a random selection of them.

Although telephone surveys are relatively inexpensive and efficient, they are not without problems. For example, to maximize the chances of reaching people at home you may need to call during evening hours and you risk reaching individuals and families at times (supper, evening TV, "quality time") when they don't want phone calls. In addition, because respondents cannot see the survey questions, they must be short and simple so that they can be readily understood over the phone.

You are also limited in the number of questions that can be asked before the respondent's patience runs out. People are usually willing to respond to reasonable research questions if they can see their legitimacy, but they may not if they believe the questions to be part of a sales pitch. A current, and likely growing, problem is the number of people, particularly young people, who have cell phones rather than land-based phones. This means that they are not reachable using phone book sampling methods.

Remember, too, that the people conducting the survey represent your employer (even if they are not your employees) and they should be well trained to ensure they represent your employer well.

Mail Surveys

Mail surveys have some unique advantages. People can complete them in their own time (a problem if their definition of time is "whenever"). Because the respondents can read the survey repeatedly and go back over it, the questions can be longer and more sophisticated than phone questions. Finally, you can use more of them.

However, mail surveys have one immediate problem. Because of the amount of mail flooding into consumer mailboxes—"junk" mail if you don't like it; "direct" mail if you're in the business—survey research has to compete with all sorts of direct mail appeals. To get people to even open the survey, the envelope must have a standout design quality.

The chief problem with mail surveys is the rate of return. In spite of incentives such as prizes and money for a rapid return, most surveys don't get good returns. For a large survey to people who are not expecting the mail, you may have to be content with a 3% return. If people find the survey relevant, you may get a 10% return.

Tricks of the trade that increase response rates include a prior mailing or phone call to alert people that the survey is coming and that it is legitimate. Follow-up phone calls or postcards are also used along with prizes or other incentives for an early return. Very high response rates are possible, but they usually happen only when the survey has been sent to a specifically targeted group to whom the survey is relevant for a reason you have spelled out in a preliminary letter or phone call. Typically, you will also have made at least one follow-up call or mailing to each individual to ensure such a high response. In the general scheme of things, most researchers are happy with something less than a 10% response.

Phone and mail methods have an inescapable bias on socioeconomic status; that is, it takes money to have a phone or an address. This makes phone and mail methods, for example, completely inappropriate if you are trying to assess attitudes of the homeless to social services that are being developed for them. This is where personal interviews come in and where debate over sampling arose with respect to the U.S. census (see www.govexec.com/dailyfed/0597/051397t4.htm or www.amstat.org/outreach/letter-congress.html).

Personal Interviews

Personal interviews refer to interviewers working through a preprinted questionnaire in a one-on-one relationship with a respondent. The method is expensive because of the labor costs, but people may be more inclined to respond to an in-person request. The interviewer can also help the respondent understand the question, but that intervention itself may potentially bias the answer.

Focus Groups

Much research has a quantitative bias—you are trying to count results. But numbers do not necessarily equate to understanding; you may not know why you got the numbers you did. For this reason, qualitative approaches such as focus groups also play a role in writing research. A focus group is a small group of participants discussing a topic of the researcher's choice. The researcher wants to understand the thinking behind consumer attitudes and decisions. If properly conducted, focus groups help you understand consumer reaction and they may well generate ideas that you had not thought of. Your task is to elicit the reasons behind the responses, and your strategy is to keep the group focused on the topic but in a relatively freewheeling discussion in which the basic instruction is, "There is no such thing as a dumb idea." A fundamental research skill is the ability to listen attentively.

Typically, you will audio- or videotape the focus group. Repeated listening, viewing, or reading of transcripts after the session usually reveals some theme or idea that will give you insight about the topic. Focus groups can also be used for writing research itself. You can use a focus group to test a proposed set of technical instructions, a new magazine layout, web page, or television public service announcement (PSA). You might elicit the participants' responses to use of language, order of presentation, metaphor or other linguistic devices, or even the point at which they got bored.

One producer of health-related PSAs argues that prelaunch focus groups are the only research method needed. You produce a PSA, focus-test to identify problems, reshoot or edit to remove the problems, pretest again, and so on until focus group research shows no negative response. At that point, you launch with confidence knowing that you have done the best possible job.

Web Surveys

An increasing number of organizations with web sites are taking advantage of the web capabilities to put their surveys online. Although you cannot expect to get a representative read on the attitudes of the general public from such a survey, you can get a fix on the attitudes of the people who actually visit your web site. It has the same limitations as a reader survey included in a publication. You can survey users or readers but you miss nonusers and nonreaders.

You can use a web survey to gather information about users' attitudes toward your organization or to assess the web site itself. Questions such as "Did you get the information you wanted from this web site?" "Was the web site easy to understand?" and "Was it easy to navigate?" will help you evaluate the contents and presentation.

These methods are all interrelated. Phone calls can prompt a respondent to answer a mail survey; a preliminary postcard can alert the recipient that a survey phone call scheduled for Saturday afternoon will be legitimate.

Mail can also be used to direct respondents to another method of phone survey: the 800 number and keypad response. This allows you to get survey data directly into your computer by having respondents key their answers in over the phone. Essentially, this is what you are doing if you book your airline tickets or do banking over the phone.

Sampling

Somewhere between asking every reader how he or she responded to your writing and asking a few friends over coffee lies the ideal number of people to ask to get the best survey results at the lowest cost in time and money. "What is the ideal number?" is a complex question that can be answered in practice by research texts or consultants.

Fundamentally, the issue is what level of uncertainty can you live with? National public opinion polls typically survey about 1,200 people, and the researchers are comfortable making generalizations to the adult U.S. population at a level of plus or minus 3%. This means that a finding that 37% of their sample would vote for Candidate X means that they are prepared to suggest that somewhere between 34% and 40% of the larger population would so vote (i.e., 3% more and 3% less than the 37% result).

This gives a useful indication of the political climate, but a problem arises when the sample shows that 49% would vote for Candidate X. With the same level of uncertainty, the candidate could lose with a 46% vote or win with a 52% vote. Under these conditions, Candidate X needs a greater level of certainty and would need a larger sample group to get it. Most research texts provide tables that will tell you sample size for a desired level of precision and statistical significance.

The second major sampling question is how to sample. The most easily understood method is random sampling. You random sample when, without looking, you pull a card from a deck or decide who is going to buy lunch by spinning a pen and letting its stopping position point to the lucky individual or by putting everyone's name in a hat and pulling names without looking at them. The essential point is that everyone has an equal chance of being selected. Conceptually, the method requires that all possible candidates for interviewing or surveying be in your initial list so that they all have an equal chance of being drawn.

Random sampling has two important benefits. Your sample is free of bias, and you are able to make extrapolations to the broader population you have sampled from. Without the precondition of random sampling or one of its relatives, you are entitled only to make generalizations about your sample population. As the whole intent of a sample is to be able to generalize to a broader population, it makes sense in principle to random sample.

Reliability and Validity

Research is evaluated by professionals on the extent to which it has reliability and validity. Reliability simply means that your questions should generate similar results from the same group of people each time they are used. For example, if 65% of respondents say that they are in favor of handgun control, you should expect approximately the same result, not 45% or 95%, from the same group a week later. If you do not get such consistency, you should wonder about the reliability of your questions.

In itself, validity deals with the concern that your research accurately captures what it set out to capture. It means that your questions measure the "reality" you are trying to measure. For some questions, validity can be established easily. For example, if you survey a cross section of the population and ask their age, the percentage telling you they are over 65 should be the same percentage that census data reveal for the overall population.

Validity is much more difficult to assess in opinion research. Subtle changes in wording can quite substantially change the results you get. For example, the aim of the questions "Should schools provide more resources for students?" and "Do you think we should spend more money on education?" may be the same, but the responses to the questions may be quite different. Which question is more valid?

Because wording can affect responses, questionnaire design may well become an ethical issue if an organization clearly wants to see a particular result or needs it for marketing purposes. Similarly, the sample—who you survey—can affect the results you get, and sampling too may have ethical considerations.

DISCUSSION 2

Identify a campus club, organization, or department that you feel could use some public relations support. Before starting your campaign, you need to identify campus opinion about this group. How will you do this? Who is/are your target public/s? What questions will you ask? What methods will you use to conduct the research? Why are these questions and methods appropriate to the public/s you have chosen?

Question Formats

There are many ways to format questions ranging from a simple yes/no to an open-ended "tell me all you know." The format you choose will be related to the method of delivery. Why waste a focus group's time on multiple-choice questions? They have come together to talk, so a well-chosen open-ended question is a necessity. Telephone surveys require simple questions that people can understand verbally and answer quickly—and that the questioner can record easily.

Researchers generally try to select a format that elicits as much specific information as possible without capturing more data than necessary and thus making the results time-consuming and difficult to analyze. Exhibit C.2 provides a simple review of several of these formats, including what they are and their advantages and disadvantages. If you conduct research often, or if you must plan and/or implement a major research project, it will pay to consult a research text for more options and more detail.

The formats discussed in this appendix are open-ended, yes/no, scaled (including Likert and semantic differential scales), and multiple choice.

Open-Ended Questions

Although open ended, "Tell me all you know about . . ." or "How do you feel about . . . ?" questions have the potential to elicit new ideas, generally, they are

Exhibit C.2   Question formats for public relations research.

Question type	Explanation/example	Used for/ advantages	Disadvantages
Open-ended	"Tell me all you know about..."or "How do you feel about...?"	Eliciting ideas or new information.	Not useful for surveys except as follow-ups such as "why/why not?"
Yes/no	"Did you read last night's newspaper?"	Speed; forces an opinion.	No neutral position. Answers are not explained.
Multiple choice or rank order	Respondents either choose one of a series of answers or rank the answers in order of importance.	You want to know which answer is most/least important.	Respondents may not see a ranking, or they may rank them equal.
Likert scale	Respond to series of statements by positioning answer on *agree–disagree scale*.	Often used in marketing to assess attitudes.	Respondents do not have the opportunity to explain their answers.
Semantic differential scale	Respondents select a position on a scale between polar opposites, e.g., good/bad, honest/ deceptive.	Useful in assessing employer against competition, for example.	Ideas to be tested are not always reducible to polar opposites.

not used in surveys because you want your research to have a focus, to be completed as soon as possible, and to get results that can be processed easily. It gets back to your research goals; if you are "fishing" for ideas, you may well want to arrange a focus group setting in which participants really are encouraged to tell everything they know and feel.

Yes/No Questions

At the other extreme is the single-choice, "yes/no" question. It is rapid and forces respondents to a position on an issue. It is appropriate for simple questions such as "Did you read last month's newsletter?" and may be widely used in national surveys that assess public sentiment. But, depending on your goals, yes/no questions may leave something to be desired. People genuinely may not know or they may have a neutral position. You may need to know the reasons behind the answer, and simple yes/no formats won't provide this information. At this point, consider the use of scaled questions that give respondents some room to move with respect to their answers.

Scaled Questions

Scales give the respondent the opportunity to relate his or her opinions to a set of questions defined by the researcher.

Likert Type Scale

Commonly used in marketing, public relations, and advertising research, the Likert scale, named after the inventor, asks subjects to respond to a series of statements by positioning themselves somewhere between agree or disagree on each statement.

Exhibit C.3 is an example of Likert questionnaire.

EXHIBIT C.3   Likert type scale questionnaire.

Survey for a reader or user survey in a publication or web site

Following are statements about the XYZ Corp. employee newsletter. Please check the response that most accurately reflects agreement with the statement.

	Strongly Agree	Agree	Neutral	Disagree	Strongly Disagree
It is easy to understand.	_____	_____	_____	_____	_____
The layout is interesting.	_____	_____	_____	_____	_____
My department is covered well.	_____	_____	_____	_____	_____
There is too much company news.	_____	_____	_____	_____	_____
The graphics are helpful.	_____	_____	_____	_____	_____

Following is an alternative way to ask the same questions, again using a Likert scale. In general, how satisfied are you with the XYZ Corp. employee newsletter?

	Very Satisfied	Satisfied	Neutral	Not Satisfied	Very Dissatisfied
Ease of understanding	_____	_____	_____	_____	_____
Layout	_____	_____	_____	_____	_____
Coverage of my department	_____	_____	_____	_____	_____
Coverage of company news	_____	_____	_____	_____	_____
Usefulness of graphics	_____	_____	_____	_____	_____

Semantic Differential Scale

The semantic differential scale, on the other hand, uses polar opposites to anchor the scale so that the answer options are always different. Good–bad, strong–weak, reliable–unreliable are examples. The scale is useful when trying to assess your

---

EXHIBIT C.4   Semantic differential scale questions.

Survey for the students and local community of a college

Following are two sets of question about Tri-State College and its students Please rank your opinion about the college and students on the following scales.

What do you think about Tri-State College?

Value for money	_____	_____	_____	_____	_____	Waste of money
Expensive	_____	_____	_____	_____	_____	Inexpensive
Too many majors	_____	_____	_____	_____	_____	Not enough majors
Friendly	_____	_____	_____	_____	_____	Unfriendly
Warm	_____	_____	_____	_____	_____	Cold
Drug-free	_____	_____	_____	_____	_____	Many drugs available
Community asset	_____	_____	_____	_____	_____	Community liability

What do you think about Tri-State College students?

Drug-free	_____	_____	_____	_____	_____	Many drugs
Alcohol-free	_____	_____	_____	_____	_____	Much drunkenness
Hard-working	_____	_____	_____	_____	_____	Lazy
Daring	_____	_____	_____	_____	_____	Timid
Friendly	_____	_____	_____	_____	_____	Unfriendly
Community asset	_____	_____	_____	_____	_____	Community liability

---

employer against other organizations or to position a product against its competition. The difficulty is that the world and its issues are not always reducible to polar opposites. Exhibit C.4 is an example of a semantic differential scale.

Multiple-Choice Questions

Frequently, you will know the answers you're looking for, but you do not know how they rank or how important they are with your publics. The American Heart Association may know, for example, that contributors expect their money to be spent on education, research, and publicity. But knowing which of these the public thinks is most/least important will have a significant effect both on how the money is spent and, more important to the public relations writer, on how any message regarding expenditures is presented.

In this scenario, multiple-choice or rank-order questions are useful. If you're responsible for assessing how to make your employee newsletter more appealing, you might decide that the following six aspects are important. You can use a multiple-choice questionnaire such as the following to get a reading on employee preferences.

For example:

1. The most important thing about the employee newsletter is that it (check one):

Is up-to-date	_____
Is mailed to my home	_____
Covers my department every issue	_____
Covers all departments every issue	_____
Has company financials	_____
Has photographs	_____

We hope that asking respondents to check only one forces a clear group preference result; however, you will learn only one preference for each respondent when they may think many things about the publication are important.

You may get a better reading on preferences if you ask people to check as many as they wish. In this case, the instruction would be the following:

1. The most important thing about the employee newsletter is that it (check as many as apply):

You will still get a preference based on number of votes for each aspect, but you will have a richer sense of where other preferences stand in relation to the "winner" (if there is one).

Of course, with the "check as many as you like" instruction, you face the possibility of no clear priority because everyone checks everything. To avoid this, you may want to force respondents to rank their preferences by numbering them. This forces them to tell you how important they consider each issue. In this case, the instruction changes to the following:

1. Please rank the most important things about the employee newsletter by numbering each choice from 1 to 5 where 1 = first choice; 5 = last choice.

You can then get a weighted score for each public that should clearly show their collective preference.

Survey Methods

With questions designed, there is now the issue of how to deliver them to respondents. "Delivery mechanisms" include phone, mail, interviews, and the Internet.

RESOURCES

Babbie, E. E. (1992). *The practice of social research* (6th ed.). Belmont, CA: Wadsworth.

Broom, G. M., & Dozier, D. M. (1990). *Using research in public relations: Applications to program management.* Englewood Cliffs, NJ: Prentice Hall.

Appendix D

Production Issues

Printing Issues

The following chart introduces many of the printing issues that you will have to deal with as a public relations writer, such as paper type, size, finish, and the printing methods that work best with each of them.

Options	Advantages	Disadvantages
8.5″ × 11″ sheet(s)	✦ Extremely flexible. You can easily print any number of pages without looking incomplete. ✦ Depending on your production method, you can print single- or double-sided. ✦ Can be produced on ink-jet and laser printers and reproduced on photocopiers, including color printers and photocopiers. ✦ Economical and reasonable quality for small quantities.	✦ Multiple pages must be stapled. ✦ Best for manual distribution as stapled pages are difficult to stuff and mail.
11″ × 17″ sheet(s) folded once to 8.5″ × 11″	✦ Very professional. ✦ Must be double-sided. ✦ Single pages of the original can be produced on ink-jet and laser printers and sent for reproduction onto the 17″ × 11″ sheets. ✦ Provides great freedom for designers and layout artists, especially for articles that run across two pages (called spreads). ✦ Because reproduction usually requires a commercial printer, you will have other options such as color, photos, and special papers.	✦ Reproduction requires a large copier or commercial printing equipment, plus a "folder." On the plus side, this may open other options such as color, photos, and special papers. ✦ You must have enough information for at least three pages or the issue will look unfinished. ✦ Unless you want a single sheet in the center, you must increase the size in multiples of 4 pages. ✦ Generally, not economical for small quantities.

(Continued)

Options	Advantages	Disadvantages
In-house photocopier	◆ Least expensive. ◆ Efficient for small print runs. ◆ Least time sensitive: Issue can be produced at any time.	◆ Relatively expensive per page for long print runs. ◆ Paper size limited to 8.5″ × 11″. ◆ Assembly of multiple pages requires stapling.
In-house or commercial copy center	◆ May allow longer print runs and larger paper. ◆ May permit colored copies.	◆ Need to ensure newsletter gets priority over other jobs to meet your deadlines. It may not.
Commercial offset printer	◆ Offers the largest range of sizes, paper choice, color reproduction, including photos. ◆ Cost-effective for large print runs. ◆ Services often include mailing and inserting inserts, such as coupons, ballots, forms, and envelopes.	◆ Generally, not cost-effective for small print runs. ◆ Production will take place on a normal printers' schedule—usually several days.

Appendix E

Grammar and Style

This appendix reviews grammar and style issues that have particular relevance to the public relations writing projects discussed in this book and that represent the most common errors. We recommend that you consult the many excellent sources on grammar, some practical, some detailed, and even some humorous. We have listed our favorites at the end of the chapter and recommend that you refer to them as you have specific questions.

Choosing the Correct Word

The following list includes words that are frequently mistaken for each other and, therefore, that are often misused. Spell check software will not identify the wrong word if it is spelled correctly. We have grouped them to make the distinctions clear. In the following cases, the problem words have similar spellings and often pronunciation. Misuse of these words will quickly mark your writing as unprofessional.

Accept ..... to receive .... I *accept* the gift.

Except ..... to make an exception.......................... Everyone *except* John will win a prize.

..... to exclude .... John should be *excepted* from the list of prize winners.

Adapt ..... o change or adjust.............................. Freshmen must *adapt* to college.

Adopt ..... to choose or take as one's own............ Many women *adopt* their husband's name.

Addition ..... an extra part... They built an *addition* on the house.

.... mathematical process. .... The *addition* of one and one equals two.

Edition ..... a new volume .... The second *edition* of this text was published in 2005.

Affect ..... a verb, to have influence .... TV *affects* children.

Effect ..... a noun, a result .... TV has an *effect* on children.

..... a verb, to bring about a resolution...... Citizens *effect* change by voting.

All ready ..... everyone/everything is prepared......... The team is *all ready* to play.

Already ..... before, previously .... The team has *already* made the playoffs.

A long ..... expressing length .... It was *a long* drive up to the house.

Along ..... in association with, together .... She went *along* with the joke.

Amount ..... cannot be counted; it is a collective .... The small *amount* of pollen

Number...... can be counted as individual pieces.... in the air affects a large *number* of people

A part ..... one section of.. The Senate is *a part* of the U.S. Congress.

Apart ..... not together, e.g., separate or broken . The mechanic took the car engine *apart.*

Assure ..... to affirm, verify .... I *assure* you I checked the spelling.

Insure/...... to make certain .... Copy editors *ensure* the grammar is correct.
ensure

Beside ..... next to .... The dictionary is *beside* the thesaurus.

Besides ..... except .... No one *besides* John is eligible to play.

..... also, in addition to .... I want to go to the fair because it's fun. *Besides,* it's free.

Cite ..... to refer to, usually as a quote .... He *cited* Mark Twain as his source.

Sight ..... vision or field of vision .... The finish line finally came into *sight.*

Site ..... location .... The *site* of the 2000 Olympics was Sydney.

Companies .... more than one business .... Ford and Chrysler are auto *companies.*

Company's .... the possessive for company .... The *company's* head office is in Akron.

Compliment ... a noun or verb conveying praise .... He paid her a *compliment.*

Complement .. a verb, to fill or complete...................... Her eyes *complement* her dress.

Eminent ..... important or outstanding .... Pasteur was an *eminent* scientist.

Imminent ..... due to occur soon .... The hurricane's arrival was *imminent.*

Its ..... the possessive of it .... A company's staff is *its* biggest asset.

It's ..... a contraction for "it is"........................ *It's* a fact.

Moral ..... noun: message or lesson .... The *moral* of the story is not to lie.

.... ethical, ethical principle .... He has a *moral* obligation to tell the truth.

Morale ..... attitude .... *Morale* was high after the company announced a bonus for all staff.

Now ..... at the present time .... The class begins *now.*

Know ..... understand, recognize .... I *know* that I should study for the test.

Passed ..... exceeded another, met a standard ...... He *passed* the exam.

Past ..... a previous time .... His leg hurt from a *past* injury.

Principal ..... most important .... Shakespeare was his *principal* source.

.... school head .... Mr. Martin was the high school *principal*.

.... sum on which interest is earned .... The loan *principal* was $2,000.

Principle ..... a basic truth .... The ten commandments are *principles.*

Personal ..... unique to oneself .... *Personal* data include sex, age, and weight.

Personnel ..... staff.. A growth in profit allowed the company to hire new *personnel.*

Perspective .... a point of view .... From the writer's *perspective.*

Prospective .... likely, in the future............................. Audiences are *prospective* supporters.

Stationary ..... not moving .... The train at the depot was *stationary.*

Stationery ..... writing paper, envelopes, etc. .... It is time to order more *stationery.*

Their ..... a possessive.. *Their* computer is broken.

There ..... an adverb indicating a place .... You will find the book over *there.*

...... an expletive .... *There* are 16 chapters in this book

They're ..... a contraction for "they are" .... *They're* about to arrive.

To ..... a preposition indicating where .... He sent the media release *to* the press.

Too ..... also, as well .... John went and Sally went *too.*

Two ..... the number .... There are *two* shoes in a pair.

Were ..... past tense of was .... The Bulls *were* three-time champions.

Where ..... what place?.. Home is *where* the heart is.

Who's ..... a contraction for "who is" .... *Who's* the owner of this jacket?

Whose ..... the possessive for who (who owns) .... *Whose* jacket is this?

Yore ..... a previous time (archaic) .... In days of *yore.*

Your ..... the possessive for you .... *Your* research paper is due next week.

You're ..... a contraction for "you are".................. *You're* late.

The above words are not the only source of common confusion. Following are additional terms and phrases you must know how to use.

Among................. Used when there are more than two choices.

Between................. Used when there are two choices.

Example................. In 1996, voters chose *between* Bill Clinton and George Bush. In 1992, they chose from *among* Clinton, Bush, and Ross Perot.

Compare................. to find the similarities.

Contrast................. to find the differences.

Example .... The SAT exam typically asks students to *compare* and *contrast* the presidencies of John F. Kennedy and Abraham Lincoln.

Caution .... Spoken English may use the two terms interchangeably; written English does not.

e.g. .... It stands for *exempli gratia*. It means "for example."

i.e. .... It stands for *id est*. It means "that is."

Example .... With controlled media, *e.g.*, the press, TV, and radio, you must always consider a third audience, *i.e.*, the editors and reporters who will determine if your story is newsworthy.

Caution .... The general trend is to prefer the English to the Latin, but e.g. and i.e. are commonly used. Check your house style for guidance. Both should be followed by a comma as in the example above.

More .... the better, greater, etc. of two, also indicated by "er" at the end of adjectives, e.g., great*er*, near*er*, smart*er*.

Most .... the best, greatest, etc. of more than two, also indicated by "est" at the end of adjectives: great*est*, near*est*, smart*est*.

Examples .... Michael Jordan was *more talented* than Scottie Pippen (compared only to Pippen). Shaquille O'Neal is *taller* than Kobe Bryant (compared only to Bryant).

.... Michael Jordan was *the most talented* member of the Chicago Bulls. Shaquille O'Neal is *the tallest* member of the Lakers (both compared to all members of their teams).

Caution .... Do not use *more* or *most* with an adjective that has the comparative "er" or superlative "est" ending, e.g., do not use "more taller" or "most tastiest."

Choosing the Right Word or Phrase

Just because you select the correct word or phrase from among those listed above (note the use of *among*, because we are referring to more than two options) does not mean it is the right word or phrase to most effectively convey your meaning. When people hear or see a word, they interpret not only its meaning but also its tone, which helps to convey the attitude of the message and improves communication.

This means that as a writer, you must choose words and phrases not only for their meaning but for their attitude as well. The right choice of words will excite, anger, or inspire your audience to behave as your employer wants. The wrong choice will at least plant seeds of doubt about your employer's credibility or relevance.

We touched on this briefly in Chapter 2 when we discussed the placement of the word "only" in the sentence "I wrote the copy" and the contents of cover letters for job applications and résumés. In particular, we discussed the differences among "heading a group," "directing a group," and "leading a group" and between "leading a group" and "leading a team." Basically, these options say the same thing, that is, that other members of a group look to you for direction. However, the words "heading," "directing," and "leading" may suggest that you are impressed by power (heading), autocracy (directing), or innovation (leading). Similarly, the choice of "team" brings with it the idea of working together, while "group" is simply a gathering of people who may or may not be working toward a single goal.

The phrase you choose will say important things about you to employers that are formal/hierarchical, on one hand, or relaxed/informal, on the other. Following are additional examples of how words and phrases convey an attitude.

Suggest	....	Provides the reader with a sense of options and the understanding of which one(s) your employer would like you to select or do.
Recommend	....	Stronger than suggest, has a connotation of you "should."
Insist	....	Getting even stronger. Has element of no choice.
Demand	....	May have legal connotations. Implies urgency and importance.
Require	....	Removes all options. The audience *must* act as stated.
Example	....	Al's friends *suggested* he might need a good lawyer to recover his money and *recommended* the firm of Morton, Morton, and Morton. Morton *insisted* that Al file a claim immediately and *demanded* that his debtor pay up, *requiring* the immediate payment of at least 50% as proof of good faith.
Talk to	....	Deliver a speech, have a one-way communication.
Talk with	....	Engage in a dialogue, have a two-way communication.
Example	....	Before the president *talked to* Congress, he *talked with* members of his cabinet to get their opinions.
Work for	....	Conveys a hierarchical rather than a team relationship.
Work with	....	Implies working together in a team relationship.
Work at	....	Carries the implication that the task is difficult for you, which may or may not be part of your message.
Work toward	....	Is forward looking, implies a goal.
Example	....	Al *worked for* Behemoth, Inc. He *worked with* Huey, Dewey, and Louie on the Smithers project. They all *worked at* assembling widgets while *working toward* the goal of someday owning their own business.

Spelling: Some Hints for Managing the Problem

In many cases, there is a fine line between choosing the wrong word and simply misspelling it. Unfortunately, neither is acceptable. Everyone should own a good dictionary, and if you are not a good speller (and many people aren't) it should be your constant companion. Even if you don't recognize the word as misspelled, a high percentage of your readership will recognize it every time, and it will annoy them.

The important issue is that you learn to identify potential problems in your writing and to be sensitive to options that may cause your writing to be misinterpreted. Consult a thesaurus, but ensure that you understand the meaning of all options before you select one. Listen closely and read voraciously. Pay attention to how you react to various word choices. Which ones make you uneasy or unsure what the writer meant? Which ones give you confidence that you and the writer are on the same wavelength? Why?

Here are a few hints to help your spelling.

Spell Check

Spell check is both an asset and a liability. There is no doubt that it will find misspellings. It will not, however, find words that are spelled correctly but that are the wrong word (e.g., *bag, beg, big, bog, bug* or *adapt, adopt* or *compliment, complement*). Be especially careful before you accept the option offered. See Appendix A.

Dictionary

Keep a dictionary handy or bookmark one of the online options. And use it. Some of the online grammar web sites even allow you to ask questions about spelling, and "bad spelling" dictionaries allow you to search for words using common misspellings on the principle that if you cannot spell it, you are unlikely to find it in a standard dictionary.

House Style Manuals

Your employer's house style manual should include the accepted spelling of all words, abbreviations, and acronyms that are peculiar to your employer or the industry or that you will use often.

Practice

When you identify the correct spelling of a word that you misspelled or didn't know how to spell, don't just insert it in the sentence and forget it. Write or type it a dozen times and really look at the spelling. Try to remember it just as you memorized your spelling words as a child.

Create Your Own Guide

Keep a personal spelling guide of words you use frequently and often misspell near your computer, even posted to the side of the monitor.

A Good Proofreader

Take advantage of the good spellers in your organization. Even if you are a good speller, another pair of eyes will often find errors you miss, especially the type missed by the spell check.

Parallel Structure

We could address many concerns with sentence structure, among them the use of phrases and clauses and dangling modifiers. We will, however, limit ourselves to the use of parallel structure, which we have mentioned again and again in the text, especially in Chapters 2 and 10. Parallel structure is the key to effective bullet points and highlights and an important element in text that flows smoothly.

Parallel structure is the process of matching, usually nouns with verbs but also singulars and plurals, verb tenses and ideas, to create units that flow smoothly and make sense. Parallel structure is not only fundamental to correct writing but also critical to polished, professional writing.

◆ *Subjects, verbs, and pronouns must match,* singular with singular and plural with plural. The professional public relations *writer proofreads* media releases carefully. Professional public relations *writers proofread* media releases carefully.

It is especially easy to err when using collective terms such as *everyone* or *the number of* that sound plural but are treated as singular. It is incorrect to write, "*Everyone* had *their* eyes on the last piece of chocolate" or "The *number* of players who scored touchdowns *have* increased annually since 1990."

Because the English language has masculine and feminine pronouns and possessives in the third person (*he/she, him/her, his/hers*), you may find yourself overwhelmed by awkward constructions when using singular subjects. For example, the sentence "When *the writer* wants *his or her* copy approved, *he or she* must submit it to the editor" is awkward. It is almost always easier to change the subject to the plural. "When *writers* want *their* copy approved, *they* must submit it to the editor," or "*Writers* who want *their* copy approved must submit it to the editor."

Collective nouns, such as *staff, team, committee,* or *faculty,* may be either singular, when you mean the group as a unit, or plural, when you refer to the individual members. Say "the *team is* heading to State University for *its* next game" and "the *team are* working on the graphics for *their* presentation next week." For clarity, it may be wise to add the word *members* when using the plural: "*team members are.*"

◆ Keep verb tenses consistent.

Shifting from present to past to future tense leaves the reader uncertain about when an event occurred. For example, in the sentence "While the players *were* on the field, they *tackle* and *will practice* returning punts and kick-offs," we are not sure when anything is happening. Assuming that the action is in the past, the sentence should read, "While the players *were* on the field, they *tackled* and *practiced* returning punts and kick-offs."

◆ Keep phrases parallel.

"The responsibilities of the public relations writer are *interviewing subjects, to proofread copy,* and *the daily fax newsletter.*" The three italicized phrases all describe the writer's responsibilities, but they are not parallel.

Following are several alternatives, each of which makes this sentence parallel:

"The responsibilities of the public relations writer are to interview subjects, proofread copy, and distribute the daily fax newsletter." (These are all infinitives with the "to" understood before "proofread" and "distribute." You can, of course, write in each "to.")

"The public relations writer is responsible for interviewing subjects, proofreading copy, and distributing the daily fax newsletter."

"The public relations writer is responsible for interviews, proofreading, and the daily fax newsletter."

✦ Be alert to pairs and make them parallel.

Paired concepts such as "either/or," "neither/nor," and "not only/but also" must be paired as well. For example, if you start a sentence with "The essay *not only was* too long" you must end it with a parallel structure such as "*but also included* many spelling errors." If you set up a choice with "either" or "neither," you must follow it with "or" or "nor." "*Neither the undergraduates nor the faculty* like early morning classes."

The same is true for the words and phrases before and after conjunctions such as "and," "but," and "or." It is incorrect to write, "Students can improve their writing by using correct grammar and choose the right word."

Politically Correct, Gender-Neutral Writing

Politically correct (PC) and gender-neutral writing is the subject of much discussion, and on many specifics the jury is still out. Theoretically, politically correct and gender-neutral writing doesn't offend anyone; that is its aim. In practice, however, because it can be awkward and obvious it has the potential to offend anyone who enjoys word specificity and the beauty of colorful, well-expressed thoughts. The sentence design and the attitude conveyed by the PC word or phrase often becomes more important than the message.

The aim of PC writing should always be a concern of the public relations writer. With a good understanding of your audience, of the meaning, and of the attitude of the words you choose, you should be able to write clear messages without excessively obvious PC constructions, such as businessperson or waitstaff. The following hints may help you deal with what will be a growing concern to professional writers in all sectors.

✦ *Never* write racial, religious, ethnic, political, or sexual slang or slurs. This is not just "PC"; it is common respect.
✦ Ask real subjects how they want to be referred to, especially if you need to describe their heritage: race, religion, or ethnic background. It seems to us that if someone wants to be referred to as African American rather than as black, or vice versa, then we owe them that courtesy. The same is true for titles, such as chairman, chairperson, chairwoman or chair, and for religions.

However, before you find yourself embroiled in a debate over such titles, ask yourself if the distinction is critical to the article. If not—and it often isn't—then don't mention it.

✦ Write sentences to avoid gender-specific pronouns.
✦ Use plural instead of singular pronouns. "They," "their," and "theirs" are gender neutral.
✦ Replace gender-specific pronouns with articles "a" or "the." "Each student must submit a paper on Friday" rather than "Each student must submit his paper on Friday."

You may have to restructure the sentence completely to avoid these pronouns, but it generally results in a more succinct sentence as well as avoiding the gender issue. This is a special problem with conditional "if" or "when" sentences. For example, "If a writer wants to avoid bias in his writing, he should try to choose plural forms" can be rewritten as "To avoid bias in writing, choose plural forms."

◆ *Use gender-neutral collectives.* Although some PC forms may interfere with your message because they are awkward and obvious, in many cases there are collectives that are easy to use and do not interfere with the communication. Learn to use them. Examples include the following:

steward/stewardess	cabin crew, flight attendant
waitress/waiter	server
chairman/chairwoman	chair, head

◆ *Use a verb instead of a gender-sensitive noun.* Instead of "Mary Smith was chairwoman/person of the committee," write "Mary Smith chaired the committee." This too is likely to result in a stronger, more active sentence.

◆ And to avoid being embroiled in specific incidents involving PC speech, it is wise to develop, debate, and adopt a house style for PC and gender-neutral speech, and then stick with it. Insist that everyone in the organization does so. We suggest the house style should be aimed at promoting thoughtful and respectful writing rather than with demanding rigid adherence to neutral but usually awkward, colorless constructions.

Punctuation for Sense and Effect

Contrary to popular opinion, punctuation was invented to help readers and writers, not to plague them. As Diana Hacker (2001) puts it, "Without [punctuation], sentence parts can collide into one another unexpectedly, causing misreadings."

For the specifics of punctuation marks and the rules that govern their use, consult the grammar book that should be on your desk beside the dictionary and the thesaurus. The following section demonstrates how punctuation can support or confuse your communication and offers tips to help you resolve some common punctuation dilemmas.

To understand the role of punctuation in communication, start by reading the following sentences aloud.

"While we ate Mandy and Marc announced their engagement."

"In a Christmas Eve, 1995, fire 23 primates died at the Philadelphia zoo." (Victims, 1998)

"Soon after we started the car began to lose transmission fluid."

Was that with or without hot peppers? Do you read "fire 23 primates" rather than "1995 fire"? Did the leak begin after you started the trip or started the car? Punctuated differently, these sentences would be perfectly clear.

"While we ate, Mandy and Marc announced their engagement."

"In a Christmas Eve, 1995, fire, 23 primates died at the Philadelphia zoo." (To avoid three commas in a row, we suggest rewriting the whole sentence to read, "Twenty-three primates died in a Christmas Eve, 1995, fire at the Philadelphia zoo.")

"Soon after we started, the car began to lose transmission fluid."

An even better example is the following anecdote that we found floating around the Web. We have attempted without success to identify the author, but we nevertheless tip our hats to him or her for a superb example.

An English professor wrote the words "Woman without her man is nothing" on the blackboard and directed his students to punctuate it correctly.

The men wrote, "Woman, without her man, is nothing."

The women wrote, "Woman! Without her, man is nothing."

Commas

Commas are a short pause like quick breaths in a sentence. Sometimes they are used for exactly that. Learn to "hear" when you need a comma. Read the sentence aloud and listen to where you are naturally taking a breath, even a small one. Chances are that a comma belongs there, but there are also rules as to when to add a comma, such as to set off a phrase.

Do use commas to

- ✦ Separate a series of nouns or phrases.
- ✦ Separate a series of coordinate adjectives. These are adjectives that all modify the subject. Rosa and Escholz (1999) suggest that you can test whether a series of adjectives need commas by changing the order of the adjectives or by trying to put the word "and" between them. If the order is interchangeable or if the word "and" is appropriate, as in the following sentence, then you need commas: "The president's speech was interesting, forceful, informative, and colorful."

  On the other hand, interchanging the adjectives in the sentence "The two red brick houses on Maple Street are for sale" does not make sense. Nor does inserting "and" between them. Commas are not necessary.

- ✦ Set off direct speech, when you quote someone.
- ✦ Set off transitions and parenthetical expressions. "Regardless of your age, you cannot avoid the driving test." "A driving test, for example, is a teenage ritual."

Although some grammarians say that you do not need a comma before "and," there are times when a comma is necessary.

Semicolons

Think of semicolons as soft periods that separate complete but related thoughts. Be sure the thoughts on both sides of the semicolon are complete. If they are not, separate them with a comma.

"We drove to the mall; the parking lot was full."

Colons

Colons are essentially directions; they point you to the words, phrases, or clauses that follow the colon and they implicitly tell you that these words, phrases, or clauses illustrate or elaborate on the clause that preceded the colon.

"At the 2004 Olympics, two American swimmers broke world records: Michael Phelps and Aaron Piersol."

Quotation Marks

The greatest confusion with quotation marks is where to place other punctuation in relation to them. The following guidelines should help.

- Place commas and periods *inside* the quotation marks.
- Place colons and semicolons *outside* the quotation marks.
- Place question marks and exclamation points *inside* the quotation marks if they apply to the quote and *outside* the quotation marks if they apply to the whole sentence.

Exclamation Marks

Exclamation marks should be reserved for special emphasis. Use them sparingly to show surprise, alarm, or excitement.

Some punctuation, especially for names and slogans, is subject to the styles of individual organizations and industries (e.g., Yahoo!). Always consult your employer's style manual or follow the style of the organization you are naming.

Apostrophes

Apostrophes have two purposes: They designate possession and they substitute for a missing letter or number. When they designate possession, they indicate an ownership or relationship. Bob's home means the place where Bob lives. General Motors' Annual Report is the report that General Motors produced. *As a general rule,* if the word does not end in s, add apostrophe and s ('s). If the word does end in s, simply add an apostrophe after the final s (s').

Be aware that there are many exceptions to this rule, the most common being the possessive of "it." There is no apostrophe in the possessive of "it." "Its" (without an apostrophe) is the possessive of "it," as in "The newspaper printed its editorial policies on the op-ed page." This is an area in which a good stylebook is essential.

When it replaces a missing letter, the apostrophe forms a contraction. "Don't" means "do not." "It's" means the same as "it is." If you are not sure whether to use an apostrophe with the word "it," try substituting "it is." If that makes sense, then you need an apostrophe. If it doesn't, you don't.

The Authors' Pet Peeves

Some grammatical problems are difficult to categorize, especially when some may be problems related to culture or changing usage. Forms and usages that were unacceptable a few years ago may be acceptable today, and some of what is unacceptable today may be acceptable tomorrow. This aside, following are some of our pet peeves.

◆ Myself

Other than for describing who has been injured, for example, "I cut myself," there is no use for the word "myself." It is not a substitute for "I," "me," or "mine," and when used to describe who did something as in "I wrote it myself," it is unnecessary. A simple "I wrote it" expresses the same thought.

◆ You or me, who comes first?

Some of what passes for good grammar relates more to common courtesy than to rules of style or structure. A case in point is the question posed above, "You or me, who comes first?" The answer is always the other person as long as he or she can be named or designated.

Wrong	I and my lab partner finished the experiment. "Me and Albert . . ." is also wrong because "me" is an objective pronoun not a subjective pronoun.
Correct	My lab partner and I finished the project.
Wrong	The server brought salads to me and my date.
Correct	The server brought salads to my date and me.

◆ Double negatives

Double negatives confuse the audience. For example, does the sentence "It isn't true that writers do not have to write clearly" mean that they do have to write clearly or that they don't? If you mean that writers have to write clearly, say so. Do not make the audience figure it out.

◆ Ain't

It doesn't matter whether "ain't" is a word or not. It is not professional. Do not use it for professional communications.

◆ Fun, funner, funnest

"Fun" is a noun. Nouns do not have comparatives and superlatives such as "funner" and "funnest." The sentence "We had a fun time" is redundant; a simple, "We had fun" is sufficient.

◆ Apostrophes and plurals

With one exception, apostrophes have nothing to do with plurals. Nevertheless, we often see them used that way, especially with short words such as TV, CD, or FAQ. Odd though it may look, the plurals of such words just have a lowercase "s" added to them: CDs, TVs, and FAQs. The *only* exception to this rule is when the word is just one letter, as in "John's fall grades were all A's and B's."

REFERENCES

Hacker, D. (1997). *A pocket manual of style* (2nd ed.). Boston: Bedford Books, p. 51.

Victims' images to go home. (1998, September). *National Geographic,* Earth Almanac.

Rosa, A., & Escholz, P. (1999). *The writer's brief handbook* (3rd ed.). Needham, MA: Allyn & Bacon, p. 193.

Glossary

1-shot.................................. in a video, shot of one person.

2-shot.................................. in a video, shot of two people.

Accordion fold.................... brochure style with at least two folds. The folds go in opposite directions so the brochure opens like an accordion.

Actuality.............................. audio material provided via tape, CD, or web to accompany a news release.

Advertising.......................... use of purchased media space or time to promote an organization's products or services. It is often used to retain full control over message content, placement, and timing.

Announcer........................... voice only.

A-roll................................... video news release (VNR) ready for broadcast.

Assets.................................. what you have. Assets include cash, securities, equipment, buildings, and merchandise.

Audio .... spoken words or sounds.

Backgrounder..................... fact sheet providing historical or explanatory information on an organization or issue.

Balance sheet..................... a snapshot of where an organization stands financially. The balance sheet is a two-column report, one column including assets (sources of revenue, increase in market value of securities, and value of tangible property) and the second column including liabilities plus owner's equity. The total of each of these columns must be the same, hence the term "balance" sheet.

Banner................................. the panel on the front page of a newsletter that contains the title, date, and volume number. Also called the nameplate.

Beat reporter...................... reporter assigned to a specific topic area, e.g., police, education, politics.

Binding................................ method of holding a multipage document together. Options include stapling, spiral binding, saddle stitching, and perfect binding.

Bio (biography).................. fact sheet about a person. May be written in bullet point, chronological, or narrative style.

Bleed .... to extend off the edge of a page. Photos often bleed.

Blog .... from *web log*. An online diary or commentary maintained by an individual.

Boilerplate.......................... standard one-paragraph description of an organization, typically placed at the end of news releases or promotional material.

Bold .... heavy, dark style of type.

Brochure .... printed sheet or sheets, usually folded, with many design elements.

B-roll .... additional video, provided as part of video news release, that local stations can edit or use for background.

Bullet point .... small symbols used to mark key points in a document.

Byliner .... article ghost-written by public relations writers and issued over the byline of someone else—usually an expert whose name will attract attention and add credibility.

Chat group .... online discussion group that takes place in real time, as a conversation.

Close-up (CU) .... in a video, shot that shows head and neck of subject.

Column .... in publication design, text bounded by white space. Books typically have one column, newspapers many.

Communication .... systematic review of communication activities to assess whether they are having their intended
    audit   effect.

Content analysis .... research method that measures the frequency of occurrence of words, visuals, or ideas.

Controlled .... media whose content and distribution do not change once they
    media   leave the public relations writer, e.g., annual reports.

Crisis .... threat or surprise of some magnitude that negatively affects an organization or individual and requires an immediate response.

Cropping .... selecting only part of a photo or piece of artwork for reproduction.

Culture .... the way groups of people collectively think and act, or the groups that act in a common way.

Cut .... sudden change from scene to scene.

Database .... information organized electronically so that a computer request can retrieve designated pieces of data. Basically, an electronic filing system.

Design .... process of positioning text and graphic elements together.

Dialogue .... two or more people talking.

Die cut .... cutting printed material to a special, nonstandard shape.

Dilution .... use of a trademark in such a way as to "dilute" or tarnish the image of the mark.

Direct mail .... mailings targeted to specific individuals. (*See also* mail merge.)

Display type .... "stand out" typeface used for major headings.

Domain name .... an organization's trade name on the Web. For example, in the URL http://www.sagepub.com the domain name is sagepub.

Drop cap .... first letter of a paragraph set into a paragraph at the height of the first two or three lines of the paragraph.

E-commerce .... commercial transactions conducted via the Internet.

Embargo .... notice on a news release that it should not be used before a designated time/date.

Emboss .... to stamp a texture or image onto paper or card.

Ethics .... standards of behavior. For members of the PRSA, expressed as the PRSA Code of Ethics.

Ethnocentric	a "we're right" position with respect to plans for overseas communication developed in the home office.
Ethos	the expression of or appeal to character or personality. The basis for source credibility.
Executive summary	brief summary provided at the beginning of a business report. Called an "abstract" in an academic/research report.
Fact sheet	printed page carrying information about an organization or topic, typically one page and relatively nondating.
Fade	gradual transition from scene to scene.
FAQ	frequently asked question.
Feature	story that focuses on human interest or background information rather than hard news.
Flame	verbal attack on a web newsgroup participant that has the effect of "igniting" responses from other participants.
Foil stamp	heat process used to apply a metallic foil with a specific design to paper or card.
Frames	in web design, frames divide the display into two or more areas (frames), each of which can show the contents of a different web page.
Gatefold	brochure fold in which the document is folded in half and then the two ends are folded to meet in the middle, forming a "gate."
Gatekeeper	one who controls the flow of information to publics: typically news editors, but also public relations practitioners.
Geocentric	communication approach based on a worldwide orientation that ignores national boundaries.
GIF	graphics format, limited to 256 colors, but can handle animation. Downloads with bitmap graphic that gets clearer.
Grant	money provided, typically by a charity or foundation, to fund projects. Usually obtained in response to a (grant) proposal.
Group shot	in a video or photo, shot of more than three people.
Gutter	inside margin of a page, where it goes into the binding.
Halftone	photograph that will be printed in one color only, usually black.
Hanging indent	style of paragraph in which the first line(s) extends to the margin while the remainder is inset.
Headshot	photograph of an individual from the neck up.
Holding statement	a news release typically used in a crisis situation announcing that detailed information will be available at a later time. It puts the media "on hold."
HTML	hypertext markup language, the language used to create web documents.
Hyperlink	in web design, a link that takes you to another section or page of the same web site when you click on it.
Income statement	also referred to as a "profit and loss statement." A snapshot of an organization's performance over time, answering the question of whether the organization made a profit for the week, month, year, etc. At its simplest, the profit and loss statement is a two-column report, one column income

and the other expenses. The difference between the two columns is the profit for the period for which the statement was produced.

internet...................................... (lowercase i) are computer networks used for the exchange of messages and files.

Internet...................................... (uppercase I) is the global network most people access, referred to as "the Web."

Intranet.................................... self-contained, limited-access network such as one linking an organization's employees and departments.

Inverted pyramid.............. the "classic" newswriting format. The story moves from most important to least important information.

ISP... Internet service provider. A company that provides access to the Internet.

Issue .... continuing problems that an organization has to respond to, e.g., environmental standards.

Italic .... slanted type.

JPEG .... graphics format capable of handling millions of colors and faster download than GIF; downloads line by line.

Justified................................. type aligned to both sides of a column. Text aligned to only one side is termed "flush" or "ragged" left or right.

Kerning................................... adjusting the spacing between letters for a finished look.

Landscape .... horizontal format.

Layout.................................... arrangement of design elements on a page or screen.

Leading.................................. spacing between lines. Leading can be adjusted to even out columns, or to squeeze in an extra line.

Liabilities............................. what you owe. Liabilities include accounts payable (for purchases you have made and that are due within a year), current liabilities, and long-term liabilities, such as loans, that are not due for more than a year.

Libel....................................... traditionally, written defamation (as compared with slander, which is oral defamation).

Likert type scale .... opinion scale that uses a standard *strongly agree–strongly disagree* format.

Line art................................. drawings, cartoons, and other artwork. This can be more easily and clearly reproduced than grayscale art (which includes screens) or photographs (halftones) that require special treatment for reproduction.

Links...................................... in web design, an active connection that takes you to another web site when you click on it.

Logo....................................... a company's or organization's identifying artwork.

Logos...................................... the expression of or appeal to reason or logic.

Long shot (LS).................... in a video, shot that shows most of the scene.

Mail merge........................... computer application that allows a file of individual information to be merged with a master document thus producing a customized document for each individual. Direct mail is a classic example.

Mailing list.......................... on the Web, it is an interest group. For direct mail, it is a list, often purchased, of names and addresses.

Masthead.............................. the panel, often on the op-ed page, that contains the newsletter name plus address, publisher, officers, and circulation information.

Media advisory .... also called an "alert." Information provided to alert the media to upcoming events—typically, in one-page, bullet-point format.

Media kit .... originally, a folder containing fact sheets, photographs, biographies, etc. provided to the media. Often includes CDs containing graphics and audio content, web links, and video. Increasingly, the same content may also be available at web sites. Packages provided via CD or web site may be known as electronic press kits.

Media scanning .... process of routinely reading, viewing, or listening to news to assess coverage of an organization or topic. May be an automated, electronic process.

Memo .... brief, internal correspondence using "To," "From," "Date," and "Topic" headings.

Meta-tag .... HTML tag embedded in the coding for a web site that is used by search engines to identify web sites that answer a search query.

Mid-shot (MS) .... in a video, waist-to-head shot of a subject.

Monologue .... one person talking.

Net income (loss) .... what is left of the revenue/gross income after expenses and cost of sales have been deducted. Net income is the "bottom line."

News determinant .... component of a story that defines it as news, e.g., relevance, proximity.

Newsgroup .... online discussion group or bulletin board, usually hosted by Usenet.

Op-ed .... (opinion-editorial) opinion of an organization or individual not on the editorial staff but published (typically) close to the editorial pages. Commercial organizations often pay to have them run as written.

Orphan .... a single word (especially a short word) that ends up on a separate line. Try to avoid orphans.

Pathos .... the expression of or appeal to emotions.

PDF .... portable document format. Created by programs such as Acrobat, PDF files allow users to share formatted content, e.g., layouts, even if they do not have compatible software.

Perfect binding .... gluing the document into a cover such as the telephone book or this textbook.

Pitch letter .... letter to journalists or editors explaining why they should cover a particular topic.

Plug-ins .... typically, software that adds a specific feature or service to a larger software package. You may have to load a plug-in to access video files, for example.

Point .... a measure of type size. Body or text copy is usually set in 10- or 12-point type, headlines in a larger point size.

Polycentric .... communication approach that assumes "they're right." Based on local, independent operations within national borders.

Portrait .... vertical format.

Position paper .... document setting out an organization's official position on an issue (that is typically timely or controversial).

Proposal .... persuasive document written to obtain funding or a contract.

Proprietary .... having ownership. Market research information is typically proprietary, i.e., confidential to the owner.

PSA .... public service announcement. Advertisements, typically promoting health or safety, carried at no charge by news media.

Public relations .... the discipline of managing relationships with publics that can affect an organization's future.

Publicity .... writing and activities aimed at gaining media attention and coverage.

Pull quote .... a line or two of type or a quote "pulled" from the text and printed as a graphic element using color or a different font.

Readability .... the level at which a piece of text can be understood. May be expressed as a school-grade level or a score.

Regiocentric .... communication approach that develops plans within regional markets rather than political boundaries.

Registration .... ensuring that two or more printing plates mesh exactly so that colors are printed exactly where they are supposed to go. You can often see this problem in newspaper supplements in which the photos are unclear, i.e., not registered correctly.

Resolution .... sharpness of an image. Referred to in DPI (dots per inch) for printers or pixels for monitors.

Revenue .... also referred to as gross income. The amount an organization has taken in before expenses are deducted.

Reverse .... light type on a dark background, usually white on black.

Roman .... type that is not italic.

Rule .... a line. The thickness of rules is specified in points.

Saddle stitching .... binding a document by stapling in the fold.

Screen .... a colored or gray panel that often forms the background for type. Screens range from 1% to 100%.

Semantic .... an opinion scale that uses polar opposites, e.g., strong-weak.
    differential

Serif .... The small lines (usually horizontal) on some typefaces. Common serif typeface families include Times, Palatino, and Schoolbook. Sans-serif typefaces such as Helvetica have no such lines.

Servicemark .... legally registered name of a service or program, designated by SM.

Signature .... a printing term for the pages printed on one sheet of paper. Always in multiples of four.

Sizing .... determining the proportions of photos or artwork that you want to print larger or smaller than the original.

Sound effects .... appropriate sounds added as background.

Split run .... producing two versions of an ad, brochure, or direct mail piece to test which version gets the better response.

Spread .... multiple-column layout.

Stock photo .... photo, usually purchased, that shows a "standard" content, e.g., children playing.

Stock .... the paper a document is printed on. Paper stock may differ in weight (thickness), texture, color, and surface (glossy or matte).

Storyboard............................ initial sketches of visual content plus copy for a video production.

Super...................................... superimposition of one picture over another, often used for slogans and logos.

Talking head........................ in a video, close-up shot of one person usually talking directly into the camera.

Text wrap.............................. text that follows the contour of artwork, photos, or even other blocks of type.

Trademark............................. legally registered name of a company or product, designated by ™.

Uncontrolled .... media whose timing, content, and distribution may change due to the actions of an outside
   media   gatekeeper, e.g., news releases.

URL.. uniform resource locator. The unique address of each document on the Web.

Usenet .... Internet bulletin board system hosting tens of thousands of online discussion groups (newsgroups),
                                            each directed at a particular topic or question.

Video..................................... action visuals.

VNR .... video news release.

Voiceover (VO) .... indicates that an announcer's voice will begin.

VRML..................................... virtual reality modeling language, the language of 3D web site design.

Web cast .... live broadcast on the Web, including streaming audio and video.

Widow................................... single line that ends up at the top of another column or page. You can usually avoid widows and
                                            orphans by kerning or editing the preceding copy.

World Wide Web .... also referred to as "the Web"; the part of the Internet capable of handling graphic files and
                                            hypertext.

XHTML.................................. extensible hypertext markup language.

XML .... extensible markup language.

Index

About the Authors

Donald Treadwell is a professor in the Department of Communication at Westfield State College. He teaches courses in public relations writing, public relations, organizational communication, communication research, and communication theory. He is the communication internship program coordinator and advisor for graduate and continuing education. He has published in *Public Relations Review, Communication Monographs, Journal of Technical Writing and Communication, Journal of the Association of Communication Administration,* and international health education journals. He is a member of the National Communication Association and the Communication Institute for Online Scholarship and has international consulting experience in agricultural extension and health communication.

Jill B. Treadwell has 30 years' experience in publications and public relations. She has managed PR campaigns for U.S. and international companies as well as for nonprofit and educational organizations. She has a background in both writing and design and has specialized in annual reports, newsletters, brochures, and proposals directed at state and federal procurement agencies. In addition to maintaining a private public relations consulting practice, she currently teaches public relations, public relations writing, and other writing courses in both classroom and online settings at Westfield State College.